Old Age in the Roman World

THE JOHNS HOPKINS UNIVERSITY PRESS

Ancient Society and History

Old Age

TIM G. PARKIN

in the Roman World

*A Cultural
and Social History*

The Johns Hopkins University Press
Baltimore and London

© 2003 The Johns Hopkins University Press
All rights reserved. Published 2003
Printed in the United States of America on acid-free paper
9 8 7 6 5 4 3 2 1

The Johns Hopkins University Press
2715 North Charles Street
Baltimore, Maryland 21218-4363
www.press.jhu.edu

Library of Congress Cataloging-in-Publication Data

Parkin, Tim G.
    Old age in the Roman world : a cultural and social history /
Tim G. Parkin.
        p. cm. — (Ancient society and history)
Includes bibliographical references and index.
    ISBN 0-8018-7128-X
    1. Aged—Rome.   2. Old age—Rome.   I. Title.   II. Series.
    HQ1064.R6 P37 2002
    305.26′0945′632—dc21

    2002003288

A catalog record for this book is available from the British Library.

In memory of Alex:
mihi cum de senectute vellem aliquid scribere,
tu occurrebas dignus eo munere
(without any implication regarding age)

Contents

Contents

Acknowledgments

Fittingly enough, this book has been fairly long in the making. My interest in older members of the Roman world began in earnest in 1985 when, as an honors student at Victoria University of Wellington, I wrote an essay entitled "The reality of old age in the Roman world." My supervisor was Alex Scobie, to whom this book is dedicated and without whom it would never have been begun, let alone written. Alex's scholarship and friendship have been a source of inspiration for me ever since; I am only sorry he did not live long enough for me to be able to hand him a copy. It was Alex who taught me to annotate my assertions. The substantial endnotes in this book are partly for his benefit. The title of my honors essay was naive on my part—there can be no such thing as a single reality in such a vast area—but the essay laid the groundwork for subsequent research. I went on to spend three years (1986–89) at St. John's College, Oxford, writing a D.Phil. dissertation with the rather more sober title of "Age and the Aged in Roman Society: Demographic, Social, and Legal Aspects." It was my great good fortune to be supervised during this period by Fergus Millar. For his advice and support, and for his encouragement and patience during the time I completed the thesis in New Zealand (it was finally submitted in 1992), I shall always be grateful. There are many others at

Oxford to whom gratitude is owed; I would mention in particular Richard Smith (now at Cambridge) for his guidance on demography; Nicholas Purcell for his willingness to guide and inspire a lost colonial; and Alan Bowman and John Rea for discussion on Roman Egypt. I was also fortunate to have in Oxford a good group of friends who provided support and distraction; I should particularly mention Franco Basso, Simon Corcoran, Richard Hawley, Geraldine Herbert-Brown, and David Jennings. My thanks also go to my two D.Phil. examiners, Jane Gardner and Barbara Levick, for their very helpful comments.

I would also like to thank Beryl Rawson of the Australian National University in Canberra for her encouragement, not least during the second and third Canberra conferences on the Roman family in 1988 and 1994, respectively. Among the many people I had the pleasure to meet at these two conferences I would especially mention Emiel Eyben of the Catholic University of Leuven, who also very kindly supplied me with a copy of Louis Berelson's unpublished dissertation on old age, and Werner Eck of the University of Cologne. The latter gave me the opportunity to turn my research into this book, by sponsoring me as an Alexander von Humboldt fellow at Cologne in 1997; he also gave me enormous help in the scientific art of prosopography, and read a draft of Chapter 4. Among the many other people it was my pleasure to meet during my sojourn in Germany, I would like to thank in particular Marietta Horster of the University of Rostock, for her friendship and help during my time in Germany.

Also deserving of special thanks for their comments on particulars are, from Australia, Elizabeth Baynham, Jane Bellemore, Brian Bosworth, and Paul Weaver. I must also thank the three anonymous readers chosen by the Johns Hopkins University Press, whose reports provided many useful criticisms.

After Oxford, I returned to Victoria University from 1989 to 1998; my sincere thanks go to all my former colleagues there, especially Arthur Pomeroy, for encouraging and humoring me over that decade.

I must express my gratitude to the Rhodes Trustees for financing my three years in Oxford, and to the Alexander von Humboldt Foundation for its very generous support in 1997. My thanks also go to the Internal Research Committee of Victoria University for providing funds toward the cost of acquiring research materials. This research could not have been undertaken without the heroic labors of the librarians at the Ashmolean Library in Oxford, especially Danny Darwish and John Taylor; of the reference staff at the Victoria University library in Wellington, especially Justin Cargill, Barbro Harris, and Anne Squire; and, more recently, of the outstanding reference staff at the University of Canterbury library: Helena Blijlevens, Janice Farrelly, Elena Frolova, and Katharine Samuel. I am also grateful for the efforts of individuals at the Johns Hopkins University Press, especially Jackie Wehmueller, Trevor Lipscombe, Michael Lonegro, and Kimberly Johnson, as well as, once again, my copyeditor Brian MacDonald.

Finally, to all my friends in New Zealand, England, Germany, and elsewhere, some but not all of whom I have already mentioned, my heartfelt thanks, especially for keeping me (relatively) young when my research into old age threatened to make a *senex* of me before my time. Above all, of course, thanks to Janet Watson. *diligat illa senem quondam.*

A number of works of relevant scholarship appeared as this book was going to press, most notably Walter Scheidel's 2001 publications on Roman demography. Although I have made some reference to these in the notes, I could not fully take them into account here. I will respond to his material more fully in a review of his work in *Bryn Mawr Classical Review.*

Old Age in the Roman World

Introduction

> When I say that I am working on a study of
> old age people generally exclaim, "What an
> extraordinary notion! . . . But you aren't old!
> . . . What a dismal subject."
> de Beauvoir (1977) 8

As the world progresses into the twenty-first century, concerns over the size and structure of national populations hold ever increasing importance, as awareness of demographic realities and of their economic and social repercussions grows. At the forefront of such "problems" is the aging population: the average age of living individuals in almost every part of the globe has been steadily increasing and the proportion of older "dependents" within such societies has grown. The phenomenon of an aging population, it should be noted, is determined more by decreasing levels of fertility than by lower levels of mortality. The significant climb in the proportion of people over the age of (say) 60 years in populations such as that of Great Britain and the United States in the course of the twentieth century has led to great concern among politicians, among others, over the social role of, and economic consequences for, this sector of society.[1] Another, more positive result of this demographic phenomenon, however, has been a

1

quite remarkable surge of interest—among both researchers and the more general public—in old age, its social, medical, and psychological contexts. As a result, great advances have been made in our understanding of the aging process and of the realities of aging in modern society. But there remains much to learn.

As part of this interest, it is only natural to ponder on the historical aspects of aging, to consider the similarities and differences between the status of old age and the position of older people then and now. This is particularly true in view of some traditional but usually unsubstantiated images we have of the older people in the past ("the good old days"), images that typically contrast the allegedly unfavorable position of old people today with that enjoyed by our ancestors.[2] More objective work has emerged, largely on demographic and sociological lines, particularly in the fields of medieval and modern European history. The focus of study, however, still tends to be the history of attitudes toward older people rather than the history of aging itself. This is perhaps unavoidable in view of the nature of the testimony, but more can and needs to be done.[3] The socioanthropological study of old age in modern-day developing societies has also provided complementary information on the role and status of older people, both males and females, within a community.[4]

While the study of ancient social history has developed over the past thirty years, the role of the private individual *as an individual* in daily life in ancient Greek and Roman societies and the realities of his or her existence (rather than the theoretical legal status) have only more recently come under detailed scrutiny. One aspect of such study has been the consideration of the position of different age-groups within ancient societies, although the focus here has been almost exclusively directed toward the young (and their parents).[5] Some study has also been made of "rites de passage," again following the lead of the sociological and anthropological literature,[6] but such interests tend to exclude the study of older people in antiquity. The passage from adulthood to old age was rarely marked by rites of transition, even in the case of older women with the onset of the menopause. The modern-day retirement celebration may be seen as one rite of passage, but there was no ancient equivalent, for reasons that will become apparent. Apart from anything else, public advertisement of decline may not have been welcomed by older people themselves. Hence, although societies past and present may assign different roles and occupations to particular age or sex categories (and as a result "category solidarity" may occur within such age or sex groupings),[7] it is a common feature of such systems that older people—provided they are still functioning members of the society—are scarcely differentiated from the general adult age-grouping, whereas greater differentiation occurs within younger age-groups.

On age-categories in society (to which we shall return presently), the classic paper is that by Linton. One of his conclusions is worth quoting, since its theme will be a recurring argument in this book: "Although certain societies ease this transition [*sc.* from adulthood to old age] by the formal ascription to the aged of a respect and authority greater than that accorded to full adults, it is an open question how far these formal patterns agree with the actual practice. It seems that even in the so-called gerontocracies age alone does not increase the individual's prestige."[8] It should also be noted that my use here of terms such as "age-classes" or "age-groups" does not imply that such divisions were ever necessarily formalized or institutionalized, only that such notions of age-categories existed.

The traditional treatment of life and customs in the ancient Roman world tended to present the picture of an upper-class male, from his first years, his education and entry into marriage and public life, culminating in his climb up the political ladder; the next time we met our Roman subject was generally at his funeral. All too often our hypothetical Roman seemed to disappear from the extant historical record once he attained the consulship; at best he might warrant a brief mention subsequently as a provincial governor. My point is not so much the broader issue—that such a career would have applied to only the tiniest subfraction of the population of the time (though this is true)—but that on attaining the consulship this Roman's life may have been perhaps only half over. What happened to him in his old age? And what of the (equally stereotyped but less often encountered) Roman woman as she grew older? The problem, of course, lies in the silence of the sources or, more fundamentally, in the interests and concerns of ancient writers and readers. When older individuals do appear, whether in ancient literature or in modern studies of antiquity, it is usually as a sideline or as a special case. A few notable old people may be mentioned (a Nestor, Sophocles, or Augustus), but the subject of old age itself seems scarcely to merit investigation.

In a similar vein the ancient accounts of old age are often little more than lists of characters, mythical and historical, who purportedly lived to a ripe old age. Such lists—to us rather monotonous—are a symptom of the ancients' predilection and fascination for the marvelous or unusual and are of little value in terms of history or demography.[9] One slightly puzzling fact is that there are relatively few examples of Romans as opposed to Greeks appearing in such ancient lists, Phlegon's being the only notable exception. Pseudo-Lucian (*Macrobioi* 29) promises a list of Roman octogenarians to parallel the Greek *exempla* given there, but, if ever written, such a list is not extant. (This may be part of the humor: the author says he will go on to compose such a list, "the gods willing"—perhaps they were not! In any event, pseudo-Lucian's list does include a few Romans.) Marcus Crassus apparently commented to Cicero that none of his (Crassus's) ancestors at Rome had ever lived beyond the age of 60 years.[10] Despite Cicero's amusement, Crassus's second thoughts about the statement, and the demographic unreality of it, perhaps *to the Romans* there was a general grain of truth behind the idea: Romans were not renowned for their old age.

The long-lived individuals, particularly in the case of the historical characters mentioned in such lists, were remembered by posterity primarily not for their old age but rather for their achievements: their age was generally irrelevant or, at best, it was remarked or inferred that they performed such feats *despite* their advanced age. This apparent lack of interest in old age in antiquity is itself important and may provide clues as to the treatment of older people in the Roman world. The reasons behind it are also important: was it simply because older people were comparatively few or, if not, then less visible within society?

Seneca the Elder, himself a long-lived gentleman (ca. 55/50 B.C.–ca. A.D. 40), has left us a collection of rhetorical exercises, designed for the use of Roman schoolboys in learning oratorical skills and in presenting both sides of an argument, a useful talent for a future lawyer. The scenarios presented, though largely fantastic, are revealing as to Roman modes of thinking—or, at the very least, the way some Romans claimed to have thought in particular circumstances. In one of these exercises (*Controversiae* 10.4), we are presented with the case of crippled beggars (*mendici debilitati*). A man used to cripple children who had been exposed, forcing them to become beggars and demanding a fee from them; he is accused of harming the state. Arguments are presented on both sides. There is much against the man: the horrors of the crippling, the fact that Romulus and Remus were foundlings, and so forth. The only point in favor of the man is that the children's parents treated them worse in exposing them than *he* did in crippling them. But one telling argument is discussed: can this man have harmed the state if he has done nothing illegal? He is allowed to do what he did, because exposed children, like slaves, do not count (*in nullo numero sunt*), "There can be no action for harming the state in the name of persons who are outside the state." Here we begin to get to the crux of the issue, as the logic is taken further. The state cannot be harmed by any marginal member of society: a woman, an old man, or a pauper. In respect of those who are not members, it is argued that the state cannot be harmed. It is one thing to state that older people were of little interest in antiquity; to what extent were they not regarded as full members of society?

If there was a lack of interest in older people in antiquity, the same is not true today. Since I started working on the subject, the amount of scholarship, particularly concerning literary depictions of old age, has become quite impressive.[11] B. E. Richardson published a book in 1933 on old age in ancient Greece, and on the whole it is useful, albeit somewhat uncritical of the sources. She studied old age in ancient Greece by attempting to bring together references in Greek literature (of all periods) to older people and to derive from them an image of the "reality" of the time. This somewhat subjective approach enabled her to convey the impression that older people (by which she seems to mean older males) in ancient Greece enjoyed something of a golden age. At least one reviewer was convinced: "In this age, when it is the tendency to focus attention on the very young, it is refreshing to turn to a nation who kept children in their proper place and paid due deference to their elders and betters."[12] Since then, while numerous studies have appeared on aspects of old age in antiquity, little has been achieved apart from a general awareness of what a particular author says about older people in his works.[13] Even less satisfactory are general papers purporting to describe in a relatively few pages the position of old people in classical times, again almost solely by use of selected literary references, in order either to confirm or (less frequently) to refute the traditional image of the golden age for older people in classical antiquity.[14] Moses Finley's brief essay of 1981 is in effect the sole example to date of a general consideration of what it might actually have meant to be old in ancient times. Much more can be said.

How, then, does one approach the study of old age in, for example, the early Roman Empire? One central problem to be confronted is the manner in which the historian may use the (mainly literary) testimony that we have—a problem of general import to the study of ancient history. The usefulness of a simple catalog of literary references to old age is limited, at least in a historical sense. The danger in studying a subject like old age (or, for that matter, childhood) in antiquity is that the result may be little more than an exhaustive but uncritical catalog of literary references, an unmade jigsaw puzzle for which, furthermore, one must wonder whether all or even most of the pieces are at hand. A mere list of quotations marks no progress from the compilation created by the fifth-century A.D. encyclopedist Stobaeus in his *Florilegium*: some ninety-five extracts from Greek authors covering a wide range of literary depictions of old age, both positive and negative (discussed in Chapter 3). I do not pretend to have assembled in this book every reference to old age in classical literature, nor do I think that such a collection would serve any particularly valid historical purpose; however, the evidence available, literary and otherwise, can serve to elucidate the position of older people in the Roman world.

As well as gathering classical "definitions" of old age, I outline the various literary images of old age, principally in literature of the classical Roman period (roughly, from 100 B.C. to A.D. 200, the period that is the focus of most of this book), though earlier (and, in a few cases, later) sources may also prove relevant and useful. My purpose in providing an overview of attitudes expressed in classical literature toward old age (Chapter 3) is principally to provide a background to more historical considerations, in particular the role of older people (both male and female, although inevitably the literary and legal sources concentrate on the men) in the world of Rome and of its empire, in both the so-called public and private spheres. Apart from the literary sources, use will be made principally of the legal corpus, papyri, and epigraphy. A detailed discussion of the depiction of old age in Roman art must be left to someone more qualified than myself.[15] On their own the sources I use are not enough in dealing with a section of society as relatively silent (about itself) as older people, and comparative material, as well as the judicious use of inference, supposition, and models, must be employed. As Moses Finley noted in 1981, the central themes of interest in the "burgeoning sociological and psychiatric literature" on old age and older people in modern society are not easily or directly applicable to the study of old age in the ancient world, largely because of a lack of awareness of, or concern about, such issues at the time and hence a dearth of explicit evidence surviving today. To quote Finley, "the ancient historian is drawn to making bricks without straw. I do not wholly despair, but I am necessarily restricted to general statements based as much on broad sociological considerations as on ancient documentation."[16]

My aim is not to make a single, definitive conclusion about "the reality of old age in the Roman world," because such reality, even if it may be discerned, will have varied from place to place, from time to time, and indeed from individual to individual. The literary sources on occasion may give subjective views of and opinions on old age, statements influenced by individual impressions as well as, perhaps, by ulterior political, social, or economic motivations and by adherence to literary or philosophical topoi. Such references cannot and should not be held to be generally representative of any time, place, or social class, if indeed of any one individual. Does a particular author—and in terms of antiquity we are almost always confined to the male view—portray the situation as it really existed (at least in his eyes), as he wanted it to exist, as he wanted others to believe it existed, or even as a patently absurd distortion of the facts for its own sake? As Falkner and de Luce astutely comment, "the texts sometimes talk *about* old age; at other times they talk *through* old age to something else."[17] Such texts, of course, may still have much of relevance to tell us.

A positive line of defense of old age by Cicero, or a negative jibe at older people by Juvenal, must be considered not just in terms of what is said, but also of *why* it is said, in the light of the author's (and the audience's) influences, motives, and expectations. Even if accurate in any specific regard, such a reference cannot be automatically assumed to reveal general opinions or practices at any one time, or to point to changes over various generations, as affected by political, social, economic, and even religious conditions. Anecdotes need not necessarily reflect a typical situation; more often, they are related for the very reason that they are unusual or remarkable. Descriptions in literature of old age or of older individuals were not written primarily to tell us objectively about old age in Roman times, but to use the concept of and images associated with old age for the writer's own purposes. When the literary sources on old age are as few and sparsely spread as they are (though not as few as one might at first suppose), this inevitably makes the interpretation of the evidence on this level doubly difficult. But the literary evidence and its interpretation are still of interest and of real historical value, provided that due caution and critical judgment are used, because they allow us to consider the avowed impression of and reaction to old age and older people by various individuals for an intended audience, both young and old, within the various genres of Greek and Latin literature. Hence I adopt a cultural as well as a social approach.

Ideally, especially as we are dealing with a vast chronological and geographical framework, one should approach this subject from a diachronic perspective, to elucidate continuity and change in the role and status of older people in antiquity. Such questions will indeed concern us in individual chapters of this book, for example, in developments in the political role of older people in the Roman world, in their social and financial commitments, and in their place within family and household structures. But I do not believe it is possible to write a history of Roman old age within a purely chronological structure; the nature of the testimony simply will not allow it. Hence the overall approach of this book is synchronic, dealing with themes in each chapter that, as far as is applicable and possible, are developed chronologically.[18] Although some scholars have pointed to change over time in attitudes toward certain age-groups, such perceived change is more likely to be the result of a change in the nature of the evidence than of real changes of attitude; apart from anything else, I do not believe that one can generalize to such an extent in terms of a society's "attitude" (as if that were one entity) toward almost anything.

Some epigraphical evidence—basically the extent to which different age-groups are recorded on tombstone epitaphs—may suggest a change in attitude in Roman times in which elders became less valued, as Brent Shaw has argued, but various cultural factors determined the propensity toward recording ages on tombstones in the first place. The lack of a statement of exact chronological age at death need not imply the undervaluation of any age-group. It should be remembered also that age is only one descriptive element on an epitaph. In fact, as is sometimes the case today, as a mark of respect, children might not be expected to know the exact age of a parent anyway. It is also less than self-evident that one's value in life is always directly proportional to the degree of attention paid to one's burial. Nor does it seem to me that a greater appreciation of the young, if indeed such occurred in later imperial times, need automatically have been balanced by a devaluation of seniority (see Chapter 4).[19] A change in attitudes in the opposite direction—that is, that a greater valuation was placed on older people in the imperial period as a result of Stoic influence and that this was fostered in time by Christianity—has also been argued, on even less convincing grounds. Although it is true that the Stoic creed advocated, for example, respect for parents (see Chapter 8), this seems to me to attribute far greater and wider influence to the Stoics than is warranted.[20] Similarly, positing a new awareness of the young from the republican to the imperial period as a result of political changes (the Roman *paterfamilias* having less political and social power) is misleading.[21]

The other ancient sources to be considered in this book—principally legal, papyrological and epigraphical—may be considered of more historical value in this context, but here too there are problems of interpretation and representativeness. The legal sources will be used primarily to consider various rules of age in public life in the empire as a whole, but the unraveling of these rules over time and place is not a simple operation: references are not in abundance and seem at times contradictory. The papyri (used here, among other aspects, to analyze the systems of specific rules of age in Roman Egypt as well as the methods of collecting and recording the ages of individuals) are similarly haphazardly extant and often liable to uncertain or ambiguous interpretation. In the same way the epigraphical evidence is manipulated to discuss aspects of ancient society for which it was never originally designed. Yet it is the task of the historian—and the ancient social historian in particular is faced with this exercise—to interpret and make judicious use of whatever genuine testimony is at hand.

In the case of "rules of age" in the Roman empire (Chapters 4–5), for example, the mode of operation of these rules is never explicitly described or explained by any primary source. The system was in general use and as such did not warrant detailed description: the people involved in various aspects presumably knew well enough how the relevant system worked, while to others it was probably of little immediate interest or importance. Statements appear in the legal corpus only when clarification or change was felt to be necessary, and it is up to the social historian to try to trace from these varying and often inadequate clues the entire system as it operated over time.

The paucity or silence of the sources becomes all the more evident when one turns to consider family life in the Roman world, especially with respect to a sector of the population (whether slaves, women, or older people) that is generally less evident in literature generated by and for a wealthy, aristocratic, male circle. Demographic considerations may reasonably lead us to conclude that a certain number of people did survive to old age but they cannot tell us the nature of these people's existence, and in this regard very real contrasts between our own times and the Roman world become striking and significant. It is necessary—though not easy—in approaching a question such as this consciously to free ourselves as far as possible from our own preconceptions and expectations, because the demographic, economic, social, and indeed "moral" situation may vary considerably between different societies. One cannot assume, for example, that an older Roman whose spouse had died would have automatically lived with his or her married offspring's family: this is only one of many possible situations.

Looking back at an era when welfare for older people, at least in our modern conception of this system, did not exist, it is of considerable interest to ask precisely what did happen to the average older Roman. Yet this question has received little attention, from ancient or modern writers. In the former case it might be suggested that this is a result of a lack of interest on the part of ancient writer and audience, who might have had no worries about such a situation in their own lives; in the latter the reason might be the lack of readily available evidence, if not also a similar lack of interest. In the face of such silence, how can one proceed? Moses Finley's reaction to the question of what happened to aged parents who were not cared for by their sons was blunt: "The answer is that we simply have no idea, and I see no virtue in idle guesses."[22] I think the evidence available does permit informed conjectures, however, as I discuss in Chapter 8. On the other hand, it is regrettable that, as a result of the nature of the testimony, it is not practical to devote a chapter of this book to the particular status and role of the older female. Women will feature throughout the book, particularly in relation to the household and family, but the Roman focus was very much upon the male.

My study is based on the conviction that questions regarding the status and the position of a social group such as older people in an ancient society are worth asking for the insight they may give us into a society as a whole, and that various aspects relating to this section of the Roman population can be analyzed and determined through the use of both primary sources and comparative material. The study of older people in the ancient Roman world, as opposed to the consideration of simply the topos of old age in classical literature, is of historical interest for the light it may throw not just on this particular age-group in its own right but also on the attitudes and reactions of the rest of the community toward this minority group of elders. We may learn something not only of the physical reality of *senectus* for older people at the time and the attitudes and experiences they faced, but also of the mentality underlying this reality. What was the emotional response of the individual as well as the deliberate policy (if any) of the state in response to the particular needs of and demands made by older members of the society, whether as dependents—willing or unwilling—or as staunchly independent individuals who wished to retain an active role in both private and public spheres of life? The point to be stressed is that older people must be considered as an integral part of the society in which they lived, not as an isolated element, however much social pressures may have wished to isolate them. Certainly these are issues of very modern concern, but they are just as relevant in any historical society in which people survived into old age in any number. Whether such a study generates reflection on contemporary society is up to the individual reader; certainly for the writer this study has generated such reflection.

PART I

UNCOVERING AGING ROMANS

One

Roman Definitions
and Statements of Age

When was a Roman "Old"?

Two millennia on, how can we investigate the old age of the ancient Romans? Terminology is an obvious starting point. The Greeks and Romans had words for "old" and "old age." In Latin *senex* means "old person" (or, more typically, "old man"), *senectus* means "old age"; such words, to which are linked the likes of *senatus* and the name Seneca, derive from the Indo-European base *sen-.[1] In Greek the usual words for old man and old age are γέρων and γῆρας respectively, derived from the root *ger-.[2] So far so good: there is no obvious problem here from a modern perspective.

Defining these terms in any more specific fashion is more difficult. One can translate them into English as "old person" and "old age," but in the process there is the risk of imposing on such terms modern connotations. What did the ancients mean when they called someone "old"? Even today, in general contexts, one does not need to know a person's exact chronological age before labeling him or her as "young," "middle-aged," or "old"; a judgment is made by appearances and circumstances, what one may term *biological* age. A myriad of social factors influences our use of such terminology, while institutions such as retirement and social welfare may furnish general indicators or turning points that to some extent determine whether we classify an individual as "old," "older," "elderly," "aged," "a senior citizen," or whatever. A figure of 60, 65, or 70 years might be used as a convenient rule of thumb for the time at which old age may be said to begin in the modern Western world, but there is no set, universally applicable age at which a person suddenly becomes old.

Are we able, then, to define terms like *senectus* with reference to a certain minimum number of years? Some scholars have thought so. For Romans "the average life was short. It was a young man's world: the word *senex* (old man) was applied to anyone over forty."[3] In other words, in antiquity people apparently grew old at what is by our standards a comparatively young age. But other scholars, more numerous, are confident that in antiquity old age began at the age of 60 years.[4] The disparity is fundamentally important in terms of our perceptions of what old age meant in antiquity; there is a significant difference between 40 and 60 years. But while it would be highly illuminating if one could say that in antiquity old age began at *x* number of years of age for men or women, in contrast or in similar fashion to modern times, reflection should make us realize that such definitions are unsatisfactory. To be sure, part of the interest in a wide-ranging study such as this is to consider what comparisons and contrasts may be drawn between then and now, and such considerations certainly emerge frequently in the chapters to follow. But first it is necessary to rid ourselves of too mathematical a definition of old age, before we make any assumptions about similarities and differences. We do not use such a universal or exact definition of old age today, and there is even less reason to suppose that the Greeks or Romans ever did.

The relevant ancient testimony at first sight does appear to provide strong mathematical clues. The literary and philosophical topos of the "ages of man" (*gradus aetatum*) has a long history, from Solon to Shakespeare and beyond. Often these systems, whether the ages are three or ten in number and whatever their relative individual length, give precise chronological breakdowns of the ages considered. Solon, for example, gave a description of human life divided into ten successive seven-year periods, up to the age of 70 years; the tenth and final age, one of decline, begins from age 63.[5] In one work in the Hippocratic corpus, the doctrine of the seven ages became established, each age itself consisting of seven years (or, in the case of the ἀνήρ [man], twenty-one years, at least in some accounts). The mathematical significance of the number seven here is the most important feature. The number nine was also regarded as significant in this context; hence ages such as 49, 63, and 81 years were later held by the Romans to be critical, *anni climacterici*.[6] The numbers seven and nine feature prominently as multiples in definitions of the commencement of old age (see Table 1 in Appendix A).

In the various accounts of the Hippocratic system, however, while the basic seven ages remain much the same, the division in years varies: the seventh stage, old age, for example, begins from the age of 42, 56, or 63 years.[7] In other Hippocratic works, four ages are standard. Very similar to and clearly influenced by the Hippocratic hebdomadal system is the description written in the second century A.D. by Claudius Ptolemaeus, where the seven stages were further linked to astrology, each stage of life (as well as its length in years) being depicted as being under the sway of a particular planet.[8] In this case old age commences from the age of 69 years; while there are seven *aetates* in Ptolemy's system, their length in years is not itself a multiple of seven. Ptolemy precedes his description of the seven ages with a comment on the wide variety of earlier treatments of the topos, and notes that one must be careful to assign the correct features to each age. This observation is important in the context of literary depictions of old age (compare especially Horace's description of older people in his *Ars Poetica*).

Censorinus, writing in the third century A.D., recorded a system of five ages, each of fifteen years' duration, described by Varro in the first century B.C. in the context of the (four) ages of Rome. Here *senectus* commences from the age of 60 years.[9] Because this age is in line with some modern conceptions of the onset of old age in ancient times, Varro's system is regularly adopted by modern scholars as definitive of Roman (and Greek) reality.[10] But there is no good reason for this, since Varro's figures are only one set in a long tradition, and it is explicitly stated by both Censorinus and Servius that the system described is Varro's, not Rome's. Saint Augustine later stated that "old age may be said to begin from the 60th year" (a sexagesimo anno senectus dicatur incipere),[11] but (i) this is also in the context of a discussion of the (six) ages of man, (ii) this figure probably reflects Varro's influence, (iii) the passage literally means an age of 59 years, and (iv) Augustine only says it *may* be. Sixty is often, however, a convenient figure with which to work when studying Roman old age. It also features in the Pythagorean system of four ages, each of twenty years' duration, which has the γέρων aged from 60 to 80 years.[12]

More than a millennium after the time of Solon there was clearly still no universally established allotment of years to any particular stage of life in this tradition. Isidorus of Seville, writing in the early seventh century A.D., states: "gradus aetatis sex sunt: infantia, pueritia, adolescentia, iuventus, gravitas atque senectus" (there are six stages of life: infancy, childhood, adolescence, adulthood, maturity, and old age).[13] In this case *senectus* begins from the age of 70 years, "for however much of life is left" (quantumcumque vitae est), though elsewhere Isidorus has *senectus* begin from as early as the age of 49 years, followed at age 77 by *senium*.[14] This twofold division of old age, active and decrepit, anticipates the modern sociological distinction between the "young-old" and the "old-old."

This is only a very brief sketch of what is a complex feature of descriptions of age, of interest in its own right and with a very long history.[15] The topos was also extended to anthropomorphizing the "life course" of a city or people (typically Rome and the Romans, as we have already mentioned that Varro did), or of history.[16] It became almost a cliché—even before Christian writers adopted the image—to talk of the world in senescence. Lucretius compares the earth, no longer producing life, to a woman past her child-bearing years ("ut mulier spatio defessa vetusto"); Aulus Gellius observes that the world seems to be aging ("quasi iam mundo senescente"), which is why men of old were apparently larger and taller (and lived longer: see Chapter 2)—in old age one shrinks.[17] But as relatively common as this image may be, it also serves to highlight further the fact that the topos of the ages of humankind is of limited use in a sociohistorical context if one is seeking to define the meaning for Romans of words describing age-groups. What the tradition of the *aetates hominum* represents is not a realistic, everyday, or universal categorization of age-classes, but a poetical and philosophical convention, influenced by mathematics, astrology, and superstition and dominated by a desire for numerical symmetry. It may be seen from Table 1 that, in deriving information from a variety of classical literary sources, *senectus* could be said to begin at various ages, ranging from 42 to 77 years. The mathematically based division of human life into various ages is a Greek rather than Roman phenomenon, with Varro, it should be added, being the notable Latin exception. Furthermore, Isidorus and Censorinus both specifically say that *philosophers* describe the life-span in this way.[18]

While the numbers for the various ages change almost by individual whim, the basic method and mathematical bases are constant. Yet one cannot envisage such systems, of varying degrees of sophistication, being used on a general daily basis, even unconsciously, as a means of defining the age-class of every individual.[19] In reviewing medieval ideas on *gradus aetatum* (derived ultimately from Greek and Roman conceptions), Peter Laslett asked: "How on earth can our ancestors possibly have believed in such a load of rubbish?"[20] Later generations may well ask the same question of, for example, certain current astrological beliefs, but it is important to remember that not everyone necessarily holds the same convictions.[21] Nor need we suppose that the various systems of *aetates hominum* were known by the general public in the ancient world. I suspect that few Romans thought that they were *senes* when they turned 60 simply because Varro defined *senectus* thus. It is a dangerous and inexact practice, as should become evident, to calculate someone's age from a passing reference to him or her being a *senex,* an *anus,* a γέρων, or a γραῦς.[22]

More general categories of age-classes certainly existed—just as, mutatis mutandis, they exist today—and perhaps better reflect contemporary, general reality, without specific age boundaries necessarily being imposed. Martial, for example, has in mind three stages in the life course when he prays for eighteen more years of life on reaching his 57th birthday:

ut nondum nimia piger senecta
sed vitae tribus areis peractis
lucos Elysiae petam puellae.
post hunc Nestora nec diem rogabo.

so that, not yet slowed down by excessive old age, but with three circuits of life's course completed, I may seek the groves of the Elysian girl. Beyond this "Nestor" of an age, I shall not ask for even another day.[23]

I would argue that classical authors typically used the terms for different age-classes—*infans, puer, puella, adulescens, vir, mulier, iuvenis, senex, anus,* and so forth (and the analogous Greek terms)—in general literary or historical contexts without implying a precise age in years or wishing the reader to associate such terms with anything more than a general sense of a stage of life.[24] In other words, *senex* means "an old man," not "a man of *x* number of years," and thus is as general as the English term in such contexts. In special circumstances age terms might convey a more specific meaning, just as, for example, "pensioner" may today. In military contexts *iunior* (17–45 years) and *senior* (46–59 years) were more specifically linked to age limits, but in more general contexts such set figures should not be imagined to have held good.[25] I do not believe that institutionalized rules of age, which we consider more closely in Chapter 4, had any great influence on Roman terminology for age-groups in terms of a set number of years. Whether what a Roman would have called an old man coincides with our own notions of old age is quite another question, to which we shall return shortly. But then again a chronological age that one person today might consider "old" another might call "middle-aged," and so on. No set, normative rules need apply, and different definitions may be used in different circumstances at different times. One's own perceptions of what is old can, of course, change as one grows older oneself; an orphaned male minor and his guardian in Egypt, for example, record in a petition against the boy's paternal grandfather's sister that she is "already extremely old: apparently she's lived more than sixty years" (ἤδη εἰς γῆρας μακρὸν ἐληλυθεῖα· ὑπὲρ γὰρ τὰ ἑ[ξ]ήκοντα ἔτη φαίνε[ται] βιώσασα). Everyone experiences old age differently.[26]

That such a word as *senex* was not strictly defined in either a general or a literary context in terms of a specific number of years may be illustrated, if not proved, by a few examples of individual perceptions that display a range of realities. Hannibal, at the battle of Zama in 202 B.C., was 44 years of age. Livy here has Hannibal call himself a *senex*, in sharp contrast to the *adolescentia* of his enemy Scipio (who was 34 years old), and to Hannibal's own *pueritia* when he first left his homeland.[27] Cicero speaks of himself in the *Philippics* (when he was 62 or 63 years of age) as having been an *adulescens* at the time of the Catilinarian conspiracy in 63 B.C.[28] So we have in these two passages the contrast between Hannibal, the defeated foe, and Cicero, defender of the state. In both cases the chronological age of the individual was around 44 years, but the circumstances were very different. Appearance and mental attitude are as (if not more) important as the number of years lived, and the contrast between generalized notions of young and old is used to good effect.

In a similar vein, Sallust describes the rivalry between Catulus and Caesar for the position of *pontifex maximus* in 63 B.C.: Catulus's *extrema aetas* is contrasted with that of Caesar the *adulescentulus,* even though the latter was in his late 30s on being elected and the difference in age between the two was only about twenty years, less than the terminology might have suggested.[29] Martial speaks of himself as a *senex* when he was at most 48 years old, and more likely about 45.[30] To give one more example of such a contrast, this time of a self-confessed *senex* as compared with his days of youth, Cicero has L. Licinius Crassus (*cos.* 95 B.C.) call himself a *senex* and compare this with his days as an *adulescens,* even though the scene is set in 91 B.C. and thus Crassus was in fact only 48 or 49 years of age.[31] Cicero would have been sufficiently aware of the fact that Crassus was of such a chronological age: *senex* should be taken in such contexts, then, as an indication more of general impressions of and attitudes toward age than of any specific position on a numerically exact age-scale. One might contrast Cicero's comment to Atticus in 44 B.C., in the preface to his *de Senectute,* that old age is now pressing on or at least approaching them both ("aut iam urgentis aut certe adventantis senectutis"); at the time Cicero was 62 and Atticus 65 years of age.[32] On the other hand Cicero a little later in the *de Senectute* has Sp. Postumius Albinus (*cos.* 186 B.C.) complain of his old age, although he died when he was only about 50 years of age.[33]

It is important to return to the question of whether people of a certain age (say, in their 50s) who today might be called middle-aged, based on physical impressions made by others and/or by themselves, might in Roman times have been considered as *senes.* The Romans seem only rarely to have used any single, clear, and common Latin tag as an approximate equivalent of the English term "middle-aged": *constans* (or *confirmata, corroborata, firmata,* or *firmior*) *aetas* may cover it, but such phraseology is both uncommon and ambiguous; use of the term *gravitas* is late. The convoluted *aetas quae media dicitur* is used on occasion, as are *medium aevum* and *media aetas,* and not always as the equivalent of *iuventus.* Seneca also recognizes a stage of life between *iuventus* and *senectus* and at one point highlights the fact that there is no single, simple tag for it: "quidquid est illud inter iuvenem et senem medium." I suggest later in this book, however, that while Latin had no single term to express the idea of middle age, the concept—relating to men (and, to a lesser extent, women) in their 40s and 50s—certainly existed.[34]

But to return to the (not unrelated) question at hand: did people get older more quickly then than they do now, whether in reality or in perception? Examples have already been seen where *senex* was used of people in their late 40s; a few more references may be helpful. Sallust, in a speech made by Gaius Aurelius Cotta (*cos.* 75 B.C.) to the Roman people, has Cotta allude to his burdensome old age (*senectus gravis*), even though he was only 50 years old at the time. Marcus Aurelius calls himself a γέρων, apparently at the age of 52 years; Dionysius of Halicarnassus, on the other hand, states (to suit his arguments) that one calls a man a γέρων from the age of 69 years.[35] Horace labels the satirist Lucilius a *senex;* Jerome records that Lucilius died in 103 B.C. "at the age of 45" (anno aetatis XLVI); the second item also means that Lucilius served in the Numantine war in 134 B.C. as an *eques* at the age of 14 years, though that is not impossible. But *senex* at 45? Is this a manuscript error, or Jerome's own error in copying an earlier source (LXVI?, LXIV?), or confirmation that in earlier times old age began at 45 years of age? It is true that Cicero in the *de Senectute* has Cato state that "in the old days old age used to be said to begin from the age of 46 years" (sex et quadraginta anni . . . ita quantum spatium aetatis maiores ad senectutis initium esse voluerunt), but this relates to the age of the *senior* in a military context, and, in any case, Horace was later than Cicero, not to mention Cato.[36] It is also worth considering that Horace may be using *senex* not as an age term but as a token of respect (*OLD* s.v. *senex* 1c) and as a mark of Lucilius's senior status (the father of satire).

Such isolated and disparate examples should not be taken as evidence that old age began, or was necessarily even *thought* to have begun, at an earlier stage in the past than it does today. The maximum potential human life-span has not significantly increased over the past two thousand years, although physically and mentally life's later years may be more comfortable today than in earlier centuries. It should already be clear that old age and the impressions and images associated with it never were and still are not thought of purely or simply in terms of the number of years lived. Physical appearance, mental attitude, circumstances, and intention also affect the way a person thinks of himself or herself and is regarded by others. One rather touching illustration of this is provided in the fourth century A.D. by Ausonius; early in his marriage he urges his wife to ignore the arrival of old age when eventually it comes and for them to always call one another *iuvenis* and *puella*: "nos ignoremus, quid sit matura senectus; scire aevi meritum, non numerare decet" (Let us refuse to know the meaning of ripe old age. Better to know Time's worth, than count his years).[37] Alternatively, age terms as labels might be used as a means of imposing authority, of showing respect, or of causing calculated affront.[38]

This subjective, impressionistic use of age terms is as evident now as it doubtless was in antiquity. Some people, then as now, may have felt older than their years—in fact, some philosophers held that debauchery in one's younger years could lead to a premature old age—and may indeed have looked older than they were. Such was a conventional complaint, for example, of poets who noticed gray hairs sprouting.[39] But this is a timeless and personal complaint, not an indication of the premature aging of the ancient world's entire population. It has been assumed, however, partly on the basis that Erasmus wrote his poem "On the discomforts of old age" when he was only 39 or 40 years of age, that in the Renaissance people in their 40s were regarded as old.[40] The point is, however, that some people might regard themselves or be regarded by others as old by their appearance or circumstances rather than by their exact chronological age. Ovid, at his lowest point in exile in his early to mid-50s, felt himself an old man before his time. On the other hand, one man who died at the age of 50 years in A.D. 247 in the province of Roman Mauretania (modern Algeria) had it recorded on his tombstone that he died "in the flower of youth" (*flos iuventutis*).[41]

A passage from Aeschines is also quite instructive for comparative purposes, displaying as it does an awareness of the fact that people of the same age may look and feel considerably different.[42] Aeschines' point here is to stress that Misgolas, who took in Timarchus as his lover, is much older than he looks:

> There are some people who by nature differ a great deal from the rest of us with respect to their age [περὶ τὴν ἡλικίαν]. For some who are young [νέοι] seem mature and older [προφερεῖς καὶ πρεσβύτεροι] than they are; others, who have lived a good number of years, seem to be mere youngsters [πολὺν ἀριθμὸν χρόνου γεγονότες παντάπασι νέοι]. Misgolas is such a man. For he happens to be the same age as me and was an ephebe with me; we are now in our 45th year. I am quite gray, as you see, but he is not.

Certainly comparative historical and medical evidence would suggest that in purely biological terms people in antiquity did not on average age at a faster rate than they do today, at least not to any significant degree. General standards of health and nutrition may have in some cases speeded up the aging process, making people both look and feel older.[43] But the opposite might also have been true; the general lack of fatty and sugar-based foods and the use of walking rather than mechanical transport might have meant that those not carried off by infection or accident looked younger thanks to a comparatively healthy life-style. Again circumstances will have varied from individual to individual. The ancient medical writers were well aware that people aged at different rates, owing to a variety of factors.[44] Indeed, if we were to try to define the commencement of old age by a set number of years it might be better to adopt the suggestion of the demographer Jacob Siegel, who remarks on the notion—in itself a useful one—that instead of considering someone old after *x* number of years from birth, we might consider a numerical value for the commencement of old age based on the average number of years *until death:* "[A]ccording to this concept, old age covers the period of life beginning with the age after which the particular [population] groups have a specified average number of years to live, say 10 to 15 years."[45] Using model life tables (see Table 3 in Appendix A and Chapter 2), one can estimate that Romans probably had on average ten to fifteen more years to live from around the age of 50 to 60 years. Any figure more precise would suffer from spurious accuracy. I am not suggesting, of course, that *Romans* defined old age in this way. Furthermore, such a definition of old age would, on an individual basis, vary widely. But it does serve to underline the fact that Romans did not necessarily or typically become old at a significantly younger age than we do today.

In conclusion, one cannot and should not define general terms like *senex* by a minimum number of years. Old age was not universally regarded as beginning after the 60th (or whatever) birthday. *Senectus* seems rather to have been characterized by the physical (and perhaps mental) state of the individual. As Moses Finley observed:[46] "Statistically, today as in antiquity, the agreed points at which to draw the line in general terms seem to be either sixty or sixty-five. In concrete terms, however, there are many lines, determined by social, economic, and political considerations, for which biology provides no more than crude limits." Even in the context of Roman law (see Chapter 4), there was no specific age set down to mark the onset of *senectus*. Rules of age did exist that affected older persons, but ages involved here might range from 50 to 70 years upward, and nothing was done to mark *senes* out as an age-class apart from adults in general. An illuminating parallel example, in this instance regarding the age-category of the *iuvenis,* is provided by the jurist Ulpius Marcellus, writing in the second half of the second century A.D., who notes a (hypothetical) case in which a man in his will bequeathed all the *iuvenes* in his service to another individual. The question is asked, "a qua aetate iuvenes et in quam intellegi debeant?"—that is, by what upper and lower limits of age are *iuvenes* to be defined? Marcellus concludes that in the case of wills people write without precision (*abusive*), and each case must be judged by its own circumstances; no strict age limits can be imposed in such contexts in regard to particular terms describing general age-categories. But then he adds that it could be thought that a *iuvenis* is someone who is between the ages of the *adulescens* and the *senior:* "ceterum existimari posset iuvenis is, qui adulescentis excessit aetatem, quoad incipiat inter seniores numerari."[47] Legal definitions of age-classes overlap with general conventions; nothing more precise is required, even by the lawyer.

So we should apply no set figure when we discuss Roman old age. If at times the age of 60 years features more than others, that is not to imply that we agree with the equation that *senectus* indicates a person of 60 years or greater. In quantitative terms a rule of thumb is convenient and 60 years of age as a dividing-line can serve that purpose, as it may sometimes (but by no means always—the age is creeping up steadily) in more recent history in terms of pensions and retirement. It is not to imply that such a turning point was more significant than any other to a Roman, or even at this stage that older people were seen as a specific age-class in the Roman world. This is a theme to which we shall need to return.

How Were Statements of Age Expressed?

Attention must now be directed toward statements of age, principally their accuracy: such considerations are, above all, a necessary prelude to an analysis of rules of age in public life but also to general awareness of and attitudes toward aging. More basic, however, is the question of exactly how ages were stated linguistically. In English, as in most modern languages, it is obvious enough: someone is 60 years old—that is, has completed 60 years—or is in his or her 61st year. Such idioms are also found in Latin (*sexaginta annos natus; sexagesimo primo anno aetatis;* also simply *sexagenarius*) and in Greek (γεγονώς ἑξήκοντα ἔτη, ἑξήκοντα ἐτῶν ὤν).[48] This should be straightforward enough, despite some confusion in languages both ancient and modern about the meaning of the ordinal phrase—that is, "in one's 61st year" means 60 years old, and *not* 61 years old. A Latin tombstone inscription from Rome, for example, is quite clear. A girl died on her birthday. She had lived six years, and so was entering her seventh year: "vixit ann. vi, obit natali suo intrans annum septumum."[49]

Further confusion has arisen, however, because of a particular question regarding fourth-century B.C. Athenian rules of age, and although such aspects are beyond the chronological scope of this book, the particular theoretical problem needs to be considered here briefly. In short, it can be (and long has been) deduced from remarks by Demosthenes that at the age of 17 years a young Athenian male "came of age" and was admitted to the register of his deme and became a citizen. It is explicitly stated in the *Athenaion Politeia,* however, that the age was 18 years (ὀκτωκαίδεκα ἔτη γεγονότες). Various attempts have been made to explain away this discrepancy, from rejecting one or the other, to suggesting an otherwise unrecorded change in the law during the fourth century or, perhaps more plausibly, by explaining that at the age of 17 years an Athenian could be enrolled in the deme and at age 18 be examined before the *boule*.[50]

Another, more radical explanation, however, is most relevant for us. J. M. Carter attempted to show, on the basis of references to the lives of Pompey, Cicero, and Caesar, and a handful of Egyptian papyri representing notices of birth or status and ephebic certificates, that when it is stated in Greek that someone ὀκτωκαίδεκα ἔτη γεγονώς, it means in fact that he is 17 years old, that is, in the 18th year, and not 18 years old.[51] This attempt to save the validity of both of the texts in question is unnecessary and unsubstantiated. The literary evidence for the dates of the lives of Caesar and Pompey is problematical, and we cannot be certain that the Greek authors (Appian, Plutarch, and Cassius Dio) knew their precise ages. Julius Caesar, for example, was born on 12 or 13 July 100 B.C. (I reject Mommsen's arguments for 102). Therefore in 44 B.C., on the Ides of March, he was 55 years old. Of the two Greek authors who give his age at death, Appian says he was in his 56th year (ἔτος ἄγων ἔκτον ἐπὶ πεντήκοντα), that is, 55 years old. The other, Plutarch, says he was, by our parlance, 56 years old (γεγονὼς ἔτη πεντήκοντα καὶ ἕξ).[52] It is quite reasonable to assume that Plutarch really thought that Caesar was 56 when he died, rather than to imagine that when he said 56 he meant 55.

We shall meet many more examples of inexact ages in ancient sources, Greek and Roman. Suetonius in his life of the emperor Tiberius states that while he, Suetonius, is quite certain of Tiberius's date of birth, because it is recorded "in fastos actaque in publica," others have come up with different figures: "nec tamen desunt, qui partim antecedente anno . . . partim insequenti . . . genitum eum scribant" (and yet there are some who record that he was born in the preceding year, others in the year following).[53] Carter's argument based on references to the life of Cicero is redundant, since Plutarch says Cicero died in his 64th year and thus agrees with the other extant sources— and with reality—in stating that he died at the age of 63 years. So far, then, no particular problem.

But the papyrological evidence is less straightforward and also of particular relevance for us here, because a not inconsiderable part of this book is concerned with such testimony. Golden dismissed Carter's use of the papyri as irrelevant: "These are official documents, and their apparent use of inclusive reckoning may well be the result of Roman or other influence on bureaucratic practice. . . . This evidence *is* of interest, however, in showing that official age-reckoning need not mirror informal methods."[54] This suggestion, even more than Carter's arguments, needs concern us. In terms of old age a year one way or the other may not seem too significant, particularly in view of what we have said already about the general meaning of terms such as *senex*. However, in dealing with specific rules of age where an age of a certain number of years is stipulated as granting exemption or eligibility, or imposing liability, then, quite apart from the question of the knowledge of exact age and the accuracy of age statements, there also needs to have been certainty about the meaning of the age laid down. If, for example, one is said to be no longer compelled to attend the senate from the age of 60 years, are we to understand (and did the Romans understand) this to mean on *attaining* one's 60th year (on turning 59) or on *completing* one's 60th year (on turning 60)? The latter alternative seems to us, familiar as we are with modern idiom, the most natural and logical, but it cannot necessarily be assumed to hold good for Roman times.

By the system of inclusive reckoning,[55] when one states "two years ago" one means, in effect, "last year." The effect of this system on the Roman calendar is familiar enough to students of Latin: one writes, for example, "A.D. V Id. Apr." for 9 April, that is, by exclusive reckoning, *four* days before 13 April. Similarly, one finds such phrases as τρίτου ἔτεος for "every other year" and *tertio quoque die* for "every other day."[56] But what effect, if any, has this on statements of age? When a certain Titus states that he is (to use the Latin) "sexaginta annos natus," does this mean that he is, by our reckoning, 59 or 60 years of age? Carter cited the evidence of four so-called birth notices from Roman Egypt where inclusive reckoning seems to have been in operation.[57] To take just one example, it is stated that an individual was born in the sixteenth year of Antoninus Pius (A.D. 152/3), and in the nineteenth year (A.D. 155/6) was 4 years old (ὄντα . . . ἐτῶν τεσσάρω[ν]), where we might have expected him to be only 3 years old (at most). From this Carter concluded: "The figure four will have to be explained by supposing that a person's age could be reckoned by official years, so that if (for example) you were born at the very end of the official year, you were officially 'two' just a few days later when the next official year began. Whether this be true or not, it is perfectly clear that the words ἐτῶν τεσσάρων here mean 'in his fourth year.'" Golden, on the other hand, cited tombstone inscriptions to show that even if Carter was right in regard to the notices of birth, the rule is not generally applicable. Is it valid, however, to assume that two different systems of age-reckoning existed, one for officialdom, another for "informal" circumstances?

I would argue that no such dichotomy existed. One's first reaction is to note that such a discrepancy would have proved very problematical and confusing, but of course that is far from proof of its nonexistence: bureaucracies are not always simple or logical in their workings. It seems to me that a more obvious explanation for the problem with the Egyptian material is to be found in attributing it not to official methods of stating age but to *Egyptian* methods as opposed to the normal Greek and Roman methods. It appears that the system of dating, in Roman times by the regnal years of the emperors, may be responsible for the discrepancy: "the second regnal year began on August 29 after the accession, that is, the Alexandrian New Year."[58] Certainly it cannot be said that the feature Carter pointed to in some Egyptian papyri is a system of the *Roman* bureaucracy. A brief consideration of methods of stating age in the Roman legal corpus illustrates this.

Ulpian notes, in the context of the minimum legal age of a manumitter, that "iam autem minor [sc. viginti annis] non est, qui diem supremum agit anni vicensimi"—that is, one who has passed the final day of his 20th year is by definition 20 years of age, not less than 20. Paul states that someone is called an *anniculus,* a 1-year-old, not as soon as he is born but on his 365th day. Ulpian again, regarding applications to the praetor, writes that *pueri* are excluded from making such applications and is here explicit on the age limit: 17 years of age. Anyone less than 17 ("minorem annis decem et septem") cannot apply—anyone, he says, who has not completed their 17th year ("qui eos non in totum complevit"). With similar logic, Ulpian states, in the context of a rule of age by which those 70 years of age and over (in Latin terminology "maiores septuaginta annis"—the converse of those "minores LXX annis") are exempt from certain obligations (*munera*; see Chapter 4), that someone who has entered but not completed his 70th year is not exempt, "because anyone who has not completed his 70th year is clearly not 70 years of age or older" (quia non videtur maior esse septuaginta annis qui annum agit septuagensimum), but rather is 69 years old.[59]

Many literary sources may also be adduced to show that Greek and Latin statements of age in this regard are akin to the modern system in English. For example, Cassius Dio gives Augustus's age at death as 75 years, 10 months, and 26 days, which is exactly right: he was born on 23 September 63 B.C. and died on 19 August A.D. 14.[60] Ordinal numbers, however, produce some confusion. Thus Aulus Gellius (15.7) states that Augustus celebrated his *64th* birthday after his 63rd (climacteric) year, when in fact it would have been his *63rd* birthday. It is definitely the birthday at which he turned 63 (23 September A.D. 1). The context alone makes this clear, but it should be noted also that Lucius Caesar is still alive: the letter of Augustus that Aulus Gellius quotes is addressed to Gaius, but Augustus uses the plural ὑμῶν at the end of the letter; by the next birthday (23 September A.D. 2) Lucius was dead.[61] The logic in this particular case may be that one's actual day of birth counted as one's first birthday (in other words, inclusive reckoning), but examples to the contrary are more common.[62]

Unfortunately, no conclusive, generally applicable answer can be given to the question at hand: the evidence is too scattered and examples may be cited on both sides. But Egypt aside, the discrepancies should, most naturally be attributed to a confusion regarding the use of ordinals as compared with cardinals, and not to any definite dichotomy in methods of expressing age. Such confusion only becomes apparent—and indeed was probably only of any importance to the Romans—when dealing with specific rules of age. In a society in which exact age may have been of less importance except in certain official circumstances, it is perhaps not surprising that some confusion arose when stating age. If nothing else, this should at least warn us to exercise caution when dealing with statements of age.

How Accurate and Important Were Statements of Age?

In societies in which specific rules of age were in operation, it might be assumed that people had an accurate idea of how old they were, but such was not the case in classical times. It has long been noticed that there was a tendency on tombstone inscriptions in antiquity to estimate ages, or at least to round the figures up or down to a multiple of five. One problem with the use of tombstone inscriptions as a source of demographic data is this "heaping" of ages, as well as the significant exaggeration of age because of either ignorance or ulterior motives. The following inscription, from the province of Noricum, provides an extreme illustration both of apparent longevity and of the rounding of ages; the predominantly Celtic individuals recorded died at the ages of 60, 100, 60, 80, 70, 80, and 50 years: "M[a]ximus Masculi an(norum) LX | et Amat(ia?) Kalandina con(iunx) | Excingomaro | Valentis f(ilio) a(nnorum) C | et Tertiae Co | mati f(iliae) ux(ori) a(nnorum) LX | Masculus Excin(gomari) | f(ilius) a(nnorum) LXXX Ecouta Sex(ti) | a(nnorum) LXX Maximilla f(ilia) | Adiutus Excingomar[i] a(nnorum) LXXX | Marcianus Masc(u)li an(norum) L." [63]

The prevalence of the phenomenon of age-rounding has been remarked upon frequently. A. R. Burn, in analyzing mortality figures using Roman tombstone inscriptions, noted a "vagueness about exact ages," and in tabulating the ages of 2,675 individuals who died over the age of 30 years as recorded on their tombstones, he calculated that 1,059 (39.6%) of the figures ended in *X,* and 684 (25.6%) in *V;* that is, 65 percent of the ages given were stated as multiples of five, where we should reasonably expect on the law of averages only around 20 percent. The exaggeration of ages on tombstone inscriptions from Roman Africa is another well-known example of this practice (see Chapter 2). Such inaccuracies in stated ages need not surprise us; one can readily point to similar misrepresentations in more modern times, even in the twentieth century.[64] Apart from anything else, it is worth observing that in expressions of age in Roman numerals (as opposed to the Greek and Arabic systems), ages as multiples of five are shorter, and therefore cheaper to inscribe: for example, XL as compared with XXXVIIII or XXXIX.

Richard Duncan-Jones analyzed in some detail the phenomenon of age-rounding in the Roman Empire and its correlation to illiteracy, using modern comparative material.[65] It is impossible to produce definite figures regarding the levels of illiteracy in antiquity: apart from basic problems of definition, our primary sources do not concern themselves with the subject. In modern societies, however, we can make reasoned statements about illiteracy, and, as Duncan-Jones notes, "there appear to be few instances in available modern evidence where heavy age-rounding is not accompanied by a significant degree of illiteracy."[66] On analyzing the substantial evidence for age-rounding in the Roman Empire, it is apparent that there is sometimes a significant link between age-rounding and illiteracy: age-rounding was more prevalent away from the cities and among women and those of lower economic status, just as must have been true as a generalization of levels of literacy (incorporating such factors as social status—with some notable exceptions—and levels of education). Other and varied factors apart from illiteracy, however, should also be taken into account: the degree of a society's Romanization or the nature of the document (e.g., official or private). Rounding of an age may be a result of the ignorance of a second party about an individual's age, and not a function of that individual's own illiteracy or ignorance. It must be stressed too that illiteracy and innumeracy are not the same phenomenon; a society may experience high levels of illiteracy but its members, for a variety of reasons but particularly as a result of the level of importance placed in knowledge of numerical age or in numerical calculations (e.g., in relation to one's livelihood), may be functionally numerate.[67]

But if one accepts that age-rounding was a widespread phenomenon in the Roman Empire, one might assume that most inhabitants of the Roman Empire had little accurate knowledge of their exact age, or at least were not unduly concerned about exactly how old they were. Further consideration and qualification will be given to this point when we come to consider rules of age, particularly in the context of Roman Egypt. For the moment a more general question is worth considering: how important (if at all) were accurate and precise concepts of age in daily life and in individual mentalities?

This is not the place to enter into a philosophical discussion of the concept of time in antiquity, a theme to which we return later;[68] what we are looking for here are more everyday notions of age accuracy and the relative importance of exact age statements in daily life. Clearly, modern-day levels of precision in the calculation of age were of less relevance in ancient times; that did not stop, of course, some examples of (spurious?) accuracy, as when age at death is given on tombstones down to months, days, and on occasion, particularly on Christian tombstones, even hours and minutes, even for alleged centenarians.[69] As Nilsson argued long ago with a wealth of comparative material, concrete time-indications (by events, generations, and relative, imprecise notions of the ages of individuals) generally precede abstract numerical counting systems of time.[70] In the *Iliad* and *Odyssey,* for example, age is expressed by generations rather than years.[71] In classical Roman times, of course, abstract numerical calculation of age was widespread, at least as the extant written record presents the situation, but had not yet acquired the importance or prevalence *at a general level* that it has for most of us today.

For the average Roman—male or female—the need to know one's exact age must have been minimal. Today one's date of birth and one's age in years are very basic pieces of information that each of us needs to know for many regular transactions. Also, and perhaps partly as a consequence of the importance of knowledge of exact age, birthdays are widely celebrated in our culture with reference to one's age. In Roman times, however, while the date of one's birth might be known, it does not appear that chronological age (the exact number of years lived) was as significant as the anniversary itself, the cult of the individual's *Genius* or *Iuno*.[72] Hence the date (month and day) of one's birthday might have been better known, especially by others, than the actual year in which one was born; in an astrological context, it was also relevant to know the (alleged) precise moment of conception or of birth in terms of month, day, and hour. Whatever the mentality underlying this neglect, it does suggest that exact age was less important, apart from in the context of official rules of age.

For diverse social groups such as women and slaves, moreover, rules of age were scarcely of any consequence. For slaves (or, perhaps more to the point, their owners), minimum age for manumission was of importance; for citizen women (or their parents), age of marriage and other rules of age in the Augustan marriage legislation (see Chapter 7). For men of any but the elite class, exact knowledge of age was probably just as inessential. As argued in Chapter 5, the bureaucratic system that existed in Roman Egypt meant that officials could calculate the age of an individual from existing records and the individual himself or herself could acquire this information from the archives if he or she needed it. In other situations the need or desire to know probably never arose. In everyday situations it was probably more than enough to have some idea of the approximate age of an individual, that is, whether he or she was young or old (*puer, puella, iuvenis, virgo, senex, anus,* and so on).

The increasing importance of rules of age in the operation of the state may have in turn increased the awareness of exact age among the population, as for example in the way that ages, though often no doubt inaccurate, only begin to appear widely on tombstones in later times, in the early empire as a rule, though it will have varied from place to place.[73] It has been suggested that knowledge of age was less important in ancient times because of high levels of mortality and shorter life-spans,[74] but this is not logical: knowledge of and significance of exact age are not directly related to length of life and, besides, many Romans did survive to an advanced age (see Chapter 2). More to the point, complications in calculating age may have deterred many from bothering. Registration of birth (discussed in Chapter 6) may have been the norm for legitimate citizen births from A.D. 4, but notices of birth—extant examples of which, even from Roman Egypt, are very scarce—were not items that every individual would need to have had readily available. Furthermore, with involved chronological systems such as dating by consuls, the calculation of one's age from such references would entail the use of a list of *fasti* and some involved finger-counting, far more complicated than modern-day methods of simple decimal addition and subtraction, and more prone to error.[75] Consider, for example, Pliny the Younger's description (*Ep.* 2.20.1) of the *captator* Regulus calculating the age of the widow Verania, and the involved discussion in Apuleius (*Apol.* 89) on the disputed age of Pudentilla: the fact that there could be alleged doubt as to whether she was 60 or about 40 years of age is quite surprising and, in this context, very illuminating (see Chapter 6). Furthermore, it is to be noted that there was no *universally used* numerical system of identifying years in the Roman period.[76]

Yet even these points in themselves are not reasons for a lack of importance in exact knowledge and statement of age: if anything, they are rather symptoms. More basically and less tangibly, the relative unimportance placed in most contexts in exact age is a result of a different mentality, a general lack of need rather than of ability. Not only was it not felt necessary to know exactly one's own age or the age of anyone else *except on an official level,* but also ages in years could be given in a historical description or biography (e.g., as a conventional part of a death notice) without the importance being placed on them that such statements have today—hence the discrepancies and errors that cause modern editors so much disquietude.[77]

In short, a tendency existed in the Roman world to generalize in terms of definitions and statements of age. There is, to be sure, a conflict here. On the one hand, knowledge of exact chronological age was of less importance than we are accustomed to today. On the other hand, exact rules of age existed and seem to have operated in a fashion very similar to that in modern Western societies. Resolving or, at least, understanding this conflict will be a recurring theme of this book. But first we need to meet some older Romans.

Two

The Demography of Old Age

f the beginning of old age cannot be defined by a set number of years, we must still consider what proportion of the population of the Roman world we mean when we use such a term as "the elderly." This chapter, in relation to age structure, tends to work with the round figure of 60 years as the minimum age to qualify as "old," without wishing to suggest that this is what ancient writers always or necessarily ever meant when they mentioned old age. I have dealt elsewhere with more general considerations of the demography of the Roman world;[1] here I focus on the subject of old age, specifically what the ancient testimony does or does not tell us about the demographic realities of old age in the Roman world; and, briefly, what light modern demographic models may throw on this question.

Ancient Evidence

Most ancient testimony that has been used to elucidate the demographic structure of the ancient world—tombstone inscriptions, mummy labels, tax receipts, legal texts, and skeletal material—is, unfortunately, all but useless. At the very best such testimony may often be said to support the notion that average life expectancy at birth in the ancient world was of the range of twenty to thirty years. This is what we would expect anyway. The Roman Egyptian census material, sparse as it is, is the best primary information that we have, and it too supports this notion, while also, after sophisticated manipulation, providing further details regarding probable levels of fertility and even, perhaps, of migration.[2] There is no room or need here to delve into this further. Of more immediate concern is what the primary evidence we have tells us about the demographic realities of old age.

Epitaphs from the Roman world commemorating elderly deceased persons present an image of incredible longevity in enormous numbers, particularly in the case of Roman Africa, where the proportion of centenarians is obviously grossly inflated. For example, in a collection of 10,697 ages at death from Roman African epitaphs, one finds that 2,835 give ages of 70 years or more (i.e., 26.50%), 317 of 100 years or more (2.96%), and 27 of 120 years or more (0.25%). Among many striking examples from Africa, it is worth citing the case of Publius Aelius Cattus, who set up a tomb for himself and his wife, along with his daughter-in-law; on the epitaph it is recorded that at the age of 104 years he was still riding around, supervising its construction, and in fine fettle (*vegetus*).[3] The fact that the epigraphic "statistics" from Roman Africa present the absurd image of an elderly population both relatively larger and older than any in the Western world today has not deterred some scholars from believing that Africans really did enjoy such longevity in such great numbers, due apparently to climatic advantages, high altitudes, and/or a healthy life-style in the countryside.[4] It is possible that there were more elderly people in the countryside than in the cities in the Roman world: evidence is lacking, but certainly the high population density of urban areas will not have been conducive to long life. It may also be argued that in an urban environment a higher valuation would have been placed in the young.[5] But apart from the fact that most of the deceased recorded on African tombstones came from urban areas anyway, no life-style—ancient or modern—is so healthy as to produce such a high proportion of people of such advanced ages. Rather what we are seeing here are biases both in the statements of age and in the custom of commemoration of different age-groups in different places.

In terms of geographical distortions the case of Africa and its centenarians highlights the extremes of the variations in life expectancy figures to be obtained from tombstone data from different regions. The inhabitants of Castellum Celtianum in Africa, for example, enjoyed an apparent average life expectancy at birth of 60.2 years (sample size = 1,258 individual ages); on the other hand inscriptions from Virunum in Noricum produce a figure of only 18.1 years (with a sample of only sixty-five ages). The sample from Castellum Celtianum consists of 494 (39.3%) ages of 70 years or more and only 6 (0.5%) under 10 years of age; Virunum, on the other hand, has 19 (29.2%) ages under 10 years and only 1 (1.5%) over 70 years of age.[6] Such distorting variations occur throughout samples for different localities. It is highly improbable that people really did live much longer lives in much greater numbers and suffer from negligible mortality rates in their early years in certain parts of the empire in sharp contrast to others. Rather, these variations reflect differences not in age-specific mortality rates so much as in customs of commemorating different age-groups. The case of Africa makes this most clear.[7] What is more, customs of commemoration differed over time and locale not only in the age-groups commemorated but also in whether age at death was recorded at all.

Census documents, on the other hand, might be expected to furnish more reliable figures. There is always the problem in censuses, however, even today, that individual declarants may be ignorant of or lie about their ages, the latter case being particularly evident when the census is for fiscal rather than purely demographic purposes. That such inaccuracies might occur in the ancient world is indicated by the figures recorded by Pliny and Phlegon, apparently derived from the Roman census of A.D. 73/4; here an incredible number of centenarians is reported for the eighth *regio* of Italy, up to the age of 150 years.[8] The data derived from these two authors are summarized in Table 2 in Appendix A.

My point is a general one: the figures from both authors would have the air of genuine authority and authenticity if it were not for two facts: (1) the authors do not agree one with the other (in Phlegon a list of individuals aged between 121 and 130 years is lacking, probably as a result of a manuscript omission rather than of a lack of alleged survivors at those ages, but even if we allow for this omission, Pliny's and Phlegon's figures never match up); and (2) such a high number of centenarians is improbable, to say the least.[9] If Phlegon's detailed list alone had survived, and if the ages stated were of a much lower order, a dismissal of the evidence would be considered ill-founded because of their (alleged) empirical basis. As they stand, few would consider these two literary sources as worthy of serious demographic consideration. Figures such as these represent, I would argue, the heightened status that might be accorded to extreme old age. In demographic terms, perhaps the evidence from Pliny and Phlegon should warn us about the efficacy of the ancient methods used in the collection of census data, if not also about the accuracy of the resulting totals, such as those that are preserved for the census of Roman citizens in the Republic and up to the time of Claudius (see Chapter 6). In the case of the Roman Egyptian census data of the imperial period, however, no such exaggeration is evident. Only one person, a male, is said to be over the age of 80 years at the time of the declaration. The age-spread of the older people registered is not perfect, to be sure, but one would not expect it to be in such a small sample. Age-rounding at older ages and so-called age-shoving (thus accounting for what seems to be remarkably low mortality levels in the seventh decade) are also typically more prevalent.[10] The utility of these figures in terms of older people is limited, however, simply by the size and scope of the sample.

If only limited information about the proportion of elderly individuals in the ancient population is available from the census material, much more might be adduced from the literary testimony. It will be useful to consider one ancient observation on population, related in particular to older people, in order to highlight the difficulties involved in interpreting literary texts. Eusebius records a letter written by Dionysius, bishop of Alexandria, to a bishop elsewhere in Egypt around A.D. 262, at the time of plague and sedition in the Egyptian capital:

> Men wonder and are at a loss as to the reason for these continuous pestilences, these chronic illnesses, all these kinds of deadly diseases, this varied and vast destruction of mankind; they cannot understand why this very great city of ours no longer bears in it as great a number of inhabitants as before, from infant children right up to the most advanced in age [μέχρι τῶν εἰς ἄκρον γεγηρακότων], as it once supported of those whom it called "hearty old men" [ὠμογέροντας]. But at that time those aged between 40 and 70 years were so much more numerous that now their num-

ber cannot be filled out when all those from 14 to 80 years of age are enrolled and counted together for the public grain distribution [τὸ δημόσιον σιτηρέσιον], and those who appear youngest have become, as it were, the contemporaries of those who in the past were the oldest. And thus, on seeing the human race on the earth constantly diminishing and wasting away, they do not tremble, though their complete obliteration is increasing and advancing.[11]

If the figures quoted here are at all accurate then we are looking at a severe decline in population numbers, so that, by Dionysius's account, in circa 262 the total number of people aged between 14 and 80 years was smaller than the number of those aged between 40 and 70 years at an earlier date. The severity of such an alleged population decline may be illustrated by supposing that, at its height, the population of Alexandria stood at half a million. A reasonable estimate of the proportion of this number aged between 40 and 70 years, male and female, if we assume for the moment a stationary population with average life expectancy at birth of around twenty-five years (e_0 = 25), would be 25 percent, that is, 125,000 individuals aged between 40 and 70 years. Now, if 125,000 was the total number of people aged between 14 and 80 years in circa A.D. 262, then this would suggest a total population (if the 14 to 80 age-group represented about two-thirds of the population) of only 190,000, a fall from the earlier figure of 310,000, or 62 percent.

This demographic use of a fairly obscure literary tidbit has a rather longer history than I had originally suspected when I wrote my book on Roman demography. Edward Gibbon used it in much the same way (and rather more elegantly) more than 200 years before me in *The History of the Decline and Fall of the Roman Empire*:

> We have the knowledge of a very curious circumstance, of some use perhaps in the melancholy calculation of human calamities. An exact register was kept at Alexandria of all the citizens entitled to receive the distribution of corn. It was found, that the ancient number of those comprised between the ages of forty and seventy, had been equal to the whole sum of claimants, from fourteen to fourscore years of age, who remained alive after the reign of Gallienus. Applying this authentic fact to the most correct tables of mortality, it evidently proves, that above half the people of Alexandria had perished; and could we venture to extend the analogy to the other

provinces, we might suspect, that war, pestilence, and famine, had consumed, in a few years, the moiety of the human species.[12]

But it is unlikely that the population of Alexandria fell from, say, 500,000 to 190,000 over a short time. The massacre in Alexandria carried out by Caracalla in A.D. 215 is perhaps as close as one might get to the type of decline Dionysius suggests. It is recorded by Cassius Dio (*Epitome* 77.22) that Caracalla all but wiped out the entire population; the author of the life of Caracalla in the *Historia Augusta* (*Carac.* 6) and Herodian (4.9.4–8) both suggest that his onslaught was particularly directed against males of military age. But even if the events of circa A.D. 262 were just as cataclysmic as that earlier episode, I doubt that this passage can be regarded as reliable evidence for such an occurrence. Gibbon makes the assumption that the figures quoted by Dionysius (as quoted by Eusebius) are authentic and exact. Perhaps they are—in several respects, they are quite unique—but their accuracy or otherwise is only one of many variables to be taken into account. Without knowing how long the grain distribution has operated in Alexandria,[13] one cannot measure the chronology of the alleged decline. Estimates of the population of Alexandria at any time in antiquity are highly speculative,[14] and the choice of the "most correct" model life tables is also open to debate. Gibbon took the demographic information one step further, by suggesting its application to the wider sphere: not just Alexandria, not just Egypt, but the Roman Empire as a whole, or indeed the entire human race. From one letter in Alexandria in circa A.D. 262 we have moved to the decline and fall of the Roman Empire. This too is an unsafe practice, albeit a tempting one in view of the paucity of primary evidence.

What makes this reference particularly interesting in this context is not so much the alleged reality of the demography of Alexandria around A.D. 262, but both the awareness of the different relative sizes of age-classes within a population (however inexact), and also the means by which a decline in population numbers has been measured. A catastrophe of this order, if it were really to occur as described, would be clearly visible to the intelligent observer, as it was apparently to Dionysius. His depiction of an aging population actually suggests a fall in fertility levels, rather than a rise in mortality rates, over the long term, unless age-specific mortality (i.e., specific to the young) on a dramatic scale is responsible. Whatever the real dimensions of this decline, however, Dionysius's discussion of its magnitude by reference to the numbers eligible for the grain distribution is in fact one way in which population numbers and large shifts in size would have been detectable at the time. Yet increased mortality and/or decreased fertility may not have been the only possible causes of such a decline in numbers of people applying for the distribution. Such factors as migration, or simply an unwillingness to apply for whatever reason, might also present the image of a decline in population size. It is unlikely that Dionysius's description of the situation in Alexandria is an accurate reflection of *long-term* demographic reality: the sort of decline he implies, over what was probably a relatively short space of time, would have been too severe for the population of Alexandria to have survived through successive generations. Perhaps a significant degree of exaggeration, to suit the argument of the letter, is to be assumed. The effects of the combined devastation brought on by plague and war may have caused a dramatic increase in mortality rates in the short term, but it is unlikely that these effects were really experienced over a protracted period in terms of mortality and fertility levels.

We cannot have complete and precise faith in everything an ancient author tells us about population sizes and demographic trends, at least not without considering the author's source of information and his purpose in giving this information. One must take into account also, of course, the notorious problem of the transmission of numerals in manuscripts. In regard to old age, we can find many extremely elderly people recorded, especially on the many tombstone inscriptions: of the circa 10,000 tombstone inscriptions from Rome contained in *CIL* 6, the oldest person recorded, a freedman, died, it is said, at the age of 113 years (*CIL* 6.6835); nine individuals in all are recorded as dying at 100 years of age or over. But there are also many instances that may be cited from classical literature. It is difficult to know for certain whether an apparent Methuselah really did live as long as a literary source or an epitaph claims. Comparative evidence tells us that the number of alleged centenarians in Roman Africa is a gross exaggeration, but that is not to say that *some* people did not survive the century mark and beyond.

Pliny the Elder, on the topic of human longevity,[15] reflects that various fabulous ages attributed to legendary figures are "uncertain" (*incertum*) because of "problems of chronology" (*inscitia temporum*). He then dismisses such legends as Arganthonius, king of the Tartesii in the sixth century B.C., living to the age of 150 years; a few paragraphs later he adds that it is an "acknowledged fact" (*confessum*) that Arganthonius reigned for eighty years, beginning at age 39. A variety of other sources highlights the confusion and diversity.[16] Whole races of people, mostly far distant if not mythical, were routinely credited with fantastic life-spans, just as were various species of animals which were synonymous with long life (the crow, crab, stag, and raven, not to mention, of course, the phoenix).[17] Figures of 300 or 500 years feature in classical literature for pseudohistorical individuals, while mythical characters, such as Tithonus, Teiresias, and the Sibyls, were attributed with lives of several centuries, if not of eternity.[18] One thinks also in this context of such individuals as Charon the ferryman, who enjoyed a "cruda viridisque senectus";[19] Aeson, the father of Jason, who was rejuvenated by Medea, and in the same context—but, by most accounts, with less success—Aeson's half brother Pelias, king of Iolcus;[20] Cadmus, king of Tyre; and from Homer such figures as Nestor, king of Pylos, the epitome of old age throughout classical times, who outlived three generations, or, as it came to be commonly understood, three lifetimes or even centuries;[21] as well as Laertes, king of Ithaca and the father of Odysseus; Anchises, the father of Aeneas; and the Trojan elder Antenor. Outdoing them all is one Makroseiris, 5,000 years old and buried on an island near Athens, according to his tombstone as recorded by Phlegon.[22] From the Old Testament we are familiar enough with fabulous ages being attributed to figures from the past. Josephus cites as authorities that the ancients lived to a thousand years such writers as Hesiod, Hecataeus, Hellanicus, Acusilaus, Ephorus, and Nicolaus.[23]

Various kings, poets and prophets of archaic times were credited with ages well in excess of a century, sometimes with spurious precision. The poet and seer Epimenides of Crete, for example, was traditionally said to have lived for 157 years—57 (Varro says 50) of which were spent asleep in a cave—although one source, Xenophanes of Colophon, gives 154, and another, apparently the Cretans themselves,

299 years (another example of pedantic squabbling for the sake of spurious accuracy).[24] Aegimius, the legendary king of Dorus, lived to the age of 200 years; Cinyras of Cyprus, to 160 years; and Dando of Illyria, to 500 years.[25] Lycurgus of Sparta is said, more modestly, to have lived to the age of 85 years ([Lucian] *Macr.* 28). Rome's second king, Numa Pompilius, and its sixth, Servius Tullius, were also held to have exceeded the age of 80 years, while Tarquinius Superbus was apparently over the age of 90 years.[26] Old age was conventionally associated with wisdom, since the time of Homer's Nestor at least (of course, Homer was himself traditionally said to have lived to a ripe old age).[27] Thus, for example, the Seven Sages of Greece were credited with extended life-spans.[28] Likewise, the somewhat nebulous figure of Pythagoras in the sixth century is usually credited with 80 or 90 years, though pseudo-Galen says he lived to his 117th year and in fine fettle, thanks to a special potion made of vinegar of squill.[29] This confusion concerning ages at death is a common one, and it is clear that the longevity of someone long dead, especially of someone notable, might be exaggerated as time passed and as circumstances suited.

There is ample historical evidence from the classical period, however, of people surviving into their 90s and beyond, and in many instances there is little obvious reason to doubt the figures quoted. It is important to remember that, despite the demographic transition following the industrial revolution and the advances in medicine in the twentieth century, people do not live significantly longer today than they did in the historical past. In classical times, dying when one was in one's 60s or beyond was regarded—at least officially—as natural; to die younger was usually seen as a harsh and unnatural fate. Hence Livy's eulogy of Cicero (frag. 60 Jal, *ap.* Seneca *Suas.* 6.22) records that he died aged 63 years, an age, we are told, that would not be considered *immatura* for death even if force had not been responsible. Statius states that his father died at an age (65 years) that was not too young nor too old: "raperis, genitor, non indigus aevi, non nimius." This is perhaps still somewhat younger than what we today might regard as a "decent" or natural age to die, and of course Statius might have said this of whatever age his father died. But the argument would not have been possible if his father had died at a much younger age.[30] Dying in old age, it was said, is like coming to the end of a journey and reaching a safe harbor, whereas the death of the young is like a shipwreck.[31] The simple demographic fact is that a greater percentage of the population survives into old age today, not that each individual lives significantly longer than elderly individuals did in past times. No precise figure can be given for the maximum potential life-span, but something around 115 (± 5?) years seems to be of the right order.[32]

To illustrate the frequency with which very aged individuals are encountered in the literary and historical record from antiquity, I have prepared a list to supplement the names we have already mentioned; I include Greeks as well as Romans, mainly because aged Greeks were of interest, even more perhaps than Romans, to our Roman authors, including Cicero in his *de Senectute*.[33] This list is intended to provide illustrative examples; it is not an exhaustive catalog. A roughly chronological order (by assumed date of death) is used; if nothing else, this serves to illustrate the fact that people survived into old age at every period of ancient history. In the archaic cases especially, of course, there is no guarantee of accuracy, and round numbers will attract suspicion. It is also noteworthy how frequently philosophers appear[34]— and how rarely women feature: this is a reflection of a male world, not necessarily of higher female mortality at younger ages.[35]

Such figures as these represent ages that range from the quite possible to the highly suspicious, and doubts remain as to their accuracy in many cases, as with the individuals listed from the census of A.D. 74 by Pliny and Phlegon. At the extreme is Zocles, a Samothracian whom, according to Pliny, C. Licinius Mucianus wrote that he saw (presumably under Nero) at the age of 104 years, having just grown a new set of teeth.[36] But while the borderlines between history, fable, and myth may at times become hazy, it does emerge both that some people in antiquity lived into extreme old age and that ancient writers were aware of the fact; indeed, they sometimes dwelt on it at some length. Notions of maximum life-span do occur in antiquity, though without any wide consensus and usually without reference to purely biological aspects of aging. As with the *aetates hominum*, discussed in the previous chapter, a certain mathematical and astrological atmosphere pervades many of the references, largely as a result of Greek influences. Favorites for maximum life-span are numbers that are multiples of seven or nine, or both (63 years was regarded by some as a limit).[37] One estimate of maximum life-span, in the astronomical view of the *secta* of Aesculapius, goes as low as the 54th year, at least for people born at certain times of the day; again the number has mathematical significance $(1 + 2 + 3 + 2^2 + 3^2 + 2^3 + 3^3)$.[38] Pliny the Younger states that one's 67th year is a good age for even the most robust constitution, and Solon speaks of a figure of 70 years, although this was later amended to 80, apparently in the light of his own experience. Four score years, indeed, is not an uncommon upper limit,[39] while the Peripatetic Staseas of Naples (second or first century B.C.) apparently added two hebdomads to Solon's system and gave 84 years as the maximum life-span.[40]

These figures are somewhat on the low side. Often, however, ancient estimates of maximum life-span are much closer to our own figure of around 115 years. Ausonius, modifying Hesiod, stated that 96 years was a limit, while 100 years was a natural favorite for many.[41] Such a limit is also reflected in the traditional timing of the secular games, every 100 or 110 years.[42] Pliny gives a variety of figures derived from "sideralis scientiae sententia," ranging from 112 to 116 years, and 124 in Italy, while a figure of 120 years also emerges as a common notion of maximum life-span.[43]

There emerges the recognition of an awareness in antiquity that some people could and did live well beyond the life-span of the average individual. While we cannot deduce from all this the number of people who lived to such advanced ages, it is clear that they were regarded as exceptional. On the other hand, individuals did survive in significant numbers to the age of (for example) 60 years, and while they may have been held to be lucky—or unlucky, depending upon one's viewpoint—they were not regarded as unique or particularly extraordinary. In order to quantify these statements regarding survival to certain ages, we need now to move from ancient evidence to modern comparative material.

Demographic Models

We enter now the realm of plausibility and probability. What we should aim to end up with are not answers to such a question as: How many elderly people were there in the Roman Empire in A.D. 100? but rather probable answers to such a question as: What was the approximate age structure of a population experiencing certain factors such as high mortality rates? In the absence of hard factual statistics (and this is true to varying degrees in all demographic history, as well as in the demography of many modern countries) we can increase our awareness of the demographic realities of the ancient world on a broad scale. General statements on population trends in the ancient world can rarely ever be proved by reliable evidence from the literary sources. They must rest on what may be held to be plausible or probable rather than on what is certain. The process does, at the very least, eradicate the impossible, as with Roman Africa's host of centenarians.

It should be understood that, while the population of the Roman world may not be directly comparable in terms of mortality and fertility levels with any single present-day or other well-documented historical population, the basic concepts in the study of demography as developed in modern times are of universal application in the trends they describe. I have argued elsewhere at greater length that modern demographic models relating to well-documented populations may be utilized in analyzing populations in earlier history.[44] In terms of many demographic variables, the ancient world had more in common with modern, so-called underdeveloped countries than with the developed, postindustrial world. Our notions of population are perhaps too greatly influenced by the nature of the societies in which we live today. From the nineteenth century onward the population structure of the developing and developed Western world has seen unprecedented and dramatic changes where the combined effect of a significant drop in mortality rates, due largely to improved hygiene and medical standards, and of an extreme decline in fertility rates, sometimes to below replacement levels, led to a quite different demographic regime than had ever been experienced before. Within recent generations most societies have experienced a phenomenal increase in the proportion and number of older people. In the United States and United Kingdom today, for example, more than 15 percent of the population is over the age of 65 years, compared with less than 5 percent a century ago, and the percentage is continuing to increase. Average life expectancy at birth in such countries is now around 80 years for females and 75 for males, and these figures too continue to rise. But it must be stressed again that this does not mean that people are living significantly longer lives today than they did some 2,000 years ago, only that *more* are surviving into old age because of a lowered risk of mortality in earlier years, and that the proportion of older people is also growing because of lower fertility rates. Average life expectancy can be a misleading concept, especially in regard to high mortality regimes where so many die in infancy. It is often useful to talk also of average life expectancy at age 5 or 10 years, that is, the average number of years lived after reaching this birthday, for this method obviates the bias produced by high infant and early childhood mortality.[45] In modern, so-called post-transitional populations, infant and early childhood mortality is minimal, and indeed the age-group of 10 to 15 years is seen as the least at risk. In ancient societies, on the other hand, as with other preindustrial populations, quite the opposite was true. While some people did live on to extreme old age, mortality was more severe throughout the earlier years, and this dramatically affected the demographic picture.

The three basic factors that determine the size and structure of all populations in purely demographic terms are mortality, fertility, and migration. The basic idea of a model life table is to provide information on populations for which data are insufficient or of dubious value, in order to test the validity or demographic plausibility of certain assumptions about the population being analyzed. The basic and proven assumption on which such model life tables work is that age *patterns* of mortality are fundamentally the same irrespective of time and place. The precise mortality rates may differ, but the overall pattern is constant: a high level of mortality in infancy (though exactly how high may differ widely), a sharp decline to lower mortality levels in later childhood and adolescence, and then gradually increasing mortality levels into old age.

Because there is no space here to discuss the construction and types of model life tables, I analyze information relevant to this book that can be derived from one such set of tables, Coale-Demeny[2] Model West.[46] One assumes a stationary population: the birth and death rates are constant over an indefinite period and are equal (the growth rate is zero), and the population is closed, that is, there is no effect from migration, and any short term fluctuations as a result of such factors as plague, war, and famine are smoothed out over the long term. The population's age composition is self-replicating and becomes fixed. The main benefit of such assumptions and of working with a stationary population is that from the basic information on age-specific mortality rates a complete life table may be constructed, and the full size and structure of the population can be analyzed. In reality, of course, no population is perfectly stationary. Nevertheless, the method provides a useful and illuminating model of population dynamics, sufficient for our purposes. It needs always to be borne in mind, however, that the information thus obtained reflects probabilities.

If we are to use the Coale-Demeny model life tables as the means for gaining an awareness of the probable population structure of the Roman Empire, we need to have an idea of the sort of population in actual terms with which we are dealing. There is every reason to believe that the average life expectancy at birth of the population of the Roman Empire as a whole was in the range of 20 to 30 years. If it fell below 20 years over a long period the population would have fallen into rapid decline. The upper limit is set on the comparative evidence of preindustrial populations in general: an e_0 in excess of 30 years would imply a quite different demographic regime, with infant mortality in particular far lower than might be anticipated with medical care, levels of nutrition, and environmental conditions being what they were. An estimate in the 20- to 30-year range is clearly right as a generalization, allowing for significant variations over time and space. With this in mind, Table 3 (in Appendix A) gives the relevant figures from Model West describing a stationary population with average life expectancies at birth ranging from 20 to 30 years. In each case the e_x column gives the various values for average life expectancies at different ages (i.e., how many more years on average an individual may be expected to live after age x), and the C_x column the proportion of the population in this age-group (i.e., $C_{30} = 7.36$ means that 7.36 percent of this stationary population at any one time may be expected to be between the ages of 30 and 34 years inclusive). Below these two columns are given the average age of the living population and the proportion of the population aged 60 years and over (C_{60+}).

What emerges is some idea of the age structure of the population of the Roman world. Various relevant—and self-explanatory—figures are set out in Table 4 (in Appendix A), where e_0 is set at 25 years. These figures will be of use in considering the realities of old age in the chapters that follow. Note in particular that while the older members of a population group of this kind may be few in number as compared with the young, their numbers are not so insignificant, particularly in the 60- to 69-year age bracket. Perhaps most striking of all, however, is just how predominant numerically the young were. It was, one might say, not just a man's world: it was a *young* man's world.

I am not suggesting that exactly 6.98 percent of the population of the Roman Empire was over the age of 60 years, but that a proportion of this magnitude, around 6 to 8 percent, is probable as a generalization over space and time. If we estimate the population of the Roman Empire at any one time to have been of the order of 60 million, the number of people one might classify as elderly would have been around 4 million, a not insignificant figure. That the proportion of centenarians in antiquity was in reality far smaller than it is in the modern world today is an obvious assumption. Model life tables would suggest that in a stationary population with average life expectancy at birth of 25 years, where the risk of dying increases sharply after the age of 50 years, only 30 to 60 individuals from an original birth cohort of 100,000 would on average survive to the age of 90 years, at which age average life expectancy would have been less than 2 years. Of this group only a handful would have reached the age of 95 years. This number would increase very slightly only if the population was in decline, that is, if fertility was relatively low.

In other words, only a very select few ancient Greeks and Romans could have genuinely boasted of passing the century mark, and demographically that is not significant, however important it may have been to those individuals at the time. While many of the "records" of ancient centenarians should be regarded as fabrications, whether on tombstone inscriptions from Africa or in census totals from Italy, there is less reason to doubt that, to take an extreme example, the orator and sophist Gorgias of Leontini did indeed live to be 108 ($\pm$ 1) years of age.[47] But it is certainly just as true that Gorgias, born around the time of the Persian Wars, must have been very aware over a century later that he was alone of his generation, even if he claimed to have no complaint against old age.[48]

One demographic statistic of particular interest in the context of this book is the so-called dependency ratio. This is a standard demographic measure, reflecting the proportion of a population under the age of 15 years and over the age of (usually) 59 years—two groups said to be economically dependent or inactive—as compared to members of the population between these two ages constituting the "productive" sector. The term "dependency" in an ancient context is not particularly valid (see Chapter 8), but the measure itself is a useful aid to reflection on the age structure of the population.[49] The dependency ratio of a modern Western population is probably of the same order as an ancient one—around 0.6 (i.e., around 40 percent of the population is under the age of 15 years or over the age of 59 years)—but for very different reasons: in the modern population cohort the percentage of those over the age of 59 years is relatively considerable, whereas in an ancient population it is the group under the age of 15 years that has by far the greater weight (see again Table 4A). In an ancient population those under the age of 15 would have outnumbered those over the age of 59 years by the order of something like five to one; in a modern Western population cohort, on the other hand, the proportions are almost equal. The ancient population was, in this sense, a very young one.

Model life tables may be further used in a computer simulation to create an imaginary life-course history, to trace individuals within a population cohort as they age (see Chapter 8).[50] The computer simulation is of great interest at one level for the Roman social historian in terms of considering the likelihood of a Roman's losing his or her parents early in life, and of a Roman male's, for example, still being *in patria potestate* as a young adult. But another striking and significant result in the context of our discussion of old age is the relative rarity in a population of this type of three generations of a family's being coexistent (let alone living in the same house). The existence in Latin of names of relatives to the sixth degree (*gradus*) in either direction of the *ego*, that is, up to great-great-great-great-grandparent (*tritavus, tritavia*) and down to great-great-great-great-grandchild (*trinepos, trineptis*),[51] is of course no indication that the extended family was the norm, any more than it indicates the likelihood that such distant kin remained alive. For example, if we assume a model in which average life expectancy at birth is 25 years and in which males marry at an average

age of 30 years, females at 20 years,[52] then it can be calculated, for example, that at birth only one in three Romans had a maternal grandfather or paternal grandmother still alive, only one in two had their maternal grandmother still alive, and, even more striking, only one in six or seven Romans had at birth a living paternal grandfather (under whose *potestas* they would normally be if he were alive). By the age of 10 years, the average Roman had only a one in two chance of having *any* of his grandparents alive. Fewer than 1 in 100 Romans of the age of 20 years would have had a surviving paternal grandfather.

The difference in terms of paternal and maternal lines is fairly easy to explain, in view of the different average marriage ages of males and females in the Roman world. A woman might become a grandmother by her daughter when the latter was in her late teens, and hence the grandmother herself was possibly not yet 40 years of age. A man would not normally expect to become a paternal grandfather, on the other hand, before the age of around 60 years. In short, at any particular moment in most Romans' life courses, living ascendants on the maternal side of the family must typically have been more common, relatively speaking, than on the paternal side. It must be added, most adult Romans would have had only shadowy memories of their grandparents, paternal or maternal. It is a fact that we encounter grandparents in the literary testimony from the Roman world surprisingly rarely, and most references are to the commemoration or listing of deceased ancestors.[53]

But even taking into account demographic considerations, grandparents feature more rarely as dedicators on commemorative tombstone inscriptions than we might have expected; the nuclear family was the focus of obligations and of affection, at least in terms of the individuals in the western empire who are recorded on epitaphs; grandparents are only mentioned in unusual cases, where, for demographic or other reasons, others were not available.[54] It is a striking fact that, when parents are not there to commemorate their children, those deceased individuals are more typically commemorated by individuals outside the extended family grouping, such as friends and dependents, rather than by grandparents (including the paternal grandfather) or by other extranuclear members (or indeed, very often, by siblings).[55]

The reality was not always quite that straightforward, however, at least in terms of an individual's entire life course. Although the traditional image of the extended family as dominant in antiquity (and beyond) has been effectively quashed by recent historians of the family, it must still be realized that it would have been inevitable that, at some points in the life cycle of a household, some more distant relatives (including grandparents, paternal and maternal, and grandchildren) often remained within the family home, especially among the lower classes and away from the city.[56] Multigenerational households, though rarely mentioned in the written sources, would not have been so very unusual. From the Roman Egyptian census material we have thirty-one examples of three-generational households (making up around 13% of reconstructable households from the data): fifteen cases of a grandmother (eleven paternal, three maternal, and one case where the grandmother is both the paternal and the maternal of the same child), nine cases of a grandfather (eight paternal, and in one case both paternal and maternal of the same children: a son and daughter, born of different mothers, have married one another and produced children), and seven cases of two grandparents in a single household (of married couples, twice are they the paternal grandparents, once the maternal, and in three cases the couple's children have married one another and had their own children, so that the grandparents are both paternal and maternal; in the other case the two co-resident grandparents are not married to one another: two sisters are co-resident and are both grandmothers, one paternal, one maternal, the son of one having married the daughter of the other, who then produced twins). In one case we have a four-generational household, where the paternal great-grandmother (who makes the declaration) is 74 years old and her great-granddaughter is 6 years old.[57] The moral duty of caring for one's aged parents (see Chapter 8) may have extended, therefore, to sharing one's roof with them—*pietas* toward parents aside, possibly the elderly relations could perform functions such as child minding,[58] although the presence of slaves in the *familia* may have both provided independent support for older family members and, conversely, made some of the traditional roles of grandparents in preindustrial societies redundant in the Roman context.[59] As a result of demographic realities, at any rate, any three-generational living arrangements would usually have been of a short-term nature anyway.

It is worth adding that living grandparents are not totally absent from our sources, nor is the focus solely on the paternal side (as the theory of the system of *patria potestas* might have suggested). It should be remembered that, in the light of relative marriage ages, one's daughters might be expected to start producing offspring much sooner than one's sons, and in a context in which grandchildren were regarded conventionally as a blessing, this must have heightened the value of such descendants.[60] Pliny was very aware that his wife Calpurnia's grandfather, Calpurnius Fabatus, was anxious to have *pronepotes*. Apart from everything else, grandchildren might be seen as *consolatio* and comfort for the loss of one's own children. Seneca offers such consolation to Marcia, the daughter of Cremutius Cordus, who had lost two sons; consolation for the loss of one of these sons is provided, according to Seneca, by the fact that that son's two daughters are still alive, and that Marcia's two daughters have themselves produced children.[61]

Maternal ascendants were held to have alimentary obligations toward their grandchildren in connection with *pietas,* even though in theory they belonged to a separate *familia.* The same was true in cases of inheritance: in the Roman aristocratic mentality it was expected that one would remember one's grandchildren, irrespective, it would seem, of whether they were the offspring of a son or of a daughter.[62] One well-known case highlights this factor, even though, as with so much anecdotal material, it presents an atypical and somewhat sinister situation. But the atypicality lies not in the involvement of an *avus maternus* but in his explicit motivations. A maternal grandfather makes his granddaughter his heiress on the condition that she is freed from the *manus* of her father (the brother of Domitius Tullus).[63] From an earlier period, we may observe that Cicero made provision for his short-lived grandson, the child of Dolabella and Tullia in 45 B.C. (so, be it noted in passing, only a year previous to the composition of the *de Senectute*).[64] This is a reflection of the reality of expected family affections, not mere theoretical legal obligations. It was not unknown, indeed, for an individual to assume the maternal name if it happened to be more distinguished than the paternal.[65]

Grandparents, where they survived, might have had a role to play within the *familia,* in particular when a child's natural parent or parents were no longer on the scene. In just such a situation, that involving children who have lost their parent(s), we most commonly meet living grandparents in the Roman testimony.[66] In the case of most Romans we know nothing of their childhood years; emperors, of course, are a noteworthy exception, albeit at the extreme end of society. The future emperor Augustus lost his father when he was only 4 years old, and his mother remarried. He was brought up at—and according to local legend he was born in—his paternal grandfather's house. This *avus* lived to an advanced age ("tranquillissime senuit"); various aspersions were hurled at Augustus on his account. At the age of 11 years, Augustus delivered the funeral oration for his maternal grandmother Julia.[67] In later life, Augustus, together with Livia, was seen to be attached to his grandchildren and great-grandchildren: he adopted Gaius and Lucius and exercised control over all his grandchildren; on the death of Lucius and Gaius, he adopted Agrippa Postumus. He also, famously, used his great-grandchildren as an example to the *equites*.[68]

Other imperial examples may usefully be adduced. Gaius Caligula, who was 7 years old when his father died, was brought up in the house of Augustus and Livia (his great-grandparents), and delivered the funeral oration at Livia's funeral; he was subsequently brought up by his paternal grandmother Antonia, before going to join Tiberius on Capri.[69] Vespasian was also raised by his paternal grandmother.[70] Antoninus Pius spent his childhood first with his paternal grandfather (T. Aurelius Fulvus, twice consul as well as urban prefect), then his maternal grandfather (Arrius Antoninus, likewise *bis consul*); Marcus Aurelius was adopted and brought up by his paternal grandfather (M. Annius Verus, thrice consul and also urban prefect), and enjoyed the influence of his mother's paternal grandfather, L. Catilius Severus (*bis consul, praefectus urbi*).[71] Nonimperial cases sometimes emerge also, and not always aristocratic. Fronto took care of one of his four grandsons while the boy's parents were away in Germany; one may also recall Fronto's strongly expressed grief in A.D. 165 at the loss of the third grandson, and the fact that he had already lost his wife and five of his six children.[72] When Quintilian's wife died, their son was brought up by his (maternal?) grandmother, described by Quintilian as "avia educans."[73]

It is worth remarking that a maternal grandmother, in support of her own daughter, might have routinely been present at a new grandchild's birth.[74] It was not uncommon, as with Augustus, for a maternal grandfather to adopt his grandchildren, should circumstances warrant it (such as an heirless grandfather, or an orphaned child).[75] There is never any suggestion that maternal grandparents should or did have any less concern for their descendants than should paternal grandparents. And as we have already seen, the chances of both sides being alive to worry about and compete over their grandchildren were minimal anyway. When, in an exercise from the declamatory school, two brothers die in the home of their father and stepmother, a maternal grandfather steps in and takes away the third brother, who is already ailing (Seneca *Controv.* 9.5). As a result the *avus* is to be tried under an *actio de vi.* In the debate over this hypothetical situation, every kind of possibility and innuendo is considered, in particular the role of the stepmother in all this, but never is it suggested that the grandfather, though described as a "violentus et inpotens senex," should mind his own business or should not have the welfare of a maternal grandson at heart. Legal definitions of responsibility might be outweighed by feelings of, and moral obligations entailed by, *pietas.* With similar logic, sometimes a grandfather may chastise and punish a grandchild (*Controv.* 9.5.7): "quaedam iura non lege sed natura nobis attributa. nepotem suum avus peccantem aliquid et inter pueriles iocos petulantius lascivientem feriet, nec iniuriarum quisquam cum illo aget" (Certain rights are given to us not by law but by nature. A grandfather may strike his grandson when the latter does something naughty and gets carried away in his childish play, without anyone suing him for damages). On the other hand, it is also worth adding that, if we apply the realities of Roman law to this case, it is never suggested—though it would suit the defense's case—that this grandfather (not, to be sure, the *paterfamilias*) had an automatic right to take the grandson. The nuclear family was the primary focus of obligations.

As unique as a Gorgias of 108 years must have been in his day, the chances of surviving to the age of (say) 60 in the ancient world were not so slim as to make people of advanced age so unusual or remarkable. Depending on one's viewpoint, one may or may not have been lucky to have survived to 60; what is certain is that there would have been plenty of other sexagenarians around with whom to discuss this issue. And discuss it they did.

Three

Old Age and the Romans:
Images and Attitudes

Much attention as has been paid to older people in ancient societies by scholars in the past century has tended to focus on the portrayal of older people in literature; items listed in the bibliography at the end of this book give some idea of the type and extent of the work done. My intention here is not to provide a detailed analysis of the literary image of old age in antiquity but only to discuss apparently prevalent attitudes and to consider their purpose and implications. It is not too difficult a task to collect and contrast references from ancient authors to present a positive or negative picture of old age and older people—a golden age in which humans lived like gods οὐδέ τι δειλὸν γῆρας ἐπῆν (and wretched old age played no part)[1] or a time of total misery—but, as I have already indicated, within the sociohistorical bounds of this study such a catalog would serve little useful purpose. The remaining chapters of this book focus on legal and social aspects of old age in the Roman world, a study that will inevitably depend to a considerable extent on the literary testimony. But first it is necessary in this chapter to provide a background picture of prevalent images and attitudes that one may detect in regard to the manner in which older people were depicted by younger generations or in which they depicted themselves, though it should be noted from the outset that attitudes expressed in literature need not always reflect the actual treatment of older individuals within a society.[2]

Old age was a reality for a significant proportion of the population in the ancient world, and one that presented itself as a potential future for the entire population. So it should come as little surprise that to varying degrees old age attracted the attention of writers in almost every genre of literature, from philosophy to comedy, from love poetry to satire. The way that ancient literary testimony may be used to present a positive or negative image of old age (as indeed many modern studies have done) is perhaps best exemplified in the collection of references on old age (περὶ γήρως) from Greek literature preserved in Stobaeus's *Florilegium* or *Anthology*, compiled in the fifth century A.D.[3] Stobaeus amassed a total of ninety-five passages from forty-two different authors (and three anonymous citations), ranging in date from the seventh century B.C. (Mimnermus) to the fourth century A.D. (Themistius); in chronological terms, citations predominate from the fifth and fourth centuries B.C. (some thirty of the forty-one datable authors). The extracts themselves are grouped under three headings:

50.1: praise (ἔπαινος) of old age (31 passages)
50.2: censure (ψόγος) of old age (55 passages)
50.3: "that good sense makes old age unburdensome and worthy of much respect" (9 passages)

Of these ninety-five passages,

30 are from Greek tragedy (11 in 50.1, 16 in 50.2, 3 in 50.3)
26 from comedy and satire (5 + 20 + 1)
25 from philosophers (13 + 9 + 3)
9 from other poets (2 + 7 + 0)
5 from other prose writers (four historians and one orator, 3 in 50.2, 2 in 50.3)

This distribution alone is quite instructive of the picture of old age one might expect according to the literary genre—in comedy, for example, a negative picture of old age comes as little surprise, whereas philosophers grappled with the problem of the role of older people in society, particularly as they themselves grew older, and presented an image with both positive and negative aspects. In tragedy the picture of the aged person might vary between the positive and the negative depending upon the individual concerned—the wise old counselor or the garrulous old fool. That under the three headings it is not so simple to classify every literary reference is well exemplified by the fact that a fragment of Sophocles (66 Radt, τοῦ ζῆν γὰρ οὐδεὶς ὡς ὁ γηράσκων ἐρᾷ, "no one loves life like the aging man") is quoted in both the first (50.1.9) and the second (50.2.72) sections.

Quite apart from the interest of the individual passages presented by Stobaeus, his collection serves to highlight the problems inherent in interpreting the position and status of older people by reference to isolated literary depictions. A literary reference may readily be found to substantiate or disprove almost any preconceived notion one might have of any feature of an ancient society. In a study of this sort it is precisely the Stobaean model that we must attempt to avoid, although in the accumulation of evidence it is easy to lose sight of this advice—at the very least, we need to be aware of the dangers as we proceed. It is almost inevitable in considering the literary testimony that a positive-negative dichotomy emerges. What we must bear in mind is that the two attitudes are not necessarily mutually exclusive, that both trains of thought are valid depending upon the circumstance of the person(s) described, the intention of the author, and the expectations of his audience. There is no easy or proper way to sift through the literature in order to present a coherent and legitimate picture of the literary depiction of old age in antiquity.

Our primary concern is with classical Roman times, but of course Greek literature, from Homer onward, is relevant in the way that literary images developed and influenced one another. An exhaustive chronological survey is not our intention and, in any case, would be distorted by the manner in which the testimony has survived. Therefore, we shall proceed guided but not bound by literary genre and the intentions—if indeed they can be detected—of the authors with whom we deal. The distinction drawn in this chapter between serious and popular traditions is, of course, highly artificial and somewhat subjective, but it is, I think, the simplest system available within the present confines, and allows for some freedom in the arrangement of what is a widely varying assortment of material. Space and a desire for comprehensibility do not permit excursions down every possible alley—our aim is quality rather than quantity—but it will be enough if the extent of the wide range of attitudes and images current over the classical period as evidenced by the extant literary record can be indicated.

Serious Traditions

Old age as a philosophical topos in antiquity had a long if undistinguished history and was related both to the observed condition of older people of the time and to the stereotypical images derived from more popular literature. Philosophical works specifically on old age were written by some; we hear of such tracts by several Peripatetic philosophers—Theophrastus of Eresus,[4] Demetrius of Phalerum,[5] and Aristo of Ceos.[6] Cicero's dialogue *de Senectute* is the only complete work of this kind extant.[7]

The tradition of philosophical writings περὶ γήρως can be traced back, however, to Plato's *Republic* (written when Plato was probably in his 50s and had more than a score of years still to live), at the beginning of which Plato has Socrates report on a conversation he had with the elderly Cephalus, the father of Lysias.[8] Socrates, himself in his late 50s in the year in which the dialogue is set, 411 B.C., says he enjoys talking to very old men, and he questions Cephalus (whose sons are in their 40s) about his old age. Cephalus notes that most old people complain about their old age, but he puts their troubles down not to old age but to their characters (τρόποι). In fact old age is in many respects a blessing, he says, because it frees one from physical desires and leaves the mind free for philosophy—not that Cephalus is a philosopher but rather a man who enjoys his leisure. Socrates teases Cephalus a little: many would say that he finds old age easy to bear because he has wealth to provide him with comforts (παραμύθια, *Rep.* 1.329e). Cephalus admits that there is some truth to this; a poor man who is good will find old age no easier to bear than a bad man who is wealthy. Cephalus tells Socrates that he uses his wealth wisely, to render to the gods and to other men their due. With that Cephalus rushes off to perform a sacrifice, his son Polemarchus takes over, and the philosophical dialogue proper begins.

Though brief, the passage is effective and important, both for the contrast it provides with the generally negative literary image of old age that precedes it from the time of Homer onward, and for the philosophical treatments of old age to follow; Cicero in particular was influenced by this passage of Plato when he came to write his *de Senectute* more than 300 years later,[9] and in chronological terms[10] this dialogue provides us with the next, substantial moralizing tract defending old age.[11]

Cicero probably wrote his *Cato Maior de Senectute* early in 44 B.C., before the Ides of March,[12] when he was 62 and Atticus, to whom the work is dedicated, was 65 years old. The dialogue is set in the past (150 B.C.), by which means Cicero hoped to give his *oratio* "maior auctoritas" and *gravitas*. There can be no doubt, however, that the views expressed are meant to reflect Cicero's own standpoint: "iam enim ipsius Catonis sermo explicabit nostram omnem de senectute sententiam" (for the words of Cato himself will now explain completely my views on old age).[13] Conversation, if it can be called that, takes place between the venerable Cato the Elder (83 years old)[14] and his two friends Scipio Aemilianus and Gaius Laelius (mere *adulescentes* in their mid-30s). In reality, however, the work represents a monologue delivered by Cato in a role very similar to that of Plato's Cephalus.

The preliminary discussion provides striking parallels with the Greek antecedent: Scipio and Laelius express their surprise at how well Cato endures his old age when most men find it a burden heavier than Mount Etna.[15] Like Cephalus, Cato replies that those who find old age a burden only have themselves to blame; anyone with any sense will prepare for old age and accept it. The man who complains of old age, he says, is a fool (*stultus*), and any faults in him are a consequence not of old age but of his own character. It is often stressed by the likes of Plato and Cicero that one retains throughout one's life particular character traits, and hence one's old age is as one deserves. But like Socrates, Laelius raises the point that perhaps it is Cato's *opes, copiae,* and *dignitas* that help him to find old age tolerable—and not many Romans are so well off ("id autem non posse multis contingere," *de Sen.* 3.8): an important point, which Cato, like Cephalus, must admit is true.[16]

After this informal *exordium* Cicero, through Cato, then proceeds to answer four specific complaints (*vituperationes*) against old age. Other complaints may spring readily to the reader's mind, but they are not rebutted here; Cicero/Cato's primary concern is with the negative aspects of old age as seen by a Roman aristocratic male who enjoys tolerably good health.[17]

First, old age takes a person away from activities, *res gerundae* (*de Sen.* 6.15–8.26). The defense is that it is only right for old men to pass from mere physical labors to more fitting, spiritual ones (political, intellectual, agricultural, and educational), because old age is marked by its good counsel and practical wisdom—an extremely common sentiment in both Greek and Latin literature, from Homer onward[18]—and the old man can provide a fine example of moderation and good sense, together with sound advice: the exemplar of Nestor is something of a cliché,[19] but other active elderly persons, Greek and Roman, are also mentioned. Cato feels that by the end of this section he has made his point (8.26): "sed videtis ut senectus non modo languida atque iners non sit, verum etiam sit operosa et semper agens aliquid et moliens, tale scilicet quale cuiusque studium in superiore vita fuit" (But you see how old age is not only not drooping or feeble, but is even active, always doing and striving for something, the kind of thing, naturally, that was each man's pursuit in his earlier life). We return to this aspect shortly.

Second, old age weakens the body. The ground covered here (*de Sen.* 9.27–11.38) is similar to that of the previous section. It is not denied that in old age physical strength wanes, but Cato states that this is no great hardship. The main reason why most people's physical strength fails in old age is that they have led a "libidinosa et intemperans adulescentia" which "effetum corpus tradit senectuti" (a lustful and intemperate youth hands on to old age a weakened body, 9.29). This is of course a perennial observation, and in a subsequent generation Seneca the Younger would make much of it: a life wasted in wine and love affairs invariably leads to an old age of incapacity, if not to an early death. Hence old age must be prepared for by a frugal way of life. Literary references to the physical weakness of older people are countless, from Homer onward; stress was typically placed on the fact that the mind may remain sound within a decrepit body, a theme that Juvenal was to develop. Seneca, like Cicero, accepted that youthful vigor (= vice) diminishes in old age, leaving the mind strong and ready for philosophy.[20] Cicero has Cato repeatedly emphasize what is said to be the best, perhaps the only way to prepare for old age—through philosophy. The enjoyment of philosophy, Cicero asserts, makes up for the loss of physical pleasures.

"There follows the third complaint against old age, namely that people say that it is lacking in pleasures" (sequitur tertia vituperatio senectutis, quod eam carere dicunt voluptatibus, 12.39–18.66). Again, the argument continues along the same lines as the previous two sections, although the rebuttal is qualified when Cicero has Cato state (14.48) that such *voluptates* are not wholly lacking—a noticeable departure from the Platonic model.[21] But that most physical pleasures, and in particular sexual desire (*libido*), are lost is not denied. Cicero/Cato asserts that this is no hardship, whatever most people might think—rather it is a marvelous boon (*o praeclarum munus!*); at the very least we should be grateful to old age for preventing us doing what we should not do (12.42). Here as elsewhere, it is stressed that one must act in a manner appropriate to one's stage of life. To support the notion that the loss of physical pleasures is to be welcomed, a long list of historical exemplars is again produced.[22] It is perhaps not entirely fair to note that neither Cato nor Cicero seems in reality to have lived up to this ideal.[23]

At any rate, it is argued, old age should be praised rather than blamed, since it gives one freedom to pursue more intellectual pursuits.[24] Cato again mentions farming as a worthwhile pursuit and here discusses it at very great length—this digression provides a marvelous example of the garrulousness of old age, as Cicero has Cato himself admit (16.55): "senectus est natura loquacior—ne ab omnibus eam vitiis videar vindicare" (Old age is by nature rather talkative—just in case I should appear to be absolving it of all faults).[25] But an even greater pleasure, the *apex senectutis,* is held to be the *auctoritas,* the prestige and respect an old man may enjoy if he has led an active public life (17.61); a telling argument and central to the theme of this book.

Cicero finally has Cato revert to the proper train of the dialogue to answer the fourth *vituperatio,* namely that old age is not far from death (19.66–23.85). The sense of Cicero's reply is, in true Stoic fashion, "Death, where is thy sting?" A mind trained in philosophy, he has Cato say, will realize that either death is complete oblivion, where there can be no unhappiness, or else it is eternal life and thus endless happiness. All this is familiar from Greek philosophy, notably with Plato's Socrates. Death is inevitable, it is argued by Cato/Cicero, and philosophy helps one to prepare for it and not fear it. Fear of death, as well as of old age, is a very common theme in both Greek and Latin literature, philosophical and otherwise; Cicero dealt with it at greater length in the first book of his *Tusculan Disputations.* From a previous generation, the third book of Lucretius's *de Rerum Natura* is also instructive, especially for its vivid depiction of the toll taken by old age on both the mind and the body; death, therefore, is of no account and is not to be feared.[26] Thus also Cato/Cicero.

The remainder of Cato's address (21.77–23.85) is devoted to the afterlife, in support of the statements he has just made, and on this philosophical note Cicero has Cato close his *consolatio* of old age with the hope that Scipio and Laelius will both reach old age and with the condition that "senectus autem aetatis est peractio tamquam fabulae, cuius defetigationem fugere debemus praesertim adiuncta satietate" (Old age is the final scene of life, just as in a play, a scene from whose tiresomeness we ought to flee, especially when we have had more than enough of it).[27]

Although Cicero states that he knows that Atticus bears the *onus* of old age "modice ac sapienter," it is *consolatio,* not praise, that is the primary aim to which Cicero alludes in dedicating the dialogue to his friend (*de Sen.* 1.1–2): "nunc autem mihi est visum de senectute aliquid ad te conscribere. hoc enim onere, quod mihi commune tecum est, aut iam urgentis aut certe adventantis senectutis, et te et me etiam ipsum levari volo" (At this time I thought I would write something for you on old age. For I want both you and myself to be relieved of this burden which I have in common with you, as old age either now presses upon us or at least makes its approach). Cicero's sincerity in this need not be doubted,[28] even if he did not himself believe all that he has Cato say in defense of old age. While following a Greek tradition that he admired greatly, Cicero did more than just produce a polished literary exercise (and it needs to be remembered that this is above all a work of literature, not a social document).[29] He also sought to provide real *consolatio* for his own old age, upset and almost overwhelmed as he was at the time by personal worries and political uncertainties.

Cicero's daughter Tullia had died in February 45 B.C., and the extent of his grief is evident from his letters of the period as well as from the *Tusculan Disputations;* he wrote at this time too a *consolatio* for himself on the death of Tullia.[30] At the beginning of the *de Senectute* (1.2) he states that "mihi quidem ita iucunda huius libri confectio fuit ut non modo omnes absterserit senectutis molestias, sed effecerit mollem etiam et iucundam senectutem" (for me at any rate the composition of this book has been so pleasant that it has not only wiped away all of old age's annoyances but it has even made old age gentle and pleasant). In a letter to Atticus written at Puteoli on 11 May 44, however, Cicero ironically complains that he should read his *Cato Maior* more often: "amariorem enim me senectus facit. stomachor omnia. sed mihi quidem βεβίωται; viderint iuvenes" (For old age is making me more cantankerous; I am irritated by everything. But I have had my time; let the young ones sort the problems out).[31] Around this period he also divorced his second wife, Publilia, allegedly because of her lack of concern at Tullia's passing.

Politically, Cicero was well aware of the turbulent times in which he was living, yet in the months before the Ides of March he was powerless to come to the aid of the *res publica*. He tells Atticus that *consolatio* in this regard is more difficult to find: "et tamen te suspicor eisdem rebus quibus me ipsum interdum gravius commoveri, quarum consolatio et maior est et in aliud tempus differenda" (And yet I suspect that you are sometimes quite seriously perturbed by the same set of affairs which is troubling me, and consolation for that is a still greater task which must be deferred until a later date).[32] Philosophy became Cicero's refuge in the mid-forties B.C., and also served as a means of expression for his greatest cares. His concern over the political situation was not centered entirely on his own position. In defending old age, he also sought to promote the status of older people, to show that *seniores* still had a role to play in the state, and a necessary role, in view of the activities of certain younger men in the dying decades of the republic—Catiline and Clodius are two obvious examples. It is worth bearing in mind that Cicero was writing at the beginning of a period when the power of the conservative senate was to be all but supplanted by that of an autocrat; the future emperor Augustus first rose to prominence (in 44 B.C.) at the age of 18 years. The collective influence of the anonymous "elderly" was in effect replaced by the executive power of the young; somewhat ironically, in the system that emerged later of the ages of Rome's history, the period from 27 B.C. was conventionally viewed as the stage of *senectus*.

As we have seen, Cicero sets his dialogue in the golden aura of the past when, he asserts, the older man held the prominence, the *auctoritas,* that he deserved and when morals were what they should have been; Cato the Censor, the *novus homo* with *dignitas* (3.8), serves as a fine exemplar, active and influential to the end.[33] The ancient system in the conservative state of Sparta—in contrast to democratic Athens in particular—is cited with approval, by Cicero as by others, for the way that precedence was given to older individuals (see Chapter 4).[34] Cicero calls for a recognition of older men's positive qualities and for them being shown due respect, the sort of respect (allegedly) accorded to them in the old days but sadly lacking, it is felt, in the present. This contrast between an idealized past and the harsh reality of the present is a common one in such contexts.[35] In an oral culture, older generations might enjoy increased prestige while still alive as repositories of traditional wisdom to be passed on to the young, whereas in a more literate culture written records might increasingly take their place. On the other hand, failing powers of memory (on which see Chapter 8, although perhaps in an oral culture memory skills deteriorated to a lesser extent) and weakened performance skills in old age could mean that the very aged had no oral role to play, whereas in classical Athens elderly authors—one thinks of the likes of Aeschylus, Sophocles, and Euripides for a start—flourished.[36] The idea, itself doubtless propagated by older people in the face of some degree of pressure from younger generations, that it is the place of the young (being rash and inexperienced) to obey, of the old (having sound judgment and practical wisdom) to rule, likewise has a long history, whatever the truth underlying it, and it was just such a message that Cicero sought to assert.[37]

This underlying line of argument in the *de Senectute* became very explicit and more extreme some 150 years later in Plutarch's pamphlet "On whether an old man should engage in public affairs" (Εἰ πρεσβυτέρῳ πολιτευτέον or, as it is more commonly known today, *An Seni Respublica Gerenda Sit*),[38] which he wrote in his old age to Euphanes, president of the *boule* of the Areopagus and a member of the Amphictyonic Council. Plutarch at the time was a priest of Apollo at Delphi, a position he held for the last thirty years of his life (*An Seni* 792f). The basic message of the treatise is very clear and repeated at length: the man of state must not retire on account of his age (783b–92f), for there are many useful tasks that he is capable of performing, *and has a duty to perform* (793a–97d).[39] Old age, it is asserted, is a time of honor, though not of excessive or vulgar ambition: much was made by some of the supposed relationship between the Greek terms for honor, γέρας, and for old age, γῆρας.[40] Length of years provides the statesman with qualities such as λόγος (reason), γνώμη (judgment), παρρησία (frankness), σωφροσύνη (soundness of mind), and φρόνησις (practical wisdom), all of which not only entitle but even require the old man to continue to serve in politics.[41] If nothing else he should at least instruct the young, who should be allowed to perform menial duties so that in time they may be ready to take over the more prestigious positions that are the realm of the elder statesmen (793c–94a, 795a–96c). For an old man to perform burdensome, trivial tasks, on the other hand, is foolish and shameful.

But even worse is for an aged man to retreat from public life entirely, argues Plutarch: this is pure laziness, befitting mere women, to slink off to one's farm when one has duties in the city to perform (the contrast here with Cicero's depiction of a fine old age is evident).[42] The career of the consul of 74 B.C., Lucius Licinius Lucullus, earns Plutarch's particular scorn. He has few kind words to write of Lucullus, who after his illustrious career declined—so it was commonly said—into a retirement of debauchery and laziness, ending in insanity: the elder Cato is a much better example, remaining politically active to the end.[43] The pleasures derived from sex, food, and drink that are lost in old age are well compensated for, it is asserted by Plutarch, by the pleasure to be derived from politics (as opposed to Cicero's philosophical pleasures). Mental powers—to answer a possible criticism and further to condemn a life of *otium*—are maintained by constant practice (792d).

After the time of Cicero—and often, no doubt, influenced by him— the philosophical, moralizing tradition regarding old age may also be detected in other works surviving only in fragments. Musonius Rufus, writing in the first century A.D. as part of the Stoic tradition, discussed the best ἐφόδιον for old age.[44] Epigraphical fragments survive of Diogenes of Oenoanda's treatise on old age, written in the second century A.D.; this is the only known Epicurean work devoted to the subject and is similar in structure (if Smith's reconstruction is correct) to Cicero's *de Senectute*.[45] Much more fragmentary are the remains of Favorinus περὶ γήρως, which we have had occasion to meet in passing several times already.[46] While parallels between such works and the other, earlier discussions on old age may be adduced, the fact that such works existed is the main point of interest to us here. Most of these works are so fragmentary, however, that it is a precarious and generally pointless occupation to try to determine whether they were attacks on or defenses of old age. Both sides of the question, perhaps in dialogue form, may have been discussed in such a philosophical framework.

Perhaps the most interesting other work of note on the subject (and of which fairly sizable sections are extant) are the extracts of a dialogue περὶ γήρως written by a certain Juncus and preserved in Stobaeus's *Florilegium*.[47] Exactly who Juncus the philosopher was remains uncertain, but his writings are conventionally dated to the second century A.D.[48] He writes, despite his very Roman name, in undatable Attic Greek, and he mentions nothing specifically Roman; the influence of Cicero, however, is detectable. Of the four quite lengthy extracts preserved by Stobaeus, one constitutes an attack (apparently by a young man) on old people, raising in the process a wide range of negative attributes associated with old age: physical disabilities and illnesses, loss of pleasures and senses, fear of death, impotence, the ridicule of younger generations, exclusion from political and military affairs—and, more originally, the specter of poverty in old age (quoted in Chapter 8). The other three passages represent the old man's replies to these attacks, to the effect that what one loses in old age is more than compensated for by the wisdom and self-control that one attains. The fear of death is answered by considering the afterlife and the pleasures (or oblivion) that will follow death. The influence of the earlier philosophical tradition, in particular Plato and Cicero, in this is clear enough.[49] To what extent, in all these moralizing works, we are dealing with simple philosophical topoi or with real, personal concerns regarding old age is less obvious. But there does emerge a very real awareness of the potential attributes of old age, both positive and negative, and underlying this depiction one can detect, it seems to me, genuine debate as to the status and role of the older members of the society, albeit at an impersonal and generalized level.

More personal and immediate discussion of old age in a serious context may be sought elsewhere: two particular writers, of the early Roman imperial period, will suffice here: Seneca the Younger (ca. 4 B.C./A.D. 1–65) and Pliny the Younger (ca. A.D. 61–ca. 112). Seneca's letters to Lucilius, written shortly before the former's death, provide several pictures of old age within a philosophical framework. They evince an awareness and certain dread of the disadvantages old age may bring even to a very wealthy man (one may recall, inter alia, that Seneca lost his only son in 41); the overall attitude toward old age and older people is sympathetic rather than optimistic. *Epistle* 12 is a particularly good example: on visiting his *suburbanum* Seneca is appalled at how run down the building and grounds are looking—all the fault of old age, the *vilicus* insists, which makes Seneca reflect on his own age, because these stones and trees are his contemporaries, if not younger![50] Meeting an aged slave is the final straw, when Seneca learns that this *decrepitus* is none other than his own former *deliciolus*: nothing is safe from old age,[51] and all around there are things to remind us of how old we are ourselves. There follows philosophical consolation: "conplectamur illam [i.e., senectutem] et amemus; plena est voluptatis, si illa scias uti" (we should embrace old age and cherish it, for it is full of pleasure, if you know how to make the most of it).[52]

In the later *Epistle* 26 Seneca refers back to these observations and reflects that he now feels even older, although it is only his body that is in decline—his mind is strong "et gaudet non multum sibi esse cum corpore" (and rejoices that it has but slight connection with the body).[53] Seneca himself suffered from a wide variety of ailments in his later years, as he is fond of mentioning.[54] Elsewhere he describes the old age of the Epicurean historian Aufidius Bassus, "an excellent man, shattered in health and wrestling with his age" (virum optimum, . . . quassum, aetati obluctantem). "Old age has begun to hang over him with its mighty, overpowering weight" (magno senectus et universo pondere incubuit), like a ship that has begun to sink or a building that is collapsing: "circumspiciendum est, quomodo exeas [sc. e vita]" (one needs to look around, to find an exit).[55] Despite Bassus's physical decrepitude, however, "his mind is sharp" (alacer animo est), and for this he has philosophy to thank. Without philosophy, one is overtaken by old age and death when one least expects it and when it is too late.[56] In all this the negative sides of old age are not glossed over: "nil habet quod speret, quem senectus ducit ad mortem. huic uni intercedi non potest. nullo genere homines mollius moriuntur sed nec diutius" (He whom old age is leading toward death has nothing to hope for; old age alone grants no reprieve. For humankind no ending is more gentle, but there is also none more lingering).[57]

In a subsequent letter Seneca speaks of his own old age in a similar fashion. He states that a man should not simply await his fate like a coward and put up with the extreme disabilities that old age may bring. Rather than praising old age, Seneca is coldly realistic: old age is only to be endured if it is endurable (one's mental condition being particularly relevant). The passage warrants quotation at length, for it is one of the most explicit and, I would assert, carefully considered and heartfelt statements surviving from antiquity by an aging man on the realities of old age as he saw them (*Ep.* 58.32–36):

> Frugal living can bring one to old age; and to my mind old age is not to be refused any more than it is to be craved. . . . So the question we need to consider is whether one should shrink from the final stages of old age [*senectutis extrema*] and not await the end, but bring it on artificially. A man who sluggishly awaits his fate is almost a coward, just as he is excessively devoted to wine who drains the jar dry and sucks up even the dregs. But we shall ask this question also: Is the final stage of life the dregs, or is it the clearest and purest part of all, provided only that the mind is unimpaired, and the senses, still sound, give their support to the spirit, and the body is

not worn out and dead before its time? For it makes a great deal of difference whether a man is drawing out his life or his death. But if the body is useless for service, why should one not free the struggling soul? Perhaps you ought to do this a little before the debt is due, lest, when it falls due, you may be unable to perform the act. And since the danger of living badly is greater than the danger of dying soon, he is a fool who refuses to stake a little time and win a hazard of great gain. Few have lasted through extreme old age to death without impairment [*paucos longissima senectus ad mortem sine iniuria pertulit*], and many have lain inert, making no use of themselves. How much more cruel, then, do you suppose it really is to have lost a portion of your life, than to have lost your right to end that life? . . . I shall not abandon old age, if old age preserves me intact for myself, and intact as regards the better part of myself; but if old age begins to shatter my mind, and to pull its various faculties to pieces, if it leaves me, not life, but only the breath of life, I shall leap from a building that is crumbling and tottering [*ex aedificio putri ac ruenti*]. I shall not avoid illness through death, so long as the illness is curable and does not impede my mind. . . . He who dies just because he is in pain is a weakling and a coward; but he who lives merely to brave out this pain is a fool.

Although in reality Seneca's suicide in A.D. 65 was forced through political circumstances rather than purely philosophical reasoning,[58] his explicit statement quoted here should be regarded not only as a conclusion based on a philosophical tradition but also as a sincere reflection on the realities of old age for one aristocratic Roman male. One thinks in this period too of Caninius Rebilus (*cos. suff.* A.D. 37), who committed suicide in order to avoid "the tortures of a sick old age" (*cruciatus aegrae senectae*).[59]

The goal was a full life—which for Plutarch meant a politically active one, for Seneca an active one at any rate—not necessarily a long one. According to Seneca (*Ep.* 93), it is not how long one lives that matters, but *how* one has lived: *vivere* as opposed to simply *esse*.[60] Plutarch would certainly have relished the story told by Seneca of the nonagenarian Turannius who, deprived of his duties as *procurator* under the emperor Gaius, had his household mourn him as if he were dead; his official position was duly restored.[61] This goal of a full life is the explicit message of Seneca's dialogue *de Brevitate Vitae*, addressed to Paulinus, who was probably related to Seneca through the latter's wife and was quite likely Seneca's father-in-law:[62] it is not that we have

a short life to live, as many complain, but that we waste much of it—
"vita, si uti scias, longa est. . . . exigua pars est vitae, qua vivimus" (life,
if you know how to make the most of it, is long. . . . The period in
which we truly live is only a small part of life).[63]

The professed ideal for Seneca, as for Cicero and no doubt for many
elderly aristocratic Roman males of the late republic or the empire, was
a healthy old age enjoyed pursuing worthwhile and rewarding activities. This may be summed up as *otium honestum,* a difficult phrase to
translate: "an honorable withdrawal to leisure" conveys some of the
force in the context of *senectus,* although of course the Roman aristocratic ideal of *otium* did not relate solely to one's later years, and, as
Cicero found, *otium* might be imposed on one at any time, however
unwilling one may be to withdraw from public life. For Plutarch, as
has been seen, any withdrawal from one's *officium,* service to the state,
was dishonorable, but Seneca viewed things somewhat differently.[64]
And it is of just such an ideal that Pliny the Younger in his letters provides concrete examples. Writing some forty years after Seneca, Pliny
was only in his 40s at this time, and died at the age of around 50 years.
Like Seneca, he displays an awareness of the negative attributes as well
as the potential positive qualities that old age may bring, as embodied
in the various elderly aristocratic mentors and friends he describes or
addresses. And like Seneca, Pliny witnessed the painful old age and
suicide of a friend: he describes the last years of Q. Corellius Rufus
(*cos.* ca. A.D. 78), who suffered from gout (*pedum dolor*) from the age
of 32 years; as he grew old the pain became increasingly acute, until
eventually he took his own life at the age of 67 years.[65] Pliny requires
consolatio; he misses his friend, but he can understand his motivation
in committing suicide. One might compare also the suicide of Silius
Italicus at the age of 75 years, which led Pliny to reflect on *fragilitas
humana* (*Ep.* 3.7.11): "quid enim tam circumcisum tam breve quam
homini vita longissima?" (For what is as fleeting and as short as the
longest of human lives?).

But the human condition is not always so wretched. Pliny also expresses his respect for elderly men who lead a full life, whether in politics or in active retirement. Cn. Arrius Antoninus earns Pliny's praise
for his political career: "quod sanctitate quod auctoritate, aetate quoque princeps civitatis, est quidem venerabile et pulchrum" (In virtue

and prestige, as well as in age, you are our foremost citizen—that is indeed a fine record, well worthy of respect), although Pliny adds that he respects him even more for his *remissiones* (recreations).[66] L. Verginius Rufus, who died at the age of 83 years (having assumed his third consulship, in A.D. 97), provides Pliny with a good model,[67] for he spent his last years "in altissima tranquillitate, pari veneratione. usus est firma valetudine, nisi quod solebant ei manus tremere, citra dolorem tamen" (living in the deepest peace and most greatly respected; his health was good, apart from a trembling of the hands, though not enough to cause him pain). The approach of death, however, was difficult and drawn-out, but he died "with a full store of both years and offices" (plenus annis, plenus honoribus), and his funeral oration was delivered by one of the other consuls of that year, Cornelius Tacitus.

Another prominent individual who wins Pliny's esteem is T. Pomponius Bassus (*cos. suff.* A.D. 94)[68] for planning and spending his *otium* in peace, living in idyllic surroundings, getting exercise on the beach, enjoying conversation and reading: "ita senescere oportet virum, qui magistratus amplissimos gesserit, exercitus rexerit, totumque se rei publicae quam diu decebat obtulerit" (This is the right way to grow old for a man who has held the highest civil offices, commanded armies, and devoted himself entirely to the service of the state for as long as it was proper for him to do so). This is the manner in which a Roman aristocrat should lead his life (*pace* Plutarch again): to devote the "prima vitae tempora et media" (first and middle stages of his life) to his *patria* and keep "the final years" (extrema tempora) for himself.[69] Yet one is reminded that, for most, *otium* was an idealized goal rather than an easy reality: Pliny wonders if he will ever get the chance to enjoy such a life of leisure. It is important to him, writing at the age of about 43 years, that people see his *secessus* not as *desidia* (as Plutarch would have) but as *tranquillitas* (*Ep.* 4.23.4).

Pliny's true ideal, however, is the old age of T. Vestricius Spurinna (*cos.* II A.D. 98): "adeo quidem ut neminem magis in senectute, si modo senescere datum est, aemulari velim" (There is no one whom I would rather take as a model in old age, if I am allowed to grow old).[70] His life in retirement, Pliny states, was well ordered and included conversation, reading, walking and other exercise,[71] writing, and bathing; he enjoyed a good, simple diet.[72] Then, and only then, are we told his age: he has passed his 77th year, "aurium oculorum vigor integer, inde agile et vividum corpus solaque ex senectute prudentia" (But his hearing and sight are strong and unimpaired, and he is physically fit and energetic; old age has brought him nothing but good sense, *Ep.* 3.1.10). Thus the ideal: after a career of distinguished service to the state, to enjoy good physical and mental health in old age, amid comfortable surroundings and with continued potential to develop one's wisdom. It is just such a goal that Pliny professes to set for himself—later. In the immediate present he has too much to do, but he instructs the addressee of this letter, C. Calvisius Rufus, to remind him of this intention later in life, when he is old enough to be able to enjoy such *otium* without being accused of *inertia* (*Ep.* 3.1.11–12).

If Spurinna provided the ideal, others around Pliny presented the image of the extreme (at least for aristocratic males) negative aspects of old age,[73] Cn. Domitius Tullus (*cos. suff.* II A.D. 98) being a prime example.[74] Despite his wealth, he is a hopeless invalid, fortunate only in that he has a wife and slaves to tend him. Even allowing for the fact that in antiquity a groom would typically have been a number of years older than his bride, the literary depiction of an elderly man with a young wife was not infrequently harsh.[75] Tullus's wife, we are told, was criticized severely for having married him in the first place, and particularly now that he is so decrepit: "divitis senis ita perditi morbo, ut esse taedio posset uxori, quam iuvenis sanusque duxisset" (a wealthy old man so wasted by illness that even a wife whom he had married when he was young and healthy could have found him repulsive). The physical and mental decrepitude of Tullus is described in brief but vivid and disgusting detail:[76]

> quippe omnibus membris extortus et fractus, tantas opes solis oculis obibat, ac ne in lectulo quidem nisi ab aliis movebatur; quin etiam (foedum miserandumque dictu) dentes lavandos fricandosque praebebat. auditum frequenter ex ipso, cum quereretur de contumeliis debilitatis suae, digitos se servorum suorum cotidie lingere.

> Deformed and crippled in every limb, he could only enjoy his enormous wealth by contemplating it and could not even turn in bed unless he was man-handled. He also had to have his teeth cleaned and brushed for him—a squalid and pitiful detail. When complaining about the humiliations of

his infirmity, he was often heard to say that every day he licked the fingers of his slaves.

It is just such a depressing image of the end of one's life, and not solely the welcome one of a Spurinna, that Pliny and his contemporaries had also to face. The negative realities, helplessness and hopelessness, could not easily be ignored.

And it should by now be apparent that not only were the evident physical shortcomings of old age to be feared, but also—and even for the upper classes—the social liabilities that such negative attributes entailed, particularly in the attitudes of society toward its elderly members. It was just such attitudes in a political sphere that Cicero and, more explicitly, Plutarch were seeking to counteract or at least redefine. Gray hair, to take a trivial instance, might be seen as a symbol of old age and its inherent nobility.[77] But gray hair alone does not make a man wise and could be taken instead as a sign of decrepitude.[78] According to an ancient proverb, attributed first to Solon, in an ideal old age one should go on learning something new every day, and this indeed, in the eyes of Plato, Cicero, and company, is seen as a requisite for a wise old age.[79] The jurist Pomponius introduced an apparently personal note in this regard: "nam ego discendi cupiditate, quam solam vivendi rationem optimam in octavum et septuagesimum annum aetatis duxi, memor sum eius sententiae, qui dixisse fertur: κἄν τὸν ἕτερον πόδα ἐν τῇ σορῷ ἔχω, προσμαθεῖν τι βουλοίμην" (For in my desire for learning, which down to my 78th year I have regarded as the single best principle for living, I am mindful of the maxim of the one who is reported to have said: "Even though I may have one foot in the grave, I want to learn something new").[80] Here too there is a negative tradition undermining the positive trait, namely the notion that learning in old age is untimely, foolish, and shameful. As Plutarch stressed in the *An Seni* in regard to politics, one must continue one's lifelong good habits in old age and not suddenly try to start from scratch when it is too late. The negative attitude expressed in regard to *opsimathia* is at times surprisingly bitter in tone, drawn as it was by those who, perhaps, felt themselves above such petty behavior.[81] Thankfully, the maxim "better late than never" features occasionally, particularly in regard to the story that Socrates learned a musical instrument late in life.[82]

Such positive-negative polarities, such ambivalent attitudes in regard to age, abound. Concurrent with the positive arguments of a Plato, a Cicero, or a Plutarch, together with the two-sided, veristic discussions by Seneca, Pliny, and Juncus, for example, we encounter a coldly negative picture even within the serious tradition. Cicero mentions in passing, only to dismiss, some negative qualities attributed by some to old age: "at sunt morosi et anxii et iracundi et difficiles senes: si quaerimus, etiam avari. sed haec morum vitia sunt, non senectutis" (But, so they say, old men are morose, troubled, prone to anger, and hard to please; if the truth be told, they are also misers. However, these are faults of character, not of old age). Half a millennium later John Chrysostom presented a rather more pragmatic list of the vices of elderly men of his own day (providing incidental evidence of the active and sociable, if somewhat undignified, old age of at least some individuals): γέρων μεθύει, ἐν καπηλείοις καθέζεται, γέρων εἰς ἱππο- δρομίας σπεύδει, γέρων εἰς θέατρα ἀναβαίνει, καθάπερ παιδίον τρέχων μετὰ τοῦ πλήθους (the old man gets drunk, he sits in taverns, he rushes off to the racecourse, he climbs up into the theater, like a child running with the crowd).[83] But it was Aristotle who dwelt on the negative traits of the character of older people at the greatest length, as he furnished for his readers rhetorical guidelines on the stereotyped image of the old man. He provided in his *Rhetoric* a clinically objective analysis of three distinct age-classes: the young (νέοι, νεότης), those in the prime of life (ἀκμάζοντες, ἀκμή), and the old (πρεσβύτεροι or παρηκμακότες, γῆρας).[84] Aristotle, who himself lived to the age of 63 years, probably wrote this account when he was in his 50s.[85] His interest, writing as he is for the orator, is in not physical attributes but character traits (and mainly male ones, it would appear) in terms of ἦθος. Hence what are described might be termed emotional and moral qualities, in a manner not dissimilar to that used subsequently by Theophrastus in his *Characters*. The young and the old have the negative extremes—one excessive, the other defective—each in direct contrast to the other; for example, the young are characterized as hot and tempestuous, whereas the aged are cold and lethargic. Those in the prime of life (defined as, physically, 30 to 35 years, and for the *psyche,* about 49 years = 7^2) embody the positive balance or mean between the two extremes.[86] One can compare [Dionysius of Halicarnassus] *On Epideictic Speeches* on how one should speak in an *epi-taphios* of one who died in what we would term middle age: "[H]e was at the prime of his life and mental powers and had given proof of his virtue; moreover he left life much desired, *not yet an object of dislike because of old age,* but in his prime."[87] This is a crucial point, as shall become apparent in later chapters. While the Greeks and Romans admired and respected men who survived fit and healthy, physically and mentally, into old age, as a generalization they revered the middle ground, those not too young or too old. As Marcus Antonius (according to Cassius Dio) said to his troops before Actium, "I am at that age when men are at their very prime [ἀκμάζουσι], both in body and in mind, and are hampered neither by the rashness of youth nor by the slackness [ἔκλυσις] of old age, but are at their strongest, because they occupy the mean between these two extremes."[88] For an old man to be charged with rash behavior, as befits a mere youth, might thus be taken as a double insult, as Apuleius was to taunt his accuser Aemilianus (*Apol.* 1): "senem notissimae temeritatis" (an old man of the most notorious recklessness).

But to return for the moment to Aristotle's categorization of older people, it is worth running through it here briefly.[89] The main factor that is stressed is the old man's wary, pessimistic manner: having lived a long life and having made many mistakes, he is overly cautious—unlike the young man who has yet to learn life's knocks and who therefore overdoes everything and lives to excess. This is in direct contrast to the traditional notion that a long life brings with it wisdom, unless one classifies such an attitude as embodying wisdom. Older people are, we are told by Aristotle, overly pessimistic, distrustful, malicious (κακοήθεις), suspicious, and small-minded (μικρόψυχοι) "because they have been humbled by life and so their greatest hopes are raised to nothing more than staying alive."[90] They lack generosity,[91] are cowardly and always anticipating danger ("old age paves the way for cowardice"),[92] and yet they also love life (φιλόζωοι) to excess, especially on their last day of life. As Lucian's Diogenes says to the aged beggar, "men as old as you are such φιλόζωοι, men who ought to be eager for death as a remedy [φάρμακον] for the evils of old age."[93]

Aristotle's diatribe continues. Older people are too fond not just of life but also of themselves (φίλαυτοι), a symptom of their petty-mindedness. Always their concern is with what is useful, σύμφερον, rather than with what is καλόν. Instead of being shy (as the young are), they are shameless, caring more for profit than for honor,[94] and taking no heed of what people might think of them. Older people, Aristotle states, dwell on and live in the past,[95] dependent on memory rather than hope—their past is long, their future short and uncertain. Thus they continually talk about the past, to the point of garrulity (ἀδολεσ-χία). They are also prone to fits of anger,[96] but even in this they are unsuccessful—such fits are feeble, because all passions (ἐπιθυμίαι) have either become feeble (ἀσθενεῖς) or have disappeared altogether; older people lead their lives more by cold logic (λογισμός, linked to utility) than by moral feeling (ἦθος, linked to ἀρετή). Pettiness is at the heart of the old man's actions and emotions. Both old and young are capable of feeling pity, but for different reasons: the young out of *philanthropia*, the old out of weakness (ἀσθένεια), because the aged man imagines that anything unfortunate that happens to another could easily happen to himself. Hence again older people's miserable pessimism: they are not witty or given to laughter or general pleasantries—old age has taken away all such qualities.

The picture Aristotle presents here is a depressing one, unrelieved as it is by any mention of positive qualities inherent in older people. It is not that he was unaware of any such positive attributes, only that in such a generalized description for rhetorical purposes of the three stages of life it is the negative characteristics that distinguish youth and old age from those at their prime. The very same viewpoint underlies a passage, written some 300 years later, in Horace's *Ars Poetica,* where there is discussed with much greater brevity, but no less chilling pessimism, the best way to portray age-classes on the stage. The portrayal, Horace stresses, must be lifelike—the influence of Aristotle is evident. The boy is playful, the beardless youth extravagant and impressionable, and the mature man (the ideal, but not idealized) active and conservative, while the old man is anything but pleasant or agreeable:

> multa senem circumveniunt incommoda, vel quod
> quaerit et inventis miser abstinet ac timet uti
> vel quod res omnes timide gelideque ministrat,
> dilator, †spe longus†, iners, <p>avidusque futuri,
> difficilis, querulus, laudator temporis acti

se puero, castigator censorque minorum.[97]
multa ferunt anni venientes commoda secum,
multa recedentes adimunt.

> An old man is surrounded by a host of troubles: he amasses money but leaves it untouched, for he's too afraid to use it, poor devil. His whole approach to life is cold and timid. He hopefully puts things off (?), is dull, and shrinks from the future. Ill-tempered and a grumbler, he is always praising the time when he was a boy, scolding and blaming "the youth of today." The years bring many blessings as they come to meet us. Receding, they take many away.[98]

The description, for all its impersonality, is brutally vivid and realistic, but its tone is serious rather than satiric. It is meant to outline the attributes one would expect to be portrayed in a *senex* on the stage (perhaps more in comedy than in tragedy). As such we are told something of the generalized attitudes that, according to Aristotle and Horace respectively, Greeks and Romans at the time had about stereotypically elderly people and about old age.

Popular Traditions

> continuos gemitus aegra senectus habet.

> Sickly old age brings endless groanings.
> Maximianus *Eleg.* 1.246

The serious literary and philosophical traditions in the description of old age have provided two main attitudes: a positive, consolatory depiction, playing down (while still accepting) the negative attributes associated with old age, in order to highlight positive qualities in, and the potential of, old age and older people; and a more negative reality, a coldly analytical, though impersonal and largely objective, depiction of the debilities and unpleasant attributes of old age—a reality of the present contrasted with an idealized past and an imagined or desired future. The depth and diversity of these descriptions of images of and attitudes toward old age and older people have made our survey up to this point a fairly lengthy one. Turning now to more popular forms of literature, the tradition, though diverse and widespread, is more straightforward to classify.

It will be useful, as well as, perhaps, inevitable, if our focus should turn first to a lengthy passage by Juvenal (*Satires* 10.188–288), in which is preserved one of the most powerful and bitter attacks on *senectus* in the literature of the ancient world, if not of all time.[99] One remembers Hamlet's reaction: "Slanders, sir: for the satirical rogue says here that old men have grey beards, that their faces are wrinkled, their eyes purging thick amber and plum-tree gum, and that they have a plentiful lack of wit, together with most weak hams: all of which, sir, though I most powerfully and potently believe, yet I hold it not honesty to have it thus set down" (2.2.195–208).

In dealing with the pointlessness and misguidedness of most people's prayers, Juvenal comes to an apparently common plea: "da spatium vitae, multos da, Iuppiter, annos" (Grant, Jove, a long life and many years, 188). But it is a prayer that he immediately rejects, for "quam continuis et quantis longa senectus plena malis" (How painful are the endless afflictions of which drawn-out old age is full, 190–91). Juvenal then proceeds to give a detailed catalog of the (mainly physical) disasters old age brings, with some pertinent examples and with considerable rhetorical distaste. Before we turn to look at these lines in some detail, we need to consider the degree of reality underlying Juvenal's profoundly negative depiction of old age. The prayer for a long life is one of five such prayers of humankind that Juvenal believes pointless: the prayers for power, eloquence, military glory, long life, and good looks (it is noteworthy that wealth plays a very minor role).[100] There is not only satire underlying Juvenal's negative view, but also philosophy; the *ira,* indignation, of Juvenal's first satire has been replaced by sympathy, a degree of *consolatio,* and rather heavy scorn.[101] The introduction to the tenth satire also points to this, through the contrast between the *personae* of Democritus with his laughter and Heraclitus with his tears.[102] Juvenal's purpose here is not purely malicious, as shall become evident. A number of other Latin authors also commented on, and typically regarded as futile if not fatuous, such a prayer for old age.[103] Persius (2.41–43) appears to accept the idea of such a prayer, but he says that for a wealthy aristocrat it is pointless, because his rich diet ensures an early grave anyway. That the prayer was also dismissed by Seneca the Younger is hardly surprising.[104] Saint Augustine too was well aware of the problems of old age and noted the absurdity of praying for *both* a long life *and* good looks.[105] Juvenal was not alone in his sentiments.

The depiction of old age in the tenth satire focuses primarily on physical manifestations, and Juvenal begins by vividly depicting five rather trivial but telling features. It will be useful and convenient to survey these features briefly in commentary form, particularly to give an indication of their pervasiveness in ancient literature (it is to be hoped that in the process the force of Juvenal's scathing and mordant humor is not entirely lost). The five features we shall focus on are wrinkles, tremulousness, baldness, a runny nose, and loss of teeth. It is particularly worthy of note, perhaps, that these features are commonly associated with elderly women more than with men.

Juvenal comments (10.191–98) on the wrinkled and sagging face of *senes*, as a result of which all old people look the same ("una senum facies"). Wrinkles were seen as an inevitable concomitant of old age, particularly in the case of women (cf., e.g., Cicero *de Sen.* 18.62; Horace *Epod.* 8.3–4, "rugis vetus frontem senectus exaret"; Ovid *Trist.* 3.7.34; Tibullus 2.2.19–20, 3.5.25; Vergil *Aen.* 7.416–17; Macedonius Consul *Anthologia Palatina* 5.233). Even old pearls get wrinkles: Pliny *NH* 9.54.109. Wrinkles were held to be a product of the dryness of the aging body (cf. Galen *de Simp. Med. Temp. ac Fac.* 2.19 [11.508K], *in Hipp. Aph.* 3.31 [17B.650K], and see Chapter 9). The Hippocratic corpus (*de Morb. Mul.* 2.188 [8.368L]) offers a recipe to remove, or at least disguise, wrinkles; Pliny *NH* 23.63.120 mentions that figs are effective in this regard, as is the application of almond oil (23.42.85), the roots of the lily (21.74.127), and the *talus,* or pastern bone, of a white bullock, boiled down to a jelly for forty days and nights (28.50.184: Pliny includes this "frivolum . . . propter desideria mulierum"). Such cosmetic attempts—or even simple denial of one's age—were typically derided by male authors: Martial 1.72, 4.20, 4.36 (dying one's hair, as also 3.43), 8.79, etc.; Juvenal 6.199 ("facies tua conputat annos"); Seneca *Ep.* 47.7, 122.7; *Anthologia Palatina* 11.310 (Lucilius); Quintilian *Inst. Or.* 6.3.73 (two telling examples of Ciceronian wit); Aelian *Var. Hist.* 7.20 (of a vain Chian man who dyed his hair because he was ashamed of his old age); SHA *Hadr.* 20.8. Eunapius (*Vit. Soph.* 16.2.5.496) mentions a woman who used a recently acquired fortune to "smooth and polish away the signs of old age" (cf. Poppaea's bath of ass's milk, "extendi cutem," Pliny *NH* 11.96.238, 28.50.183). Another way a woman might protect her own vanity, we are told, was to surround herself with "old women and maids uglier than herself": [Lucian] *Amores* 39. Cf. Pollux *Onom.* 4.150–51 for the dramatic masks used to represent old women, with an emphasis on wrinkles.

Juvenal notes the shaky voices and limbs of older people, 10.198; cf. 10.267 (with Vergil *Aen.* 2.509–10) and 6.622–23, of Claudius ("senis tremulumque caput . . . et longa manantia labra saliva"); Ennius *Ann.* 1.34 ("cita . . . tremulis anus . . . artubus"); Calpurnius Siculus 5.12–13, 7; Ausonius *Epist.* 6.31 Green; Galen *de Sympt. Caus.* 2.2 (7.157–58K), *de Trem. Palp.* 3 (7.587K). Plutarch *Mor.* 650e notes the similarity between symptoms of old age and of drunkenness (see Chapter 9 note 67): trembling limbs, stammering tongue, excessive talking, irascible temper, forgetfulness, and a wandering mind. For the trembling *vox*, cf. also Terence *Eun.* 229–31 (with the etymological observations of Eugraphius *ad loc.*: "decrepiti dicuntur magis senes, si qui longa senectute vix loqui possunt et tantummodo fractis vocibus exprimunt quae loquantur ac sunt quasi quaedam crepitacula"; cf. Festus 62L s.v. *decrepitus*); Ovid *Fasti* 6.399; and also Shakespeare's *As You Like It,* 2.7.161–63, for the sixth stage of life.

Juvenal also draws attention to old people's bald heads, 10.199. Celsus *de Med.* 6.1.1, in line with the theory that baldness results from the cooling and drying process of old age (see Chapter 9), comments that nothing can prevent people becoming bald through old age (cf. Aristotle *Hist. An.* 3.11.518a, *de Gen. An.* 5.3.782a; Galen *de Temp.* 2.5–6 [1.621, 640- 41K]). In this case, however, prayer might actually help, if we believe *CIL* 11.1305 (= *ILS* 3135): "Minervae memori Tullia Superiana restitutione facta sibi capillorum v.s.l.m." (see also Richardson 1933: 9 n. 74). Hippocrates *de Morb. Mul.* 2.189 (8.370L) offers advice to bald and balding women; for baldness concomitant with the growth of facial hair in women after the cessation of menstruation, see Pliny *NH* 11.94.230. Pliny, among numerous recipes to avert hair loss, mentions bear grease mixed with ladanum and maidenhair; grayness can be prevented with "cinere genitalis asini" (*NH* 28.46.163–64). For baldness in old age and attempts to disguise it,

see also Martial 5.49, 10.83, 12.7, etc.; Pliny *Ep.* 3.6 (see note 73);
Suetonius *Dom.* 18; Lucian *Alex.* 59, *Dial. Meret.* 11.3; and several tales
in the Aesopic corpus, where baldness is used for comic purposes.
Seneca *de Brev. Vit.* 12.3, on men's concerns with making the most of
the remaining hairs on their head, has a timeless ring to it. Artemidorus *Oneirocrit.* 1.21 (and cf. 1.49) states that "if anyone dreams
that the back part of the head is hairless, he will endure ἐν τῷ γήρᾳ
πενίαν καὶ ἀπορίαν, for the entire back part of the head signifies the
future." Conversely, gray hair might be regarded as an unwelcome indication of one's age and one to be removed (cf. Tibullus 1.8.41–46;
Phaedrus 2.2.3–4; less trivially, for childbirth and offspring as indicators of age and, it is alleged, therefore despised and shunned by many
women, see Seneca *Cons. ad Helv.* 16.3 and [Quintilian] *Decl. Min.*
277.10). It was also noted that in old age, paradoxically, some people's
eyebrows become bushier: Aristotle *de Part. Anim.* 2.15.658b; Maximianus *Eleg.* 1.139–40.

   With the old man's driveling nose (10.199), a feature of old age that
Lucian also points to (*Dial. Mort.* 6.2, 9.2), Juvenal explicitly evokes
the common notion of old age as a second childhood, as the ancient
scholiast on line 199 explains ("ut infantibus"; see Chapter 8). For
such watery discharges, a result of the collection of an overflow of su-
perfluous humidity (τὰ περιττώματα, which is also why old men
cough and spit), see Galen *de Temp.* 2.2 (1.580–81K), *de San. Tuenda*
5.8, 6.3 (6.350–51, 396–97K = *CMG* 5.4.2.151, 174), *de Marc.* 4
(7.679–80K), *de Simp. Med. Temp. ac Fac.* 1.8 (11.396K), *in Hipp. Aph.*
3.31 (17B.651K), and further Chapter 9; note also Maximianus *Eleg.*
1.137–38. On the other hand, in the weakened state of old age sneez-
ing is both difficult (because old people's brains are heavy, according
to Gabriele Zerbi in the fifteenth century, *Gerontocomia* ch. 40) and
dangerous: cf. [Aristotle] *Probl.* 33.12.962b; Theophrastus frag. 348
Fortenbaugh *ap.* Pliny *NH* 28.15.57.

   And then there are their toothless gums, 10.200: "frangendus mis-
ero gingiva panis inermi"—Juvenal does not merely list the stereotypes but, here as elsewhere, brings to them an original touch. Toothlessness is an often noticed feature of old age, especially in women: cf.
Plautus's *edentulae* (e.g. *Most.* 275); Horace *Epod.* 8.3 ("dens ater");
Martial (Howell 1980: 149–50); *Priap.* 12.9; Lucian *Dial. Mort.* 6.2,

9.2; Seneca *Ep.* 12.3, 83.4; Tacitus *Ann.* 1.34; Diocles frag. 14 Kock
(= Bekker, *Anec. Graeca* 1.339); *Anthologia Palatina* 11.374 (Macedonius Consul: the woman who disguises her wrinkles with white lead
but then makes the mistake of smiling); Pollux *Onom.* 2.16 (νωδο-
γέρων); Galen *de Comp. Med. Sec. Loc.* 5.4 (12.851K); Jerome *Comm.
in Amos* 2.pr. (*PL* 25.1021–23 = *CCSL* 76.255), including among a
list of *senectutis mala:* "nudi gingivis dentes, et inter cibos cadentes."
Paul *Dig.* 21.1.11, indicates how common a feature (and stereotype)
it was: "cui dens abest, non est morbosus: magna enim pars hominum
aliquo dente caret neque ideo morbosi sunt; praesertim cum sine den-
tibus nascimur nec ideo minus sani sumus donec dentes habeamus—
alioquin nullus senex sanus esset" (Someone who is missing a tooth is
not "diseased." For the majority of people lack some tooth or other but
are not "diseased" on that account. This is especially true in view of
the fact that we are born without teeth and we are not thereby less
healthy until we have teeth—otherwise no old person would be
healthy).

As a result of such unsightly infirmities the old man (and here the focus is on the male) is offensive both to his family and to himself;[106]
even the *captator,* whose job it was to fawn over ailing aristocrats, finds
the old man disgusting, a cleverly vicious, though perhaps exaggerated, effect. Juvenal then moves on to more significant and pervasive
disabilities associated with older people (many of which we shall meet
again later when we consider medical aspects of old age). Juvenal first
considers the loss of pleasures and of senses, a feature that Cicero had
already noted as a typical *vituperatio* against old age.[107] No longer can
one find enjoyment in food and wine, and sexual activity has long
since been forgotten.[108] Other pleasures are also lacking: the old man
can no longer enjoy singing, music, or the theater—for a start, he is
deaf.[109] This leads on to geriatric illnesses; the old man's chilly frame
can be warmed only by a fever; another clever image, albeit unorigi-
nal.[110] The diseases old age brings are countless,[111] along with its
other physical shortcomings, to shoulders, loins, hips, and eyes; like
a swallow's chick (*pullus hirundinis*), the old man cannot even feed
himself.[112] Finally, as an endnote to add to the misery, mention of

mental failings is also introduced, and they are held to be the worst feature of all.[113]

From this unrelievedly vicious attack, Juvenal turns next to consider drawbacks suffered by older people, negative features of a more emotional and sentimental nature. Even if his mind retains its vigor ("vigeant sensus animi"), yet the aged man must endure the cruel fate of burying a beloved wife or a child, a brother or a sister: "haec data poena diu viventibus" (this is the price of longevity)—a very real and touching side of old age of which, as we have seen, Cicero himself was all too well aware when he wrote his *de Senectute* and one that Juvenal shows real sensitivity (whatever his motives) in portraying.[114] Many ancient literary and epigraphical sources make the point that it is unnatural for parents to have to bury their children; Herodotus has Croesus note it as one of the characteristics of wartime.[115] The two surviving fragments of Demetrius of Phalerum's work περὶ γήρως deal with such a fate befalling Anaxagoras and Xenophanes. Lucian, however, is much more cynical than Juvenal. In the *de Luctu* a son at his own funeral is imagined as responding to his aged father's grief, pointing out the positive features of dying young: he will not have to grow old, to look like his father (head bald, face wrinkled, back bent, knees trembling, wasted [σαφρός] through time); by dying young he will not be scorned in old age, nor will the sight of him offend the young.[116]

Juvenal next presents rhetorical exempla of some elderly gentlemen: Nestor, Peleus and Laertes, Priam, Marius, and Pompey (the latter, it may be noted, died at the age of 58 years, which might suggest that we are dealing with biological as opposed to chronological age again) with a passing reference to Mithradates and Croesus, and a bizarre twist at the end: the Catilinarian conspirators Lentulus (though he was consul in 71 B.C., so must have died at the age of at least 50 years) and Cethegus, as well as Catilina himself, were fortunate, we are told, to have died so young.

In these lines, Juvenal's treatment of old age is unpleasantly vivid, brilliantly harsh, unforgivingly cruel, and, above all, powerfully portrayed. The message is clear enough: what one should pray for is not "spatium vitae," but, as we are told at the end of the satire, "mens sana in corpore sano," which "spatium vitae extremum inter munera ponat naturae."[117] This is one possible response to the realities of old age. There is realism in Juvenal's diatribe as well as rhetorical exaggeration; what is lacking, to be sure, is a genuine concern for the plight of the older people described.

But negative images and attitudes are common enough, even simply as asides or passing references. Standard epithets in Latin literature to describe old age, many of which we have already seen and which will recur, include *curvus, decrepitus, egens, fessus, gravis, ignavus, invalidus, madidus, saevus,* and *tardus.* The satiric-comic tradition is the harshest, directed especially against women. If Juvenal provides the strongest overall picture of the elderly individual, then others have left us the most offensive and devastating indictments of the aged female. Highly unpleasant portrayals of the *anus deformis deliraque* abound: from Latin literature one thinks in particular of two epodes by Horace, a score of poems by Martial, and several among the *Carmina Priapeorum.*[118] The stereotyped old woman is, in sum, a disgusting, haggard, stinking, toothless, and sex-crazed *fellatrix.* As marginalized members of society, old women were especially set apart. Past the age of the menopause and therefore no longer able to perform their duty as reproducers, they might easily become stereotyped—by men—as dysfunctional members of society. Hence it is not uncommon in classical literature to meet elderly females as brothel madams,[119] as superstitious crones or even evil witches,[120] or as alcoholics;[121] the last role one especially finds depicted in art of the Hellenistic period, in turn copied by the Romans.[122] John Chrysostom remarked that gossiping and alcoholism are particular faults of women and older people.[123] One of the Greek magical papyri offers a remedy for an old woman's excessive gossiping and drinking: chop up some pine (πίτυς) and put it in her drink.[124] All these negative attributes said to be found in elderly women are epitomized in, for example, Petronius's aptly named *crudelissima anus* Oenothea: a priestess of Priapus and an adept in magical practices, she and her equally aged assistant Proselenus are overly and aggressively fond of wine and young men ("aniculae . . . solutae mero ac libidine"), not to mention money.[125] On the other side of the coin, a handful of poems *in praise of* older women highlights the very atypicality of such an approach; this is the novel point of such exercises, attempting to persuade the reader of the possibility of finding such women sexually attractive.[126] What degree of reality—if any—underlies all these stereotypical images, so antithetical in every respect to the depiction of the *gravis senex,* is a question to which we return in later chapters.

The bitterly negative, often extremely personal indictment of old age, especially in satirical and erotic poetry, had a long history, which the Roman writers of the early empire adopted willingly and enthusiastically; the tradition in Latin literature extends in painful, clinical, and—in my view—rather dreary detail to the six elegies on old age and love written in the sixth century A.D. by Maximianus, probably a contemporary of Boethius (Maximianus addresses him at one point in his poems), although almost certainly not a Christian himself.[127] Maximianus was popular in the Middle Ages, not least, perhaps, because of the somewhat misogynistic attitudes he sometimes avers. His poems, heavily influenced by the Roman love elegists, are also at times quite racy, which makes his use as a medieval school text more surprising.

Invective against old age, then, has a very long history.[128] It may be traced back almost as far as Homer—and some have found it in Homer too.[129] Mimnermus in particular dwells, with heavy and sentimental self-pity, on the flight of time, the loss of youthful pleasures, and the hatefulness of old age.[130] In Greek tragedy and comedy alike, old people (especially women) regularly—though of course not invariably—come in for unflattering, if not harsh, treatment in their depiction.[131] On the Roman stage, particularly in the plays of Plautus, the advice given by Horace many years later (quoted above) can be seen to have been already in operation; every conceivable negative quality associated with old age is highlighted, with special emphasis on the old man's sexual, though impotent, proclivities.[132] One of the stock figures of the *fabula atellana* was Pappus (from the Greek πάππος, grandfather), whom Varro called "the most ridiculous old man the Latin stage has ever seen"; Cicero remarked that "in fabulis stultissima persona est improvidorum et credulorum senum" (in stage plays the stupidest character is that of the old men, who lack foresight and who are easily deceived).[133]

The negative images pervade almost every popular branch of classical literature; one may also delve into the Aesopic fables to find lessons on the harshness of old age.[134] As with Juvenal, it is the evident physical disabilities on which all such literature tends to focus, highlighting the immediate concerns and fears of what old age will bring, as well as the humor to be derived therefrom, more than on the more "philosophical" *vituperationes* that concerned the likes of Cicero. In more serious literature, even in the midst of *consolatio,* the same concerns, however, are also evident, as has already been noted. Early Christian poetry, for example, has more than a little to say on the subject of old age; the views expressed are highly derivative and mostly negative, often as a means of stressing the temporality of human existence and the desirability of death.[135] Other instances may be adduced.

In the pseudo-Platonic *Axiochus* (traditionally said to date from the first century B.C.),[136] for example, *consolatio* is required for Axiochus as he is on the point of death. As one of his arguments, Socrates states, quite conventionally, that death should not be feared but rather welcomed, because no age in life is exempt from pain and hence death is a blessed release. As part of this argument, he quotes from a discourse given (we are told) by the sophist Prodicus, in which are described the effects of nature on the aged frame, a force that it is pointless to resist (367b):

εἶτα λαθὸν ὑπῆλθε τὸ γῆρας, εἰς ὃ πᾶν συρρεῖ τὸ τῆς φύσεως ἐπίκηρον καὶ δυσαλθές. κἂν μή τις θᾶττον ὡς χρέος ἀποδιδῷ τὸ ζῆν, ὡς ὀβολοστάτις ἡ φύσις ἐπιστᾶσα ἐνεχυράζει τοῦ μὲν ὄψιν, τοῦ δὲ ἀκοήν, πολλάκις δὲ ἄμφω. κἂν ἐπιμείνῃ τις, παρέλυσεν, ἐλωβήσατο, παρήρθρωσεν.

Then, undetected, there steals over you old age, into which all things pernicious and deadly in nature flow together. And if you do not hasten to give up your life as a debt due, Nature, like a petty usurer, steps in and grabs her pledge—your sight, your hearing, often both. And if you hold out, she paralyzes you, mutilates and tears asunder.

Again it is the physical disabilities associated with old age that are stressed, although Socrates goes on to comment on afflictions of the mind as well, with the comment that old age is a second childhood (see Chapter 8). In similar vein but with added complaints, Xenophon has Socrates in his *apologia* at the age of 70 years declare that his *dai-*

mon had not offered any sure defense for the simple reason that it was not in Socrates' interests to survive any further into old age because of all its negative attributes: loss of hearing and sight, no longer being able to learn but becoming forgetful, general discontent—"old age, on which all troubles, all privations of comfort, concur to fall. . . . the most burdensome part of life."[137] Even Plutarch in his treatise *An Seni Respublica Gerenda Sit* admits the existence of such illnesses and disabilities, but, like Plato's Cephalus and Cicero's Cato, he puts such faults down not to old age but to a lax life.[138] Like Socrates and Juvenal, Pliny the Elder argues that a short life is nature's greatest gift. How can old age even be considered a part of life, he asks, with all the disabilities associated with it?[139] And this is perhaps the dominant underlying attitude toward or image of old age to emerge from the literary sources, both serious and popular, whether by a Cicero (in defense) or by a Juvenal.

Literary portrayals, then, concentrate almost exclusively on a stereotypical old person, generalizing mainly on the physical infirmities old age brings.[140] Plutarch apart, perhaps, there seems very little attention to the social framework. The emphasis is on the way older people are to be pitied (a poor *apologia*) or are derided, and on how old age is to be feared or at best endured. Realities of old age are disguised beneath literary topoi. It is to the realities that we return in the following chapters, but throughout it may be seen that this literary background reflected or perhaps even shaped much of the treatment of older people and the social construction of old age in Roman times.

PART II

OLD AGE IN PUBLIC LIFE

Four

Rules of Age in the Roman Empire

V arious rules relating to age, instituted either by law or by custom, were in operation in the Roman world during the later republic and principate. In this chapter I consider the role of old age—and to some degree age in general—in Roman public life. In Chapter 5, more detailed analysis is made of specific public rules of age in a specific province, Roman Egypt, and in Chapter 6 certain practicalities that such rules of age imply are discussed.

First, however, it is worth considering briefly some basic rules of age which are important in regard to both private and public life and which are of relevance to our theme of the status of older people—at least to the extent that they show that *senectus* featured rarely in legal definitions. It may be seen, for example from the writings of the jurist Paul *ad Edictum,* quoted in the *Digest* under rules of *ius antiquum,* that from an early period age might be a factor taken into account in legal contexts, even if not strictly defined in terms of a set number of years: "fere in omnibus poenalibus iudiciis et aetati et imprudentiae succurritur" (in almost all penal cases both age and ignorance are a defense)—presumably the reference is to youth. More advanced age makes an appearance already in the Twelve Tables: "si morbus aevitasve escit, iumentum dato" (If there is disease or age, he [the plaintiff] is to provide a yoked beast of burden).[1] But otherwise it rarely features in the republican period.

The most basic distinction in terms of age in Roman law, under the republic and the empire, was that between *minores* and *maiores,* which seems to have been formally introduced by the *lex [P]laetoria* in circa 200 B.C. The term *minores* in this context means, in effect, those under the legal age of 25 years ("minores viginti quinque annis"), whereas a *maior* is one who is 25 years of age or older. Persons under the legal age were regarded in terms of Roman law as being incapable of maintaining their own affairs and were, if *sui iuris,* therefore entrusted to the care of *tutores* or *curatores:* in the case of persons *sui iuris, tutores* were appointed for males below the age of puberty and for women, and *curatores* might be appointed for males over the age of puberty, for *furiosi,* and for *prodigi,* although in time the distinction between *tutela* and *cura* virtually disappeared.[2] Over the legal age a male was considered legally capable unless he was in some way disadvantaged, as was the case with *furiosi, prodigi,* and the deaf.[3] For males over this legal age no further similar legal distinctions were made with regard to age, even for *senes.* While *minores* were further differentiated as being *infantes, impuberes,* or *puberes, maiores* were not similarly distinguished; one remained a *maior* until death.

There is no need to discuss here the subdivisions of *minores,* but one point is worthy of note in the context of rules of age. Males gained full legal competence at the age of 25 years, that is, on completion of the 25th year.[4] But under later classical law, if not earlier, it was possible to attain restricted legal independence before one's 25th birthday. By an imperial rescript of the early A.D. 320s, in carefully defined circumstances *adolescentes* were given the opportunity of being granted by the emperor the status of *maiores* at the age of 18 and 20 years in the case of females and males respectively. This age, in legal terms between that of *adulescentia* and *legitima aetas,* was given the tag *firmata aetas.*[5] Individuals had to prove both their age and that they were "honestate morum praediti" (endowed with noble manners). This innovation, like the imposition of an age of minority in the first place, was intended to protect or assist young individuals,[6] and enabled *minores* to undertake transactions of their own accord, an obvious expedient in certain cases. It is hardly surprising, therefore, that the opposite could also hold true. From at least the reign of Diocletian and Maximian, provision was made for the age of minority to be extended as protection during the formal institution of a suit.[7] This adaptation of rules of age, dependent upon circumstances, is noteworthy.

A quite different aspect of age definitions operated in the case of military life, that of the *iuniores* and *seniores*.[8] Our basic source of information on this age definition is Aulus Gellius, who cites Aelius Tubero (first century B.C.) and records that the division was made by Servius Tullius:

> Tubero in Historiarum primo scripsit Servium Tullium regem, populi Romani cum illas quinque classes <seniorum et> iuniorum census faciendi gratia institueret, "pueros" esse existimasse qui minores essent annis septem decem, atque inde ab anno septimo decimo, quo idoneos iam esse reipublicae arbitraretur, milites scripsisse, eosque ad annum quadragesimum sextum "iuniores" supraque eum annum "seniores" appellasse.

> Tubero, in the first book of his *Historical Researches,* wrote that King Servius Tullius, when he divided up the Roman people into those five classes of older and younger men for the purpose of conducting the census, counted as "boys" those who were under 17 years of age. After the 17th year, at which age they were considered suitable for public service, he enrolled them as soldiers, and up until their 46th year called them "younger men"; beyond that age they were called "older men."[9]

A Roman was, in military terms, a *iunior* from the age of 17 years (i.e., having completed 17 years) until the end of the 46th year (i.e., on turning 46 years of age). As was seen in Chapter 1, figures often tend to become confused and contradictory, especially when ordinals are involved, but the age of 17 years as the beginning of military service, or at least of eligibility, seems clear enough.[10]

On the age at which a Roman became a *senior* the relevant literary sources are somewhat less straightforward, but the problem is, I believe, linguistic rather than historical. As we just noted, Tubero, as recorded by Gellius, refers to military service normally being completed at the end of the 46th year, and this figure finds support in other authors.[11] Dionysius of Halicarnassus, in describing the reforms of Tullius, makes an explicit distinction between those of military age and those older than 45 years of age (τοὺς ὑπὲρ τετταράκοντα καὶ πέντε

ἔτη γεγονότας), by which may be meant those who have completed
at least 45 years (just as *maiores XXV annis* means those 25 years of age
or over, as opposed to *minores XXV annis*).[12] And Varro, in his description of the "ages of man,"[13] states that "in tertio gradu qui erant
usque quinque et quadraginta annos, iuvenes appellatos eo quod rem
publicam in re militari possent iuvare" (in the third stage, those up to
the age of 45 years were called *iuvenes* because they were able to help
[*iuvare*] the state in military affairs), whereas after that age, up to the
60th year, men were called *seniores*. Yet it must be remembered that
Varro was intentionally working with multiples of fifteen years as part
of his mathematical pattern and, in any case, his system would imply
that the stage of the *iunior* began from the age of 30 years. Again, the
problem is that we are looking for greater precision than our limited
sources are prepared to give. The definition recorded by Aulus Gellius
is accurate and precise enough: in military terms, a man was a *iunior*
from the day he turned 17 years of age until he turned 46, at which
time he became a *senior* and was no longer normally called up for military service. In times of emergency, however, those up to the age of
50 years could be called upon.[14]

We must turn now to rules relating to age in regard to the offices of
state, both at Rome and elsewhere, and to the duties that the state imposed on its citizens and subjects. Our focus is on the *maximum* ages
set, but with a brief consideration of the minimum ages for eligibility
or liability as well, both because the evidence for such ages tends to
be more plentiful (if nothing else because more people are involved)
and because such minimum ages provide further evidence for the application of rules of age in the Roman world.

Minimum Ages in the Senate

Although a consideration of the minimum age regulations for the senatorial *cursus honorum* is beyond the scope of a study of old age, the
system underlying such regulations provides a very good illustration
of and an introduction to the way that rules of age worked, especially
as it is for these specific rules that the most detailed evidence exists. I
have chosen not to consider the equestrian *cursus,* if there ever was
such a thing, because it seems certain that there was no fixed system

of age rules in operation here as there was with its senatorial counterpart. Only in one sphere of the equestrian "career," that of the *iudex,* do we have any significant data for rules relating to age, material that is considered later in this chapter in the context of *munera et honores.*[15]

Despite the traditional image of the early senate, it seems that before the second century B.C. no definitive rules laid down the minimum age before which an office could be held. Tacitus, in discussing the quaestorship, states that:

> Among our ancestors [the quaestorship] had been the reward for *virtus,* and every citizen who had good qualities to support him could stand for office. In fact there used to be no distinctions made even in regard to age [*aetas*]: nothing prevented a man in his early youth [*prima iuventa*] from taking up the consulship or a dictatorship.

And Cicero, in arguing at the beginning of 43 B.C. that Octavian should be allowed to hold the consulship at an early age (he was 19 years old at the time), notes that:

> An older age [*grandiorem aetatem*] was set by the *leges annales* for the consulship in the past because people were afraid of the rashness of youth [*adulescentiae temeritatem*]. But Gaius Caesar, young as he is [*ineunte aetate*], has shown by his excellent and outstanding qualities that it is not necessary to await any "coming of age" [*progressum aetatis*]. And that is why our earlier ancestors had no *leges annales;* such laws were introduced many years later as a result of rivalry [*ambitio*], so that the rungs on the political ladder were reserved for those of the same age-group [*ut gradus essent petitionis inter aequalis*].

Cicero goes on to cite some famous examples of men of earlier times who had held the consulship at a relatively early age, including M. Valerius Corvinus.[16] Although such cases do not prove the absence of specific rules of age in this context, not until the second century B.C. does definite evidence for the introduction of *leges annales* emerge.

The motivations underlying the introduction of such laws, and in particular the *lex Villia annalis* of 180 B.C., were probably various: an attempt both to reduce the number of candidates for more senior offices at a time when there was a significant surplus, and also, though perhaps less important, to prevent *adulescentes* (which might mean men even in their 30s) from rising up through the ranks of the senate at too meteoric a pace.[17] For such had been the case, for example, with the elder Scipio Africanus, who, according to Livy (38.51.11), had been allowed to assume office from the age of 17 and who was consul in 205 B.C. at the age of 30 years. Develin maintains that this second aspect, the too swift advancement of young men within the senate, was not related to the purpose of the *lex Villia* at all, and certainly he seems right in arguing that the law's main aim was to reduce the overall number of candidates. Evans and Kleijwegt stress that the focus of the *lex* was on the more senior positions in the *cursus* and they also argue, quite rightly, for the *lex* to be considered in the context of other legislation of the period, particularly regarding electoral corruption.[18] The two alleged aims of the *lex,* however, are not mutually exclusive, and certainly it would (or rather should) have accomplished both, as Cicero understood (see the passage from the *Philippics* quoted earlier). In fact the *lex Villia* did not accomplish either: one may note, for example, a surplus of candidates in 174 B.C. (Livy 41.28.4) and observe the younger Scipio for an example of a meteoric career. But as with the Augustan marriage legislation, subsequent failure to succeed need not refute possible original aims and objectives.

The minimum age qualifications for senatorial offices through to imperial times, as set by convention and by *leges annales,* are summarized in Table 5 in Appendix A. There is no space here to discuss the derivation of these figures, but it must be noted that even in this area, where one might expect our knowledge to be quite extensive, the matter is much disputed, for references in historians such as Livy and Appian give only tantalizing clues as to the full tenor of the laws, and much must be deduced from the reconstructions of individual careers. The figures in Table 5 are what may be considered the most plausible in the light of available evidence.[19] Exceptions to the rules existed, not least in the principate and in regard to the imperial family. Although we cannot focus here on the intricacies of these rules of age, two aspects under the early empire are of particular relevance to the themes of this book.

The minimum ages for holding the quaestorship and praetorship in this period were 25 and 30 years respectively, but these ages could be lowered in various ways, quite apart from adlection. The *ius liberorum* affected many spheres of both private and public life in the principate. In regard to the republican magistracies, one may note that certain advantages applied to candidates with children. As well as the senior consulship being decided by the number of children each consul had and precedence being given to candidates for office who had the *ius*,[20] according to an interpretation by Severus the minimum age qualification for office could be lowered by one year for every (living) child the candidate had: "quod enim legibus cavetur, ut singuli anni per singulos liberos remittantur, ad honores pertinere divus Severus ait, non ad rem suam recipiendam" (For the provision of the laws, that one year is remitted for every child, relates, according to the divine Severus, to offices and not to the receiving [sc. from *curatores*] of their property).[21] The historical context shows clearly that this was in practice from an early stage, probably even before the relevant laws came into operation. Obviously in such cases, honorary grants of the *ius liberorum* became very important and sought after.

Another enactment that effectively lowered the minimum age in this context was the legal fiction that "a year begun is a year completed" (*annus coeptus pro pleno*). It is stated most explicitly by Ulpian in relation to the age of 25 years and *munera et honores:* "annus autem vicensimus quintus coeptus pro pleno habetur: hoc enim in honoribus favoris causa constitutum est, ut pro plenis inchoatos accipiamus" (The 25th year once begun is regarded as completed; for it has been laid down as a favor in terms of offices that we should accept years as completed once begun), provided that no property of the community is to be entrusted to the care of the 24/25-year-old. The same rule may be seen in operation elsewhere in regard to *munera*. Paul mentions a constitution of Hadrian "in qua quantum ad munera municipalia iusserat eum annum, quem quis ingressus esset, pro impleto numerari" (in which he had ordered that where municipal *munera* were involved, the current year of a person's age was to be reckoned as completed).[22]

The important point to draw from this brief overview of minimum rules of age for senatorial offices is that these ages were set precisely as early as the beginning of the second century B.C. and were redefined several times over the following centuries, depending upon, inter alia, the political climate. The precise ages set might suggest that the Romans had exact and accurate knowledge of individuals' ages. These figures are also of interest for the insight they give into the way the Roman political system worked. One may wonder, for example, how experienced a patrician consul of some 32 years of age could be (or, for that matter, needed to be). And in the light of our discussion of Roman demography (Chapter 2), one may consider the chances of a young man of 25 years, political considerations aside, surviving long enough to hold the consulship and from there to go on to a proconsular career.[23] The fact that the consulship could be held at what is, by modern standards, a remarkably young age might reflect the realities of the shortness of life at Rome. But there is more to it than that; my underlying contention in what follows is that in reality the Roman state, especially in its republican constructs, accorded most power not to the oldest individuals as such but to older generations; if we had to quantify this, we might say as a generalization that most power (as opposed to less tangible respect) lay not with those over the age of 60, but with those in their 40s and 50s, *integerrima aetas.*[24]

Old Age and the Senate

Some senators *did* survive to a relatively advanced age, those who had already qualified in terms of age for the various magistracies: how numerous were they and what was their position in old age? Our discussion covers a broad span of history, in particular as it was envisaged by Romans of the late republic and early empire.

The conventional Roman view of the most ancient senate is well summarized by Ovid, in the speech he gives to Urania on the origin of the name of the month of *Maia:*

> magna fuit quondam capitis reverentia cani,
> inque suo pretio ruga senilis erat.
> Martis opus iuvenes animosaque bella gerebant
> et pro dis aderant in statione suis.
> viribus illa minor nec habendis utilis armis
> consilio patriae saepe ferebat opem.
> nec nisi post annos patuit tunc curia seros,
> nomen et aetatis mite senatus erat.
> iura dabat populo senior, finitaque certis
> legibus est aetas, unde petatur honor,

et medius iuvenum, non indignantibus ipsis
    ibat et interior, si comes unus erat.
verba quis auderet coram sene digna rubore
    dicere? censuram longa senecta dabat.
Romulus hoc vidit selectaque pectora patres
    dixit: ad hos urbis summa relata novae.
hinc sua maiores tribuisse vocabula Maio
    tangor et aetati consuluisse suae,
et Numitor dixisse potest "da, Romule, mensem
    hunc senibus" nec avum sustinuisse nepos.
nec leve propositi pignus successit honoris:
    Iunius a iuvenum nomine dictus habet.

Great of old was the reverence for the hoary head, and wrinkled old age was valued at its true worth. Martial exploits and doughty wars were work for youths, who in defense of their own gods kept watch and ward. In strength unequal, and for wars unfit, age often stood the country in good stead by its advice. The senate house was then open only to men of mature years, and the very name of senate signified a ripe old age. The elders legislated for the people, and certain laws defined the age at which office might be sought. An elder man used to walk between younger men, at which they did not repine, and if he had only one companion, the elder walked on the inner side. Who would dare to talk bawdy in the presence of an old man? Old age conferred a right of censorship. This Romulus perceived, and on the men of his choice he bestowed the title of fathers: on them the government of the new city was conferred. Here I incline to think that the elders gave their own name to the month of May, and that in doing so they had their own age in view. And Numitor may have said, "Romulus, grant this month to the old men," and the grandson may not have been able to resist his grandfather. No slight proof of the proposed honor is furnished by the next month, the month of June, which is named after young men.[25]

But in fact the conventional image of the Roman senate as a body of white-haired elder statesmen, an image that persisted through to imperial times (and indeed beyond), is misleading and was probably never true. Other assumptions that Ovid makes are clearly false: apart from the etymologies of the months of May and June, Ovid's reference to *leges annales* is, as we have already seen, anachronistic. But it was conventionally believed that Romulus set up the senate, originally with 100 senators, all men of older years. The very name *senatus* seems to support this last contention. Mommsen for one was convinced: "Die uralte Benennung *senator* fordert das Alter nicht bloss des *senior,* sondern des *senex* und es muss also wohl in ältester Zeit in den Gemeinderath nur aufgenommen worden sein, wer das sechzigste Lebensjahr überschritten hatte."[26] This is based on the false assumption that *senex* must refer to a man of at least 60 years (see Chapter 1); indeed, if we were to believe Cicero's Cato, *senex* had in early times (i.e., well before 150 B.C.) referred to a man of 46 years or more.[27] But it is clear from Aelius Tubero *apud* Aulus Gellius (quoted earlier) that the age of 46 years never marked the onset of old age as such, but the age after which, in terms of the reforms of Servius Tullius, a *iunior* became a *senior;* the *aetas senioris*—or, in later terminology, *gravitas*[28]—is generally the age described as coming before *senectus* (i.e., *senior* is the comparative of *senex* but has the meaning "*less* old [sc. than a *senex*]").[29] In any case, a survey of the evidence leads to a different conclusion than Mommsen's: *senator* was more closely linked, at least in some Romans' minds, with *senior.* What in reality this image of the past represents is a typically Roman one: in the old days, as opposed to contemporary society, older people got the respect and authority they deserve.

Various etymologies for *senatus* were given in antiquity, but the link to age is usually evident enough. The range of opinions, from the sensible to the bizarre, is well represented by Servius's comment on Vergil *Aeneid* 5.758: "senatores autem alii a senecta aetate, alii a sinendo dictos accipiunt: ipsi enim agendi facultatem dabant per senatus consulta" (some derive the name "senators" from "old age," others from "permitting," since they used to give permission to do something through senatorial decrees), and on *Aeneid* 1.426: "legitur apud quosdam . . . eum ordinem senatum appellatum quod una sensissent, quod patricii essent" (some writers assert that the senatorial order was so called because they were of one accord, all being patricians).[30] The *patres* received their name, we are frequently told, on account of their status as older, respected members of the state; that they were older is highlighted by the use of the phrase "maiores natu" in the ancient fetial formula, quoted by Livy.[31] The parallels between the purported ancient Roman senate and the Spartan *gerousia*—the latter much admired by Cicero and his ilk, as we have seen, for its positive implications for old age—are evident enough, and indeed the similarity in etymological meaning, often remarked upon, is far from accidental.[32] That need not automatically mean, however, that Roman senators, like Spartan *gerontes,* were therefore ever over the age of 60 years. Nor am I arguing that a permanent senate on the later model (i.e., from the fifth century B.C. onward) existed from the eighth century B.C.; the significance for us here is that Romans of the later republic and empire, such as Cicero and Ovid, expressed the belief that it did, and that it was made up of those of mature years.[33]

Cicero, in fact, in his *de Senectute* makes the link between *senatus* and *senex* most explicitly: he refers, in regard to the time of Cincinnatus, to "senatores, id est senes," and also speaks of *consilium, ratio, sententia* "quae nisi essent *in senibus,* non summum consilium maiores nostri appellassent senatum" (Had the faculties of planning, thinking, and advising not been present in old men, our ancestors would not have called the highest body of advisers the senate).[34] The idea is also taken up by Florus (*Epit.* 1.1.15) for the time of Romulus: "iuventus divisa per tribus in equis et armis ad subita belli excubaret, consilium rei publicae penes *senes* esset, qui ex auctoritate patres, ob aetatem senatus vocabantur" (The young men were divided into tribes and were to keep guard with horses and arms against unexpected attacks; the policy of the community was to be in the hands of the old men, who were called "fathers" from the authority which they exercised, and "the senate" on account of their age). But there is no particular need to regard this as authoritative, nor for that matter need it be imagined that by *senes* in these contexts the two authors meant men over the age of 60 years. In any event it was in the interests of Cicero's argument to allege a senate of *senes,* on the Spartan model. Most other authors understand the word *senior* rather than *senex* in this context, as the following passages indicate:[35]

Eutropius *Brev.* 1.2: "Romulus chose 100 from the older men [*ex senioribus*], to make use of their advice in all his actions, and he called them senators on account of their age [*propter senectutem*]."

Ovid *Fasti* 5.65: from the time of Romulus "the older man [*senior*] issued laws for the people."

Justin *Epit.* 43.3.2: In the time of Romulus "a senate was set up of 100 older men [*seniorum*], who were called *patres.*"

Servius *ad Aen.* 8.105: "'iuvenum primi pauperque senatus': totam ostendit aetatem . . . nam per senatum *seniores* significantur" ("The leading young men and the poor senate": this shows the full range of ages . . . for by *senatus* are signified the older men).

Isidorus *Orig.* 9.4.8: "The senate derived its name from age [*aetas*], for they were older men [*seniores*]."

In other words, an assumption such as Mommsen's, that the early senate was composed of (or was even later thought to have been composed of) members over the age of 60 years, is based on inadequate evidence. This is more than just pedantry on my part; while I have argued already that a specific number of years should not be allocated to such words denoting age-classes or -groups, it would be fair to say as a generalization that *senior* denotes a wider sense of age than does *senex*—just as in English "older men" is more general than "old men." We have already seen in the context of Servius Tullius's military reforms that *senior* was used to denote a man between the ages of 46 and 60 years. In a literary context *senior* is less specific, and could in fact be used of men over the age of 60 (perhaps euphemistically or flatteringly). But it is also clear that it could readily be used of someone well under 60, especially in contrast or comparison to a *iunior*. In short, this testimony suggests to me that Romans thought of senators of early history in terms of older or mature men (as Ovid put it, "annos patuit tunc curia seros"), rather than strictly old men.

There is no reason, therefore, to think of the Roman senate as ever being composed, or ever having been generally envisaged as having been composed, solely of *senes*. Certainly, to turn to more historical times, the minimum (and regular) age for entry to the senate was 25 years in the principate, or even earlier as a result of remissions, and life expectancy, as discussed in Chapter 2, was relatively very low, so that many who entered the senate at age 25 would not have survived into advanced old age. In relation to the age composition of the senate in the principate, model life tables can be used to come up with probable figures.[36] Taking as a model a stationary population with an average expectation of life at birth of 30 years, it emerges that, of 100 individuals at age 25, around 77 will probably survive to the age of 40 years, 46 to age 60, and only 6 to age 80. The probable age breakdown of the imperial senate in my model is: 25–29 years, 14–16%; 30–39 years, 25–28%; 40–49 years, 22–23%; 50–59 years, 17–19%; 60–69 years, 11–13%; 70+ years, 5–6%. Using these figures, it may be estimated that only about 17 percent of senators at any one time (i.e., around 100 out of 600) would have been 60 years of age or older, while something of the order of 65 percent (around 400 out of 600) would have been under the age of 50 years. Conversely, it might be noted, a fair number of senators *did* survive to age 60, but it is only the "successful" ones we tend to hear about, thus conjuring up the image, perhaps, that all older senators were prominent. It is worth bearing in mind also that at any one time many of the older senators, especially those of plebeian status, would have been absent from Rome on provincial duties.[37]

The exact figures are less important than the realization that any picture of the Roman senate of republican and imperial times as a body of wise *old* men is a false one, as prosopographical work has also made evident. It was an image, however, of which the Romans were also aware and a stereotype that apparently their art also fostered. Cassius Dio, for example, mentions a dream that the future emperor Trajan had in which he saw "an *older* man [ἄνδρα πρεσβύτην] in a tunic and purple-bordered clothing and with a crown upon his head, *as the senate is represented in pictures* [οἷά που καὶ τὴν γερουσίαν γράφουσι]."[38] The depiction of the senate on coins of the imperial period supports this idea.[39] It is not that this was the true image of a *typical* senator, but that such was the stereotypical image of the senate collectively, in which the older—not necessarily the old—held sway. In a later period Ammianus Marcellinus expresses the apparently common view that white hair carries with it authority, and as such, senators are owed reverence: "ubique patrum reverenda cum auctoritate canities." Plutarch too refers to gray hair as the crown of old age, "a prized symbol of the high dignity of leadership"—one is reminded of Cicero's *apex senectutis* again.[40] This idea that old age brought with it practical wisdom is, as we have already seen, a common feature of

ancient literature, particularly in rhetoric. One need think only of Homer's Nestor to realize how traditional this argument was; the old man
is held to be of great use still for the advice he can give.[41]

What degree of reality underlies this idealized picture in the late republic or early empire? Even if the senate was in reality composed of
senators of a variety of adult ages, is the stereotypical image a result of
the fact that the older members were held in particular esteem—or,
more to the point, held particular authority? According to Richard Talbert, "the House in fact showed respect for age," and he cites as evidence for this the observation that "whenever it was free to choose an
emperor, its candidates were all men over retirement age—Galba,
Nerva, Pertinax, Balbinus and Pupienus."[42] There is some point to Talbert's remark, but it is far from conclusive. Much more to the point
would be if they chose the *oldest* senator, but that is not stated to be
the case; nor should the senate be thought of as a body so unified in
its choice. Certainly, however, these emperors were old. Galba was
probably 69 years old on becoming emperor, Nerva 60 or 65,[43] and
Pertinax 66. The ages of the two emperors of 238, Pupienus (*cos.* II
234) and Balbinus (*cos.* II 213)—chosen from among the senators of
age and repute (τῶν ἐν ἡλικίᾳ καὶ ἀξιώματι προυχόντων), according to Herodian—are uncertain: Zonaras states that Pupienus was 74
years of age at accession, and Balbinus 60. The second figure is certainly wrong, because Balbinus must have been older than 35 years
when he held his second consulship in 213; in fact, one would suspect he was older than Pupienus.[44] But the most obvious emperor Talbert might have cited is Tacitus. Allegedly chosen by the soldiers *and*
senate in A.D. 275—so something of a novelty by this time—his old
age was, it would seem, praised to excess. According to the *Historia
Augusta,* Tacitus claimed before the senate that he was too old to serve:

> I am amazed, senators, that in place of Aurelian, a most valiant emperor,
> you should want to make an old man [*senem*] emperor. . . . I can hardly
> perform the functions of a senator, I can hardly speak the opinion to which
> my position constrains me. Observe with greater care my age [*aetatem*],
> which you are now sending out from the shade of the chamber into the
> cold and the heat. And do you think the soldiers will welcome an old man
> [*senem*] as their emperor?

But the senators are adamant:

> Thereupon there were the following acclamations from the senate: "Trajan also came to power as a *senex.*" This they said ten times. "Hadrian also came to power as a *senex.*" This they said ten times. . . . "Who can rule more ably than a *senex?*" This they said ten times. . . . "We have chosen as emperor a *senior,* one who will watch over all like a father. From him we need fear nothing ill-considered, nothing overhasty, nothing cruel [*nihil ab hoc inmaturum, nihil praeproperum, nihil asperum formidandum est*]."

It is a wonderful example, and the last sentence is particularly revealing. The author, rather surprisingly, contrasts the wisdom of the "elderly" Trajan (41 or 44 at accession), Hadrian (41), and also Antoninus (51), with the rashness of the youthful Nero (16 years at accession), Heliogabalus (13–15 years), and Commodus ("seu potius semper Incommodus"—he was 18 years old when Marcus Aurelius died).[45] The emperor Tacitus was not quite in the same league as the likes of Trajan and Hadrian; he was, it would seem, in his 70s on becoming emperor and lasted barely six months.[46] As illuminating as the account in the *Historia Augusta* may appear, it is, unfortunately, pure fiction.

But then so may be the logic that choosing an old senator as emperor is a sign that old age was held in the greatest respect. An old man may be chosen not because it is felt that he will be a "good" emperor but simply as a stopgap or as someone who may be easily swayed by the senate ("nihil inmaturum, nihil praeproperum, nihil asperum"). Furthermore, Galba, proclaimed by his troops in Spain, can hardly be said to have been chosen freely by the Roman senate, and judging by Tacitus's comments, not all respected his old age.[47] In the five cases Talbert cites, the reigns were remarkably brief: all but Nerva held imperial power for one year at most, their downfall being a result of the actions of the praetorian guard and not of their own old age. Nerva reigned for a little over sixteen months and died of natural causes, it is true, but he too might have met with an earlier end at the hands of the praetorian soldiers had he not made quick moves to parade a successor; Cassius Dio (68.3.4) states that Nerva found himself held in such contempt by the praetorians because of his old age that he adopted Trajan—a wiser choice than Galba had made.

What is most problematic with Talbert's statement, however, is the general impression it advocates that the Roman senate of the principate not only showed due respect to old age but even granted to it, when the opportunity arose, the greatest authority. Certainly this is a viewpoint elderly senators would have promoted, but this need not mean that it was true in reality. In regard to Roman emperors, it might be fairer to say that neither youth nor old age was prized. The middle ground, in the 40s or early 50s, was the ideal. In one of the lives of the *Historia Augusta* it is observed that an emperor must not be too old nor too young: too old and he is "past it," too young and he is too impetuous.[48] Dio has Hadrian remark of Antoninus Pius, aged 51 years in A.D. 138, that he is not too young to be reckless or so old as to neglect anything (μήθ' ὑπὸ νεότητος προπετὲς μήθ' ὑπὸ γήρως ἀμελὲς ποιῆσαί τι δυνάμενον).[49] Those thus suited by age, if not by other qualities, included Tiberius (54 years of age at accession), Titus (39), Vitellius (53 or, more likely, 56), and Trajan (41 or 44).[50] Claudius's *composita aetas* (he turned 46 years of age in A.D. 37)—but not his *imminuta mens*—was suitable for a successor to Tiberius.[51]

Age was not, however, the only, or indeed the primary, factor to consider in choosing or revering a leader. Even given the choice, what seems more likely is that preference was shown to rank and experience, not to mere age (though the two might tend to coincide). That old senators did foster an image of their usefulness is clear enough and easy to understand. One can detect in Cicero's *Cato Maior de Senectute,* for example, the underlying conviction that the aging man—including Cicero himself—still had a prominent part to play in the state. As was discussed in the previous chapter, Cicero set his dialogue in the golden aura of the past, choosing as his principal advocate the aged censor Cato, the upholder of traditional, conservative morals, the *mos maiorum.* Through Cato, the reader is given numerous examples of elderly men who have led an active political life. Cicero emphasizes the respect that old age should be shown, quoting with approval the ancient system in Sparta. In the *de Senectute* he also draws attention to the college of augurs and, in another work, to the Syracusan *senatus* as praiseworthy examples of precedence and honor being accorded to old age.[52] The implication must be that in Cicero's own day and in Cicero's estimation the Roman senate failed to live up to such ideals. This timeless notion that respect is the *apex senectutis* is also implied by Plato's Cephalus, as well as by Pericles when Thucydides has him say in the funeral speech that "it is the love of honor, not gain, that gladdens the heart of age and helplessness."[53]

In Cicero's *de Senectute* and more explicitly (and in tedious detail, as we have seen) in Plutarch's *An Seni Respublica Gerenda Sit,* we find the argument put forward in vigorous fashion that the old man has a vital role to play in the administration and government of the state, and that he should not retire into a life of idle luxury. As point of contrast Plutarch notes the active, if ultimately unsuccessful, old age of Pompey and the extravagant last years of L. Licinius Lucullus.[54] Like Cicero and others, Plutarch also invokes the example of the Spartans with their *gerousia,* where "men grow old most nobly" because they retain an active and ever increasing role in the political affairs of the state (*Mor.* 795f). As has been mentioned already, the minimum age qualification for the Spartan *gerousia* was 60 years and the office was held for life—a practically unique ancient example of, at least in theory, a gerontocracy.[55] Even in the more democratic *polis* of Athens,[56] older men had an official function: there is slight evidence for priority in speaking being given to age in the assembly before the fourth century B.C.,[57] and from the fourth century male citizens served as mediators at the age of 59 years.[58]

So did old senators at Rome really enjoy the respect and authority that Cicero, Plutarch, and Talbert would have us believe they did? Cicero's and Plutarch's very need to stress this aspect of old age might lead us to suppose that in some cases they did not. In fact, in the case of Sparta, Aristotle provides an interesting contrast as well as making a valid point: old age may conventionally be credited with wisdom, yet in practice old men in power could harm rather than benefit the state. He refers to the Spartan *gerousia* in particular: "Nor are they well served by the arrangements for the office of the Elders [τὴν τῶν γερόντων ἀρχήν]. One would probably say that provided they are respectable men, adequately educated with a view to manly virtue, the office is an asset to the state—yet their lifelong sovereignty in important trials is a point for debate; for the intellect too has its old age, just like the body [ἔστι γάρ, ὥσπερ καὶ σώματος, καὶ διανοίας γῆρας]."[59] There is evidence, furthermore, that in antiquity old men, including those prominent in the state, did *not* always enjoy the respect to which they may have felt they were entitled (and which was allegedly shown to older people in the days of Romulus: see again the lines from Ovid's *Fasti,* quoted earlier).

Then too there must be considered the fact that, apart from the actual perils of relatively high mortality levels, it was regarded as difficult anyway for people in the loftiest echelons of political life to attain a ripe old age, at least in some periods—suspicious deaths were notoriously common. Tacitus notes with some surprise that the *pontifex* L. Calpurnius Piso (*cos.* 15 B.C.) died a natural death, a rare thing in court ("rarum in tanta claritudine"), and attributes it to the tact that Piso showed in his dealings with his associates.[60] It was apparently proverbial that the only way to survive in the political arena was to show such diplomacy and to keep one's mouth shut. Seneca the Younger tells a story, apparently well known ("notissima vox"), of how one man achieved "rarissima res in aula," namely old age: by taking the knocks and expressing gratitude for them ("iniurias . . . accipiendo et gratiam agendo"). One might also cite the case of Juvenal's Crispus, to be identified with L. Iunius Q. Vibius Crispus (*cos.* II 74), who, if we are to believe the satirist, lived to his 80th year ("iucunda senectus") by agreeing with the emperor in everything. Juvenal notes that Crispus was the exception and that he himself would prefer to be a nobody.[61]

But there is, of course, ample evidence for the existence of old senators. Various examples, drawn from the long course of Roman history, of aged senators still holding office may be adduced, some of whom we have already met, such as M. Valerius Corvus, who held his sixth consulship in 299 B.C. at over 70 years of age; L. Caecilius Metellus, consul at the age of 70 in 251 B.C. and consul again in 247 (he lasted to the age of 100 years); and Marcus Perperna, consul in 92 B.C., who died in 49 B.C. at the age of 98 years.[62] Such cases abound: L. Quinctius Cincinnatus, consul in 460 B.C. and (by some accounts) dictator for the second time in 439 when he was apparently 80 years old;[63] M. Fabius Buteo (*cos.* 245, censor 241, dictator 216), in 216 the oldest living *homo censorius;* and of course Cato the Elder (*cos.* 195, censor 184) who died at the age of 84 or 85 years and who was politically active to the end. Under the empire many more cases may be noted. There are also the particularly striking examples of L. Volusius Saturninus who, having been consul in A.D. 3, went on eventually to become *praefectus urbi,* the office he held when he died in A.D. 56 at the age of 93 years; and of C. Manlius Valens, consul for the first (and only) time in A.D. 96—and *consul ordinarius* at that—at the sprightly age of 89 years and who died in the same year. A first consulship at such an age is certainly unique; for the imperial period (see Figure 1 in Appendix B), the closest in age, but still thirty years or so younger, are the former Antonian (which explains a lot) Cn. Cornelius Cinna Magnus (*cos. ord.* A.D. 5), at around age 60; and the future emperor Gordian I, who was apparently born circa 159 and who was not consul till circa 222. Closer in date to Valens, and also noteworthy, is C. Iulius (Plancius Varus?) Cornutus Tertullus, suffect consul in A.D. 100 with Pliny the Younger, and later (116/17 or 117/18) proconsul of Africa; he must have been in his late 50s already in 100. If Cornutus's career is to be classed as sluggish, Valens's was all but stagnant.[64]

But these examples, interesting though they may be, are only isolated cases that tell us very little about the general or typical position of *senes* within the Roman senate. Those from early Roman history, strikingly frequent, are perhaps more a sign of the ancient interest in historical details of this kind, as we have already discussed in our Introduction. It needs also to be stressed that old age in itself did not grant automatic authority or superiority. Thus, for example, the order of speaking in the Roman *curia* was by the later republic determined not by the criterion of age per se, but by seniority in office, with *consules designati* being called first, followed by consulars (presumably beginning with the one who held the office earliest).

In this context we need to consider further for a moment the historical development of the workings of the senate in the republican era to understand better the place of elderly senators and of old age in general within the *curia,* then and later. Livy provides some clues as to perceived change over time, in particular to changing attitudes in the late third–early second century B.C., and it will be useful to take a snapshot of the years 211–209 B.C.; this may also serve to highlight, perhaps, related interests of the Augustan era at the time when Livy was writing. In Livy's overall account of republican politics we hear much of the *sententiae* of *primores patrum: consulares, censorii,* and *dictatorii.*

It may be inferred that what mattered most regarding influence and power in the senate in this period (and, it might be said, into imperial times) was rank and inherited status, not age as such. On occasion, however, in Livy's account debate is centered around age-groups, and in the early period the *auctoritas seniorum* usually prevails.[65] One example, coming as it does at a crucial period in Roman history, may illustrate the traditional ideal. T. Manlius Torquatus (*cos.* 235, 224 B.C., censor 231, dictator 208, *pontifex* from before 212 down to 202) apparently refused—because of *oculorum valetudo*—to stand for the consulship of 210 B.C., despite the support of the *iuniores* of the Voturia tribe, who were voting first. The *iuniores* consulted the *seniores* as to for whom they should vote, a practice that Livy finds highly commendable and which he regrets is no longer followed: "But that a century of the *iuniores* wished to confer with the *seniores* on the question to which persons they should, by their vote, entrust a high command, should seem to us scarcely credible—this is owing to the cheapened and diminished authority [*vilis levisque auctoritas*] even of parents over their children in our day."[66] However unrealistic this dichotomy on account of age may appear in historical terms, its significance to our understanding of later perceptions of the workings of the earlier senate is important. For the traditional mechanisms were seen to have changed subtly and slowly, but fundamentally, in this time of increasing crisis—the Second Punic War and the threat of Hannibal.[67]

Livy again provides us with clues as to the change, in this case regarding the choice of *princeps senatus* by P. Sempronius Tuditanus (*cos.* 204) and M. Cornelius Cethegus (*cos.* 204), the two censors of 209 B.C.—that is, only two years after the elections of the consuls for 210, and a telling contrast. By tradition the *princeps senatus*, he whose name came first in the roll of senators and who had the right to express his opinion first in debate, was the one from among the living patricians in the senate (probably of the *maiores gentes*) who had held the censorship the earliest. In other words, precedence had traditionally been given to a combination of inherited status, rank, and seniority. But in 209 B.C. this tradition was successfully challenged. Merit, rather than simple chronological age, was to be taken into account:

> The revision of the list of the senate was delayed by a dispute between the censors in regard to the choice of a *princeps*. The choice belonged to Sem-

pronius; but Cornelius said that they must follow the traditional custom of the senate, namely, to choose as *princeps* the man who, among the living, had been censor first. That was T. Manlius Torquatus. Sempronius claimed that if the gods had given a man the choice by lot, they also gave him an unrestricted right; he would make the choice according to his own judgment, and would choose Q. Fabius Maximus, whom he could prove, even with Hannibal as judge, to be at that time the first citizen [*princeps*] of the Roman state. After the war of words had lasted a long time, his colleague began to give way, and Sempronius chose Q. Fabius Maximus, the consul, as *princeps senatus*.[68]

The change in the method of choosing this post reflects, I would argue, the ongoing change in the degree of precedence given to age. Both Torquatus and Fabius Maximus were elderly; the former was first consul in 235 and censor in 231, the latter first consul in 233 and censor in 230.[69] But in terms of seniority and presumably age Torquatus held the edge. By traditional rights the title of *princeps senatus* should have been his. But it was not to be. It is a subtle but important evolution; to be sure, it is no revolution, but an isolated episode. The automatic precedence due to seniority, once eroded, may continue to decline, even in the face of strong conservatism. The later history of precedence in the senate also points to this: after Sulla, who may have abolished the office of *princeps,* priority was given to the consuls designate (or, in their absence, to a consular, and not necessarily in order of age). Late in the first century B.C. this practice too was modified; Augustus made himself *princeps senatus* in 28 B.C., at the age of 35 years.[70]

But let us return briefly to the period of the Second Punic War and its aftermath. In 205 B.C. the question arose as to whether the province of Africa should automatically go to the consul Scipio Africanus Maior, aged 30 or 31 at the time; his meteoric rise we have already had cause to mention. He had received consular *imperium* in 210—clearly a critical year for our purposes—to command in Spain, the first to get it without having been praetor or consul. Fabius Maximus spoke against his command in Africa, and was, according to Livy (28.40–43), supported by the older senators (*seniores*) in particular. So the *auctoritas seniorum* is still important, but so is the fact that there was debate. Eventually Scipio was given Sicily, with permission to cross to Africa: a compromise in Scipio's favor. But it is in the ensuing period (ca. 197

to ca. 177 B.C.), after the Second Punic War, that the *leges annales* were introduced, as we have already mentioned, perhaps inter alia as a (fruitless) attempt to quell the tide of change.[71] In 172 B.C. another significant and not, I think, unrelated event took place in the senate. Livy presents the conflict of opinion over the innovative diplomatic strategy of Q. Marcius Philippus (*cos.* 186, 169, censor 164), a conflict between "the majority of the senate" (magna pars senatus—which supports Marcius) and "the older, more conservative senators" (veteres et moris antiqui memores . . . seniores). In this case the former—not the *seniores*—prevailed.[72] That year, 172, was also the first in which both consuls were plebeian; interestingly enough, two plebeians were elected first in 215 B.C. (during another period of social and political change), but the election was declared invalid for religious reasons (Livy 23.31).

This detour into one short span of mid-republican political history does not do justice to the period, but it does highlight one factor in the evolution of Roman political life, as it was later perceived. The traditional and automatic rights owing to the age of a senator were being challenged and changed. In hindsight this is perceptible, and its effects would be felt for the following centuries, however subtly. This is not to deny, however, the continued authority that age, with experience and the tenure of offices, brought.[73] Imperial sources still show that respect and precedence in given circumstances would be expected of the younger toward the older senators. For example, Pliny the Younger praises the young Iunius Avitus, recently deceased, for the respect he had shown Pliny; note that Pliny regards such a characteristic as somewhat atypical in his day:

> Such was his affection and respect for me that he adopted me as his moral guide and, so to speak, instructor. This is rare in the young of today [*rarum hoc in adulescentibus nostris*]; for very few of them will yield to age [*aetati*] or authority as being their superior. They straightaway know and understand everything; they neither respect nor follow the example of anyone, but set their own standards. Avitus, however, was quite different.[74]

This contrast between past and present is very traditional—*mos maiorum* sums it up quite effectively—and very Roman. Aulus Gellius made a rather astute observation in this connection:

Among the most ancient Romans [*apud antiquissimos Romanorum*] neither birth nor wealth was generally more highly honored than age. Older men [*maioresque natu*] were treated with reverence by their juniors [*minoribus*], almost like gods and like their own parents, and in every place and in every kind of honor they were given preference and more importance. From a dinner party too, as it is written in accounts of antiquity, *seniores* were escorted home by the *iuniores*—it is recorded that the Romans adopted this custom from the Spartans, among whom, following the laws of Lycurgus, greater honor in every respect was paid to greater age [*aetati maiori*]. But after it was seen that progeny were needed for the state and use was made of rewards and inducements to increase the population's fecundity, then in certain respects those who had a wife and those who had children were preferred to older men [*seniores*] and to those who did not have children or wives. Thus, in chapter 7 of the *lex Iulia,* priority between the consuls in assuming the *fasces* is given not to the one who is older [*qui pluris annos natus est*] but to the one who has more children (either in his *potestas* or lost in war) than his colleague.[75]

The contention that the Augustan legislation brought less deference to age is particularly telling. It will be recalled that it was under Augustus that the senate was opened up to younger men, and that many offices could thenceforth be held at younger ages. This is to be seen as one more step in a gradual but definite progression: age was perceived as carrying less sway, less automatic respect or authority, than it had traditionally enjoyed in the more conservative—and somewhat nebulous—past, the era idealized by the likes of Cicero.

One mark of continued influence and/or prestige for elderly senators would be the tenure of important offices. It is certainly true that particular positions were available after the consulship; in the imperial period, a very honored band might achieve a second or even third consulship in later life (see Table 6 in Appendix A). Such an honor was usually held at least a decade after the first tenure and, on occasion, three decades or more.[76] This is clearly a sign of distinction, typically reserved for those of very senior status (and, inevitably, age), such as sons of former *ordinarii* who had only been suffect consuls previously, as well as those with some relationship to the imperial house. Apart from provincial governorships, there were also *praefecturae* and curatorships.[77] In no case is there evidence for a minimum age qualification. Some posts, such as those of the *curator alvei Tiberis* and the *cu-*

ratores operum publicorum, were generally held by new consulars, but other positions, notably that of the *praefectus urbi,* were held by more senior men who might remain in the position for a number of years, if not till death. Unfortunately, though we know the names and approximate dates of office for more than sixty *praefecti* from 26 B.C. to A.D. 270, for very few can age be determined; the interval after the first consulship provides better indication, albeit less precise than might be desired (see Table 7 in Appendix A). Senior men also held the *cura aquarum,* but it is clear that this was not the most prestigious (only one *nobilis,* and all suffect consuls) or demanding of posts.[78] The censorship, under the principate a position commonly reserved for the imperial family, in the later republic was generally held (if at all) within a decade of the consulship.[79] Many provincial governorships under the early principate were typically held before the age of 50 years, but the interval between consulship and proconsular command inevitably increased—a result not of increased prestige being accorded to those of older years but of the fact that more proconsular candidates were available.[80] The proconsulships of the public (senatorial) provinces of Asia and Africa, typically depicted as the crowning glory of a long and distinguished career, were generally held (for one year) by a select few a good number of years after their consulship. It was generally the case that the proconsulship of Africa or Asia marked the end of a senatorial career; occasionally, another consulship or the post of *praefectus urbi* might follow.[81]

Figure 2 (in Appendix B) assembles the available evidence to show apparent trends in the interval between first consulship and tenure of the proconsulship of Africa and Asia for those who were selected in the course of three centuries. Under the Julio-Claudians, not least under Tiberius, a definitive pattern is elusive. But in the latter part of the first century these most prestigious of posts were typically held around a decade after the consulship, with much individual variation; from circa A.D. 80 through to 230 a clear pattern emerges, rising from ten to fifteen or sixteen years. A longer interval is very rare; the absolute maximum is twenty years, which seems to have occurred on only two occasions—if then—over three centuries: M. Aemilius Lepidus, who was *consul ordinarius* in A.D. 6 and proconsul of Asia perhaps as late 26/8 (even then he was still only about 53 years old);[82] and M. Aufidius Fronto, who was *consul ordinarius* in 199 and proconsul of Asia around 219, having been prevented by Macrinus from taking up the proconsulship of Africa a few years earlier, according to Dio (78.22.4).

Typically, then, these very senior men, particularly if of patrician status, will in fact often have tended to be in their 40s and 50s. As has been seen (Table 5, and see again Figure 1), patrician senators during the principate might expect to reach the consulship as much as a decade before their less "dignified" peers. It is logical to deduce that, typically, the older a man was when he held a proconsular command, the later in life he had held his first consulship[83] and—by implication and other circumstances notwithstanding—the lower, relatively speaking, his inherited status within the senate. With most individuals we cannot be certain of age, which makes the inquiry more difficult. But to take some concrete examples: the future emperor Galba (*cos. ord.* A.D. 33) was no more than 46 or 47 years old when in A.D. 44 or 45 he was sent to Africa.[84] M. Iunius Silanus, who we know was born in A.D. 14 (he was Augustus's *abnepos*), was *consul ordinarius* in A.D. 46 and proconsul of Asia in A.D. 54, at the age of 39 or 40 years. As a later example, the patrician Q. Pompeius Sosius Priscus, *consul ordinarius* in A.D. 149 at the age of 32 years (or possibly a few years older), was probably only in his mid to late 40s when he served as proconsul of Asia (ca. 163/4). Older but still under 60 years was, for example, P. Mummius Sisenna Rutilianus, who died circa A.D. 174 at the age of 70,[85] so that he was around 42 years of age as suffect consul in 146 and in his mid to late 50s as proconsul of Asia (ca. 160/1); similarly M. Didius Severus Iulianus (emperor A.D. 193 at the age of 60 years, *cos. suff.* in 175?) was probably 55 or 56 years old on his appointment as proconsul of Africa (ca. 189/90).

In other words, the fact that some individuals held the proconsulship of Africa or Asia at advanced ages need not signify honor to old age, but may rather point to their slow advancement, for whatever reason; the future—at the age of 66—emperor Pertinax, who turned 49 years of age in his first consulship in 149, was 62 years old as proconsul of Africa, but, however illustrious, his was not a typical or steady career.[86] Figure 3 in Appendix B illustrates the attested ages of these proconsular governors in the Julio-Claudian period. Only two cases, both of *novi homines,* are attested over the age of 60 years. It is true that in the next centuries the chances of a proconsul of Africa or Asia being over the age of 60 years were greater as the interval after the first consulship increased. For example, Q. Voconius Saxa Fidus, *consul suffectus* in 146 at around 50 years of age, was *proconsul Africae* circa 161/2, at the age of about 65 years; the case of Cornutus we have already noted. But such was not, I would suggest, the norm. Even if a first consulship was held in a man's early to mid 40s, he might still expect to be governor in Africa or Asia—if at all—before he turned 60 years of age.

To summarize, it is inevitable that we find men of quite advanced years holding these posts, and in some cases such select positions, together with priesthoods,[87] might be seen as a tribute to a long career. But the crucial factors for election to most senior positions were undoubtedly experience and imperial patronage, rather than old age per se.[88] Being the oldest candidate by no means ensured success: it is worth remembering that one's married status and number of living children could bring preferment and more rapid advancement. Indeed an infirm old age might deter or disqualify a senator from the performance of such duties. Such may have been the case with Cornelius Fronto and the proconsulship of Asia in A.D. 157. Dio mentions the intriguing case of C. Iulius Asper (*cos.* II *ord.* 212 and *praefectus urbi* around that time), who "received" the province of Asia from Macrinus in A.D. 217. Apparently Asper asked not to be sent, but Macrinus insisted. Then, on his way to Asia, Asper was recalled—Macrinus, we are told, had heard that Asper had made some improper remarks—and Q. Anicius Faustus (*cos. suff.* ca. 198) was sent to Asia in Asper's place. Dio comments that it was as though Asper had made a second request to be relieved "on account of old age and illness" (διά τε γῆρας καὶ νόσον).[89]

But in one area of imperial affairs at least, as *amici principis,* advisors or counselors of an emperor, quite elderly senators did play a leading role. And not only senators: in this context one thinks in particular of the equestrian C. Turannius, whom we met briefly in the previous chapter and who was an *amicus* of Augustus, Tiberius, Gaius, and Claudius; he was prefect of Egypt 7–4 B.C., and apparently *praefectus annonae* A.D. 14–48, which means he died in office close to the age of 100 years.[90] John Crook remarked in his comprehensive and still fundamental study of the subject of imperial *amici* that "[t]he imperial service seems to have had no tendency to force men into retirement while they had a spark in them, and in any case retirement from administrative duties might be the beginning of a man's most valuable period as a counsellor."[91] But this second notion, logical as it might sound, is not borne out by what we know of *amici*. Emperors used the services of those still "in office," senators in particular. If "retired" men continued in this function, the evidence is strikingly sparse. Certainly, at any rate, there is plentiful evidence for older *amici,* and a representative prosopographical catalog will be of some service, updating Crook in the process. Most precise ages remain uncertain (relevant information is given where possible), so the list cannot claim anything approaching completeness; more to the point, it is rarely clear from the literary sources whether a man served as an *amicus* or not, because neither the title nor the post was official. But the catalog may also serve to present some of the better known elder statesmen of imperial times, some but by no means all of whom we have already met. For the sake of some brevity, the most familiar of literary names, such as Seneca, the two Plinies, Quintilian, Fronto, and Cassius Dio, are omitted. A roughly chronological order is followed.

T. Statilius Taurus (*amicus* of Augustus)
Cos. I 37 B.C., *cos.* II *ord.* 26 B.C., *praef. urbi* 16–13 (?) B.C. *Novus homo.* Tacitus *Ann.* 6.11 notes his "provecta aetas" as *praef. urbi.* Perhaps the brother, or better father (or uncle?), of "Statilia," who was 99 years old under Claudius (Pliny *NH* 7.48.158). *PIR* S 615.

L. Tarius Rufus (*amicus* of Augustus and Tiberius)
At Actium (Dio 50.14); *cos.* 16 B.C., *curator aquarum* A.D. 23–24, i.e., 53 years after Actium (thus Frontinus, although Syme 1986: 223–26 has raised the possibility, inter alia, of changing this to A.D. 8–13: "complicated, hazardous, and vulnerable"; cf. Bruun 1991: 156, 177–79). *Novus homo. PIR* T 14; *RE* 4a.2320–23.

L. Calpurnius Piso (Pontifex) (*amicus* of Augustus and Tiberius)
Born 48 B.C. *Cos. ord.* 15 B.C., *praef. urbi* A.D. 13 (17?)–32. Died in his 80th year (Tacitus *Ann.* 6.10); cf. Seneca *Ep.* 83.14–15. *PIR*[2] C 289; Syme (1986) ch. 24.

C. Asinius Gallus (*amicus* of Augustus and Tiberius)
Born 41 B.C. *Cos. ord.* 8 B.C., *procos. Asiae* 6–5 B.C. Died A.D. 33.
PIR[2] A 1229.

Cn. Calpurnius Piso (*amicus* of Augustus and Tiberius)
Cos. ord. 7 B.C. Died in A.D. 20 after "quinque et quadraginta annorum obsequium" (Tacitus *Ann.* 3.16), including as *procos. Africae. PIR*[2] C 287; Eck et al. (1996) 71–77.

L. Volusius Saturninus (*amicus* of Augustus, Tiberius, and Claudius)
Born 38 B.C. *Cos.* A.D. 3, *procos. Asiae.* Died age 92 or 93 as *praef. urbi* (apparently from A.D. 40/1), in A.D. 56. Cf. Pliny *NH* 11.90.223 (exceeded his 90th year), 7.14.62, 7.48.156 (he outlived all senators who had been there in his consulate); Tacitus *Ann.* 13.30.4: he departed "egregia fama," 93 years old, having enjoyed the unbroken friendship of so many emperors (reading *amicitia* for *malitia*). See J. Reynolds, *JRS* 61 (1971) 142–43 (= *AE* 1972: no. 174; cf. Eck 1996: 125–45) for the family inscription, lines 4–5: "in ipsa praefectura obiit nonagesimum et tertium annum agens" (i.e., 92 years of age). *PIR* V 661. Columella 1.7.3 (writing in the early A.D. 60s) refers to a "P. Volusius," an old and wealthy ex-consul whom he has met—probably this man (*pace* the *praenomen* and Loeb editor; cf. Syme 1958: 448 n. 8, and *RE Suppl.* 9.1862).

C. Poppaeus Sabinus (*amicus* of Augustus and Tiberius)
Cos. ord. A.D. 9, *novus homo,* governor of Moesia 11/12–35 (in A.D. 15 Achaea and Macedonia were added): Tacitus *Ann.* 6.39 ("par negotiis"), 1.80; cf. Dio 58.25.4. Died A.D. 35. *PIR*[2] P 847.

Ti. Plautius Silvanus Aelianus (*comes* of Claudius, *amicus* of the Flavians)
Born circa A.D. 11 (no later). *Cos. suff.* 45, II *suff.* 74, *procos. Asiae* under Nero (ca. 55/6), *praef. urbi* circa 70 (?)–*ante* 79 (apparently died before Vespasian). *PIR*[2] P 480.

M'. Acilius (Glabrio?) Aviola (*amicus* of Claudius, Nero, Vespasian, and Domitian)
About 80 years of age under Domitian, if this is the same man as

in Juvenal 4.94–103 ("prodigio par est in nobilitate senectus"), which not all accept. *Cos. ord.* 54, *procos. Asiae* 65–66, *curator aquarum* 74–97 (?)—Bruun (1991) 179 suspects a shorter tenure. *PIR*² A 49, 62.

L. Iunius Q. Vibius Crispus (*amicus* of Nero, Vitellius, and the Flavians)
Born circa A.D. 13? *Cos.* I circa 61 (?—much debated; unlikely to be later, but possibly in the previous decade, ca. 54), II 74; III 83 (?); *curator aquarum* 68–71; *procos. Africae* circa 71/2; legate of Hispania Citerior circa 73/4. Died before A.D. 93. Cf. Juvenal 4.81–93 ("Crispi iucunda senectus," in or over his 80th year [presumably at death]). *PIR* V 379 (outdated); Eck, *RE Suppl.* 14.852. We have already met Crispus several times.

L. Verginius Rufus (*amicus* of Nerva)
Born circa A.D. 14. *Cos.* I *ord.* 63 (so already close to 50 years of age), II 69, III *ord.* 97. Died A.D. 97, 83 years old: Pliny *Ep.* 2.1.4. *PIR* V 284. See Chapter 3.

Cn. Arrius Antoninus (*amicus* of the Flavians, Nerva, and Trajan)
Cos. I 69, II 97 (?), *procos. Asiae* 78/9 (?). Pliny *Ep.* 4.27.6 ("gravissimus senex"), cf. 4.3.1 (to Arrius): *princeps civitatis* in terms of his *sanctitas, auctoritas, aetas. PIR*² A 1086.

Q. Iulius Cordinus C. Rutilius Gallicus (*amicus* of Domitian)
Born circa A.D. 24. *Cos.* I 71/2, *cos.* II 85; *procos. Asiae* 82/3–83/4?; *praef. urbi* circa 89–91/2? Cf. Statius *Silv.* 1.4; Eck (1985b); Syme (1988: 514–20; 1991: 623–29); *PIR*² R 248.

Sex. Iulius Frontinus (*comes* of Domitian, *amicus* of Nerva and Trajan)
Born ca. A.D. 35? *Cos.* I 73 (?), II 98, III *ord.* 100, *procos. Asiae* ca. 84–85, *curator aquarum* 97–ca. 103/4. *Novus homo. PIR*² I 322; see Eck (1982b) and Bruun (1991).

T. Vestricius Spurinna (*amicus* of Nerva and Trajan)
Born A.D. 24/5. *Cos.* I 73 (?), II 98. Died aged 80+ (past his 77th year: Pliny *Ep.* 3.1.10), in or after A.D. 105. For the governorship of Germania Inferior in A.D. 97, see Eck (1985a) 152–54. *PIR* V

308 comments, not very astutely, "sed homini tres et septuaginta annos nato provinciam bellicosissimam creditam esse non est probabile." Cf. Syme (1958: 634–35; 1991: 541–50).

A. Didius Gallus Fabricius Veiento (*amicus* of Nero, the Flavians, Nerva, and Trajan).
Cos. I ca. 74 (?), II 80, III 83 (?). Still alive in A.D. 97 (Pliny *Ep.* 4.22.5). Cf. Juvenal 4.113. *PIR*² F 91; Syme (1958: 633; 1991: 533–34).

Q. Corellius Rufus (*amicus* of Nerva)
Born ca. A.D. 31. *Cos.* 78 (?). Pliny *Ep.* 1.12.11: he completed his 67th year. *PIR*² C 1294; cf. Chapter 3.

L. Iulius Ursus Servianus (*amicus* of Trajan and Hadrian)
Born ca. A.D. 46/7. *Cos.* I 90, II *ord.* 102, III *ord.* 134. Died in A.D. 136, at Hadrian's behest, at age 89 or 90; cf. Pliny *Ep.* 10.2.1; Dio 69.17.2; SHA *Hadr.* 15.8, 23.8, 25.8. *PIR*² I 631; cf. also Chapter 3 note 71.

M. Lollius Paullinus D. Valerius Asiaticus Saturninus (*amicus* of Trajan and Hadrian)
Cos. I 94, II *ord.* 125, *procos. Asiae* ca. 108/9; *praef. urbi* (*ante* 125–*non ante* 134). *PIR*² L 320.

L. Catilius Severus Iulianus Claudius Reginus (*amicus* of Trajan and Hadrian)
Cos. I 110, II *ord.* 120, *procos. Africae* 124/5, *praef. urbi* ca. 134–38. *PIR*² C 558.

M. Servilius Silanus (*amicus* of Marcus and Commodus)
Cos. I 152, II *ord.* 188. Killed under Commodus. *PIR* S 428 is outdated.

Ti. Claudius Pompeianus (*amicus* of Marcus, Commodus, and Pertinax)
Cos. I 167 (?), II *ord.* 173. Retired into private life: cf. Dio 73.3.3–4 (age and bad eyes used as an excuse to absent himself from the city under Commodus and after Pertinax). *PIR*² C 973.

M'. Acilius Glabrio (*amicus* of Commodus and Pertinax)
Cos. I 173 (?), II *ord.* 186. Cf. Dio 73.3.3–4 (cited earlier concerning Pompeianus). *PIR*² A 69.

C. Ceionius Rufius Volusianus (*amicus* of every emperor from Carinus to Constantine)
Cos. I 311, II *ord.* 314, *procos. Africae* ca. 305/6, *praef. urbi* 310–11, 313–15. *PLRE* 1.976–78 (Volusianus 4; *PIR*² R 161).

The list is striking; a fair stream of relatively aged men enjoyed close contact with the emperor and a position of undoubtedly high preference. Some *amici*—not, it should be added, all elderly—went on to be emperors themselves: Galba, Otho, Vitellius, Vespasian, Nerva, Hadrian, and Pertinax are noteworthy cases. This is only reasonable to expect, because these men would have gained valuable experience and expertise, not to mention ambition, under their predecessors. But it would be misleading to infer from this catalog of older *amici* anything approaching a gerontocracy. It is both practical experience and imperial patronage that count (note the frequency, for example, of features we have already noted, such as the office of *praefectus urbi* and proconsular commands in Africa or Asia), not mere age, though experience and age will naturally coincide in time with most individuals if they survive long enough. It is also clear that these men remained useful because they were still active, at least in terms of tenure of offices; they had not "retired."

Crook rightly stresses the continuity and stability in the composition of counseling bodies under different emperors. If an *amicus* served well and did not put a foot wrong, there was every reason to expect him to serve until he was incapable, or unwilling; in retirement he might retain the *amicitia* of an emperor without actively serving as a recognized or active *amicus* in the full political sense. Typically, furthermore, as *amici* grew old in the job, they were less commonly appointed as *senes*. Volusius Saturninus is a good example: at Augustus's death, he would have been only 51 years old and had already done good service as an *amicus*. Verginius Rufus, on the other hand, was a *novus homo* (a fairly recurring feature) and a late starter. Ideally, an elderly emperor would have built up a large collection of experienced friends on whom he could draw; many would already be serving as *amici*. Nerva is a striking case, with the likes (some of whom we have also met in the previous chapter through the correspondence of Pliny the Younger) of Verginius Rufus, Spurinna, Fabricius Veiento, Arrius Antoninus, Frontinus, and Corellius Rufus to support him. But even here it is not the case that the empire was being governed just by a "small cabal of elderly nobles who formed [Nerva's] entourage."[92] New, younger men increasingly played a role, ensuring the continuity of the system.[93] And as for the *comites* who accompanied the emperor on provincial visits, incapacity may well have limited the viable participation of the more aged.[94]

It must be borne in mind that, in general, the longer a person lived, the greater the chances of his name being preserved for history, whether in literary or epigraphical testimony, and thus appearing in the historical record as an *amicus;* in any event, a perusal of Crook's list of *amici* will dispel the notion that they were *all* elderly gentlemen. In fact it is striking how rarely old age is mentioned in the context of *amici*. The only explicit case is highly unusual: when Severus Alexander attained the throne in A.D. 222 at the tender age of 12 or 13 years, Herodian states, sixteen senators were chosen, men "of the greatest dignity in years [ἡλικίᾳ σεμνοτάτους] and the most moderate way of life"—nor were these sixteen the entire *consilium*.[95] When Cassius Dio has Maecenas advise Augustus on the creation and use of such a council,[96] he makes no reference at all in this context to age. To Dio at least, age was not a primary factor: what mattered was ἀρετή, excellence. From what little we know of the order of procedure within the council (no doubt affected by the whim of the emperor), it is clear that precedence was typically given not to age but to rank or *dignitas*.[97] It is perhaps also worth noting, as Crook does, that in regard to the business handled by Nerva's council "their triviality is the most significant thing about them."[98] *Amici* may have enjoyed close contact with the emperor and all the trappings that went with this, but it is another matter always to assume real imperial powers. Besides, an emperor might be wary of too eminent an *amicus* who had proved *capax imperii*, and withdrawal might well be provident; Seneca the Younger for one was aware of the dangers.[99]

To broaden the picture somewhat, we may now consider the presence of elderly senators in the *curia.* Were they free to attend the senate for as long as they wished or was a maximum age limit in operation, in the same way that minimum ages were set for the various magistracies? At first sight it would be natural to say that no maximum age was in force: how otherwise could someone like Valens have become consul as a nonagenarian? There is evidence that a *voluntary* age limit, a sort of retirement age, was set, however, at least in the principate. But it needs to be stressed first that "retirement" is not a good term to use, because modern connotations of this word, implying as it does pensions and the like, have no place in the ancient world and its use of words like *otium.* This need not surprise us, for compulsory and widespread retirement is a modern phenomenon developed in industrial societies. Nevertheless, "retirement" is a convenient word to use here, so long as it is remembered that in the Roman world there was no such institutionalized notion, nor was it compulsory at any age. The only sorts of retirement we tend to hear of are basically voluntary ones, such as individuals from political life, under discussion here, or the cessation of campaigning for soldiers (discussed later). Any other ancient reference to retirement, if it does not mean a gradual process of withdrawal and cessation of labor through inability to perform (in which case "retirement" is a euphemism), is simply the situation of someone with the required means choosing to withdraw from earlier activities, or wishing it could happen (as we have seen with Pliny the Younger).[100] Poets are a case in point, expressing their wish to retire to their hometowns.[101]

But to return to the question at hand, what of the presence of elderly senators in the *curia?* A Roman senator, at least from the fourth century B.C., held this position for life.[102] There are some isolated references, however, to the opportunity for senators to withdraw from attendance in the *curia* at a certain age. Dio implies that a law (νόμος), instigated by Augustus, laid down who had to attend the senate, and this law may have set down a maximum age after which attendance was not compulsory, or it may have decreed certain times of the year during which, owing to the strain of a long day in the house or to other commitments, members might be excused. The main purpose of the law, however, appears to have been to *improve* levels of attendance, not to provide excuses not to attend.[103] Pliny, in one of his letters, provides further evidence that some sort of optional retirement age was established in the early principate. In addressing the aged T. Pomponius Bassus (*cos. suff.* A.D. 94), Pliny, as we saw in the previous chapter, praises him for his style of life: "[T]his is the right way for a man to grow old" (ita senescere oportet virum), to be active in politics and then to enjoy a quiet life of *otium* in one's last years, "as the laws themselves encourage by returning the older man to his leisure" (ut ipsae leges monent, quae maiorem annis otio reddunt).[104] Likewise it is stated by pseudo-Quintilian that certain privileges are granted to old age ("ius senectutis") as opposed to youth, such as the fact that "the consul does not summon a senator to meetings for his whole life" (non perpetuo senatorem citat consul).[105] If, therefore, as seems likely, such laws did exist, what age was laid down after which attendance for senators was not compulsory?

Evidence is sparse. The Elder Seneca, quoting the Augustan rhetorician Publius Asprenas, states quite categorically that the age of 65 years (i.e., the completion of one's 65th year) was the "retiring" age: "A senator is neither forced nor forbidden to attend the house after the 65th year" (senator post sexagesimum et quintum annum in curiam non cogitur, non vetatur).[106] There is no problem here. The difficulty is that Seneca's son mentions in the same context the 60th year: "audies plerosque dicentes: 'a quinquagesimo anno in otium secedam, sexagesimus me annus ab officiis dimittet' . . . lex a quinquagesimo anno militem non legit, a sexagesimo senatorem non citat" (You will hear most people saying: "From my 50th year I'll withdraw into leisure; my 60th year will relieve me from public duties." . . . The law does not draft a soldier from his 50th year, it does not summon a senator from his 60th).[107] The discrepancy may be explained by positing that Augustus instituted a maximum age of 65 years, which was subsequently lowered to 60 years "unter oder vor Claudius."[108] Another possibility is that Seneca the Elder (or Asprenas) was mistaken in giving the age as 65 and that it was in fact originally set at 60 years—this is possible but even more difficult to prove. But exactly why such a measure should have been introduced is unclear; was it because senators from their early 60s wanted to be granted leave to absent themselves, or alternatively because younger members of the house believed that senators in their early 60s were more of a hindrance than a help to proceedings? It has been argued that it was indeed Claudius who lowered the age as part of his moves to ensure the "regularity and efficiency" of the senate,[109] but there is no definitive proof of this date or of this motivation.

It must be mentioned in passing that some scholars have argued that the "retiring age" under the principate was first set at 70 years and subsequently lowered to 65 and then 60 years.[110] This supposed first age of 70 years is, however, erroneous. It depends on a passage from the Augustan edict of 4 B.C. to Cyrene that states (5.112–13) that in the appointment from the senate of special judges to preside over extortion cases, no one aged 70 years or older is to be selected. This has nothing whatsoever to do with the age after which senators were not compelled to attend meetings of the senate. Rather it is derived from the maximum age laid down for judges (and for *munera* in general) in the empire.[111]

Although we may accept, then, that 65 and later 60 years were introduced as the ages after which a senator was not compelled to attend meetings, nonetheless the age itself is not as significant as the minimum ages we have already mentioned, for the simple reason that this upper age limit was not compulsory. Elderly men, as has been seen, could continue to be active in politics, though perhaps not as active as many would have liked to have been, as Cicero and Plutarch seem to have been aware. The practicalities of a retiring age are obvious: Aristotle for one drew attention to the possible negative repercussions of having aged men in charge (quoted earlier). It is perhaps worth remarking that Plato in his ideal state would have imposed a compulsory retirement age of 70 years for the senior magistracies.[112] But such a compulsory system, for whatever reason, did not come into existence in the Roman senate; perhaps older senators were at least able to exact this much respect for their status. Yet the drawbacks of old age were well known, in this as in other aspects of Roman life. Some elderly senators, for example, were apparently known to suffer from problems of deafness.[113] But still the notion of the wise old man continued to be fostered, and men of advanced age were not infrequently called upon in affairs of state for the practical wisdom and guidance they were believed to be able to impart.[114] One must conclude, therefore, that, apart from an optional retirement age—to use the modern terminology—being in operation by law under the principate, and perhaps by convention before this, there exists no evidence to suggest that there was any maximum age limit in the Roman senate to match the minimum age requirements set by the *leges annales.*

Yet at the same time it may be argued that the existence of an optional age of retirement is not simply an honor or privilege accorded to old age. Rather it may be seen as a nudge in the right direction, a guide to accepted or expected behavior. We saw in the previous chapter the type of old age that Pliny the Younger eulogized: a man who has been active in earlier years seeks tranquillity, *otium,* in his old age. It is worth recalling once more the words Pliny wrote to T. Pomponius Bassus:

> This is the right way to grow old [*ita senescere oportet*] for a man who has held the highest civil offices, commanded armies, and devoted himself entirely to the service of the state for as long as it was proper for him to do so. For it is our duty to give up our youth and manhood [*prima vitae tempora et media*] to our country, but our last years [*extrema*] should be our own; this the laws themselves suggest in permitting the older man [*maiorem annis*] to withdraw to leisure [*otio*]. I wonder when this will be permitted to me—when shall I reach the age which will allow me to follow your noble example of a graceful retirement [*pulcherrimae quietis*], when my withdrawal [*secessus*] will not be termed laziness but rather a desire for *tranquillitas?*

One thinks again also of Vestricius Spurinna, and Pliny's observation in that context: "a certain amount of chaotic disturbance is not unsuitable for the young [*iuvenes*], but in the case of old men [*senibus*] everything should be calm and orderly: their time of public activity is over, and ambition only brings them into disrepute."[115] The implication, emergent over the course of Roman history, as has been sketched here, is that old senators have had their day and, with all due respect, should to an extent leave it to the younger ones to get on with the current business.[116] It is not that elderly senators had no role to play— far from it—but that their claim to authority, as opposed, perhaps, to respect, was far from automatic. A senator of any age needed to prove his enduring capabilities, physical and mental, if he were to attain and maintain a position of authority.[117] For aging senators this meant restraining, or concealing, the negative effects of old age for as long as possible. Otherwise, *otium,* whether desired or not, was expected. In any case, asks Seneca, "adeone iuvat occupatum mori?" (Is it really such a pleasure to die in harness?).[118] Archilochus, seven centuries earlier, had put it rather differently: "An idle life is good for older people, especially if they happen to be simple in their ways and prone to be stupid or talk nothing but nonsense, as is typical of aged individuals."[119]

Honores, Munera, and Rules of Age

We move now beyond the senate house at Rome to consider another aspect of rules of age in public life in the Roman world, an aspect that would have been much more relevant and immediate to the average inhabitant of the Roman Empire but one which has been much more rarely analyzed by legal and social historians. Throughout the Roman Empire practically every living adult male was obliged to fulfill certain duties (*munera*) on behalf of his community and, in certain cases, to carry out public offices (*honores*). *Munera et honores* form a complex part of municipal life in the Roman world. Our primary area of interest here will be the way that the age of the individual, among other considerations, may or may not have gained him exemption or immunity (*excusatio, immunitas*) from these otherwise compulsory duties.[120]

It is important first, however, to emphasize that these *munera* did indeed, at least on occasion in the imperial period and in some localities, become "burdens" in every sense, especially financial. Furthermore, original *honores* increasingly came to be regarded by many as *munera* themselves, as the original honor or dignity of rank began to disappear, to be replaced by crippling financial commitments under the guise of a title. Thus, to take the most obvious case, the decurionate was originally regarded as an *honor.*[121] Yet *munera* and *honores* came more and more to be assimilated.[122] Even as early as the Flavian Municipal Law of A.D. 82–84 there is evidence that compulsion could be used to fill offices if there were insufficient candidates, and the same is true during the reign of Trajan. It is clear from this that compulsory public duties might be regarded as a burden from quite early in the principate.[123] This would have been true even of the decurionate, in cases where there was a shortage of candidates with adequate means to carry out the office. Anyone who fled the office could be forcibly brought back and such a fugitive was, by the terms of a rescript of Constantine, forced to serve for two years instead of the usual one.[124] So although the distinction between *munera* and *honores* remained important in theory, particularly in cases of exemption, in practice the two seem to have become alike regarded by some as financial, and on occasion physical, burdens to be avoided whenever and howsoever possible. Old age might provide some relief.

In regard to *munera* themselves, further distinctions were drawn in later times by the jurists, although these distinctions are not as clearly defined or as definitive as they may at first appear. We are not dealing here with a static situation, and differences resulting from chronological, geographical, and circumstantial factors further complicate the issue.[125] The distinctions are, however, important in terms of applications for exemption on the grounds of age. Firstly, there were *munera publica,* with which we are principally interested here, and *munera privata,* duties such as *tutela* and *cura. Munera publica* were further subdivided by the jurists into *munera patrimoniorum,* in essence a form of taxation on a person's estate and as such involving a purely financial commitment, and *munera personalia,* involving initially not expenditure but personal labor (hence the terms *munera corporalia* and *sordida*), but with a financial commitment becoming more and more necessary as well (*munera mixta*). Examples of *munera personalia* where physical labor was involved are the maintenance of public roads and buildings and the compulsory duties of transportation. Depending on the financial resources of a city, expenditure might also be expected from those enlisted to *munera personalia,* but at an early stage a maximum of five days' service annually was set as a limit for any individual to serve.[126] Furthermore, some individuals were considered as naturally exempt from such physical labor: women, for example, were originally regarded as incapable of such tasks.[127] Age too naturally granted exemptions from such *munera,* but it is important to stress that age did not bestow an automatic or universal immunity, particularly in regard to duties that involved only a financial burden. Thus exemption from *munera patrimoniorum* and *honores* is extremely rare, granted only and in certain cases to the poor.[128]

In broad terms—and this is nothing more than a convenient rule of thumb—exemptions from *munera personalia* on the grounds of age were granted to *minores viginti et quinque annis* and to *maiores septuaginta annis*.

The case of exemption for *minores* is stated most plainly by Ulpian, who notes at the same time that this immunity is a temporary one applying only to administrative duties (*honores* and *munera personalia*), not to *munera patrimoniorum*.[129] The minimum age of 25 years for *munera* and *honores* became the established rule only under Justinian;[130] before that time, even though it was accepted that persons of a younger age should be exempt, in practice, especially if a sufficient number of candidates were not available, they could be admitted (even without the principle of *annus coeptus* being taken into account) and specific provision was made for this.[131] On several occasions it is accepted that males under the required age will serve, to make up for a shortage of eligible candidates.

Turning now to rules imposing a maximum age after which the performance of duties of state was not compulsory, one finds the same basic regulations as in the case of *minores,* namely that exemption may be granted from *munera personalia* but not as a rule from *honores* or *munera patrimoniorum.* The normal age for exemption appears to have been 70 years and older, that is, from the end of one's 70th year (as opposed to *annus coeptus*), as Ulpian makes explicit: "maiores septuaginta annis a tutelis et muneribus personalibus vacant. sed qui ingressus est septuagensimum annum, nondum egressus, hac vacatione non utetur, quia non videtur maior esse septuaginta annis qui annum agit septuagensimum" (Those who are over 70 years of age are exempt from tutelages and personal *munera*. But someone who has begun but not yet ended his 70th year may not make use of this exemption, since someone in his 70th year does not seem to be over 70 years of age).[132] In no other text is the 70-year maximum so carefully defined. This maximum age is mentioned frequently enough, however, to leave little doubt that from the age of 70 years an individual was not compelled to undertake *munera personalia.*[133] The exemption, it is often stressed in the legal texts, applied only to *munera personalia,* not to *honores* or to the *munera* thereby involved.[134]

This is stated most explicitly, early in the reign of Septimius Severus, by Callistratus, who opens with the assurance that "*senectus* has always been revered in our *civitas*" and that in regard to *munera municipalia* exemption is granted to *senes* as a matter of honor.[135] He proceeds, however, to note exceptions to this general principle, and one can perhaps understand from this why in his opening comments he has gone to some trouble to stress the honor old age receives. What we seem to have here is not a statement of the actual legislation regarding exemption through old age but rather an expression of opinion on how the legislation is to be interpreted. As such, it may be more than just the opinion of Callistratus and may reflect the operation of the laws in practice. The shortage of available persons at certain times and in certain places to fulfill *munera* that were financially burdensome, one imagines, necessitated the enlistment of some older people, particularly the wealthier among them: "But it can be said that a man who has become wealthy in old age (*in senectute locuples*) without having previously undertaken any public *munus* is not exempted from this burden by the privilege of age (*privilegio aetatis*), especially if the administration of the *munus* imposed involves not so much physical disturbance as expenditure of money, and if he belongs to a *civitas* in which men of adequate means to perform public *munera* are not easily found." One may see from this how in time *senectus* might be considered as less than a perfect excuse; certainly old age usually provided no *vacatio* from purely financial burdens.[136]

One finds a considerable body of testimony regarding the office of the decurionate, and at first glance the evidence appears somewhat contradictory. First, the decurionate is treated in certain regards as a *munus*: whereas no upper age limit existed for *honores* in general, the decurionate was restricted, presumably because of the duties involved. It is stated by Callistratus that not only the young (those of "tenera aetas") but also older people ("qui grandes natu sunt") are debarred from becoming decurions, an exclusion that is permanent. According to Callistratus, however, the 70-year rule was not in operation here: he states that "those who have passed the age of 55 years" cannot be made decurions, although he notes that changes to this rule could be made when the "long-established custom" (*longa consuetudo*) of a particular *municipium* warranted it. It might be inferred from this that the maximum age for the decurionate was 55 years, at least in the third century.[137] But in the light of other references to higher ages, that was clearly not the case.

Ulpian offers a clue for solving this dilemma. Consider what he has to say, remembering that he is writing as a close contemporary of Callistratus (*Dig.* 50.2.2.8): "Those who are older than 55 years of age [*maiores annis quinquaginta quinque*] are prevented by constitutions from being called on for the office of decurion against their will. But if they have agreed to this, they ought to hold the office, even if they are over 70 years of age, though they are not forced to perform civil *munera*." From this one may infer that, while an individual could not be nominated for the office of decurion *against his will* once he had reached the age of 55 years,[138] nonetheless he was still liable to the duties that the decurionate involved if he had already been drafted into the *curia* before the age of 55 years. Perhaps, at least at certain periods or in certain places, a voluntary age of retirement for decurions existed, as in the case of the senate at Rome but without quite so much flexibility. It is stated in a rescript issued by Diocletian and Maximian, furthermore, that "it is a clear rule of law that those over 55 years of age cannot be called to perform personal *munera* against their will" and that therefore the person addressed in this case is to be excused; the case is complicated by the fact that the individual in question is over the age of 70 years anyway ("cum itaque septuagenario maiorem te esse profitearis").[139] On the other hand, the same Augusti respond in another rescript to a certain Iulius that "because you undertook the office of decurion voluntarily, you cannot be released from the roll, even though you state that you are advanced in years [*annosum*]."[140] In other words, while a person could not be drafted against his will in old age, once he had undertaken the office of his own free will he had to fulfill his obligations even in old age.[141]

Furthermore, it must be stressed that even when extreme old age did constitute a valid excuse from office, it was not an automatic exemption.[142] Proper application had to be made and due process followed. Also a successor had to be found,[143] which, judging by the variety and number of applications for immunity as well as of fugitives from office, may not have ever been a simple matter. Furthermore, valid exemptions already granted might be universally annulled in special circumstances, and rules might vary. Despite the possibility of exemption from the age of 55 years from the decurionate at least, the general rule for applicable liabilities and duties must have laid down the age of 70 years;[144] and it was expected that the sons of the *senex* would perform the relevant *munera* on his behalf: "Even if someone is over 70 years of age [*maior annis septuaginta*] and the father of five living children and is therefore exempt from civil *munera,* nevertheless his sons are obliged to assume the corresponding *munera* on his behalf. For the appropriate reward of immunity is thus given to fathers on account of their sons, because they will undertake the *munera.*"[145] There is no testimony as to what happened to the elderly individual who had no living descendants to assume duties on his behalf. One interesting case, however, is presented to us in a letter by Saint Basil (*Ep.* 84) written in A.D. 372 to a ἡγεμών, presumably the governor of Cappadocia, on behalf of a "miserable old man" (ἄθλιος γέρων). The old man's complaint is that, although an imperial decree (γράμμα) had earlier exempted him from public burdens (τῶν δημοσίων), he now finds that he is being "dragged back" because his two-year-old grandson (he is "not yet in his fourth year") has been elected to the local *bouleuterion*—that is, his grandson is no longer nominally able to take his place in the performance of a liturgy. He states that, even before the imperial decree, old age itself had granted him the necessary release (αὐτὸ τὸ γῆρας ἔδωκεν αὐτῷ τὴν ἀναγκαίαν ἀτέλειαν), and he goes on to note that such exemption is only prudent, ὡς ἂν μὴ ἀνθρώπῳ παρανοοῦντι διὰ τὸν χρόνον κινδυνεύοι τι τῶν κοινῶν (lest any public interest should be put at risk by a man whose mind is becoming deranged through age). Otherwise ἀνάγκη πάλιν τοῦ ἀθλίου γέροντος τὴν πολιὰν καταισχύνεσθαι (it will be necessary for the hoary locks of the miserable old man to be put to shame once more). Basil implores the governor to take pity upon the ages of both: the younger who has been bereft of his parents from birth, the older who "has been dished up such a long life that he has escaped no form of misfortune."

Acting as a *iudex* was a duty that also seems to have come to be regarded as a *munus.*[146] In the case of *iudices,* there is a similar variation in the maximum age limit. Under the republic we find reference to the age of 60 years. This ties in with isolated references to the age of 60 years as granting a reprieve from public duties in the late republican period.[147] In 4 B.C. the upper age limit for judges (selected from among the *consulares*) was set at 70 years. Late in the first century A.D. the age appears to have reverted to 65 years.[148] Whether the differences are a result of the passing of time or to individual decisions in differing circumstances is difficult to determine; what is clear is that here again old age was seen as a valid excuse. The same is true of illness in certain cases. Ulpian expressly states that one's *valetudo* was taken into consideration in the appointment of *iudices*. The legislation on illness as conferring exemption from *munera* in general is complex and confused, but the overall impression is that such exemptions, though possible in theory, were seldom easy to obtain.[149]

As for *munera privata,* the age of 70 years is explicitly stated several times as excusing the individual from undertaking the burdens of the tutorship and curatorship. This provides further confirmation that the usual legal definition of exemption on the grounds of old age was indeed 70 years.[150] The only legal text that explicitly states that the age limit was ever lower than 70 years is in the *lex Romana Burgundionum,* where it is stated (36.6) that exemption is granted from *tutela* at the age of 60 years. It is argued in the next chapter that in practice, in Roman Egypt at any rate, the age limit *was* lowered from the legal rule of 70 years. But this reference from the *lex Romana Burgundionum* cannot be taken as conclusive evidence of this. For a start this legal text dates from circa A.D. 500 and, though based on earlier Roman legal texts, it clearly contains elements of law applicable only to the Burgundians. In the same sentence it is stated that having four sons ("quattuor masculi filii") also confers exemption from *tutela,* which is either an erroneous interpretation of the *ius liberorum,* a late and otherwise unattested alteration, or a Burgundian peculiarity.

The case of veterans and their immunity (or otherwise) from *munera* and also, unlike other categories of people, from *honores,* is relevant here also.[151] From Octavian's edict on veterans' privileges it is clear that from an early stage veterans enjoyed exemption, at least in theory, from *munera* and that they could not be appointed to office against their will.[152] Some 350 years later we find Constantine assuring angry veterans that they will continue to enjoy immunity from

civilia munera and *opera publica*, "ut integra beneficia eorum sub saeculi nostri otio et pace [*sic*] perfruantur et eorum senectus quiete post
labores perfruatur" (so that in the peace and repose of our era they may
enjoy their privileges unimpaired and in their old age they may enjoy
tranquillity after their exertions).[153] Clearly veterans in the interven-
ing period had not always enjoyed the privileges to which they were
in theory entitled, and these privileges were being encroached upon.
From Karanis in Egypt, for example, we have the urgent complaints in
A.D. 172 of one veteran, a former auxiliary who describes himself as
now "an elderly man on his own" (ἄ[ν]θρ[ω]πος πρεσβύ[τη]ς καὶ
μόνος τυγχ[άν]ων); he addresses his petition to the local *strategos*: "It
has been decreed, my lord, that after their discharge veterans should
have a five-year period of rest. In spite of this regulation I was mo-
lested two years after my discharge and arbitrarily nominated for a
liturgy, and from then till now I have been on duty without a break."[154]
He goes on to petition for the privileges that he claims are due to him.
The official reply is, unfortunately, not preserved. This fellow appears
to have been discharged after a full term of service. Men could be discharged at an earlier time on the grounds of old age, however, and in
such a case were entitled to complete privileges.[155] In cases where
men simply deserted, however, length of years (*annositas*) afforded no
excuse.[156]

Furthermore one detects here, as elsewhere, the apparent situation
that, although old age did afford an excuse from *munera et honores,* it
might not always in practice be an easy matter to obtain such exemption. Immunity, as has been stressed, was far from automatically
granted. Exemptions were of necessity difficult to obtain and became
increasingly so as time progressed. Not only was it imperative to fill
unpopular positions but the more exemptions granted, the greater the
burden placed on others, both financially and physically. These factors, underlying the system of exemptions by age, are further explored
in the next chapter, when we consider the specific situation of Roman
Egypt in this regard, in particular the practicalities behind the rules,
aspects that do not emerge from cold legal texts. What the legal corpus does reveal in the context of rules of age, however, is that some allowance was made for old age. The age of 55 years limited liability to
some extent, but there remained significant areas of liability between

55 and 70 years, and even after the age of 70 an elderly man could not expect total immunity from civil duties.

It may be true as a generalization that in most societies, in public and in private, more respect is generally accorded to advanced age than to youth, and more trust typically placed in the older than in the younger generations. We may take a relatively trivial example from Roman law as a useful illustration: according to Ulpian in regard to the question of with whom a will should be deposited, the *senior* should be preferred to the *iunior,* just as the person of higher *honor* should be preferred to one of lower status, and the male should be preferred to the female, the freeborn to the freed.[157] This is scarcely surprising, particularly in a relatively conservative society. But this need not translate in reality into a significant level of tangible authority or influence for older people. What we have seen in this and the previous chapter suggests rather that in the elite Roman society of the late republican and the imperial period authority and prestige, as opposed to more passive respect, lay with those in their 40s and 50s—the older generations, rather than the oldest. But just as important as chronological age, or rather overriding it, in this context were the questions of physical and mental capabilities, themes to which we return in later chapters.

Five

Rules of Age in Roman Egypt

τῶν κατὰ τὴν Αἴγυπτον πραγματειῶν . . .
πολύτροποι δ'εἰσὶ καὶ ποικίλαι, μόλις τοῖς ἐκ
πρώτης ἡλικίας τὸ ἔργον ἐπιτήδευμα πεποιημένοις
γνωριζόμεναι.

Egyptian affairs are intricate and diversified, hardly
grasped even by those who have made a business of
studying them from their earliest years.
Philo *in Flaccum* 3

The comparatively abundant evidence from Roman Egypt permits us to review in some detail the rules of public life relating to old age, in particular regarding liturgies imposed on individuals by the state and the poll tax paid by a particular age-group of the population; and to consider briefly, but in a more far-reaching fashion than we can for the rest of the empire, the actual workings and practicalities of such rules of age. What were the realities underlying these rules? For example, how accurate were the records of age held by the authorities, and did ordinary individuals know precisely what their age was? Even if people over a certain age could gain release from burdens imposed on them by the state, how many would ever have survived to an age to be able to enjoy such privileges? In other words, why bother having such rules of age in the first place?

In this chapter we are interested not only in individual rules of age but also in how such rules were viewed and put into effect. The rules involve the responsibility of individuals in the workings of the state, in terms of both financial and corporeal commitments. Although the bureaucracy of Roman Egypt was more complex than anything visible in the rest of the empire, it was still directed toward one main aim: keeping the state functioning, especially in its role as a primary producer for Rome. As a rule the Romans tended not to impose a vast administrative machine on their subject states but to maintain as far as possible the status quo. It so happens that in Egypt they inherited from the Ptolemies a machine that was already well developed, and perhaps necessarily so, considering the agricultural wealth the country as a whole enjoyed. Because of this all-pervading bureaucracy and, more fundamentally, the fact that the Egyptian sands have preserved for us such a varied selection of records of the administration's inner workings, it is possible to get a glimpse not only of what rules were imposed but also of how these rules were put into operation and—even more revealing—how the people of Roman Egypt reacted to these rules on a practical level. Although Egypt cannot be taken automatically as being generally representative of the empire as a whole and the papyrological evidence does not provide a complete or necessarily cohesive picture, nevertheless we are given interesting clues as to how rules of age were imposed and received in the imperial period.

Records of Age in Roman Egypt

In the Roman Empire Egypt appears as a special case in certain regards, not least in its administrative framework. Not only was it apparently more complex in its administrative procedure than the other provinces, both western and eastern, but it was based on a quite different infrastructure.[1] From the central record offices in Alexandria to the smallest village, comprehensive information about property and persons was regularly collected and, it would seem, consulted. Space precludes a detailed analysis of the workings of the Egyptian bureaucracy—the officials whose job it was to amass the information and the means of collating, storing, and using the data collected—but brief reference to the census is relevant, in terms both of this chapter and of age-awareness in Roman times.

In the offices of the administrative districts of Roman Egypt, the *nomoi,* were contained fairly detailed records of each individual inhabitant of the land, not only in official correspondence and papers, but also in tax returns and census lists, the latter being ordered according to household, with quite full details of the status, origin, age, and financial standing of the owner and inhabitants or tenants. In theory, therefore, officials could trace the history of any individual, alive or dead. Furthermore, on the payment of a fee, private individuals could make use of the official records for their own purposes, to substantiate a claim concerning their hereditary status, for example. Thus, in submitting a declaration for the *epikrisis* (an investigation by officials to determine the status of an individual) of their 14-year-old son in the hope of gaining for him immunity from the poll tax, two parents draw on the records to trace his gymnasiarchal ancestry back through seven generations, a time span of more than 250 years.[2] Such archive searches were clearly in the individual's interest, because proof of non-Egyptian (i.e., Roman, Greek, or—at least originally—Jewish) origin conferred, among other things, a reduction in the amount of poll tax due each year, if not a complete exemption from payment.

But archive offices were not established, at least not primarily, for the personal profit of the inhabitants. They were in effect the best means available to the state to ensure the effective administration of the province with the end in view of the collection of taxes, both in money and in kind. Roman Egypt apparently required a mass of diverse records to maintain its effective running. Yet such a system where records are carefully preserved may also have benefits for the individual, when he or she can find a way through the formalities. There is evidence that ordinary people in Roman Egypt had some form of access to their records; this has already been seen in cases where individuals refer back to earlier census records to use them to their own advantage. On the payment of a fee a file search could be made.[3] Furthermore, private documents, while not normally filed in the public archives, could be given the force of law by being deposited among the official records—again on payment of a fee.[4]

The underlying purpose behind this archival system was the proper collection of taxes from every liable inhabitant of the land. To ensure that every such individual was taxed was a formidable task that required quite prodigiously exact knowledge of who lived where. Such was the theoretical result achieved by the census, held every 14 years. People declared themselves: their status, their occupation, their place of residence, and—most important in the context of this study—their age. The fairly sizable number of papyrological documents relating to the census in Roman Egypt provides a good idea of how this nationwide survey operated.[5] It was incumbent upon all inhabitants of Roman Egypt to be declared on a census return. In most cases the householder, the owner of the property, would declare all the members of his house, as well as property, including slaves.[6] In some cases, where tenants inhabited the house of another, they themselves made the declaration and had it endorsed by the owner.

The declaration having been made, copies went to various officials.[7] In some cases declarations are addressed to more than one official at once. Most are directed to the *strategos* of the nome or to his deputy, the *basilikogrammateus*. At the *metropolis* (the mother-city, or nome capital) the records were collated in a central office, to which lists from the local notarial office or *grapheion* would also have been forwarded. The two central offices of the nome, the *bibliotheke demosion logon* or *demosia bibliotheke,* and, from the second half of the first century A.D., the *bibliotheke enkteseon*, the register for "real property," were under the direct supervision of the *bibliophylakes,* a liturgical office and one that, interestingly enough, seems to have been imposed not infrequently on older people. One finds the case of a 71-year-old man holding the post; the prefect Mettius Rufus had pronounced that candidates for liturgical office must be suitable "not only from the point of view of possessing property but also of age and way of life, all that should be found in men entrusted with imperial business." Perhaps older people were felt to possess the required abilities to perform the duties of official registrar. Unfortunately for their families, however, if they died in office the burden passed to their widows and children.[8]

Individual returns were pasted together and numbered; this can still be seen with, for example, *P.Brux. inv.* E.7616, a roll of eighteen returns with numbers at the head of each declaration. Two from one village are numbered 98 and 99, while sixteen from another village are numbered from 92 to 107. Clearly each complete roll contained many declarations. Such τόμοι, grouped according to village or toparchy, could then be checked with the summary lists of population (*ana-graphai*) drawn up from previous censuses. Once this process of scrutinization (*exetasis*) was complete, new summary lists could be drawn up, providing an enumeration of persons and their property which could then be directly used for fiscal as well as legal purposes. Such a list is extant in *P.Lond.* 257–59, a table of men liable to poll tax in the year A.D. 94, that is, following the census of A.D. 89/90.[9] It is clear from this that the lists were updated not only every fourteen years with each new census, but also annually, on the basis of documents such as notices of births and deaths received in the interim.

Another document of particular interest here is a tax list, dated to A.D. 72/3 and apparently drawn up by the amphodarch, a subofficial of the *metropolis* of the Arsinoite nome who worked under the direction of the *basilikogrammateus*.[10] The document provides us again with a clear example of just how voluminous the paper work must have been: the first column of this roll is numbered 31 (λα), implying that many such lists existed in the many offices around the province. The whole roll as we have it preserves lists of individuals of various types. First, there are the names of 385 men in the local area with the amount of the poll tax they have paid, including 47 men who were totally exempt. A postscript to this list adds that a copy has been deposited with the *basilikogrammateus*. There follows a list of male minors registered as being between the age of one and two years at the time of the census of A.D. 61/2, and therefore coming up to the age of liability to poll tax (14 years) in A.D. 72/3. Allowance is made in the list for the addition of those registered late and for changes for those who have since died. The document continues with various other lists of individuals of different statuses—slaves, Roman and Alexandrian citizens, women, Jews, and members of certain professions—regarding their liability to taxes. Next comes a γραφὴ ὑπερετῶν καὶ ἀσθενῶν, a list of those classified as being exempt through age and sickness. Thirteen males from 63 to 80 years of age are listed, as the document records, by express order of the prefect, though none of them is liable to the poll tax.[11]

Here are also lists of young males who have been examined in an *epikrisis* within the past twenty years. The total document as extant extends to forty-five columns, probably little more than half of the whole roll.[12]

The age at which men became liable for payment of the poll tax was 14 years. Because a definite age was set, the authorities seem to have taken it for granted that they would be able to compute exactly who were liable and when their liability commenced. This is precisely what the census documents enabled them to do. Furthermore, in the archives the administration had notices of birth (ὑπομνήματα ἐπιγεννήσεως) submitted by the parents. From these they could calculate when males were of the age of liability.[13]

The operation of the *epikrisis,* another potential source of information for the administrative officials on the age of the inhabitants, shows a similar objective. Performed by local officials under the supervision of the *strategos* and his subordinates, it was concerned with the liability of individuals to compulsory services, military duty, and taxes. The particular *epikrisis* on which we have the fullest information and which need particularly concern us here was the examination of 14-year-old males regarding their liability to the payment of poll tax. As will be seen presently, certain privileged individuals—Roman and Alexandrian citizens as well as members of specific professions—could be totally exempted from payment of this tax, while other persons, most notably the "Greeks" of the *metropoleis,* paid poll tax at a lower rate than the average Egyptian. Young males at the time at which they were liable to poll tax might therefore present themselves before the *epikrisis* commission in the hope of being entered in the lists of these privileged persons, following formal application by their parents (as noted). Such persons listed as privileged were termed ἐπικεκριμένοι, as opposed to those who were liable to the full amount of the tax, the λαογραφούμενοι.[14]

The officials therefore had three potential sources of information on the ages of the inhabitants of Roman Egypt: the declarations of the census, together with the summary lists drawn up from such declarations in previous censuses; notices of births and deaths; and the records of the *epikrisis.*[15] One final question is whether these records concerning age were accurate. Could individuals falsify their ages with impunity?

One thing that we can be sure of is that, periodically at any rate, efforts were made not only to keep the records up-to-date but also to ensure that declarations were made by all and that they were genuine reports. From the *Gnomon of the Idios Logos,* a second-century list of rules that were also in operation in the first century, we have examples of such efforts.[16] Fines were imposed on those who failed to register in the census, including the registration of Romans and Alexandrians, slaves (a failure that could result in the confiscation of the slave), and the families of soldiers.[17] One example of a person being prosecuted for failure to furnish a census return may be found in *PSI* 1326 (A.D. 181–83), where a peasant is ordered by the prefect to be arrested for failing to be registered; he claims that his parents had died when he was a small child and before they had had a chance to register him.

The multiple number of returns filed and the cross-checking carried out by various officials also may have served to eliminate many errors in the system. On the whole the bureaucratic system of recording the inhabitants of Roman Egypt strikes us as a relatively complex and involved process. The administration of Roman Egypt, more perhaps than in any other place or period of time in the ancient world, had complete records of its people for the primary purpose of ensuring the universal collection of taxes at all levels and of enforcing on everyone who was liable the performance of duties imposed by the state.

Rules of Age in Roman Egypt

LITURGIES

It was seen in the previous chapter that definite rules were in theory set down in the Roman world for the age at which individuals were liable to the performance of liturgies—that is, compulsory duties exacted by the state, of either a pecuniary or corporeal nature. Certain definitions, drawn largely from the legal writers of the third century A.D., were given there to illustrate the types of *munera* imposed, namely *munera personalia* and *munera patrimoniorum,* both of which may be classed as *munera publica,* public duties, as opposed to *munera privata,* such private duties as *cura* and *tutela.* The relevant rules of age were focused particularly on *munera publica* or, more precisely, on *munera personalia,* because very few exemptions were granted to the performance of *munera patrimoniorum.*

The rules of age discussed earlier were seen to apply to the Roman Empire in general, and the basic rule as far as *munera personalia* and old age were concerned was that older people might be exempt from the age of 70 years; as noted, some individual exceptions to this general principle existed. In the case of Roman Egypt various papyrological documents, principally records of individuals appealing against their nomination to a particular liturgy, allow us to see the operation of compulsory public services in practice instead of through the writings of later jurists, and thus we may further define rules of age in this context. Of course, such conclusions can only be held to apply to Roman Egypt and not necessarily to the empire as a whole; furthermore, the situation in Egypt itself may not have been uniform, with possible variations in different localities, over different periods in history, among different classes (such as bouleutic or nonbouleutic), and between types of liturgies,[18] as well as perhaps in differing individual circumstances.

At the most basic level the evidence we do have allows us to classify types of liturgies[19] as they operated in Roman Egypt as follows:

(i) ἀρχαί = *honores,* duties carried out by the upper-class *metropolitai.*

(ii) Ordinary liturgies, largely *munera personalia* and *munera patrimoniorum,* of which three types should be distinguished:

    (a) Bouleutic liturgies, performed by members of the bouleutic class following the institution by Septimius Severus in A.D. 199–200 of the *boulai.*

    (b) Metropolitan liturgies, performed by members of the *metropoleis* who were not *bouleuteis.*

    (c) Village liturgies, performed by nonmetropolitans who had the required means.

(iii) Compulsory labor, performed by those who were classified as ἄποροι, that is, lacking the financial means to carry out the pecuniary commitments of an ordinary liturgy. Such compulsory tasks, including dike work and agricultural labor, the legal writers were to call *munera sordida.*

We are dealing here principally with the ordinary liturgies, although our evidence overlaps into all three main definitions of compulsory public services.

Exemptions, whether permanent or temporary, were in theory granted on various grounds.[20] Among those granted exemption were Roman citizens (though as time passed they became increasingly liable, and from A.D. 212 their privileged status lost its exclusiveness), *metropolitai,* veterans, members of certain professions and occupations, women, fathers of five children, the sick, and people of a certain age. It is on this last category that we focus here, analyzing the age at which older people in Roman Egypt were considered exempt from the performance of liturgies. Was it the same as for the empire as a whole?

Before we consider the actual age at which older men might be exempted from compulsory public services, it is worth looking at the actual procedure by which they applied for and were granted exemption, a factor the reality of which the legal sources do not make clear. It was stressed in the previous chapter that such exemption was far from an automatic privilege but had to be applied for with due bureaucratic practice observed. In the case of Roman Egypt we are given a glimpse of such red tape. The process of the *epikrisis* has already been mentioned, particularly in the context of young males coming up to the age of 14 years, the age when liability to payment of the poll tax began. It appears probable that a similar examination was carried out to determine the right to exemption from such liabilities as poll tax and liturgies in the case of those ὑπερετεῖς (over-age).

Proof would have to have been presented to show that the individual in question was indeed over the age of exemption. Presumably such proof consisted of records drawn from the archive office: former census lists and, where available, notices of birth in particular. As already noted, ordinary individuals had, on payment of a fee, access to public records. How carefully such attestations of age were scrutinized by the officials it is difficult to know, but certainly they would have had the means at their disposal to check claims that someone had reached the required age (though with how much precision is debatable). Evidence of such an examination, though not specifically linked to old age, may be seen in one papyrus, where it is expressly stated that "the *komogrammateis* are to present under oath the names of those who are infirm [τῶν ἐπισινῶν] or who wish to be released on other grounds, with the *strategos* supervising."[21] Apparently from such examinations, just as was the case with those who were declared as dead, lists were drawn up of those classified as exempt on the grounds of old age or infirmity.[22] Such exemption, as stated earlier, applied only to physical and not financial burdens.

The papyrological evidence for the age at which exemption was granted from compulsory public services in Roman Egypt shows, as has already been noted, that over time immunity became more difficult to obtain. In addition, the rules themselves changed, exhibiting a lowering of the age, whether for practical or conciliatory reasons. Although some documents cannot be dated with precision, the most useful approach is to consider the testimony in chronological order. Our evidence begins early in the Roman era—one must bear in mind that the liturgical system was very much a Roman innovation in Egypt, a system that began to take shape only in the first century A.D.

The earliest piece of evidence we possess—earlier in fact than any of our extant legal texts on the subject—is *P.Flor.* 312, from the late first century (A.D. 91/2). Even at this early stage in the history of liturgies in Roman Egypt it is clear that exemption could be granted, or at least claimed, on the grounds of old age and ill health. From the Hermopolite nome on the banks of the Nile opposite the future site of Antinoopolis, this papyrus records the orders of an unnamed official, possibly the *strategos* of the nome or even the prefect of the whole of Egypt, that individuals are to be freed from λειτουργίαι on the grounds of old age and illness (διὰ γῆρας καὶ ἀσθένιαν).[23] The fragmentary text appears to be a petition addressed to the *dioiketes* claiming exemption from compulsory services. We do not know whether the appeal was successful, nor is any definite age stated; from later evidence one might suppose that the age set at this time was 70 years, although at this early date perhaps no definite age limit had been set.

The next piece of testimony likewise provides no definite age, although the general term γῆρας has been replaced by the more technical term ὑπερέτης. In *P.Phil.* 1, in which is preserved a fragment of an edict by the prefect Vibius Maximus (A.D. 103–7), it is ordered (line 29) that those ὑπερετεῖς ἐπισινεῖς ἐπικριθέντε[ς (over-age and feeble) be exempted from the physical performance of liturgies. The term *epikrithentes* further reinforces the theory that an *epikrisis* was necessary before exemption could be granted; in the case of ill health this entailed a medical examination,[24] whereas for older people it must have involved establishing the age of the claimant, as described earlier. Among the list preserved in this papyrus of those exempted by the edict (the text of which is, again, only fragmentary) are priests, physicians, and members of various other professions. It is stated expressly, however, that those who would otherwise be exempt are still liable "if they own private land and their wealth is established to exceed one talent."[25] Even at this early stage it would appear that there was a dire need to find enough people with the required means to perform certain burdensome duties.

Not until the mid-second century is there mention of a specific chronological age in this context. In *P.Leit.* 4, a very fragmentary text dating to circa A.D. 161 and of uncertain provenance, a man nominated to a liturgy addresses a petition to the *strategos* (or perhaps *epistrategos*) claiming exemption on the grounds that he is 72 years of age.[26] In his petition he refers to an appeal he has already addressed to the prefect; this earlier petition is cited and followed by the prefect's subscription that the (*epi-*)*strategos* decide the case. Again we are given no clue as to the official's decision, nor do we know whether the individual in question claimed exemption on the grounds that he was over a certain specific age (perhaps 70 years) or simply that he was an old man.

That the grounds for exemption from compulsory public services were becoming more strictly defined and more restrictive becomes apparent from evidence from the late second century onward. Very revealing is one of the *apokrimata* of Septimius Severus concerning exemption through physical disability: **Κρονίῳ Ἡρακλείδου· αἱ πρόσκαιροι νόσοι τῶν πολιτικῶν οὐκ ἀπαλλάσουσιν λιτουργιῶν, καὶ οἱ ἀσθενεῖς δὲ τῷ σώματι λιτουρ[γ]οῦσιν ἐὰν τῇ φροντίδι τῶν οἰκίων πραγμάτων ἐξαρκῖν δύνωνται.** (To Kronios son of Herakleides. Passing illnesses do not afford release from municipal liturgies, and those who are physically sick are subject to liturgies if they have the mental capacity to conduct domestic duties).[27] As Westermann noted, extant demands for exemption reach a high point in the principate of Septimius Severus,[28] though it is worth remarking that a large proportion of our documents of the Roman era surviving on papyri appears to date from this period anyway.[29] One papyrus, *P.Flor.* 382 (= *P.Flor.* 57, Hermopolis Magna), well exemplifies the preciseness of rulings from this time. Itself a petition of circa A.D. 222, it includes no fewer than six earlier decisions (probably five private rescripts and one edict) of Septimius Severus and Caracalla concerning, inter alia, the liability of elderly and infirm individuals to compulsory public services. These six rulings, forming part of the petition of one Aurelius Heron addressed first to an acting *epistrategos* and then to the prefect, date from A.D. 199/200 to 216; four of them state that from the age of 70 years release from liturgical service is to be granted to individuals.[30] This exemption from the age of 70 years is subsequently repeated throughout the petition (lines 29–30, 55–57, and 62–65, the last adding a reference to the petitioner's poor eyesight). Heron also claims exemption on the grounds of his being an Alexandrian and of his general *aporia;* this enumeration of several grounds for exemption in a petition will be seen again.

P.Flor. 382, then, incomplete though it is, provides conclusive evidence for the existence of a rule of age at this time, namely that those of 70 years of age and over were in theory to be granted exemption from compulsory public services. This supports the evidence from the legal corpus, predominantly from the first half of the third century, cited in the previous chapter. Further support is provided by *P.Oxy.* 4068 (A.D. 200), where it is stated that the age of 70 years confers exemption from municipal liturgies (πολιτικαῖς λειτουργίαις)—but not from *munera patrimoniorum*—according to (three) rescripts of Severus and Caracalla, and by *PSI Congr.* 20.13 (Oxyrhynchus, A.D. 260/1), where, in very similar fashion again to *P.Flor.* 382 but almost forty years later than that petition, the age of 70 years is several times mentioned as granting exemption from a λειτουργία, namely φυλακία. Here too the petitioner, Aurelius Ptolemaeus, who has apparently already been granted exemption on the grounds of old age but, it would seem, to no effect, quotes for the benefit of the prefect an imperial rescript (lines 7–10) to support his case. In reply, the *strategos* is ordered to enforce the exemption.

Another document of relevance, dating to a few years prior to the first of the constitutions mentioned in *P.Flor.* 382, is *PSI* 1103, a petition addressed to the *epistrategos* of the Heptanomia by an individual residing in the Arsinoite nome.[31] We would expect this petition of the late second century to adhere to the rule of 70 years. At first sight it does. The petitioner is over the age of 70 years (lines 10–11) and, so he claims, has been assigned to a liturgy in error by the *basilikogrammateus*. That such errors might occur is interesting in itself; perhaps the fault lay more with the petitioner himself, because the administrative system depended on the individual bringing the grounds for exemption to the notice of the officials, not vice versa. At any rate, what is of more interest to us here is the mention made by the petitioner of the age of 65 years (lines 12–13) as in some cases conferring exemption from liturgies. What the petitioner seems to be saying (presuming we can believe him) is that, "while the mandatory age of exemption remained at 70, prefects and *epistrategoi* exercised discretionary power to release men after the age of 65,"[32] or at least people believed that they had this power. The date of this papyrus implies both that the age was in practice being lowered at a very early stage and that the original rule was, so to speak, made to be broken, despite the collection of imperial constitutions submitted later by, for example, Heron in circa A.D. 222. The letter of the law remained the same: the age of exemption was 70 years, and 65 years in theory conferred no exemption, as Ulpian states explicitly.[33] But in practice, in Roman Egypt if not elsewhere, dispensations must have been given to individuals at an earlier age on something approaching a regular basis, regular enough to give the impression of a new rule of age of 65 years. This is certainly what our petitioner in *PSI* 1103, *himself over the age of 70 years,* believes and what he complains about (as well as being impoverished and "physically ill with terrible eyesight"—line 14) to his *epistrategos* in A.D. 192–94.

That the age of exemption was being gradually lowered is further evidenced in the few relevant papyri that follow, though even as late as A.D. 294 we still find an imperial constitution assuming that the theoretical age of exemption remained at 70 years.[34] Of the four papyri left to consider in regard to liturgies, two make no mention of specific ages of exemption. *P.Wisc.* 3, to be dated to A.D. 257–61 and of unknown provenance, is a fragment of a petition made by an 83-year-old (lines 11–12) who complains of his physical weakness and poor eyesight (lines 22–24, 28–30), and who applies for exemption from the burden of *munera personalia,* an exemption that was clearly due to him at his age anyway. In fact, as he states in his petition, he has previously been granted exemption by the prefect already on the grounds of old age (lines 6–15) but has since been renominated for a liturgy. He therefore applies again now (to whom we do not know), adding the fact that his health is poor. That such additional grounds for exemption, as well as that of old age, should need to be stated has already been seen in other examples, and it points to the fact that old age in itself might often be, despite previous rulings, an unsatisfactory reason on its own. Also noteworthy is the fact that, while the petitioner applies for release from the physical duties of the liturgy, he states that he will continue to "contribute to expenses" (line 30); old age, as has been seen already, only afforded immunity from physical, not financial burdens. It is of interest, incidentally, to read in the petition that this individual has kept records of his earlier grant of exemption by the prefect (lines 24–27); clearly, in this bureaucratic system, written records were of fundamental importance.

Mention should also be made of *P.Panop.* 29 (= *SB* 11222), a papyrus of A.D. 332 from Panopolis and chronologically the last extant papyrus that deals with old age and liturgies.[35] In it the petitioner, one Aurelius Pasnos, whose age we are not told apart from the fact that he calls himself a γέρων, requests from two different officials release from a bouleutic liturgy on the grounds of his old age. Again we have here an example of complicated procedure and of inefficiency (whether accidental or intentional) in the system: Aurelius had obtained release from liturgies from the *praeses* Flavius Quintilianus, but the official's order was subsequently violated and Aurelius must now reapply to the *exactor* for a new hearing by the *praeses,* a request that was eventually granted.[36] The application for exemption obviously proved to be a lengthy and involved process, which, even if successful in the end, might be subsequently violated. Bureaucracies can prove frustrating for the ordinary individual.

So much for these two papyri, *P.Wisc.* 3 and *P.Panop.* 29, neither of which states a definite age of exemption. Two other papyri of the fourth century, however, do provide us with further information: first,

PSI 685, a fragment of a petition addressed to the prefect Aurelius Apion by one Aurelius Silbanus of Oxyrhynchus, a weaver by trade who applies for release from a λειτουργία. Unfortunately we cannot date the papyrus with precision, apart from stating (mainly from palaeographical evidence) that it belongs to the first half of the fourth century.[37] The petitioner, who talks of his own old age (lines 8, 13), is apparently over 60 years of age[38] and is claiming exemption from σωματικαὶ λειτουργίαι (*munera corporalia*) both on this ground and by reason of his profession.[39] It would appear from this that early in the fourth century the age of exemption may have been further lowered to 60 years. Further support for this theory appears in our last piece of papyrological evidence.

P.Oxy. 889 contains a petition "addressed to the *boule* of, no doubt, Oxyrhynchus, by a man who probably wished to be let off some municipal burden on the score of old age and ill health."[40] The man describes himself as being in his 73rd year (line 17) and claims the exemption granted to those who have passed their 60th year (line 16). What then of the date of this petition? What remains of the date (lines 11–12) is too fragmentary to read, but what does provide more evidence is the opening section of the papyrus, which is in the form of an imperial edict prefixed to the petition. The original editors, Grenfell and Hunt, stated that "the authors of the present decree are clearly Diocletian and Maximian" and they dated it on the evidence of the consuls mentioned to A.D. 300. The petition that follows, they said, "no doubt falls within the 50 years following A.D. 300."[41] So it was long assumed. But in more recent times two scholars have independently shown that the decree belongs to December A.D. 324 and is an edict not of Diocletian and Maximian but of Constantine; the petition itself probably belongs to A.D. 325.[42]

What the edict in substance says is that, owing to the emperors' *philanthropia* (line 5), at the age of 60 years (line 9) men are to be granted exemption, a statement picked up and reiterated by the petitioner (line 16). Barnes argues that the exemption being referred to is from the poll tax, although he concedes that it may refer to liturgies; certainly in its context the latter case seems more likely. Barnes further suggests that Constantine lowered the age of exemption (for both the poll tax and liturgies) to 60 years in A.D. 324 after Licinius had raised the age to 70 years in 321. But in fact, as has been seen here, the age of exemption from liturgies before the fourth century was legally 70 years anyway; and there is no evidence that the age of exemption from poll tax was ever as high as 70 years.[43] What *P.Oxy.* 889, together with *PSI* 685, does suggest is that the age of exemption from compulsory public services in Roman Egypt was lowered to 60 years in the first half of the fourth century. It has already been seen that in A.D. 192–94 the age of exemption, while in theory still 70 years, could be lowered by special dispensation to 65 years (*PSI* 1103). Some 130 years later it was lowered by law to 60 years; perhaps such an age of exemption had operated in practice before this time, both in Egypt and in the empire as a whole.[44]

It was seen in the previous chapter that a rule of age of 55 years was also in operation in the late third and early fourth centuries, at least in the case of the decurionate if not of *honores et munera personalia* in general, whereby a man over the age of 55 years could not be forced to serve against his will but must continue to serve until at least the age of 70 years if co-opted before he had turned 55 years of age.[45] This rule may also have applied to the members of the *boulai* in Roman Egypt, but if so the papyri remain silent on the subject.[46]

The papyri we do have, however, in regard to old age and liturgies, while perhaps not numerous enough to provide conclusive proof, support and supplement the evidence of the legal texts. Although one must also allow for local developments, and though the situation in Egypt may have evolved in different ways from elsewhere in the empire, there are indications of consistency over different parts of the empire. The evidence—literary, legal, and papyrological—discussed in this and the previous chapter regarding the age of exemption from compulsory public services is summarized in Table 8 in Appendix A. The age of exemption was in general 70 years but over the course of time the age was progressively lowered in individual cases and eventually the practice seems to have been given the force of general law.[47]

Furthermore, old age appears to have become something of an unconvincing ground for exemption on its own, as shown by the comparative frequency of instances where grounds supplementary to old age are cited, whether they are related (such as ill health and poor eyesight) or—arguably—largely separate (such as one's profession or poverty). Cases have been seen where exemptions already granted to elderly men were subsequently ignored by officials, perhaps for the same reason. If the rules actually stated that a person was to be released from liturgical services at the age of *x* years, then why was there the apparent need for extra grounds for exemption and why should such legal releases sometimes have been ignored?

One possible reason is that when nominees for liturgies were more difficult to find, whether through individuals' lack of means or through their simple flight, those who might normally have been excused were actually forced to serve—hence the natural inclination, if not the legal compulsion, to give several grounds for exemption rather than just one. The jurist Modestinus provides two interesting pieces of information in relation to claims for exemption from *munera privata*. He states that someone who has a number of alleged grounds for exemption, none of which is individually legally valid (such as having two children, not five, or being 60 years of age, not 70), will not be granted exemption; clearly there was some question about this. Elsewhere he notes that *all* grounds for exemption must be stated in one's application.[48] Another reason that might be suggested for multiple grounds being given in a petition is that actual statements of age, despite the bureaucratic system of the census and related documents, might have been difficult or too time-consuming to substantiate and could be falsified. Clearly it would have been in the interests of a 69-year-old to say that he was 70, and who would have been able to refute him? As a result of such factors as these, it is easy to see how theoretical dispensation at a certain age and actual practice might have meant two different things. Such considerations as these, among others, we shall return to later in this chapter. First we need to look at another aspect of rules of age in Roman Egypt, that relating to the poll tax.

THE POLL TAX

One of the chief purposes underlying the operation of the bureaucratic "machine" in Roman Egypt was the collection of taxes, and the tax system in Egypt at this time was as complex as the bureaucracy created to ensure its collection.[49] Practically every facet of daily life had its associated levy: the government exacted its due on land, grain, wine, vegetables, oil, property, animals, professions, business transactions, and so forth, whether paid in money or in kind. The liturgical system itself played an important part in the tax structure at every level, particularly in the collection of money and the transportation of levied produce. Massive amounts of "paper work" were also involved, not least in the form of receipts (often multiple copies) on *ostraka*. The burden of taxation on the average Egyptian, just as with the burden of compulsory public services, led some to flee from their liabilities or collapse under the weight.

The most general tax and the one we know most about was the *laographia,* poll tax, exacted at varying rates from practically every male inhabitant of the land. Many receipts relating to this tax have survived, and from these it is possible to build up a picture, albeit far from complete, of how the tax system worked in this area. Exemptions from payment, again as was also the case with exemptions from liturgies, were both sought after and rare, applying (up to the third century) only to the most privileged Roman citizens primarily, as well as to members of the "Greek" cities, certain high priests and important non-Roman officials. Some others paid the tax at a lower rate: in Arsinoe, for example, at twenty drachmas instead of the usual forty. Such was the case with members of the higher classes in the *metropoleis*. The average Egyptian male, on the other hand, paid the full amount for most of his life; women did not pay the poll tax.

Liability to the poll tax began for males at the age of 14 years, and for this basic reason the census was held every 14 years. From the census documents lists of those liable to the poll tax were drawn up. We need now to consider the age at which the Egyptian male under the Roman principate ceased to be liable for the payment of the poll tax. Again, caution is necessary as we proceed. It is clear enough that the actual amount of tax paid varied from nome to nome.[50] Evidence, such as it is, for the age of exemption appears contradictory, as will be seen presently, and it is possible that different age limits were set in different regions. Likewise over the course of time the age may have been changed, as we have seen occurred with the age of exemption from compulsory public services. Certainly the geographical problem is a considerable one: in relation to *laographia* most of our papyri come from the Arsinoite and Oxyrhynchite nomes, and Upper Egypt has left us almost no evidence at all. For Middle Egypt we do have definite evidence that in old age men could be exempted from payment of the poll tax. As to exactly what that age was, the papyri with which we deal indicate different figures. As yet no consensus among scholars has been reached; often no awareness of the ambiguity is evident. Therefore, it is necessary to look in some detail at the pieces of testimony that we have.

First, it must be stressed that there are no grounds for supposing that the age of exemption from the poll tax was ever the same as the age of exemption from compulsory public services.[51] Likewise evidence from one part of the empire cannot be assumed to have been valid for another part, however close geographically. Ulpian, writing in the early third century and himself originally from Tyre, makes the following statement about the age of exemption from *tributum capitis* in Syria:

> aetatem in censendo significare necesse est, quia quibusdam aetas tribuit, ne tributo onerentur: veluti in Syriis a quattuordecim annis masculi, a duodecim feminae usque ad sexagensimum quintum annum tributo capitis obligantur. aetas autem spectatur censendi tempore.

> It is necessary to indicate age in compiling censuses, because age confers on some people exemption from the payment of tax, for example, in the provinces of Syria males are bound to pay poll tax from the age of 14 years, females from the age of 12 years, in both cases up to the 65th year. The relevant age is that at the time of the census operation.[52]

It was supposed by Wilcken that this rule of age also applied to Roman Egypt,[53] but this was clearly not the case; for a start, we know that in Egypt only men paid the poll tax, although women were subject to certain other taxes. As for the maximum age of 64 years, papyrological evidence suggests that the age of exemption from poll tax in Roman Egypt was in fact lower than this.

The most important text in this context is a document first published by Kenyon in 1898 as *P.Lond.* 257–59.[54] What this document represents is a long list of men liable to payment of the poll tax in the Arsinoite nome in the year A.D. 94; the list is based on the declarations of the census of A.D. 89/90 and of previous censuses. What is striking about the list, which contains the ages of some 270 individuals, is that throughout it no person is mentioned whose age exceeds 60 years. This fact led Kenyon to say that "[i]t cannot be merely an accident," with which I agree, and he concluded that "the upper limit of age was sixty," with which I disagree.

Line 64 of *P.Lond.* 259 is crucial. In Kenyon's published text, lines 63–65 read as follows:

> . . . σαγ εις απαι^τ τωι ιγL   ομ^ο αν^δ χκθ
> υπερ τ̣ο̣ Lξα   ε
> [τε]τε^λ ιγL   β   αν^δ χλς

From this it appears that five individuals (further described in lines 75–91) were "over the age of 61 years" and therefore exempt from the poll tax. As Wallace rightly pointed out,[55] the text as it stands would in fact suggest an age of exemption of 62 years, that is, on completion of one's 62nd year when one was indeed "over the age of 61 years" (line 64). What Wallace overlooked, however, was the following amended text produced by Wilcken shortly after Kenyon's text appeared:[56]

> ἤχθη]σαν εἰς ἀπαίτ⟨ησιν⟩ τῷ ιγ ⟨ἔτει⟩ ὁμό⟨λογοι⟩ ἄνδ⟨ρες⟩ χκθ
> ὑπὲρ ιγ ⟨ἔτους⟩ ⟨ἐτῶν⟩ ξα   ε
> [τε]τελ⟨ευτηκότες⟩ ιγ ⟨ἔτει⟩   β   ⟨γίνονται⟩ ἄνδ⟨ρες⟩ χλς

What we have in substance here is a summary of those cited in the preceding lists: 629 (χκθ) men were liable to pay the poll tax in this year, the 13th (ιγ) year of Domitian; five (ε) are described as being 61 (ξα) years old and two (β) others have died in the course of the year, bringing the year-end tally to 636 (χλς) men. According to Wilcken the poll tax was only paid up to the age of 60 years at this time; the five 61-year-old individuals listed here were, Wilcken assumed, over the age of exemption.[57]

When Kenyon published his text in 1898 the existence of the word ὑπερετής (over-age) was not known; it was only when Grenfell and Hunt published *P.Oxy.* 478 in 1903 that the word was recognized (line 35). When in 1905 Wessely published the roll of *P.Lond.* 260 and 261 together with *P.Rainer,* the word was also seen to occur there (line 208); not until 1964, however, was the true reading of *P.Lond.* 259.64 finally arrived at, by Youtie:[58]

> ὑπερ⟨ετεῖς⟩ ιγ ⟨ἔτει⟩ ⟨ἐτῶν⟩ ξα   ε

As Youtie realized, ὑπερ here, as often elsewhere, is the standard abbreviation for ὑπερετής. Thus the text now reads that five men were "over-age" and 61 years old. Does this mean that the age of exemption from the poll tax at this time was indeed from after the age of 60 years, that is, having completed one's 61st year and turning 61 years of age?

It is my hypothesis that it was not. What *P.Lond.* 259.63–65 does tell us is that 629 men were liable to poll tax, five others were 61 years old and described as "over-age," and another two had died during A.D. 94, bringing the total number of individuals listed to 636. We have not actually been told, however, that the five over-age men were exempt from the tax: why should they be listed if they were? It is my contention that in fact all 636 people listed here were actually liable to payment of the poll tax. It may, of course, be wondered how two dead men could pay tax. In fact, however, it would appear that if a man died in the course of a year his immediate heirs were liable for the poll tax he would have paid in that year. Furthermore, if a person died in the second half of the year the entire amount of the poll tax was due, just as if he had been alive throughout the course of the entire year.[59] Thus the two individuals here described as τετελευτηκότες still owed poll tax. The same was true in this period of those 61 years of age, I believe. This was to be their last year of liability and as such they were listed separately, in preparation for the final *epikrisis* examination in the following year; after this their names would have been transferred to the lists of those exempt as being 62 years of age or older.

This line of argument finds support in *P.Coll.Youtie* 20, published in 1976. This papyrus is a summary list very similar in character to *P.Lond.* 259.63–65; it is from the same area (Philadelphia) but some forty years earlier in date (ca. A.D. 56), and contains the scribblings of the tax official Nemesion regarding the numbers of men liable to the poll tax in that year. The text is not completely intact but it is preserved well enough for us to see in outline how the systems of liability and exemption operated. Out of a total of 782 men, 210 are described as excused (on what grounds we are not told, but certainly not on the grounds of age, as the rest of the document makes clear) and another 9 are described as being exempt by being ὑπερ⟨ετεῖς⟩ (line 5). Nemesion then retotals his figures and with the two deductions made comes up with a new total of 563. To this he then adds 57 further men: 9 as being 14 years of age and therefore newly liable, 36 as ἀφήλικες who were now liable,[60] 6 other individual cases of liability, and 6 who are liable as being ὑπερ⟨ετεῖς⟩ ξα (line 8). It is this last reference that is crucial. That these six 61-year-old men were liable to the poll tax cannot be doubted: they are added into the new and final total of those from whom tax is to be exacted, a total of 620 men (i.e., 782 − 219 + 57), and they are quite separate from the 9 individuals listed as "over-age" in line 5 and thereby exempt. This must mean that, at least in the Arsinoite nome at this time, 61-year-old men were not exempt from payment of the poll tax and that the age of exemption was 62 years, that is, on the completion of one's 62nd year. Likewise *P.Lond.* 259.64–65 refers not to those exempt from the poll tax but to those who were liable to the poll tax for the last time in that year. It would seem from this that a separate list of such individuals was drawn up each year.[61] *P.Lond.* 259.75–91 appears to be just such a list.[62]

The problem remains, however, as to why 61-year-old men should have been described as "over-age" (ὑπερετεῖς) when in fact they were not over the age of exemption. It is my belief, though at this stage impossible to prove, that initially in Roman Egypt the age for exemption was 60 years and that the original terminology remained in use even after the age had been raised. This is suggested by one fragmentary papyrus,[63] a petition of 5/4 B.C. addressed to the prefect (our friend C. Turannius, whom we have met in the previous two chapters) by a Jew living in Alexandria, one Helenus, claiming exemption from *laographia*. Helenus's primary claim to exemption is that he is an Alexandrian citizen, though this had perhaps been put in doubt: the scribe writing the document changed "Alexandrian" to "a Jew of Alexandria" (line 2). Helenus adds the argument that he should be granted exemption from the poll tax διὰ τὸ τῶν ἑξ⟨ή⟩κοντα (line 22), which seems to mean, as Schubart takes it, "das Privileg der 60. Jahre,"[64] though the text is very fragmentary and the exact context remains uncertain. If Helenus really was an Alexandrian citizen, the plea of old age is irrelevant—he would have been legally exempt anyway—but, as has already been seen, the mentality seems to have been that the more excuses one could find the greater the chance of gaining exemption.[65] This isolated piece of evidence does suggest, however, that at this time, in Alexandria at any rate, the age of exemption from the poll tax was 60 years.

But there are further complications to be noted. *P.Grenf.* 1.45–46 (= *W.Chr.* 200), 19–18 B.C., are some sort of census declarations (the term ὑπόνημα is used) by a "royal farmer" of Theadelphia. Very strange: why declarations in consecutive years? No certain answer may be given. What is of real interest to us here also is that the farmer declares himself as 63 years of age in 19 B.C., 64 in 18, and that he states in the former document (45.8) that he is declaring himself θέλων σύνταξιν—even stranger. Amending θέλων to τελῶν, as most scholars want to do, makes some sense, but why is he paying poll tax? The simplest solution is that the reference is not to poll tax, but "a simple capitation tax of local significance."[66] But I would wish to defend the original reading θέλων and to reinterpret σύνταξιν. The problem lies, I would suggest, not in a scribal error but in our incomplete knowledge of the range of meanings of this noun. Our farmer presumably knew what he was doing: he is seeking a pension, not wanting to pay a tax.

Some fifty years later there is the evidence provided in a register for tax being paid by a 62-year-old man in Philadelphia.[67] If, as I believe, the age limit had been raised in the interim from 60 to 62 years, why was a 62-year-old paying the tax, when in fact his liability had ended on turning 62? One possible explanation is that the tax had been due in the previous year but that he had paid it later in the next year, by which time he was over the age of liability but would still have owed tax due when he had been 61 years old.[68] But we cannot even be definite that this register relates to the poll tax: the term συντάξιμον rather than λαογραφία is used and it is not certain that the two terms are synonymous.[69] Here we cannot be sure that the age of liability for the two taxes was exactly the same (though the συντάξιμον seems also to have been due, like the λαογραφία, from the age of 14 years). At any rate, this papyrus on its own is of dubious value as evidence for the age of exemption from poll tax at this time.

Evidence from the second century A.D., however, does point to an age of exemption from the poll tax of 62 years, just as the evidence of *P.Coll.Youtie* 20 implies such an age limit for the mid-first century. In A.D. 178/9 a man of 62 years of age from Socnopaiou Nesos is described in a tax list as ὑπερετὴς πεπληρωκὼς τῷ ἐνεστῶτι ιθ ⟨ἔτει⟩ ⟨ἔτη⟩ ξβ,[70] whereas in A.D. 189 a census return from the Arsinoite nome (*P.Tebt.* 322.17) records a donkey-driver of 61 years of age as still liable for the poll tax (λαογρα⟨φούμενος⟩ ὀνηλ⟨άτης⟩ ⟨ἐτῶν⟩ ξα). It is also worth pointing out that with the thousands of Theban tax receipts studied in relation to life expectancy, no example of anyone paying the poll tax over the age of 61 years appears, and of all the taxes no one over the age of 62 years.[71] Furthermore, in the tax rolls from Karanis, a certain "Priscus, also known as Pasoxis" appears in the year A.D. 71/2 paying the poll tax at the age of 60 years, and he goes on to pay the tax until he has completed 62 years.[72] This much supports our hypothesis.

A recently published papyrus from Arsinoe, however, seems to provide evidence for exemption from the poll tax after the age of 60 years. In a copy from the census register of A.D. 131/2, one Apronius, son of Marcus, *eques,* is described as ὑπερετὴς ἀπολύσιμ⟨ος⟩ τῆς λαο-γρ⟨αφίας⟩ ιε ⟨ἔτει⟩ ⟨ἐτῶν⟩ ξα (past the age, released from the poll tax in year 15 [sc. of Hadrian = A.D. 130/1], 61 years of age).[73] But something is amiss here. For in the census register of A.D. 117/18, also quoted, Apronius is declared as 48 years of age (line 47); fourteen years later one would in fact expect him to be 62 years of age (and therefore ὑπερετής). Of the individuals listed in both registers, two age by 14 years, two by 13, and one by 24 years![74] In short, this papyrus, if anything, supports the notion that the age of exemption from the poll tax was 62 years.

Another papyrus from Hermopolis, however, adds still further complications.[75] In it we find a 64-year-old man in the *metropolis* paying the poll tax at a rate of twenty drachmas (col. 2 line 9). This is the reduced rate, but whether the reduction is as a result of status or of something else is unknown; it is unlikely to be age alone, because other individuals recorded as paying at this reduced rate are aged 17, 18, 27, 33, 50, and 52 years. In any event: why so old and still paying? Two other over-age individuals are listed (but without mention of any payment), one of 65 years, another of 69 years (col. 1 line 2; col. 2 line 18). The date of the papyrus is important. Wessely dated it paleographically to the first half of the second century; Wallace argued for a date at the end of the second or beginning of the third century on the grounds that, unless it was an example of extortion, the 64-year-old should not have been liable in the early second century.[76] It now seems certain, in fact, that the papyrus dates to the mid-third century.[77] Perhaps at this time the age limit had increased to 65 years (which would tie in, incidentally, with Ulpian's statement for Syria) or even 70 years in this part of Egypt, but if so, this is the only piece of evidence that we have for it. Another possibility is that it does not refer to the poll tax at all.[78]

At any rate, a theory has been tentatively set out here as to the age of exemption from the poll tax in Roman Egypt. Originally (i.e., from the time of Octavian) the age limit may have stood at 60 years but that very shortly thereafter, within the next half century, it had been raised to 62 years (perhaps as a single, deliberate legal innovation, but more probably as a gradual process of evolution and interpretation of the rules), and remained as such until at least the end of the second century. This is, however, little more than a hypothesis designed to suit the limited testimony that we have. Certainly more evidence is needed before anything more conclusive can be presumed.

There remains the possibility that the age of exemption varied from one nome to another. Our evidence is certainly far too scanty to make any presumptions about this,[79] but it is worth presenting one more piece of relevant testimony: P.Oxy. 984A. This census register from *Upper* Egypt (probably Ptolemais or Lycopolis), dating to A.D. 91/2, records two individuals as ὑπερετεῖς.[80] The age of one (line 133) is preserved: he is 60 years old. This might be taken as an indication that the upper age limit in Upper Egypt was 60 years, whereas in the Arsinoite nome a few years later a man is not described as ὑπερετής until he is at least 61 years of age. But the Upper Egypt list is not internally consistent: another 60-year-old in the list (line 162) is *not* described as ὑπερετής. The ages preserved in this list suffer from marked rounding, far more than in the many examples of such lists from Middle Egypt. What we perhaps have here, then, is a geographical difference not in rules of age but in precision of stated ages and in concern about precise rules of age; more probably, it seems to me, we have here an isolated case of inaccuracy and error in terminology. It should serve to warn us again, however, of the difficulties of determining general rules from such scanty pieces of evidence.

What can be said with confidence is that, as with compulsory public services, an age of exemption from the poll tax was applied at least in theory and that it was the responsibility of the individual affected to apply for release from the burdens imposed by the state.[81] It remains now to consider certain practicalities related to the rules of age seen here.

Realities of Rules of Age in Roman Egypt

STATEMENTS OF AGE

It has been seen in both this and the previous chapter that definite rules of age were in use in the Roman Empire, stating that after a particular age a person was held to be eligible to perform certain functions or liable to certain duties or, at the other end of the age-scale, was exempt from them. This must presuppose, one might think, that such a person knew how old he or she was, in terms of years at least, if not also of months and days. Yet in fact such was clearly not the case in classical times, and, as was discussed in Chapter 1, the tendency to estimate ages appears to have been quite widespread and common. One clear sign of this is the occurrence of age-rounding.

In the case of Roman Egypt, as for elsewhere in the empire, it might be natural to infer that in fact "most of the inhabitants . . . had no accurate knowledge of how old they were."[82] What then was the point of definite rules of age, if no one knew his or her real age? If, for example, a male was by law exempt from the payment of the poll tax once he had reached his 63rd year, how could he claim such exemption if he did not know whether he was 60 or 65 years old? Lewis assumes this to have been the reason why, as we have already noticed, claims for exemption regularly stated grounds supplementary to that of old age, such as poor health or poverty. But such multiple reasons for exemption, I would argue, are due more to a natural desire to ensure the acceptance of one's application: why cite only one legitimate reason to be let off when one could give several and thus perhaps increase one's chances? In periods when eligible candidates for public duties became difficult to find, otherwise exempt people could be forced to serve all the same.[83] It would have been more sensible wherever possible in such circumstances to provide a whole range of reasons for being granted immunity from financial and/or corporeal burdens, rather than pinning all one's hopes on a single factor, however valid.

I would argue that in Roman Egypt, if not elsewhere in the empire, at an official level the bureaucratic system enabled people to get an accurate idea of their age. That is not to say that they achieved (or were necessarily interested in achieving) as high a level of accuracy as we are accustomed to find in modern archival records. Instances can be and have been found of marked misrepresentations of age in Roman Egypt. Where rules of age regarding public duties were concerned, a degree of accuracy was possible and necessary; on a private level such accuracy may have been seen as of less importance. The average Egyptian male may have told his family and friends that he was "60 or so" years old, but when he came to his local public office and claimed exemption from a particular duty because he had just turned 62, his claim needed verification as a first step, and the bureaucratic apparatus of Roman Egypt provided the means of establishing this.

So much for the theory. We shall review actual evidence for the extent of age-rounding in Roman Egypt shortly. First, however, we need to return to the question, mentioned in Chapter 1, of illiteracy. There is little point denying that a high level of illiteracy existed in Roman Egypt, as elsewhere in the empire. The evidence speaks for itself. In an important series of articles, Herbert Youtie considered various aspects of the phenomenon.[84] We cannot give precise figures for the levels of illiteracy among the population, of course, but its presence, at least in terms of the Greek language, seems clear enough, particularly in the large number of papyrological documents where an individual can scarcely sign his name to a document written for him by a scribe "because he does not know letters."[85] Some people could not write at all, others are described as "slow writers," that is, they could do little more than painstakingly scrawl their names at the bottom of a document; interestingly such people were not classed as "unlettered." Youtie convincingly elucidated several points relating to illiteracy in Roman Egypt: first, when someone is described as "unlettered" it sometimes means only that the individual cannot read and write Greek, the language of public transactions. Egypt at this time can be seen to have been a bilingual society (quite apart from Roman citizens writing in

Latin). An unlettered person in fact often may have been quite capable of reading and writing his or her own native tongue, the language of everyday life.[86] Such people had no real need to be fluent in Greek; such circumstances as required a knowledge of the language of bureaucracy were entrusted to a *hypographeus,* a scribe who may have been a personal acquaintance or a paid professional.[87] When we talk of high illiteracy in Roman Egypt, therefore, we need to bear this factor in mind. Second, there was apparently no embarrassment or shame attached to illiteracy.[88] It was practical and desirable on a public level to be literate but there were "no implications of social superiority" in being lettered.[89]

Although a large proportion of the overall population of Roman Egypt would have been incapable of writing or reading Greek, the actual administrative system could still operate efficiently with Greek as its primary means of communicating and recording information. In the light of the amount of bureaucratic practice evident in the administration of Roman Egypt, Brunt concluded that "this passion for paper work obviously presupposes a degree of literacy among the subjects that must have been uncommon in the more barbarous north."[90] This is not necessarily true. The "subjects" as a whole may have been "unlettered" in Greek, but the officials producing and handling the written work clearly were not—or, at least, not usually.

One effect that general literacy at an official level might have would be a lowering in the tendency to age-round. Among the many documents that the *grammateis* had and used were the census declarations and the notices of birth on which were recorded the ages of individuals. Once the year of birth had been recorded, whether directly by notice of birth or by declaration in the first census after birth, followed by *epikrisis* in youth, the age of an individual was in the archives, to be consulted whenever necessary in future. It was on this system that, at a public level, the precision or otherwise of statements of age depended. What then do we know of the tendency toward age-rounding or of general age miscalculation in Roman Egypt?

Several specific examples of obvious age miscalculation in documents from Roman Egypt may be highlighted, but at most these prove only that a few private individuals made mistakes, whether intentionally or through ignorance.[91] One factor that does seem to point to a more general lack of precision in statements of age is the frequency with which ages are expressed in the papyri as ... ὡς ἐτῶν, "about *x* years old." It has been suggested and it is widely assumed that the significance of this phrase was that, because many individuals had no precise idea of their actual ages, officials had to make guesses for them.[92] This is to some extent probably true: many people, as has been seen already, would have had no accurate knowledge or any particular interest in their exact age. But I would argue that in most cases the officials should not have had to make guesses; they would have had the relevant information about the individual in their archives already. It is perhaps just as likely that the officials in question added the ... ὡς for the same reason that they often wrote as part of their notation on the documents drawn up for illiterate people "I have written for so-and-so because *he says* that he is unlettered," a typically bureaucratic way of avoiding responsibility if records were subsequently found to be fraudulent,[93] remembering that the Roman Egyptian system ensured consistency over time in the age as initially recorded but could not precisely verify the age when it was first recorded. One might compare too the phrase *citra causarum cognitionem,* in the sense "without investigation," which occurs in the majority of the Latin notices of legitimate births (*professiones*) that are extant, apparently as a means of avoiding responsibility for the authenticity of the information contained in the notice.[94] Also of interest is *P.Oxy.* 715, a registration of house property in the Heracleopolite nome for the year A.D. 131, where the *bibliophylax* appends a note stating that the return has been entered on the register κινδ⟨ύνῳ⟩ τῶν ἀπογρα⟨φομένων⟩ μηδενὸς ⟨δ⟩ημοσίου ἢ ἰδιωτικο⟨ῦ⟩ καταβλαπ⟨τομένου⟩ (at the risk of the declaring parties, with no public or private interests being harmed, 36–37).

I would suggest, therefore, that in the phrase ... ὡς ἐτῶν the sense of ... ὡς is more "allegedly" than "approximately." At any rate, one must also admit that while officials had the relevant information on ages stored away in their archives, more was involved in retrieving these data than just the press of a button. Total precision and efficiency may well have often been sacrificed in the interests of a quick and easy result. Nonetheless the phrase ... ὡς ἐτῶν, though alien to modern-day standards of accuracy and precision, does not in itself prove universal ignorance concerning age in Roman Egypt.

In his study of age-rounding and illiteracy in the Roman Empire (see Chapter 1), Duncan-Jones pointed to evidence for what appear to have been high levels of illiteracy in Roman Egypt, and he assumed that age-rounding here was as prevalent as elsewhere in the empire. In a subsequent article specifically on Egypt, however, he modified his views somewhat, dealing with age-rounding as attested from various sources:[95] in Ptolemaic sources and in Roman examples on nonofficial documents (such as tombstones and mummy labels) levels of age-rounding appear high;[96] however, in official documents of the Roman era a significant difference is noted, and this in particular seems to me to support the theory of the existence of a very real ability at an official level in Egypt to cite ages accurately when using archive records as derived from census declarations and the like. In dealing with papyri and *ostraka* that record Roman legal transactions and tax payments, Duncan-Jones comments on "a marked improvement in age-awareness in the Roman period." In regard to tax records in particular there is almost no age-rounding tendency at all.[97] For example, in the tax lists preserved in *P.Lond.* 257–58, only 20.8 percent of the ages stated are multiples of five, almost exactly on average the proportion one would expect in normal circumstances. Such precision is very striking. The editors of the Theban tax *ostraka* note a similar precision in census declarations,[98] but they seem unwilling to accept that at an official level such precision was possible. This is, I feel, largely unjustified. Duncan-Jones's conclusion is worth citing here, for it supports exactly the basis of my argument, namely that the bureaucracy of Roman Egypt was capable of furnishing exact statements of age: "The Roman authorities were capable of compiling age-data at the local level which were effectively free from rounding error. . . . Since liability to the poll tax depended on the taxpayer's age, it was vital to both parties that the age-records should be kept accurately for this purpose."[99] Villagers may not have known or cared exactly how old they were, except perhaps when it came to possible exemptions from state duties, but in official records age-rounding is almost wholly absent. Bureaucracy appears to have fostered age awareness at an official level, to a degree that was perhaps significantly higher than in most parts of the Roman Empire.[100]

One final word of caution, however. Does such apparent precision necessarily mean that we can assume accuracy? On this point one cannot answer with certainty. All the testimony does support our conclusions, however, that the system of administration and record keeping in Roman Egypt was in theory capable of producing precise and consistent statements of an individual's age, to counteract any ignorance or fraudulent intent on the part of the individual; and that the system appears to have worked in practice when one compares the very low tendency for age-rounding in official documents with the high levels in private documents and in sources from the rest of the empire.

WHOM DID THE RULES AFFECT?

A fundamental question in the context of rules of age needs now to be considered. If there were in existence in Roman Egypt regulations that in theory granted exemption to individuals in old age from the burdens imposed by the state, how many people survived to such an age? That such rules did exist is clear from what has been said already; but on reflection the ages set by these rules, in the range of 60 to 70 years, seem surprisingly high in the light of the discussion in Chapter 2 of the demographic realities of the time.

In modern times, somewhat similar rules of age exist in most societies: for example, retirement and pensions at 60, 65, or 70 years of age. Although there was no such concept as retirement in ancient times (as was noted in the previous chapter), at least as we understand this term today, some concessions and privileges seem to have been granted to some individuals in their old age. But though the ages set both in ancient and modern times are similar numerically, the situations are not in reality comparable. A primary consideration here is the average life expectancy of the ordinary individual. Today the chances of a person surviving from the time he or she enters the work force until the time he or she might be expected to leave it, in his or her 60s, are very high. In the ancient world, of course, the chances of surviving from one's teens until one's 60s were much lower. It is necessary to consider rules of age in this light.

At the beginning of their study of longevity in antiquity, Samuel et al. state: "It would be interesting to know whether 62 could have been seen in antiquity as some sort of 'retirement age,' or whether, in fact, so few would have reached that age as to make the benefit virtually meaningless."[101] In fact neither option seems to me to reflect reality very well. At age 60 the upper classes could, if they chose, enjoy some freedom from duties of the state, but for most of the population such an age limit would have meant very little, especially if they had to continue to support themselves. At age 62 in Roman Egypt, liability to the payment of the poll tax ended, it is true, but liability to liturgies probably continued for several more years, and financial burdens in this regard remained till death.

The demographic aspect is not so straightforward either. I have argued elsewhere that Samuel et al. grossly overestimate age-specific mortality rates in Roman Egypt.[102] In actual fact, if one survived to age 14, the age at which liability to payment of the poll tax began for males, one had a quite good chance of surviving into one's 60s, as is shown in Table 9 in Appendix A. In approximate and generalized terms, one can see from this table that something like 30–35 percent of those who began to pay the poll tax at age 14 years would have survived to enjoy exemption at age 62 years. What *is* true is that the chances of surviving from birth to the age of 14 years were much lower: fewer than half achieved this. As was pointed out in Chapter 2, it was the early years that were so dangerous. Once one had survived into one's teens, the chances of surviving into old age were quite good (though nothing like as good as they are in the Western world today). In other words, the exemption granted to those in their 60s from the poll tax, for example, was far from "meaningless."

It is clear, then, that the exemption from some liturgies and from the poll tax in Roman Egypt in old age did have a very real application for some members of the society, real enough for them to go to some length to petition for such exemption. The question remains as to *why* such exemption was granted. In the case of liturgies of a corporeal nature the answer may be apparent enough: old people were generally considered incapable of performing physical duties and were therefore put in the same grouping as women, the very young, and the ill. So the exemption here may be seen as purely practical and not inspired by benevolent or humanitarian motives on the part of the state. Older people were not, it should be remembered, exempt from liturgies of a purely financial nature (*munera patrimoniorum*). But then they were exempt from payment of the poll tax, which was itself a purely financial burden. Why did the state in this case grant such an exemption, thus forgoing a not insignificant source of tax revenue?

We do not know the mentality underlying the legislation, but we can at least conjecture. It may be relevant to point out that *munera* and *honores* were duties carried out for the local community, whereas the poll tax or *tributum* was in a sense an "external" burden, imposed on the members of a community by the ruling power of the empire as a whole. Hence the rules of age in both cases may have been quite different, and different liabilities for different social classes or age groups may have operated. It was suggested earlier in this chapter that the age of exemption from the poll tax in Roman Egypt may have increased from 60 to 62 years at some point in the first century A.D. This may have been seen as one way of increasing the tax income (especially if many men in their late 50s were declaring that they were 60 years of age!), albeit a small one. On the other hand, the age of exemption from liturgies appears to have been progressively lowered in the later principate. One possible cause may have been the protests of older people themselves, and the lowering of the age of exemption may have been in effect, therefore, a concession to old age.

It is worth recalling here a passage from the legal corpus where Callistratus is discussing the liability of older people to *munera*: "semper in civitate nostra senectus venerabilis fuit: namque maiores nostri paene eundem honorem senibus, quem magistratibus tribuebant. circa munera quoque municipalia subeunda idem honor senectuti tributus est" (Old age has always been revered in our state; for our ancestors used to accord almost the same honor to elderly individuals as to magistrates. In regard also to the liability to municipal *munera,* the same honor has been accorded to old age).[103] I suggested earlier that Callistratus, expressing his own interpretation rather than recording actual legislation, made this statement as a precursor to his assertion that *senes* should undertake financial commitments when they had sufficient means; in other words, he begins with compliments to make his main point, that old age should still be liable to some burdens. What we have here in effect is an attempt to make such an argument more palatable, presumably to older people themselves. But it may also be the case that old age was indeed granted such exemption in the first place as an *honor* in the sense of a benefit. It is probably correct to view the imposition of the poll tax on the Egyptian population as in part a mark of the subjugation or degradation of the race. It is worth pointing out, for example, that Cassius Dio wrote of the "enslavement" of Egypt in 30 B.C. Tertullian, in fine rhetorical style, expressed the imposition of taxes thus: "sed enim agri tributo onusti viliores, hominum capita stipendio censa ignobiliora—nam hae sunt notae captivitatis" (But lands subject to tribute go cheaper and people assessed under the poll tax are less "noble"—for these are the marks of servitude). As Tcherikover noted, in an excellent discussion of the purposes of the poll tax, a "special act of kindness on the part of the authorities is needed to exempt a person, or a group of persons, from this invidious and expensive obligation."[104] Seen in this light, the granting of immunity to older people was indeed a mark of esteem, in the same way that exemption was granted to certain privileged classes of the population. In this sense the exemption granted to older people from the poll tax was quite different from their continued liability to *munera patrimoniorum.* Their exemption from so-called *munera sordida,* duties involving physical labor, may then be seen not as any form of benefit but simply as a practical necessity, elderly individuals being considered incapable of such tasks.

There is some evidence, then, in the Roman world for what may be called—to use modern terminology—tax relief for the elderly.[105] That it was seen in antiquity purely as such is probably unlikely: we must be wary of imposing our own notions on the motives of the Roman legislators. To treat such benefits as a form of retirement is unrealistic; there was certainly no universal, deliberate social program of help and support for older people in antiquity (see Chapter 8). The *gerousia* in Egypt (and elsewhere in the eastern empire, possibly as a Hellenistic legacy, centered as it appears to have been around the gymnasium) might be regarded as a means of support, at least for selected (wealthy and well-born) elderly individuals, but its role is a controversial and complex question that has much occupied scholars this century and which we can touch on here only briefly.[106] Papyri from Oxyrhynchus have shed new light on the *gerousia* there. Four papyri, dating from A.D. 225/6, present the image of membership in the *gerousia* being sought after as a sign of prestige (the number of members was probably fixed) as well as a means of support in old age (τὴν τῶν τρεφομένων ἡλικίαν). Furthermore, age is shown to be an important criterion for admission; again we find census documents being used to prove age. The *minimum* age remains uncertain: perhaps in one's early or mid 50s, almost certainly no later, but this age limit may well have varied from town to town throughout the relevant parts of the empire. Social status, however, seems to have remained an important consideration too. To quote the editor of these papyri, John Rea: "It was in part an old age pension scheme, and one which followed the tradition of Greek and Roman charities in being confined to those who could prove, not their need, but their inherited social status."[107]

Hence this type of *gerousia,* despite its name, is of limited interest in the context of this chapter; if anything, it is of more relevance to the previous chapter, in terms of the political influence and public prestige of older males, because these eastern *gerousiai* not infrequently (and, it seems to me, not surprisingly, in view of their wealthy and, presumably in many cases, leisured members) might play a quite prominent role in the public, religious affairs of communities.[108] But to return to the theme of this chapter: what we have seen here does suggest that the "ordinary" elderly inhabitants of Roman Egypt (and no doubt elsewhere: note again the age of exemption from *tributum* in Syria, mentioned earlier in this chapter), while they might expect no tangible form of social welfare or pension, were in some respects granted a privilege, albeit a minor one, after a lifetime of paying tax and performing compulsory public duties. This too is a theme that we shall see recurring, on occasion, in the remaining chapters of this book.

Six

The Realities of Rules of Age: Proofs of Age

It was seen in the previous two chapters that definite and specific rules existed in the public sphere of the Roman world regulating the age at which an individual was allowed or was required to commence or terminate the performance of a particular civil function, be it as a senator at Rome or as a taxpayer in Roman Egypt. One key fact to emerge from these chapters has been that, although the ages specified in the rules might have changed over time and perhaps also varied over space, the figures arrived at were far from approximations but were in most cases specific and seem to have been designed to be enforced. This aspect of rules of age may be considered as somewhat paradoxical in view of the conclusion reached in Chapter 1 that, at an everyday level, exact age was considered of minor importance. It appears often to have been of little critical concern when erecting someone's tombstone, for example, to get the age at death exactly right.

The central and underlying argument in the previous two chapters has been that at an official level, however, precise and accurate knowledge of age should in theory have been important, for the very reason that specific and exact age regulations were in operation over a wide sphere of public and private aspects of life. It was argued in Chapter 5 that the bureaucratic system of Roman Egypt enabled such rules of age to have operated effectively, at least in terms of the recording of ages. But such rules, it has been seen, are also in evidence elsewhere in the empire. Yet we have no evidence for a similarly advanced system of archives over the empire as a whole; Egypt remains quite unique in this regard.

That age was important in Roman law cannot be doubted. The dividing line between the *minor* and the *maior,* for example, the age of 25 years exactly, determined a man's capacity to act independently and, as such, must have been pivotal for many individuals, not least those of the upper classes. In the private sphere rules of age might on occasion play a part in the lives of most, if not all, individuals: age determined such factors as the time at which a person could enter into a legally recognized marriage, manumit or be manumitted, or adopt under the system of *adrogatio.*[1] How, then, were such rules of age put into operation, if, outside of Roman Egypt, adequate means of checking an individual's age were not available? When a certain Marciana sent a petition to Diocletian and Maximian seeking some favor on the grounds that she had not yet reached the age of 25 years, they replied: "cum te minorem quinque et viginti annis esse proponas, adire praesidem provinciae debes et de aetate probare" (Since you allege that you are under 25 years of age, you should appear before the governor of the province and prove your age).[2] How did Marciana prove her age?

The most obvious way to substantiate age was to produce a notice of birth, as Apuleius famously did in the case of Pudentilla (*Apol.* 89). Mention has already been made in passing of the existence of notices of birth or status in the Roman world and it is appropriate at this stage to discuss more fully their existence and the use to which they were (or were not) put in terms of identification and age clarification in Roman times. As well as notices of birth, one obvious source of information on the ages of individuals is the census. It was seen in Chapter 5 how essential the census was to the efficient and effective collection of taxes in Roman Egypt; it was also mentioned at that point that concrete evidence for the operation of the census outside Egypt in Roman times is sparse. It will be necessary, therefore, to consider briefly such evidence as there is and to see what use, if any, was made of any census data, as well as of other archival material related to age, collected outside of Roman Egypt. The main point of this chapter is to see how, at a general level and in comparison with Roman Egypt, rules of age could possibly have operated. Two questions need to be considered: *could* archival material such as birth notices and census declarations have been used in order to determine an individual's age, that is, was the employment of such documentation widespread and did it carry the required information; and *was* such material so used?

Registration of Births

Elsewhere, in considering the so-called Ulpianic life table, I discussed whether an empirical basis for such a table could be found to have existed in the Roman world, namely through the registration of deaths,[3] and I concluded that no such statistical source was available. Apart from anything else, the registration of the death of a Roman citizen was not obligatory, nor indeed usual. Registrations of death only survive from Roman Egypt and there only for the native Greco-Egyptians,[4] not for Roman citizens. In the case of the registration of births, however, there is evidence from Roman Egypt of such notifications by both Roman citizens (in Latin) and by Greco-Egyptians (in Greek); the two types of registration must be carefully differentiated, since in legal terms they are quite unrelated, and they will be treated separately here. The most important question with which we must first deal is whether registration of birth in either case was compulsory.

REGISTRATION OF BIRTH BY GRECO-EGYPTIANS

I know of thirty-four notices of the registration of birth by Greco-Egyptians over a span of some 270 years and of varied provenance. The documents follow a fairly standard pattern: addressed to an official, the registration was made on the initiative of the father or another close relative and gave the name and current age of the individual concerned.[5] Such registrations of the birth of Greco-Egyptians supplemented the information gathered by the census, because it allowed officials to calculate in what year an individual would become liable to the poll tax at the age of 14 years. However, the census itself, held every 14 years, also provided this information, and this fact alone tells against the registration of such births being compulsory. On the other hand, a notice of birth could be used by the parents as proof at the *epikrisis* if an individual was eligible for exemption from tax, or was liable for a lower rate of tax, because of his privileged status (such as gymnasiarchal ancestry).

The question of whether the registration of the birth or of the death of a Greco-Egyptian was compulsory is a complex one. For some it was clearly an advantage to have had their birth registered, because, as has already been said, it might provide proof of their status; indeed, it is something of a misnomer to call these papyri notices of birth, because they are more certification of status than of birth. The same motive is true for the registration of death: one would tend to notify the authorities of the death of a (male) member of the family in order to cancel his continued liability to taxes and compulsory duties—hence the fact that extant copies of notices of death were often found among collections of tax documents. But one peculiarity, if registration of death was carried out simply to remove someone from the lists of those liable to such burdens and was not obligatory, is that we have certificates for those who would have gained no benefit by having them, most noticeably men over the age of liability (ὑπερεταί).[6] This need not constitute proof, however, that such registration was compulsory; it merely points to the fact that some people acted without our logic or felt that they *should* make such a declaration. It may also be the case that people of the age-groups who were exempt from the poll tax were liable to the payment of other taxes. One should note, furthermore, that registration of birth was left in some cases until individuals were in their teens,[7] whereas if birth registration was compulsory one would have expected it to have been enforced somewhat earlier. It has been suggested that notices of births and deaths had a more general purpose and were used to update the general lists of population, which included everybody, irrespective of age and sex,[8] but it should be noted that all ninety-four extant notices of death relate to the deaths of males alone.[9]

To us today it might appear logical for birth and death registration to have been compulsory, to facilitate the effective running of the administrative process, but this argument, based on logic and argued from silence, is far from being conclusive or convincing. Taubenschlag made the very relevant point that if birth and death certificates were required by law, one would expect a phrase such as κατὰ τὰ κελευσθέντα to appear, as it routinely does in census declarations but never does in extant birth and death registrations.[10] Browne argued that the phrase ἵν ᾧ ἀναίτιος καθάπερ καί εἰμι, which occurs on one papyrus, proves that the registration of death was compulsory; he translates the word ἀναίτιος as "free from guilt," that is, by registering the son (although even this need not mean that the man had had to declare the death of his son by law, simply that he felt it to be his "moral" duty); the original editor, on the other hand, took the phrase as a whole to mean "so that I may not be responsible, as indeed I am," that is, for payment of the son's tax, which makes better sense of the phrase καθάπερ καί εἰμι, and which does not mean that the declaration had had to be made.[11]

Hopkins states that certificates of birth and death were probably submitted compulsorily, but he admits that the number surviving is very small and he suggests that "perhaps compliance was intermittent."[12] Montevecchi has argued that the registration of birth was obligatory for a certain number of years after a census but not in the years immediately preceding a census,[13] but the evidence for this is slim (the number of declarations surviving making such conclusions unwarranted), and it may simply be that people felt that the need to make a declaration was more pressing when the census was not due for some considerable time. It has already been noted that some individuals were declared when they were already in their teens; so either they had already been declared in a census or they were born immediately after a census but were not declared until just before the next census. Death registration Montevecchi believes was also obligatory, though she notes that no time limit is apparent.

More recently Casarico has argued that death registration was obligatory, but she assumes that birth registration was not. Her comments in the latter regard are worth quoting here:

> Because the poll tax was paid from the 14th year, the census held every fourteen years was sufficient to ensure that no one escaped. Birth notices between one census and the next were not necessary for this purpose (because of the very high infant mortality level many of them would have been shortly followed by death notices). And in fact it does not appear that there was any obligation to declare births. We do have a certain number of declarations of birth but these relate to children of privileged categories. Notices of birth served as supporting evidence for the petition, made when

> boys attained the age of 13–14 years, for them to be granted admission to
> the same privileged status. In such petitions one requested the *epikrisis* . . .
> for the boy, furnishing the documents which proved his right.[14]

I think this is essentially right. That the registration of death in this
context was obligatory, however, is a possibility but impossible to
prove; the evidence we have is simply not sufficient to be certain. The
fact that we have significantly more death than birth notices extant
(94:34) may be due merely to chance, or may reflect the fact that registering a death was more financially beneficial to the family than was
the notification of a birth, and not necessarily that the former was
obligatory while the latter was not.

What seems apparent, however, is that the system of the registration of the births and deaths of Greco-Egyptians operated with less efficiency or thoroughness and was less universal than was the application of the census. Such notices of registration as were made may have
supplemented the operations of the census, but it was on the lists
drawn up from the census that the bureaucratic machine principally
relied. There is no evidence for notices of birth being used in this context to prove one's age; rather they might be used to indicate one's status and ancestry in situations where such a pedigree might be of advantage, in the *epikrisis* in particular.

REGISTRATION OF BIRTH BY ROMAN CITIZENS

In the corpus of Roman law it is of course with the Roman citizen that
the legislator was primarily concerned; this is particularly evident in
the rules of age discussed in Chapter 4. Here the whole procedure,
purpose, and legal significance of registration are quite different from
the situation for the local population in Roman Egypt. With the *lex
Aelia Sentia* of A.D. 4 and the *lex Papia Poppaea* of A.D. 9 Augustus introduced a system of birth registration for Roman citizens. The reasons
behind the introduction of such a system we shall consider shortly.
First we must look briefly at the evidence that exists for the system itself.[15]

We have, mainly from Roman Egypt, twenty-one documents in
Latin, both on papyri and on *tabulae ceratae,* recording individual notifications of birth by Roman citizens, where the date of birth of the
individual is recorded. Ranging in date from A.D. 60 to 242, fourteen

of these documents appear to be the *professiones* of the birth of legitimate children, either as originally recorded or as copied from the public register, and seven the *testationes* of the birth of illegitimate (or, in one case, legitimate) children.[16]

It needs to be stressed that in the case of the fourteen *professiones,* ten are copies from the public *album* (i.e., "descriptum et recognitum ex tabula professionum"). So the majority of our examples are cases where individuals have paid a fee to have a copy of the registration made, presumably for their own purposes. The use made of such "certificates" will be considered shortly. First, however, we must consider the question of whether Roman citizens were legally bound to register a birth. As with the registration of birth by Greco-Egyptians, the question of obligation is important to our discussion, because an efficient system of proof of age through the use of such documents must depend primarily on whether every individual was able and was expected to have such proof available.

Augustus's social legislation introduced various rules of age, such as the minimum age at which a person could generally manumit or be manumitted, the age by which he or she was expected to have married and produced legitimate offspring, or the age after which such "requirements" no longer applied. Along with and to accommodate such measures, Augustus introduced a system for the registration of births by Roman citizens. According to one late and generally historically untrustworthy source, the *Historia Augusta,* this innovation is to be attributed to Marcus Aurelius, but it is almost universally recognized today that the system of Roman birth registration dates to the time of Augustus; it is more likely that Marcus Aurelius made it permissible for *illegitimate* free children to be registered.[17] It is also usually assumed that the registration of births by Roman citizens was obligatory, but this is less certain, as Gardner for one has pointed out.[18] The modern assumption that it was compulsory for Roman citizens to register births from the time of Augustus probably relies on the passage from the *Historia Augusta* just mentioned; yet other statements in that passage relating to the registration of birth, such as the idea that it was introduced by Aurelius or that it had to be done within thirty days of birth, have been shown to be false.[19]

There is ample evidence for penalties being laid down for failure to register in the census, yet no such penalties are known to have existed in regard to the failure to register a birth. On the other hand, we do hear of cases where individuals have not had their births registered, or of people who do not have notices of their births available to them, and yet in terms of the law they are not at a disadvantage. An imperial rescript of A.D. 239, for example, states that failure to register children should not deprive them of their right to legitimacy.[20] Diocletian and Maximian inform an individual that "statum tuum natali professione perdita mutilatum non esse certi iuris est" (It is a well-established rule of law that though a declaration of birth has been lost, your status is not adversely affected).[21] Even when a declaration of birth was available it does not seem to have been regularly regarded as the sole or even as the best form of evidence as to a person's age or inherited status. Part of the reluctance to accept declarations of birth as *probatio,* apart from the fact that they were apparently not obligatory or universally available, may have arisen from the fact that it was recognized that mistakes could appear in such *instrumenta,*[22] and further that such declarations may be fraudulent.[23] A case even arises where a person makes a mistake in computing his own age from documentary evidence: a certain Livius had stated that he was a *maior* but had subsequently discovered that he was still a *minor;* Diocletian and Maximian state that the *praeses* of the province is to reconsider the evidence of the *probationes* furnished.[24] The complications and difficulties in calculating age even when the date of birth is known we have already considered; of course, Livius may have had ulterior motives for misrepresenting his age. But it is worth pointing out also that the legal discussions on the forgery of documents relate almost exclusively to clauses in wills. If declarations of birth were important elements in cases of *probatio,* one might expect more evidence for the falsification of such documents.[25]

Although declarations of birth, when available, could be used as proof of age or status, it is clear enough that such documents were not always regarded as sufficient proof in themselves, nor were they necessary,[26] so long as some proof could be furnished. Hadrian, for example, stated in a rescript that when the age of an individual was at issue, *all* proofs of age should be furnished and a decision reached based on the most credible evidence.[27] Modestinus, in stating that the age of 70 years conferred exemption from *munera personalia,* notes that in making application for such an exemption "age is proved either by notices of birth [ἐκ παιδογραφιῶν] or by other customary [*or* lawful] evidence [ἐξ ἑτέρων ἀποδείξεων νομίμων]."[28] What other types of evidence could be used? It would appear that at most times any *probatio* supporting an individual's claim might be considered. In applying, for example, for *venia aetatis,* that is, assumption of the age of "majority" before completion of the 25th year, persons must, according to Constantine, provide witnesses to their good morals, and witnesses or *instrumenta* to their age.[29] This use of different types of evidence, oral and written, may be seen more clearly in cases where status must be proved, because it is with this factor, rather than with age, that the legal texts are principally concerned. Under the early principate oral evidence might still be preferred to written documentation,[30] whereas in classical law it appears that written and oral testimony were held to be of equal value.[31] But as the law evolved greater credence was in time given to written evidence.[32] By the third century it would appear that written evidence was regarded as preferable to oral testimony, although both types of evidence remained admissible.[33]

At any rate, the use of notices of birth as proof of age or of status never became obligatory, and any appropriate *probatio* might be employed. In the case of the age of legal independence, even physical appearance might constitute proof, albeit an imprecise one.[34] In short, documents such as birth notices were a useful tool when factors such as age or status needed to be proved,[35] but they were not seen as essential or necessarily conclusive. This fact distinguishes them from the use made of certificates of birth today.[36] One cannot assume that every Roman citizen carried around with him or her or even had at home a copy of the registration of his or her birth to be produced whenever the need arose. In most cases, when age was in question, a Roman might state his or her age, and this statement would be accepted without further investigation, *citra causarum cognitionem.*[37] When necessary, further proof might be sought, whether from oral testimony or from the archives, although there would be no guarantee that such evidence would be available. Potential sources for such information, apart from notices of birth, need now to be considered. With Roman Egypt it has been seen that such information came primarily from the census. What, then, of the census elsewhere in the empire?

The Census

This is not the place for a detailed analysis of the operation and function of the census in the Roman world, though such a study is needed.[38] My primary purpose here is to consider the importance of statements of age in this context and to determine whether the census, whether of citizens or of local inhabitants of the provinces, provided accessible information for the calculation and verification of statements of age.

A very basic, but too easily overlooked, distinction must first be drawn. It was seen in regard to the registration of birth that two very separate categories are evident: the registration of births to Roman citizens, and those to *peregrini*. In the case of the census a similar distinction must be noted. From republican times we have quite substantial evidence for the census of Roman citizens, that is, the counting of citizens, for political, military, and financial reasons. From the time of Augustus, provincial censuses were carried out by the Romans, primarily to facilitate the collection of taxes; the census of Roman Egypt falls into this second category, although it is a special case in many ways, because aspects of its mode of operation were inherited from the Ptolemaic period.[39] Provincial censuses, however, seem to have been universal, and possibly regular even outside of Egypt, in the imperial period. Each census was based in the province and was not, *pace* Luke's gospel (2.1), empire- (or world-)wide, nor indeed necessarily held at the same time in each province.[40] The Roman census, on the other hand, became increasingly irregular in the late republic, and seems last to have been held in the first century A.D. It is with the Roman census that we shall be principally interested here, though not with every aspect. Our primary interest is in the census as a means of enumerating the citizens of the Roman world, not as a means of regulating morals (*regimen morum*) or of classifying the citizen body into classes or ranks according to property ratings.[41] Nor are we concerned here with the reliability of the census totals, a question that has occupied scholars greatly over the past century.[42]

What does concern us here is age. It is evident that in the Roman census a citizen's age was recorded,[43] just as age was also recorded in the provincial census.[44] In the latter case the reason for recording a person's age is clear enough: for calculation of an individual's liability to tax, as Ulpian states and has been seen in the case of Roman Egypt. For Roman citizens, age needed to be known, at least originally, in order to classify persons according to their military and political class, as *seniores* or *iuniores,* for example.[45] In time, however, such categories became less important as Italians became generally exempt from direct taxation and as the army became increasingly a professional force voluntarily recruited rather than conscripted. Originally the Roman census had been designed to be held on a regular basis, "quinto quoque anno," but from the first century B.C. no such regularity is apparent.[46] The Roman census was revived by Augustus, presumably as part of a general move to restore Roman traditions and apparently for purely demographic reasons, if there was any functional purpose behind it at all. Three censuses were carried out under his reign.[47] Claudius also carried out the census, in A.D. 47/8, and the last instance occurred in Italy in A.D. 73/4 under the censorship of Vespasian and Titus.

It is commonly stated[48] that until Augustus introduced a system for the registration of births by Roman citizens, the census "was the only regular means by which a Roman citizen could establish his identity and be recognized as a citizen," or indeed prove his age by the use of documentary evidence. This all presupposes, of course, that such evidence was needed. It is noteworthy, for example, that in Acts 22, Paul has only to state that he is a Roman citizen for the required action to be taken; at no stage is it recorded that he needed to prove that he was what he said he was.[49] It needs also to be stressed that enrollment on the census list was not in itself proof of Roman citizenship; it showed only that the person registering himself considered himself to be a citizen, or even just wanted to be considered as one.[50] Again, it is the case of a drafted document being accepted *citra causarum cognitionem.* We have already seen that declarations of birth were not regarded as definitive or essential proofs of age, status, or identity, but was registration in the census? First it is necessary to consider again the question of obligation.

It seems certain enough that, in theory at least, all Roman citizens had to be registered in the census: "censa sunt capita civium tot."[51] It is probable that this means only adult *male* citizens, though this remains unclear, as we have already noted, and the situation may have varied over time. Those under *patria potestas* had no property of their own, and therefore would not have featured separately in the census lists; young men under *patria potestas*, however, still needed to be listed, at least in theory, for military service. *Orbi orbaeque,* widows and orphans, on the other hand, appeared on a separate list, since they might own property in their own right and thus be liable for tax.[52] What is clear is that very strict penalties originally existed for those who failed to register, as Dionysius of Halicarnassus makes plain when discussing the legendary institution of the census by Servius Tullius: τῷ δὲ μὴ τιμησαμένῳ τιμωρίαν ὥρισε τῆς τ' οὐσίας στέρεσθαι καὶ αὐτὸν μαστιγωθέντα πραθῆναι· καὶ μέχρι πολλοῦ διέμεινε παρὰ Ῥωμαίοις οὗτος ὁ νόμος (If any failed to give in their valuation, the penalty Servius established was that their property be forfeited and they themselves whipped and sold for slaves. This law continued in force among the Romans for a long time).[53] Yet it needs to be noted that we know of no cases where such penalties were inflicted, whether because the laws were not enforced, or because everybody registered, or merely because our sources are incomplete.[54] It is clear from the testimony, however, that it was generally expected that everyone would be enrolled in the census, whereas the same expectation is absent in the case of the registration of births. It must be the case, just as we know it was in the provincial census, that registration in the Roman census was obligatory, and that it was assumed that everybody would register.[55]

But it has already been seen that the census was held only on isolated occasions in the late republic and under the empire, so this potential source of information on the age of Roman citizens, while in theory it appears useful in this context, in practice cannot have been so relevant, at least in the period of the principate. Certainly the extensive use made by the bureaucratic machine of Roman Egypt of data on age and status derived from the census there has no parallel in the workings of the census of Roman citizens in the late republic or early empire. With this qualification in mind, it is worth looking at the evidence that does exist for the limited use made of census data in establishing or checking statements of age.

Census records, where available, might be used as a source of information on the alleged wealth of individuals within a community; this possibility is dramatically portrayed by Dio in his account of how the emperor Gaius, when losing at dice, made use of the *apographai* of Gaul to select wealthy people from whom he could instantly "inherit" by having them done away with.[56] On a more mundane level, census documents seem to have had some value as evidence in a court of law, as an otherwise unattested *senatus consultum* of unknown date indicates: "census et monumenta publica potiora testibus esse senatus censuit" (The senate resolved that census records and public documents prevail over witnesses).[57] It may be that the reference here is to the use of previous census declarations to substantiate one's claim to a particular status, but age may also have been relevant.

One particular and rather unusual example of the use of census data to furnish information specifically on age does survive, and it is one that is particularly relevant to this book as a whole; indeed we have already met it in a quite different context.[58] The census carried out in A.D. 73/4 by Vespasian and Titus provided both Pliny the Elder, writing only a few years after the census had been taken, and Phlegon, writing in the time of Hadrian, with details of alleged centenarians from the eighth region of Italy, between the Apennines and the Po (Gallia Cispadana, Aemilia).[59] It would appear that Phlegon was not simply following Pliny in this; at the very least he must have had another source as well, because his list is far more detailed than Pliny's. Only one individual is named by both, "L. Terentius M. filius" of Bononia, who in A.D. 74 was, apparently, 135 years old. Is it purely by chance that both Pliny and Phlegon use census material from the same region? That is unlikely: it may be that Phlegon was influenced by Pliny and followed his lead, or that the centenarians of this region were renowned.[60] It can hardly be coincidental that Pliny's only other use of census data also derives from the eighth *regio* of Italy: T. Fullonius of Bononia, recorded in Claudius's census of A.D. 47 as being 150 years of age—and therefore born around 104 B.C.[61]

Pliny's and Phlegon's use of the census data is extremely interesting but rather mysterious. Both authors claim to have consulted the relevant census records. Pliny says, in introducing his figures, that it was not necessary to ransack all the records ("nec sunt omnia vasaria excutienda"),[62] meaning to imply, I imagine, that he could have scrutinized them all if he had so chosen. Instead he looked only at the figures from the eighth *regio*. Pliny does not burden us with a list of the over ninety individuals he reports as being at least 100 years of age from this area at the time of the census. Instead he summarizes the total figures, picking out the names of only a few noteworthy cases; these statements of age he regards as certain ("in re confessa," *NH* 7.49.164). Phlegon, on the other hand, insists on listing many of them, together with examples of aged individuals from Macedonia, Pontus and Bithynia, and Lusitania. It is noticeable that women also appear in his list; this does not necessarily mean, however, that women were routinely registered in the census: women of extreme old age may well have been *orbae* and therefore would have been recorded anyway. His source of information for the Italian names, Phlegon states, is the census lists (ἐξ αὐτῶν τῶν ἀποτιμήσεων), which he studied with some care (οὐ παρέργως). He arranges his list first in order of decades, that is, those who were recorded as being 100 years old, from 101 to 110 years, and so on. This may be Phlegon's reworking of the figures as given in the census data, or—perhaps more likely, in view of the fact that Pliny also summarizes the data by age-groups—Phlegon's source grouped the figures thus. What is more mysterious is the order of the first forty-two names in the group of those who are recorded by Phlegon as being 100 years old. All eight Lucii are grouped together, then eight Gaii, six Marci, nine Titi, and so forth; they are ordered by *praenomina*. I can see no logic behind such a system of ordering and I find it difficult to imagine that they were ordered thus in the original census lists.[63] One would expect names to be arranged (if any sort of alphabetical arrangement is used at all) by *nomina*; in the *Tabula Heracleensis* of late republican date, it is stated, in the context of the local Italian census, that people are to declare first their *nomen,* then their *praenomen,* and subsequently their *cognomen.* Presumably this reflects the order in which the names were recorded and archived. From Flavian times comes a striking example of such ordering by *nomina:* the lists of *iuniores* of the Succusanan tribe at Rome preserve hundreds of names, arranged in alphabetical order by *nomina.*[64] It must be the case that Phlegon has rearranged the data available to him, but exactly why he does it as he has is unclear. Perhaps because of his Hellenic background? Intriguing as the point is, however, what is more important in this context is the very fact that Pliny and Phlegon could have had access to the information in the first place. I am reluctant to disbelieve both authors and to assume that both copied from another literary source. But even if that were true, there is still the fact that *someone,* contemporaneous with Pliny, drew on the census records. The information that could be derived from these data was both an individual's name, and his or her age.

This fact is important, but before we can assume from this that in ordinary circumstances people could consult the archives for such details, some qualifications must be made. It is one thing for an author to use census data as a source of information for a list of centenarians (or for an emperor to consult the lists, as Gaius did), quite another for an individual to obtain information on his or her own age in an isolated instance. It may be that, as was seen to be the case in Roman Egypt, a certified copy of a declaration could be obtained from the archive office for a fee, but we have no evidence for such a thing having occurred routinely outside of Egypt.[65] Second, as has already been stressed, the Roman census operated only irregularly in this period— indeed Phlegon only had the census of A.D. 74 to draw upon, because no other census of citizens had occurred since. So it was only in Pliny's time that such records were up-to-date, and this fact alone undermines the value of the census as a source of information for the administrative machine. In the second or third centuries A.D., no such source was available. It should also be noted that, quite apart from the fact that it is unlikely that so many people lived to such an extreme old age, these (alleged) centenarians of A.D. 74 were born well before Augustus introduced the system of birth registration, so how (if at all) could they have proved their age at the time of the census? Presumably *citra causarum cognitionem* again.

The use made by Pliny and Phlegon of the census data remains fascinating but puzzling, and of limited value in our search for an accurate means of checking and corroborating ages where rules of age were concerned. One further source of information remains to be considered, that relating directly to citizens. Did there exist a register of Ro-

man citizens which, though from what we have said here it clearly
could not have been updated regularly by census declarations, at least
contained sufficient information to establish the age of a Roman citizen?

A Register of Roman Citizens?

From letters written between Pliny and Trajan it is evident that *commentarii* existed in the principate recording certain grants (*beneficia*)
by the emperors to individuals.[66] Trajan states that a grant of the *ius
trium liberorum* to Suetonius is to be recorded "in commentarios
meos," and likewise that grants of the *ius Quiritium* to Latin freedmen
who had been entrusted in a will to Pliny as patron were to be similarly recorded.[67] When Pliny asks Trajan about the status of freeborn
persons who had been exposed after birth and who had subsequently
been raised as slaves, the emperor states (*Ep.* 10.66) that no decision
can be found on the matter in "the *commentarii* of my predecessors"
(commentarii eorum principum qui ante me fuerunt). And when
Pliny requests from Trajan (*Ep.* 10.6) the granting of Roman citizenship to that individual, part of the process involves giving details of
the person's "age and property holdings" (annos eius et censum). Until
recent decades no further details were available to us regarding such
archives.

The *Tabula Banasitana,* discovered in 1957 and first fully published
in 1972, has provided us with documentary evidence of just such detail. A public record or memorial rather than a personal certificate,[68]
it includes an authenticated extract from the register of persons
granted Roman citizenship by the emperors, "commentarius civitate
Romana donatorum" (from Augustus to M. Aurelius and Commodus,
excluding Otho and Vitellius). In this extract, dated to A.D. 177, are
given the names and ages of the family of Julianus, chief of the Zegrensians, dwelling on the border with the Roman province of Mauretania Tingitana (present-day northern Morocco): "Faggura uxor Iuliani principis gentis Zegrensium ann<o>s XXII, Iuliana ann<o>s VIII,
Maxima ann<o>s IIII, Iulianus ann<o>s III, Diogenianus ann<o>s II,
liberi Iuliani s<upra> s<cripti>" (Faggura, wife of Julianus, chief of the
Zegrensian tribe, 22 years old; Juliana, 8; Maxima, 4; Julianus 3; Dio-

genianus 2—the children of the aforementioned Julianus). This is the only extant example of such an extract. Apart from anything else, it provides conclusive evidence for the existence of a *commentarius civitate Romana donatorum* in the first two centuries A.D.,[69] a register of all new citizens by individual grants from which certified copies of the entries could be obtained.[70] It thus appears that included in each entry was the individual's age—one assumes primarily as a means of identification.[71] Potentially, therefore, this archive could provide details of an individual's age for use as a *probatio.*

But, quite apart from the fact that there would be no obvious and accurate means to verify the ages as given, it is clear that only special, individual grants were so recorded, in chronological order. Those who were Roman citizens by birth would not have been thus listed, and those who received citizenship as part of a general grant to an entire community would similarly not have been individually enumerated. These *commentarii*, therefore, were *not* registers of all Roman citizens, such as a regular program of censuses would have provided. While the remote possibility remains that a *commentarius* of *born* citizens did exist, there is absolutely no evidence to support such an assertion.

One must conclude, therefore, that no reliable or universal means were available for the calculation or substantiation of statements of age, such as have been seen to have existed in Roman Egypt in the first three centuries A.D. This conclusion is in line with what has already been said in earlier chapters regarding the relative importance of statements of age in Roman life and law. Basically, the system of rules of age in the Roman world relied on an individual's own statement of his or her age. That such a mechanism might be regarded as insufficient today is largely irrelevant. The system that operated outside of Roman Egypt may not have been as exact or as precise as we would expect it to have been in order to be administratively efficient, but nevertheless rules of age did exist and operate over a wide sphere of activities. A person's age was accepted as stated, *citra causarum cognitionem.* A person was as old as he or she acted.

PART III

OLD AGE IN PRIVATE LIFE

Seven

Old Age, Marriage, and Sexuality

> Shall I never see a bachelor of three-score again?
> Benedick, in Shakespeare's
> *Much Ado about Nothing* 1.1.209

The social legislation enacted by Augustus over the course of his long reign has been the focus of considerable scholarly attention in recent decades. In regard to his legislation concerning marriage and the bearing of legitimate children, our direct sources of information are somewhat fragmentary and even the purpose underlying the legislation has been much debated.[1] This is not the place for a general survey of the legislation's content and aims; it is enough to say that broadly speaking the ostensible aim of the legislation was to encourage both legitimate, lasting marriage and large families, in particular among the upper classes, through a system of penalties for the unmarried and/or childless, and privileges for those married *secundum legem Iuliam et Papiam Poppaeam,* with extra privileges for those married with children; the greater the number of legitimate offspring, the greater the benefits for the parents.

Here we shall consider only one aspect of the legislation, an aspect that has particular relevance to other social questions regarding age at marriage and of fertility. The evidence for rules of age in Augustus's marriage legislation will be applied to the information we have in regard to the age of menopause in women in classical times, and similarly the age up to which males were considered capable of fathering children. While it is not possible to ascertain with total precision or accuracy the age at which such conditions generally occurred in antiquity (and of course to some degree the age would have varied from individual to individual), nevertheless we may deduce the ages at which the Romans themselves, or at least some of them, believed that these medical phenomena occurred. The ages at which men and women were held to be no longer capable of reproduction are of particular interest here, for such information may help to broaden the picture of attitudes toward old age described in previous chapters. If the aged man or woman was unable to fulfill the function of begetting or bearing children, in what light were elderly married couples seen? What was the place of such elderly people in society? These are broad questions for which the laws discussed here cannot be expected to provide anything like full answers. Yet the marriage legislation does give us an insight into certain legal and social concepts of age.

Under the terms of the *lex Iulia,* unmarried persons, *caelibes* (i.e., unmarried as defined by the laws), were incapable of taking either inheritances or legacies. Married persons who had no children, *orbi,* could take no more than one-half of either inheritances or legacies.[2] Originally this basic principle seems to have applied only to those of a certain age, namely to men between the ages of 25 and 59 years, and to women of 20 to 49 years of age. Apart from questions of age, others were also exempted from the limitations imposed on the capacity to inherit, namely relatives, *cognati,* to the sixth (and in a certain case to the seventh) degree, as well as those in the *manus* or *potestas* of such relatives.[3] As well as the barriers enforced on the right of unmarried and/or childless individuals to receive in wills, restrictions were placed specifically on the capacity of inheritance between husband and wife. Previously, by the *lex Voconia* of 169 B.C., a woman had in effect been unable to receive more than half of her husband's estate. Under the Augustan legislation a husband and wife could enjoy complete capacity to inherit if, apart from rules of age, they were otherwise related to within the sixth degree, or the husband was absent for a certain period of time (a temporary privilege), or the couple had a living *communis* child or a certain number of children who had survived to certain ages,[4] or they had otherwise been granted the *ius liberorum*. If the married couple could not claim under any of these conditions, then they were normally capable of taking only one-tenth of the estate of the other.

The Augustan marriage laws laid down strict definitions of *matrimonium iustum*. Apart from questions of relative status, the crucial concept was that marriage *secundum legem Iuliam et Papiam Poppaeam* was undertaken in order to produce legitimate children (*liberorum procreandorum causa*). By the original terms of Augustus's laws, as has been said, such marriage was defined within certain age limits. That is to say, below the lower or above the upper ages (25 and 59 years for men, 20 and 49 years for women) individuals were not legally required to be married or to have children in order to enjoy the benefits associated with such states, nor were they liable to the penalties associated with *caelibatus* and *orbitas*.

This dispensation for old age, however, subsequently disappeared, though later it was partly restored. The history of this particular measure I have discussed elsewhere; our evidence for it comes largely from the *Epitome* of pseudo-Ulpian:

> aliquando vir et uxor inter se solidum capere possunt, velut si uterque vel alteruter eorum nondum eius aetatis sint, a qua lex liberos exigit, id est si vir minor annorum XXV sit, aut uxor annorum XX minor; item si utrique lege Papia finitos annos in matrimonio excesserint, id est vir LX annos, uxor L . . . . qui intra sexagesimum vel quae intra quinquagesimum annum neutri legi paruerit, licet ipsis legibus post hanc aetatem liberatus esset, perpetuis tamen poenis tenebitur ex senatus consulto Persiciano. sed Claudiano senatus consulto maior sexagenario si minorem quinquagenaria duxerit, perinde habebitur, ac si minor sexaginta annorum duxisset uxorem. quod si maior quinquagenaria minori sexagenario nupserit, "inpar matrimonium" appellatur et senatus consulto Calvisiano iubetur non proficere ad capiendas hereditates et legata [dotes], itaque mortua muliere dos caduca erit.

> Sometimes husband and wife can receive from each other the entire inheritance, for example, if both or either of them are not yet of the age by which the law requires children, that is, if the husband is less than 25 years

or the wife is less than 20 years of age; also if both have in the course of their marriage exceeded the ages set as limits by the *lex Papia,* that is, the husband 60 years, the wife 50. . . . A man who has conformed to neither law within his 60th year, or a woman who has not done so within her 50th, although after this age exempt according to the laws themselves, will still be liable to the standing penalties by reason of the *senatus consultum Persicianum.* But by the *s.c. Claudianum* a man over 60 who marries a woman under 50 will be treated just as if he had married while under 60 years of age. But if a woman over 50 is married to a man under 60, the marriage is styled "unequal," and by the *s.c. Calvisianum* it is ordered that such a case is of no avail in the taking of inheritances and legacies. Therefore on the woman's death her dowry will lapse [i.e., go to the *fiscus*].[5]

The basic reasoning was that aged couples were incapable of producing children, as "required" by the Augustan legislation, and therefore originally were not penalized for not having children (or, in the case of aged individuals who were single, widowed, or divorced, for not being married) but, within a short time, became liable to the penalties incurred through *orbitas* and *caelibatus.* The laws set the upper age limits at 60 years for males, 50 for females. Why?

We need to turn to the medical evidence, in particular for the age of the onset of the menopause in women.[6] Menopause marks the end of the reproductive years with the permanent cessation of menstruation, though, as with menarche, the process is a gradual one, with "a transition period of several years during which female fecundity gradually approaches zero."[7] In the modern Western world menopause usually occurs in the late 40s, though individual cases can range from below the age of 40 up to almost 60 years. In classical sources the observed age of menopause varies from 35 to 60 years.

While there is evidence to show that the age of menarche has decreased over the course of history, it is uncertain whether the average age of menopause has correspondingly increased. Aristotle, our earliest source on the subject, states that in women menstrual discharge ends usually about their 40th year, "but with some it goes on even to their 50th year, and women of that age have been known to bear children. But beyond that age there is no case on record."[8] An isolated reference in the Hippocratic corpus[9] gives 42 years as the average age of menopause in women, but this figure is undoubtedly influenced by the seven-year cycle of the ages of mankind found so frequently in classical literature, as we have seen.[10] The medical writer Soranus refers to the belief of Diocles (a physician contemporary with Aristotle) that menopause may occur as late as the 60th year; Soranus himself adds that for most women it occurs between the 40th and 50th years.[11] Other medical references, like Soranus, all postdate the Augustan legislation but must nevertheless have been influenced to a certain degree by earlier writers. Pliny the Elder states that "mulier post quinquagensimum annum non gignit, maiorque pars XL profluvium genitale sistit" (a woman does not bear children after the 50th year, and with most women menstruation ceases with the 40th year). In this he is closely followed by the third-century writer Solinus: "post annum quinquagesimum fecunditas omnium [sc. mulierum] conquiescit" (after the 50th year the fertility of all women grows dormant).[12] In later writers—heavily dependent on earlier work—the 40–50/60 year range is extended as low as 35 years in the case of obese women, though whether diet has any significant influence on the age of menopause remains open to debate.[13]

These various references are of interest, to be sure, but they should be treated with caution and not necessarily regarded as definitive; they are too general to enable us to reach a final conclusion about the "exact" age of menopause in classical times and its relation to the age of menopause today. Furthermore, it should be remembered that the information given by these authors may only relate to specific sectors of the population. What can be said is that there appears to have been a real (and unsurprising) awareness of the fact that fertility among women decreased after the age of 40 years, and for most women ended by about the age of 50, the age laid down by the Augustan legislation as the maximum limit after which a woman was not expected to bear children.

The age of 50 years is also borne out by one late legal source. Justinian, in a rescript dating to 532, allows for the unusual possibility of a woman over the age of 50 years bearing a child; that such a possibility was considered exceptional is evident: "We have been asked by the office of the imperial advocate, if a woman over 50 years of age [*maior quinquagenaria*] should have a child, whether it should be recognized as its father's legitimate offspring and should succeed to him.

We decree that, although a birth of this kind is extraordinary [*mirabilis*] and rarely occurs, nevertheless nothing which is known to be plausibly produced by nature should be rejected."[14] Clearly this was written with direct reference to the Augustan legislation and implies that the age of 50 years was instituted for the precise reason that women were not normally expected to bear children from this age. The link between sterility (i.e., when a woman is incapable of producing a live birth) and the age of 50 years and over is explicitly made elsewhere, in the case of a pregnant slave woman whose child is sold in the expectation of its live birth: "If a man sells the offspring of a slave woman who is *sterilis* or over the age of 50 years [*maior annis quinquaginta*], and the buyer does not know this, the seller is liable for the purchase."[15] This evidence, both medical and legal, may not be as extensive as we might wish but it does make it clear that the Augustan legislation in this regard was based on the realistic assumption that women from the age of 50 years were generally incapable of bearing children. The age of 50 appears as a logical round figure at which to set the limit; it also appeared elsewhere in the marriage legislation as the age after which a freedwoman was not compelled to perform *operae* for her patron.[16]

In the case of men an age after which reproduction is biologically impossible is more difficult to set; the same problem must have faced the Augustan legislators. As stereotypical as an impotent old age was, cases were cited in antiquity where elderly men had fathered children; two notable exemplars were King Masinissa of Numidia (ca. 239/8–148 B.C.), who reigned for some sixty years, lived to be at least 90, and had a child at the age of 86 (by some accounts his fifty-fourth son);[17] and Cato the Censor (234–149 B.C.), who died at around the age of 85 after fathering a child at the age of 81 years.[18] A contemporary of the Augustan legislation whom we have already met was L. Volusius Saturninus, who died while holding the office of *praefectus urbi* at the age of 93 and who had a child after the age of 62 years. Aristotle stated that men were usually sexually potent until they were 60, though some continued up to the age of 70 years.[19] Pliny the Elder takes this further, and for once reference is made outside of the upper classes (though with how much real basis it is difficult to be sure); he states that "usque ad LXXV apud ignobiles vulgaris reperitur generatio" (procreation is found among the lower classes right up to the 75th year).[20] Solinus, who relied on both Pomponius Mela and Pliny, notes that "men can father children till their 80th year" (in annum octogesimum viri generant).[21]

The age of 60 years in the case of men, therefore, seems less precise, medically speaking, than the age limit of 50 in the case of women. Legally, however, 60 years may have been regarded as the age up to which a Roman male was expected to fulfill certain responsibilities, among them that of fathering children. Dealing with *adrogatio,* for example, Ulpian states that the adrogator should normally be at least 60 years of age, because before that age "magis liberorum creationi studere debeat" (he should rather be attending to begetting his own children), unless illness prevents this.[22] Whether this statement is itself a reflection of the age limit laid down by the *lex Papia* or is linked to the same reasoning that instituted the age of 60 years in the Augustan legislation in the first place, it is impossible to be certain. But it is of interest that Cornelius Nepos, writing some years before the legislation, mentions that Atticus, when the civil war broke out, made use of the fact that he was about 60 years old and took no part in public life, using the *aetatis vacatio* granted to him. This might imply that from the age of 60 years Roman men were allowed a very far-reaching release from the activities and liabilities of civil life, just as in the early empire 60-year-old senators were excused attendance at the *curia* and 60-year-old males, as early as the republic, were excused from other more specific duties.[23]

It would appear, then, that men, unlike women, were regarded as being capable in some cases of producing children after the age laid down by the Augustan legislation. This in itself helps to explain the change made by Claudius to the original terms of the law, by which a man from the age of 60 could undertake a legitimate marriage *liberorum procreandorum causa* with a woman under the age of 50, whereas the opposite case, a woman of 50 or more years marrying a man under the age of 60, was not regarded as valid. By the terms of the law a man of 60+ years was capable of being a father, but a woman of 50+ could not be a mother. This might not have been true in all cases, but as understood by the legislation it was a set rule of age.

Finally, one further aspect of "late" marriages is worth mentioning, since it may have influenced the view of contemporary Romans on the legal consequences of marriage from the age of 50 or 60 years. This is the picture to be derived from classical literature regarding marriage and sexual intercourse in general among elderly people. The overall feeling throughout the classical period appears to have been that in old age sexual activity is limited and, in some cases, is a fit object for ridicule and disgust as being unnatural. Ovid's famous statement, "turpe senilis amor," sums it up well enough, and a range of literary musings from practically every period of antiquity reflects this long-standing and rather depressing attitude, that older people are fit neither to initiate nor to participate in amorous encounters. Publilius Syrus remarked that "amare iuveni fructus est, crimen seni" (having a love affair is a boon for a young man, a crime for an old man), Menander that γέρων ἐραστὴς ἐσχάτη κακὴ τύχη (an aged lover is the worst form of misfortune). Plautus's young Eutychus would outlaw all old men's love affairs. Much earlier, Mimnermus and Anacreon seem to have felt the drawbacks of old age in this regard quite strongly and personally. Propertius will turn to serious study in his old age (so he says), when old age has put a stop to love affairs—Cicero would approve, but not of the late start. Martial is almost as derisive of old men engaged in sexual activities as he is of elderly women. Sextus Empiricus is very blunt: οὐθεὶς γὰρ γερόντων . . . ἐρᾷ (old men don't fall in love), and according to the third-century B.C. lampoonist Timon of Phlius, ὥρη ἐρᾶν, ὥρη δὲ γαμεῖν, ὥρη δὲ πεπαῦσθαι (there is a time to love, a time to marry, and a time to rest). The point is well made by pseudo-Lucian: the highly heterosexual Charicles has no adult males in his house; the only males are an infant boy and an aged cook, of such an age as to invoke no sexual jealousy.[24]

Cicero expresses the philosophical view that the loss of physical urges should be regarded as a blessing, freeing one as it does from the vices of youth and allowing one to concentrate on allegedly higher, more worthwhile practices such as philosophy and farming.[25] This line of argument, which is by no means original and which continues to be voiced by later writers,[26] may or may not have been convincing to an elderly Roman at the time. Certainly some appear not to have followed this advice (did Cicero himself, for that matter?), judging by the widespread appearance in Latin literature of the *senex amator* (and not only of the male gender), who is a constant source of amusement and a perennial target of abuse. On the Roman stage, especially in the comedies of Plautus, in the Latin love elegy, in the merciless satire of writers such as Juvenal and Martial, and in the coldly analytical judgments of, for example, Pliny the Elder and Seneca the Younger, the overall impression is that sexual excess in old age is inappropriate, if not repulsive. Medical opinion of the period seems to have promoted little dissent from such a view.[27] And it has taken a very long time for attitudes to change significantly, if indeed they have: in the twelfth century Andreas Capellanus maintained on medical grounds (the loss of heat and the increase [sic] of *humiditas*), and in line with concepts of courtly love, that, although sexual intercourse is still possible, men from the age of 60 and women from the age of 50 years are incapable of love.[28]

If the image of an active sexuality in old age was viewed with some disdain and scorn in ancient times, the ideal of an aged married couple was not, at least not before late antiquity.[29] The image of the husband and wife together in old age, spending their last years united in tranquil "retirement," is not frequently encountered but when it is— almost invariably among the upper classes—it tends to warrant a positive depiction. Such was the hope expressed for himself by Pliny the Younger, and by Martial—not usually so optimistic regarding old age—for two of his friends.[30] This ideal, realistic perhaps for some, was originally fostered by the *lex Iulia et Papia Poppaea:* a wedded couple of or over the age of 50/60 years was freed from liability to the penalties involved if it was childless, and instead could enjoy complete capacity to inherit from each other. But the subsequent *senatus consultum* under Tiberius in effect penalized elderly married couples who were still childless, with the only hope of relief coming from the remarriage of the husband to a younger wife, as allowed under the *s.c. Calvisianum.*

Overall, however, the rules of age laid down by the Augustan legislation allowed a fairly considerable length of time, in relative terms, before a man or woman was required to marry and have children: 25 and 20 years respectively. Whether they did so or not was entirely up to them. At the other end of the age-scale, the 50/60-year age rules throw interesting light on Roman notions of the age of fertility and of "retirement," if one can call it that in this context. It was the rules of inheritance encompassed in the *lex Iulia et Papia Poppaea* that became the focus of attention in subsequent years. The laws remained in force throughout the period of the high empire, and, despite their apparent failure to achieve their ostensible and ultimate aims, they do serve to highlight the concerns and attitudes of the early empire, both toward marriage and morals and, in the aspect discussed here, toward age.

Eight

Aging and the Roman Family

ἐκεῖνος [sc. ὁ γέρων] . . . πολλῆς
δεῖται θεραπείας, τοῦ γήρως
ἐξασθενοῦντος αὐτόν.
The old man needs a great deal of care
when old age exhausts him.
John Chrysostom *in Epist. ad Hebraeos* 4.7.4,
PG 63.66

ὁ υἱὸς, ἂν ἐπιπολὺ ζῶντα τὸν
πατέρα ἴδοι, βαρύνεται.
The son, if he sees his father living
to a ripe old age, gets annoyed.
John Chrysostom *in Epist. ad Coloss.* 1.1.3,
PG 62.303

How sharper than a serpent's tooth it is
To have a thankless child.
Shakespeare *King Lear* 1.4.312–13

In Chapters 4 and 5 we focused on the ways that a person's age played a part in his (and, to a lesser extent, her) life as determined by rules of age. These rules were of a public nature, by which it is meant that specific age limits were imposed by the state on certain public functions, duties, or liabilities. We have also seen in those chapters isolated examples of more public forms of aid to older people, both direct, such as membership in the *gerousia* in Egypt for a select few, and indirect, such as freedom from liability to the payment of some taxes or to the performance of certain *munera*. In this chapter, as in the preceding one, however, we need to consider more private aspects of the ancient world, aspects in which the state did not necessarily play such an active role. Our primary concern here will be with older people in the family and with their means of livelihood, and their degree of dependence in differing circumstances.[1] What ties of affection and duty existed between adult offspring and their aged parents? How different was the life of the aged male head of a wealthy family, for example, from that of an impoverished, elderly widow with no surviving descendants? I shall first consider the expectations and rights people had with regard to forms of support or welfare in their old age, and then the effect old age itself might have had on such rights.

Welfare for Older People—Ideals and Realities

In any society welfare aid toward older people, as toward other sectors in society, may be of various types, depending in part on the kinship system operative in that society, and may be given on a formal, institutionalized, and regular basis, or at an informal, individual level, as a single act. Again, it may take different forms, through the provision of food and goods, of money or housing, of medicine and nursing, or less directly as exemption from certain financial burdens or the granting of certain privileges. It may even take the form of "moral support" or the enhancement of status. In the modern Western world, there are institutionalized pension schemes and the like, and an increased awareness both of the problems faced by older people and of the contributions they can make to society—not to mention their voting power. As a consequence most older people today can expect some form of welfare aid independent of their own or their families' resources, though some may still live within the family group. In the ancient world the situation was very different. Furthermore, the situation in ancient Greece, or, more specifically, in classical Athens, contrasts sharply with that in the Roman world, and it will be useful to consider the differences between the two classical societies.

THE DUTY OF ONE'S CHILDREN

The precept of honoring one's parents is an ancient one, common to most civilizations and to most periods of history.[2] Among the Romans *pietas* expressed this virtue very well. It was epitomized in the character of Aeneas, himself a father, and his "dutifulness" toward his aged father Anchises.[3] Pausanias, in discussing paintings by Polygnotus in a temple at Delphi, describes a scene on the banks of the Acheron where there is depicted the punishment of those undutiful to parents. This leads him to reflect that in the old days parents were treated well, and he mentions the story of the so-called Pious Ones (*Eusebeis*) of Catana in Sicily, who, when Etna erupted, saved not their property but their parents; the lava caught them up but went round them.[4] *Pietas*, it must be remembered, was a reciprocal arrangement: parents had the duty of bringing up their children, and the children in return were expected to repay this "debt," of both life and nurture, by providing support for their parents when they in their turn were in need—in their old age. This expectation, frequently expressed in Greek literature also and reinforced throughout the education of the young Greek or Roman, may sound coldly calculating, bereft as it is of any notion of familial love.[5] But in reality this expected reciprocity may be seen as a form of old-age security, operated privately but promoted at a public level, sometimes by legislation. In view of recent new trends in expectations regarding the welfare state in the modern Western world, the phenomenon of childbearing as a form of old-age security in various modern societies has increasingly become a renewed object of investigation. It has been discovered, indeed, that over time fertility levels often increase in such societies, apparently in order to ensure security in later life.[6] It is of considerable interest to investigate whether such a system of welfare for older people operated effectively in the ancient world.

In ancient Greece the notion of a debt owed to one's parents for having been reared that must be repaid in their old age (by providing food and shelter, and burial when they died) is at least as old as Homer and continues throughout the classical period and beyond.[7] To take a trivial example: Pollux, as synonyms for παῖδες (children), includes νοσοκόμοι, γηροτρόφοι, τροφεῖς, and ταφεῖς—children care for the sick and elderly, and bury the dead.[8] The same notion of the debt owed by children to parents may be found among the Romans too, particularly under the influence of the Stoic creed.[9] The idea was commonly expressed, indeed, that one motivation for a couple to have children was just so that they might have someone to tend them in their old age. Lucretius stated that a couple had children "so that they could fortify their old age with offspring" (*ut possent gnatis munire senectam*); Cornelius Nepos preserves a letter allegedly written by Cornelia to her sole surviving son, Gaius Gracchus, upbraiding him for causing trouble when it should have been his duty to see to it "that I had the least possible anxiety in my old age" (*ut quam minimum sollicitudinis in senecta haberem*).[10] Certainly a common lament at the death of one's offspring was for the loss of support in one's old age, and the prospect of being childless was regarded as most unfortunate, especially because a potential source of solace and welfare in one's old age had been lost.[11] This could be criticized in antiquity as a rather selfish sentiment on the part of parents: pseudo-Plutarch asserts that parents who mourn for those who die young mourn selfishly if their grief is because of the fact that "they have been cut off from some gratification or profit or comfort in old age" (ὅτι τῆς ἀπὸ τῶν τεθνεώτων ἡδονῆς ἢ χρείας ἢ γηροβοσκίας ἐστερήθησαν), while Seneca the Younger states that it is sheer stupidity to marry and have children in order to ensure the immortality of one's name, to secure heirs, and to have help in old age: it matters little when you are dead, and in any case a son may die before you or else be unwilling to help.[12]

There was also some philosophical debate as to whether a child's devotion toward his or her parents was a result of natural feelings or of a sense of obligation.[13] At any rate, as we have already seen, individuals who lived to see several generations of descendants born were regarded as particularly fortunate, both because they were sure to have someone to tend their old age and because they could die in the secure knowledge that their name would live on. Such is the fond wish of a father for his daughter: App. Claudius Iulianus (*cos.* II A.D. 224) gives his daughter a house, from the walls of which, he hopes, she as a *pulchra anus* (the only instance of which I am aware of these two words together) will in time look down upon her offspring.[14] Pliny the Elder presents three useful case studies in this context. One of the many exceptional circumstances connected with *divus Augustus* was that he lived to see his granddaughter's grandson (*neptis suae nepotem,* namely M. Iunius Silanus, *cos. ord.* A.D. 46), born in the year of Augustus's death. At a somewhat less elevated but still remarkable level, in 5 B.C. a freeborn plebeian of Fiesole, C. Crispinius Hilarus, had in his procession twenty-seven grandchildren and eighteen great-grandchildren. Also Pliny notes that Q. Caecilius Metellus Macedonicus (*cos.* 143 B.C.) died leaving six children and eleven grandchildren.[15] The examples highlight their very rarity. Other alleged cases may also be noted, for example, in an anonymous poem in the *Anthologia Palatina* that commemorates a woman who lived to 105 years, having borne twenty-nine children, all of whom survived her. Not impossible, but improbable.[16]

What is of particular interest at this stage is to discover whether such a "duty" of care was merely hoped for or expected from one's offspring, or whether it was in fact directly imposed on children by the state. It was commonly regarded as a law of nature and of the gods that children should treat their parents well. Nature, indeed, provided a model for this in the way that some animals were believed to nurse their old parents, in particular the stork (*ciconia,* πελαργός), a bird that came to symbolize filial piety by—so it was believed—voluntarily caring for its elderly parents by providing them with food and shelter.[17] It was felt that humans too often failed to live up to the model that nature provided. For even if one's children lived long enough themselves, there was always the possibility that they would be financially unable or unwilling to support their aged parents. One way round this problem might be to force offspring to see to the welfare of their elderly parents. In classical Athens legislation existed to ensure just that: children had a *legal* as well as a moral obligation to maintain their parents in their old age. Having said that, however, it is important to remember that this need not imply that a legal obligation had more force than a moral one or an unwritten law. The opposite could in fact be true, especially if a law is imposed to mend a breakdown in social sanctions.

The Athenian statute, attributed to Solon, stated that he who did not support (τρέφειν) his parents was to be ἄτιμος, deprived of citizen rights. Children accused of maltreatment of parents were liable under a charge of γονέων κάκωσις, a charge that (uniquely in the case of a *graphe*) any third party could bring without the risk of penalty if it withdrew the case or failed to secure at least one-fifth of the votes. Furthermore, "do you treat your parents well?" was one of the questions asked a candidate for the archonship and for other public offices.[18] Athenians seem to have taken their duty seriously.

Nor was it simply a case of refraining from maltreating one's parents: positive services were also expected, such as the provision of food and shelter, and the observation of due rites after death. Such a duty, we are told, was laid on all offspring, with very few exceptions.[19] Hence, with an eye to the future, there was every motivation to have children or, failing that possibility, to adopt them.[20] Certainly this (moral) duty persisted, as the second-century A.D. Stoic philosopher Hierocles makes clear in his ethical fragments, discussing proper conduct toward parents: "For our parents, therefore, we should provide food freely, and such as is fitting for the weakness of old age [τὴν ἀσθένειαν τοῦ γήρως]; besides this, a bed, sleep, oil, a bath, and clothing—in short, general physical necessities, so that they should never lack any of these things; thus we imitate the care they took in rearing ourselves when we were infants." In another passage, he discusses the benefits of marriage, among which is the fact that it produces children "who help us now while we are strong, and when we are worn out, crushed by old age [κάμνουσιν ὑφ᾽ ἡλικίας καὶ γήρᾳ πιεζομένοις], they will be fine allies."[21]

But there were potentially negative aspects to such a system as well as beneficial ones: older people could be seen to be totally dependent on the younger generation and lose their power when they no longer held the purse strings. Such, for example, is the situation described in Aristophanes' *Wasps,* where the son Bdelycleon is depicted as the master of the house and his aged father Philocleon is reduced to childlike dependency. Bdelycleon promises support for his father, but there is a marked lack of any filial respect here: "I'll support him, providing everything that's suitable for an old man [ὅσα πρεσβύτῃ ξύμφορα], gruel to lick up, a soft thick cloak, a goatskin mantle, a whore to massage his prick and his loins." As Philocleon later complains, he is being treated like a child by his own son—a complete reversal of roles: "At the moment I'm not in control of my own property, because I'm young [νέος γάρ εἰμι]; and I'm closely watched; my little son keeps his eye on me and he's mean-tempered, and a cress-paring-cumin-splitter into the bargain."[22] This is of course a scene from comedy, not a direct depiction of real life, but its "humor" surely lies at least in part in its underlying reality, that an aged father could be treated in this way by his own son. Philocleon's complaint of being treated like a child is reminiscent (as an ancient scholiast to the passage also realized) of a common proverb, to be found not only in Attic comedy but in classical literature in general, that old age is a second childhood (δὶς παῖδες οἱ γέροντες, *bis pueri senes*). The life course, in other words, has come full circle. The logic behind such a metaphor, if indeed any underlying logic is to be expected, may be partly explained by the observation of the physical and mental decline experienced by many elderly individuals and the dependence on others brought about by this; it is, of course, a timeless metaphor, still current today.[23] In Athens, in economic terms at any rate, old people may have been seen as children for the very reason that they had lost their independence and, like Philocleon, felt themselves to be prisoners in their own (or rather their children's) homes.

While actual legislation did exist in Athens of the fourth century and apparently earlier that aimed to enforce the moral precept of treating one's parents well, particularly in their old age, the legislation may not have been conceived of or implemented *purely* in the interests of older people, but also to secure the welfare of the *oikos* as a whole. Athenian legislation in effect made the son (and in some cases, perhaps, the daughter—or rather her husband) the head of the household; at times, no doubt, this happened against the wishes of the father. With the effects of senility in old age, it will be seen that just such a situation as that of which Philocleon complained was a potential legal reality.

According to Vitruvius, the comic poet Alexis stated that the Athenians deserved praise, "because the laws of all the other Greeks compel children to maintain their parents, but those of Athens applied only to parents who had taught their children a trade."[24] If the first part of this statement is true we lack good evidence for it, but perhaps that is not so surprising since our sources are primarily concerned with Athens. There does survive, however, an inscription of the late fourth or early third century B.C. from Delphi that records the law that "if anyone does not support [τρέφειν] his father and mother, this is to be reported to the *boule,* which will bind the 'nonprovider' and send him off to prison."[25]

From an earlier period, Herodotus (2.35) reports that in Egypt "sons need not support their parents unless they choose, but daughters must, whether they choose to or not." The main point here is clearly to contrast the situation with that in Athens, where it would naturally have been conceived of as the son's duty; how true it was in Egypt at the time is impossible to know. From Roman Egypt, however, we have more substantial evidence for the care expected from children by their elderly parents,[26] though no legislation seems to have enforced such welfare. Often it appears to have been the case of parents negotiating with their children. The papyri preserve cases where the elderly father, and sometimes mother, promise to leave their property to their children after their death on the condition that they care for them in their old age and provide proper burial for them when they die.[27] Normally the changeover in legal ownership is explicitly stated to take place only after the death of the donor, but sometimes, in practice if not also in theory, during their own lifetime parents hand over ownership entirely to their children and become dependent on them.

Thus, for example, in A.D. 42 a father in Tebtunis, Orseus by name and "allegedly" (. . . ὡς) 65 years old, divides his property among his four children (three sons and one daughter); it is stated that the division is to take place after Orseus's death, but in effect it takes place immediately. One son (probably the oldest), Nestnephis, is to receive most of the property. In return, for the rest of Orseus's life Nestnephis is to provide his father with twelve artabas of wheat and twelve silver drachmas annually for food, clothes, and other expenses, and is to pay the tax due on the land and Orseus's trade taxes as a flute player. For his part Orseus promises to keep the property intact until his death and not to give it to anyone else. In an example (also from Tebtunis) a few years later, on the other hand, there is no mention of the legal changeover of ownership taking place after the death of the father: here Psuphis, "allegedly" 69 years old, and his wife Tetosiris, "allegedly" 60 years, divide their property (individually) among their sons, daughters, and a grandson (the son of a deceased third son). Possession is immediate, and in return the offspring are to provide food and money, pay any debts, and furnish burial for the elderly parents when they die. And to cite a third, much later case, from Ptolemais Euergetis in A.D. 213, a mother gives almost all her property to her son, to take effect the day *before* her death![28]

This transfer of property to offspring in return for care may be seen to have been a function under Roman law of the *donatio mortis causa,* a gift in contemplation or anticipation of death, and of the *donatio inter vivos,* in this circumstance less common.[29] Strictly speaking, a *donatio mortis causa* was made where the donor felt himself to be in imminent danger of death, including being "worn out by age" (aetate fessus).[30] The *donatio* facilitated the exchange of property without recourse to a *testamentum,*[31] but it could also be used to strike a bargain with the donee. *Donationes* from the *paterfamilias* to those in his *potestas,* as to his wife, were generally forbidden, because those in *potestas* were *alieni iuris* and therefore were incapable of owning property apart from their *peculium* while their *paterfamilias* remained alive.[32] But a *donatio* to a person under the donor's power was valid if confirmed in the will; in the meantime, it would appear, the donor had the right to revoke the gift. Hence perhaps it acted as a guarantee of good and dutiful behavior on the part of the donee.

At any rate, there is no evidence from Egypt, at least in the first centuries of Roman rule, to suggest that the duty of caring for one's aged parents was compulsory. Some elderly fathers saw the need to make an official complaint or take personal revenge when they felt that their children were not performing their (moral) duty; it must be noted, of course, that we most often tend to hear about welfare provision when it fails to work. In one case, in Tebtunis in A.D. 138, a father in his 70s who is in the process of distributing his property all but disinherits his oldest son because of the son's allegedly undutiful behavior; instead he leaves most of his estate to his other two sons and his granddaughter. In another case, a veteran in the third century A.D. complains to the acting prefect of Egypt about his daughter, charging her with ingratitude for not caring for him in his old age (⟨γεγ⟩ηροβοσκηκέναι με). With this case one may also compare a petition to Ptolemy Philopator, almost half a millennium earlier, in which an infirm old man of the Arsinoite nome complains that his daughter provides no support for him, even though she had previously sworn (in writing) to give him twenty drachmas a month and, instead, despises his old age. The complaint is timeless. In a much later case (Antinoopolis, A.D. 567–68), an eldest son defends his right to take most of his deceased father's estate on the grounds that he spent a small fortune on his father's debts and maintenance when he was alive (his father, we are told, had gone blind and needed taking care of), and after his father's death paid for his burial and maintained the rest of the family at his own expense.[33] One first-century papyrus provides a neat example of a father both seeing to his own old age and making sure his son learns a trade (just as the law in Athens would have required): he sends his son off to serve as an apprentice to a weaver for a year and receives in return from the weaver a set amount for food and clothing for himself.[34]

Roman Egypt provides us with one more intriguing piece of information in this context. In a poll tax register dating to the first half of the first century A.D., mention is made of men from the Oxyrhynchite and Cynopolite nomes who, as sons, have been "chosen by their parents to support them in old age [εἰς γηροβοσκίαν]."[35] The implication is that such sons, by performing this service, received partial if not full exemption from the poll tax: if this was the case it is our sole piece of evidence for such compensation, and it may be a legacy of the Ptolemaic period that did not endure under Roman rule.[36] This does not necessarily mean, however, that sons were *compelled* to render such a service to their parents,[37] only that those who did so apparently enjoyed some privilege from the state.

What, then, of classical Roman society? The contrast is striking. To put it quite bluntly, the Roman legislators do not seem to have given much thought as to how parents in their old age might look after themselves or be looked after. The reasoning behind this is probably not too difficult to find. Under Roman law, as opposed to the situation in Athens, the oldest male relative, be he father or grandfather or even great-grandfather, in theory retained power, *patria potestas,* until death, and as such should have retained control over the purse strings.[38] As for the elderly female, her situation must have varied depending upon her status: whether her husband was alive or dead, whether she was married with or without *manus,* whether she had children surviving (and cooperative) or not, and in particular whether she owned property or not. Widowed or divorced women without children, or for that matter never-married women—the latter presumably relatively few in number—must have had the most difficult circumstances if they did not have control over inherited property and their own means of support.[39] In *P.Oxy.* 1794 (late second century A.D.), anonymous hexameter lines in Greek (originally, no doubt, of the third century B.C.), an old woman complains of the mutability of fortune: she had been rich, but is now poor and alone, an uncared-for vagrant in the city. About such individuals in "real life" the literature is virtually silent. There is, however, some testimony from the Roman world for *pietas* toward aged parents working in practice. Indeed, it might be argued that a further motivation for the state to increase the legitimate birthrate would be so that there would thus be more offspring to provide for their parents.

Evidence for the intervention of the state in the treatment of parents by their offspring (short of parricide) is negligible before the second century A.D. Dionysius of Halicarnassus mentions (*AR* 20.13.3) that in the earlier republican period the Roman censors, as one of their invasions into the privacy of citizens, made sure that children were not disobedient to their aged parents. Perhaps such scrutiny did come under the aegis of the *cura morum,* though no concrete evidence for such intervention survives. Extant declamatory speeches, however, show that the maintenance of parents by their children was an issue, in ethical terms at least, of some interest and perhaps debate. The relationship such *declamationes* may have to legal reality, however, is less clear. A "law" requiring that "children maintain their parents or be imprisoned" (liberi parentes alant aut vinciantur) is frequently debated in such exercises.[40] There is even a case where it is recognized that such maintenance for older people brought with its immediate benefits a loss of independence and power for one old man who is made to say to his son: "ad te legem meam transfero: licet alliges, et alas" (I transfer my rights to you; go ahead and bind me, but please feed me too).[41] Were the rhetoricians simply arguing about theoretical niceties, quite divorced from the reality of Roman life but influenced by what was known to have been the case in Athens at any rate, or did such a law actually exist from the time of Seneca the Elder?[42]

Only in the second century A.D. do we begin to find discussion in the legal corpus (itself, it must be remembered, only compiled several centuries later) of the duty of parents toward children and vice versa in terms of maintenance (*alimenta*).[43] An undated rescript of Antoninus Pius states that "parentum necessitatibus liberos succurrere iustum est" (it is right for children to look after the needs of parents); that is, it is just and befits *pietas,* but is not necessarily compulsory. The "moral" obligation is reciprocal.[44] A few years later Marcus Aurelius and Lucius Verus inform a certain Celer that "competens iudex a filio te ali iubebit, si in ea facultate est, ut tibi alimenta praestare possit" (The competent judge will order that you be maintained by your son, if he has the means to be able to provide support for you).[45] In other words, the son is expected to maintain his father if he has the means to do so, but the obligation is not automatic: a judge must order the son to perform this duty if he feels the situation calls for it.[46]

Ulpian in the *Digest* makes the position clearer. In a lengthy extract from his *Libri tres de officio consulis,* a work written in the reign of Caracalla[47] and therefore practically contemporaneous with the passages from the *Codex* just cited, the obligations of parents toward their children and vice versa are discussed. It is first stated that "si quis a liberis ali desideret vel si liberi, ut a parente exhibeantur, iudex de ea re cognoscet" (if anyone wishes to be supported by his children or children ask to be maintained by their parent, a judge will look into the matter);[48] the duty of maintenance, not an automatic one (though some families may have treated it as such), is seen as reciprocal and treated in the same context. Subsequently Ulpian discusses specific circumstances: for example, a son may have a natural obligation toward his *paterfamilias,* but what if the son had been emancipated while still an *impubes?* He is no longer in *potestas* and therefore, technically, under no obligation to his father. Ulpian states that in such a case a son may be compelled (sc. by the *iudex*) to support his father if the former is financially able and the latter is in need ("patrem inopem alere cogetur"). The duty is seen again as a moral or natural one, rather than one strictly required by the letter of the law.[49]

Similarly, a son serving in the army, if he is in funds, Ulpian notes, has a duty of *pietas* to support his parents.[50] Another rescript that Ulpian cites states that, while a son might support his father out of a sense of *pietas,* if the son dies his heirs should not be compelled to provide maintenance for the father if they are unwilling to do so, "unless the father is reduced to extreme poverty [*summa egestas*]"—presumably this son had been emancipated, or perhaps the reference is to the inheritance of his *peculium castrense* (discussed later). Since one was not legally under the *potestas* of one's ascendants on the maternal side (such as the *avus maternus,* but also one's mother), it was asked whether *pietas* should extend to the maintenance of such elderly people; Ulpian states that the *iudex* should give consideration to these relatives' physical and financial position, "cum ex aequitate haec res descendat caritateque sanguinis" (since this obligation is based on justice and affection between blood relations). Similarly the question was raised as to whether ascendants on the female side have a duty to support descendants; Pius replied that an *avus maternus* must support his grandchildren.[51] This ties in with our observations in Chapter 2 regarding grandparents.

The legal duty of a daughter in this regard is more difficult to trace, though it is in line with *pietas* that she should, if circumstances warrant it, care for a parent. Thus Diocletian and Maximian tell a father that his daughter should offer him not only respect but also a livelihood, and that the provincial governor will enforce this if required: "filia tua non solum reverentiam, sed et subsidium vitae ut exhibeat tibi, rectoris provinciae auctoritate compelletur". It was apparently legitimate cause for a wife to have the dowry returned to her if she needed to maintain a needy parent or sibling.[52] It should also be noted that in all this we are of course typically dealing only with *matrimonium iustum,* but Ulpian does state at one point that a mother should support her illegitimate children, and they should support her, on the basis of justice and affection (and on the decision of a *iudex*).[53]

In short, therefore, the care of older people within the Roman family was felt to lie naturally with one's children, but direct legislation to impose this obligation, such as has been seen to have existed in Athens (and as was set down, for example, in the English Poor Law Act of 1601, and in Singapore in 1994), was never introduced at Rome. The institution of *patria potestas* in theory meant that the *paterfamilias* could expect total and immediate support from his dependants for as long as he lived and continued to control the purse strings. The position of elderly relatives, such as the mother and the maternal grandparents, who did not carry such sway in legal terms, is less straightforward, and the expectation that they would receive support seems to have rested on general feelings of *pietas,* at times enforced by the decision of a *iudex.* Exactly what sort of care should be provided was not made explicit, but it seems to have been limited to financial aid, expected if the son was financially capable and the elderly parent was in need.

The Romans, perhaps influenced by Greek ideas and practices, may have debated the duties owed by children to their parents, particularly in the rhetorical schools, but in reality the laws did not secure the welfare of older people. The contrast here with the situation in classical Athens is striking, and one may wonder about the general validity of the well-known passage from Dionysius of Halicarnassus, himself a Greek,[54] where he describes the Roman institution of *patria potestas* as being far superior, in terms of ensuring the obedience and dutifulness of children toward their parents, to that which had obtained among the Greeks. Certainly the *paterfamilias* may have been happy, but what of others? *Patria potestas* revolved around the male head of the family, perhaps to the detriment of other aging members. Whether the *paterfamilias* himself was concerned with the welfare of such other elderly relatives probably depended upon the individual and his circumstances; what is clear is that the Roman legislator, unlike Solon and his successors, saw no need to intervene for their benefit.

OTHER POTENTIAL SOURCES OF WELFARE
FOR OLDER PEOPLE

Thus far we have focused exclusively on the expectation that a father and mother will be supported in their old age by their children. What (if any) other sources of maintenance might have been available to the elderly person? Here it must be admitted from the outset that we are practically clutching at straws, seizing on any reference which might provide us with a clue, but without knowing if such evidence as we might come upon can be held to be of general application. The very paucity of the evidence suggests two possibilities, not exclusive: our sources are not particularly concerned with how older people were cared for (we may presume that many elderly aristocratic Roman male readers felt quite secure in their own means); and there was no widespread availability of any form of care for older people. Both possibilities, I believe, are true for the Roman world. What degree of care elderly individuals did receive, if their children were unable or unwilling to help, or if they had no surviving children in the first place, was dependent primarily on the initiative they themselves showed and the authority they possessed. We need to consider briefly the theoretical opportunities for welfare that presented themselves, and their applicability in reality.

In much of the modern Western world, at least until very recently, it has been the expectation that the welfare state will provide care for older people, particularly for those in need, in the form of pensions and the like. Personal initiative is also expected, and lauded, such as investment in private pension and medical schemes with an eye to the future, and it is usually presumed that society as a whole, not just the immediate family, will provide assistance, through organized charities as well as through general attitudes. In coming to the ancient Roman situation we must put aside all such notions. For a start, a secular, institutionalized system of old-age welfare was unknown at any general level.[55] True, certain privileged citizens might receive benefits from the state, but age per se had nothing to do with it. We hear, for example, of exceptional cases where individuals allegedly received lifetime maintenance at the expense of the classical Athenian *polis;* perhaps the most famous reference to this possibility is when Plato has the 70-year-old Socrates sarcastically declare at his trial that his sentence should be lifelong provision of meals (σίτησις) in the *prytaneion* at public expense. Normally such an honor was reserved for Olympic victors and other celebrities, though apparently also for "an athlete exhausted by old age."[56] Another example of maintenance at state expense, from Rome, is of a *humilis* plebeian woman whose mother was in prison and was forbidden food. The daughter, we are told, fed her with her own milk. On being caught in the act, the mother was freed and both women received *perpetua alimenta* as a reward for this show of *pietas.* The tale, told in the period of the late republic and early empire, belongs, however, to the dim and distant past: the site of the prison was consecrated in 150 B.C.and a temple of Pietas built there, where the theater of Marcellus now stands. Although the story is not historical

(it is actually Greek in origin), it clearly appealed to the Romans—
artistic and literary depictions survive from Pompeii—and that is its
significance for us here.[57]

But as a group the elderly of the ancient world, and in particular
those most in need, the impoverished, were never felt to warrant institutionalized help. In democratic Athens only those who had lost
children in war, as well as those who were regarded as war invalids,
were deemed worthy of state assistance en masse, and this was seen as
a privilege rather than as a basic or necessary form of social welfare.[58]
Legionary veterans at Rome were similarly in a privileged position, at
least to the extent of receiving, in some periods (and never automatically), blocks of land on which to retire or a lump sum of money after
a lifetime of service, as well as exemption from *munera*. Elderly citizens at Rome might expect to receive the privileges granted to all
adults, such as free distributions of corn or other forms of largesse,[59]
and also to be granted exemption from public duties on the grounds
of their age, but as an age-class they were never in receipt of any general state aid. That in a well-ordered, utopian state such social welfare
should be available was at least raised as a possibility: Aelius Aristeides, in his speech to the Rhodians περὶ ὁμονοίας (A.D. 149), asserts
that in an ideal state governed by concord all ideals will be met: one
can marry whom one wants, children are raised and educated well,
women are safe, guests are welcome, the gods are worshiped, state
business is run in an orderly fashion, there are enjoyable events such
as processions and choruses and other pleasures of life, the poor are
supported, the wealthy are allowed to enjoy their possessions, the
young lead an orderly life, senior citizens are maintained in their old
age (πρεσβύταις γηροκομηθῆναι), "and, as they say, all things are held
in common, just like the light of the sun, under whose sway we are
kept safe."[60] An idealistic picture; in reality no such utopia existed outside of the imagination of some rulers and philosophers. The only exception, such as it is, is worthy of mention: Aelian records that on
Chios, the so-called Harbor of Old Men (γερόντων λιμήν) is full of
tame fish, there to feed the oldest (τοῖς πρεσβυτάτοις—perhaps, as
with the function of the *gerousia*, applicable only to the most honored)
citizens.[61] More typically, however, the duty of maintaining older peo-

ple remained one either expected from or imposed on the immediate family.

Nor were there regular public charities to help older people in Roman times. The closest one comes is when some wealthy benefactor, being public-spirited or seeking publicity, saw fit to bestow a gift on his native city that could be used to support those in need: the jurist Paul, in discussing the giving of legacies "conducive to the honor and embellishment of the *civitas*" (quod ad honorem ornatumque civitatis pertinet),[62] such as money for public games and feasts or for erecting buildings, adds the fact that money might be given to be used to provide *alimenta* for those of *infirma aetas,* such as *seniores* or young boys and girls (but not necessarily those in financial need), and that such gifts are also held to be conducive to the honor of the *civitas.* We know of no specific examples, however, of such largesse being directed toward older people; presumably a new building, a sumptuous feast, or extravagant games held more immediate appeal as a means of advertisement and of winning public approval than did help for marginalized groups. Consciously or unconsciously, a public old-age welfare system depends on the assessment by those in power of whether the relative cost of supporting old people is worth the investment in terms of older people's contribution to the society as a whole or to the ruling group itself. It is only later in Christian times that the possibility of any tangible form of social and medical welfare for older people is raised, and even then evidence is limited; Tertullian mentions a Christian fund for *domestici senes,* and from the sixth century A.D. terms such as γηροκομεῖα and γεροντοκομεῖα (old-age homes?) appear in the legal corpus.[63]

So if no welfare on a concerted, public scale was available to older people, to whom else, apart from one's children, could one turn? It might be said that that is what friends and neighbors are for. Certainly a utilitarian motive underlying friendship had long been recognized in antiquity, for older people in particular.[64] One particular friend, if he can be called that, that the wealthy Roman elderly had was the *captator* (inheritance hunter), a favorite target of the satirist. Many literary (but not legal) references to *captatio,* particularly from Martial, Juvenal, and Lucian, may be adduced.[65] It certainly became proverbial that wealthy and childless old men and women could expect a large host of "friends" to surround them, in the expectation that they would look kindly on these flatterers in drawing up a will and would not live too long after performing this duty. For all the odiousness and deceit of such an alleged practice, any reality underlying it would at least mean that such an elderly person had someone to tend to his or her every need and whim. As Seneca the Younger states, with evident disapproval and irony, childlessness now has its advantages, and loneliness is no longer a curse to be endured by older people; in fact, even if they do have children, they tend to ignore them.[66] *Potentia* could indeed be a tempting incentive for an elderly man to enter into such a bargain, if he was faced with the alternative of total dependence on his children, as also for a childless (wealthy) widow with no one else to attend to her.[67] But not all old people may have succumbed to such moral reprehensibility. Cn. Domitius Tullus, an otherwise apparently despicable character whose own old age we have already had cause to mention and who cultivated the flattery of many a *captator*, we are told, disappointed them all in his will and left his wealth to his wife and descendants—a praiseworthy, if somewhat surprising, display of *pietas*, remarks Pliny.[68]

For the wealthy such scavengers may have provided companionship, but the poor had no such alluring bait to proffer. At least membership in a funeral *collegium* secured one's burial after death, but such institutions as the *gerousiae* in the Greek cities typically offered a place only to the upper classes (see Chapter 5). Slaves in their old age might find support from a kind master, and eventual burial; one thinks particularly of Pliny's old—and anonymous—nurse, who was given a farm on which to retire.[69] But in terms of economic reality such generosity may not have been common. Aged slaves, if no longer capable of performing their physical duties—as has been noted, they might still be useful as child minders or *paedagogi*—may have been seen as a liability or a nuisance for their owners.[70] One way around this would have been to sell them, if any buyer could be found; Cicero's exemplar for a fine old age, Cato the Elder, apparently regarded it as sound policy to sell off old, useless slaves, along with anything else surplus to requirements, such as old cattle and farm tools.[71] One wonders who would want to buy them, and why. Cato, of course, should not be re-

garded as typical.[72] Another expedient would have been to manumit
older slaves and let them take care of themselves (or be partially maintained at state expense through the grain distribution).[73] Manumitted
slaves owed their former masters a debt of gratitude in the form of *operae,* services,[74] and masters also retained a right to their property after the freedmen's death; thus for slave owners a double benefit: rid-
ding themselves of the expense of keeping some slaves and possibly
providing themselves with some form of service in their own old age.[75]
On the other hand, patrons may remember their freedmen in their
wills as a reward for services rendered, hence helping them in their old
age. The jurist Scaevola mentions the case of a woman who added a
codicil to her will asking that her "liberti senes et infirmi" should be
allowed to grow old in the places which they then occupied.[76]

But when slaves could offer a living master no hope of any return,
a third option in the treatment of elderly or infirm *servi inutiles* was
open to him: simply to dump them and let fate take its course. Sick
and feeble slaves at Rome were left routinely, it would seem, on the *in-
sula Tiberina,* a practice that Claudius was the first to attempt to counteract in an edict of A.D. 47, perhaps more to control the masters than
to save the slaves.[77] On the other side of the coin, it is worth adding,
an old master might need to be wary of his slaves. The jurist Marcian
discusses the case of slaves using force to compel their owner to manumit them; one wonders what happened when a *dominus* on his own
became too old or feeble to control his own slaves. Columella (in an
agricultural context) notes that a master must always maintain disci-
pline among his slaves, so that when he grows old they will not despise him.[78]

But still we have not properly answered the question of what happened to the poor, freeborn Roman citizen in his or her old age. There
can be no doubt that the care of such individuals as survived into old
age was a matter of private rather than public concern. It has been seen
that the duty of caring for elderly parents lay primarily with the children, whether naturally, morally, or in strict legal terms, and such support must have been particularly needed by the poorer classes. For the
wealthy members of society for whom we have the most evidence the
need would usually have been far less urgent, though not insignificant.
When such a source of welfare failed, whether through never having

had children, having lost children, or having undutiful children, a Roman had only two possible venues to which to turn: a spouse or oneself.

The probable demographic regime of the ancient world meant that a "typical" marriage, if it did not end in divorce,[79] was terminated after less than twenty years by the death of one of the couple. Remarriage was permissible, however, and was deliberately encouraged under the terms of Augustus's marriage legislation.[80] It would therefore have been perfectly feasible still to have a husband or wife in one's old age, even if one's children were no longer living. The idea that a spouse could provide comfort, if not also material support, in one's old age is regularly raised. Indeed, one of the encouragements to marriage that Dio (56.3.3) has Augustus express to the assembled equestrians in A.D. 9 is that a wife will "temper the untimely harshness" of old age. It is a commonly expressed wish in Latin poetry that a couple may grow old together; an elderly couple, even of slender means, might be regarded as happy and fortunate.[81] Pliny expresses his contentment at the fact that his young third wife, Calpurnia, will love him, even though he will grow old: it is not his years or his body—"which are gradually aging and dying" (quae paulatim occidunt ac senescunt)—that she loves, but his reputation (*Ep.* 4.19.5). Pliny was probably only about 40 years old at the time and, of course, did not live to an advanced age.

Nature again provides a model in the way that the male kingfisher, when it becomes too old to fly and support itself, is carried by the female and fed by her.[82] Aelian, in citing this example, states that human beings fail to live up to the ideal: women, he says, despise their old husbands and chase after young men, while elderly husbands ogle girls and ignore their elderly, lawfully wedded wives.[83] Ulpian (*Dig.* 24.3.22.8) discusses the case of a wife who suffers from *saevissimus furor* but who receives no form of support from her husband; in such a case, he says, the woman's *curator* (i.e., she should be under *cura furiosi*) or *cognati* should either force the husband to care for her or else take back her dowry and let the woman provide for herself. Normally a husband would have been on average some ten years older than his wife, and they might—other factors notwithstanding—have grown old together and provided comfort and perhaps support for one another.[84] No legislation, however, forced a man or woman to provide for an elderly spouse; again, it was felt that a natural sense of obligation should ensure that this happened. If death, divorce, or desertion meant that in old age a person was on his or her own, only one other source of maintenance was available: oneself.

The notion that one should make provision for one's own old age was a commonplace with a long history, even though most of our authors need have had relatively few financial worries themselves in that regard. Xenophon has Socrates advise a certain Eutheros to prepare for his old age by getting a job that will pay. The *strategos* Timotheus, as defendant in court in circa 362 B.C., was apparently concerned (and had sworn in the assembly to the effect) that he had not sufficient εφό-δια for his old age; Apollodorus in response pointed out his sizable estate.[85] In a papyrus letter of the second century B.C., a Greek mother congratulates her son on having learned demotic and having thereby opened up for himself a career in teaching as an εφόδιον for his old age.[86] One of the *Declamationes Maiores* of pseudo-Quintilian deals with a father who sold everything in order to ransom his captive son, keeping nothing even for his own old age, and who subsequently found that he could not support himself; he states that his old age, poverty, and *languor* could have excused him from providing a ransom, and he stresses that his indigence entitles him to support from his surviving son.[87] A son, it could be added, might also, stereotypically, spend the savings a father has made for his own old age.[88] Horace describes how all sorts of people—farmers, soldiers, and sailors—work all their lives and endure untold hardships in order that, like ants, they may have a nest egg to depend on in old age, while some misers take it to extreme lengths and live in abject poverty for fear of finding themselves impoverished in old age.[89] A tombstone inscription from Ravenna, dated palaeographically to the first century A.D., is indicative of just such a mentality; this Parthian's life was an eventful one, to judge from this account:

C. Iul<ius> Mygdonius | generi Parthus, | natus ingenuus, capt<us> | pubis aetate, dat<us> in terra<m> | Romana<m>. qui, dum factus | cives R<omanus>, iuvente[90] fato collocavi arkam, dum esse | annor<um> L. peti<i> usq<ue> a publertate senectae meae perveni|re; nunc recipe me, saxe [*sic*], libens; | tecum cura solutus ero.

> Gaius Iulius Mygdonius, a Parthian by race, born a free man, captured in youth and given over into Roman territory. When I was made a Roman citizen, at fate's command I collected up a nest egg for the day I should reach 50 years of age. I sought from puberty to achieve my old age; now receive me, rock, willingly; with you I shall be released from care.[91]

No family is mentioned. The man's primary concern in life—and the compulsion here may not sound entirely foreign to some modern readers—was to secure a nest egg for the day he reached 50 years of age.

The dread of a combination of old age and poverty is one strongly expressed in the extant literature, even though for our writers no such combination would have been a realistic prospect. In theory a wise man did not need wealth to enjoy a profitable old age.[92] But as we have seen, even Cicero, in his consolation for old age, has Cato admit, when asked by Laelius whether it is not true that old age is more tolerable for him only because of his wealth and position ("opes et copias et dignitatem") which many others lack, that "nec enim in summa inopia levis esse senectus potest, ne sapienti quidem, nec insipienti etiam in summa copia non gravis" (An old age of extreme poverty cannot be tolerable even for a wise man, nor can it fail to be burdensome, even in the greatest wealth, for a fool).[93] In the same dialogue Cicero states that the two greatest burdens of life are thought to be *paupertas* and *senectus,* a sentiment shared by many; both factors in combination must have proved highly unfortunate, as is quite regularly mentioned by ancient writers.[94]

But the literary sources, on which we are dependent for testimony, fail to furnish us with reliable and realistic depictions of the life of the elderly poor, despite the fact that we may assume that some 5–10 percent of the overall population of the Roman world at any one time would have been over the age of 60 years and that the vast majority of them would not have been affluent, to say the very least. The concern of the literature remains within the elite circle of the writer and his contemporary audience who, like Cicero's Cato, were assumed to have the power and resources—if not also the mental fortitude—to find consolation and support in old age.[95] Nor does the legal corpus concern itself overly with the impoverished elderly members of society. The poor could of course turn to mendicancy in old age (one notes the fears of Juvenal's Naevolus) and one late legal "concession" made to aged beggars may be seen in the statement from the later fourth century that all beggars are to be tested concerning their "integritas corporum et robur annorum"; if they have not been reduced to *mendicitas* through any *debilitas,* they are to become the slaves of those who report them and are to be taken off the streets. In other words, the only "legal" sort of beggar came to be one who was old and/or physically handicapped.[96]

Only in a passage from the second-century A.D. philosopher Juncus do we find the admission, without it being developed for satirical or humorous purposes, that for some members of society old age might present an impossible burden. In dealing with the hardships of later life, Juncus notes the additional miseries that true poverty would bring:

> εἰ δὲ καὶ πενία πως ἀνδρὶ γεγηρακότι ξυμπέσοι, αὐτὸς ἂν ἐκεῖνος εὔξαιτο ἀπαλλαγῆναι τέλεον τοῦ βίου διὰ τὸ ἄπορον ἐπὶ πᾶσιν, οὐχ ἡγεμόνος ὁδοῦ τυγχάνων, οὐ τροφέως, οὐκ ἐσθῆτα τὴν αὐτάρκη περικείμενος, οὐ στέγης εὐπορῶν, οὐ τροφῆς, ἔστι δὲ ὅπη καὶ ὕδατος οὐκ ἔχων τὸν ἀρυσόμενον.

> If moreover poverty happened to befall a man when he had become old, he would himself pray to be freed totally from life: this is because of his deprivation in all respects, not having anyone to guide him, nor a source of support, not having adequate clothing, and lacking shelter and food. There are times when he does not have anyone to draw even some water for him.[97]

This is held to be the most horrible reality of old age, "an oppressive, painful, grievous and decrepit spectacle: in short, an *Iliad* of woes," to use Juncus's own words.[98] There is some realization here that true poverty does not mean merely the inability to be comfortable in old age, to enjoy *otium honestum;* it is the grim reality of complete destitution without the basic necessities of life such as shelter and sustenance, not to mention self-respect. And it is a condition for which there can be no relief, except in death; neither the state nor the wealthier members of society provided any tangible aid. In this passage, whatever Juncus's motives in writing it, we have a depiction that begins to go beyond the philosophizing platitudes of a Cicero, beyond the derogatory and wry remarks of a Martial, and there emerges, however distant, a picture of the real misery, degradation, and helplessness that old age might bring to the less-privileged members of an ancient society.

We have been dealing here with means of support for older people, contrasting in particular the situations in Athens and Rome at different periods (a contrast that is not made in any extant Roman text). In the Roman context it would appear that the duty lay primarily with a man's or woman's immediate descendants, as part of a sense of *pietas,* but it was only in the second century A.D. that such a duty found expression in law. While no form of direct public aid or welfare was ever available, help might be expected from other family members or from powerful friends, always supposing that such people were alive and willing. Eventually the old person must look to his or her own resources, and the pervasive mentality that one's lot was what one deserved—a sentiment with something of a modern ring to it—left little room for genuine interest or sympathy. This negative conclusion is, of course, a subjective generalization, to be gleaned as much from inference as from the inadequate ancient sources, but it is, I believe, a necessary antidote to a long-standing myth that in past cultures, both in antiquity and in more recent history, older people enjoyed a life of prestige, comfort, and respect—with an implied contrast to the present day.[99] That some did is certain. That most did not should be recognized.

Older People in the Family: The Threat of Senile Dementia

GENERATIONAL CONFLICT

Hesiod depicts the fifth age of humankind, the Iron Age, as a time of misery, marked by disputes within the family, where men dishonor their aged parents and are so degenerate that even infants are born with gray hairs on their heads.[100] The notion that children should be dutiful to their aged parents has been seen earlier in this chapter, where some indication was also apparent that it was felt that some offspring failed to perform their duty. This aspect of generational conflict is a theme that frequently appears in classical literature.[101] It is not, however, an aspect in which I wish to become too embroiled here, for the simple reason that an exhaustive collection of literary references to the conflict between the young and old would achieve little more than making us aware of something that should be obvious enough, that the young and the old do not always see eye to eye.[102] That much seems to be universal to every society. In classical literature most depictions of this conflict fall into one of two categories: moralizing by older people on how the young should (but apparently do not) behave; and comic descriptions, not necessarily written by the young, of the struggle of a rebellious son against a conservative—or in some cases even more rebellious—old father.

What is of more interest in the context of this chapter are the reasons why this conflict of generations arose, if in fact the conflict is more than just a literary motif or a sign of the paranoia of some older people, and the repercussions such a conflict might have had on the household. Two types of generational conflict need to be differentiated, something most of the modern literature on the subject fails to do. The conflict within a family, between father and son (or mother and daughter, and so on), may be common to any household at any time; most cases of family generational conflict in classical literature, especially in tragedy and comedy, focus not on everyday, mundane disagreement, but on crucial moments, such as the marriage of the young son or daughter.[103] The potentially more serious conflict of the younger generation of a society with the elder members is a public one that breaks out in particular during times of crisis, as for example in the conflict between Nicias and Alcibiades (the latter, it may be noted, would have then been close to 40 years of age) before the Sicilian expedition, made good use of by Thucydides.[104] The narration of this conflict has a long history, and has often in the process not been kind to Nicias: his name was used as a nickname for Saturninius Secundus Salutius, praetorian prefect in the East in the 360s A.D., because of his slothfulness (βλα-κεία) in old age.[105]

The former, intrafamilial type of conflict in its extreme manifestation may result in family disintegration; the latter, more political dissension may lead to civil strife. Before we consider one particular product of intrafamilial generational conflict, namely the threatened usurpation by a son of the control held by a father, we must first discuss an aspect of old age rarely mentioned in the ancient testimony or, for that matter, in modern discussions of ancient old age—the legal and social effects of senility on the elderly person. By the term "senility" I mean primarily the potential *mental* repercussions of old age (in other words, senile dementia), as opposed to the strictly physical ones, though the English word may carry both senses—and indeed the two may be interrelated. To what extent were the mental disabilities that might accompany old age recognized in the ancient world? Our primary concern here is with the awareness at a more general social level, as evidenced in literary and legal sources (rather than in the medical literature, which is discussed in relation to old age in Chapter 9).

MENTAL ILLNESS IN OLD AGE

Sir Moses Finley noted in his brief survey of the status of older people in the ancient world that "I can find hardly any reference [sc. in classical literature] specific to mental illness in old age, and then only of the most casual kind."[106] This is true enough, because the emphasis in the literature is, as we have said, on the easily visible, physical drawbacks suffered in old age. But an awareness of the mental shortcomings is still there, as a brief survey of the testimony reveals.

In the imperial period *senium* was regularly differentiated from *senectus* or *senecta,* general terms for old age, with reference to particular negative aspects.[107] This tradition is made very clear in the following comment by Isidorus, in describing the sixth and final age of human life:

> *Senium* is the final stage of *senectus,* so called because it is the end of the sixth age. . . . Now *senectus* brings with it many things, some good, some bad. Good, since it frees us from the most violent of masters: it imposes a limit on pleasures, it smashes the force of lust, it increases wisdom, and it grants wiser counsels. Bad, however, because *senium* is most wretched in terms of both the disabilities it inflicts and the loathing it incurs [*miserrimum est debilitate et odio*].[108]

Loss of mental prowess was one negative feature of old age that was recognized. As Juvenal puts it, after describing all the physical horrors of old age as he saw them, "sed omni membrorum damno maior dementia" (but worse than all bodily ills is madness). He lists such features as forgetting the names of one's slaves, and not recognizing the faces of old friends and one's own children—the second recognized today as one symptom of Alzheimer's disease (premature senility), as opposed to shrinkage of the brain, which occurs with normal aging. Galen remarks on people forgetting the alphabet and even their own names in extreme old age (γῆρας ἔσχατον), symptoms coinciding with Thucydides' description of the Athenian plague, Galen notes; Galen also refers on several occasions to the phrase εἰς τὸ λήθης γῆρας, used by Plato.[109] Assorted references, most of them casual, may be collected to illustrate this general awareness of the fact that in old age the mind may fail. This is particularly true, not surprisingly, of comic and satirical literature, Greek and Roman, which makes much of elderly individuals' deranged minds, but references may also be found in more serious literature.[110] Cicero attributes "ista senilis stultitia quae deliratio appellari solet" (that senile foolishness which they call "dotage") to a character fault in some old people, but he does not deny its existence.[111] One particularly interesting reference—and far from casual—is to be found in a passage by the first-century A.D. pneumatist, Aretaeus of Cappadocia,[112] where, in discussing mental illness, he differentiates primarily between depressive melancholy and *mania,* and subsequently between (inter alia) *mania* and λήρησις, the latter being "the misfortune of old age," which is "a numbness or deadness of the senses" and "a benumbing of the *gnome*[113] and of the *nous* through cooling," unlike *mania. Leresis,* he goes on to say, begins in old age and, again unlike *mania,* does not go away, but dies with the person. To contract *mania* one needs to be vigorous, remarks Aretaeus; hence the young, who have much heat and blood, are susceptible, not older people.

We have already seen one image of the mental disabilities associated with *senectus* in the proverb that old age is a second childhood, which relates to both physical and mental debilities among older people. The loss of memory in old age, also remarked upon, is another feature of relevance here.[114] M. Valerius Messalla Corvinus (*cos.* 31 B.C.) is a particularly noteworthy case. Pliny the Elder states that he forgot his own name; in his *Chronicle* Jerome provides further details: "Messala Corvinus orator ante biennium quam moreretur ita memoriam ac sensum amisit, ut vix pauca verba coniungeret, et ad extremum ulcere sibi circa sacram spinam nato inedia se confecit anno aetatis LXXII" (The orator Messalla Corvinus, two years before he died, lost his memory and intellect to such an extent that he could scarcely string a couple of words together. In the end, when he developed an ulcer around his sacrum, he finished himself off through starvation; he was in his 72nd year).[115] An aging man suffering from such disabilities might be felt by the younger members of his family, whether through genuine concern or for more selfish reasons (control of property meaning power), to be incapable of retaining authority over the household. It is just such a situation that we must now consider, not as a literary motif but as a legal reality.[116]

SENILITY AND LOSS OF POWER

What happened in an ancient society when an aged man who, as oldest male member of the family, controlled the social and economic life of his household became incapable through perceived loss of mental faculties of performing effectively this function and furthermore acted recklessly in dealing with the family property? In Athens an action[117] for παράνοια (insanity) existed, which a son could bring against his father in such circumstances, aimed primarily at preventing the old man from squandering and thereby dissipating the estate of the *oikos*. Although no concrete evidence for such a charge ever having been brought by a son against his father exists, the existence of the law is clear enough and is frequently referred to in the literature.[118] Indeed, one very famous account, doubtless fictitious, of a son prosecuting a father on just such a charge had long currency in antiquity, that of Sophocles accused by his son or sons; what is more, Cicero in mentioning this case implies a Roman parallel.[119] The Athenian action existed as a possibility and as a potential threat in old age; the fact that we know of no genuine case from the period may be due either to our own inadequate knowledge or to the fact that the existence of the law meant that sons in many cases almost automatically took over control of the *oikos* in their father's old age, whatever the latter's mental condition.[120] When an Athenian son married, at around the age of 30 years, this may have been seen as the appropriate time for control of the household to pass to him, it being his duty to care for his aged parents if they were still alive.[121]

What then of the Roman situation? The contrast again is apparent.

The only suggestion that a Roman son took over control of the family property at the age of 30 years comes from the declamatory school: in one exercise it is stated that when a son reaches the age of 30, his father must divide his property with him: "cum tricenario filio pater patrimonium dividat". The old man, having given his estate to his sons, is described as helpless and alone ("solus, senex, inops"—a revealing triad). In this case, however, there seems to be no relationship to Roman reality.[122] It was a well-known feature of Roman law that the *paterfamilias* retained control of the household until his death, and of this unique feature the Roman legal system was insistently proud.[123] Despite the system of *donationes,* noted earlier, it was the norm under Roman law that property devolved only at the death of the *paterfamilias.* Daube has presented a well-known caricature of the repercussions of this legal situation:

> Suppose the head of a family was ninety, his two sons seventy-five and seventy, their sons between sixty and fifty-five, the sons of these in their forties and thirties, and the great-greatgrandsons in their twenties, none of them except the ninety-year-old Head owned a penny. If the seventy-five-year-old senator or the forty-year-old General or the twenty-year-old student wanted to buy a bar of chocolate, he had to ask the *senex* for the money. This is really quite extraordinary.[124]

It certainly is. Demographic realities, as we have already noted, meant that many, in fact most, Roman males of about the age of 30 years did not have a father—let alone a grandfather or great-grandfather—still alive and so were no longer *in potestate.* But the fact remains that *some* did remain under the complete control of the elderly male members of their family well into their adult life. That such a situation might lead to very real intrafamilial conflict, at least when there was property for the *paterfamilias* to control, should be obvious enough (though much modern discussion seems to assume that such direct control would have lead to familial harmony). Indeed the specter of parricide finds room for an appearance here, particularly when a *filiusfamilias* was in debt to a moneylender and had no means of repaying the debt while his father remained alive.[125]

In terms of Roman law, as opposed to the earlier situation in Athenian society, there is no testimony that it was the norm or indeed that it was even considered appropriate for an elderly father to hand over practical control of the family property to his sons, though this would have been one way in which the potential conflict engendered by the system of *patria potestas* might have been eased. The fact that a *filius-familias* could hold a *peculium,* and, from the time of Augustus, a *peculium castrense* independent of his father's property,[126] may have made the situation slightly more tolerable, as would the possibility of division of the father's property in anticipation of his death.[127] While a young Athenian male in the classical era became independent (i.e., no longer under the control of a *kurios*) on being entered on the deme's register at the age of 18 years, a Roman remained *in potestate* even after reaching the age of 25 years. *Emancipatio* of a son *in patria potestate,* though often discussed in the legal texts, seems not to have been a common reality in classical times.[128] Such a dramatic move as allowing Roman children total independence as a matter of course from, say, the age of 25 years (when they became *maiores*) might have served to ease a great deal of tension. But the suggestion probably never arose, except perhaps in the minds of some particularly rebellious young sons. In wealthier circles a young male may commonly have left the family home to set up his own residence and family,[129] but ordinarily it must often have been the case that a son stayed at home, ready and waiting to take over his share of the family estate on the death of the father.

Such, then, very briefly, is the generalized Roman situation. But what if the father was regarded as mentally incapable of running the household effectively and there was a perceived danger of the family estate being lost? The old man would retain his legal status as *paterfamilias,*[130] but did he in practice retain all his rights? The Roman institution of the *cura furiosi et prodigi* is relevant here. From the time of the Twelve Tables[131] it was admitted that a *furiosus* or a "prodigal" should not be considered capable of looking after his own property and that therefore a *curator* should be appointed for him (as with the *cura* of *minores* and of women *sui iuris*) until his madness or prodigality abated. This duty was traditionally assigned to the agnatic relatives; failing this a suitable *curator* might be appointed by the praetor or *praeses.*[132] It is expressly stated under later law that a son who is *probus* may be the *curator* of his own father (or mother).[133] In such cases the son effectively gained control over the family property, while still remaining *in potestate*. Such cases are not, of course, restricted to elderly parents, and in fact the old age of the parents is not specifically mentioned as a factor in the legal texts.[134] But it may be assumed, in the light of what we have said already about the observed mental incapacity associated with old age, that a father suffering from senile dementia may indeed have been assigned to the *cura* of his son on the latter's application.

There is a problem of terminology here: the man suffering from *furor* may be assigned a *curator*, while the mental disability experienced by older people is generally termed *insania* or *dementia*. Not too much should be made of this, however.[135] The main difference appears to have been that while a *furiosus* of younger years may have lucid intervals and may be expected to recover eventually, the *insania* of old age generally persists without interruption and until death.[136] In both cases the same action lay open to the *sani* relatives. It may be to this action, rather than just interdiction of a prodigal by a magistrate, that Cicero was referring when he said that the measures taken by Sophocles' son Iophon had a parallel in Roman times.

This brings us again to the declamatory school. A specific action for *dementia* is mentioned several times, usually in bizarre circumstances, where a son prosecutes a father. A few examples may serve to exemplify the unusual nature of these scenarios. We hear in one exercise of a rapist winning over the father of a girl he has raped, but not his own father, so he accuses his father of *dementia*. That is bizarre enough but quite rudimentary compared with other cases. In another situation a man disinherits his son; the latter has a child by a prostitute, whom he acknowledges; the son falls ill, calls his father, and entrusts the *nepos* to the grandfather; the son dies, the grandfather adopts the child, and is accused of *dementia* by his other son. One more of interest may be cited: a man began to lead a life of debauchery (*luxurians*), his son already doing so; the son accuses his father of *dementia,* on the grounds that debauchery belongs to youth, not old age.[137]

The extreme and convoluted nature of these plots apart, it is difficult to judge what if any degree of *legal* reality underlies such exercises.[138] It seems to me most probable that in these exercises the declaimers had in mind both the Greek action for παράνοια and the Roman institution of *cura* for the *furiosus*.[139] But it must be pointed out that the praetor or *praeses* would presumably only have placed a father in *cura* for *furor* or prodigality in extreme cases,[140] whereas the situations the declamatory exercises portray are in most cases bizarre but trivial. It should also be noted that only in one case has the father been accused of leading his children into poverty ("liberos tuos ad egestatem"); in the other examples, the son accuses his father of *dementia* for some decision or action he has made that adversely affects the rest of the family—or, more typically, just the son.[141] In "real life," furthermore, accusing one's father of insanity is an extreme step, and not one that the legal system regarded lightly; indeed the Praetor's Edict forbad bringing one's father or mother to court without the praetor's permission.[142]

Whatever the degree of reality underlying the *scholastica materia,* however, it seems most probable that the theoretical possibility of an action for insanity being brought by a son against his aged father might be enough, in both Athens and Rome, for a compromise to be reached out of court and within the home (at Rome, no doubt, in a family *consilium*), but without such an agreement being legally binding. That the Roman system of *patria potestas* was in cold legal terms much harsher than the situation in Athens is clear enough. But in reality it might be expected that the Roman *filiusfamilias* was not totally subject to the whims of a despotic old father. Senile dementia was at least recognized, if not dwelt upon, in antiquity, and the Roman son's capability to act as *curator* for a *furiosus* or *prodigus* father opened up one legal loophole whereby a son might in practice succeed to his father's position while the latter was still alive.

On the other side of the coin, however, one must remember the position of the elderly parent in this relationship. From what has been said in this chapter, the implication appears to have been that older people in the family could be in many respects in a position of almost childlike dependency. But the absence of wage earning as a fundamental element in the structure of Roman life, and with it the absence of a notion of institutionalized retirement, meant in effect that an elderly person, so long as he or she possessed some means of financial independence—be it a patch of garden[143] or a slave—would not be totally helpless. The words Cicero has Cato speak must have rung true with many elderly Romans: "Ita enim senectus honesta est, si se ipsa defendit, si ius suum retinet, si nemini emancipata est, si usque ad ultimum spiritum dominatur in suos" (Old age will only be respected if it fights for itself, maintains its own rights, avoids dependence on anyone, and asserts control over its own to the last breath).[144] When a person's failing state of physical and mental health led to total inability to be self-supporting, then, in the absence of effective medication (a topic to which we shall turn shortly), dependence on others may have been short-lived anyway.

PART IV

PUTTING OLDER PEOPLE IN THEIR PLACE

Nine

The Marginality of Old Age

I n the previous chapters of this book, in regard to varied aspects of aging and old age in the Roman world, two extremes in attitude toward older people have been seen to recur, explicitly or implicitly, in the testimony: that they have a definite and appropriate role to play and contribution to make; and that they are an unwelcome burden and at best must be tolerated. These are gross generalizations, but the awareness of the fact that such attitudes, at both extremes, may coexist, rather than be mutually exclusive, is important. People at different times under different circumstances may hold one view or the other, or a mixture of both (if they hold any attitude at all) about different aged individuals. It is the aim of this final chapter, by way of bringing together the varied aspects we have already considered as well as of introducing some new ones, to consider the extent to which the Roman elderly were perceived as an integral part of their society or were in some way excluded from full participation; in other words, to what extent were older people marginalized or set in a liminal position of "otherness"? This question has already concerned us at some length in considering the depiction of old age in literature, the part *senes* played in public affairs, and the position of older people within the family and household. In these earlier discussions it was at times inevitable that old people were considered as one homogeneous group, though some allowance was made for class and, more especially, gender. That older people were never in reality such a united body, however, needs now to be considered in greater depth.

Just as quite distinct attitudes toward older people may be discerned, so the differing circumstances, economic and social, personal and public, of each individual older person may have led to very different attitudes by other members of society toward him or her. My underlying argument in this final chapter is that the extent to which old people in ancient society were an integral part of that society or were in some way excluded from full participation depended to a large extent, apart from questions of gender and status, on the degree of capability of the individual; that individual would not be wholly marginalized so long as he or she was still capable of performing some useful function, be it as a statesman or as a child minder. In other words, the prestige enjoyed, the part played, the actual status of an aged person in the Roman world depended more on the person than on the general fact that he or she was old.[1] Just as Plato's Cephalus and Cicero's Cato, among others, stated that the faults found in an old person were due not to old age but to that person's character, so it may be said that society's view of an elderly Roman was dictated by the extent to which that individual continued to find a niche in that society. Old people were not automatically accorded a role or privileged position—hence, perhaps, the insistence of some ancient authors that, for example, old men still have an important part to play in public life.

Crucial in this context is the physical and mental well-being of older people, and another distinction in our definition of old age needs to be borne in mind, between the healthy and the decrepit elderly, that is, between those who enjoy a robust old age during which they are capable of continued activity, physical and/or mental, and those who, as a result of the natural consequences of senescence, are no longer able to function as society would wish or expect.[2] Indeed we have already met such a distinction, that drawn between *senectus* and *senium*.[3] There is some slight evidence for further distinctions being drawn between different stages of old age at various times in classical antiquity, particularly in a medical context. In one of his works Galen asserts that there are three parts to old age: in the first, τῶν ὠμογερόντων, people can still take part in public life (τὰ πολιτικὰ πράττειν); in the next stages, the age of the σῦφαρ (wrinkle or sloughed-off skin) and the final stage, dubbed πέμπελος ("very old," allegedly linked etymologically to the idea that extreme old age is on the way [πέμπεσθαι] to Hades!), decline and disability take over. Such a system explicitly takes into account the differing realities of old age for different people, and not simply in terms of chronological span.[4]

The Liminal Status of Older People

In the Roman world, especially in terms of political and public life but also in relation to the family, old people were not automatically accorded a role. For example, as was discussed in Chapters 3 and 4, Cicero and Plutarch argued forcefully that elderly men still have a vital part to play in the running of the state. Implicit in their argument is the fact that some people did *not* think older people had such a role. In most preindustrial societies in the past and in many contemporary societies studied by anthropologists,[5] the active adult male group sets the norms, and other sectors of society—children, women, old men, and the disabled or sick (to which groups one might add for antiquity slaves and foreigners)—are regarded as in some respects on the margins of this cultural ideal. In terms of ancient societies the traditional norm may be seen as the adult male warrior,[6] and membership of this privileged minority depends on physical capabilities as well as inherited status. All other individuals are to some degree distanced from this ideal image. It needs to be noted further that members of such a marginalized body may be of differing circumstances and the degree of marginality may differ markedly (although similarities were certainly evident, as with old age being regarded as a second childhood). The young, for example, will in time grow up, and through rites of transition will enter into the elite group, whereas older men have had their time at the helm (though to some extent they might rebel against their exclusion) and no "rite de passage" is left apart from death.

One difficulty in analyzing the position of marginal groups within a historical society is that by their very nature such marginal sectors tend to be the focus of very little attention and therefore leave little in the way of historical record. One *advantage,* however, with studying the Roman elderly is that, unlike other groups on the fringe such as women and slaves, they have left us testimony, particularly in the form of literature, in which they do indeed stress their continued role. The social realities behind this assertion need now concern us at greater length. We look first at the marginalized status of elderly males, and then at the doubly marginalized status of females in old age.

A recurring theme in classical literature (as we have already seen) is that war is for the young, advice for the elderly; this is a natural consequence of the physical deterioration evident in many old people, but assumes continued mental capabilities, an assumption that, as we saw in Chapter 8, was not always safe. To be old is not enough; one must have positive attributes to outweigh the perceived negative ones (a recurring theme in Chapter 3). To be sure certain positive qualities were well appreciated, and not just by older people themselves: the experience gained through longevity, the social contacts, cultural understanding, and traditional *mores* "stored" in old people. But one factor did forcefully exclude elderly individuals, as it did younger women and children, from the active citizen body, and that was their perceived lack of any active military capability, at least in terms of actual fighting. Historians, orators, and epic poets regularly made the observation that the young men go out to fight while the women, children, and elderly are left behind at home.[7] Exceptions to this rule are highlighted for the very reason that they are foreign to normal, "civilized" practice (e.g., among the Germans), or are necessitated by highly unusual circumstances, as when Crassus enlisted old veterans for the campaign against Spartacus in 72 B.C., selecting "all those who, though their bodies were aged [*senecto corpore*], still had an *animus militaris*."[8] Marginalized individuals, especially the very young, the old, and women of any age, are often grouped together, particularly to contrast them with active adult males.[9] In a court of law the figures of women, fatherless children, and old men could be used to invoke pity, "even in a *rectus iudex*," as Quintilian notes; the technique is perhaps most familiar from Plato's *Apology*, when Socrates refused to follow what seems to have been a common practice, but some Roman orators were clearly not averse to or unskilled at such practices.[10] An old man might also be used by an author to invoke pity or, if the *senex* is maltreated, outrage, as in Livy's account where an old soldier, impoverished and whipped, is the catalyst for the plebeian revolt of 495 B.C.[11] The various roles of the age-groups, similar to those later described by Aristotle in his *Rhetoric* and by Horace in the *Ars Poetica,* are neatly, if somewhat cynically, summed up by the proverb (and note the reference to middle age again): "Deeds belong to young people, council to those of middle years, prayers to old people" (ἔργα νέων, βουλαὶ δὲ μέσων, εὐχαὶ δὲ γερόντων).[12] The point in most literary examples of such stereotypical attitudes toward old age is to highlight the pathos of the situation, the misery and helplessness of those left behind, rather than to imply that older people are a burden or cowardly.[13] But the social reality still meant that old people were not normally called to arms and were not seen in the same light as the younger, stronger men. Ovid put it most bluntly: "turpe senex miles" (an old soldier is a disgusting thing).[14]

If, like Nestor, the old man accepted—albeit grudgingly, perhaps—that his best fighting days were in the past, the argument could still be made that he had a vital role to play in this sphere as adviser and/or leader.[15] More broadly, to follow the arguments of the likes of Cicero and Plutarch again, older people's role in government, as citizens of the state, might be held to make up for their lack of participation in military affairs. There is no need to reiterate here the arguments we have already outlined in Chapters 3 and 4 in this regard, but we do need to consider further the extent to which an old man was regarded as a complete member of the political body, the *polis* or the *civitas.* Aristotle, in defining the nature of citizenship, considers various categories of persons who may not be deemed citizens in the fullest sense. Factors he mentions include residence, rights under private law, and age:

> Minors who by reason of youth have not yet been enrolled, and old men [τοὺς γέροντας] who have been exempted, must not be called quite simply "citizens," but rather citizens "of a kind," with addition of the words "not yet full" [τοὺς ἀτελεῖς] or "superannuated" [τοὺς παρηκμακότας] or the like—it does not matter what, since what is being said is plain. Similar difficulties can be raised and solved about exiled and disfranchised persons. But we are looking for the citizen proper, who is free from every such charge calling for correction.[16]

One should note again that while the young will in time overcome the "defect" of age and thus become citizens in the full sense, older people will not. Of course, with Aristotle's definition we are dealing with theory, not necessarily practice, nor with the Roman world. Yet the feeling if not the rule in Greek and Roman times seems often to have been that the old man had outlived not only his military but also his political usefulness. The point is made explicitly many centuries after Aristotle by Juncus, who lists among the many negative attributes of old men their exclusion from political and military affairs:

> If the old man has the audacity to enter the *agora,* he provokes the laughter of those who see him, for he cannot see properly and cannot hear when people shout. Trying to make his way forward he trips and falls. He is accused of getting in the way and of using up [*or* spoiling] the common air of the city [ἀφανίζειν τὸν κοινὸν τῆς πόλεως ἀέρα]. For when he appears in the assembly, he is not included among the ranks of the tribes, nor is he capable of holding office, on account of the aforementioned disabilities: he is bowed and withered, misshapen and feeble, and in spirit, as the saying goes, has become a child again [κυφός τε ὢν καὶ ῥικνὸς καὶ ἄμορφος καὶ ἀδύνατος τῇ τε ψυχῇ κατὰ τὴν παροιμίαν παῖς πάλιν γεγονώς]. In war (for this too should be mentioned) he is exempt from service and is left naked and defenseless, since he is not enlisted in the infantry or cavalry, nor indeed as a rower on a ship nor as a marine.[17]

The conclusion is almost inevitable, that old age is useless, *inutilis,* an epithet that is not irregularly attached to *senectus.*[18] Cicero, for example, denigrates L. Calpurnius Piso (*cos.* 58 b.c.) by comparing him to "parvo puero aut . . . imbecillo seni aut debili" (a small boy or a weak and feeble old man)—both marginal members of society.[19] In old age a man is not what he was, much of his usefulness is gone, and in some respects, or in some people's eyes, he would be better off dead.[20] This side to old age, not just one of physical or even mental disability but also one of diminished status and of lowered social estimation, is one which we have already frequently mentioned, because it is occasionally alluded to in the literary depiction of old age and older people. The lesson is there, for example, in a fable by Phaedrus (1.21), where the lion, "defectus annis et desertus viribus" (worn out through years and bereft of strength), is insulted by the other animals over whom he had previously lorded it: "quicumque amisit dignitatem pristinam ignavis etiam iocus est in casu gravi" (Whoever has lost the prestige he once had becomes in his dire state an object of ridicule even to cowards). Cicero in his *de Senectute* mentions—very much in passing—that one problem older people might face is the fact that they are shunned by others and treated with scorn and disdain;[21] but, as we have seen, such problems Cicero puts down to character, not to old age per se. Maximianus also noted the ridicule suffered by the elderly individual, and his lines, written some 1,000 years after the time of Aristotle, offer a powerful if pitiful insight into the position of an elderly man:

> iurgia, contemptus violentaque damna secuntur,
>   nec quisquam ex tantis praebet amicus opem.
> ipsi me pueri atque ipsae sine lite puellae
>   turpe putant dominum iam vocitare suum.
> irrident gressus, irrident denique vultum
>   et tremulum, quondam quod timuere, caput.
> cumque nihil videam, tamen hoc spectare licebit,
>   ut gravior misero poena sit ista mihi.

> Insults, contempt, and violent losses follow, and where once there were so many friends, now none comes forward to offer help. The very boys and girls themselves, indisputably, think it disgusting to call me now their master. They snigger at my gait, they even snigger at my face, and my trembling head, which once they feared. And though I can see nothing, yet this I may behold—so it makes that penalty itself harder for me, poor wretch, to bear.[22]

If some old men were disadvantaged by their marginal status, double marginality may have incurred twice the problems. The motif of the *puer senex* (and *puella senex*), the ideal of late paganism and early Christianity in particular whereby the young were precociously invested with (positive) qualities of old age such as practical wisdom and moderation—the stuff of saints—is one artificial example of such double marginality, with positive implications, at least for the young. Cicero, for example, describes one young man as "serious, with an old man's judgment" (adulescens gravis, senili iudicio); it is worth remembering that this is meant as a compliment. With similar logic, Pliny the Younger describes a girl deceased at age 13, Minicia Marcella, as displaying before her untimely death the good sense of an old woman and the seriousness of a Roman matron, while at the same time retaining a girl's charm and a virginal sense of propriety ("nondum annos xiiii impleverat, et iam illi anilis prudentia, matronalis gravitas erat et tamen suavitas puellaris cum virginali verecundia"). On a Greek tombstone from Rome, probably to be dated to the third century A.D., it is stated that a boy who died at the age of 2 years, 8 months, 15 days, and 5 hours, had an intellect worthy of gray-haired old age; on another Roman (verse) epitaph, that of an 11-year-old boy, we are told that the deceased was indeed young in years, but exhibited the seriousness of an old man ("annis parve quidem, sed gravitate senex"). In like fashion Ausonius describes the full life of the 16-year-old *mater* Anicia: "aetatis meritis anus est, aetate puella" (in terms of age's achievements she is an aged woman; in age itself, a girl).[23]

The double marginality, in terms of both gender and age, of the older woman, however, is not so positive. It has already been seen that the depiction of the old woman in Greek and Latin literature was almost monotonously negative and at times grotesque and cruel.[24] It is a well-known feature of classical Athenian society (as depicted in extant evidence) that women, especially of the upper classes, enjoyed very little freedom outside the home. After the menopause, however, a woman was apparently granted the freedom to go outside the family confines—thus, for example, the law of Solon that the only women allowed to take an active part in funerals were close relatives and those over the age of 60 years.[25] One may note also the traditional use, at least in some societies, of older women (i.e., past the age of reproducing) as midwives.[26] As widows in particular, in both the Greek and the Roman world, women in old age might in fact have enjoyed considerable authority, in practice if not also in legal theory, because they controlled the family wealth to some limited extent[27]—always supposing, of course, that the family had wealth in the first place. It was seen in Chapter 8 that an elderly woman might derive some security through the fact that she had offspring dependent on her, although the reverse might also be true. But it must be realized that any benefits (in our eyes) accruing to a woman through her old age were not a result of any privileged or enhanced status, but rather quite the opposite. Because a woman past the menopause could no longer perform her primary function as a producer of legitimate offspring, it became of little concern to the adult male who made or enforced the "rules" or social norms whether or not an old woman followed the conventions of society or not. As a doubly marginalized member of society an older woman became an object of minimal interest, sexually and otherwise, so far had she strayed from the center of attention, the world of the adult male citizen.[28] The curse Ovid invokes on the aged *lena* Dipsas (Thirsty) may sum up well the fate of many an old Roman woman, as well as the callous view many a Roman male may have taken: "di tibi dent nullosque lares inopemque senectam | et longas hiemes perpetuamque sitim" (May the gods grant you no home and a needy old age and long winters and everlasting thirst).[29] To most other members of society, however, such marginalized individuals would have been of little interest. In two areas, however, some interest is expressed in older people (or at any rate in some of them) in their own right: in the realms of medicine and religion.

Old Age and Medicine

ἀκμὴ ἡλικίης πάντα ἔχει χαρίεντα,
ἀπόληξις δὲ τοὐναντίον.

In the prime of life everything is lovely,
in the decline it is the opposite.
Hippocrates *Praec.* 14 (9.270L)

There are many references in the ancient medical writers to elderly patients,[30] typically commenting on the various ailments suffered by older people and offering little in terms of what we understand today by geriatric medicine. It was something of a commonplace in antiquity to state that old age was itself a disease.[31] In the second century A.D. Galen for one disagreed: he states that while diseases are contrary to nature (παρὰ φύσιν), old age is not; it is a natural process, just as to die of old age is natural, as was generally accepted.[32] Therefore, Galen insists, old age, despite what some say, is *not* a disease; it is also not complete health either, he adds, but rather there is a state of health peculiar to old age (contrast, e.g., Cicero *de Sen.* 11.35). In this regard Galen was certainly ahead of his time; indeed whether aging is a physiological or pathological process is still debated today.[33]

But Galen was no modern-day scientist or gerontologist either, and the significance of his contribution to what we would call today geri-

247

atric science or medicine, or the health of older people, should not be exaggerated. There is, as we have seen, no lack of reference, in medical and general literature from antiquity, to the physical disabilities of old age, and the mental drawbacks were also touched upon. But while references to older people abound, there was no specialized focus on geriatric medicine such as has been seen within the past century; indeed, the medical science of geriatrics is a twentieth-century phenomenon. In one key passage Galen does comment on the "gerocomic" field of medicine, but it is clear from his comments that this was no more than the observation of the "symptoms" of old age and the theoretical study of means of prolonging life; it was not a study of old age nor gerontology in its own right:

τὸν δὲ τοῦ γήρως μαρασμὸν ἀδύνατον δήπου καταλῦσαι, βοηθεῖσθαι δὲ ὡς ἐπιπλεῖστον ἐκταθῆναι δυνατόν, καὶ τό γε γηροκομικὸν ὀνομαζόμενον μέρος τῆς ἰατρικῆς αὐτὸ τοῦτ᾽ ἔστι, σκοπὸν ἔχον ὡς ἡ τοῦ πράγματος ἐνδείκνυται φύσις, ἐνίστασθαι καὶ διακωλύειν ὡς οἷόν τε, μὴ ξηρανθῆναι τὸ σῶμα τῆς καρδίας εἰς τοσοῦτον, ὡς ἐνεργοῦν ποτε παύσασθαι. τοῦτο γὰρ δὴ τὸ πέρας ἐστὶ τῆς ζωῆς, παῦλα τοῦ τῆς καρδίας ἔργου, ὡς μέχρι ἂν ἥδε κινῆται κατὰ τὴν ἑαυτῆς ἐνέργειαν, ἀδύνατον ἀποθανεῖν τὸ ζῷον. εἰ μὲν οὖν οἷόν τέ ἐστιν ὑγρότερον ἐργάσασθαι τὴν οὐσίαν αὐτοῦ τοῦ τῆς καρδίας σώματος, ἢ καὶ νὴ Δία τοῦ ἥπατος, ἐγχωρεῖ τὸ γῆρας ἐπισχεῖν· εἰ δὲ μηδεὶς ἱκανός ἐστι μήθ᾽ ἧπαρ ὑγρότερον ἑαυτοῦ ποιῆσαι μήτε καρδίαν, ἀλλ᾽ ἀναγκαῖον ἐπὶ προήκοντι τῷ χρόνῳ ξηρότερα γίνεσθαι σφῶν αὐτῶν οὐ τὰ σπλάγχνα μόνον, ἀλλὰ καὶ τὰς ἀρτηρίας καὶ τὰς φλέβας, κωλῦσαι μὲν τὸ γῆρας ἀδύνατον, ἐπισχεῖν δὲ τὸ τάχος αὐτοῦ δυνατόν.

It is thus impossible to prevent the *marasmos* [i.e., the wasting or dying away through dryness] of old age but it is possible to aid in the augmentation of the length of life. This is precisely what is the part of medicine which is called "gerocomic"; it has as its goal the explanation of the nature of the problem of aging and, to as great a degree as possible, the resistance to and the prevention of the aging process, so that the mass of the heart does not dry out to the point of ceasing to function. That is the end of life, the cessation of cardiac activity. For as long as the heart remains active with its own energy, it is impossible for the living creature to die. If there is a means of humidifying the substance of the heart or, indeed, that of the liver, it is possible to check the aging process. But if no one is capable of making the liver or the heart more humid, then it is inevitable that, with the passage of time, not only their innards become more dry but also their arteries and veins; in such a case, it is impossible to prevent aging, although it is possible to retard its progress.[34]

Thus the doctor's interest in old age seems to have been purely in the sphere of taking the age of patients into account (together with their occupation, the climate in which they lived, and so on) in making a diagnosis.[35] Or at least this is what the ancient doctor was meant to do. Our only way of testing the likelihood of age being taken into account is by looking at the collection of case studies from northern Greece preserved in the Hippocratic *Epidemics* (5.72–468L), relating to circa 410–350 B.C. The results of such a survey are not encouraging. The age of the patient is very rarely taken into account, or at least it is not mentioned. Of 388 individuals recorded,[36] the vast majority is signified only by name; 261 are male, 127 (i.e., less than a third) female. Of the females, a clear majority is of reproductive age (not stated directly, but implied from reference to menstruation and childbirth)— an indication, perhaps, of the doctors' interests and/or of the patients' expectations of what can be treated, if not also of the prevalence of gynecological problems. In terms of age, general terms for age-groups are used rarely: γέρων occurs once (*Epid.* 4.2 [5.44L]), πρέσβυς and πρεσβύτης once each (4.42, 55 [5.182, 194L]), γραίη twice (4.30, 7.105 [5.172, 456L]), and πρεσβυτέρη once (7.8 [5.378L]), as well as an occasional reference to a patient being young.[37] I have found only 15 cases (i.e., less than 4% of patients) where age in years (or months) is given: a 2-month-old infant (7.106 [5.456L]); boys aged about 6 years (7.122 [5.466L]; Littré's punctuation and therefore translation are probably wrong), 11 (5.16 [5.214L]), 12 or 13 (5.23 [5.222L]); a girl aged about 12 (5.28 [5.226L]); men aged nearly 20 (4.15 [5.154L]) or about 20 (1.2.2 [2.688L], 3.1.8 [3.56L]), about 25 (6.8.29 [5.354L], 7.68 [5.430L]), about 30 or a little less (5.22 [5.220L]), and about 50 (7.112 [5.460L]); and women aged about 17 (3.1.12 [3.66L]), 20 (5.50 [5.236L]), and 60 (5.25 [5.224L]). The level of age-rounding is noteworthy.[38]

If elderly patients were consulting their doctors, they have generally become assimilated into the basic adult grouping, age unspecified. Geriatric patients seem to warrant no special mention, at least in this period. Things may have changed in later centuries, but there is no indication of this. Indeed Alexander of Tralles (sixth century A.D.), following the influence of Galen and ultimately of the Hippocratic corpus, wrote that since old age as a natural condition is incurable, doctors must consider whether to treat aged patients: through a sense of compassion a doctor should not abandon all such patients but offer what help he can, unless the case is truly hopeless, in which event the doctor should seek to protect his own reputation.[39] One might compare the saying of the emperor Tiberius, recorded by Plutarch, that a man of 60 years of age who holds out his hand to a physician is ridiculous, the implication being that at that age either a man should be able to look after himself or he is not worth looking after.[40] Galen notes that some people are in such bad physical condition from an early age that even if Asclepius himself were to treat them, they would not survive to their 60th year.[41] Such attitudes, if they were widespread, would hardly have been conducive to the treatment or the welfare of older people. As Celsus (writing under Tiberius) commented, "medicina . . . vix aliquos ex nobis ad senectutis principia perducit" (Medicine . . . scarcely protracts the lives of a few of us to the verge of old age).[42]

Whether or not ancient doctors routinely took into account their patients' age, it is certainly true that the observations derived from the Greek doctors continued to govern the medical treatment of older people for well over a 1,000 years. The first practical manual to be printed that was devoted to the medical problems of old age and their treatment was the Italian physician Gabriele Zerbi's *Gerontocomia* (or, more precisely, *Gerentocomia* [sic], *scilicet de senium cura atque victu*). Published in Latin in 1489, it is heavily and explicitly dependent on Galen, among many others (most notably Aristotle and Cicero); Zerbi's range of quotations from classical as well as later sources is staggering. It is particularly striking that he drew on sources that were both medical (especially for the theory of the humors) and astrological (e.g., for the influence of Jupiter and Saturn); he clearly considered the two areas interrelated and as of almost equal significance. One may note too that Zerbi, as was presumably true also for the Greco-Roman medical authors, was writing for a wealthy and leisured audience: when discussing diet, he remarks that "it is of course understood that those old people who earn their living with their hands should have additional food. Our present *gerontocomia* does not extend to them. They prefer to live contented with plain fare."[43] The ideas of the classical authors on whom Zerbi drew are worth considering briefly here, both because they add something to our picture of the realities of old age in the ancient world and because they serve to highlight the marginalized status of older people. First, however: what, according to the ancient physicians, causes old age?

The afflictions old age may bring were well appreciated by the ancient medical writers, who provide many details. But regarding causes the literature is less pragmatic. The faults of old age that Cicero put down to character, Plutarch, to further his argument that *some* old men are still fit to lead the state, ascribed to disease and πήρωσις, general disablement or mutilation,[44] but this is effect rather than cause. The most common theory to be found in the extant ancient literature, both medical and philosophical, on the cause of aging was that the body in time loses its innate heat and fluid, its life force, so that the infant is warm and moist while the old person, like a corpse, is cold and dry.[45] In other words, aging is a cooling and drying process, and the desiccation of the heart and liver leads to death, as Galen asserts (quoted earlier); as in illness, the balance of the four humors has been lost. As heat dissipates, the body takes longer to recover from illness and injury, but for the same reason symptoms such as fever become less acute in older people,[46] as does activity in general. The theory, mentioned frequently by Aristotle, as well as by Theophrastus and by a number of Stoics,[47] is discussed at most length by Galen, who takes it for granted that the aged person is cold and dry.[48] Another theory, that the old person is cold but *humid* or moist (and therefore requires a regimen of health that warms and dries), is mentioned twice in the Hippocratic corpus,[49] but is soundly refuted by Galen;[50] the mistake is due, he remarks, to the external appearance of moisture about the old person—coughing, a runny nose, and the like—but these are merely an abundance of external, phlegmatic secretions (τὰ περιττώματα φλεγματικά) or residue of humidity, and are not to be taken as an indication of the innate condition of the elderly individual.[51]

This idea that old age is cold often recurs in general literature also, as we have already seen.[52] As for its dryness, old age is often described as *exsanguis*, ὀλίγαιμος, or ἄναιμος, drained of the moist (and hot) *humor* of blood.[53] What blood the aged body does have is icy cold, an image Vergil well evokes in the person of Entellus: "gelidus tardante senecta sanguis hebet" (my blood is chilled and dulled by sluggish old age). Isidorus of Seville remarked that, according to the *physici,* "men of colder blood are stupid, those of warm blood wise; hence, old men, in whom the blood is now cold, and boys, in whom the blood is not yet warm, have less sense" (physici dicunt stultos esse homines frigidioris sanguinis, prudentes calidi: unde et senes, in quibus iam friget, et pueri, in quibus necdum calet, minus sapiunt).[54] Indeed Galen himself noted that the coldness of old age affects not only the body but also the mind: "So why do many people become demented [παρελη-ρήθησαν] when they reach extreme old age [εἰς ἔσχατον ἀφικνο-ύμενοι γῆρας], an age which has been shown to be dry? We shall maintain that this is not a result of dryness, but of coldness. For this clearly damages all the activities of the soul."[55] Furthermore, because aging was conventionally seen as a process of desiccation, those who were by nature very humid were held to have the greatest chance of a long life.[56] With similar logic it was stated that men, being warmer, age more slowly than women and hence live longer (the latter observation may well have been often accurate in the ancient world, though for other reasons).[57] Part of the theory was that one felt best in the season appropriate or complementary, that is, opposite, to one's age (in a system of four ages). It was a literary commonplace that old age is like winter, at least in its coldness—winter is rarely described as dry, however!—and that therefore winter was a dangerous time for older people.[58] So it was observed that summer and early autumn were the seasons in which older people might thrive, and winter was the season to avoid as best one could.[59] In regard to climate and environment, pseudo-Aristotle pondered the question of why people age more quickly in damp places and noted that people in hot climates live longer.[60] To counter the dryness and coldness of old age, it was necessary to seek to restore the balance of the humors, to give warmth and humidity to the aged frame. Such was the principal aim of the "gerocomic art."

While Galen did not believe that old age was a disease, he did stress that there is a state of health peculiar to old people that may be maintained through a moderate life-style. Hence it was apparently common

practice for physicians to recommend a particular regimen or δίαιτα
that older people should follow, and in the fifth book of his *de Sanitate
Tuenda* Galen provides abundant material on the subject, considerably
more detailed than anything that precedes it and of enormous influence on treatments of the subject over the following centuries and,
through Arabic sources such as Avicenna, into later times.[61] Galen's
recommendations incorporate massage, gentle exercise,[62] the right
amount of sleep, and tepid baths,[63] in order to warm the aged frame
and to retain what warmth it still had. Bloodletting might even be
used, though it was not recommended for the very young or elderly,
especially as the latter needed every drop of blood that they had.[64]
Particular attention was paid to diet: some foods were recommended
(plums are good as laxatives, according to Galen), others (such as
cheese, hard-boiled eggs, snails, lentils, mushrooms, and many vegetables) were regarded as dangerous.[65] The same was true of bev-
erages: water was not recommended, nor was milk for most elderly
individuals—it apparently rots aged teeth and gums.[66] Wine was particularly commended, and in the name of science Galen devoted much
study to the question of which wines were best for medicinal purposes
(sweet wines rather than, of course, dry were said to be best suited for
older people).[67] Wine could have positively rejuvenating effects; indeed it was apparently proverbial that wine makes an old man dance,
even against his will.[68] Concrete examples of the benefits of wine
drinking may also be found: Augustus's wife Livia attributed her long
life to the wine of Pucinum in northern Italy, and Romilius Pollio, an
otherwise unknown centenarian from the time of Augustus, credited
his aged vigor (as well as, perhaps, his succinct wit) to honeyed wine
within and oil without ("intus mulso, foris oleo").[69] Worthy of note
also is one C. Domitius Primus, who on his tombstone from Ostia
records that "balnia [*sic*] vina Venus mecum senuere per annos" (baths,
wine, and love aged with me through the years).[70] Before her death in
1997, the world's oldest living person, Jeanne Calment of France, on
her 122nd birthday in that year attributed her longevity to cooking
with olive oil, eating lots of garlic, and drinking a daily glass of port;
she gave up smoking in 1992. We have long recognized the benefits,
for example, of a glass of red wine for one's heart. It is now emerging
that alcohol, in moderation, may also protect against cognitive deteri-

oration in later life—something, perhaps, that Galen and company were not totally unaware of themselves.[71]

In effect, then, recommended treatment for older people in classical antiquity was as much for the (presumed and stereotypical) causes of old age as for the observable symptoms experienced by individual patients. Medical science of the period did, however, extend beyond such generalized and optimistic recommendations for health in order to observe the particular ailments endured by the (stereotyped) elderly. The Hippocratic corpus preserves one comprehensive list, which in the first century A.D. Celsus repeats with some variation:

> τοῖσι δὲ πρεσβύτῃσι, δύσπνοιαι, κατάρροιαι βηχώδεες, στραγγουρίαι, δυσουρίαι, ἄρθρων πόνοι, νεφρίτιδες, ἴλιγγοι, ἀποπληξίαι, καχεξίαι, ξυσμοὶ τοῦ σώματος ὅλου, ἀγρυπνίαι, κοιλίης καὶ ὀφθαλμῶν καὶ ῥινῶν ὑγρότητες, ἀμβλυωπίαι, γλαυκώσιες, βαρυηκοΐαι.

> In older people there occur difficulty of breathing, catarrhal coughs, strangury, painful urination, arthritis, kidney disease, dizziness, apoplexy, cachexy, violent itching over the whole body, insomnia, watery discharges from the bowels, eyes, and nostrils, failing sight, blindness from glaucoma, and deafness.

> in senectute spiritus et urinae difficultas, gravedo, articulorum et renum dolores, nervorum resolutiones, malus corporis habitus (καχεξίαν Graeci appellant), nocturnae vigiliae, vitia longiora aurium, oculorum, etiam narium, praecipueque soluta alvus, et quae secuntur hanc, tormina vel levitas intestinorum ceteraque ventris fusi mala.

> In old age there occur breathing and urinary difficulties, choked nostrils, joint and renal pains, paralysis, the bad habit of body which the Greeks call *cachexia*, insomnia, the more chronic maladies of the ears, eyes, also of the nostrils, and especially looseness of the bowels with its consequences, dysentery, intestinal lubricity, and the other ills resulting from bowel looseness.[72]

Few physical ailments remained undetected by the medical authors; there is much detail but little help or relief is offered, and the prevailing theme again is the weakness and debility of old age.[73] To cite two particularly unpleasant observations noted by Celsus in the first century A.D.: gangrene is held to be a characteristic of old age, and uncomfortable advice is given on how to cure an elderly male patient's difficulty in urinating (presumably owing to an enlarged prostate).[74] At a more conventional level, various ailments and disabilities associated with old age frequently recur, in the medical as in more general ancient literature. Dental problems and inadequacies we have already seen to be a stock literary motif for older people. Another example is problems with sight (along with the loss or impairment of the other senses), especially cataract diseases and general dimming of vision.[75] The sexual impotence of the elderly male we have also often seen reference to, not least in Juvenal; sexual intercourse is typically said to be unsuitable (it expels much-needed moisture, especially in the case of males) if not impossible in old age.[76] Gout and arthritis also figure prominently as afflictions of older people, particularly of the wealthy old.[77] Difficulties with the digestion and evacuation of food (as Hippocrates and in particular Celsus, as we have seen, noted) are mentioned on occasion.[78] It was thus important to ensure as part of a regimen of health that older people evacuated their bladders and bowels at least once a day; Galen recommends that, rather than using drugs to effect this purpose, it is better to employ parsley, honey, or (once again) wine.[79] Sciatica and sleeplessness, also problems familiar enough to many older people today, warrant mention, albeit briefly.[80] Diseases of the kidney were regarded as particularly common, and difficult to treat, in old age.[81] It is probable that degenerative cardiovascular and pulmonary diseases (especially tuberculosis) were also common.[82] We also hear of older people suffering apoplexies or strokes, typically resulting in partial or complete paralysis; in such cases the condition tended to lead to a rapid demise.[83]

The visible, physical disabilities of old age, then, are the focus of the medical literature, just as we have seen them to be of much general literature. It is perhaps nowhere more graphically visible than in the common image of bowed old age, *curva senectus*.[84] One may recall again Juvenal's words, rejecting the utility of a prayer for long life: "quam continuis et quantis longa senectus plena malis" (How painful are the endless afflictions of which drawn-out old age is full).[85]

This brief survey of the medical literature in regard to old age highlights the fact that, while some discussion of and concern for old age and its associated ailments did exist, there was no separate field of geriatric medicine. Medical science in antiquity, and up until the past century, concerned itself, when it turned to older people at all, with the possibilities for the prolongation of life—or rather, perhaps, for not shortening its duration—through a regimen of diet and exercise, and with the observation of ailments; in other words, the emphasis was diagnostic and dietetic. In the face of the dearth of systematic treatment of gerontology in the classical Greek world, Robert Garland has observed: "The general lack of medical interest in the elderly may be explained as a reflection partly of the small number of geriatrics in the population and partly of professional helplessness in the face of the degenerative processes brought on by old age. It not only suggests that old people received little attention from doctors but hints as well at their emarginated social status."[86]

It might be argued that things improved for older people in the Roman world but this is only relative. Galen has more to say than any of his (extant) predecessors, but the progress is, in my view, minimal by comparative standards.[87] In simple quantitative terms, Galen's discussion of elderly patients and of the symptoms of old age (including much repetition) constitutes only some 0.6 percent of his extant works, by my rough calculation. Furthermore, it could be said that old age features in the ancient medical literature partly in order to fill out the picture, as it were: the dominant focus, in this sphere as elsewhere, is on the young and those in their prime; old age is added to provide the antithesis of the positive attributes of the adult male.

In view of the fact that older people constituted a not insignificant proportion of the population, we are left again with the conclusion that, as a marginal sector of society, older people—even those fortunate enough to be in a position to avail themselves of such a contingency—could expect little comfort from the doctor. Death is the only sure cure for the *insanabilis morbus;* Pliny the Elder sums the case up well:

> natura vero nihil hominibus brevitate vitae praestitit melius. hebescunt sensus, membra torpent, praemoritur visus, auditus, incessus, dentis etiam ac ciborum instrumenta, et tamen vitae hoc tempus adnumeratur.

> It is certainly true that Nature has granted to humankind no more precious gift than shortness of life. The senses grow sluggish, limbs grow numb, sight, hearing, walking, even teeth and the digestive tract, all die before their time—and yet people count this as a part of life.[88]

Old Age in Myth and Religion

Another area of Roman life in which old age figures is religion, in particular in the mythological ideas which the Romans inherited from the Greeks. In Rome "Youth," personified and deified as *Iuventa, Iuventas,* or *Iuventus*, was worshiped or at least glorified and was one center of attention and enthusiasm for the young.[89] Old age enjoyed no such prestige. The Romans inherited a personification of *Senectus* from the Greek Γῆρας, first explicitly attested in Hesiod.[90] The references in literature are several, and virtually identical: old age is one of a hideous troupe, incorporating all the malevolent features of life: grief, misery, disease, hunger, discord, envy, fear, poverty, greed, war, and the like, normally relegated to the Underworld but all too often unleashed on frail mortals.[91] The contrast with desirable youth could not be more evident; old age is feared rather than worshiped. The only known exception to this, remarked on twice in later antiquity solely for its uniqueness, is the altar of Γῆρας said to have been found in Gades, and possibly suggesting a cult. Apparently the people there were "excessive in religion," evidenced by the fact that they also sang paeans to death and had shrines to Πενία and Τέχνη, Poverty and Craft.[92] The exception proves the rule, itself not overly surprising, that old age as a personified concept to the Greeks and Romans merited not worship but awe, if not dread.

Old age, as the final stage of life rather than as a personality in its own right, does feature in the mythological depictions of mortal heroes and villains, but not of gods, who are held to be ageless and immortal, an honor on rare occasions also accorded to privileged mortals.[93] Many grotesque figures from mythology are old and haggard for the very reason, however, that this will invoke fear in the hearts of mortals; some of the most fearsome and loathsome creatures might in fact be classified as old spinsters, a sign of their complete isolation or marginality from "normal" society.[94] On the other hand attempts at rejuvenation and immortality by mortal men are frequently remarked upon, and both have been aspirations of humankind throughout history.[95] Galen mentions the intriguing case of a contemporary sophist who had, at the age of 40 years, published a book on how to avoid the effects of old age and remain perpetually young. By the time this fellow turned 80 years of age, however, age had indeed taken its toll, making him appear shriveled and dried out, and earning him general mockery. He then revised his book and brought out a second edition, stressing that only *some* individuals may enjoy eternal youth and that it is necessary to prepare from the earliest years; this sophist declares that, while he himself unfortunately started the process too late to save himself, he is prepared to undertake such a task for the benefit of the children of his fellow citizens—presumably for a substantial fee.[96] From the time of Homer mortals have wished for their old age to be scraped from them,[97] just as they observed that the snake sheds its wrinkled skin (also called γῆρας or *senectus/a*) and appears young again.[98] The prayer for a long life—and its pointlessness—has already been seen. Beyond prayers and doctors recourse might also be had to magic, in the hope of discovering "drugs to ward off ills and old age" (φάρμακα δ᾽ ὅσσα . . . κακῶν καὶ γήραος ἄλκαρ).[99]

If the participation of the aged person in public affairs was at times debated, his or her role in religious practices was not, and this again is a mark of marginalization, as Thomas Wiedemann has well remarked:

> Classical society relegated children, together with women, old men, and slaves, to the margins of community life. While that gave each of these groups an intermediate position between being fully human and being a beast, it might also give them a position intermediate between the human world and that of the gods. . . . The relative physical weakness of the child, the old man, and the woman, meant that these three groups were thought to require, or deserve, particular support from the supernatural. . . . It is because they are excluded from the political process or from social influence that they have no other way to express their concerns than by reference to powers outside the political community, controlled as it usually is by "rational" adult males. . . . It was this powerlessness that lay behind the assumption that "marginal" groups were more likely to be in touch with the divine world than were adult male citizens. . . . The old are thought to be particularly numinous.[100]

The religious role of elderly women has already been remarked upon earlier in this chapter, and we have seen in Chapter 3 how old females might be stereotyped as witches. Prophets and seers in literature were often depicted as marginal members of society: women and aged men.[101] Plato and Aristotle both remarked that in their ideal states religious duties would be reserved for those in old age.[102] In the Roman state the *paterfamilias,* as the senior male member of the household, had the duty to observe the customary religious rites, the worship of Lares, Penates, and ancestors. Priests at Rome need not be old, though the office normally lasted for life,[103] and, in line with traditional ideas of respect for age, seniority would normally be expected to be given to the oldest member of the college, or at least to the individual who had belonged to the college the longest.[104]

The impression remains, however, here as elsewhere, that the continued activity of older people depended on their own proven capability to perform the duties required. As marginal members of society any rights they held were far from automatic but had to be won and maintained through continued performance and incessant pressure. What may appear at first sight as privileges, such as the greater degree of freedom for women in later life, in many cases should be more closely defined as a diminution of status and a lack of concern by other sectors of society. As the capability or right to execute some functions in society disappeared, other functions had to be found if old people were not to be dismissed as *inutiles* and therefore, like Cato's aged slaves, as surplus to requirements. This potential threat to older people, implicit in much of what has been seen here, is perhaps nowhere more menacing than in one proverb current in the late republic and early empire. The feeling that old people, if no longer useful, should be disposed of is an extremist view rarely voiced explicitly in any "civilized" society (though voluntary euthanasia may be seen by some as a step in this direction). But the Romans had a proverb that could be interpreted as just such a threat, and with this proverb we shall close this chapter.

Sexagenarios de Ponte

There is a story of a New Zealand chief who, questioned as to the fortunes of a fellow-tribesman long ago well known to the enquirer, answered, "He gave us so much good advice that we put him mercifully to death." The reply, if it was ever given, combines the two views which barbarous men

> appear to have taken at different times of the
> aged. At first they are useless, burdensome, and
> importunate, and they fare accordingly. But at a later
> period a new sense of the value of wisdom and
> counsel raises them to the highest honour. Their
> long life comes to be recognised as one way of
> preserving experience.
> Maine (1883) 23–24

Sir Henry Maine's dichotomy is, to say the least, simplistic in modern anthropological terms, but it remains thought-provoking. It has already been seen that from around the age of 60 years a Roman male, willing or otherwise, could expect to be relieved of certain public duties. In some "primitive" preindustrial societies old people may be relieved even of the right to life, particularly if they are no longer held to be of much use in that society. The Greeks and Romans were aware of this practice, and ancient writers quite often remarked upon it; it was generally regarded as totally foreign, a contrast to their own civilized way of life. But it could also be seen as somewhat humorous, as in Herondas, when Gryllus is told, at the age of 60, to die and become ashes, or in Lucian, when Peregrinus of Mysia strangles his 60-year-old father, on the grounds that the latter has lived long enough.[105] Examples of a less jocular nature may also be found where a society's elderly voluntarily commit suicide or are sacrificed by the younger members of the society. A concise survey of such alleged cases of senicide, though widely spread not only geographically but also chronologically, is useful here.[106]

Some accounts are simply the stuff of legend. The Hyperboreans, a fabled race usually said to live in the far north, disposed of their elderly at the age of 60 years. According to Hellanicus, the Hyperboreans took their 60-year-olds outside the gates and killed them. Pomponius Mela, on the other hand, states that the elderly Hyperboreans, on achieving a full life ("vivendi satietas magis quam taedium"), quite cheerfully leapt from a certain rock into the ocean. Thus, an interesting discrepancy between forced and voluntary euthanasia. As a result of such a practice, at any rate, as Pindar noted, no age-related debilities or diseases affected the Hyperboreans![107] Around the globe, on a legendary island in the south (Sri Lanka? Utopia?), as Diodorus Siculus, summarizing the Hellenistic writer Iambulus, records, "the people are said to be extremely long-lived, living to the age of 150 years and being for the most part free from disease. If one of them becomes crippled or suffers from some physical infirmity, they force him, in accordance with an inexorable [ἀπότομον] law, to remove himself from life. And there is also a law among them that they should live only for a set number of years, and that at the completion of this period they should make away with themselves voluntarily" (by lying on a plant which makes them fall asleep). Diodorus goes on to note that the oldest male in each group rules until his death at the end of his 150th year, then the next oldest succeeds.[108]

In a more historical context, to turn first to the west of the classical world, Julius Caesar (*Bell. Gall.* 7.77) presents a speech by Critognatus, who cites the earlier example of the Gallic *oppida* besieged by the Cimbri and Teutones and who urges the people of the besieged town of Alesia (in 52 B.C.) to support themselves by eating those who seem "aetate ad bellum inutiles." His suggestion is left as a last resort, and those "valetudine aut aetate inutiles bello" were instead sent out of the town; reinforcements shortly thereafter arrived. In this case the action of senicide, mooted but rejected, was a one-off option. On the other hand, the Ligurians of southern Gaul routinely threw their parents, whenever they were no longer useful because of old age, off a cliff.[109] A similarly enforced system of euthanasia allegedly operated among the Heruli of Germany; Procopius (*Bell. Goth.* 2.14.2–5) reports that "they observed many customs which were not in accord with that of other men. For they were not permitted to live either when they grew old or when they fell sick [οὔτε γὰρ γηράσκουσιν οὔτε νοσοῦσιν αὐτοῖς βιοτεύειν ἐξῆν], but as soon as one of them was overtaken by old age or by sickness [ἐπειδάν τις αὐτῶν ἢ γήρᾳ ἢ νόσῳ ἁλώη], it became necessary for him to ask his relatives to remove him from the world as quickly as possible." The old man was stabbed to death and burned on a pyre. In Spain, according to Silius Italicus (*Pun.* 1.225–28), when a man has passed "florentes viribus annos" (the years flourishing in strength), rather than live on he scorns any acquaintance with old age ("impatiens aevi spernit novisse senectam") and ends his own life. Silius later (*Pun.* 3.328–31) describes the Cantabrians of northwest Spain and their distaste for a life of peace; "cum pigra incanuit aetas," they cut short the *inbelles anni* with death.

But it is from the more mysterious east that most reports of senicide come. The Padaeans of India, according to Herodotus (3.99), put to death and eat old people and anyone who is sick (whether they admit to being sick or not). Herodotus comments wryly that few Padaeans survive to old age, since all who are sick are killed before they have any chance of growing old. One may note also Pomponius Mela, who reports on a class of Indians who, "ubi senectus aut morbus incessit, procul a ceteris abeunt mortemque in solitudine nihil anxii expectant" (when old age or illness has set in, go off a distance from the others and await death in solitude and free from care); Philo provides similar details on the Indian *gymnosophistes* who perform self-immolation when illness or "the long and incurable disease of old age" makes its presence felt.[110] Further west, the Trogodytes,[111] a nomadic people of "Ethiopia" (around southern Egypt and northern Sudan), apparently routinely killed their elderly. Diodorus Siculus (3.33.5–6) records that among the Trogodytes, "those who can no longer accompany the flocks on account of old age [διὰ τὸ γῆρας] tie the tail of an ox tightly around their own necks and so put an end to their lives of their own free will; and if a man puts off his death, anyone who wishes has the authority to fasten the noose about his neck, as an act of goodwill, and, after rebuking the man, to take his life." The disabled (πηρωθέντας) and the terminally ill are similarly done away with, "for they consider it to be the greatest disgrace for a man to cling to life [φιλοψυχεῖν] when he is unable to accomplish anything worth living for. As a result, one can see every Trogodyte sound in body and still robust in years, since none of them lives beyond 60 years."

From the central Asian continent come many accounts of senicide. Among the Massagetae, in the north, beneath the Aral Sea (modern Turkestan), ἐπεὰν γέρων γένηται κάρτα (when a man has reached a very great age), according to Herodotus, all the relatives gather round and make a sacrificial offering of him; killing animals along with him, they boil the flesh and have a feast. Diseased deaths are not eaten but buried; it is regarded as a misfortune not to be so eaten.[112] South of the Massagetae lived the Bactrians and Sogdians, in the northeastern limits of Alexander's empire (northern Afghanistan and further north to southern Turkestan). According to Onesicritus, the old and sick there were thrown to specially trained dogs, "the undertakers," and hence the streets were strewn with bones. Alexander, the "civilizing" agent—and as a result of whose conquests many of these tales, no doubt, arose and spread—put a stop to the practice.[113] The Derbiccae, east of the Caspian sea and north of Parthia, also killed their male kin over the age of 70 years and ate them; their aged women they merely strangled and buried.[114] The Hyrcanians, southeast of the Caspian Sea, immediately south of the Derbiccae (i.e., in northwest Iran), left their (living) aged parents to be devoured by birds and dogs.[115] Similarly the Caspians, west of the southern end of the Caspian sea (i.e., north of the Armenians, and to the south of the Caucasus Mountains), shut in their parents who were over 70 years of age and let them starve to death—a practice more tolerable, Strabo says, than outright murder. They left the corpses to be consumed by birds and dogs.[116] Somewhat more dramatically, the Tibarenians, to the south of the Black Sea (northern Turkey), threw their aged relatives alive from the top of a precipice.[117] And finally from the east, the Iazyges of Sarmatia, who originally dwelt east of the Tanais but who moved west over the course of the last three centuries B.C. to settle to the east of Pannonia and the Danube, had "no acquaintance with gray-haired old age" (expertes canentis aevi), according to Valerius Flaccus (*Argon.* 6.122–28), for when their "strength became icy" (vires gelidae) and they could no longer use their weapons, they followed a custom inherited from their "great-hearted ancestors" (magnanimis . . . avis) and gave a sword to their children to dispatch them, thus avoiding a slow death. Claudian (*in Rufin.* 1.328) reports that the Huns love to swear oaths by their murdered parents; one assumes from the context that the offspring have murdered them.

All very barbaric, but it is important to stress that such practices were not just reported in classical times as having occurred in the wild west or in the far distant and illusory east. Sidonius Apollinaris reported that in Thrace "consummatamque senectam non ferro finire pudet" (it is a shameful thing not to put an end with the sword to an old age which has run its course, *Carm.* 2.44–45). In Sardinia, according to the historians Timaeus (*FGH* 566 F 64) and Demon (*FGH* 327 F 18), whose accounts were quoted and embellished by numerous later authors, *scholia*, and *lexica*,[118] sacrifices were made "to Cronus" (= "because of old age"?), in which the Sardinians killed their fathers after the latter had reached 70 years of age, by hitting them with clubs and throwing them over a cliff. Hence, according to this version, the Sardonic smile: either the insane grin of the victim, or the laughter of the younger Sardinians.

The island of Ceos provides perhaps the most famous example. It was well known in antiquity that there was a custom or law determining that older people (by most accounts, those over 60 years of age) drink hemlock. Apparently it was particularly common among women, at least according to one source: οὔσης δὲ ὑγιεινῆς τῆς νήσου καὶ εὐγήρων τῶν ἀνθρώπων, μάλιστα δὲ τῶν γυναικῶν, οὐ περιμένουσι γηραιοὶ τελευτᾶν, ἀλλὰ πρὶν ἀσθενῆσαι ἢ πηρῶθεναί τι, οἱ μὲν μήκωνι οἱ δὲ κωνείῳ ἑαυτοὺς ἐξάγουσι (Since the island has a healthy climate and men and especially women reach a fine old age, they do not wait for death when they are old, but before they become ill or disabled in any way, some poison themselves with poppy, others with hemlock).[119] The "law" is elsewhere cited with particular reference to the siege of Ceos by the Athenians, when the Ceians voted that the oldest be put to death so that there might be enough food for the rest.[120] Vestiges of the practice remained even down to Roman imperial times, at least in terms of voluntary euthanasia. Valerius Maximus relates that in the town of Iulis on Ceos, a noble and very healthy lady of 90 years ("ultimae iam senectutis. . . . nonagesimum annum transgressa cum summa et animi et corporis sinceritate") was about to take hemlock with the citizen body's approval; Sex. Pompeius, on his way to take up the proconsulship of Asia (ca. A.D. 27), tried to deter her, but on hearing her arguments he was finally persuaded and she did away with herself.[121]

In short, an abundance of material relating to senicide and euthanasia exists. Many features recur: the need to dispose of older people (or have them dispose of themselves) in order to save food (and in a few cases create food),[122] or the wish to dispose of them, particularly if they are physically decrepit, because they are regarded as useless. On the other hand, there appears in some cases the idea that as people enter their 60s or 70s[123] they should, as it were, quit while the going is good; the focus, here as elsewhere, tends often to be on males, but that reflects, I would argue, the nature of the sources, and not a special status for women. The ubiquitous principle is neatly summed up by Menander:[124] ὁ μὴ δυνάμενος ζῆν καλῶς οὐ ζῇ κακῶς (he who is unable to live well should not live badly), and its implicit logic, not seen as barbaric, is familiar from Stoic doctrines also.[125] More often than not the slaying is a public affair, with religious overtones of human sacrifice, although as a propitiary offering one can imagine that an aged individual might not always be seen as the greatest sacrifice.[126] At any rate, the practice of senicide is typically seen as foreign, antithetical to classical practices and beliefs, although some of the examples cited above seem to be uncomfortably close to home. Throughout the narratives, furthermore, one may detect the writer's fascination with, if not revulsion at, the subject. But as Livy maintained, human sacrifice was far from Roman ("minime Romano sacro"), and Pliny the Elder argued that one of Rome's great contributions to civilization was the abolition of such *monstra*.[127]

Yet testimony survives to suggest that the concept, if not the practice, of the disposal of older people was considered at Rome, in the form of a rather mysterious (to modern scholars as well as to Romans at the time) proverb, that 60-year-olds should be thrown from the bridge. A catalog of references, in approximate chronological order, is called for.

L. Afranius frag. 301 (*Repudiatus* 8), *ap.* Festus 452L (quoted below).[128]

Varro *ap.* Nonius Marcellus 316L and 122L (*Menipp.* 493–94 Astbury, *Sexagesis* 18–19):[129]

"acciti sumus ut depontaremur. murmur sit [fit?] ferus" . . . vix ecfatus erat, cum more maiorum ultro carnales[130] arripiunt, de ponte in Tiberim deturbant.

"We were summoned so that we might be thrown from the bridge. Let there be a wild outcry" . . . Scarcely had he spoken out, when, following the custom of our ancestors, of their own accord the executioners [?] grab them and toss them from the bridge into the Tiber.

Varro *ap.* Nonius Marcellus 842L (cf. Chapter 4 note 147):

sexagenarios per pontem mittendos[131] male diu popularitas in-
tellexit, cum Varro de Vita Populi Romani lib. II [frag. 71 Riposati
= 87 Semi] honestam causam religiosamque patefecerit: "cum in
quintum gradum pervenerant atque habebant sexaginta annos, tum
denique erant a publicis negotiis liberi atque otiosi. ideo in prover-
bium quidam putant venisse, ut diceretur sexagenarios de ponte de-
ici oportere id est, quod suffragium non ferant, quod per pontem
ferebant."

For a long time popular opinion has misunderstood the proverb that
the 60-year-olds should be sent over the bridge, although Varro made
clear the respectable origin, a devout one . . . : "When they had entered
the fifth age-grade and were 60 years of age, then at last they were released from public duties and permitted a life of leisure. Hence some
believe that it became proverbial, so that it was said that 60-year-olds
should be thrown from the bridge, that is that they should not have
the right to the vote, which they used to carry over the bridge."

Cicero *pro Rosc. Amer.* 35.100, on T. Roscius Capito and his various
modes of murder (80 B.C.):

habeo etiam dicere quem contra morem maiorum minorem annis
sexaginta de ponte in Tiberim deiecerit.

I can even tell you of one man whom, contrary to the custom of our
ancestors, he threw from the bridge into the Tiber, even though he
was not yet 60 years of age.[132]

Catullus 17: the bridge at "Colonia" (Verona?) on which dancing
takes place and from which Catullus wishes a certain (presumably
cuckolded) fellow *municeps* to be thrown headlong into the mud.
There is no explicit reference to him as a *sexagenarius,* but it is likely
that Catullus has the proverb in mind.[133]

Ovid *Fasti* 5.623–24, 633–34:

corpora post decies senos qui credidit annos
missa neci, sceleris crimine damnat avos . . .
pars putat, ut ferrent iuvenes suffragia soli,
pontibus infirmos praecipitasse senes.

He who believes that after 60 years men were put to death, accuses
our forefathers of a heinous crime. . . . Some think that, in order that

the young men alone should have the right to vote, they used to hurl the feeble old men from the bridges.

Festus 450–52L = 334M:[134]

sexagenarios <de ponte olim deiciebant,> cuius causam Mani<lius [?] hanc refert, quod Roma>m qui incoluerint <primi Aborigines, aliquem> hominem, sexaginta <annorum qui esset, immola>re Diti patri quot<annis soliti fuerint.> quod facere eos de<stitisse adventu Her>culis; sed religio<sa veteris ritus observatione> scirpeas hominum ef<figies de ponte in Tiberim antiquo> modo mittere <instituisse.

alii dicun>t, morante in Italia <Hercule, quod quidam e>ius comitum habitave<rint secundum rip>am [haberi] <Tiberis ?>, atque Arga<eos se a patria voca>verint Ar<gis>, quorum pro<pagatam memori>am redintegrari eo ge<nere sacri.

alii, e Graeci>a legatum quondam Arga<eum temporibus antiqu>is[si] Romae moratum esse. [h]is ut <ex vita excesseri>t, institutum a sacerdotibus, ut <effigies s>cirpea ex omnibus, cumque publicae < . . . . nu>ntiavisset, per flumen ac mare in patriam remitteretur.

sunt, qui dicant, post urbem a Gallis liberatam, ob inopiam cibatus, coeptos sexaginta annorum homines iaci in Tiberim, ex quo numero unus, filii pietate occultatus, saepe profuerit <pa>triae consilio, sub persona filii. id ut sit cognitum, ei iuveni esse ignotum, et sexsagenaris [sic] vita concessa.[135] latebras autem eius, quibus ar<c>uerit senem, id est cohibuerit et celaverit, sanctitate dignas esse visas, ideoque Arcaea appellata.

sed exploratissimum illud est causae, quo tempore primum per pontem coeperunt comitiis suffragium ferre, iuniores conclamaverunt, ut de ponte deicerentur sexagenari, qui iam nullo publico munere fungerentur, ut ipsi potius sibi quam illi deligerent imperatorem: cuius sententia<e> est etiam Sinnius Capito. vanam autem opinionem de ponti Tiberino confirmavit Afranius in Repudiato.

In the past they used to throw 60-year-olds from the bridge. The explanation for this Manilius [?] gives as follows: the first natives who lived at Rome were accustomed to sacrifice every year a man who was 60 years of age to Dis Pater. They stopped doing this on the arrival of Hercules; instead there was established, as the sacred observation of the old rite, the throwing of bullrush effigies of men from the bridge into the Tiber, in the ancient manner.

Others say it is because, while Hercules was lingering in Italy, certain of his companions were living on the bank of the Tiber and they called themselves Argei after their native land of Argos [?], and their memory might be revived and maintained by this type of ancestral rite.

Others say that in ancient times an Argive legate from Greece once stayed at Rome. When he died a rite was set up by the priests, in which a bullrush effigy, after . . . had publicly announced it, was . . . from everyone and he was sent back to his native land by river and sea.

There are those who would say that after the city had been freed from the Gauls, because of the shortage of food, men of 60 years began to be thrown into the Tiber. One of them, hidden through the piety of his son, often served his country well with his advice in the guise of his son. When this fact was discovered, the young man was forgiven and the 60-year-olds were given the right to live. His hiding place where he had "treasured" the old man, that is, kept and concealed him, seemed worthy of sanctity, and so was called Arcaea.

But the best-researched explanation is that at the time that they first began to cast their votes over the bridges at the assemblies, the younger men exclaimed that the 60-year-olds should be thrown from the bridge, since they no longer performed any public duty; hence they, the younger men, and not the old men, should choose a leader for themselves. This is the opinion also of Sinnius Capito. Moreover, that the opinion about the Tiber bridge is groundless Afranius established in his *Repudiatus*.

Paulus *ex* Festus 66L:

> depontani senes appellabantur, qui sexagenarii de ponte deiciebantur.

> Old men used to be called *depontani,* in that 60-year-olds used to be thrown from the bridge.

Lactantius *Inst. Div.* 1.21.6–7 (cf. Schiebe 1999):

> apparet tamen anticum esse hunc immolandorum hominum ritum, siquidem Saturnus in Latio eodem genere sacrificii cultus est, non quidem ut homo ad aram immolaretur, sed ut in Tiberim de ponte

Mulvio[136] mitteretur. quod ex responso quodam factitatum Varro
auctor est: cuius responsi ultimus versus est talis: καὶ κεφαλὰς
Ἀίδη[137] καὶ τῷ πατρὶ πέμπετε φῶτα. [id est hominem.] quod quia
videtur ambiguum, et fax illi et homo iaci solet.

Nevertheless it is clear that this rite of sacrificing human victims is
ancient, if indeed Saturn was honored in Latium with the same kind
of sacrifice—not indeed that a man should be slain at the altar, but
that he be thrown from the Milvian bridge into the Tiber. And Varro
relates that this was done in accordance with an oracle, the last verse
of which is as follows: "And offer heads to Hades, and to the father
a man/lights." Because this appears ambiguous, it is the custom for
both a torch and a man to be thrown to him.

Lactantius, quoting Ovid "in Fastis," goes on to note that Hercules,
returning from Spain, put a stop to the practice (compare this with
Festus above), and that *imagines e scirpo,* images made from rushes,
replaced human beings. The link with *sexagenarii* is only made in
the *Epitome* 18.2:

etiam ante Saturno sexagenarii homines ex persona [sc. responso]
Apollinis de ponte in Tiberim deiciebantur.

Even earlier, in honor of Saturn, men of 60 years of age, according
to the oracle of Apollo, were thrown from a bridge into the Tiber.

Fortunatianus *Ars Rhet.* 1.14 (*RLM* 92.23–25):

more quem ad modum fit? "mos apud Scythas[138] fuit, ut sexagenarii per pontem mitterentur: Scytha Athenis sexagenarium patrem
per pontem deiecit, reus est parricidii." hic enim se dicit gentis suae
more fecisse.

How is it done according to custom? "It was the custom among the
Scythians that 60-year-olds were sent over the bridge: a Scythian at
Athens throws his 60-year-old father over the bridge, he is charged
with parricide." For this man says he did it according to the custom
of his race.

Prudentius *contra Symm.* 2.291–95 (on the barbarity of *primi homines* and the dangers of returning to such customs):

inmanes quondam populi feritate subacta
edomiti iam triste fremant iterumque ferinos

269

> in mores redeant atque ad sua prisca recurrant.
> praecipitet Scythica iuvenis pietate vietum[139]
> votivo de ponte patrem (sic mos fuit olim).

> Let races that were once barbarous but had their savagery subdued
> and became civilized once more issue their harsh cries and return
> to their wild ways, going back to their former state. Let the young
> man, with Scythian piety, fling his wrinkled father as an offering
> from the bridge (for such was once the custom).

Macrobius *Sat.* 1.5.10:

> et heus tu hisne tam doctis viris, quorum M. Cicero et Varro imita-
> tores se gloriantur, adimere vis in verborum comitiis ius suffragandi,
> et tamquam sexagenarios maiores de ponte deicies?

> And when it comes to voting in the elections of words, would you
> disenfranchise such learned men as these, whom Cicero and Varro
> boast that they imitate, and would you throw them from the bridge
> as our ancestors did 60-year-old men?

This body of testimony offers many interesting glimpses of a proverb familiar enough for both Cicero and Catullus to refer to it allu-
sively, and for neologisms such as *depontare* and *depontani* to enter the
language. Festus offers the most detailed explanations of the origin of
the proverb, but the fragmentary nature of the text hampers progress.
As a result modern scholarship on the subject has been free to make
what presumptions it will, finding in the proverbial activity traces of
ancient religious, military, or political practices;[140] but "eine plausible
Erklärung steht aus."[141] Most scholarly attention has been focused on
the question, as formulated by Varro, Ovid, and Sinnius Capito (*ap.*
Festus), of whether Romans in the past actually *killed* their 60-year-old
men by throwing them from a bridge into the Tiber, or deprived them
of the right to vote in the *comitia,* symbolized by casting them down
from the voting bridge. The latter interpretation, favored by the three
ancient authors mentioned, must surely be seen, to quote Frazer, as "a
pious antiquary's attempt to save the credit of his barbarous forefathers."[142] At any rate, even if this version of the story were correct, it
would prove only that old men did *not* lose the vote.

But the other popular interpretation, that older people at Rome were
killed, perhaps when the city was under siege by the Gauls around 390

B.C. (Festus's fourth explanation), seems to me to hold no greater historical credibility. What we have is a proverb, not a statement of fact. It is possible that it was Afranius, in the second century B.C., who invented the saying in the first place, as part of a comic representation, and that his idea was developed by Varro (again in a comic context, at least in part); thence the saying became so well known that some explanation had to be found as to its origin. Néraudau has pointed out the chronological coincidence of many of the relevant details:[143] bridges were used for voting from the later part of the second century B.C. (the period of the *leges tabellariae*), roughly the time when Afranius was writing; Cicero's and Varro's contributions both date to the first half of the first century B.C.; Manilius, the name conjectured at the beginning of the Festus passage, was quite probably the same individual who claimed to have seen the oracular pronouncement from Dodona (on which see Lactantius, quoted earlier); he may be identified, furthermore, with a senator of 97 B.C. who, according to Pliny the Elder, wrote on the phoenix, itself the very paragon of long life.[144] On closer analysis, however, cracks in this tidy argument begin to appear. The oracle from Dodona, for example, makes no mention of 60-year-olds, and Dionysius of Halicarnassus in quoting the pronouncement actually reads Λεύκιος Μάμιος, the *nomen* being routinely amended to Μάλλιος.[145] Our man might just as likely, or unlikely, be Manius Manilius, the consul of 149 B.C., who was a famous orator and jurist as well—hence, perhaps, an interest in the voting rights of older men.[146] I would like to note in passing another Manilius with an apparent interest in old age: Varro quotes a two-line poetical fragment by one Manilius containing the word *cascus* twice and referring to the wedding of an aged couple.[147]

In any event, the notion that the proverb was invented in the later republic makes much sense; by the time of Sinnius Capito, under Augustus, perhaps a sociological explanation for a comic invention was required. Although there is, it seems to me, a problem with the fact that the antiquity of the proverb is assumed already by Varro and Cicero (*mos maiorum,* though that need not mean the too distant past), it is on the other hand somewhat striking that Plautus makes no reference to the proverb where he well might—but of course it is pointless to argue from silence.[148]

The relationship of the proverb to the Argei, the straw puppets thrown into the Tiber, on first sight also appears strong, and certainly the similarities were noted (i.e., by Ovid and Festus, and in the *Epitome* of Lactantius).[149] But again the coincidences are probably a result of later attempts at explanation and not of original links. In accounts of the Argei there is nothing to suggest old men, and the number of puppets, twenty-seven (or, by Dionysius of Halicarnassus's account, thirty), has no association with *sexagenarios de ponte* either.[150] Too many scholars have too readily connected two different proverbs.[151]

It is not that senicide could never have occurred in Rome's past,[152] simply that the existence of this proverb cannot be taken as evidence for such a practice. The siege by the Gauls offered later writers a plausible historical context in which to place the proverb,[153] but it is clear from the testimony we have that Romans had no more definite historical explanation for *sexagenarios de ponte* than we do.[154]

But the proverb remains of interest to us here because it yet again points to older people being to some degree set aside or marginalized from the rest of society. Whatever the real origins of the saying, the fact that it was interpreted in various ways, all negative in import in regard to *sexagenarii,* is significant in itself. With the underlying sentiment that turning 60 years of age brings with it a different or lesser role in the life of the city, it may be seen that the proverb represents a further potential threat to older people's position, it being interpreted at the time either as a feeling that *senes,* because they no longer perform an active military function, should lose the right to vote, or that *senes,* because they are a burden on society, should lose the right to live. The Romans, like the Greeks, recorded with detailed and prurient horror the barbaric practices of euthanasia among other, "less civilized" societies, yet the possibility that in the past they themselves had not shown old age the respect some held it warranted was not excluded.

Final Remarks

Reconnaissons toutefois qu'un travail d'érudition
prend, au moins pour celui qui l'exécute, un intérêt
singulier, s'il le peut rattacher à un problème qui,
étudié dans une époque déterminée, avec les
caractères propres à cette époque, trouve encore un
écho dans les consciences contemporaines.
Roussel (1942) 132

A knowledge of aging in the past . . . is evidently
necessary in order to recognize how novel the
situation now is in the advanced countries. There is
no other way of grasping that fact.
Laslett (1995) 3

My aim in this book has been to present various aspects of aging and older people in the Roman world. The chapters have looked at definitions for old age, ancient and modern, and the means of recording age; the proportion of the population who might be classified as "elderly" (in spite of low expectation of life at birth, a not insignificant percentage of the adult population was in its 60s or 70s); what the literature can (and cannot) tell us about attitudes toward old age and older people; the role of older people in public and private life and the extent to which age was an important factor in public and private concerns; and the varied realities of life for older people, both within the household and within the community. Although discovering the realities of life for the poorer classes (as well as for females in general) will always be difficult, certain factors have been discussed here, in particular with regard to the life of the family, which show the perils that old age could hold for rich and poor, male and female, alike. In public life and in literature the focus inevitably centers around the wealthy minority, although Roman Egypt has allowed us to go beyond this limitation. From all such evidence an overall impression of many aspects of the life of elderly people in the ancient Roman world may be gleaned. In tying together many of these themes, as well as introducing some new ones, Chapter 9 serves in many ways as a conclusion to this book. But I would like to finish with a few further remarks.

One aspect of the study of age that has not featured at any length in this book—because it was never a feature of the Roman world—is that of age-class systems. Anthropologists have studied in depth the occurrence of such institutionalized and formally graded age-groupings in African societies in particular,[1] and some features of such a system may also be said to have operated in selected ancient Greek *poleis,* in particular Sparta and Crete, as well as to a certain extent in Athens.[2] A fundamental aspect of such age-class systems is their function as a means of distributing and rotating power; it may be summed up in the simple sentiment—one that, as has been seen, was regularly expressed in antiquity but, in Rome at least, not always followed—that it is the place of the young to obey, of the old to rule. The absence of such a system in the ancient Roman world, where the social structure was aligned more in terms of male kinship groups, or in patronage (and, to some extent, wealth), is itself important. We have found that age-grading existed at Rome only in a very limited fashion: as part of the philosophical topos, inherited from the Greeks, of *gradus aetatum;* and as a military distinction between *iuniores* and *seniores.* In a broader sphere no such formal age distinctions occurred. The rules of age we have discussed operated at a much more limited level, dictating for practical purposes at what ages an individual was eligible for, liable to, or exempt from certain privileges or duties. Age-class systems did not operate in Rome and its empire, any more than they do in modern Western societies, and in this respect, therefore, it should be noted that, in the study of the Roman elderly, anthropological studies of modern, developing societies are of less use for comparison than historical material from, for example, early modern Europe. If an age-class system had operated in Rome, the likes of Cicero may have felt more secure in the knowledge that political leadership (and with it esteem) was reserved for older people; it was precisely this aspect that Cicero and company admired in the Spartan system, while deploring the disengagement which their own society fostered.[3]

If elderly Roman males felt that they did not wield the power in the state that they should, at home the situation may not have been entirely different, for male and female alike. In spite of the theoretical dominance of the *paterfamilias,* it has been suggested here that in reality the aged members of the family were often in a situation of dependence on the younger generations, and a dependence without security at that, because the obligation to support elderly parents rested more on *pietas* than strict law and, from at least the time of Plautus, was implicitly called into question.

The various aspects discussed in the chapters of this book have individually built up a quite detailed picture, where old age is seen by all but elderly individuals themselves as a threat in the future. It is also an age that older people themselves might see as a time not so much to be enjoyed (a golden age) as to be endured,[4] while ensuring that privileges are accrued rather than that their rights are taken away. We must always be sensitive to the possibilities of differences over time and space, subtle differences upon which the available testimony will not allow us to elaborate. But I believe it is fair to close with a generalization of this sort, that although criteria of age played an important part in public and private life alike, old age, the inevitable conclusion of a long life and the precursor to death, was not accorded in practice the esteem or authority that people such as Cicero and Plutarch in their own old age felt it merited. Whatever the scattered expressions of reverence for old age might suggest, there is nothing to indicate any significantly positive role for "the elderly" as a group in the Roman world, whether as decision makers or as advisers. Privileges granted to old age generally took the form of *exemptions* from duties (not always freely given at that), rather than positive benefits. The feeling was, to put it in very general terms, that old age was a time not of power or authority but of acceptance of the realities of aging and, when necessary, of withdrawal, with the minimum of fuss. As one maxim of the Delphic canon had put it, γῆρας προσδέχου—accept old age.[5] The primary factor that ultimately determined an older person's place in the society was the health, mental and physical, that that person did or did not enjoy: in short, his or her social "worth."[6] While we might talk of someone of advanced years reaching "a good age," to the Romans it was those of younger years who enjoyed a *bona aetas;* old age, by contrast, had been known as the *mala aetas.*[7]

It must be added, however, that for the Romans old age was less of a "problem," at least for men, than all too often it is regarded by us today. By this I mean not that old age was a more comfortable state then than now; what we have seen here precludes such a general assessment. Rather it is the case that old age in Roman times was not seen formally as a different or distinctive stage of the life cycle to the same extent that it is in modern Western societies. It is not that the ancients had not "discovered" old age but that in the absence of wage labor as the standard way of life and of a retirement age in general life, people were expected simply to go on doing whatever they had always done until they dropped. While they had no geriatric skills to speak of, the Romans did not in reality seek to shorten the life course. Old age, with all the negative features it might entail, was still regarded as part of the natural course of adult life. In that sense systematic and deliberate marginalization of older people did *not* occur.

As we enter the twenty-first century, the "over-60s" constitute close to 20 percent of the total population of most developed nations. This "problem" of the aging population has meant that much attention has focused on old age. If we are to learn practical lessons from history it is from the failings as well as the glories of the past. If nothing else, history can lead us to reflect on comparisons and contrasts between our own conceptualization of old age and elderly individuals and that of the Romans. There is a world of differences between the two—in realities and in ideals—but at the same time there is so much that rings as true now as it did then. And that continuity is surely cause for reflection.

Haec habui de senectute quae dicerem: ad quam utinam perveniatis, ut ea quae ex me audistis re experti probare possitis.

Appendix A

Tables

Table 1

Gradus Aetatum: The Age at Which "Old Age" Commences

Age in Years	Source
42	Hippocrates *de Hebd.* 5 (*schol. ad* Pollux *Onom.* 2.4)
46	Cicero *de Sen.* 17.60: ("ita quantum spatium aetatis maiores ad senectutis initium esse voluerunt") (but see Chapter 4 note 27)
48	*Anthologia Palatina* 14.127 (Metrodorus)
49	Galen *in Hipp. Aph.* 3.29 (17B.643K); Isidorus *Diff.* 2.19.74–76
56	Hippocrates *de Hebd.* 5 (Philo *de Opif. Mundi* 36.105; Censorinus *de Die Nat.* 14.3; *MS. Cod. Phil.* 1529, 8.633L; Boissonade *Anec. Graec.* 2 p. 456); cf. Philostratus *Vit. Soph.* 1.25.543
60	Hippocrates *de Articulis* 41 (4.182L); Varro *ap.* Censorinus *de Die Nat.* 14.2; Pythagoras *ap.* Diogenes Laertius 8.10
63	Hippocrates *de Hebd.* 5 (*Paris MS* 7027, 8.636L; *schol. ad* Hesiod *W&D* 447; Boissonade *Anec. Graec.* 2 p. 455; *Cod. Ambros.* G 108f., 9.436L); Hippocrates *Coac. Praenot.* 5.30.502 (5.700L); Philo *de Opif. Mundi* 35.104 (Solon); Censorinus *de Die Nat.* 14.15–16
69	Dionysius of Halicarnassus *Din.* 4; Ptolemy *Tetrabiblos* 4.10.206–7
70	Isidorus *Orig.* 11.2; Macrobius *Comm.* 1.6.76
77	Staseas and the Etruscan *libri fatales* (Censorinus *de Die Nat.* 14.5–6, 10); cf. Isidorus *Diff.* 2.19.74–76 (beginning of *senium*)

Table 2

Centenarians in the Eighth *Regio* of Italy in A.D. 73/74

Age in Years	Number of Individuals in	
	Pliny	Phlegon
100–109	54	63
110–19	14	5
120–29	10	1
130+	12	1
Total	90	70

Table 3
Different Mortality Levels in a Stationary Population:
Coale-Demeny² Model West levels 1–5 Female

Age	(1) e_x	(1) C_x	(2) e_x	(2) C_x	(3) e_x	(3) C_x	(4) e_x	(4) C_x	(5) e_x	(5) C_x
0	20.00	3.81	22.50	3.48	25.00	3.21	27.50	2.98	30.00	2.78
1	30.32	10.50	32.61	9.98	34.85	9.53	37.04	9.12	39.21	8.75
5	36.59	11.24	38.35	10.87	40.06	10.53	41.75	10.21	43.40	9.91
10	34.30	10.55	35.92	10.27	37.50	10.00	39.05	9.74	40.58	9.50
15	31.23	9.87	32.75	9.66	34.24	9.46	35.70	9.26	37.13	9.07
20	28.52	9.06	29.93	8.94	31.31	8.81	32.67	8.68	34.00	8.55
25	26.14	8.18	27.43	8.15	28.69	8.10	29.93	8.04	31.14	7.97
30	23.83	7.29	25.00	7.34	26.14	7.36	27.25	7.37	28.34	7.37
35	21.61	6.42	22.64	6.53	23.65	6.62	24.64	6.69	25.61	6.75
40	19.34	5.59	20.25	5.76	21.13	5.91	22.00	6.03	22.84	6.13
45	16.92	4.82	17.71	5.04	18.48	5.22	19.23	5.39	19.97	5.53
50	14.26	4.06	14.96	4.30	15.64	4.52	16.30	4.71	16.94	4.89
55	11.80	3.26	12.40	3.52	12.99	3.75	13.56	3.97	14.11	4.17
60	9.43	2.41	9.94	2.67	10.44	2.91	10.93	3.14	11.40	3.35
65	7.55	1.58	7.96	1.80	8.37	2.03	8.76	2.25	9.13	2.46
70	5.80	0.88	6.13	1.05	6.45	1.23	6.75	1.41	7.05	1.59
75	4.39	0.37	4.64	0.47	4.88	0.58	5.11	0.70	5.33	0.83
80	3.22	0.10	3.40	0.14	3.57	0.19	3.73	0.25	3.89	0.31
85	2.31	0.02	2.43	0.03	2.54	0.04	2.66	0.07	2.76	0.09
Average age	25.49		26.41		27.27		28.09		28.87	
C_{60+}	5.36		6.16		6.98		7.82		8.63	

Table 4

Older People as a Proportion of the Population:
Based on Coale-Demeny[2] Model West level 3 Female: $e_0 = 25$ Years

(A)	Number in Age-Group in a Population of				
Age-Group	10,000	25,000	50,000	100,000	500,000
<20 years	4,273	10,683	21,365	42,730	213,650
20–59 years	5,029	12,572	25,145	50,290	251,450
≥60 years	698	1,745	3,490	6,980	34,900

(B)	Number Surviving at Age				
Age-Cohort	40	50	60	70	80
100,000 at birth	31,208	24,389	16,712	7,934	1,644
100,000 at age 10	61,006	47,676	32,669	15,509	3,214
100,000 at age 20	68,238	53,328	36,542	17,348	3,595
100,000 at age 30	80,820	63,161	43,280	20,547	4,258

(C)	Age-Groups as a Percentage of the Total Population				
Age-group (years)	60–64	65–69	70–74	75–79	80+
% of total poulation	2.91	2.03	1.23	0.58	0.23
Age-group (years)	60–64	60–69	60–74	60–79	60+
Cumulative % total	2.91	4.94	6.17	6.75	6.98

Table 5

Minimum Ages for First Magistracies

	Quaestorship	Aedileship	Praetorship	Consulship
Before 180 B.C.				
Patrician	25	33	33–37	37–40
Plebeian	30–	35	36– 40	40+
180–81 B.C.				
lex Villia annalis	(25–30?)	36	39	42
Evidence from careers	29–30	36–37	39–40	42–44
80–ca.49 B.C.				
Patrician	30	34	37	(40?)
Plebeian	30	36	39	42
Principate				
Patrician	24/25		29/30	32–34
Plebeian	24/25		29/30	(39–42?)

Table 6

Iterated Consulships in the Principate (Omitting Imperial Consulships)

	Cos. I	Cos. II	Cos. III	Gap
T. Statilius Taurus	37 B.C.	26 B.C. *ord.*		11
Q. Sanquinius Maximus	A.D. 21/2	A.D. 39		17–18
L. Vitellius	34 *ord.*	43 *ord.*	47 *ord.*	9, 4
C. Sallustius Passienus Crispus	27	44 *ord.*		17
M. Vinicius	30 *ord.*	45 *ord.*		15
D. Valerius Asiaticus	35	46 *ord.*		11
L. Salvius Otho Titianus	52 *ord.*	69		17
L. Verginius Rufus	63 *ord.*	69	97 *ord.*	6, 28
C. Licinius Mucianus	64?	70	72	6?, 2
T. Flavius Sabinus	69	72		3
Ti. Plautius Silvanus Aelianus	45	74		29
L. Iunius Q. Vibius Crispus	61?	74	83?	13?, 9?
T. Clodius Eprius Marcellus	62	74		12
Q. Petillius Cerialis Caesius Rufus	70?	74		4?
L. Tampius Flavianus	44/5	75?		30–31?
M. Pompeius Silvanus Staberius Flavianus	45	75/6?	83? *des.*	30–31?, 7–8?
A. Didius Gallus Fabricius Veiento	74?	80	83?	6?, 3?
Q. Petillius Rufus [or same as cos. II 74?]	73?	83 *ord.*		10?
T. Aurelius Fulvus	70	85 *ord.*		15
Q. Iulius Cordinus C. Rutilius Gallicus	71/2	85		13–14
M. Arrecinus Clemens	72/3?	85		12–13?

L. Valerius Catullus Messallinus	73 *ord.*	85		12
M. Cocceius Nerva	71 *ord.*	90 *ord.*		19
A. Lappius Maximus	86	95		9
Cn. Arrius Antoninus	69	97?		28?
Sex. Iulius Frontinus	73?	98	100 *ord.*	25?, 2
T. Vestricius Spurinna	73?	98		25?
L. Iulius Ursus	84	98	100	14, 2
Cn. Domitius Tullus	?	98		?
L. Licinius Sura	?	102 *ord.*	107 *ord.*	?, 5
L. Iulius Ursus Servianus	90	102 *ord.*	134 *ord.*	12, 32
M'. Laberius Maximus	89	103 *ord.*		14
P. Metilius (Sabinus) Nepos	91	103?		12?
Q. Glitius Atilius Agricola	97	103		6
Sex. Attius Suburanus Aemilianus	101	104 *ord.*		3
Ti. Iulius Candidus Marius Celsus	86	105 *ord.*		19
C. Antius A. Iulius Quadratus	94	105 *ord.*		11
Q. Sosius Senecio	99 *ord.*	107 *ord.*		8
A. Cornelius Palma Frontonianus	99 *ord.*	109 *ord.*		10
C. Iulius Proculus (see Birley 1997: 231–36)	?	109 suff. ?		?
L. Publilius Celsus	102	113 *ord.*		11
L. Catilius Severus Iulianus Claudius Reginus	110	120 *ord.*		10
M. Annius Verus	97	121 *ord.*	126 *ord.*	24, 5
M. Lollius Paullinus D. Valerius Asiaticus Saturninus	94	125 *ord.*		31
L. Nonius Calpurnius Torquatus Asprenas	94 *ord.*	128 *ord.*		34
L. Neratius Marcellus	95	129 *ord.*		34

(continued)

Table 6
Continued

	Cos. I	Cos. II	Cos. III	Gap
P. Iuventius Celsus	117?	129 ord.		12?
C. Bruttius Praesens	118/9	139 ord.		20–21
Sex. Erucius Clarus	117?	146 ord.		29?
Q. Iunius Rusticus	133	162 ord.		29
L. Venuleius Apronianus	145?	168 ord.		23?
L. Sergius Paullus	151?	168 ord.		17?
Cn. Claudius Severus	167?	173 ord.		6?
Ti. Claudius Pompeianus	167?	173 ord.		6?
T. Vitrasius Pollio	151?	176 ord.		25?
M. Flavius Aper	155/60?	176 ord.		16–21?
P. Martius Verus	166	179 ord.		13
Cn. Iulius Verus	151?	180 des.		29?
C. Bruttius Praesens	153 ord.	180 ord.		27
C. Aufidius Victorinus	155	183 ord.		28
M'. Acilius Glabrio	173?	186 ord.		13?
P. (?) Seius Fuscianus	151?	188 ord.		37?
M. Servilius Silanus	152	188 ord.		36
P. Helvius Pertinax	174/5	192 ord.		17–18
C. Domitius Dexter	before 183	196 ord.		≥14
P. Cornelius Anullinus	174/5?	199 ord.		24–25?

P. Septimius Geta	191?	203 ord.	12?
L. Fabius Cilo	193	204 ord.	11
C. Iulius Asper	180/92	212 ord.	≥20
D. Caelius Balbinus	before 200?	213 ord.	≥14?
P. Catius Sabinus	before 210	216 ord.	≥7
Q. Tineius Sacerdos	192	219 ord.	27
L. Marius Maximus	199?	223 ord.	24?
App. Claudius Iulianus	200/210	224 ord.	≥14
Ti. Manilius Fuscus	196?	225 ord.	29?
C. Aufidius Marcellus	205?	226 ord.	21?
Q. Aiacius Modestus	198/204?	228 ord.	24–30?
L. Cassius Dio Cocceianus	205?	229 ord.	24?
M. Clodius Pupienus Maximus	?	234 ord.	?
C. Octavius Appius Suetrius Sabinus	214 ord.	240 ord.	26
C. Fulvius Aemilianus	223/235	249 ord.?	14– 26?
L. Valerius Maximus	233 ord.	256 ord.	23
P. Cornelius Saecularis	?	260 ord.	?
C. Iunius Donatus	?	260 ord.	?
(M.) Nummius (Ceionius?) Albinus	?	263 ord.	?
(Aspasius ?) Paternus	245?	268 ord.	23?
Flavius Antiochianus	?	270 ord.	?
(. . .) Pomponius Bassus [. . .]stus	259 ord.	271 ord.	12
Aemilianus	?	276	?
Nonius Paternus	?	279	?

Table 7
Praefecti urbi under the Principate (to A.D. 270)

M. Valerius Messalla Corvinus, 26 B.C.	L. Pedanius Secundus, 56(?)–61
cos. 31 B.C. (cf. Chapter 8 note 115)	*cos.* 43
Held office for a few days at age 33 or 38	Assumed office at least 13 years after consulship
T. Statilius Taurus, 16–13 (?) B.C.	(T.) Flavius Sabinus, between 56 and 69 (under Nero, Otho, and Vitellius)
cos. I 37 B.C., *cos.* II *ord.* 26 B.C.	*cos.* 45 or 47?
Assumed office 21 years after first consulship	A. Ducenius Geminus, appointed by Galba, 68–69
L. Calpurnius Piso (Pontifex), A.D. 13 (17?)–32	*cos.* before 62
cos. ord. 15 B.C.	Assumed office at least 7 years after consulship
Held office from age 60 or 64 to age 79	Ti. Plautius Silvanus Aelianus, 70(?)–*ante* 79
L. Aelius Lamia, 32–33	*cos.* 45, II 74; *procos. Asiae* 55/6?
cos. ord. A.D. 3	Assumed office 25(?) years after first consulship, aged late 50s/early 60s
Assumed office 29 years after consulship	[L.? Plo?]tius Pegasus, *ante* 79–ca. 85
Cossus Cornelius Lentulus, 33–36	*cos.* ca. 73
cos. ord. 1 B.C.	Assumed office ca. 5 years after consulship
Assumed office 33 years after consulship	?T. Aurelius Fulvus, ca. 85–*ante* 89
L. Calpurnius Piso, 36–38/9	*orn. cos.* 69, II *ord.* 85
cos. ord. 27	Q. Iulius Cordinus C. Rutilius Gallicus, ca. 89–91/2
Assumed office 9 years after consulship; subsequently (39/40) *procos. Africae*	*cos.* I 71/2, II 85
Q. Sanquinius Maximus, 38/9–40/1	Assumed office ca. 17 or 18 years after first consulship, aged about 65 years
cos. I 21/2, II 39	M. Arrecinus Clemens, *post* 89–*ante* 96
Assumed office 17/18 years after first consulship; subsequently (46) *legatus* in Germania Inferior	*cos.* I 72/3?, II 85
L. Volusius Saturninus, 40/1–56	Syme would put him before Gallicus
cos. A.D. 3	Assumed office ca. 18 years after first consulship
Held office from age 77 or 78 to age 92 or 93	

(*continued*)

Table 7

Continued

Q. Glitius Atilius Agricola, ca.104– ca.105?
cos. I 97, II 103
Assumed office ca. 7 years after first consulship

Ti. Iulius Candidus Marius Celsus, ca. 105–?
cos. I 86, II *ord.* 105; cf. RE *Suppl.* 14.207 (Eck)
Held office ca. 19 years after first consulship; still alive in 109/10, dead before 117

? Q. Fabius Postuminus, ca. 113(?)– 14 (*ante* 117)
cos. 96
Assumed office ca. 17 years after consulship

Q. Baebius Macer, *post* 113–17
cos. 103
Assumed office ca. 11–13 years after consulship

M. Annius Verus, ca. 121–*ante* 125
cos. I 97, II *ord.* 121, III *ord.* 126
Assumed office ca. 24 years after first consulship; resigned; still alive in 135

M. Lollius Paullinus D. Valerius Asiaticus Saturninus, *ante* 125–*non ante* 134
cos. I 94, II *ord.* 125; *procos. Asiae* ca. 108/9
Assumed office ca. 30 years after first consulship

L. Catilius Severus Iulianus Claudius Reginus, ca. 134–38
cos. I 110, II *ord.* 120; *procos. Africae* ca. 124/5
Assumed office ca. 24 years after first consulship

Ser. (Cornelius) Scipio Salvidienus Orfitus, 138
cos. ord. 110
Assumed office 28 years after consulship

C. Bruttius Praesens L. Fulvius Rusticus, 138(?)–140
cos. I 118/9, II *ord.* 139; *procos. Africae* 134/5
Assumed office ca. 19 or 20 years after first consulship

Sex. Erucius Clarus, 140(?)–146
cos. I 117?. II *ord.* 146
Assumed office ca. 23 years after first consulship

Q. Lollius Urbicus, ca. 146–60
cos. 135?
Assumed office ca. 11 years after consulship

Q. Iunius Rusticus, ca. 160–67/8?
cos. I 133, II *ord.* 162
Assumed office ca. 27 years after first consulship

L. Sergius Paullus, ca. 168
cos. I 151?, II *ord.* 168
Assumed office ca. 17 years after first consulship

C. Aufidius Victorinus, ca. 179–83
cos. I 155, II *ord.* 183
Assumed office ca. 24 years after first consulship

P. (?) Seius Fuscianus, ca. 188
cos. I 151?, II *ord.* 188
Assumed office ca. 37 years after first consulship

M. Servilius Silanus, 188–90(?)
cos. I 152, II *ord.* 188
Assumed office 36 years after first consulship

(continued)

Table 7
Continued

P. Helvius Pertinax, 190(?)–92
  cos. I. 174/5, II *ord.* 192
  Held office from age 64(?) to age
    66
T. Flavius Claudius Sulpicianus, 193
  cos. under Antoninus Pius or M.
    Aurelius
Cornelius Repentinus, 193
  cos. before 193 (in 188?)
(Vibius?) Bassus, 193
  cos. before 193
C. Domitius Dexter, 193–96?
  cos. I before 183, II *ord.* 196
  Assumed office at least 11 years
    after first consulship
P. Cornelius Anullinus, around 199
  (from 196?)
  cos. I 174/5?, II *ord.* 199
  Assumed office ca. 21+ years af-
    ter first consulship?
L. Fabius Cilo, before 204–11?
  cos. I 193, II *ord.* 204
  Assumed office ca. 10 years after
    first consulship?
C. Iulius Asper (Iulianus), 211–12?
  cos. I under Commodus, II *ord.*
    212
M. Oclatinius Adventus, 217
  cos. II *ord.* 218
L. Marius Maximus Perpetuus Aure-
  lianus, 217–18
  cos. I 199?, II *ord.* 223
  Assumed office 18? years after
    first consulship
P. Valerius Comazon Eutychianus,
  219–23
  cos. II *ord.* 220

(Domitius?) Leo (Procillianus?),
  220–?
  cos. 207?
  Assumed office 13(?) years after
    first consulship
Fulvius, ?– 222
Severus, 223
App. Claudius Iulianus, 223–24
  cos. I 200/10, II *ord.* 224
  Assumed office 13– 23 years after
    first consulship
M. Clodius Pupienus Maximus, ca.
  234
  cos. I?, II *ord.* 234
Sabinus, ?–238
Vettius Sabinus, 238–?
L. Caesonius Lucillus Macer Rufini-
  anus, under Gordian III (?); after
    239
  cos. ca. 230?
  Assumed office ca. 10(?) years
    after first consulship
(C.?) Flavius Iulius Latronianus, ca.
  243
D. Simonius Proculus Iulianus, ca.
  245–49?
  cos. 238/9
  Assumed office ca. 6–7(?) years
    after consulship
A. Cae[cina?] (Tacitus?), between
  241 and 253?
—us Paulinus, ca. 254
Fl(avius) Lollianus, ca. 254
L. Egnatius Victor Lollianus, 254
  cos. ca. 230
  Assumed office ca. 24 years after
    first consulship

(*continued*)

Table 7
Continued

L. Valerius Maximus, 255
  cos. I. *ord.* 233, II *ord.* 256
  Assumed office ca. 22 years after
    first consulship
(M.) Nummius Ceionius Albinus,
  256, 261–63
  cos I?, II *ord.* 263
C. Iunius Donatus, 257
  cos I?, II *ord.* 260
P. Cornelius Saecularis, 258–60
  cos. I?, II *ord.* 260
(M.) Nummius (Ceionius?) Albinus,
  261–63
  cos. II *ord.* 263

(Aspasius ?) Paternus, 264–66
  cos I 245?, II *ord.* 268
  Assumed office ca. 19 years after
    first consulship (cf. Peachin
    and Preuß 1997).
L. Petronius Taurus Volusianus,
  267–68
  cos. ord. 261
  Assumed office 6 years after con-
    sulship
Flavius Antiochianus, 269–70, 272
  cos. I?, II *ord.* 270

Table 8
Age of Exemption from Compulsory Public Services

Source	Date	Age of Exemption	Exemption from
lex Repetundarum	123/22 B.C.	60 years	*iudex*
Varro	Mid-1st cent. B.C.	60 years	*publica negotia*
lex Urso.	44 B.C.	60 years	*munitiones*
Corn. Nepos	Late republic	60 years	(*aetatis vacatio*)
Festus	Late republic/early empire?	60 years	*munera publica*
Cyrene Edict	4 B.C.	70 years	*iudex*
Flavian Munic. Law	A.D. 82/4	65 years	*iudex*
P.Flor. 312	A.D. 91/2	Old age	λειτουργίαι
P.Phil. 1	A.D. 103–7	"Over-age"	λειτουργίαι
P.Leit. 4	Ca. A.D. 161	72 years	λειτουργίαι
Fronto	Ca. A.D. 165	70 years	*omnia munera*
PSI 1103	A.D. 192–94	65 years	λειτουργίαι
P.Oxy. 4068	A.D. 200	70 years	πολιτικαὶ λειτουργίαι
Dig. 50.2.11	Ca. A.D.200	55 years	decurionate
Dig. 50.6.6.7	Ca. A.D.200	70 years	*munera municipalia*

Source	Date	Age	Category
Dig. 50.2.8	Early 3rd cent. A.D.	55/70 years	decurionate, munera civilia
Dig. 50.4.3.6	Early 3rd cent. A.D.	70 years	munera civilia
Dig. 50.4.3.12	Early 3rd cent. A.D.	70 years	cura frumenti comparandi
Dig. 50.5.2.1	Early 3rd cent. A.D.	70 years	munera civilia
Dig. 50.6.4	Early 3rd cent. A.D.	70 years	munera personalia
Dig. 27.1.2.pr.	Early 3rd cent. A.D.	70 years	ἐπιτροπὴ καὶ κουρατορία
Dig. 27.1.15.11	Early 3rd cent. A.D.	70 years	ἐπιτροπή
P.Flor. 382	Early 3rd cent. A.D.	70 years	λειτουργίαι
P.Wisc. 3	A.D. 257–59	Old age	λειτουργίαι
PSI Congr. 20.13	A.D. 260/1	70 years	λειτουργία
Cod. Iust. 10.32.10	A.D. 294	70 years	munera personalia
Cod. Iust. 10.50.3	Diocletian & Maximian	55 years	munera personalia
PSI 685	Early 4th cent. A.D.	60+ years	λειτουργίαι
P.Oxy. 889	A.D. 324	60 years	λειτουργίαι (?)
P.Panop. 29	A.D. 332	Old age	λειτουργίαι
Macrobius	Ca. A.D. 400	49/70 years	omnia officia et munera
lex Rom. Burg.	Ca. A.D. 500	60 years	tutela

Table 9

Of 100 Individuals Surviving to Age 15 Years, Number That Would
Probably Survive into Their 60s

Age	Number Surviving if $e_0 =$			
	20 years	25 years	30 years	60 years
0	262	212	185	113
15	100	100	100	100
60	34	39	45	74
65	24	29	35	66
70	14	19	24	55

Notes: The figures are derived from the Coale-Demeny[2] Model Life Tables, averaging the values for the West and South models, and a stationary population is assumed (see Chapter 2, and Parkin 1992: ch. 2).

The table is designed to give an idea, principally, of the probable chances an individual had of surviving from age 15 years into his (or her) 60s, specifically to illustrate the probability of an Egytian male at age 14 years (i.e., when he began to pay the poll tax) surviving to age 62 years (when liability to payment of the poll tax ended), as discussed in Chapter 5.

For example, if $e_0 = 25$ years, of 100 individuals at age 15 years, the probability is that 39 will survive to age 60, 29 to age 65, and 19 to age 70 years. If life expectancy at birth was lower, fewer would have survived into old age; if higher, more would have survived. It should also be noted that, if the population was growing (i.e., $r > 0$), the proportion of those in old age would be lower, and, conversely, if the population was in decline ($r < 0$), the proportion of those over age 60 years would be higher than in a stationary population.

The table also shows that, where, for example, $e_0 = 25$ years, if 100 individuals survive to age 15 years, this would suggest an original cohort size of 212 individuals; that is, in this hypothetical population, the chance of survivng from birth to age 15 years is approximately $100/212 = 0.4717$.

For further comparison, to indicate the difference much lower mortality levels would make, the final column shows the probable numbers surviving to these ages where $e_0 = 60$ years.

Appendix B

Figures

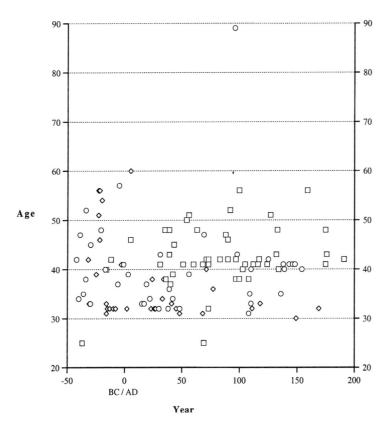

Fig. 1. Known ages (estimated) at first consulship, 42 B.C.–A.D. 200 (for data, see especially Morris 1964)

296

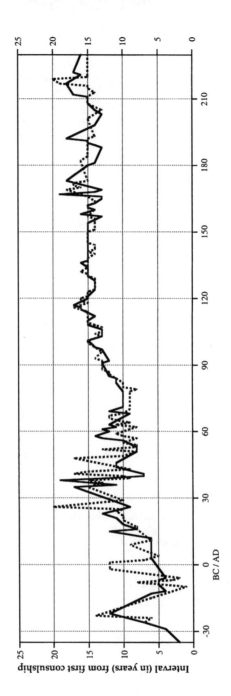

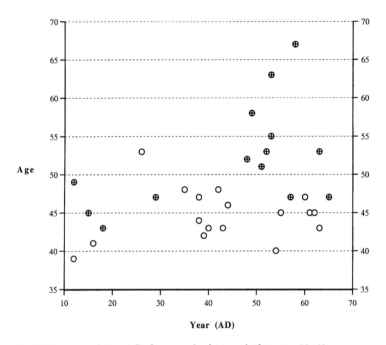

Fig. 3. Known ages (estimated) of proconsuls of Asia and Africa, A.D. 12–68

Fig. 2. Interval between first consulships and proconsulships of Asia and Africa

Appendix C

Some Stages of Old Age

It was noted in Chapter 9 that Galen in one of his works (*de San. Tuenda* 5.12 [6.379–80K = *CMG* 5.4.2.167]) divided old age up into three stages: the age of τῶν ὠμογερόντων, the age of the σῦφαρ, and the final stage, dubbed πέμπελος. It will be appropriate to comment on such a system, rare as it may have been; a number of ancient grammarians make remarks about terms for different stages.

The term ὠμογέρων is as old as Homer (*Iliad* 23.791; cf. also *schol. ad Iliad* 13.361 on μεσαιπόλιος: Odysseus is ὠμογέρων while Nestor is γέρων), of a "raw," fresh, or sprightly old age. For its use as an age-grade, in much the sense that we have seen of *senior* or πρέσβυς, note also Galen *in Hipp. Prog.* 18 (18B.221K); Apollonius Sophista *Lex. Hom.* 171.7 Bekker; Lucian *de Merc.* 20; Aristeides *Orat.* 28.30, 33; Eusebius *Hist. Eccl.* 7.21.9–10 (see Chapter 2 note 11); Hesychius Ω 196–97; *Suda* A 2855, M 642, Ω 95. On occasion ὠμογέρων means instead "prematurely gray" (cf. West on Hesiod *W&D* 705): Arrian *Ind.* 9.7 (of the Indians); *Anthologia Palatina* 5.264 (Paulus Silentiarius); Herodian *Partit.* 100 Boissonade. At *schol. ad* Euripides *Med.* 1209, however, ὠμογέρων is given as a synonym for τυμβογέρων (on which see below).

For the reading σῦφαρ in the Galen passage, see *LSJ* s.v. σύμφορος III and σῦφαρ; it is worth adding that the linking of σῦφαρ and πέμ-

πελος as stages in old age is noted several times by Eustathius (ad Iliad 23.791, ad Odyss. 14.223ff., 15.472). For πέμπελος and its alleged
etymology (noted in Chapter 9), cf. Lycophron Alex. 682, 826, with
schol. to both citations (and note line 793 for σύφαρ); Suda Π 958;
Hesychius Π 1381; Herodian de Orth. 489.35 Lentz. Eustathius (who
uses the term πέμπελος frequently) ad Iliad 1.250 suggests that πεμπέλος may be defined as someone over the age of 60 years, but Galen
et al. clearly thought otherwise. Note also τριπέμπελος (Plutarch Mor.
1071c; argumentum to Aristophanes Plut.) and εὐπέμπελος (Aeschylus Eum. 476 with schol.).

In such a system of stages of old age the final step might also logi-
cally be termed ἐσχατόγηρως vel sim.: among many examples note, in
a medical context, Aetius Lib. Med. 3.159 (CMG 8.1.328.29) and Galen in Hipp. Aph. 1.14 (17B.403K), as well as Diodorus Siculus 15.76.4,
20.72.2; Plutarch Pomp. 64.4; M. Aurelius Med. 9.33.

For three stages to old age in a medical context, note also Marcellinus (second century A.D.?) de Puls. 25 (Schöne 466.356–59), who follows the Hippocratic system of seven ages but makes the last three
those of the γέροντα καὶ πρεσβύτην καὶ γηραιόν. Cf. similarly An-
thologiae Palatinae Appendix 3.254 (seven ages, the final three being
those of the ὠμογέρων, γέρων, and πεμπέλος), Eustathius ad Iliad
8.518 (seven ages, the final three being those of the ὑποπόλιος/ὠμο-
γέρων, γέρων/πρεσβύτης, and ἐσχατόγηρως), Aristophanes of Byzantium (as at Chapter 1 note 2: identical to the previous "system"), and,
somewhat differently, Meletius de Natura Hominis (Cramer Anec. Graec.
3 pp. 12–13): τέσσαρες εἰσὶν ἡλικιαὶ καὶ τοῖς ἀνθρώποις· πρώτη
μὲν ἡ τῶν νέων· δευτέρα ἡ τῶν ἀκμαζόντων· τρίτη ἡ τῶν μέσων· καὶ
τετάρτη ἡ τῶν γερόντων· εἰ καὶ ἄλλας προστιθέασιν οἱ ἰατροί· τὴν
τῶν παίδων, τὴν μειρακιῶν, καὶ τῶν ἐσχατογήρων.

It is intriguing that Theophrastus apparently divided old age into
at least five stages; this at any rate seems to be the sense of the lexico-
graphical entry at Suda T 1160: τυμβογέροντες· πέμπτη ἡλικία γερόντων, ὡς καὶ Θεόφραστος (a previously unrecognized fragment of his
περὶ γήρως?—see Chapter 3 note 4). Τυμβογέρων as a comic, perjo-
rative term for an elderly person (noted in Chapter 3 note 26) had a
long history: cf. Aristophanes frag. 55 (Demianczuk, Suppl. Comic.)
and Comica Adespota (Kock, CAF 3) frag. 1172; Procopius Bell. Goth.

4.12.33; Pollux *Onom.* 2.16; Eustathius *ad Iliad* 23.91–92 and 791, *ad Odyss.* 2.16. Note also that Hesychius **T** 1632, *Suda* **T** 1219, and *schol. ad* Aristophanes *Clouds* 908 and 998, have τυμβογέρων and ἐσχατόγηρως as synonyms (cf. *Suda* **T** 1157 for τυμβογέρων, πέμπελος, and ἐσχατόγηρως used synonomously).

It is worth adding, finally, that *schol. ad* Aristophanes *Clouds* 998 has as synonyms for Ἰαπετόν (the Titan Iapetus's name, like that of Cronus, Nestor, and Tithonus, might be used of any very old person: Eustathius *ad Iliad* 23.791) both ἐσχατόγηρων and λῆρον (cf. similarly Hesychius **T** 1632 and see further Chapter 8 note 113 on senile dementia).

Abbreviations

The names of Greek and Latin authors are given in full; the titles of their works are generally abbreviated as in *LSJ*[9] and *OLD*. Abbreviations for papyrological collections are as in J. F. Oates et al., *Checklist of Editions of Greek and Latin Papyri, Ostraca And Tablets*[5], *BASP*, suppl. 9 (2001).

AAN	*Atti della Accademia di Scienze morali e politiche della Società nazionale di Scienze, Lettere ed Arti di Napoli.*
A&S	*Ageing and Society*
AC	*L'Antiquité classique*
ADH	*Annales de démographie historique*
AE	*L'Année épigraphique*
AJAH	*American Journal of Ancient History*
AJPh	*American Journal of Philology*
Annales ESC	*Annales (Economie, Sociétés, Civilisations)*
ANRW	*Aufstieg und Niedergang der römischen Welt*
AS	*Ancient Society*
ASR	*American Sociological Review*
BASP	*Bulletin of the American Society of Papyrologists*
BHM	*Bulletin of the History of Medicine*
BICS	*Bulletin of the Institute of Classical Studies*

BIDR	*Bullettino dell' Istituto di Diritto romano "Vittorio Scia-loja"*
BMCR	*Bryn Mawr Classical Review*
CA	*Classical Antiquity*
CAH	*The Cambridge Ancient History,* 1st ed. (Cambridge, 1923–39)
CAH^2	*The Cambridge Ancient History,* 2nd ed. (Cambridge, 1961–)
C&M	*Classica et Mediævalia*
CB	*Classical Bulletin*
CCSL	*Chronique d'Égypte*
CGL	*Corpus Glossariorum Latinorum*
CIL	*Corpus Inscriptionum Latinarum*
CJ	*Classical Journal*
CLE	*Carmina Latina Epigraphica,* ed. F. Bücheler (Leipzig, 1897–1926)
CMG	*Corpus Medicorum Graecorum*
Coale-Demeny^2	A. J. Coale, P. G. Demeny, and B. Vaughan, *Regional Model Life Tables and Stable Populations*^{2} (New York and London, 1983)
CPG	*Corpus Paroemiographorum Graecorum,* ed. E. L. Leutsch and F. G. Schneidewin (Göttingen, 1839–41; suppl. vol., Hildesheim, 1961)
CPh	*Classical Philology*
CQ	*Classical Quarterly*
CR	*Classical Review*
CRAI	*Comptes rendus de l'Académie des Inscriptions et Belles-lettres*
CSEL	*Corpus Scriptorum Ecclesiasticorum Latinorum*
CSSH	*Comparative Studies in Society and History*
CW	*Classical World* (previously *Classical Weekly*)
D&S	C. Daremberg and E. Saglio, *Dictionnaire des antiquités grecques et romaines d'après les textes et les monuments* (Paris, 1877–1919)
DE	E. de Ruggiero et al., *Dizionario epigrafico di antichità romane* (Rome, 1886–)
EMC	*Échos du Monde classique/Classical Views*

ERE	*Encyclopaedia of Religion and Ethics,* ed. J. Hastings (Edinburgh, 1908–21)
FGH	*Fragmente der griechischen Historiker,* ed. F. Jacoby (Leiden, 1923–)
FIRA²	*Fontes Iuris Romani AnteIustiniani,* ed. S. Riccobono et al., 2nd ed. (Florence, 1940–43)
G&R	*Greece and Rome*
GCS	*Die griechischen christlichen Schriftsteller der ersten [drei] Jahrhunderte*
GL	*Grammatici Latini,* ed. H. Keil (Leipzig, 1855–1923)
GRBS	*Greek, Roman and Byzantine Studies*
GVI	*Griechische Vers-Inschriften, I: Grab-Epigramme,* ed. W. Peek (Berlin, 1955)
HRR	*Historicorum Romanorum Reliquiae,* ed. H. Peter (Leipzig, 1906–14)
HSCPh	*Harvard Studies in Classical Philology*
ICS	*Illinois Classical Studies*
IGRom.	*Inscriptiones Graecae ad res Romanas pertinentes,* ed. R. Cagnat et al. (Paris, 1901–27)
ILS	*Inscriptiones Latinae Selectae,* ed. H. Dessau (Berlin, 1892–1916)
Index	*Index. Quaderni camerti di studi romanistici*
Index Interpolationum	*Index Interpolationum quae in Iustiniani Digestis inesse dicuntur,* ed. E. Levy and E. Rabel (Weimar, 1929–35)
JAC	*Jahrbuch für Antike und Christentum*
JEA	*Journal of Egyptian Archaeology*
JHM	*Journal of the History of Medicine and Allied Sciences*
JHS	*Journal of Hellenic Studies*
JJP	*Journal of Juristic Papyrology*
JRA	*Journal of Roman Archaeology*
JRS	*Journal of Roman Studies*
L&S	*A Latin Dictionary,* ed. C. T. Lewis and C. Short (Oxford, 1879)
LEC	*Les études classiques*
LIMC	*Lexicon Iconographicum Mythologiae Classicae*

LSJ⁹	*A Greek Lexicon,* ed. H. G. Liddell and R. Scott, 9th ed. (Oxford, 1940; with new suppl., 1996)
MEFRA	*Mélanges de l'École française de Rome: Antiquité*
MGHAA	*Monumenta Germaniae Historica, Auctores Antiquissimi*
MGH Leges	*Monumenta Germaniae Historica, Leges*
MH	*Museum Helveticum*
Mnem.	*Mnemosyne*
MRR	T. R. S. Broughton, *Magistrates of the Roman Republic* (New York, 1951, 1952, 1986)
NP	*Der neue Pauly. Enzyklopaedie der Antike,* ed. H. Cancik and H. Schneider (Stuttgart, 1996–)
OCD³	*The Oxford Classical Dictionary,* 3rd ed., ed. S. Hornblower and A. Spawforth (Oxford and New York, 1996)
OGI	*Orientis Graeci Inscriptiones Selectae,* ed. W. Dittenberger (Leipzig, 1903–5)
OLD	*Oxford Latin Dictionary,* ed. P. G. W. Glare (Oxford, 1982)
Palingenesia	O. Lenel, *Palingenesia Iuris Civilis* (Leipzig, 1889)
P&P	*Past and Present*
PBA	*Proceedings of the British Academy*
PBSR	*Papers of the British School at Rome*
PCPhS	*Proceedings of the Cambridge Philological Association*
PG	*Patrologiae Cursus, series Graeca,* ed. J.-P. Migne (Paris, 1857–66)
PIR	*Prosopographia Imperii Romani,* 1st ed., ed. E. Klebs et al. (Berlin, 1897–98)
PIR²	*Prosopographia Imperii Romani,* 2nd ed., ed. E. Groag et al. (Berlin and Leipzig, 1933–)
PL	*Patrologiae Cursus, series Latina,* ed. J.-P. Migne (Paris, 1844–65)
PLM	*Poetae Latini Minores,* ed. E. Baehrens (Leipzig, 1879–1935)
PLRE	*Prosopography of the Later Roman Empire,* ed. A. H. M. Jones et al. (Cambridge, 1971–92)
PMG	*Poetae Melici Graeci,* ed. D. L. Page (Oxford, 1962)

PS	*Population Studies*
QUCC	*Quaderni urbinati di cultura classica*
RAC	*Reallexikon für Antike und Christentum*
RAL	*Rendiconti della Classe di Scienze morali, storiche e filologiche dell'Accademia dei Lincei*
RCCM	*Rivista di cultura classica e medioevale*
RE	*Paulys Real-Encyclopädie der classischen Altertumswissenschaft,* ed. G. Wissowa et al. (Stuttgart, 1893–1980)
REA	*Revue des études anciennes*
REG	*Revue des études grecques*
REL	*Revue des études latines*
RHDFE	*Revue historique de droit français et étranger*
RhM	*Rheinisches Museum*
RIDA	*Revue internationale des droits de l'Antiquité*
RLM	*Rhetores Latini Minores,* ed. C. Halm (Leipzig, 1863)
RRC	M. H. Crawford, *Roman Republican Coinage* (Cambridge, 1974)
RSA	*Rivista storica dell' Antichità*
Schanz-Hosius	M. Schanz, *Geschichte der römischen Literatur,* rev. by C. Hosius et al. (Munich, various dates)
SEG	*Supplementum Epigraphicum Graecum*
Sel. Pap.	*Select Papyri, II: Non-Literary Papyri—Public Documents,* ed. A. S. Hunt and C. C. Edgar (London and Cambridge, Mass., 1934)
SHM	*Social History of Medicine: The Journal of the Society for the Social History of Medicine*
SO	*Symbolae Osloenses*
Suppl. Hell.	*Supplementum Hellenisticum,* ed. H. Lloyd-Jones and P. Parsons (Berlin and New York, 1983)
SVF	*Stoicorum Veterum Fragmenta,* ed. H. von Arnim (Leipzig, 1903–24)
TAPhA	*Transactions of the American Philological Association*
Thesleff	*The Pythagorean Texts of the Hellenistic Period,* ed. H. Thesleff (Abo, 1965)
TLL	*Thesaurus Linguae Latinae*
VIR	*Vocabularium Iurisprudentiae Romanae*

WS	*Wiener Studien*
YCS	*Yale Classical Studies*
ZPE	*Zeitschrift für Papyrologie und Epigraphik*
ZRG	*Zeitschrift der Savigny-Stiftung für Rechtsgeschichte (Ro-manistische Abteilung)*

Notes

Introduction

1. The literature is vast. For informative introductions to important aspects, see Eekelaar and Pearl (1989), Laslett (1996).
2. Laslett (1977, 1996), Haber (1983), Freer (1988).
3. Specifically on the cultural history of old age, the most comprehensive work to appear is that by Minois (1987), of interest in its wide scope but also too sweeping, and particularly weak on antiquity; note the comments of Mattioli (1989). For a cultural and social approach, see now the collections of papers in Conrad and von Kondratowitz (1993) and Johnson and Thane (1998), as well as, most recently, the masterly survey by Thane (2000). For methodology, see esp. Laslett (1977: 174–213; 1996), and Kertzer and Laslett (1995) for the emerging study of the historical demography of aging. Troyansky (1989) makes excellent use of available evidence, literary and historical, for a particular period and place (eighteenth-century France) to elucidate the position of and attitudes toward older people of that society; see further Troyansky (1996) and note too Bourdelais (1993) for demographic history. Other influential studies of old age in history include Subrenat (1987), and Pelling and Smith (1991). There is some validity to Simone de Beauvoir's comment (1977: 100) that it is "impossible to write a history of old age." Apart from anything else, each culture and society require separate treatment. For a particularly useful study of old age in the Middle Ages, see now Shahar (1997); I received a copy of this work as I was in the later stages of completing this book,

and it is both gratifying and fascinating to see the parallels in both approach and conclusions between that study and this.

4. Spencer (1990), esp. 1–34, a clear introduction to the subject. Note also Simmons (1945), Fry (1980, 1981), Kertzer and Keith (1984), Philibert (1984). For excellent overviews of sociological aspects of age, see van den Berghe (1973), O'Donnell (1985), Riley (1987); some key texts are collected in Gubrium and Holstein (2000). Maddox et al. (1995) is of use in any study—literary, historical, anthropological, or sociological—of old age. See also the collection of sociological and historical papers (including a French translation of Finley 1981) in *Communications* 37 (1983).

5. On aspects of the young in Roman society, see esp. Eyben (1972b, 1977, 1981, 1993) and Kleijwegt (1991); note also Néraudau (1979, 1984), Wiedemann (1989), and most recently Rawson (1997a); on Athenian society, Koliadis (1988), Golden (1990), and Garland (1990); earlier bibliography in Karras and Wiesehöfer (1981).

6. The classic work is van Gennep (1909). The standard study of such rites in a classical society remains Gagé (1958); note also Brelich (1969) 98–100, and the papers in *MEFRA* 102 (1990) 7–137.

7. For the ancient version of the "birds of a feather flock together" proverb, particularly with reference to older people, see Plato *Rep.* 1.329a and Cicero *de Sen.* 3.7; other references in Otto (1890) no. 1335 (with Häussler 1968: 62, 77, 197, 242) and Powell (1988) 114–15.

8. Linton (1942) 602–3.

9. Valerius Maximus 8.13 (and much too in 8.7, *de studio et industria*); Pliny *NH* 7.48.153–49.164; Phlegon *Macrobioi* (*FGH* 257 F 37; see further Chapter 6); [Lucian] *Macrobioi* (of uncertain date: ca. A.D. 160 or ca. A.D. 212–13 are plausible); Censorinus *de Die Nat.* 15.

10. Plutarch *Cic.* 25.3. Note P. Licinius Crassus (*cos.* 205 B.C., *pont. max.* 212–183, *cens.* 210) as *exemplum senectutis:* Cicero *de Sen.* 9.27.

11. See Eyben's bibliographical article in Falkner and de Luce (1989) 230–51, and Suder (1991), to which add in particular David (1991), Falkner (1995), and Mattioli (1995).

12. E. Dobson, *Antiquity* 8 (1934) 365–66. Compare the rather more penetrating review by W. Schmid, *Gnomon* 10 (1934) 529–32. The only comparable work on old age in Roman society is the unpublished (and, it must be said, unsatisfactory) dissertation by Berelson (1934).

13. This remains true of most of the essays in Mattioli (1995). Happily the study of the literary depiction of old age is becoming much more sophisticated, at least in some quarters: see most recently Falkner (1995).

14. Rather than single out the unsatisfactory, I would note that Kirk (1971) on Greek old age is one of the more successful attempts, although the focus remains on literary images, and that Gnilka (1983) is an insightful overview of old age in ancient times, though his focus is on early Christianity and his coverage of the Roman world is sparse. Garland (1987;

1990: ch. 6) offers a good introduction to aspects of old age, literary and otherwise, in ancient Greece; note also most recently Byl (1996). Suder (see bibliography) has produced a number of useful studies of aspects of old age and demography in the Roman world; unfortunately (for me), the most pertinent work on the Roman life course, Suder (1994), is in Polish.

15. The most comprehensive coverage on the Greek side remains that by Richardson (1933), in part making up for her treatment of the literary testimony. For aspects of the depiction of older people in Greek art note also Meyer (1989), and Zanker (1995) for the use of the image of old age to enhance or reinforce the air of an intellectual, esp. 14–22 and 52–57 for depictions of Homer and Euripides respectively; as Zanker notes (22), "In the Greek imagination, all great intellectuals were old," though it might be added that that need not mean that all old people were intellectuals! On the Roman side, note especially the so-called veristic period of the later republic, in which the wrinkles and creases of old age—and/or by implication, perhaps, of a hardworking life—are emphasized (see Gruen 1992: ch. 4, with, most recently, Stevenson 1998). By contrast note, e.g., the idealized image of Augustus (as well as of Livia) in statuary and the reality of his physical appearance in later years, as described by Suetonius (*Div. Aug.* 79–80).

16. Finley (1981: 165).

17. Falkner and de Luce (1992) 4.

18. Thus, while I am in sympathy with the views expressed most recently, for example, by Pomeroy (1997) 1–4, I tend toward the line of, e.g., Golden (1992) and Saller (1994) 4–8, in adopting a synchronic approach; see also Golden and Toohey (1997), esp. the chapters by Dixon and Golden.

19. Shaw (1991a); for ages on epitaphs, see Sigismund Nielsen (1997), and for useful discussion on epigraphical evidence for attitudes, see Giacomini (1992–93). On knowledge of parents' ages, cf. Ausonius *ad Patrem de Suscepto Filio* 25–30, with Ovid *Fasti* 2.625 and Statius *Silv.* 5.3.254–55; the topos of *captatio,* on which see Chapter 8, is the primary concern in these texts.

20. See esp. the work of Gnilka (1972, 1983)—and contrast Minois (1987) 133.

21. Cf., e.g., Néraudau (1987) 206–7, following Veyne.

22. Finley (1981) 168.

Chapter 1. Roman Definitions and Statements of Age

1. Pokorny (1959) 907–8; Slusanski (1974). On *senecta* (sc. *aetas*), cf. Servius *ad Aen.* 11.165; Charisius *Ars Gramm.* 1.15; Slusanski (1974) 567–68; Oakley (1997) 464–65. For the noun *senex* as masculine, note Isidorus *Orig.* 11.2.28: "senex autem tantum masculini generis est, sicut

anus femini; nam anus dicitur sola mulier." For the rare use of *senex* (as an adjective?) for a woman, see Tibullus 1.6.82 (with Évrard 1978) and Papinius *ap.* Varro *de Ling. Lat.* 7.28. The only different (ancient) etymology that I know of for *senex* is from Isidorus *Diff.* 2.21.84, and should not be taken too seriously: "senes autem quidam dictos putant, eo quod *se nes*ciunt, et per nimiam aetatem delirent atque desipiant. unde et Plato: in pueris crescit sensus, in iuvenibus viget, in senibus minuitur."

2. Pokorny (1959) 390–91. For Greek words for age-groups, male and female, see also Aristophanes of Byzantium frags. 37–90 (Slater = frag. 1 Nauck), and cf. Pollux *Onom.* 2.12–13.

3. Wilkinson (1974) 26. Similarly, A. S. L. Farquharson, in his edition of Marcus Aurelius's *Meditations*[2] (Oxford, 1952), *ad Med.* 2.2 (cited below), states that "in Roman eyes a man became *senex* at 40." In a piece published in *CW* 23 (1930) 103–4, entitled "Mr Fabian Franklin on old age," ancient and modern examples are given of individuals over the age of 40 years who have made a contribution to society; cf. Ullman (1933–34) for the same assumption that old age = 40+ years. Such assumptions may in part be a result of the mistaken reference in *L&S* s.v. *senex,* where Aulus Gellius 10.28.1 is cited as evidence that a man is *senex* "from the latter half of the fortieth year onward"; I assume what is meant is from the age of 46 years. Cf. Grasby (1975) 124: "[I]n the Republic a man was *senex* over [*sic*] the age of 46"; similarly, Reinhold (1988) 106: "In Roman practice, a man over 45 was officially called *senex*"; Christes (1998) 73. Presumably they mean *senior,* or they are taking Cicero *de Sen.* 17.60 (to be discussed presently) too literally and as too representative of later times. For the age of 40 years as the perceived ἀκμή of a career, see below; for 40 years taken as a generational length (longer than is typical), see Laroche (1986). For the persistent view in some modern scholarship that in antiquity people aged more quickly than they do today, see, e.g., Nisbet and Hubbard (1970) 358, on Horace *Odes* 1.31.19; Raepsaet (1971) 90; Sande (1995) 48; Cameron (1995) 176. By way of contrast, note Pelling and Smith (1991) 7.

4. E.g., Jacoby (1902) 45; Berelson (1934) 4–7; Byl (1974) 114; Néraudau (1979) 118–19; Powell (1988) 2 n. 8, 100, 231; Dixon (1992) 150; cf. also Cameron (1995) 175. Few argue that Roman old age began at 50: Orth (1963) 22 assumes it began with the 50th year, while de Luce (e.g., 1993: 230–31) has old age beginning at age 40 for women, 50 for men.

5. Solon frag. 27 West (*ap.* Philo *de Opif. Mundi* 35.103–4 and Clement of Alexandria *Strom.* 6.16.144.3–6); on Solon's poem, see most recently Falkner (1990 = 1995: ch. 4) and Musti (1990). Compare Solon frag. 20 (see Chapter 2); Herodotus 1.32 (Solon to Croesus: 70 years a maximum); Censorinus *de Die Nat.* 14.4, 7. Macrobius *Comm.* 1.6.70–76 uses a similar system to Solon's, but seems to define *senectus* (he does not use the term) as beginning at age 70—on this see further Chapter 5 note 34, and

note also Chapter 2 note 39 for a system of twelve hebdomads. Jones
(1853) 169 observed that "[h]ad Solon lived at the present time, he would
most probably have allowed man a longer period for the full use of his
faculties than the age of sixty-three; nor would he have condemned him
to death at three score years and ten. But there were no temperance societies in the days of Solon."

6. On the significance of the number 7, note Philo *de Opif. Mundi* 30.89–
43.128; Varro *ap.* Aulus Gellius 3.10; Macrobius *Comm.* 1.6; and cf.
Seneca *de Ben.* 7.1.5. For modern discussion, see Roscher (1903, 1904,
1906, 1911, 1913, 1919)—classic works, albeit with much repetition
and at times rather idiosyncratic; Boll (1913) 112–18; Slusanski (1973)
103–4; Eyben (1973a) 228. On *anni climacterici,* note Aulus Gellius
3.10.9, 15.7 (on Augustus's 63rd year, see below); Censorinus *de Die Nat.*
14.9–15.3 (14.11: "quadrati numeri potentissimi ducuntur"); Firmicus
Maternus *Math.* 4.20. On the avoidance for superstitious reasons of the
numeral 7 in age statements in Roman Egypt, see Scheidel (1996a) 65–
66.

7. Hippocrates *de Hebd.* 5: *schol. ad* Pollux *Onom.* 2.4 (old age from the age
of 42 years); Philo *de Opif. Mundi* 36.105 (old age from 56); *MS. Cod. Phil.*
1529, 8.633L (from 56); Censorinus *de Die Nat.* 14.3 (from 56); Boissonade *Anec. Graec.* 2 pp. 454–56 (a compilation of various lists of *aetates,* two of them—δ and ζ—stated to be Hippocratic: old age from 56
or 63); *Paris MS* 7027, 8.636L (from 63); *schol. ad* Hesiod *W&D* 447 (from
63); *Cod. Ambros. G* 108f., 9.436L (from 63). Cf. Ambrose *Ep.* 44.10–12
(*PL* 16.1139–40 = *CSEL* 82.222–23, with Lamirande 1982) on Hippocrates and Solon, and note that Plutarch *Mor.* 392c assumes seven ages,
very similar to the structure of the Hippocratic system; cf. also Jerome
Comm. in Amos 3.6.2/6 (*PL* 25.1061 = *CCSL* 76.304) for seven ages, attributed to Philo. On the Hippocratic work, see further Roscher (1911;
1913: 9–10; 1919); Boll (1913) 117, 137–45; Jones (1946) 6–10; Mansfeld (1971); West (1971). Note that opinions vary markedly on the date
of the Hippocratic work, Mansfeld allocating it to the first century B.C.,
West, more conventionally (and in my view correctly), to the fourth, and
Roscher to the sixth or fifth century; Jones considers it "early."

8. Ptolemy *Tetrab.* 4.10.204–7; Boll (1913) 105, 118–28.

9. Censorinus *de Die Nat.* 14.2 (for Censorinus's sources—chiefly Varro—
see Dahlmann and Heisterhagen 1957: 26–28; Mansfeld 1971: 185–92).
Compare Servius *ad Aen.* 5.295, 5.409, 6.304 (though note that Servius
ascribes different age-classes to Varro than does Censorinus); Nonius Marcellus 842L (cited in Chapter 9). Further discussion also in Slusanski
(1973); Deschamps (1987); Lehmann (1991); Stok (1991). Tacitus *Agr.*
3.2 describes fifteen years (the length of Domitian's reign) as the span of
time from *iuventus* to *senectus* and from *senectus* to "ipsi exactae aetatis ter-
mini."

10. Indeed Mommsen (1887–88) 2.408 n. 2 stated that "in technischen Sinn (Varro bei Censorinus)" *senex* means someone 60 years of age or older.

11. Augustine *de Div. Quaest.* 58.2 (*PL* 40.43 = *CCSL* 44a.107).

12. Diogenes Laertius 8.10; Diodorus Siculus 10.9.5; Boissonade *Anec. Graec.* 2 p. 455; cf. Ovid *Met.* 15.199–236; Boll (1913) 102–3. Note also Iamblichus *de Vit. Pythag.* 11.56 for four ages of women. Mosshammer (1976) would change the Pythagorean ages from 20/40/60/80 to 25/40/64/80 as more mathematically beautiful. Lucian *Catapl.* 5 seems to equate *gerontes* (who are unmourned at death and look like raisins) with those over the age of 60 years; cf. also Theophrastus *Char.* 27.2.

13. *Orig.* 11.2.1; the Latin terms cannot readily be put into directly comparable English. Cf. Augustine *de Div. Quaest.* 58.2 (*PL* 40.43 = *CCSL* 44a.106) and *Ep.* 213.1 (*PL* 33.966) for the same six ages (with Eyben 1973b: 161).

14. Isidorus *Orig.* 5.38.5 and 11.2.32 lists only three ages (*infantia, iuventus, senectus*; for *senectus* from age 70, see *Orig.* 11.2.6–7). At *Diff.* 2.19.74–76 (*PL* 83.81) and *Liber Numerorum* 7.31 (*PL* 83.185), Isidorus has six ages (*infantia, pueritia, adolescentia, iuventus, senectus* [from age 49], and *senium* [from age 77]). For old age having no set upper limit in terms of number of years, cf. Cicero *de Sen.* 20.72: "senectutis autem nullus est certus terminus"; St. Augustine *de Genesi contra Manich.* 1.42 (*PL* 34.193, on the six ages of man), and *Ep.* 213.1 (*PL* 33.966). Contrast Isidorus *Orig.* 11.2.8 (discussed further in Chapter 8) and *Diff.* 2.19.76.

15. The classic work is Boll (1913); see further Eyben (1973b; 1977: 5–40) for Latin authors and especially for Christian treatment of the topos, and Néraudau (1979) 91–143. For its continuation into later thought, literature, and art, see also Wackernagel (1862); Harcum (1914); Hofmeister (1926)—a mine of information; de Ghellinck (1948); Vessey (1973); Lamirande (1982); Burrow (1986); Dove (1986); Sears (1986); Covey (1989; 1991: ch. 2); Roueché (1993).

16. See esp. Seneca (whether father or son is uncertain, and possibly Lactantius did not know there were two; I favor the senior) *ap.* Lactantius *Inst. Div.* 7.15.14–16; Florus *Epit.* pr.4; Ammianus Marcellinus 14.6.4. For the theme of *Lebensaltervergleich* and its later blossoming, see Schmidt (1955–56); Richter (1961) 310–15; Häussler (1964); Cameron (1970) 365–66; Alonso-Núñez (1982); Bartelink (1983); Burrow (1986) 79–92; Havas (1992); Zocca (1995).

17. Lucretius *de Rer. Nat.* 5.827; Aulus Gellius 3.10.11 (cf. Pliny *NH* 7.16.73). Political systems might also be compared to the stages of life: on oligarchy as old age in Plato, see Meulder (1991).

18. Isidorus *Orig.* 11.2.8: "in his igitur sex spatiis philosophi vitam discripserunt humanam"; Censorinus *de Die Nat.* 14.9: "medici ac philosophi . . ." (if anything Censorinus 14.7 thought Solon's system fitted

closest to nature, as did Aristotle *Pol.* 7.1336b40–1337a1). Note, e.g., Manilius *Astr.* 2.82–105 and Ausonius *Ecl.* 25 Green, as well as Ptolemy (above), for the astrological influence on the human life-span.

19. On stages of life in the legal sense—*infantes, impuberes,* and so forth— which may have been more generally applicable and of wider use in daily life, see Chapter 4.

20. Laslett (1987) 103. Cf. Laslett (1990) 462, reviewing Minois's history of old age: "It demonstrates all over again what little relevance what our ancestors thought about ageing has to our present position. . . . The hell with the seven ages of man!" I would agree at least that in terms of social history, the *aetates hominum* have little historical value.

21. Burrow (1986) 36 makes the point also that there is no particularly valid reason for the enduring system of *four* seasons of the year.

22. For such an exercise, see, e.g., Jones (1978) 133 ("past his prime" = 50– 60 years?), and, at great length, Hamblenne (1969); note also Griffin (1976) 35–36 regarding Seneca the Younger's *senectus.* Roesch (1982) 323–39 highlights the problems in defining νεανίσκος in terms of number of years. In 1862 Migne made the point forcefully in discussing John Chrysostom's use of age terms: Chrysostom could speak of his mother at age 46 as γεγηρακυῖαν but of himself at age 40 as μειρακίσκον, a mere lad (on the wide range in terms of years to which μειράκιον may apply, from παῖς to ἀνήρ, see Gomme and Sandbach 1973: 140 on Menander *Dys.* 27; but, all the same, Chrysostom is pushing his luck). Migne observed (*PG* 48.691–92): "Iam sane ostendimus hoc computandi genus aggressos viros doctos frequenter lapsos esse. Uno verbo concludam . . . ab huiusmodi temporis notis prorsus abstineamus oportet." In fact Chrysostom made the point himself (*in Isaiam* 3.2, *PG* 56.42): a man is called a γέρων not simply because of his chronological age (50 years) but also because of his attributes (good sense and gray hair).

23. Martial 10.24.8–11. For the *tres areae* (the reading of the Aldine text of 1517, widely accepted, though Housman suggested "arcubus"), cf. Ovid *Fasti* 4.9–10. *Area* in this sense is probably derived from the imagery of the racecourse—fitting for the *cursus vitae* (note, e.g., Cicero *pro Cael.* 31.75). For the long and enduring tradition of three ages, see, e.g., Pindar *Nem.* 3.72–74; Aristotle *Rhet.* 2.12–14 (discussed in Chapter 3); Cicero *de Sen.* 2.4; Aulus Gellius 10.28; Martianus Capella 1.76 (with which cf. Macrobius *Sat.* 1.18.10 and Prudentius *Psych.* 845–48, both with four ages). Seneca *de Brev. Vit.* 10.2 has an even simpler and more practical system: "in tria tempora vita dividitur: quod fuit, quod est, quod futurum est." For four ages, also standard, cf. Horace *Ars Poet.* 156–78 (discussed in Chapter 3); Hippocrates *de Victu* 1.33 (6.512L—see also Chapter 9), *Aph.* 3.18 (4.494L); Galen *in Hipp. de Sal. Vict. Rat.* 7 (15.186K = *CMG* 5.9.1.94–95), *in Hipp. Aph.* 3.29 (17B.643: by implication old age begins

at age 49, i.e., 7^2); [Galen] *Def. Med.* 104 (19.373–74K); Manilius *Astr.* 2.844–55; and the Pythagorean system of four ages (noted above) to correspond to the four seasons (old age = winter; on this see Chapter 9).

24. Servius *ad Aen.* 5.553: "poetica licentia confundit aetates, ut modo pueros, modo iuvenes dicat." And it need not be only poetic, as we shall see.

25. For the "military" definitions of *iunior* and *senior*, see Aulus Gellius 10.28, discussed further in Chapter 4, and note the difference from Varro's ages. Contrast, e.g., Aulus Gellius 15.7.1–3, where *senior* is used of a man in his 63rd year.

26. *P.Sakaon* 40.12–13 (Theadelphia, A.D. 318–20). Cf. Seneca *Cons. ad Marc.* 21.4: "non una hominibus senecta est."

27. Livy 30.30.10 (note also 30.28.5, and cf. 30.37.9). Claudian *de Bell. Goth.* 149 also calls Hannibal a *senex*. Lucilius talks of Hannibal as "that old wolf" (frag. 826M, "veteratorem, illum vetulum lupum"). Cicero *de Sen.* 4.10 (echoed by Jerome *Ep.* 105.3) describes Hannibal as "iuveniliter exsultantem" as he charged into Italy in 218 B.C., aged 29, in contrast to the *patientia* of the *senex* Q. Fabius Maximus (Cunctator).

28. *Phil.* 2.46.118: "defendi rem publicam adulescens, non deseram senex." See further Axelson (1948) and Delgado (1961) on Cicero's use of the term *adulescens*.

29. Sallust *Cat.* 49.2. Cornelius Nepos *Att.* 16.1 and Suetonius *Tib.* 70.1 provide examples of a difference of twenty-two to twenty-eight years between a *senex* and an *adulescens*.

30. Martial 1.108.4; Howell (1980) *ad loc.* Martial, born around A.D. 40, had his first book published in 86.

31. Cicero *de Orat.* 2.4.15; Licinius was born in 140 B.C.: see Sumner (1973) 94–97. Macrobius *Sat.* 2.5.2, on Julia, daughter of Augustus, is surprising: "[S]he was in her 38th year, the time of life, if she had kept her wits about her, which is verging on *senium*" (annum agebat tricesimum et octavum, tempus aetatis, si mens sana superesset, vergentis in senium; cf. 2.5.7 for her prematurely gray hair, which she was in the habit of having plucked out).

32. Cicero *de Sen.* 1.2. A little later Cicero is blunter: "ad senem senex de senectute scripsi" (*de Amic.* 1.5).

33. Cicero *de Sen.* 3.7; Powell (1988) 116.

34. *Constans* (etc.) *aetas*: Cicero *de Sen.* 10.33; *TLL* 1.1129.5–37; Eyben (1973b: 166–67; 1977: 16–19), Powell (1988) 171. *Gravitas*: see Isidorus *Orig.* 11.2.1, quoted above, and 11.2.6 ("quinta aetas senioris, id est gravitas, quae est declinatio a iuventute in senectutem"), with Chapter 4 notes 28–29. "Aetas quae media dicitur": Cicero *de Sen.* 20.76; cf. Plato *Epist.* 3.316c. *Medium aevum:* Pliny *NH* 7.2.28; Martial 8.77.7; Phaedrus 2.2.3; *TLL* 1.1166.75–76. *Media aetas:* as early as Plautus *Aul.* 159, 162 (of men and women); *CIL* 12.861.10 = *CLE* 1192.10, *CIL* 5.1493.2

= *CLE* 1472.2; *TLL* 8.589.7–16. Cf. Martial 10.32.3: "mediis annis" (between the ages of the *iuvenis* and the *senex*). Seneca *Ep.* 70.2 (here quoted), 22.14, *Oed.* 776; contrast *Cons. ad Marc.* 21.6. Ovid *Met.* 12.464–65 has Nestor say of the centaur Latreus: "huic aetas inter iuvenemque senemque, vis iuvenalis erat, variabant tempora cani." This is precisely what we today would term "middle-aged" (cf. *Met.* 15.226 for the *medii temporis anni* between *iuventa* and *senecta*). For the situation in Greek, see Garland (1990) 242–43.

35. Sallust *Hist.* 2.47M; Marcus Aurelius *Med.* 2.2 (cf. Rutherford 1989: 123-24); Dionysius of Halicarnassus *Din.* 4 (with Dover 1968: xxvi). Various other items of related interest may also be adduced. Metrodorus, *Anthologia Palatina* 14.127, has γῆρας beginning from age 48 (cf. also John Chrysostom *in Isaiam* 3.2, *PG* 56.42, on the age of 50 years, cited in note 22). In *SEG* 9.1.20–25 (with *SEG* 18.726 = *SB* 10075; ca. 322/1 B.C.) the γέροντες of Cyrene are to be chosen from among those 50 years of age or older (see further Chapter 4 note 24). The emperor Macrinus at age 53 is γέρων, to heighten the contrast with Elagabalus (ca. 13 years old), Dio *Epit.* 78.40.4.

36. Horace *Sat.* 2.1.34; Jerome *Chron.* p. 148H; Cicero *de Sen.* 17.60 (on which see further Chapter 4); cf., e.g., Eyben (1977) 381–83; Rudd (1986) 45–46; Christes (1998) 71–74; Herbert-Brown (1999). For "Kinderkarrieren," see now Horster (1996). Krenkel (1972) 1250–57 would put Lucilius's life at 180–133 B.C., but this is to accept one part of Jerome (the age) and not the other (the date, on the basis that Jerome confused the consuls of 148 B.C. with those of 180 B.C.). For discussion of what Jerome himself apparently understood by the term *senex*, note Hamblenne (1969) and Kelly (1975) 337–39—not entirely convincing. As in the case of Lucilius, there is considerable modern debate about Jerome's date of birth: as early as A.D. 330, or as late as 347/8; for the latter date, see Booth (1979).

37. Ausonius *Epigr.* 20 Green. Ausonius's wife was to die when she was only 27 years old (*Parent.* 9).

38. Of particular interest in the light of what we shall have to say in Chapter 4 is Donatus's comment *ad* Terence *Phorm.* 378: "est haec auctoritas in senibus, ut minores aetate appellatione pueri vel adulescentis vel iuvenis minores etiam ostendant auctoritate, ut hoc de nomine illis quidem detrahant, sibi vero auctoritatem attribuant."

39. Philodemus, *Anthologia Palatina* 11.41 (at 37 years of age); Horace *Epod.* 17.23, *Odes* 3.14.25, *Epist.* 1.20.24: *praecanum* (writing in his late 30s or early 40s); Pliny *Pan.* 4.7 (of Trajan, in his mid-40s); Ovid *Trist.* 4.8 (at the age of 50; Falkner and de Luce 1989: 200–201, de Luce 1993: 233–34). Prudentius, writing at the age of 57 years, notes (*Praef.* 23) that at that age "inrepsit subito canities seni." For some interesting research on the possible correlation between gray hair and chronological age—ap-

proximate at best—see Keogh and Walsh (1965); Ebling (1980) 226; Orentreich and Orentreich (1994) 381–83. It is noted by Ebling, for example, that in modern-day male Caucasians, white hairs around the temples first appear at the age of 34.2 ± 9.6 years, and that by the age of 50 years half the male population has at least 50% of their hair gray; figures for females are virtually identical. Incidentally, Pliny *NH* 7.2.12 (citing Isigonus of Nicaea) and Aulus Gellius 9.4.6 mention that men in the far-distant (and aptly named) land of Albania "canescant in pueritia"; they can also see better at night than during the day. Cf. Ctesias *FGH* 688 F 52 = Pliny *NH* 7.2.28, with Solinus *Coll. Rerum Mem.* 52.28, for the Pandae of India who have white hair in their youth and black hair in old age (see further Chapter 8 note 100). Phlegon *Mirab.* 32 (*FGH* 257 F 36.32) cites the case of one male who apparently went through the whole life cycle in only seven years. One might attribute this to the very rare progeria or Hutchinson-Gilford syndrome, except that within the seven years the individual apparently married and begot children. For similar alleged cases in antiquity, see Hansen (1996) 167–70, and for the motif of the *puer senex,* see Chapter 9.

40. Gilbert (1967); see further Covey (1992), and Shahar (1997) ch. 1.
41. Ovid *ex Pont.* 1.4.20; *CIL* 8.9158 = *ILS* 8503.
42. Aeschines *in Timarchum* 49 (345 B.C.); whether the age of 44 years is accurate makes no difference to our argument here. Cf. Aelian *Var. Hist.* frag. 110 Hercher for the 91-year-old Isidorus, who apparently looked 60 at most, thanks to exercise (on this theme see Chapter 9). Note too Plato *Lysis* 207c where two young friends are unsure which of them is the older.
43. Garland (1995) 26.
44. E.g., Galen *de San. Tuenda* 5.9, 6.3 (6.356–57, 398K = *CMG* 5.4.2.154, 175). I agree with Byl (1983: 86; 1988b: 83) that Hippocrates and Galen envisaged old age "d'un point de vue beaucoup plus qualitatif que quantitatif," and I would add that the same could plausibly be said of the attitude of most people in antiquity in general.
45. Siegel (1980) 346.
46. Finley (1981) 156; note also Dover (1968) xxvii; Philibert (1984) 16–19.
47. *Dig.* 32.69.1. Note again that there is no Latin term here for "'middle-aged'"; one progresses directly from *iuvenis* to *senior.* In the second century A.D. the Christian theologian Irenaeus *adv. Haereses* 2.33.3 stated, with somewhat spurious precision, that "quia autem triginta annorum aetas prima indolis est iuvenis, et extenditur usque ad quadragesimum annum, omnis quilibet confitebitur; a quadragesimo autem et quinquagesimo anno declinat iam in aetatem seniorem."
48. On Latin *Zahlwörter* and expressions of age, see Kühner and Stegmann (1955) 1.284, and Hofmann and Szantyr (1965) 42, 210–14. The use of the ordinal in Greek appears to have been less common, but note for Roman times, e.g., [Lucian] *Macr.* 22; Plutarch *Philop.* 18.1, *Cic.* 48.4.

49. *CIL* 6.8517 = *ILS* 1660.
50. Demosthenes 27.4–6; [Aristotle] *Ath. Pol.* 42.1. Sealey (1957), citing earlier discussions; Welsh (1977); Golden (1979). Note also the comments of Tazelaar (1967) 128–29, Rhodes (1981) 497–98, and Crowther (1988) 306.
51. Carter (1967).
52. Appian *Bell. Civ.* 2.149 (likewise Suetonius *Div. Iul.* 88); Plutarch *Caes.* 69.1. On Pompey's age at death, note esp. Velleius Paterculus 2.53.3–4, who reports that some ("nimium occupati") have miscalculated his age by a *quinquennium*—thus Valerius Maximus 5.2.9 and, later, Tacitus *Ann.* 13.6.
53. Suetonius *Tib.* 5; Levison (1898) 11. See too Aulus Gellius 15.28, noting errors in various calculations of Cicero's age by Cornelius Nepos and by Fenestella (*HRR* 2.84, and cf. Quintilian *Inst. Or.* 12.6.4). On Suetonius's method of stating ages, see Levick (1966) and Sumner (1967). Note also Sumner (1973) 155–58 on Cicero's calculation of the ages of orators in the *Brutus,* and cf. Chapter 1 note 76, on Galba.
54. Golden (1979) 25–28.
55. Brief treatment in Richardson (1985) 11.
56. Herodotus 2.4.1; Celsus *de Med.* 3.5.3; see further Howard (1958), who concludes that inclusive reckoning is not always adopted with this type of phrase, although it is usual when small numerals are involved, and Beaujeu (1975). Compare (i) the confusion caused by intercalation "quarto quoque anno" at the end of the first century B.C.—the extra day was added every *third* year instead of every fourth (Macrobius *Sat.* 1.14.13–15; Solinus *Coll. Rerum Mem.* 1.45–47), and (ii) the Roman census being held every fourth year originally (at least in theory) but in the second century B.C. every fifth year (Chapter 6).
57. Carter (1967) 53–54: *P.Gen.* 33 (the example I cite here), *BGU* 28, 110, 111; see now also Kruit (1998), who broadens the scope of the investigation, finding evidence for inclusive reckoning in regard to age in years in ephebic registers and census returns from Egypt. On birth or status notices, see Chapter 6.
58. Bickerman (1980) 66. See also Schulz (1942) 89 (amended readings): "According to the Egyptian style the imperial year began with the 29th or (after leap years) the 30th August. The second year of an emperor began with the first 29th or 30th August after his accession."
59. *Dig.* 40.1.1, 50.16.134 (on *anniculus,* see further Gaius *Inst.* 1.29–31; [Ulpian] *Epit.* 3.3; and cf. *Frag. Vat.* 371: "minor anniculo"), *Dig.* 3.1.1.3 (with Mommsen 1887–88: 1.506 n. 2), 50.6.4 (also quoted in Chapter 4). For other explicit and exact statements of age in the legal corpus, note *Dig.* 4.4.32 (Paul), 48.5.16.6 (Ulpian); *Cod. Theod.* 2.16.2 (= *Cod. Iust.* 2.52.5; A.D. 319?), 12.1.19 (A.D. 331); *Cod. Iust.* 5.60.3 (A.D. 529), 5.4.24 (A.D. 530).

60. Dio 56.30.5 (the precision is typical of Dio); cf. Suetonius *Div. Aug.* 100.1; Velleius Paterculus 2.123.2; Jerome *Chron.* p. 171H.
61. Date of Lucius's death (20 August A.D. 2): *PIR*² I 222. Note, however, that Russell (1990) 91 assumes that the letter is to be dated to A.D. 2, taking ὑμῶν as "my grandson and other family." But it is worth pointing out that Firmicus Maternus *Math.* 4.20.3 also assumes that the climacteric year is the 63rd, not the 64th.
62. On Augustus as "annos undeviginti natus" (*Res Gestae* 1.1) after the Ides of March (at the age of 18, as both Velleius Paterculus 2.61.1 and Dio 45.4 are aware), see Lauffer (1983). One further complication is the legal fiction that "a year begun is a year completed"—for its limited applicability, see Chapter 4. On ordinal-cardinal confusion, see also Reinhold (1933); Halkin (1948—useful for citation of examples but probably wrong re Vergil *Ecl.* 4); Waltz (1949); Levick (1966) 238. On such confusion and the increasing importance of numerical age in Tudor and Stuart England, see K. Thomas (1976) 206–7.
63. *CIL* 3.11711 = *Inscriptionum Lapidarium Latinarum Provinciae Norici* (Berlin, 1986) 1794; see further Parkin (1992) 14.
64. Merrill (1900); Burn (1953) 14, 19; Hopkins (1966–67) 249. Howell (1986) has a useful discussion on the problems for anthropologists of age determination. Among many case studies of value for comparative purposes, note the censuses held in the Russian cities of Tula and Viatka in 1715 and 1720. Interesting data on levels of age-awareness emerge: while many people age by five years between the two censuses, "some reports in 1720 actually supplied ages several years *younger* than those reported in 1715; at the other extreme were those who estimated as many as 33 years having passed" (Kaiser and Engel 1993: 827).
65. Duncan-Jones (1977; 1979; 1980; 1990: 79–92). In the context of Roman Egypt, see further Chapter 5.
66. Duncan-Jones (1977) 334; also (1990) 91–92. Cf. Harris (1989) 271–72; Thomas (1989) 79 n. 207.
67. Cf. Bagnall and Frier (1994) 46 (note the apparent increase in the incidence of age-rounding among older age-groups); Scheidel (1996a) 89–90. Harris (1989) has little to say on numeracy, but there is useful discussion in Horsfall (1991) 64–65 and Hanson (1991) 183–87.
68. Note Thornton and Thornton (1962), Chevallier (1976), Sorabji (1983).
69. E.g., *CIL* 6.17420, 6.25302, 6.27124, 9.1746. Kajanto (1968) 18–19 assumed that such precision means that exact age was known, but that need not be true at all; on the other hand, however, astrological influence may have meant the precise hour of one's birth—or of conception—was necessary knowledge. Regarding Christian exactness in recording age at death on tombstones, see also Shaw (1996) 103.
70. Nilsson (1920), esp. 98–108 on ignorance of exact age.

71. For generational reckoning, see Samuel (1972) 241–45, esp. for reference to work by Molly Miller; Nash (1978) 1–21; Laroche (1986). Note also Fortes (1984), who asserts (114) that "chronological age becomes significant when the political and legal framework takes precedence over familial and kinship relations for determining citizenship." In the Athenian context, now see Robertson (2000).
72. On ancient birthdays, see W. Schmidt in *RE* 7.1135–49, and further Schmidt (1908), with Argetsinger (1992). A. Stuiber's piece in *RAC* 9.217–43 is predominantly on Christian aspects; note further Shaw (1996) 103.
73. Kajanto (1968) 9–13 (there are mistakes in his figures at some points however: see Parkin 1992: 8–9). Age at death as well as the number of years of service often appears on soldiers' tombstones, but because service usually started around the age of 17 or 18 years, evidence of so basic a calculation to produce a figure for length of life is hardly significant.
74. Néraudau (1984) 40.
75. For the complexities of calculating age in Roman Egypt, complexities that increased as one aged, see Hanson (1991) 184.
76. This may, for example, account for the fact that in his life of Galba (4), Suetonius says that Galba was born in the consulship of M. Valerius Messalla and Cn. Lentulus, i.e., 3 B.C., but later Suetonius states (23) that Galba died in his 73rd year, whereas in fact, if he was born (on 24 December) in 3 B.C., he was only in his 71st year when he died (on 15 January) in A.D. 69. If the manuscript readings are to be trusted, then it seems to me more likely that Suetonius got the year of birth right, based on annalistic sources, and miscalculated the age at death, than vice versa. But having said that, it must then be assumed that others also got it wrong, for all other extant sources suggest a birth year of 6 or 5 B.C.: Dio 64.6 states that Galba was aged 72 years and 23 days at death, and [Aurelius Victor] *Epit. de Caes.* 6.4 records that he died in his 73rd year. It is implied that he became emperor in his 73rd year (and therefore died in his 74th year) by several sources: Suetonius *Nero* 40.3, Plutarch *Galba* 8, Eutropius 7.16. Tacitus *Hist.* 1.49 gives him 73 years at death. *PIR* S 723 comments: "fieri potest, ut fama Galbae aliquot annos addiderit." This is probably right; in other words, despite the abundance of literary references to 6 or 5 B.C. (copying each other's mistakes?; cf. Syme 1958: esp. 674–76, 683), Galba was most likely born in 3 B.C.
77. For example, 40 years of age is a common assumption for an individual's floruit: see Jacoby (1902) 41–51 for 40 years as the ἀκμή of a career in Apollodorus's *Chronica* (a basic source of information on *makrobioi*), with Mosshammer (1976), who, like Jacoby, stresses the Pythagorean influence. Even Tacitus may slip up on ages occasionally: Syme (1958) 746, Gallivan (1974).

Chapter 2. The Demography of Old Age

1. Parkin (1992); some material from there, particularly on longevity, is further discussed here. The most significant studies to appear on aspects of the demography of the Roman world since 1992 are Bagnall and Frier (1994) and Scheidel (1996a); note also Shaw (1996) and Bagnall et al. (1997). Of particular importance on a related theme is Saller (1994) pt. 1. Scheidel (2001a–c) and B. Frier's chapter in *CAH*[2] 11 appeared too late to be considered in depth here.

2. Bagnall and Frier (1994), discussed further in Parkin (1995); important critical assessment is now to be found also in Scheidel (2001b).

3. Macdonell (1913); Leschi (1957) 297–99. From Africa note also the illuminating case of Titus Flavius Pudens Maximianus (83 or 100 years old?; Parkin 1992: 14–15), that of Q. Iulius Castus (75 or 81?; *CIL* 8.26933 = *CLE* 1873, Thugga), and of Masinissa, king of Numidia (see Chapter 7).

4. Harkness (1896) 68; Macdonell (1913) 375–77; Berelson (1934) 82; Étienne (1959) 419; Lassère (1977) 527, 537, 562–63; Morizot (1989) 666–68. Literary support has been found in such texts as Sallust *Bell. Iug.* 17.6. Outside of Africa, one thinks too of Claudian's so-called old man of Verona (*Carm. Min.* 20; cf. Horsfall 1991–92). Note also Pliny *Ep.* 5.6.5–6 on the healthy air in Tuscany, conducive to long life, and Ammianus Marcellinus 27.4.14 on the longevity of the Thracians, a result of such factors as "aurae purioris dulcedo" (on which see the curious little article by Damsté 1929). Brogan (1962) cites several cases of individuals recorded as dying as centenarians in Roman Africa (including one of the third or fourth century A.D., *AE* [1964] no. 194, whose tombstone records that "vixit annorum CX et supra") and concludes that "Africans of the second and third centuries, by and large, found that life was worth living."

5. Dyson (1992a: 212, 1992b: 374); Shaw (1991a). On environment and climate allegedly affecting the aging process, see also Chapter 2 note 43 and Chapter 9, esp. note 60.

6. Clauss (1973) table 10; Parkin (1992) 8.

7. See Shaw (1973, 1982, 1991b) on the persistently high status of older people—or at least of some older males—in Roman African society, as evidenced by epigraphical testimony for *seniores* and the *undecimprimi.*

8. Pliny *NH* 7.49.162–64; Phlegon *FGH* 257 F 37. These data and their derivation are discussed further in Chapter 6, and in Parkin (1999) 155–57.

9. It is also of some interest that extant epitaphs from this region of Italy (in *CIL* 11 and subsequent publications) record no one dying over the age of 83 years, and indeed relatively few (compared with most other *regiones*) over the age of 60 years. By contrast, from Aquileia in the tenth region we

find a woman recorded as dying at the age of 135 (*CIL* 5.8595) and a male over 110 (5.8294).

10. See esp. Bagnall and Frier (1994) 43, 46–47, 104–9, with Parkin (1995) 91. Further discussion and bibliography in Chapter 5.
11. *Hist. Eccl.* 7.21.9–10. Cf. Rea (1972) 1–2; Bienert (1978) 149–53, 157–62; Andresen (1979) 414–28; Parkin (1999) 153–54.
12. E. Gibbon, *The History of the Decline and Fall of the Roman Empire*, ch. 10. Cf. Parkin (1992) 63–64.
13. Jones (1964) 1045 is clearly wrong in dating it from as late as the time of Diocletian; see also Garnsey (1988) 254, and now Haas (1997) 77, 392 nn. 68–69 (possibly as early as the end of the first century A.D.).
14. Delia (1988); cf. Bagnall and Frier (1994) 53–56. Haas (1997) 45–47, 375–76 n. 3 prefers a lower figure; I disagree, but in any case it makes little difference to our arguments here.
15. *NH* 7.48.153–49.164. For Pliny's use of Varro, Verrius Flaccus, and Valerius Maximus, see Münzer (1897) 105–18, 137–295, 299–321; Rabenhorst (1907); Ranucci (1976); note also Kádár and Berényi-Révész (1986) 2214–16.
16. Pliny *NH* 7.48.154. Most other sources attest a life-span of 150 years for Arganthonius: Phlegon *FGH* 257 F 37.98; [Lucian] *Macr.* 9–10 (noting that some consider it a fable); Censorinus *de Die Nat.* 17.3—all misquoting Herodotus; so too Appian *Hisp.* 63. But Herodotus 1.163 and Cicero *de Sen.* 19.69 state that Arganthonius lived 120 years, and Valerius Maximus 8.13.ext.4 (quoting Asinius Pollio) gives 130. The earliest source, Anacreon 16 *PMG,* quoted by Strabo 3.2.14.151, implies a *reign* of 150 years. At any rate, Arganthonius was traditionally believed to have lived a long time—he became almost as proverbial as Nestor (e.g., Ausonius *Epist.* 4.6 Green, Themistius *Or.* 2.38a, Libanius *Or.* 25.23, *Ep.* 1406). The exact age probably was of little more than pedantic concern: Silius Italicus 3.396–98 has him at 300 years old.
17. For a sample of human races, see Pliny *NH* 7.2.27–30 and [Lucian] *Macr.* 4–5, with Garland (1990) 247. According to Ctesias (*FGH* 688 F 45.43 = Photius *Bibl.* 48b), the Indian Κυνοκέφαλοι live to 170 or even 200 years, and are thus the longest-lived of all humans. On long-lived Indians, see also Ctesias *FGH* 688 F 45.32 = Photius *Bibl.* 47a (120, 130, 150, and even 200 years) and 688 F 52 (with Valerius Maximus 8.13.ext.5 and Solinus *Coll. Rerum Mem.* 52.28), Onesicritus *FGH* 134 F 11 (Pliny *NH* 7.2.28) and F 24 (Strabo 15.1.34.701), and Crates of Mallos (Pliny *loc. cit.*; see *RE* 11.1634–41); on the Μακρόβιοι of Taprobane (Sri Lanka), see Chapter 9. For *short-lived* Indians (old age from the age of 30, maximum life-span of 40 years), see Arrian *Ind.* 9 with Pliny *NH* 7.2.29 (Megasthenes, *FGH* 715 F 13). For the animals, see Richardson (1933) 230.

18. Tithonus: *Homeric Hymn to Aphrodite* 218–38; Plutarch *Mor.* 792e; Cicero *de Sen.* 1.3 (Powell 1988: 101); *Suda* T 578; see also King (1986), Brillante (1987), and Chapter 9. On Varro's Menippean satire, *Tithonus* ἢ περὶ γήρως, see Chapter 3. Teiresias: seven, or even nine (says Tzetzes), times the normal human life-span (or, less dramatically, generation): Hesiod frag. 275–76; [Lucian] *Macr.* 3; Phlegon *FGH* 257 F 36.4; Hyginus *Fab.* 75; Lactantius Placidus *Comm. in Statii Theb.* 2.95; *Scriptores Rerum Mythicarum Latini* 2.84; Tzetzes *ad Lycophr.* 682. Cf. Roscher (1916–24) 180; McCartney (1925) 40; Brisson (1976); Ugolini (1995) 36–65. Sibyls: Phlegon *FGH* 257 F 37.99 (Sibyl of Erythrae), just short of 1,000 years, in her tenth *saeculum* (note also *Die Inschriften von Erythrai und Klazomenai* 2 [Bonn, 1973] no. 224: 900 years); Ovid *Met.* 14.142–49 (Cumae), 700 years when Aeneas met her, and she lived another 300 years. Cf. Parke (1988) 20 n. 15, 63; Potter (1990) 116 n. 59.

19. Vergil *Aen.* 6.304; Apuleius *Met.* 6.18, following Vergil, describes Charon as *squalidus senex*. See further Sourvinou-Inwood (1995) ch. 5.

20. Aeson: see Chapter 9. Pelias: Powell (1988) 262–63 on Cicero *de Sen.* 23.83.

21. Homer *Iliad* 1.250, 2.373; *Odyss.* 3.245. More than two generations (i.e., over 60 years old), *schol. ad Iliad.* 1.250. In his third century, Ovid *Met.* 12.187–88. Cf. [Lucian] *Macr.* 3: outlasted three generations; Laevius *Poet.* frag. 8 (Courtney 1993: 124) *ap.* Aulus Gellius 19.7.13 ("trisaeclisenex"); Cicero *de Sen.* 10.31 (Powell 1988: 166); Plutarch *Mor.* 788b, *Cato Maior* 15; Artemidorus *Oneirocrit.* 2.70 (90 years); *Anthologia Palatina* 7.144.2 (Anonymous: τριγέρων). The ancient scholiast to Juvenal 10.246 states that Nestor lived to the third *aetas*, "id est trecentos annos." Note also Martial 10.24.11, quoted in the previous chapter.

22. *Mirab.* 17 (*FGH* 257 F 36.17), citing Apollonius the grammarian.

23. *Ant. Jud.* 1.3.9.108 (*FGH* 1 F 35, etc.), with John Lydus *de Mens.* 3.5. Note also the lengthy discussion in Saint Augustine *de Civ. Dei* 15.9–14, using Pliny *NH* 7; Augustine argues that the fabulous ages attributed to figures from the Old Testament are to be believed, despite the incredulity of many (one "obscura et non necessaria quaestio" with which Augustine must deal in this context is that men "primi saeculi" by implication abstained from sexual intercourse for the first hundred or so years of their lives, 15.15). At 16.28 Augustine reports that in the days of Genesis people "adhuc tamdiu vivebant ut centum anni nondum facerent hominem decrepitae senectutis." Note also Diodorus Siculus 1.26.4–5; Censorinus *de Die Nat.* 19.4; Lactantius *Inst. Div.* 2.12.21- 24 and *Epit.* 22.5 (dismissing Varro's opinion that this was because Egyptians counted months as years; cf. Augustine *de Civ. Dei* 15.12–13 on, inter alia, Pliny *NH* 7.48.155, and see also Ogilvie 1978: 51–52 on Lactantius's use of Varro here).

24. Diogenes Laertius 1.111 (Phlegon *FGH* 257 F 38; Xenophanes 21 B 20 D-K); Varro *de Ling. Lat.* 7.3, *Menipp.* frag. 491 Astbury (*Sexagesis*); Va-

lerius Maximus 8.13.ext.5 (Theopompus); Pliny *NH* 7.48.154, 7.52.175; Plutarch *Mor.* 784a; *Suda* E 2471 (a life-span of 150 years, with 90 years asleep); Roscher (1904: 91; 1906: 207). Pseudo-Lucian is particularly fond of listing aged and distant but allegedly historical monarchs, such as Hyspausines, "the king of Charax and the country on the Red Sea" (*Macr.* 16), 85 years of age at death, and various of his successors, such as Tiraeus (92 years) and Artabazus (king at age 86 years, according to *Macr.* 16); Artaxerxes, king of Persia and brother of Gosithras, 93 years of age when assassinated (*Macr.* 15, citing Isidorus the Characene historian, *FGH* 781 F 3–4); Ateas, king of the Scythians, over 90 years of age when he fell fighting (10); Camnascires, king of the Parthians, 96 years (16); Goaesus, king of Omania, died at the age of 115 years (17, again following Isidorus); and Teres, king of the Odrysians, 92 years (10, quoting Theopompus).

25. Pliny *NH* 7.48.154 (Anacreon), 7.48.155; Valerius Maximus 8.13.ext.7 (Alexander Polyhistor). Cf. Valerius Maximus 8.13.ext.6 and Pliny *NH* 7.48.154 (Damastes), for Pictoreus or Litorius of the Epii in Aetolia (300 years); and Censorinus *de Die Nat.* 17.3: Ephorus "tradit Arcadas dicere apud se reges aliquot ad trecentos vixisse annos." On Illyrian and Celtic longevity, cf. Grmek (1958) 38–39.

26. [Lucian] *Macr.* 8 (note the Roman exempla); Plutarch *Numa* 21; Dionysius of Halicarnassus *AR* 6.21.3.

27. Cf. Cicero *de Sen.* 7.23.

28. The obscure Myson of Chen: 97 years (Diogenes Laertius 1.108). Pittacus: variously 70 to 100 years ([Lucian] *Macr.* 18; Diogenes Laertius 1.79). Cleobulus of Lindos: 70 years (Diogenes Laertius 1.93). Periander of Corinth: 80 years (Diogenes Laertius 1.95). Solon: usually 80 years (Diogenes Laertius 1.62; *schol. ad* Plato *Rep.* 10.599; cf. Plutarch *Mor.* 794f, *Solon* 31–32; Cicero *de Sen.* 20.72; and note 39), though [Lucian] *Macr.* 18 says 100 years. Thales: 78, 90, or 100 years (Diogenes Laertius 1.38; [Lucian] *Macr.* 18).

29. [Galen] *de Rem. Parab.* 3 (14.567K)—apparently πᾶς αὐτοκράτωρ also used this potion; in fact squill does have a digitalis-like effect on the heart. See Diogenes Laertius 8.44 for more "established" figures for Pythagoras's life-span: Heracleides son of Serapion gives 80 years, but most authorities say 90 years (for the latter see also *P.Herc.* 1788 [D-K 14.13] and *schol. ad* Plato *Rep.* 10.600b). Cf., however, the anonymous *vita ap.* Photius *Bibl.* 438b (Thesleff p. 237) for Pythagoras living 104 years. Georgius Syncellus *Ecl. Chron.* 469 gives 95 years, with a variant (Apollodorus?) of 75 years. See further Jacoby (1902) 215–27; *RE* 24.179–87.

30. Statius *Silv.* 5.3.252–54 (cf. 72–73), and note Plutarch *Mor.* 113d–e. The grief of Claudius Etruscus at the death of his father, at the age of almost 90 years, might have seemed excessive, it is said, for such an old man: Statius *Silv.* 3.3.8–12; compare *CIL* 8.11594 = *CLE* 1328 (Ammaedara).

For the *naturalis mors* of *senes*, cf. Isidorus *Orig.* 11.2.32: "tria sunt autem genera mortis: acerba, inmatura, naturalis. acerba infantum, inmatura iuvenum, merita, id est naturalis, senum" (cf. Chapter 9 note 20).

31. Cicero *de Sen.* 19.71 (Powell 1988: 244–45); Stobaeus *Flor.* 50.1.27 (Juncus), 29 (Themistius). On *mors immatura,* see Parkin (1992) 181 n. 20, with references to earlier discussions, and Sigismund Nielsen (1997) 198–202.

32. For interesting discussion, see Kannisto (1988), esp. 402–4, with the papers in Jeune and Vaupel (1995, 1999).

33. The list can be found at http://www.clas.canterbury.ac.nz/oldancients.html. The only modern list of elderly Greeks of antiquity, that in Richardson (1933) 215–22, is plagued with errors.

34. Note also, for the flourishing old age of sophists, Philostratus *Vit. Soph.* 1.25.543 (56 years is young), and for that of philosophers in general, Jerphagnon (1981), particularly good on types of death. Eunapius and Philostratus mention many aged sophists who are usually otherwise unknown; note the age-rounding in what follows: Aedesius of Cappadocia (over 70), Alypius, Antiochus of Aegae (70 or almost), Apollonius of Athens (about 75), Apollonius of Naucratis (70), Aristocles of Pergamon, Aspasius of Ravenna, Chrysanthius (about 80), Damianus of Ephesus (70), Heliodorus, Hellespontius, Heracleides of Lycia (over 80), Hippias of Elis, Hippodromus of Thessaly (about 70), Nymphidianus of Smyrna, Onomarchus of Andros, Pausanias of Caesarea, Philiscus of Thessaly (67), Phoenix of Thessaly (70), Priscus, the Theoprotian or Molossian (over 90), Proclus of Naucratis (at least 90), Ptolemy of Naucratis, Quirinus of Nicomedia (in his 70th year), and Rufus of Perinthus (61).

35. Hallett (1992) 342–47 remarks on the striking rarity of women in Cicero's *de Senectute;* this is a very valid observation, and Hallett makes some suggestions regarding reasons (see also de Luce et al. 1993: 367), but I think the public nature of the topic as Cicero deals with it is the most important factor (see Chapter 3). On aged females, note also Pliny *NH* 7.48.158–59, and Syme (1991) 511; on Sammula, who according to Pliny died at the age of 110, see Syme (1983b) 108 n. 44.

36. *NH* 11.63.167 (*HRR* 2.105); Mucianus is also Pliny's source (7.48.159 = *HRR* 2.103) for a certain Tempsis, of Mount Tmolus in Asia Minor, living to 150 years. Aristotle *Hist. An.* 2.4.501b (and cf. Pliny *NH* 11.63.166) notes that the wisdom teeth (οἱ κραντῆρες) may emerge in both men and women as old as 80 years or more. Old age was traditionally associated with toothlessness (see Chapter 3 on Juvenal 10.200), but an abundance of teeth was taken as a sign of longevity: Hippocrates *Epid.* 2.6.1 (5.132L); Aristotle *Hist. An.* 2.3.501b; [Aristotle] *Probl.* 34.1.963b; Pliny *NH* 11.114.274. Pliny *NH* 7.16.71 mentions further that men have more teeth than women (likewise Isidorus *Orig.* 11.1.53), an idea which is perhaps tied in with the notion that men live longer than women (see Chap-

ter 9). Gabriele Zerbi, in his *Gerontocomia* of 1489 (discussed further in Chapter 9), ch. 17, observed that not chewing food properly shortens one's life, and hence those with few teeth lead shorter lives.

37. See Chapter 1, with Aulus Gellius 3.10, 15.7 and Censorinus *de Die Nat.* 14. Seneca *de Brev. Vit.* 3.5 states, to suit his argument, that few (*pauci*) survive beyond the age of 50 or 60 years; cf. Cicero *de Sen.* 19.67: "pauci veniunt ad senectutem."

38. Pliny *NH* 7.49.161: "longiora tempora" are "rara." Note also Plutarch *Mor.* 415e on 54 years as the limit of the *middle* years of human life (μεσούσης ὅρον ἀνθρωπίνη ζωῆς).

39. Pliny *Ep.* 1.12.11; Solon frag. 27.17–18 (= Philo *de Opif. Mundi* 35.104: 70 years); note also Macrobius *Comm.* 1.6.76 (70 as the *meta vivendi* and the terminus of the *vitae humanae perfectum spatium,* which commences from age 49; cf. Chapter 1 notes 5–6 and Chapter 5 note 34). Diogenes Laertius 1.60–61 (Mimnermus frag. 6: 60 years; Solon frag. 20: 80 years), and cf. Herodotus 1.29–33, 3.22; Dio Chrysostom 17.20; Augustine *de Civ. Dei* 15.14 (people nowadays live 70 or 80 years "vel non multo amplius"); *Psalms* 90.10.

40. Censorinus *de Die Nat.* 14.5, 14.10. The Etruscan *libri fatales,* which Varro for one must have consulted, also employed a system of twelve hebdomads and mentioned maximum human life-span: *de Die Nat.* 11.6, 14.6.

41. Ausonius *Ecl.* 22 Green, with Plutarch *Mor.* 415c–f; cf. Ausonius *Griphus Ternarii Numeri* 4–6 for 81 years, i.e., 9^2 (Plato's age at death). 100 years/100th year: Pliny *NH* 11.70.184 for the Egyptian tradition; Plato *Rep.* 10.615b; Varro *de Ling. Lat.* 6.11 (quoted in the next note); Seneca *de Brev. Vit.* 3.2; Lucian *Herm.* 50; *Digest* 7.1.56, 33.2.8 (Gaius), and cf. 5.1.76 (Alfenus); Artemidorus *Oneirocrit.* 2.70; Jerome *Ep.* 10.1; *CIL* 8.11594 = *CLE* 1328 (Ammaedara). Note also Diodorus Siculus 1.26.4 (καὶ γὰρ νῦν . . . οὐκ ὀλίγους ὑπὲρ ἑκατὸν ἔτη ζῆν), and Lactantius *de Opif. Dei* 4 (*PL* 7.21 = Usener, *Epicurea* frag. 372), criticizing the Epicurean view.

42. Censorinus *de Die Nat.* 17 has the most detail; cf. Varro *de Ling. Lat.* 6.11: "seclum [sic] spatium annorum centum vocarunt, dictum a sene, quod longissimum spatium senescendorum hominum id putarunt" (contrast *de Ling. Lat* 5.5). Generally *saeculum* refers to a life-span, *aetas* to a generation (i.e., the time a man takes to be born and to reproduce himself, in classical times usually held to be between twenty-seven and forty years), though the two were frequently confused (as in the case of the life-span of Nestor, mentioned earlier): cf., apart from the passages from Varro just cited, Pliny *NH* 16.95.250 and Juvenal 10.248–49. According to Servius *ad Aen.* 8.508, a *saeculum* was variously calculated as 30, 110, or 1,000 years. For 110 years as the χρόνος ἀνθρώποισιν ζωῆς, see Phlegon *FGH* 257 F 37.5.4 (the Sibylline oracle).

43. Pliny *NH* 7.49.160, for 112 years, the view of Epigenes of Byzantium (second century B.C.?), and 116 (CXVI), that of Berosus of Babylon, third

century B.C. (cf. Censorinus *de Die Nat.* 17.4); Servius *in Aen.* 8.51. The figure of 124 years belongs to the Egyptians "Petosiris and Necepsos" (Nechepso; second century B.C.?): the "system of the quarters," says Pliny. For 120 years, cf. Censorinus *de Die Nat.* 17.4; Tacitus *Dial.* 17.3; Arnobius *adv. Nat.* 2.71; Servius *in Aen.* 4.653 (nature allots 120 years, four revolutions of Saturn; fate reduces it to 90); SHA *Claud.* 2.4; Augustine *de Div. Quaest.* 58.2 (*PL* 40.43 = *CCSL* 44a.107); Lactantius *Inst. Div.* 2.12.23–24, 2.13.3, *Epit.* 22.5; note also Grassl (1978–79) on *CIL* 3.5389. For the old age of Britons *beginning* at 120 years (because they live in a colder climate, as opposed to the Ethiopians, who, because of the heat of the sun, grow old in their 30th year), cf. Asclepiades *ap.* [Galen] *de Hist. Phil.* 33 (19.344–45K = Diels, *Dox. Graec.* p. 648) and [Plutarch] *Plac. Philosoph.* 5.30 (*Mor.* 911b; Diels pp. 443–44); Pliny *NH* 6.35.195 says that *pars quaedam Aethiopum* do not exceed their 40th year. Contrast Herodotus 3.22–23 (with 3.17, 21, 97, 114; also Pomponius Mela *de Chorographia* 3.9.85, Valerius Maximus 8.13.ext.5, Pliny *NH* 7.2.27, *schol. ad* Juvenal 10.150, etc.) for the "long-lived" Ethiopians; cf. Last (1923). According to Pliny *NH* 8.75.199, even animals live longer in Ethiopia.

44. Parkin (1992) ch. 2; see also Saller (1994) ch. 2.
45. Compare Chapter 1, for old age being defined as beginning when e_x = 10–15 years.
46. While reference is made here to Model West "female," it should be stressed that these figures need not be related to a single, specific sex. On the stable and stationary population models, see Parkin (1992) ch. 2. It must be stressed again that model life tables are used here only to illustrate probable (as opposed to improbable) variables and orders of magnitude. Scheidel (2001a–c) has argued vigorously against the use of the Coale-Demeny model life tables in the context of Roman history. There is no doubt that one cannot assume a close fit to any exact model in any one place at any one time in the Roman world. What we are using the life tables for, as I emphasized in Parkin (1992), is simply a generalized perception of population structure, and unfortunately we do not have sufficient evidence to fit any ancient population with more precision. It is certainly true that we cannot assume infant mortality levels from adult mortality, but we have insufficient basis to "splice" model life tables to allow for lower infant mortality levels, for example. But since the publication of Coale-Demeny[2] in 1983, new model life tables for higher mortality regimes have been designed that actually allow for the sort of criticisms Scheidel subsequently made of Coale-Demeny[2]; they allow for lower levels of infant mortality and higher mortality levels for ages 15–65 years than in the relevant Coale-Demeny tables: see Preston et al. (1993), who specifically state that their tables may be used in conjunction with Coale-Demeny[2] "[f]or populations with life expectancies [at birth] between 20

and 32 [years]" (p. 153). The resulting figures, however, make little significant difference to our conjectures for calculations relating to Romans over the age of 60 years; in a stable population model. For example, where life expectancy at birth is in the band of the low- to high-20s (see my Table 3 in Appendix A), life expectancy at age 60 years is of the order of 9–11 years, and the proportion of a stationary population over the age of 60 years (C_{60+}) remains in the 5–7% range.

47. Philostratus *Vit. Soph.* 1.9.494 (108 years); Censorinus *de Die Nat.* 15.3 (108); [Lucian] *Macr.* 23 (108); Pliny *NH* 7.48.156 (108: "indubitatum est"); *schol. ad* Plato *Phaedr.* 261c = Hermias Alexandrinus *ad Phaedr.* 261b (108, stressing the parallel with Nestor, as had Plato *Phaedr.* 261c); Cicero *de Sen.* 5.13 (107 years); Valerius Maximus 8.13.ext.2 (still alive in his 107th year); Quintilian *Inst. Or.* 3.1.9 (109); Diogenes Laertius 8.58 (Apollodorus, *FGH* 244 F 33: 109); *Suda* Γ 388 (109); Olympiodorus *ad* Plato *Gorg.* 447a (109). I know of only two significantly dissenting voices: Pausanias 6.17.9 says 105 years (amended to 109 by Wilamowitz), and Clearchus (frag. 62 Wehrli) *ap.* Athenaeus *Deipn.* 12.548d says Gorgias was σχεδὸν π̄, nearly 80—this is usually amended to read ρ', 100, or ρι', 110 years. On these figures see also Jacoby (1902) 261–66. One further item might arouse some suspicion: Plutarch *Mor.* 415e gives 108 years as the length of a γένος (cf. note 38). The fact that early references to Gorgias's longevity (Plato *Phaedr.* 261c, Isocrates 15.155) cite no specific age also makes one wonder.

48. Cicero *de Sen.* 5.13, Valerius Maximus 8.13.ext.2. Gorgias's health apparently never deteriorated (though note Aristotle *ap.* Stobaeus *Flor.* 51.28 W-H); one of his secrets for long life was said (by [Lucian] *Macr.* 23) to be that he never accepted an invitation to dinner; another, according to Clearchus and Demetrius of Byzantium *ap.* Athenaeus *Deipn.*12.548d, was that he never did anything for pleasure or, if we trust the manuscript reading, for anyone else either. Gabriele Zerbi, in his *Gerontocomia* of 1489 (see Chapter 9), ch. 15, credits Gorgias's 108 years to living on an island.

49. Parkin (1992) 85, with tables 7–8 and 12; see also Saller (1994) 11 n. 3.

50. Such an exercise has been carried out by the Cambridge Population Group (CAMSIM; see the useful overview in Laslett 1988, with Smith and Oeppen 1993), and its methods used by Richard Saller in the Roman context. The figures I cite here are derived from Saller (1994) 48–65 (tables 3.1–3), though there are some problems with the figures, as Saller is himself aware (46, 67–69 on remarriage); I also do not subscribe to the sex-specific use of model life tables. But for our purposes the figures are, in my opinion, both of the correct magnitude and very valuable as indicators of probable reality.

51. For the list, see, e.g., Plautus *Pers.* 57 and *Dig.* 38.10.10 (Paul).

52. If one assumes younger average marriage ages ("senatorial" ages, on av-

erage 25 years for males, 15 for females), the resulting figures change slightly; the difference is only of any significance in terms of the somewhat greater likelihood of having a grandparent alive in later years (by age 16, in this case, one in two Romans would have had no grandparents living).

53. To take just one example of commemoration, Ovid *Fasti* 5.426: at the festival of the Lemuria, a grandson pays his respects to the tomb in which his grandfather is interred ("compositique nepos busta piabat avi"). In the context, it is interesting to note Hopkins (1983) 205–6, discussing the relative rarity of family tombs that contain more than two generations; for an exception, see *CIL* 11.4978 (*CLE* 1848, Spoletium): "hic aviam neptemque locus post fata recepit . . ."

54. This is not to deny, of course, that one's extended ancestry and lineage matter, not least for some Romans in the imperial period in terms of qualification for the rank of senator or *eques*. Note too, conversely, that descendants might bring dishonor: e.g., according to Pliny the Elder (*NH* 7.28.104), the good name of Marcus Sergius, though he himself was long dead, was brought into disrepute by the actions of his *pronepos* (greatgrandson), Catilina.

55. Saller and Shaw (1984) 136–37; Saller (1986) 16. In response to the critique of Martin (1996), see Rawson (1997b). I intend to produce at a later date a study of the status and role of grandparents in Roman law and life; there is some useful material in Wiedemann (1989) and Gardner (1998). For ancient Greece, see the general account by Corvisier (1991), part of a collection of papers on grandparents in history from a demographic perspective, though Corvisier's focus is literary.

56. Cf., e.g., Plutarch *Crass.* 1, *Aem. Paul.* 5; Valerius Maximus 4.4.8; *Dig.* 7.8.4–6 (Ulpian, Paul). See Dixon (1988: 14–15; 1992: 6–7, 22, etc.); Bradley (1991), esp. chs. 6–7; Treggiari (1991) 410–12; Gardner (1998) 67–74. For comparative purposes, cf. Laslett (1977: ch. 5; 1983: ch. 4; 1996: ch. 8); Mitterauer and Sieder (1982) ch. 7; and the excellent study by Wall (1995).

57. Basic information at Bagnall and Frier (1994) 146–47, with further cases from Bagnall *et al.* (1997), to which add also *P.Bodl.* 17 col. 5. The fourgenerational household is *BGU* 2.577 (Karanis, A.D. 203).

58. Note Arnobius *adv. Nat.* 5.14 on myths (or, quite literally, "old wive's tales"—see Chapter 3 note 120): "cum historias, quaeso, perlegitis tales, nonne vobis videmini aut textriculas puellas audire taediosi operis circumscribentes moras aut *infantibus credulis avocamenta quaeritantes anus longaevas* <* ?> et varias fictiones sub imagine veritatis expromere?" Likewise Lactantius *Inst. Div.* 3.18.16: "videlicet senex vanus, sicut otiosae aniculae solent, fabulas tamquam infantibus credulis finxit." *Avia,* incidentally, need not always have positive connotations: note Persius *Sat.* 5.92 with *schol.*: "veteres avias dicit aut aniles ineptias aut inveteratam stulti-

tiam" (and Persius *Sat.* 2.31 for a stereotypically superstitious grand-mother; the passage also provides incidental evidence of the grandmother assisting in child rearing).

59. Tacitus *Dial.* 28.4 has Messalla comment that in the "good old days" an older female relative would have had charge over the young children of the house; now slaves take control. Note the *famula decrepita,* stern child rearer through several generations in the home of Saint Augustine's maternal grandfather, and *sagax anus* honored in this Christian home "propter senectam ac mores optimos" (*Conf.* 9.8).

60. Treggiari (1991) 84. For the blessing of grandchildren, see, e.g., Catullus 68.119–24 (and note that it concerns the son of a *daughter;* Crook 1986:73–74, with Gardner 1998: 33), Pliny *Ep.* 3.3.1, and see further Chapter 8.

61. Pliny *Ep.* 8.10; Seneca *Cons. ad Marc.* 16.6–8 ("respice tot nepotes").

62. Much has been made of the linguistic differences in archaic Latin between the maternal and paternal sides of the family, particularly with reference to the word *avus:* for discussion, see Bremmer (1976, 1983b) and Hallett (1984) 127–32, with Bettini (1984: 487–90; 1991: ch. 3). But whatever the truth of that—I am skeptical—what I am suggesting here is that the realities of life in the Roman world of the classical period meant that no significant variation between the paternal and maternal side existed in this regard (though it did in some other, legal respects, to be sure); *avus* was used for both sides, only on occasion being further defined as *paternus* or *maternus.* The jurist Paul is unambiguous (*Dig.* 38.10.10.13; likewise Festus 12L): "avus, hoc est patris et matris pater. item avia, similiter tam paterna quam materna." For linguistic differentiation between paternal and maternal, note *patruus/amita* as opposed to *avunculus/matertera.*

63. Pliny *Ep.* 8.18.4; Dixon (1988) 60; Treggiari (1991) 395–96; Gardner (1998) 105. Tullus, whom we shall have occasion to mention several times in the chapters to follow, found a way round this. Note also the case of Ummidia Quadratilla, who left two-thirds of her estate to her grandson (a close friend of Pliny the Younger), the other third to her granddaughter, "honestissimo testamento." It remains uncertain whether she was their maternal or paternal grandmother. At any rate, the grandson was brought up in her house, and she asked Pliny to see to his training; she was also careful not to let her *pantomimi* perform in his presence: Pliny *Ep.* 7.24. For (alleged) sinister behavior by a grandfather in Roman Africa, similar to Tullus's case, see also Apuleius *Apol.* 68: Pudentilla's husband Sicinius Amicus dies; the two sons remain in the *potestas* of their paternal grandfather, but they are brought up by their mother; the grandfather tries to orchestrate a new husband, and threatens to disinherit his grandchildren if Pudentilla marries outside the family. She must wait for the grandfather to die.

64. Cicero *ad Att.* 12.18a.2, 12.28.3, 12.30.1. Cf. *Dig.* 23.2.67.1 (Tryphoni-

nus) for *affectio avita* (paternal). At *Dig.* 24.3.45 (Paul), a *maternal* grandfather has provided a dowry for his granddaughter "quae erat in patris potestate"; see also Gardner (1998) 235 on generous maternal grandmothers.

65. Tacitus *Ann.* 13.45: Poppaea Sabina adopts her maternal grandfather's name; Hallett (1984) 106–9; Gardner (1998) 139.

66. Most detail, which I need not rehash here, in Krause (1994–95) 3.57–62, 67–73, esp. in the context of Roman Egypt; see also Dixon (1988) 132–33, and note too Paulus *ex* Festus 201L s.v. *Opiter.*

67. Suetonius *Div. Aug.* 2–4, 6, 8; cf. Nicolaus *Bios Kais.* 3.5 = *FGH* 90 F 127, and Syme (1939) 112.

68. Suetonius *Div. Aug.* 64–65, 34. Note Suetonius *Gaius* 7 for Augustus's and Livia's grief at the loss of a great-grandson. Of course grandparenthood was not always blissful or revered: note Suetonius *Div. Claud.* 3.2 for Livia being scornful of her grandson Claudius (Claudius lived with her for a long time, according to Dio 60.2.5), and Suetonius *Div. Aug.* 65 for Augustus disinheriting Agrippa Postumus (with *Tib.* 15; and posthumously having him executed?: *Tib.* 22; Tacitus *Ann.* 1.6, however, records that "neque mortem nepoti pro securitate privigni inlatam credibile erat"), banishing his granddaughter Julia, and refusing to let her child be acknowledged or reared. Augustus was regarded as fortunate in surviving to see the birth of his great-great-grandson (see Chapter 8).

69. Suetonius *Gaius* 8, 10; Tacitus *Ann.* 5.1. Note in this context also the positive reference to the "discipulinae avi eorum [Germanicus's sons and Claudius] et patrui et Iuliae Aug." in the *s.c. de Cn. Pisone patre* 149–50 (Eck et al. 1996: 48, 247).

70. Suetonius *Div. Vesp.* 2; his mother may have still been alive.

71. SHA *Ant. Pius* 1.9, *M. Aur.* 1.10, and cf. M. Aurelius *Med.* 1.1, 1.4, 1.17.

72. Fronto *de Nepote Amisso* 1–2. Fronto stresses his old age (2.7, 2.8). *Suda* Φ 735 has him "around 60 years"; Champlin (1980) 137–42 suggests a longer life-span, of ca. A.D. 95–ca. 166/7. See also Wiedemann (1989) 93–99; Saller (1994) 77; and van den Hout (1999) 63–64, 379–80, 533.

73. Quintilian *Inst. Or.* 6 pr. 8; compare *CIL* 6.1478, dedicated to an "avia carissima et educatrix dulcissima." Note also *CIL* 6.20938, commemoration by an *avia* and a *nutrix,* and *Dig.* 33.9.7 (Scaevola), children living with their grandmother.

74. Paucity of explicit evidence in such a context is of little surprise, but note Aulus Gellius 12.1.5, of a senatorial family.

75. *Dig.* 37.4.10.1 (Ulpian), 38.17.2.6, 19 (Ulpian); see further, again, Chapter 8, and Gardner (1998) 139. Note also Valerius Maximus 7.1.1: Q. Metellus (see Chapter 8 note 15) takes in his three daughters' offspring ("earum subolem sinu suo exciperet"). It is important to note in the legal context that the term *liberi* could include grandchildren (just as male designation might include females as well): see esp. *Dig.* 50.16.220 (Callis-

tratus); note also 50.16.50 (Ulpian), 51 (Gaius: *parens* can also include *avus* and *proavus,* etc.), 104 (Modestinus), 136 (Ulpian), 146 (Terentius Clemens), 201 (Julian); Gaius *Inst.* 2.129; etc.

Chapter 3. Old Age and the Romans

1. Hesiod *W&D* 113–14 (on which see most recently Most 1997).
2. See Fry and Keith (1986), and esp. Glascock and Feinman (1986) 283; more generally, note Hazan (1994) for the dangers of studying older people solely from the point of view of ideas expressed *about* them rather than *by* them; hence works like de Beauvoir (1977) assume "a nexus between 'us' and 'them'" (Hazan 1994: 94).
3. *Flor.* 50 Wachsmuth and Hense = 115–17 Meineke, Gaisford. References here are to Hense's edition (W-H vol. 5 [1912] 1020–65). For other early collections of Greek quotations—not just classical but also biblical—*de senectute,* note pseudo-Maximus Confessor *Loci Communes* 41 (*PG* 91.916–20) and Antonius Melissa *Loci Communes* 17–18 (*PG* 136.1053–57).
4. Theophrastus (ca. 371–ca. 287 B.C.): Diogenes Laertius 5.43; at 5.40 Theophrastus is said to have died at age 85, "not long after he had relinquished his labors." In the preface to Theophrastus's *Characters* the author says he is 99 years old, but the preface may not be by Theophrastus. To complicate matters, Jerome *Ep.* 52.3 states that Themistocles died at the age of 107 years, regretting having to die just as he was beginning to grow wise. Editors have changed this to Theophrastus, on the basis of Cicero *Tusc. Disp.* 3.28.69 (Theophrastus on his deathbed) and of the fact that Themistocles is usually said to have died around the age of 65 years. Some editors have used this as evidence that Theophrastus therefore *did* write the preface to the *Characters*! For a possible fragment from Theophrastus's περὶ γήρως, see Appendix C.
5. Demetrius (born ca. 350 B.C.) frag. 82–83 Wehrli = *FGH* 228 F 37–38: Diogenes Laertius 2.13, 5.81, 9.20.
6. Aristo of Ceos, the third-century B.C. Peripatetic (less likely, the aged Stoic Aristo of Chios—see Powell 1988: 101–2, 269–72; cf. Gnilka 1983: 1022): Cicero *de Sen.* 1.3.
7. For Democritus on old age, see Herter (1975). By most ancient accounts Democritus died a centenarian: 104 years: [Lucian] *Macr.* 18, Phlegon *FGH* 257 F 37.79; less than 108 years (i.e., less than Gorgias): Censorinus *de Die Nat.* 15.3; over 100: Diogenes Laertius 9.39 (Antisthenes); nearly 109 years: Diogenes Laertius 9.43 (Hipparchus); 90 years: Diodorus Siculus 14.11.5. For important discussion of the philosophical tradition in regard to old age, note also Hense (1909) introd. and Powell (1988), esp. 24–30.
8. *Rep.* 1.328b–331d; useful comments in Silk (1995) 199–203. Accord-

ing to most of our sources, Plato lived to be 81, which pleased the mathematically minded, being $(3^2)^2$. Regarding old age in Plato's works, Forest (1944) is little more than a summary of these opening chapters of the *Republic;* better but still brief is Rankin (1964) 113–19; note also Philibert (1986). Plato's last work, the *Laws,* has quite detailed consideration of old age; see Roussel (1942) 149–53, 187–96; Powell (1994) 274–84.

9. See Powell (1988), esp. 5–6, 111–13. At *de Div.* 2.59 Cicero mentions having a copy of the *Republic* at home.

10. Varro's Menippean satire, *Tithonus* ἢ περὶ γήρως, probably predates Cicero's work (see Cèbe 1972: 31 n. 4; 1999: 2035–37), but only five fragments survive (544–48 Astbury), and in any case from these it cannot be determined (*pace* Cèbe, and Powell 1988: 27) that a favorable view of old age was expressed. See also Dahlmann (1959).

11. The excellent—in all respects, particularly linguistic and literary—commentary by Powell (1988) largely superseded what had for so long been the standard edition, the Budé text and translation by Wuilleumier (three editions, appearing in 1940, 1955, and 1961); an Italian edition by P. Venini also appeared in 1959. With such authoritative editions available, I see little point in my analyzing the dialogue at too great a length; for our purposes, specific points will be stressed. Of other recent discussion of the *de Senectute,* of particular interest is the innovative series of essays by de Luce et al. (1993), approaching the text from a variety of perspectives.

12. Allen (1907); Wuilleumier (1961) 9–10; Powell (1988) 267–68.

13. Cicero *de Sen.* 1.3; cf. *de Amic.* 1.4–5.

14. Cicero *de Sen.* 10.32. Cato died in the next year, aged 84 or 85: Cicero *Brut.* 20.80 (85); Valerius Maximus 8.7.1 (85); Pliny *NH* 29.8.15 (84; Pliny also mentions Cato's regimen of health, which brought him "usque ad longam senectam"). Livy 39.40.12 states that he was in his 90th year, while Plutarch *Cato Maior* 15 says he lived 90 years; presumably they are rounding up. See also Astin (1978) 1 n. 1.

15. *De Sen.* 2.4; for Aetna, see Euripides *Herc. Fur.* 637; Otto (1890) no. 33.1, with Häussler (1968) 52; Powell (1988) 104. In somewhat similar vein, the 84-year-old slave Syra complains of the *onus* of her years weighing her down: Plautus *Merc.* 673; cf. Ovid *Met.* 9.437-38 ("senectae pondera"). *Gravis,* a common epithet for *senectus,* can of course have two meanings in the context of *senectus*—the burden of old age (cf., e.g., Ovid *Met.* 7.478; Seneca *de Ben.* 3.37.1: "gravem senio" of Anchises, being carried by Aeneas; *de Brev. Vit.* 20.4; Sallust *Hist.* 2.47M [Chapter 1 note 35]), or the "gravity" of older people (Cicero *de Rep.* 1.43.67, *pro Cael.* 6.13: "cum senibus graviter"; Pliny *Ep.* 6.20.12: his mother, "annis et corpore gravem," 6.26.1: "puer simplicitate comitate iuvenis senex

gravitate"; Maximianus *Eleg.* 1.105–6; but note Cicero *de Sen.* 10.33: "et infirmitas puerorum, et ferocitas iuvenum, et gravitas iam constantis aetatis [see Chapter 1 note 34], et senectutis maturitas").

16. A further qualification is also made later: Cato states (20.72) that the best type of old age is one "cum integra mente certisque sensibus." As will be seen shortly, old age was generally noted for exactly the opposite features; Seneca was to remark that "paucos longissima senectus ad mortem sine iniuria pertulit" (*Ep.* 58.34).

17. Cf. similarly Musonius Rufus 17.

18. See the passages collected in Stobaeus *Flor.* 50.1, e.g., Sophocles frag. 664 Radt; also Cicero *de Sen.* 6.17, 20 (Powell 1988: 144, 147); Plutarch *An Seni Respublica Gerenda Sit* (discussed below); Seneca *Ep.* 68.14; Jerome *Ep.* 52.3 (Linn 1934). It was said by tradition to be the place of the young to obey and of the old to rule: e.g., Plato *Rep.* 3.412c, 5.465a, *Laws* 3.690a, 11.917a; Aristotle *Pol.* 7.1332b35–41. For older people as teachers of the young, cf. Plato *Laws* 2.659d; Cicero *de Off.* 1.122–23, *de Sen.* 9.29; Pliny *Ep.* 8.14.4 (a thing of the past); Quintilian *Inst. Or.* 12.11.4–7; Plutarch *Mor.* 790e–791c. See also Schofield (1986), Eyben (1972b). Silk (1995) 204 n. 45 makes the point, in relation to Greek literature, that "the wisdom old men may lay claim to . . . is more a matter of good counsel . . . than of sophistication."

19. Indeed Plutarch compares Cato to Nestor, *Cato Maior* 15 (however, he gives Cato more years than in fact he lived).

20. Seneca *de Brev. Vit.* 1.3–4, 7.1–2; *Ep.* 26, 58.29–36, 68.13; note also Xenophon *Mem.* 2.1.31; Bion *ap.* Diogenes Laertius 4.50; [Lucian] *Macr.* 2; Juvenal 1.144 (although the meaning of "intestata senectus" has long been debated—see esp. Cloud 1989: 57–58, rightly challenging the traditional view established by Housman; Courtney 1980: 114, however, would prefer to read "intemptata"). For physical weakness, regularly counterbalanced by intellectual abilities, cf., e.g., *Iliad* 4.314, Powell (1988) 160 on Cicero *de Sen.* 9.27–11.38, and Oakley (1997) 583.

21. Saint Augustine *Sermo* 128.11 (*PL* 38.718–19) noted that while "the enemy," *concupiscentia,* becomes weaker in old age, it must still be fought against. *Anthologia Palatina* 10.56.15–16 (Palladas) remarked that "not even old age has peace from the goads (οἴστρων) of Aphrodite." Conversely, it would appear that one cult title of Aphrodite in Sparta was Ἀμβολογήρα, "Postponer of old age" (Pausanias 3.18.1)—presumably on the "only as old as you feel" principle.

22. The story of Sophocles, taken from Plato *Rep.* 1.329b, is perhaps the most familiar; see Powell (1988) 198–99 for references, to which add Ammianus Marcellinus 25.4.2–4. Contrast the view of Epicurus *ap.* Plutarch *Mor.* 1094e. One might also note the tradition that Sophocles took mistresses in his old age: Athenaeus *Deipn.* 13.592a–b. For the ad-

vantages allegedly accrued as a result of the loss of sexual desire in old age, see also Favorinus frag. 13 Barigazzi, Juncus (discussed below) *ap.* Stobaeus *Flor.* 50.1.23, 27 (1025.9–12, 1027 W-H), and Diogenes of Oenoanda frag. 149 Smith. Plutarch mentions (*Mor.* 199a15, 784a, 829f; *Cato Maior* 9) a saying attributed to Cato to the effect that, because old age has so many odious things connected with it, it is only right not to add the *odium* that comes from vice (cf. also Aristotle *NE* 4.9.1128b). For an example of such aged *odium,* see Dio 75.8.2: Septimius Severus tells the senate of seeing at Ostia a consular γέρων publicly playing around (ἔπαιζεν) with a prostitute "who imitated a leopard"—the point is that Commodus's slaying wild beasts in the arena is not so bad! And as will be seen below, elderly women en masse were not uncommonly stereotyped (by men) as being sex-mad.

23. Note Lucian *Apol.* 7 for the hypocrisy of an elderly person who criticizes youth for its vices and then indulges in them himself. For Cato's late and (at the time) surprising marriage, see Plutarch *Cato Maior* 24 (and *Comp. Arist. et Cat.* 6, for Plutarch's disapproval), with Astin (1978) 105. In 46 B.C. Cicero, at the age of 60 years, married his young and wealthy ward Publilia, after having divorced his wife of twenty-nine years, Terentia (Plutarch *Cic.* 41, citing the invective of M. Antonius; Quintilian *Inst. Or.* 6.3.75 records that Cicero was criticized as a sexagenarian for marrying a virgin; his reply: "cras mulier erit"). Note also Fufius Calenus's invective against Cicero in 43 B.C. (Dio 46.18.3–4), including the allegation that Cicero (ὑπεργήρως) in turn divorced the παρθένος Publilia in order to carry on with the elderly Caerellia who, if we are to believe Calenus, was over 100 at the time (see *RE* 3.1284 for more established evidence); it is a great pity that nothing at all substantial of Cicero's correspondence with this aged friend has survived.

24. Cf. Seneca *Ep.* 12.4: old age is "plena . . . voluptatis, si illa scias uti" (discussed further below); 12.5: "quam dulce est cupiditates fatigasse ac reliquisse!"; Favorinus frag. 15 Barigazzi *ap.* Stobaeus *Flor.* 50.1.25; Jerome *Comm. in Amos* 2.pr. (*PL* 25.1023 = *CCSL* 76.255). For Cicero and Seneca, this pleasure is to be found in philosophy. It is assumed that a man will reach old age with knowledge and learning to feed upon (*de Sen.* 14.49); on the folly and disgrace of "late learning," see below.

25. The agricultural foray, at *de Sen.* 15.51–17.60, is most dependent on Xenophon's *Oecon.* (see Powell 1988: esp. 224–26), which Cicero translated/adapted in his youth. Here again Cicero failed to follow his own advice: note, e.g., Plutarch *Cic.* 32, 40. On garrulous old age, note also Horace *Epist.* 1.20.18: "balba senectus"; Dio Chrysostom 7.1; Plutarch *Mor.* 505b; Lucian *Dion.* 7; Macrobius *Sat.* 7.2.14–16; Maximianus *Eleg.* 1.108, 201–4; Maltby (1979) 141–43 (old men's long-winded expressions in Terence; "senilis μακρολογία," as Donatus observes *ad* Terence

Adel. 68); Silk (1995) 181 n. 14 (with 171 on Nestor, *contra,* e.g., Falkner 1995: 18). Old age is also, according to Cicero/Cato, boastful: *de Sen.* 23.82 and cf. 9.30.

26. Fear of old age/death: cf. Juvenal 11.45; Mimnermus frag. 4; Anacreon 50 *PMG;* Musonius Rufus 17 (Stobaeus *Flor.* 50.3.94 [W-H p. 1059]); Seneca *Ep.* 12.6. From Lucretius *de Rer. Nat.,* note esp. 3.37–93, 451–71, 772–74, 824–30. Seneca's Pacuvius (*Ep.* 12.8, and cf. 30.10) and Petronius's Trimalchio provide extreme cases of the fearful. On the closeness of death to old age in a medical context, note particularly Galen *de Temp.* 2.2 (1.582K): ὁδὸς ἐπὶ θάνατόν ἐστι τὸ γῆρας (and cf. *de Marc.* 4, 7.680K). For the "fact" that old age is close to death being used as a taunt in court, see Apuleius *Apol.* 64. In a variety of literary genres older people were not uncommonly equated with corpses and tombs, as in nouns such as τυμβογέρων (on which see also Appendix C): e.g., [Plutarch] *Mor.* 13b (of a father, κρονόληρος καὶ σοροδαίμων, "coffin ghost"); Lucian *Dial. Mort.* 6.2 (ἔμψυχον τάφον), *Dial. Meret.* 11.3; Chrysippus *ap.* Plutarch *Mor.* 1039a (*Frag. Mor.* 211 = *SVF* 3.50: δυσθανατώσης γραύς—cf. *Frag. Mor.* 274 = *SVF* 3.67, with Algra 1990); *Anthologia Palatina* 11.425 (anonymous), for an old woman with money being a πλουσία σορός; Plautus *Pseud.* 412 ("sepulcrum vetus"), *Mil.* 627–28 (an older man regarded as an "Acherunticus" and as *capularis*—for the latter adjective, cf. *TLL* 3.382.22–29 and Apuleius *Apol.* 66); *Priap.* 57.1 ("vetus bustum"). On a related theme, Lucian relates that a man saw on the legs of the aged Cynic Demonax (who was said by Lucian to have died almost a centenarian) "a discoloration of the sort that is natural to old people [τοῖς γέρουσιν], and inquired: 'What's that, Demonax?' With a smile he said: 'The ferryman's toothmark! [Χάρων με ἔδακεν]'" (*Demonax* 45, tr. Harmon). For old men and women with one foot in the grave, see Chapter 3 note 80.

27. *De Sen.* 23.85. Suetonius *Div. Aug.* 99.1 uses the same metaphor, in Greek lines delivered by Augustus on his deathbed. Cf. also Seneca *Ep.* 77.20 and Wackernagel (1862) 26.

28. *Pace,* e.g., Haynes (1963) 33.

29. See Powell (1988) 3–4 for some judicious comments, and for appreciation of the work by gerontologists, see Hübener (1957) and de Luce et al. (1993). Laslett (1996) 48 is too dismissive: "From the Greek and Roman classics we have sententious lucubrations in the manner of Cephalus . . . and Cicero's garrulous and imperceipient discourse." This overlooks the authors' intentions, not to mention the historical and social contexts. But each to their own: cf. W. A. Falconer's introduction to his Loeb translation of Cicero, p. xi. Ullman (1933–34) 456 was struck by the fact that the *de Senectute* "is so up to date" (cf. Twigg-Porter 1962–63: 4: "modern in its scope"). Zeman (1944–45) 302 regards it as "rep-

resentative of the opinion of aging Romans" but also notes that it is "unique in its optimistic tone"; Lind (1988) 312 considers it "the best essay on old age ever written," while the gerontologist Mildred Seltzer (in de Luce et al. 1993: 374) describes it as "a gerontological document par excellence." Wuilleumier (1961) 57 cites Montaigne as the source for the comment that the *de Senectute* gives the young "l'appétit de vieillir"; in fact, Montaigne makes no such comment, as I have discovered after an extensive search and as Jonathan Powell has confirmed to me; Jean-François de la Harpe in his *Lycée, ou Cours de littérature* (Paris, 1799) refers to the fact that "on a dit qu'il [sc. le traité de la vieillesse] faisait appétit de vieillir" (vol. 3.2, p. 157) but I have not found an earlier citation anywhere.

30. Cicero *ad Att.* 12.14.3 (March 45); cf. Plutarch *Cic.* 41.8.
31. Cicero *ad Att.* 14.21.3; cf. also 12.46, and *de Div.* 2.3.
32. *De Sen.* 1.1. Cf. also *de Orat.* 1.1.1 for earlier reflections.
33. Cf. Cicero *Verr.* 2.5.70.180, *de Amic.* 1.4; Plutarch *Cato Maior* 24.7. Cato himself wrote (frag. 141 Peter; cf. *de Sen.* 8.26) "qui tantisper nulli rei sies, dum nihil agas." Cicero was no doubt well aware of how much he and Cato had in common, both personally (e.g., Cato had lost a son: note Cicero *de Sen.* 19.68, and cf. also Chapter 3 note 23) and politically (as *novi homines*). Cicero found another good example in the augur Q. Mucius Scaevola (*cos.* 117 B.C.; he lived from ca. 157 to at least 88), who led an active political life, though "summa senectute et perdita valetudine" (*Phil.* 8.10.31), as well as instructing a young Cicero (*de Amic.* 1.1). Note also what Cicero has himself say are his hopes for his own old age, *de Leg.* 1.3.10: he is looking forward to *vacatio aetatis.*
34. *De Sen.* 18.63 ("honestissimum domicilium senectutis"); cf. similarly Herodotus 2.80.1; Xenophon *Mem.* 3.5.14–15, *Lac. Pol.* 10.1–2; Valerius Maximus 4.5.ext.2; Plutarch *Mor.* 232b–f, 235d, 795f; Aelian *de Nat. Anim.* 6.61 (elephants do even better); Aulus Gellius 2.15.2; Nicolaus *ap.* Stobaeus *Flor.* 2.25 (*FGH* 90 F 103z.3; *Paradoxographus Vaticanus* 62.1 Keller = 57.1 Giannini): Λακεδαιμόνιοι τοὺς γέροντας αἰσχύνονται οὐδὲν ἧττον ἢ πατέρας.
35. For the sentiment that respect is owed to older people and is (to use Cicero's term) the *apex senectutis,* cf. Thucydides 2.44.4; Cicero *de Inv.* 1.30.48 ("commune est quod homines vulgo probarunt et secuti sunt, huiusmodi ut maioribus natu assurgatur"; for such practices, see further Gnilka 1983: 1036–37, Powell 1988: 234); Valerius Maximus 2.1.9–10.
36. Kirk (1971) 148–52. Garland (1990) 286 stresses the differences between "a largely illiterate society such as Sparta" and "[p]rogressive and highly literate societies such as Athens" in their respective treatment of older people. But one should not, I think, overemphasize the literate na-

ture of classical societies in this regard; as Syme (1986) 328 observed, "Old men's memories were a precious source for historians." Cf. Ober (1989) 181 and Crichton (1991–93), for the use Athenian orators made of old memories (and for older people in the courts, note, besides Aristophanes' *Wasps,* Libanius *Decl.* 12.8).

37. Cf. Chapter 3 note 18; note also Plato *Laws* 3.690a; Ovid *Fasti* 5.61–62; Apuleius *Met.* 5.25; Plutarch *Mor.* 789e. Contrast Juvenal 14.57–58, 251; [Cato] *Dist.* 1.16.

38. *Mor.* 783b-97f. Cuvigny's edition (1984) has a useful introduction (pp. 49–78); note also the very full commentary by Stamatakos (1957), the remarks of K. Ziegler in *RE* 21.820–22 and of Swain (1996) 184, and the chapter by A. Cacciari in Mattioli (1995) 1.361–95, as well as Byl (1977b).

39. Fornara (1966) argues that Plutarch was answering a specific negative argument, that of the Stoic Aristo of Chios (cf. Cicero *de Sen.* 1.3, with Chapter 3 note 6; see also *RE* 21.821 on Aristo of Ceos as a source), and that Plutarch had as a source the work by Demetrius of Phalerum (see note 5). Neither argument I find compelling; we do not know enough about the literature on old age, nor is it necessary to believe that Plutarch had any specific work in mind: the negative-positive traditions themselves would have provided ample material with which to work (including, undoubtedly, Cicero's *de Senectute*) and it was within just such a general tradition, together with genuine convictions (an attempt to dissuade Euphanes from retiring, perhaps), that Plutarch wrote; cf. Cuvigny (1984) 55–65.

40. See, e.g., Plutarch *An Seni* 789f, with Homer *Iliad* 9.422; Zonaras *Lex.* 1.435 Tittman; Roussel (1942) 171. Note also the famous statement in Pericles' funeral speech (Thucydides 2.44.4) that it is love of honor (τὸ τιμᾶσθαι), not gain, that marks old age, and that this should not extend to overambition (cf. also, e.g., Plutarch *Lucull.* 38). In the late Roman and Byzantine dream books it is said that to dream of an old man is to foretell honor for oneself (e.g., in Oberhelman's ed.: Astrampsychus *Oneirocrit.* 10, Achmet 17–18, Nicephorus 61, Germanus 29).

41. See esp. *An Seni* 797e–f, and cf. Democritus 294 D-K *ap.* Stobaeus *Flor.* 50.1.20 (ἰσχὺς καὶ εὐμορφίη νεότητος ἀγαθά, γήραος δὲ σωφροσύνη ἄνθος); Aristotle *Pol.* 7.1329a14–15. For *seniles artes* in politics—a rather more cynical way of looking at it—note Tacitus *Ann.* 3.8.4.

42. Cf. *An Seni* 784a, 785c–e, 788a–b, 789c, 790c. Cicero comes closer to Plutarch's view, it seems to me, in *de Off.* 1.123 (the shamefulness in old age of *luxuria, languor, desidia,* and *libidinum intemperantia*). The unpopularity of public service (further discussed in Chapter 4) is implied by Plutarch (787b, 795a).

43. Plutarch *Lucull.* 39–43, *Comp. Lucull. et Cim.* 1.3; *Cato Maior* 24.7; *An*

> *Seni* 785f–86a, 792b–c. See van Ooteghem (1959) 166–99 for a rather more objective picture of Lucullus, with Keaveney (1992) 164–65 and Hillman (1993), and cf. Chapter 3 note 76, Chapter 4 note 54, and Chapter 8 note 110.

44. Musonius Rufus 17 (= Stobaeus *Flor.* 50.3.94).

45. Diogenes of Oenoanda frags. 137–79 Smith; cf. Clay (1990) 2519–26; Smith (1993; 1996: 196–232; 1998). On the reconstruction, see esp. Smith (1993) 566–68. For Epicurean views on old age, cf. also Plutarch *Mor.* 1094e–1095b.

46. Favorinus frags. 9–17 Barigazzi; see now also the edition by Amato (1999), attributing another seven fragments. In the context note too *P.Schub.* 38 (first–second century A.D.), with a "substantial parallel" to Cicero *de Sen.* 7.21: Powell (1988) 29, 149; cf. Frösén and Westman (1997) 30–41.

47. *Flor.* 50.1.27, 50.2.85, 50.3.95, 53.35. What proportion of the original work is preserved by Stobaeus is uncertain.

48. On Juncus, see briefly *RE* 10.953–54 (Kroll, Juncus 1) and Hirzel (1895) 2.252–54, and, most important, Wilhelm (1911). Dyroff (1937; 1939: esp. 80–137) stresses the Aristotelian element in both Cicero's and Juncus's writings on old age, but unconvincingly identifies Juncus with Aristo of Ceos (third century B.C.—see above; Dyroff's view is, however, followed, e.g., by Roussel 1942: 128). The second-century A.D. date is based primarily on the reasonable hypothesis that he belongs to the Second Sophistic movement. Oliver (1967) 53–54 argues that our author was L. Aemilius Iuncus, suffect consul in A.D. 127 (*PIR²* A 355) and mentioned by Juvenal (15.27); this is possible but unprovable. It could just as likely, or as unlikely, be Aemilius Iuncus's son (*cos. suff.* A.D. 154?), or another descendant, the *cos. suff.* of A.D. 179. *PIR²* lists four Aemilii Iunci; cf. *NP* 1 (1996) 183 (Aemilius II.4–5); Alföldy (1976) 269. What most interests us here is the writing rather than the man, though of course a date of composition would be valuable in order to place the work within the tradition.

49. And is spelled out in Wilhelm (1911).

50. Cf. Claudian *Carm. Min.* 20.15–16, the "old man of Verona" (cf. Chapter 2 note 4), for more positive reflections along these lines: "ingentem meminit parvo qui germine quercum aequaevumque videt consenuisse nemus." Re Seneca's views on old age, note also Crisafulli (1953); De Caria (1977) 7–44; and O. Fuà in Mattioli (1995) 2.210–38.

51. Cf. Seneca *Nat. Quaest.* 6.10.1: "nec quicquam tutum a senectute est." As Ovid *Fasti* 6.771 noted, "tempora labuntur, tacitisque senescimus annis." It was a common complaint; cf. Cicero *de Sen.* 2.4: "obrepere aiunt eam citius quam putavissent" (see Powell 1988: 106 for other citations).

52. *Ep.* 12.4, in true Ciceronian fashion; cf. Chapter 3 note 24, with *de Rem. Fort.* 4 (with similar terminology as *Ep.* 12.6).

53. *Ep.* 26.2; cf. 66.1, of Claranus, *condiscipulus meus:* "senem, sed mehercules viridem animo ac vigentem et cum corpusculo suo conluctantem."
54. See, e.g., *Nat. Quaest.* 1.pr.4; *Ep.* 67.2. For his regimen of health, note esp. *Ep.* 83.3–6.
55. *Ep.* 30.1–2. For the image of the sinking ship, see also Chapter 2 note 31; for that of the collapsing building ("in putri aedificio"), note too *Ep.* 58.35, quoted below, *de Ira* 2.28.4, *Nat. Quaest.* 6.10.2; Cicero *de Sen.* 20.72; Aristotle *ap.* Stobaeus *Flor.* 51.28 (of Gorgias); Maximianus *Eleg.* 1.171–74. On Bassus see *PIR*² A 1381 and *RE* 2.2290–91. On suicide, note Seneca's well-known seventy-seventh letter, and the discussions of ancient attitudes toward suicide and euthanasia in Carrick (1985) and Brody (1989). Van Hooff (1990), using eighty-seven recorded cases from antiquity of self-killing among the old, provides a wealth of analytical detail on older people's means (starvation being the most common) and motives (most notably *inpatientia, pudor,* and *taedium vitae*); cf also Elders (1983). In the context it is also interesting to note the suicide of M. Pomponius Bassulus, apparently through *taedium* and probably in old age: *CIL* 9.1164 (= *ILS* 2953 = *CLE* 97, with *PIR*² P 698 and van Hooff 1990: 153–54, 259 n. 75; early second century A.D.?).
56. Cf. *Ep.* 13.16–17 ("quid est autem turpius quam senex vivere incipiens?"), 76, *Nat. Quaest.* 1.17.4, *de Brev. Vit.* 7.3, 9.4, 11.
57. *Ep.* 30.4. Cf. Cicero *de Sen.* 19.68: "at senex ne quod speret quidem habet"; Saint Augustine *Ep.* 213.1 (*PL* 33.966): "senectus autem aliam aetatem quam speret, non habet."
58. The "retirement" speech Tacitus, *Ann.* 14.53–54, has Seneca deliver, however, is instructive, and one thinks too of the suicide in 37 of L. Arruntius, *cos.* A.D. 6 and *capax imperii* (*PIR*² A 1130), to escape the insults and perils to which the likes of Sejanus and Macro subjected his *anxia senectus,* and the promise of worse tyranny to come, *Ann.* 6.48 with Dio 58.27.4.
59. Tacitus *Ann.* 13.30 (sharp contrast to Volusius Saturninus); *PIR*² C 393.
60. Cf. in somewhat similar vein Democritus 160 D-K; Martial 1.15, 6.70; Pliny *NH* 7.50.167.
61. Seneca *de Brev. Vit.* 20.3, quoted in the next chapter.
62. *Dial.* 10. The date of composition is uncertain. The favorite remains A.D. 49, although Griffin (1962) has put forward plausible reasons why A.D. 55 might be right, namely (to state it briefly) that Seneca was writing to his father-in-law, at the time *praefectus annonae,* with a practical end in view: to provide Paulinus with a face-saving means of leaving political life (as there was pressure for him to do), and to get himself out of the embarrassing situation of having a duty to preserve his father-in-law's position in the court (see also Griffin 1976: 22, 317–21, 398, 401–7). The other date sometimes put forward (most recently by Nicolova 1986:

99–103, arguing on stylistic grounds) is A.D. 62. Cf. at most length Hambüchen (1966), although he dismisses Griffin's arguments too lightly.
The question is important for us, since it would be of interest to know,
for example, whether Seneca was writing in his 40s or his 60s. On this
dialogue, see most recently André (1989) 1747–56, and Motto and
Clark (1994), who regard Seneca's advice to Paulinus to "retire" as humor; note also Armisen-Marchetti (1995).

63. *De Brev. Vit.* 1.3–2.2; cf. 3.2–3, 7.7, 7.10 ("non est itaque quod quem-
quam propter canos aut rugas putes diu vixisse; non ille diu vixit, sed
diu fuit"), *Ep.* 49, *de Tranq. An.* 3.8 ("saepe grandis natu senex nullum
aliud habet argumentum quo se probet diu vixisse praeter aetatem").
Seneca would have appreciated the case of Sulpicius Similis (in turn prefect of the grain supply and of Egypt, and praetorian prefect under
Hadrian); he spent his last seven years in the countryside, and had in-
scribed on his epitaph, says Dio 69.19.2, Σίμιλις ἐνταῦθα κεῖται βιοὺς
μὲν ἔτη τόσα, ζήσας δὲ ἔτη ἑπτά.

64. Note Seneca *Ep.* 13.17, 36.1–2, 101.4; *de Otio,* esp. 2; *de Brev. Vit.* 12.4:
"non habent isti otium, sed iners negotium"; 12.9; 20.1–4: "adeone iuvat occupatum mori?" Indeed, at *de Brev. Vit.* 20.4 Seneca has in mind
those who put forward the very view that Plutarch later espoused:
"senectutem ipsam nullo alio nomine gravem iudicant, quam quod illos
seponit"—cf. also *Ep.* 36.2. For Cicero and Seneca philosophy is the ultimate activity in, as well as refuge from, old age (cf. *de Brev. Vit.* 14.1:
"soli omnium otiosi sunt qui sapientiae vacant, soli vivunt"; 15.2). *Otium*
as the most honorable aim in old age, and the most worthwhile *consolatio,* is referred to repeatedly in the *de Brev. Vit.,* even if in reality it could
not be achieved (*de Brev. Vit.* 4.2–5, of Augustus; 17.6: "otium num-
quam agetur, semper optabitur"). On the concept of *otium* as an intellectual and elite ideal, especially in relation to Seneca's writings, see the
still valuable work by André (1962), and, for the earlier period, André
(1966); see now also Toner (1995) ch. 4 for more general, and practical, discussion. For the more complex notion in Cicero of *otium cum dignitate,* cf. *ad Fam.* 1.9.21, *pro Sest.* 46.98, 49.104, 66.139; note also *Brut.*
2.8, and see Wirszubski (1954) for a review of scholarly opinion to that
date.

65. *Ep.* 1.12. Rufus (*PIR²* C 1294) was born ca. A.D. 31 and died in 97 (cf.
1.12.11: "implevit . . . annum septimum et sexagesimum, quae aetas
etiam robustissimis satis longa est"); see also Pliny's eulogy of Rufus, *Ep.*
4.17.6: "quamquam et inbecillus et senior, quasi iuvenis et validus con-
spiciebatur." On gout in old age, see Chapter 9. Some discussion of
Pliny's views on old age may also be found in Kebric (1983).

66. *Ep.* 4.3; *PIR²* A 1086.

67. *Ep.* 2.1, and cf. 6.10, where nine years later Pliny visits the home in

Etruria in which Rufus lived in his last years (*nidulus senectutis*); *PIR* V 284; Syme (1991) 512–20.

68. *Ep.* 4.23 (written in A.D. 104/5); *PIR*² P 705, with Syme (1983c) 254.

69. *Ep.* 4.23.2–3, "ut ipsae leges monent"—see Chapter 4. For such hoped-for *otium,* cf. also, e.g., Martial 4.25, 10.23, 10.44; Suetonius *Tib.* 24; Ovid *Trist.* 4.8.30; and Chapter 3 note 64.

70. *Ep.* 3.1.1 (note Pliny's personal proviso again); for Spurinna, see also 2.7, 3.10; *PIR* V 308; Syme (1991) 541–50 (with the observation, 547: "a bland and benevolent character").

71. Namely ball playing (3.1.8), "nam hoc quoque exercitationis genere pugnat cum senectute"; cf. Martial 14.47; Petronius *Satyr.* 27.2; Plutarch *Mor.* 793b. Contrast Cicero *de Sen.* 16.58, and note too Sidonius Apollinaris *Epist.* 1.8.2 on Ravenna, "in qua palude indesinenter rerum omnium lege perversa," including the fact that "student pilae senes aleae iuvenes." See also Champlin (1985) and Schmidt (1999) for the intriguing case of the *senex* Ursus and the glass-ball game. On exercise for older people, see also Chapter 9.

72. *Ep.* 3.1.2–3 ("senibus placida omnia et ordinata conveniunt"). For the *vita disposita,* cf. *Ep.* 4.23.1; we return to this theme in the next chapter. Pliny's own life on holiday sounds similar: *Ep.* 9.36, 40.

73. Compare Pliny's very vivid description, *Ep.* 3.6, of a Corinthian bronze statue of a *senex* (male or female? As we have stated, *senex* is usually masculine; Sherwin-White *ad loc.* takes it as a woman, perhaps because *papillae* are mentioned, although one would assume a man is meant). Contrast this with the statue of the elderly Homer, described by Christodorus of Thebes in the fifth–sixth century A.D. at *Anthologia Palatina* 2.311–50 (and cf. Lilja 1978: 60–62), and note also Pliny's ghost (*Ep.* 7.27.5): "senex macie et squalore confectus, promissa barba horrenti capillo."

74. *Ep.* 8.18 (A.D. 108?); on Tullus, probably in his late 60s when he died, see *PIR*² D 167 with Konrad (1994) 141, and also Chapter 3 notes 106, 112; Chapter 8 notes 68, 75, 84.

75. For earlier attitudes, cf., e.g., Theognis 457; Euripides *Phoenix* frag. 807, *Danae* frag. 317; Aristophanes frag. 600 Kock = 616 Kassel and Austin; Stobaeus *Flor.* 22.5.109–17 W-H; note also Plutarch *Solon* 20.4–5. See also Chapters 7 and 8, and cf. Treggiari (1991) 102–3.

76. *Ep.* 8.18.9 (trans. adapted from Radice). Compare the similarly decrepit and dependent old age of an elderly man described by Lucian *Dial. Mort.* 6.2, and that of Lucius Licinius Lucullus as described by Pliny the Elder *NH* 28.14.56 (cf. Chapter 3 note 43).

77. Plutarch *An Seni* 789e (see also Chapter 4); Pliny *Pan.* 4.7 (cf. Chapter 1 note 39; Pliny stresses Trajan's gray hair ["ornata caesaries"] as a sign of premature old age—would Trajan have been pleased?); and John Chrysostom *in Epist. ad Hebraeos* 4.7.4 (*PG* 63.66): τὴν πολιὰν τιμῶμεν,

οὐκ ἐπειδὴ τὸ λευκὸν χρῶμα τοῦ μέλανος προτιμῶμεν, ἀλλ᾽ ὅτι
τεκμήριόν ἐστι τῆς ἐναρέτου ζωῆς, καὶ ὁρῶντες ἀπὸ τούτου στοχα-
ζόμεθα τὴν ἔνδον πολιάν.

78. Cicero *de Sen.* 18.62 (Powell 1988: 233); Menander frag. 553.1 K-T (=
Monost. 618 Jaekel) *ap.* Stobaeus *Flor.* 11.8 W-H; Menander *Monost.* 661
Jaekel; Democritus 183 D-K; Cleanthes *ap.* Diogenes Laertius 7.171;
Herondas *Mim.* 1.67–68; *Anthologia Palatina* 11.419 (Philo), 11.420
(anonymous; cf. Brecht 1930: 71); Seneca *de Brev. Vit.* 7.10: gray hair
and wrinkles signify a long life, not a full one; Publilius Syrus *Sent.*
590W: "sensus, non aetas invenit sapientiam" (and, for the same logic,
cf. Varro *Menipp.* frag. 5: "nec canitudini comes virtus" [see further Cèbe
1972: 31–35], and *The Book of Wisdom* 4.7–15, with Ambrose *Ep.* 16.5
[*PL* 16.960 = *CSEL* 78.69–70]). For gray hair characterized by comic
poets as the "mildew" or "mold" (εὐρώς) and "frost" (πάχνη) of old age
("hoary locks"), see Aristotle *de Gen. An.* 5.4.784b20 and [Alexander of
Aphrodisias] *Prob.* 4.78 (Usener 17.26 = *Poetae Comici Graecae, adespota* 76 Kassel and Austin). Gray hair was, conversely, said to be a result
of dryness (of the brain) in old age: Aristotle *de Gen. An.* 5.1.780b6 and
Plutarch *Mor.* 364b; note also Aristotle *ap.* Athenaeus *Deipn.* 15.692b–c
and Hippocrates *de Nat. Puer.* 20 (7.510L).

79. Solon frag. 18 ([Plato] *Amat.* 133c); Plutarch *Solon* 2.2, 31.3; Aeschylus
frag. 396 Radt; Plato *Lach.* 188b–189a, 201a–b, *Rep.* 7.536d; Cicero *de
Sen.* 8.26, 14.50; Valerius Maximus 8.7.ext.14; Seneca *Ep.* 26.3, 76.1–
2; Pliny *Ep.* 4.23; [Cato] *Dist.* 3.1, 4.27; Zenobius 3.4, Diogenianus 3.80,
Gregorius Cyprius *Cod. Leid.* 1.79 (*CPG* 1.58, 229; 2.65); cf. Otto (1890)
nos. 563, 1627, with Häussler (1968) 41–42, 102, 157, 211, 235, and
Menu (1992) 176–77. For γεροντοδιδάσκαλος, a regular term of
abuse, note Plato *Euthyd.* 272c, Pollux *Onom.* 2.13, and Varro's Menippean satire of that name (frag. 181–98 Astbury; Lenkeit 1966; Cèbe
1980: 831–921; Powell 1988: 159).

80. *Digest* 40.5.20, Pomponius' *Epistulae* book 7; it is a fairly remarkable coincidence that another Pomponius who wrote *epistulae,* Cicero's friend
Atticus, died at the age of 78 years. For the argument that Pomponius
the jurist is not quoting himself, however, see *PIR²* P 694. For the notion of old age having one foot in the grave, cf. Lucian *Herm.* 78: one
foot ἐν τῇ σορῷ; similarly Lucian *Apol.* 1: one foot ἐν τῷ πορθμείῳ.

81. Aristophanes *Clouds* 129–30; Theophrastus *Char.* 27 (the old man acting like a youngster; cf. Lucian *de Salt.* 33); Cicero *ad Fam.* 9.20.2, *pro
Quinct.* 56; Horace *Sat.* 1.10.21; Aulus Gellius 11.7.3, 15.30.1; Seneca
the Elder *Controv.* 1.pr.4; Seneca the Younger *de Tranq. An.* 2.6 ("senectus ad novandum pigra"), *Ep.* 36.4 ("turpis et ridicula res est elemen-
tarius senex [on the later use of this phrase, see Burrow 1986: 151–
56]: iuveni parandum, seni utendum est"), 33.7; Apuleius *Apol.* 10,
36.

82. Valerius Maximus 8.7.ext.8; Sextus Empiricus *adv. Math.* 6.13; cf. Plato *Euthyd.* 272b–d; Cicero *de Sen.* 8.26; Quintilian *Inst. Or.* 1.10.13; Diogenes Laertius 2.32. Cleobulus seems to have made the point succinctly (*ap.* Stobaeus *Ecl.* 3.1.172α, although the reading is disputed): ὀψιμαθῆ ἢ ἀμαθῆ. Cf. also Lucian *Herm.* 84. For setting the foundations in youth, see Cicero *de Sen.* 3.9, 18.62 (Powell 1988: 121, 233, cites further examples), and previous notes in this chapter.

83. Cicero *de Sen.* 18.65; John Chrysostom *in Epist. ad Hebraeos* 4.7.3 (*PG* 63.65), and cf. *in Epist. ad Titum* 2.4.1 (*PG* 62.681–82).

84. *Rhet.* 2.12–14 (1388b31–1390b13); for varied discussion, see Burckhardt (1908) 414- 15; Boll (1913) 99–101; Dyroff (1939) 15–34; Gigon (1968); Koumakis (1974); Mette (1982) 263–68; Grimaldi (1988) 191–211; Garver (1994); Silk (1995), esp. 178–81. Such delineation of characteristics by age-classes clearly had an effect on later treatments: cf. Horace *Ars Poet.* 156–78 (discussed below), and Seneca *Ep.* 121.15–16: "unicuique aetati sua constitutio est, alia infanti, alia puero, <alia adulescenti,> alia seni. . . . alia est aetas infantis, pueri, adulescentis, senis . . ."

85. On his age at death, the ancient sources are almost unanimous: Diogenes Laertius 5.6, following Eumelus, says 63 years (cf. 5.10, following Apollodorus: about 63); Dionysius of Halicarnassus *Ep. ad Amm.* 1.5 (63); Censorinus *de Die Nat.* 14.16 (63); Aulus Gellius 13.5.1 (on Aristotle's sick old age at age 61 or 62); the anonymous *vitae* give 63 years or the 63rd year (Rose pp. 428, 441, 444, 449); but *Suda* A 3929 has 70 years.

86. *Rhet.* 2.14.1390b9–11; compare *Pol.* 7.1335a29, 1335b32–35 (with explicit reference to the hebdomadal system); Plato *Rep.* 5.460e–1a; Dionysius of Halicarnassus *AR* 4.29.3 (cf. 4.31.4).

87. [Dionysius of Halicarnassus] *On Epideictic Speeches* 282–83 (tr. Russell and Wilson; emphasis added).

88. Dio 50.17.3 (tr. Cary). Antony was being a little optimistic (or naive, intentionally so by Dio?): he was about 52 years old at the time (cf. Chapter 4 note 49).

89. *Rhet.* 2.13 (1389b13–1390a27). For some contrast between the views of Plato and Aristotle (on which see also Chapter 4), see Roussel (1942) 187–203, with Fuà (1979–80). But on many points the two philosophers agree (as indeed a rereading of the opening to Plato's *Republic* alongside Aristotle's *Rhetoric* makes clear): see further Byl (1974) and Elders (1983) 98, *contra* de Beauvoir (1977) 122.

90. Cf. John Chrysostom *in Epist. ad Titum* 2.4.1 (*PG* 62.682): μικροψύχους γὰρ τὸ γῆρας ποιεῖ. See also Chapter 3 note 57 on older men having few hopes.

91. Cf. *NE* 4.1.1121b14; Plautus *Rud.* 937 (Gripus); Horace *Sat.* 2.3.117–23 (cf. Chapter 4 note 53 and Chapter 8 note 89, on miserliness in old age); [Cato] *Dist.* 3.9.

92. Cf. Valerius Flaccus *Argon.* 6.283–84 for cowardice on the battlefield:

"quae vos subito tam foeda senectus corripuit fregitque animos atque abstulit iras?" and Plutarch *Brut.* 12.2 for Cicero's γεροντικὴ εὐλάβεια before the Ides. Contrast one brave old senator, Q. Considius, in ca. 59 B.C., Plutarch *Caes.* 14.8: με ποιεῖ μὴ φοβεῖσθαι τὸ γῆρας· ὁ γὰρ ἔτι λειπόμενος βίος οὐ πολλῆς ὀλίγος ὢν δεῖται προνοίας (cf. Plutarch *Solon* 31.1, and *Pomp.* 64.4). Cicero *ad Att.* 2.24.4 describes Considius in 59 as "fortissimus senex." In some circumstances old age's bravery might be said to be a result of the fact that older people have little to lose: in A.D. 58 P. Suillius Rufus (*cos.* 44), for example, attacks Seneca with the outspokenness that *extrema senectus* brings (Tacitus *Ann.* 13.42)—not that he had been particularly restrained in his younger days.

93. Lucian *Dial. Mort.* 27.9. Cf. Sophocles frag. 66 Radt (quoted at the beginning of this chapter); Euripides *Alc.* 669–72; Democritus 199–206 D-K; Seneca *de Brev. Vit.* 11.1; Aesop *Fables* 60 Perry; [Quintilian] *Decl. Maior.* 5.23: "vivacissima senectus." Further material in Powell (1988) 246–47, on Cicero *de Sen.* 20.72.

94. *Rhet.* 2.13.1390a1–3; cf. 2.13.1390a15: they are "slaves to gain" (δουλεύσι τῷ κέρδει). This is in direct contrast to what Thucydides has Pericles say of older people (see Chapter 3 note 40, and further Chapter 4 note 53).

95. Phaedrus 5.10.9 (an old dog): "quod fuimus lauda, si iam damnas quod sumus." By implication, older people also avoid the present and ignore the future (note Horace's "<p>avidusque futuri" below, and Lucan 2.232–33: "sic maesta senectus praeteritique memor flebat metuensque futuri"). One symptom of this feature of old age, perhaps, is a tendency toward archaism in language (cf. Grasso 1995 on Menander and Maltby 1979: 138–41 on Terence), and an avoidance of neologisms (for Roman times, note Varro *de Ling. Lat.* 6.59).

96. Cicero *de Sen.* 18.65 (quoted above); Horace *Ars Poet.* 173–74 (see below; the *senex iratus* is something of a staple in comedy); Seneca *de Ira* 1.13.5 ("iracundissimi infantes senesque et aegri sunt"—all marginalized groups), 2.19.4, 3.9.4; Plutarch *Mor.* 457b (said to be a symptom of weakness of soul, as also with females and the sick; cf. 788f); Ammianus Marcellinus 27.7.4 (*mentis mollitia*); Macrobius *Sat.* 7.6.21; John Chrysostom *in Epist. ad Titum* 2.4.1 (*PG* 62.681–82).

97. For "censorious" old men as an ideal (one, of course, thinks of Cato Maior—cf. Cicero *de Sen.* 18.65: "severitatem in senectute probo"), note *CIL* 3, p. 962 no. 2 (= *CLE* 34): "senem severum semper esse condecet" (for the stereotype, cf. also Catullus 5.2, "senes severiores"; Propertius 2.30.13, "duri senes"; Ovid *Fasti* 4.310, "rigidi senes"). Pliny *NH* 14.28.144 mentions Tiberius "in senecta" as *severus* but also *saevus*.

98. *Ars Poet.* 169–76; see Brink (1971) 228–44, esp. on textual difficulties and on Peripatetic influence; cf. also Colmant (1956) and Hohnen

(1988). Notice that in his depiction of the (in this case four) age-classes, Horace, unlike Aristotle, follows chronological order: *puer,* lines 158– 60; *iuvenis,* 161–65; *vir,* 166–68; *senex,* 169–74. On the influence of this passage on later medieval literature, see the classic article by Coffman (1934), though strangely he makes no mention of Juvenal. Maximianus *Eleg.* 1.195–210 is strikingly similar in many respects. For Horace's usually negative depiction of old age (especially that of women), cf., e.g., *Odes* 2.14, 2.18, 3.15, 4.1; *Epist.* 2.2.55–57, 205–16, and elsewhere in this chapter. It is instructive to compare again Cicero's list of old age's faults (*de Sen.* 18.65, quoted above).

99. Highet (1954) remains the best general discussion, at least on Juvenal's influence on later literature; see esp. 14, 125–29, 275–78. The most recent commentaries, Ferguson (1979) and Courtney (1980), are of little help as regards the study of the depiction of old age in this passage; older commentaries, particularly Mayor (1878–80) 2.134–55, provide some useful illustrative material, which we shall attempt to complement here. On *Satire* 10, see most recently Fishelov (1990), esp. 377–80, and note also Tengström (1980), of some use regarding the rhetorical nature of the tenth satire.

100. Cf. Socrates on such prayers, Valerius Maximus 7.2.ext.1, with [Plato] *Alcib.* 2.142e–143a.

101. See Courtney (1980) 446, and 448–51 on Socratic, Democritean, and Stoic influences. For the argument (which I do not believe) that Juvenal was specifically seeking to answer Cicero's *de Senectute,* see Rebert (1926). But of course Juvenal was aware of the positive tradition, and Juvenal 9.128–29 ("dum bibimus . . . obrepit non intellecta senectus"; cf. also Ausonius *Epigr.* 14.3 Green) certainly puts one in mind of Cicero *de Sen.* 11.38 ("non intelligitur quando obrepat senectus"). Highet (1937) 486–87 (cf. 1954: 14) assumes that *Satire* 10 was written in Juvenal's old age (note also 11.203; Juvenal was most likely close to 60 years old at the time that his fourth book appeared: see in the context, from the fifth book, 13.16–17, with, inter alia, Syme 1958: 775) and that the sentiments expressed reflect Juvenal's personal feelings. Such assumptions, though now unfashionable, may nonetheless be correct.

102. Juvenal 10.28–30. An *erroris nebula* (10.4) surrounds each prayer that men utter—indeed, the cloud remains, even in spite of Juvenal's castigation of the prayer in the tenth satire, when at 12.128–29 he, rather ironically, wishes for Pacuvius a long life and great wealth (Braund 1988: 189).

103. Cf., e.g., Statius *Silv.* 1.3.110, 1.4.125–27, 2.3.72–74, 3.1.174–75, 3.4.103–5; Tibullus 1.10.43–44; Ausonius *Ecl.* 19.15–17 (quoted in Chapter 3 note 111). For Greek prayers, see Nan Dunbar's comments on Aristophanes *Birds* 606. Cf. also *Comp. Men. et Phil.* 3.47–48 Jaekel (= Philemon frag. 178 Kock; rather ironically, Philemon himself is said

to have survived to the century mark or thereabouts, both physically and mentally sound): "He errs who prays to the gods for old age, for extreme old age [τὸ πολὺ γῆρας] is full of the worst evils"; Publilius Syrus *Sent.* 212W; Antiphanes frag. 94 *ap.* Stobaeus *Flor.* 50.2.58. Lucilius, *Anthologia Palatina* 11.161 has a boxer go to an astrologer to inquire as to whether he will live to old age; one can imagine such a query being typical (cf. Artemidorus *Oneirocrit.* 2.70; note also that question 44 of the *Sortes Astrampsychi* was "Will I live a long life?"—of ten variant answers, five are negative and five positive; one of the positive answers (33γ) has the addendum that a long life will bring much pain to the feet).

104. Seneca *de Brev. Vit.* 11; *de Const. Sap.* 17.2; *Cons. ad Marc.* 20; *Ep.* 49, 101.10–14.

105. Augustine *Tract. in Iohann. Evang.* 32.9 (*PL* 35.1647 = *CCSL* 36.305): "decrepitam senectutem, quam omnes optant antequam veniat, omnes de illa cum venerit murmurant [a very common sentiment: cf. Cicero *de Sen.* 2.4, with Otto 1890: no. 1624 and Powell 1988: 105 for other parallel examples]. . . . vult esse pulcher, et vult esse senex; ista duo desideria sibi invicem concordare non possunt; si senex eris, pulcher non eris; quando senectus venerit, pulcritudo fugiet; et in uno habitare non possunt vigor pulcritudinis et gemitus senectutis." Cf. *Sermo* 81.8 (*PL* 38.504): "querelae multae in senecta: tussis, pituita, lippitudo, anxietudo, lassitudo inest. ergo senuit homo; querelis plenus est."

106. Juvenal 10.201; one is reminded again of Domitius Tullus (Chapter 3 notes 74 and 112).

107. For emphasis on the impairment or loss of the senses in old age, see also Pliny *NH* 11.115.277; Diodorus Siculus 20.72.2; Galen *in Hipp. Epid.* 6 *Comm.* 3.1 (17B.5–6K = *CMG* 5.10.2.2.126); Juncus *ap.* Stobaeus *Flor.* 50.2.85, pp. 1050–51 W-H; Diogenes of Oenoanda NF 133 (Smith 1998: 163–65); John Chrysostom *in Epist. ad Titum* 2.4.1 (*PG* 62.681–82); Maximianus *Eleg.* 1.119–22; and further in Chapter 9.

108. Juvenal 10.204–9. Cicero *de Sen.* 14.46 has Cato note that old age removes the *aviditas* for food and drink. Macrobius *Sat.* 7.13.4 states that old people have little appetite for food because they are cold and there is no fire to nourish (cf. Galen *in Hipp. Aph.* 1.13–14, 17B.400–415K). The scholiast to Juvenal 10.204 aptly quotes Vergil *Georg.* 3.97, "frigidus in Venerem senior." For other references in Latin literature to the coldness of old age, see Eyben (1972a) 681; Oakley (1997) 588–89; and further Chapter 9. With lines 205–6, cf. Martial 11.46.3–4, and Lucilius frag. 331–32M: "quod deformis, senex, arthriticus ac podagrosus est, quod mancus miserque, exilis, ramice magno." Pliny *NH* 22.38.81 offers some helpful advice for the old man whose sexual virility is flagging. But even if the old man's flesh is willing, it is felt that no woman would want to go near him (cf., e.g., Tibullus 1.9.73–74, and Chapter 7).

109. On hearing problems in old age, see Chapter 4 note 113.
110. Juvenal 10.217–18; cf. Martial 3.93.16–17. Hippocrates observed that in older men, as a result of the coldness of their bodies, fevers are less acute than in younger individuals (*Aph.* 1.14 [4.466L], followed by Galen in his commentary [17B.413–14K]; cf. also Hippocrates *Progn.* 22 [2.174L], *Coac. Praenot.* 2.6.185 [5.624L], *de Morb.* 1.22 [6.184–86L]). For a *gelidus-frigidus* old age, see Chapter 9.
111. Juvenal 10.218–26, with a wonderful list of comparisons. Cf. Ausonius *Ecl.* 19.15–17 Green: "ipsa senectus, expectata diu, votisque optata malignis, obicit innumeris corpus lacerabile morbis." For old age itself being regarded as a disease, see Chapter 9.
112. Juvenal 10.231–32; note Domitius Tullus again (and Syme 1979: 253).
113. Juvenal 10.232–39, on which see further, Chapter 8.
114. Juvenal 10.240–45 (with Courtney on 240). On this factor in old age, note de Beauvoir (1977) 408. On the grief of parents at the death of an offspring being based on allegedly utilitarian grounds, see Chapter 8.
115. Herodotus 1.87; also Polybius 12.26.7. In relation to the topos note also Valerius Maximus 5.10, *de parentibus qui obitum liberorum forti animo tulerunt.*
116. Lucian *de Luctu* 16–17 (for the last feature, note the passage from Juncus quoted in Chapter 9); Byl (1978).
117. Juvenal 10.356–58. The final phrase quoted must mean "counts long life the least of nature's gifts" (*extremum* being predicative). Worthy of note in the context is T. Raecius Severus, who, it is recorded, died at the age of 90, "[pla]cidus in membris, oculis et corpore sano" (*CIL* 8.15569, *in regione el-Khrîb*). Cf. also Horace *Odes* 1.31.17–20 and Synesius *Hymn* 7.15–18.
118. Horace *Epod.* 8, 12 (with Fitzgerald 1988, Suárez Martínez 1994); *Priap.* 12, 32, 57, 83 (Buchheit 1962: 88–91); Martial 3.93, as well as 1.19, 1.72, 3.32, 3.76, 4.5.6, 4.20, 7.75, 8.33.17, 8.79, 9.37, 10.8, 10.67, 10.90, 11.29, 11.87, 14.147. Cf. also, e.g., *Anthologia Palatina* 5.21 (Rufinus); 11.65 (Parmenion), 66 (Antiphilus of Byzantium), 67 (Myrinus), 68–69 (Lucilius), 70 (Leonidas of Alexandria), 71 (Nicarchus), 72 (Bassus of Smyrna), 73–74 (Nicarchus), 256 (Lucilius), 408 (Lucian), 417 (anonymous), 425 (anonymous). For modern literature on the subject, note Brecht (1930) 62–65, 71; Grassmann (1966) 1–46; Colton (1977); Kay (1985) 134–35, 248; Bremmer (1987); the essays by Bertman and Esler in Falkner and de Luce (1989); Richlin (1992) 52, 68, 109–16; Rosivach (1994); Mattioli (1995), esp. the papers by Bonvicini; and Wortley (1998) 55–61. See also Opelt (1965) 27, 49, 259, for abuse directed against old women, and 153, 173, 231, for abuse against older people in general.
119. For the old bawd, cf. esp. Ovid *Amores* 1.8 and Propertius 4.5, with Myers (1996).

120. Cf., e.g., Tibullus 1.5.12, 1.8.18; Lucian *Dial. Meret.* 4 (an old, wine-drinking, Syrian witch); Apuleius *Met.* 2.20, 2.30, 9.29; note also Pliny *NH* 28.12.48 for the use of the names of widows in magic spells. Compare also Ammianus Marcellinus 29.2.26, and, for the case of Trotula, the aged sorceress and procurer, Rowland (1979); also the proverbial "old wives' tales" and Latin *superstitiones/fabellae aniles,* Greek μῦθοι γραῶν (cf. Chapter 2 note 58; Cicero *de Nat. Deor.* 2.2.5; Otto 1890: nos. 120–21, with Häussler 1968: 96, 134, 261; Massaro 1977; Bremmer 1987: 200–201; and Tosi in Mattioli 1995: 2.368–70). In general see further Scobie (1983) 91–94; Henderson (1987) 126–27; Bremmer (1987) 204–6; Rosivach (1994) 112–13. For some fascinating comparative material, Burstein (1949) and Billault (1980); cf. Rowlands (2001).

121. Along with many examples of drunken old women to be found in ancient literature, note "anus recocta vino trementibus labellis" (Petronius frag. 21; cf. Catullus 54.5, "seni recocto," and Chapter 9 on rejuvenation); Plautus *Curc.* 76–161 (the *vinosissima* Lenaea); Ovid *Fasti* 3.541–42 with Paulus *ex* Festus 281L; and the proverb "anus [rursus] ad amphoram/armillum": Lucilius frag. 766–67M; Apuleius *Met.* 6.22, 9.29; Phaedrus 3.1; Ovid *Fasti* 3.765 ("vinosior aetas"); Otto (1890) no. 123; Oeri (1948) 13–18, 39–46; Musso (1968); Byl (1977a) 70 n. 110; Henderson (1987) 119–20; Bremmer (1987) 201–2; Fowler (1989) 71–72; Arnott (1996) 503–4. Aristo, *Anthologia Palatina* 7.457, has an old woman drowning in a wine vat; cf. also 7.353 (Antipater of Sidon).

122. Cf. Pliny *NH* 36.4.32 (the *anus ebria* type—not *anus inebria,* as Richardson 1933: 168 would have it!), Salomonson (1980), Pfisterer-Haas (1989), Zanker (1989), Sande (1995), Schneider (1999).

123. John Chrysostom *in Epist. ad Titum* 2.4.1 (*PG* 62.683), and cf. *in Act. Apost.* 31.4 (*PG* 60.234) for the proverbially abusive tongue of the shameless, drunk old woman. Note too Plautus *Cist.* 149: "utrumque haec, et multiloqua et multibiba, est anus." On alcohol and old age, see also above on Juvenal 10.198, and Chapter 9.

124. *Pap. Graec. Mag.* 7.174–75 = *Die griechischen Zauberpapyri*², ed. K. Preisendanz et al. (Stuttgart, 1973–74) 2.7.

125. Petronius *Satyr.* 134–38; cf. Apuleius *Met.* 6.25: "delira et temulenta . . . anicula," and Ovid *Fasti* 2.571–82.

126. *Anthologia Palatina* 5.13 (Philodemus), 48 (Rufinus), 62 (Rufinus), 258 (Paulus Silentiarius), 282 (Agathias Scholasticus); 7.217 (Asclepiades); cf. Maximianus *Eleg.* 2.25–32.

127. *PLM* 5.313–48. For a brief introduction to Maximianus, see Schanz-Hosius 4.2.76–78; even briefer: *OCD*³ 941 or *PLRE* 2.739–40 (Maximianus 7); note also Wilhelm (1907); Curtius (1953) 50; and Nitecki (1990). See the commentaries by Webster (1900) and Spaltenstein

(1983), and the English translation by Lind (1988). There is a useful discussion in Szövérffy (1967), who regards Maximianus as a satirist—wishful thinking, I fear, though see now also Öberg (1999). On some medical aspects of Maximianus's depiction of old age, note Neuburger (1947). Of more recent scholarship, cf. esp. Schetter (1970) and Ratkowitsch (1986, 1990—attempting, inter alia, to date Maximianus to the ninth century). For full concordance, *loci similes,* and recent bibliography, see Mastandrea et al. (1995).

128. For negative imagery associated with old age in other early cultures, note esp. Ptahhotep *Maxims* 4.2–5.2 (in Lichtheim 1973: 1.62–63); probably the earliest extant text to deal with old age, the passage shows remarkable similarities in imagery to that of Juvenal. Cf. also *Ecclesiastes* 12.1–8; the papers in *Saeculum* 30.4 (1979), esp. for biblical times; Curchin (1980); and now Harris (2000).

129. For discussion of the treatment of old age and older people in Homer, Hesiod, and the early lyric poets—a rich field—see Schadewaldt (1933); Jeanmaire (1939) 11–26 (stressing Spartan parallels); Roussel (1942) 171–74; Kirk (1971); Byl (1976); Preisshofen (1977); the essays by Falkner and King in Falkner and de Luce (1989); Corvisier (1985b) 58–59; Yamagata (1993); Falkner (1995); and a number of papers in Mattioli (1995) vol. 1, esp. that by Burzacchini.

130. Mimnermus frags. 1–6; 3–5 are contained in Stobaeus *Flor.* 50. For discussion see esp. Preisshofen (1977) 86–90, with Schmiel (1974) and Falkner (1995) 128–39. Note too Poseidippus's elegy on the misfortune of old age, preserved on two writing tablets: Lloyd-Jones (1963) = *Suppl. Hell.* 705, with Gow and Page (1965) 482 and Cameron (1995) 183–84. For Sappho on old age ("a jaundiced view"), cf. Friedrich (1978) 115, with Falkner (1995) ch. 3.

131. See especially the thorough treatment of the subject of old women in Greek comedy by Oeri (1948). Apart from individuals, one thinks too of the ineffectual choruses of old men. Discussion also in Richardson (1933); Kirk (1971); MacCary (1971); Byl (1975, 1977a); Vílchez (1983); Corvisier (1985b); Falkner (1985; 1995: chs. 6–7); Silk (1987); Thury (1988b); the essays by Hubbard, Falkner, and van Nortwick in Falkner and de Luce (1989); Crichton (1991–93); Handley (1993); the chapters by Paganelli and Tammaro in Mattioli (1995) vol. 1; Escalante Merlos (1998).

132. Some illustrative examples of the roles of the old man (*senex amator* et al.) in Roman comedy: Plautus *Bacch.* 816–21, *Cas.* (see Cody 1976), *Menaec.* 756–60, *Merc.* 264–315, 1015–26; Terence *Adel.* 64, 833–34, 870–71, 953–54. See further Duckworth (1952) 242–49; Estevez (1966); Seaman (1969); Maltby (1979); Ryder (1984); Segal (1987) 37, 117–21, 157, 217; and the chapter by Minarini in Mattioli (1995) vol.

2. On sexual impotence in old age, see Chapters 7 and 9. It is a common satirical theme that impotent old men must turn to practicing oral sex: e.g., Martial 4.50, 6.26, 11.25, and cf. Suetonius *Tib.* 44.

133. Varro *Menipp.* frag. 51 Astbury (Cèbe 1974: 234–36); Cicero *de Amic.* 26.99–100, and cf. *de Sen.* 11.36 and Austin on *pro Cael.* 16.37. Note Pollux *Onom.* 4.143–44, 149, on comic masks for Pappus.

134. For example, the aged horse (Babrius 29 = 318 Perry: πολλοῖς γὰρ τὸ γῆρας ἐν κόποις ἀνηλώθη). In antiquity the horse's old age was proverbial, with both positive (Cicero *de Sen.* 5.14; Otto 1890: no. 604, with Häussler 1968: 102) and negative (Waters 1922) connotations; cf. also Foulon (1986), Perelli (1993), Wortley (1997) 189–90. Philostratus *Vit. Soph.* 2.23.606 records that the sophist Damianus of Ephesus died at the age of 70 years, weak of body but not of mind: he resembled the horse in Sophocles *Electra* 23–28, appearing sluggish from old age, but in discussions he recovered the vigor of youth. For the old age of the horse (including one aged 75 years), see Pliny *NH* 8.65.162–66.163, 11.47.131, 11.64.169. Pliny also notes, 11.63.167, that horses are unique in that their teeth get whiter with age.

135. For a representative sampling (cf. Wilhelm 1907: 606), see Orientius *Comm. Carm.* 1.417–34, 2.213–54 (*CSEL* 16.1.220, 235–37); Columbanus *Carm.* 1.32–93 (*PL* 80.285–87); Eugenius Toletanus *Carm.* 14–15 (*MGHAA* 14.243–45 = *PL* 87.362–64); Hrabanus Maurus (Raban Maur) *Carm.* 1.29 (*PL* 112.1606–8); Marbod *Liber Decem Capit.* 5 (*PL* 171.1702–4). Note also the opening lines of Boethius's *de Cons. Phil.*, and two late Latin poems *in senectutem*: *Anthologia Latina* 929 ("utilis es nulli, cunctis ingrata, senectus . . ."), and Boutemy (1939) 192; the latter, an anonymous twenty-five-line poem in dactylic hexameters lamenting old age, is one of the most clichéd and depressing pieces I have ever read on the subject.

136. But note Powell (1988) 11, who implies it may be earlier. It is certainly later than Plato.

137. Xenophon *Apol.* 6, 8; similarly *Mem.* 4.8.1, 8.

138. *Mor.* 791d; cf. Cicero *de Sen.* 11.36, Juncus *ap.* Stobaeus *Flor.* 50.1.27 (p. 1028 W- H), and Chapter 8 note 111.

139. *NH* 7.50.167–68 (see also Chapter 9). Compare *CIL* 5.5320 (from Comum, as it happens; = *CLE* 1203) for a similar philosophy; one thinks again also of Seneca's *de Brev. Vit.* Maximianus *Eleg.* 1.143–44 reflects that "nec credere possis hunc hominem, humana qui ratione caret"; cf. 1.265.

140. For a valuable comparative study of stereotypes of older people held by different age-groups, including older people themselves, in modern Western societies, see Hummert et al. (1994, 1995).

Chapter 4. Rules of Age in the Roman Empire

1. Paul, *Dig.* 50.17.108; *XII Tables* 1.3 (Crawford 1996: 587). Much later Scaevola, *Dig.* 22.5.8, notes that *senes* cannot be compelled to give evidence against their will, although the reference may be to only those who are *valetudinarii*.
2. Kaser (1971–75) §§ 20–22, 85–90, 231–35. The age definition of a *minor* as being under the age of 25 years (i.e., not having completed his 25th year) is further complicated in some contexts by the rule of "annus coeptus," on which see below. On the *lex [P]laetoria*, cf. Watson (1967) 157, Néraudau (1979) 106–8, and Evans (1991) 190; on *cura* note also the comments of de Zulueta (1953) 53–54. For the age for *tutela* being extended on the testamentary request of a parent, see Saller (1994) 176.
3. Summarized in Justinian *Inst.* 1.23.3–4.
4. Ulpian, *Dig.* 4.4.1; Justinian *Inst.* 1.23.pr.
5. For this instance of *venia aetatis,* see *Cod. Theod.* 2.17.1, *Cod. Iust.* 2.44.2; Kaser (1971–75) 2.119; Arjava (1996) 177; and compare the case of Melania and her husband at the beginning of the fifth century: Gorce (1962) 138 n. 1.
6. See, e.g., *Cod. Iust.* 2.21.8 = *Cod. Theod.* 2.16.3, A.D. 414.
7. See *Cod. Theod.* 2.16.2 (= *Cod. Iust.* 2.52.5, A.D. 319), *Cod. Iust.* 5.74.1–3 (A.D. 290, 293, 529), *Lex Rom. Burg.* 36.5. Eventually the system of allowing changes to the *legitima aetas* appears to have got out of hand: *Cod. Iust.* 2.44.4 (A.D. 530).
8. For this question in relation to age classifications in general, see Chapter 1. On the possible division in the early principate of *equites* into *cunei iuniorum et seniorum,* see Tacitus *Ann.* 2.83 and Rawson (1987) 105–6, with Nicolet (1976) 36–37, and cf. Chapter 4 note 103. For epigraphical evidence of *seniores* and *iuniores* in the *curia* and *tribus,* see *CIL* 6.199 (= *ILS* 6050), 6.200 (*ILS* 6049), 6.33997 (*ILS* 6053), 6.10215 (*ILS* 6057), 8.2714, and *DE* 2 (1910) 1398. For the possibly ancient division between young and old among the Salii, note Vergil *Aen.* 8.285–87 (with Servius *ad Aen.* 8.288) and Diomedes *Ars Gramm.* 3 (*GL* 1.476), with Néraudau (1979) 222–24.
9. Aelius Tubero *HRR* 1.309, Aulus Gellius 10.28.1. For the full "historical" context, see Thomsen (1980) ch. 5, and cf. Livy 1.43 with the comments of Ogilvie (1965) *ad loc. cit.*
10. *Dig.* 3.1.1.3 (Ulpian); Livy 22.57.9, 25.5.8, 27.11.15; Plutarch *C. Gracch.* 5.1, *Cato Maior* 1. I fail to see any difficulty here, *pace* Mommsen (1887–88) 1.506 n. 2 and Néraudau (1979) 116–17 (cf. 299–310). In the fourth century A.D., however, it would appear that the sons of decurions had to enter service by the age of 18 years, but this is unrelated to the earlier status of *iuniores:* see, e.g., *Cod. Theod.* 12.1.7 (A.D. 320) and 12.1.58.2 (364), with 7.13.1 (353); Evans Grubbs (1995) 25. *Cod.*

Theod. 12.1.19 (331) provides a good illustration in this context of confusion between ordinals and cardinals ("decimum et octavum annum aetatis"); note too that *minores* in this passage means something different in terms of age than in the distinction between *minores* and *maiores* we have just seen. This observation alone should warn us against insisting that any word denoting an age-category need have attached to it in any historical context a specific or exact number of years.

11. Livy 43.14.6; Polybius 6.19.2–3; Cicero *de Sen.* 17.60.

12. *AR* 4.16.3. For a similar confusion (relevant in this context: cf. Cicero *de Sen.* 17.60) between 45 and 46 years, compare the case of M. Valerius Corvus, noted below. Very rarely is the English phrase "a person of x years or over" rendered in Latin as "is x annorum maiorve": e.g., Livy 25.5.8; Flavian Municipal Law 86, 87.

13. See Censorinus *de Die Nat.* 14.2, and Chapter 1.

14. Livy 40.26.7, 42.31.4, 42.33.4 (cf. 10.21.4); Quintilian *Inst. Or.* 9.2.85; Dionysius of Halicarnassus *AR* 2.21.3; Appian *Bell. Civ.* 2.150; Seneca *de Brev. Vit.* 20.4 (discussed below). Calling up men as old as 65 years is seen as extreme, if not downright evil, as in the case of Clearchus, tyrant of Heraclea: Polyaenus 2.30, Whitehead (1991) 138 n. 16. On the old soldier, see further Chapter 9.

15. For some discussion of equestrians in relation to rules of age, see esp. Pflaum (1950) 210–14, with Birley (1988) 147–72; also Millar (1977) 102, 284–90, and Nicolet (1966: 77–83; 1984).

16. Tacitus *Ann.* 11.22; Cicero *Phil.* 5.17.47 (cf. *pro lege Manil.* 21.61). On Octavian and his early consulship, in the context of age, see Eyben (1981) 340–41, with references. M. Valerius Corvus (the name "Corvinus" was only assumed by his son) is an interesting case in several respects (*MRR* 1.129–30, 170, 173): he allegedly lived to be 99 (ca. 371–271 B.C.), and first held the consulship at the age of 23 years (in 348 B.C.: Livy 7.26.12), going on to hold the office another five times, the last in 299, i.e., an interval of 48 years, though the literary sources make it 45 or 46 years: Cicero *de Sen.* 17.60 (with Powell 1988: 231); Valerius Maximus 8.13.1 (with 8.15.5); Pliny *NH* 7.48.157; Plutarch *Mar.* 28.6. Corvus also held the dictatorship, probably thrice, and was *interrex* and censor on occasion. Some would now argue that two Valerii, father and son, have become assimilated: see Rilinger (1978) 295–96. But Tacitus *Ann.* 1.9 displays no doubt.

17. See Develin (1979), esp. 82–83. In the 180s B.C. in particular electoral competition was severe: Jones (1960) 32; Rögler (1962) 116–19; Evans and Kleijwegt (1992) 184–86. For the *adulescentes*, see Scullard (1951) 172–74; Eyben (1981) 331–32; Alföldy (1985) 49.

18. Develin (1979); Evans and Kleijwegt (1992).

19. For republican figures and controversies, see Mommsen (1887–88) 1.523–36; Afzelius (1946); Astin (1958); Rögler (1962); Badian (1964)

140–56; Develin (1979); Evans and Kleijwegt (1992); Ryan (1996). Badian's thesis on the *cursus* from 81–49 B.C. seems to me the most plausible; Astin remains the best for the earlier period. See Sumner (1971) for an analysis of the years 49–44 B.C., particularly the ways in which the *leges annales* were violated or ignored, not least in 45 and 44. On figures and evidence for the principate, see still Morris (1964–65), together with Syme (1958) 652–56; Eck (1974); Alföldy (1977); Birley (1981) 4–35; Talbert (1984) 9–27; Jones (1984). Morris's arguments are followed here, but with the serious reservation that he is overly confident that offices were routinely held *suo anno* (1964: 322, 324, 335; 1965: 27).

20. Aulus Gellius 2.15.4–5; Tacitus *Ann.* 15.19. Note also the Flavian Municipal Law 56 and ch. B.

21. Ulpian, *Dig.* 4.4.2. For references to the practice from, e.g., Dio, Tacitus, and Pliny, see Morris (1964) 317 nn. 11–12.

22. *Dig.* 50.4.8; 36.1.76.1. Note again what was said, Chapter 1, regarding confusion between ordinal and cardinal numbers.

23. Hopkins (1983) 148.

24. For this kind of nontechnical phrase, see, e.g., Cicero *pro Cael.* 24.59 (Metellus Celer at about 43 years of age); Tacitus *Agr.* 44.3 (Agricola at 53 years); Suetonius *Tib.* 10 (Tiberius at 36); *TLL* 7.1.2074. Evans and Kleijwegt (1992) 189 remark that "ancient society and in particular the Roman senate had a strong preference for experienced men in middle age to lead public affairs. In actual fact, there was a certain distrust of youngsters in the Roman world" (cf. also Kleijwegt 1991: 189). Distrust by older generations, it needs to be said. This need not imply "gerontocratic preferences" (to use their term), however. Rome with its senate was no gerontocracy (*pace*, e.g., Hallett 1984: 37, 330; Kleijwegt 1991: ch. 7: "The Roman senate: a perfect gerontocracy"). Like Aristotle in his *Rhetoric* (see Chapter 3), the middle ground was preferred by the Romans. For a somewhat similar situation, see Chapter 9 note 102, for Ptolemy I's edict to Cyrene (*SEG* 9.1, late fourth century B.C., probably 322/1; cf. Chapter 1 note 35), where it is stated that the 500 members of the *boule* and the 101 γέροντες, as well as five of the *strategoi* (the sixth is to be Ptolemy himself), the ephors, priests of Apollo, and—presumably, though the age here is lost—*nomophylakes,* are to be chosen from those not younger than 50 years of age; in times of shortage, councillors may be selected from those 40 years of age or over (cf. Roussel 1942: 145–49); according to Heracleides Lembus *Excerpta Politiarum* 63, Chalcis also had a minimum age requirement of 50 years for state positions. For reference to the interesting and suggestive case of the council of late medieval Venice, see Kleijwegt (1991) 198–208; Evans and Kleijwegt (1992) 189–90.

25. *Fasti* 5.57–78; on May and June, see Frazer's comments *ad loc.* (I append

here his translation), with Varro *de Ling. Lat.* 6.33 and Macrobius *Sat.* 1.12.16 (cited below, note 35). Plutarch (*Numa* 19.3, *Mor.* 285a–b) prefers derivation from Maia and Juno.

26. Mommsen (1887–88) 3.874; cf. Mommsen (1903) 74–79.

27. Cicero *de Sen.* 17.60; note also Venini (1960).

28. See Chapter 1 note 34, with Augustine *Enarr. in Psalm 70 Sermo* 2.4 (*PL* 36.894 = *CCSL* 39.962–63), *Ep.* 213.1 (*PL* 33.966), *de Div. Quaest.* 58.2, 64.2 (*PL* 40.43, 55 = *CCSL* 40a.106, 137), and *de Ghellinck* (1948). Note also Paulus *ex* Festus 85L s.v. *gravastellus*. Ambrose *Explan. Psalm.* 1.9.3 (*PL* 14.925 = *CSEL* 64.8) and *Ep.* 44.10 (*PL* 16.1139 = *CSEL* 82.222) uses *veteranus* to describe the age-class between *vir* and *senex*. In Greek, *senior* = πρέσβυς; cf. Galen *in Hipp. Aph.* 3.31 (17B.648K: see Chapter 9 note 3); Augustine *de Genesi contra Manich.* 1.39 (*PL* 34.191); Isidorus *Orig.* 7.12.20, 11.2.6.

29. In the grammarians, it is true, *senior* is used somewhat more flexibly. Hence: Varro *ap.* Servius *ad Aen.* 5.409 ("senior non satis senex"), 6.304 ("senior est virens senex"); Isidorus *Orig.* 11.2.6 ("quinta aetas senioris, id est gravitas, quae est declinatio a iuventute in senectutem; nondum senectus sed iam nondum iuventus . . ."), 11.2.25–26 ("senior minus sene"). But we also find: Priscian *Inst. Gramm.* 3.14 ("*senioris* . . . pro *senis*," as well as "senior minus sene"); *Commentum Einsidlense in Donati Artem Minorem* 152 (= *GL* suppl. [1870] 232.19–23): "*senior* dicitur qui intra senectutem est, *senex* vero qui ad ultimam iam pervenit aetatem." In other words, *senectus* was defined loosely by some as the age of both the *senior* and the *senex* (cf. Néraudau 1979: 100). Augustine seems to me to sum up well the likely reality (*Quaest. in Gen.* 35, *PL* 34.557 = *CCSL* 33.14): "seniorum aetas minor est quam senum, quamvis et senes appellentur seniores" (cf. *Quaest. in Gen.* 70 [*PL* 34.566 = *CCSL* 33.26–27]).

30. Also Isidorus *Orig.* 9.4.8: "alii a sinendo dictos accipiunt senatores." For the true etymology of *senatus* see Walde and Hofmann (1954) 514 and Ernout and Meillet (1959) 613, and see also note 32.

31. Livy 1.32.10. For *senatus* linked to age (along with such concepts as respect, honor, and responsibility), see also Quintilian *Inst. Or.* 1.6.33 ("'senatui' dederit nomen aetas, nam idem patres sunt"); Livy 1.8.7; Sallust *Cat.* 6.6 (on early Rome: "imperium legitumum, nomen imperi regium habebant. delecti, quibus corpus annis infirmum, ingenium sapientia validum erat, rei publicae consultabant; ei vel aetate vel curae similitudine patres appellabantur"); Cicero *de Rep.* 2.8.14, 2.20.35. Cf. also Philo *in Flaccum* 80 (τὴν γερουσίαν, οἳ καὶ γήρως καὶ τιμῆς εἰσιν ἐπώνυμοι). See further Bonnefond (1982) 175–76.

32. On *senatus* and γερουσία, see Cicero *de Rep.* 2.9.15, 2.28.50; Plutarch *Rom.* 13.3, *Mor.* 789e; Servius *ad Aen.* 1.426. Dionysius of Halicarnassus *AR* 2.12.3 is more cautious. Note Porzig (1956) 322 for the uncon-

ventional view that *senatus* is not derived from *senex* (or **senare*) but is "eine Nachbildung, eine Lehnübersetzung" or calque from γερουσία.

33. See most recently Cornell (1995), esp. 247–49, on the archaic senate as an ad hoc *consilium* for the king (cf. Festus 290L; Mommsen 1887–88: 3.1028–29). For assumptions and difficulties, note *CAH* 7 (1928) 413 (H. Stuart Jones, "The primitive institutions of Rome"): "The Council of Elders, whose existence in a primitive community we should be obliged to assume, even were it not attested"; and Ogilvie (1965) 63: "A Council of Elders (*senatus,* γερουσία) is as old as society and its origins at Rome cannot profitably be investigated."

34. Cicero *de Sen.* 16.56, 6.19; cf. *de Rep.* 2.28.50.

35. Note also Macrobius *Sat.* 1.12.16, citing Fulvius Nobilior: "Romulus, after he divided the people into *maiores* and *iuniores,* so that the former should protect the state with their counsel and the latter with arms, honored each class by calling this month *Maius* and the month that followed *Iunius.*" Clearly *maiores* here has the same sense as *seniores.* Also relevant, albeit problematic, is Festus 454L: "senatores a senectute dici satis constat; quos initio Romulus elegit centum, quorum consilio rempublicam administraret. itaque etiam <pa>tres appellati sunt; et nunc cum senatores adesse iubentur, 'quibus in senatu[m] sententiam dicere licet'; quia hi, qui post lustrum conditum ex iunioribus magistratum ceperunt, et in senatu sententiam dicunt, *et non vocantur senatores ante quam in senioribus sunt censi.*" For *senioribus* should *senatoribus* be read? Or is this anachronistic? Or is it that all senators of whatever age were classified as *seniores* rather than as *iuniores?* The most plausible suggestion is that the reference is to office-holding equestrians (compare Varro *ap.* Aulus Gellius 3.18.5–6): see Mommsen (1887–88) 3.874; Nicolet (1976) 25; Bonnefond-Coudry (1989) 668. Note the use here of both *senectus* and *seniores,* as also in the passage quoted from Eutropius.

36. Hopkins (1983) 146–49 (followed by Talbert 1984: 150) makes these calculations, using the United Nations life tables and assuming e_0 to be 30 or 32.5 years. My figures, using Coale-Demeny[2] Models West and South Level 5 female, where $e_0 = 30$ years, are not significantly different.

37. Morris (1964) 336; Eck (1997) 75; and cf. Talbert (1984) 134–52.

38. Dio 68.5.1; note that πρέσβυς (= *senior*), not γέρων, is used.

39. E.g., Mattingly (1923) 359, no. 260a (Vespasian), which shows on the reverse "the senate, represented as an elderly man," and Mattingly (1940) 31, no. 204 (Antoninus Pius), depicting an elderly senator with the words *GENIO SENATUS.* See further Talbert (1984) 217–18, and the bronze statue from Spain of the *genius senatus* (100–101). Note also Béranger (1964), esp. 78.

40. Ammianus Marcellinus 14.6.6; Plutarch *Mor.* 789e; likewise *Proverbs* 16.31: "The hoary head is a crown of glory." For *canities* as a metonymic

figure for old age, compare Isidorus *Orig.* 11.2.29. For refutation of the traditional equation of "white/gray hair = wisdom," see Chapter 3.

41. E.g., *Iliad* 3.150, 4.321–23; note *Odyss.* 7.155–57 and 11.342–43 for the oldest Phaeacian γέρων Echeneos, "wise in old things." See Chapters 3 and 9, for further examples, and esp. Cicero *de Orat.* 1.45.199–200 (L. Licinius Crassus: in his late 40s, as we saw in Chapter 1). As Syme (1991) 533 notes, "Senior statesmen like to parade in the role of a Nestor. Thus Statius on Vibius Crispus, 'Nestorei mitis prudentia Crispi.'" On Crispus, see below.

42. Talbert (1984) 153.

43. Dio 68.4.2 states that Nerva became emperor at the age of 65 years, 10 months, and 10 days, but [Aurelius Victor] *Epit.* 12.11 has him dying in his 63rd year. On the other hand, Eutropius 8.1.2 and Jerome *Chron.* p. 193H record that he died in his 72nd year. Cf. *PIR*^{2} C 1227, Syme (1958) 653. On Nerva as a desirable choice to the senate for a variety of reasons, see Syme (1958) 2–3; Jones (1992) 195.

44. Herodian 7.10.3; Zonaras 12.17; Syme (1971) ch. 10; Dietz (1980) 99–103, 129–34.

45. SHA *Tac.* 4–6. Contrast, e.g., Tacitus *Ann.* 13.6, where the young Nero is contrasted favorably with Claudius (emperor at age 49, died aged 63), "invalidus senecta et ignavia." On old age in SHA, see also Hartke (1951) 190.

46. Zonaras 12.28 says he was 75 when he was acclaimed emperor, but may well be wrong; he also says Tacitus was proclaimed by the troops, and this is probably right, as even SHA seems to admit (8.5). See Syme (1971) ch. 15, esp. in regard to Tacitus as a military emperor (and 245 on his age). The *Chronicon Paschale* 1.509.1 Dindorf has Aurelian dying in A.D. 275 at age 75—a mistake for Tacitus's age(?) (as noted by Gibbon, *Decline and Fall* ch. 12).

47. As Syme (1988) 675 remarks, the septuagenarian Galba was a disaster. Tacitus *Hist.* 1.7: "ipsa aetas Galbae inrisui ac fastidio erat" (and 1.5 for unfavorable comments on Galba's "senium atque avaritiam," with 1.22 and 2.1; 1.6: Galba as *invalidus senex*). According to Suetonius *Galba* 17 (with 20–21, Plutarch *Galba* 13, and Dio 64.3.4, on his old age), Galba thought that it was his *orbitas* that was criticized rather than his *senectus* (similarly Plutarch *Galba* 19.1), hence in part his adoption of Lucius Piso (and note Tacitus *Hist.* 1.15: Piso is not chosen on the basis of seniority). Suetonius also notes (14.2) the influence over Galba of T. Vinius, Cornelius Laco, and the freedman Icelus, calling them his *paedagogi*—an inference, perhaps, of Galba returning to a state of childhood; for old age as just that, a second childhood, see Chapter 8 (and in similar vein Juvenal 10.92: a *tutor* for Tiberius the *senex*).

48. SHA *Quad. Tyr.* 10.3: "omnis aetas in imperio reprehenditur: senex est quispiam: inhabilis videtur; at iuvenis: ardet furore."

49. Dio 69.20.4; compare 50.17, of Marcus Antonius at his prime (in fact no younger than 52 years old—cf. Chapter 3 note 88), unhampered by the rashness of youth and the slackness of age. Note also [Dionysius of Halicarnassus] *On Epideictic Speeches* 282–83, also quoted in Chapter 3, and, again, Tacitus *Hist.* 1.15 (Piso is not too young).

50. Tacitus *Ann.* 1.4 notes that Tiberius was "maturus annis" and in that regard suitable as *princeps;* Suetonius *Vitell.* 7 has Vitellius as "aetate integra," in contrast to Galba (but compare Tacitus *Hist.* 3.65–66 on Vitellius's end: "invalidus senecta . . . ipsum sane senem" at the age of 57; it is striking how often old age is described as *invalidus* in Tacitus). On the right age for an emperor, note the apposite comments of Syme (1958) 45: "The Caesars since Augustus ran to extremes—young princes wild and unteachable, old men sad and sorry, imprisoned by their experiences or debilitated by various infirmities. . . . Popularity and long life were hardly compatible"; see also Syme (1988) 674–75, 699.

51. Tacitus *Ann.* 6.46.

52. Cicero *de Sen.* 18.63 (Chapter 3 note 34), 18.64 ("ut quisque aetate antecedit, ita sententiae principatum tenet"); *Verr.* 2.4.64.142 ("quisque aetate et honore antecedit").

53. Plato *Rep.* 1.329b; Thucydides 2.44.4 (also quoted in Chapter 3 note 40). But compare, e.g., Aristotle *Rhet.* 2.13 (Chapter 3 note 91), *NE* 4.1.1121b14; Terence *Adel.* 833–34; Lucilius frag. 413M; and Plutarch *Mor.* 786b (Simonides, with *P.Oxy.* 1800 frag. 1.40 and Stobaeus *Ecl.* 3.10.61), for the proverbial meanness and greed (closely related) of older people—hence, perhaps, their proverbial love of gambling: Cicero *de Sen.* 16.58; Juvenal 14.4: "senem iuvat alea"; Powell (1988) 223; Meulder (1991). On miserly, penny-pinching old age, note also Cicero *de Sen.* 7.21 (with Powell 1988: 149), 18.65–66 ("avaritia senilis"), and Chapter 8 note 89.

54. Plutarch *Mor.* 785f–86a and again 792b–c; see Chapter 3 note 76 for further references.

55. Plutarch *Lyc.* 26.1, Polybius 6.45.5. Of course, in Sparta the (presumably typically younger) ephors from an early period held much effective power. For other similar bodies of *gerontes* before the time of Alexander the Great, note Aristotle *Pol.* 2.1272a–b (Crete and Carthage), 5.1306a (Elis); Strabo 10.4.18.481 (Ephorus, *FGH* 70 F 149: Sparta and Crete); Diodorus Siculus 16.65.6 (Corinth). See further J. Miller, *RE* 7.1265–67; David (1991) 15–36; Powell (1994) 274–84. It would appear that by Roman times the minimum age for the Spartan *gerousia* had dropped, possibly to as low as 40 years: Cartledge and Spawforth (1989) 192 (and 51–52, 146–47, on reforms of the *gerousia* under Cleomenes III). For the *gerousia* of Cyrene (*gerontes* over the age of 50 years), see Chapter 4 note 24. On the *gerousia* in the East under the Roman Empire, see Chapter 5.

56. And therefore, it would seem, less accommodating to the older politician: cf. Chapter 8 note 104. Only in the oligarchic coup of 411 B.C. did the older age-group, or some of them, dominate (Thucydides 8.1; [Aristotle] *Ath. Pol.* 29.2)—hardly a high point.

57. Aeschines 1.23 (precedence to those over 50 years) and 3.2–4 (in order of age—in sharp contrast to Aeschines' own day); but this may be mere wishful thinking on Aeschines' part: cf. particularly Griffith (1966) 119–20; Hansen (1987) 91, 171; Lane Fox (1994) 147–49.

58. The Athenian *diaitetai* (instituted from 399/8 B.C.) were in their 60th year (thus [Aristotle] *Ath. Pol.* 53.4; Bekker, *Anec. Graeca* 1.235.23–24; *schol. ad* Plato *Laws* 920d), though even here there is confusion in the sources, worthy of note. Pollux *Onom.* 8.126 and the *Lexicon Patmense* (*schol. ad* Demosthenes 22.27 = *Bull. Corres. Hell.* 1 [1877] 13) say they were over 60, Hesychius Δ 1032 says "around 60," and other sources say they were either 50 years of age (Psellus *de Act. Nom.* 25 [*PG* 122.1013d]) or over 50 (*Suda* Δ 887; Bekker, *Anec. Graeca* 1.186.1; *schol. e Codice Bavarico ad* Demosthenes 21.83). Possibly the age limit was lowered by Demetrius of Phalerum—the same who wrote on old age (see *FGH* 228 F 13 with Kahrstedt 1936: 19), but more likely it is another case of confusion over numbers in the sources, in particular the lexicographers. "In their 60th year," i.e., 59 years old, is clearly right, in view of the 42 age-classes (cf. Wilamowitz-Moellendorff 1893: 224–25; note also *Suda* T 998, presumably confusing dikasts with *diaitetai*).

59. *Pol.* 2.1270b35–41 (tr. T. J. Saunders), applied also to the Cretan system. Contrast Plato *Laws* 3.691e, and see also Gigon (1968) 191.

60. Tacitus *Ann.* 6.10.3; on Piso, who died in his 80th year, see Syme (1986) ch. 24, and later in this chapter on *amici principis*.

61. Seneca *de Ira* 2.33.2. For a similar train of thought, see Diogenes Laertius 1.37, of Thales, and Dio Chrysostom *Or.* 6.41: οὐ ῥάδιον μὲν γὰρ ἄνδρα γηρᾶσαι τύραννον, χαλεπὸν δὲ τυράννου γῆρας. Cf. too, perhaps revealingly, Seneca *Herc. Fur.* 198, "venit ad pigros cana senectus," with Degl'Innocenti Pierini (1996). For Crispus (discussed below on *amici principis*), see Juvenal 4.81–98, and note 4.97 of Acilius: "prodigio par est in nobilitate senectus." Crispus, of course, also had wealth on his side (Martial 4.54.7; Tacitus *Hist.* 2.10). On the other hand, compare Tacitus *Ann.* 3.57 for the "foedissima adulatio" of the orator Q. Haterius (ca. 63 B.C.–A.D. 26, *cos. suff.* 5 B.C.; *PIR*² H 24, Syme 1986: 145–46) in A.D. 22, a cause of ridicule and *infamia* for a *senex*, with Jerome *Chron.* p. 172H: "Q. Haterius promptus et popularis orator usque ad XC prope aetatis annum in summo honore consenescit."

62. On Perperna, see esp. Valerius Maximus 8.13.4, Pliny *NH* 7.48.156, and Dio 41.14.5.

63. Cicero *de Sen.* 16.56, with Powell (1988) 219.

64. Saturninus: see below re *amici principis*. Valens: Dio 67.14.5, *PIR*² M 163,

RE 14.1212–13 (Groag); that his *praenomen* was Gaius, not Titus, is confirmed by the *Fasti Ostienses* (96.13 Vidman). Note Syme (1983a) 134 on Valens: "selection of that relic could scarcely have been taken by the high assembly as other than affront and contempt." Contrast Eck (1970) 67: "Offensichtlich hoffte Domitian, dadurch daß er diesen alten Mann ehrte, sich in manchen Kreisen des Senats Sympathien zu erwerben." For Cinna see *PIR²* C 1339; on Gordian, see below; and on Cornutus, promoted to praetorian rank by Vespasian in A.D. 73/4 (*CIL* 14.2925 = *ILS* 1024; Eck 1970: 72), see *PIR²* I 273. On iterated consulships, see further below.

65. E.g., Livy 31.48.2–6: *maiores natu* (it is unclear in this instance whether this includes *consulares* or whether they are separate; cf. 38.53.6: "a consularibus senioribusque"), as opposed to *magna pars senatus.* In his commentary Briscoe *ad loc.* comments: "Livy represents the conflict as one between age-groups. . . . This seems unlikely." The latter observation may be true enough (cf. also Bonnefond 1982: esp. 198–99), but it is *Livy's* perception that interests us here. Note also 38.50.2 (187 B.C.): "auctoritas seniorum valuit." For an overview of the history relevant to the period we are here briefly discussing, see Briscoe in *CAH²* 8 (1989) ch. 3, esp. 67–74.

66. Livy 26.22.15. See also 10.13.6–7 for Q. Fabius Maximus Rullianus (*cos.* 322, 310, 308, 297, 295 B.C.; dictator 315, [313?]; censor 304) unwilling as a *senex* to be consul in 298; Oakley (1997) 583.

67. The time also, it is worth remarking, of Plautus (see Chapter 3) and of the *lex [P]laetoria* (Chapter 4 note 2).

68. Livy 27.11.9–12. Cf. Scullard (1951) 70, who suggests that the custom of seniority might have already been set aside in 220 B.C. Note also p. 69: "But the political scene was changing. War casualties, old age, and iteration of the consulship had combined to thin the ranks of the *consulares* to an astonishing extent: not more than a dozen survived and of these some were probably useless through incapacity or old age." Neither censor in 209, it should be noted, had held the consulship thus far. Of related interest to the passage we are discussing here is Livy 25.5.2–4, where P. Licinius Crassus (censor 210 B.C., *cos.* 205) in 212 defeats Torquatus and another senior consular, Q. Fulvius Flaccus, for the post of *pontifex maximus*; Livy comments, "hic senes honoratosque iuvenis in eo certamine vicit." On the *princeps senatus,* see Suolahti (1972), and (better) Bonnefond-Coudry (1993) and Ryan (1998) pt. 2. Bonnefond-Coudry stresses the association of ἀξίωμα and *gravitas* with the position; it is *dignitas,* not just years, that mattered; cf. Ryan (1998) 225–32. Note also that it would appear that in 136 B.C. App. Claudius Pulcher (*cos.* 143, censor 136) was appointed *princeps* (by himself?) in preference to his foe P. Cornelius Scipio Aemilianus (*cos.* 147, 134, censor 142): Bonnefond-Coudry (1993) 112, and see further Ryan (1998) 183–85.

69. Q. Fabius Maximus Verrucosus (Cunctator), *cos.* 233, 228, 215, 214, 209; censor 230; dictator (221?), 217; *pontifex maximus* 216–203; augur for 63 (Pliny *NH* 7.48.156) or 62 years (Livy 30.26.7, Valerius Maximus 8.13.3; cf. *MRR* 1.283, 3.88; this may possibly be a conflation of two Fabii); he was reappointed *princeps* in 204 (Livy 29.37.1). On Fabius, see also Cicero *de Sen.* 4.10–12; Soverini in Mattioli (1995) 2.252–58; and Sumner (1973) 30–32, particularly for date of birth—not many years prior to 265 B.C.(?); contrast Powell (1988) 275–76: 285 B.C. or a few years later; the median, ca. 275 B.C., is actually a good compromise in the light of available evidence. On Torquatus see above, regarding the consular elections for 210 B.C.

70. Aulus Gellius 14.7.9 (time of Varro); Dio 53.1.3. A new order of speaking was introduced by a *lex Iulia* in 9 B.C., the details of which remain uncertain (see further below), though seniority certainly played a part, as did in practice the emperor's wishes. Cf. Aulus Gellius 4.10.1–4; Suetonius *Div. Iul.* 21; Mommsen (1887–88) 3.965; *MRR* 2.130 n. 1; Talbert (1984) 240–48; Bonnefond-Coudry (1989: 487–88; 1993); Tansey (2000).

71. Note the resistance of the *tribuni plebis* when T. Quinctius Flamininus put himself forward for the consulship of 198 B.C., at the age of no more than 30 years: Livy 32.7.8–12, Plutarch *Flam.* 2.1–2.

72. Livy 42.47.9. On the historical context, see *MRR* 1.413 and Briscoe (1964).

73. Nor should it be inferred, on the other side of the coin, that before this period of republican history seniority always won the day: cf. Livy 1.3.10, "plus tamen vis potuit quam voluntas patris aut verecundia aetatis."

74. Pliny *Ep.* 8.23.2–3; on Avitus, *PIR*[2] I 731. Note similarly Fronto *Ep. ad Verum Imp.* 1.6.2 van den Hout, A.D. 163: "a prima aetate sua me curavit Gavius Clarus [*PIR*[2] G 97] familiariter non modo iis officiis, quibus senator aetate et loco minor maiorem gradu atque natu senatorem probe colit ac promeretur . . ."

75. Aulus Gellius 2.15.1–4, and see also sections 5–8. Cf. Tacitus *Ann.* 3.31.6 (the conflict between Domitius Corbulo and L. Sulla in A.D. 21); Juvenal 7.209, 13.54–55; Ovid *Fasti* 5.57–58 (quoted above); Callistratus, *Dig.* 50.6.6.pr. (some striking parallels; this text is discussed later in this chapter and in Chapter 5). It is a timeless complaint: cf. the seventeenth-century essay (in the form of a dialogue) "Of the want of respect due to age" by Edward Hyde, Earl of Clarendon and Lord High Chancellor of England (ed. M. W. Brownley, Augustan Reprint Society no. 227 [Los Angeles, 1984]), owing much to Cicero, as well as to Bacon's essay "Of youth and age." For older people in every generation harping on the "good old days," cf., e.g., Cicero *ad Fam.* 2.16.6 ("aetatis vitium"), and Horace *Ars Poet.* 173 (the old man as "laudator temporis acti"), discussed in Chapter 3.

Notes to Pages 115–116

76. E.g. (all dates are A.D.), L. Verginius Rufus, *cos.* I *ord.* 63, II 69, III *ord.* 97 (but, as Pliny *Ep.* 2.1 comments, he was living "in altissima tranquillitate" before the third consulship at the age of 83; cf. Plutarch *Galba* 10.7); M. Pompeius Silvanus Staberius Flavinus, *cos.* I 45, II 75/6?, III *des.* 83?; L. Iulius Ursus Servianus, *cos.* I 90, II *ord.* 102, III *ord.* 134; M. Lollius Paullinus D. Valerius Asiaticus Saturninus, *cos.* I 94, II *ord.* 125; L. Nonius Calpurnius Torquatus Asprenas, *cos.* I *ord.* 94, II *ord.* 128; L. Neratius Marcellus, *cos.* I 95, II *ord.* 129; P. (?) Seius Fuscianus, *cos.* I 151 ?, II *ord.* 188 (also *praef. urbi;* see Alföldy 1977: 159–60 on A.D. 151); M. Servilius Silanus, *cos.* I 152, II *ord.* 188. See also Eck (1974) 222–23.
77. For a clear outline of complex matters, see Eck (1974) 206–28, with (1979).
78. On the *praefectus urbi,* a post not infrequently held in close conjunction with a second consulship, see Vitucci (1956), with the review in *JRS* 49 (1959) 152–60 by T. J. Cadoux; Eck (1974) 209–10; Vidman (1982); Syme (1988) 608–21. On relative lack of prestige for the *cura aquarum,* cf. Syme (1986) 220–26; note, however, how many *amici principis* held the post (see below). Cf. Eck (1974) 208–9 ("ein alter, erfahrener Konsular"), Bruun (1991), esp. 184–87, and below on L. Tarius Rufus, apparently a very aged *curator aquarum.* As Syme (1980) 101 observed in this context, "Titles are more important than work."
79. Suolahti (1963) 555–77. Appius Claudius Caecus held the censorship in 312 B.C. (note Cicero *de Sen.* 6.16) before the consulship, but such a practice became extremely rare.
80. On the *legati Augusti pro praetore* in the "imperial" provinces, see Mommsen (1887–88) 2.250–54; Syme (1958) 665; Thomasson (1991) 26–54. Of imperial legates in the age of Augustus, only two may have been over the age of 60 years: Cn. Cornelius Lentulus, *cos.* 18 B.C. (*PIR²* C 1378) or 14 B.C. (*PIR²* C 1379), probably legate of Pannonia early in the Christian era; and L. Volusius Saturninus, *cos.* 12 B.C. (*PIR* V 660), legate of Syria in A.D. 4–5. Most legates were under the age of 50 years.
81. Eck (1974) 221–22. For the typical modern view, see, e.g., Birley (1953) 204: "I need hardly stress that the two proconsular provinces of Asia and Africa . . . were often reserved to crown the career of a man whose whole active life had been spent in the emperors' service." Also Morris (1965) 24: "the proconsulates of Asia and Africa, dignities proper to those who survived to the age of 60 or thereabouts"; Talbert (1984) 393: "reserved for senior consulars and frequently represented the pinnacle of a man's career." I do not dispute the claim that these governors were senior, only the implication that they need be, say, over 60 years of age—*senior* rather than *senex* again, to put it crudely. For what follows on the proconsulships of Africa and Asia, and for the information from which Figure 2 (in Appendix B) is derived, see esp. Thomasson (1960, 1984, 1996), Vogel-Weidemann (1982), Eck (1982a, 1983), Alföldy (1977), Syme

363

(1953a,b, 1986), Leunissen (1989). Figure 2 incorporates all individuals for whom probable and specific dates for first consulship and proconsulship may be surmised. No significant difference in this respect between Africa and Asia can be discerned. For the data for Figure 3 (in Appendix B), see Vogel-Weidemann (1982) 510–12.

82. Syme put Lepidus's proconsulship so late, in my view correctly, though others would put it earlier in the decade and others even as late as 29: Vogel-Weidemann (1982) 268.

83. E.g., C. Iulius Cornutus Tertullus (*cos. suff.* A.D. 100), mentioned above. Note also that those who held an ordinary as opposed to a suffect first consulship often rose through the subsequent "ranks" more quickly.

84. But of course this was far from the end of his career; indeed he was governor of Hispania Tarraconensis for some eight years before becoming emperor—though "per octo annos varie et inaequabiliter provinciam rexit. . . . paulatim in desidiam segnitiamque conversus est" (Suetonius *Galba* 9).

85. Lucian *Alex.* 34 (Alexander promised him 180 years of life); Alföldy (1977) 44; Dietz (1993) 305.

86. The same might be said of Q. Curtius Rufus, *cos. suff.* A.D. 43/4 (?), *procos. Africae* ca. 58/9 (?), in his old age: Tacitus *Ann.* 11.21; cf. Vogel-Weidemann (1982) 184–88. As for Gordian I, allegedly proconsul of Africa at the surprising age of about 79 years in A.D. 237/8 (see Herodian 7.5.2; Zonaras 12.17; SHA *Gord.* 9.1; see above), Grasby (1975) argues that he was in fact 59 or 60 (i.e., born ca. 178). Grasby's case, however, is weak and overlooks some inscriptional evidence; see Birley (1981) 181–86. Better to assume, with Syme (1971) 167, that Gordian I was born "in 159 (or perhaps a year or two later)," and that his career was severely retarded (see Barnes 1968: 594–96 for cogent suggestions in this regard); he was *legatus Augusti pro praetore* in Britannia Inferior in 216, and consul ca. 222.

87. Seneca *de Ira* 3.31.2. Cf. Tacitus *Hist.* 1.77: "Otho pontificatus auguratusque honoratis iam senibus cumulum dignitatis addidit" (Chilver in his commentary *ad loc.* is very cautious: "*honoratis iam senibus* is perhaps contemptuous"; note *Hist.* 1.88, also under Otho: "primores senatus aetate invalidi").

88. See esp. Saller (1982) ch. 3. Mommsen (1887–88) 2.252 commented: "es hat auch nachweislich nicht selten der jüngere Consul vor dem älteren die Consularprovinz erhalten."

89. For Fronto (who himself reflected that "senectus crepusculum est, quod longum esse non potest," *Ep. ad Amic.* 2.7.18 van den Hout), see *Ep. ad Ant. Pium* 8; Champlin (1980) 82, 164 n. 13; van den Hout (1999) 392–93. For Asper, Dio 78.22. Cf. *CIL* 9.5533 (= *ILS* 1011): Salvius Liberalis (under Trajan) "sorte [procos. fac]tus provinciae Asiae se excusavit."

Note Mommsen (1887–88) 2.253 n. 2 in reference to proconsular commands: "Wahrscheinlich bestanden noch andere Ordnungen, namentlich um die allzu alt gewordenen Personen auszuschliessen."

90. Turannius: Tacitus *Ann.* 1.7 ("C. Turranius"), 11.31 ("Turranius"); Seneca *de Brev. Vit.* 20.3: "Sex. Turannius [*sic* Reynolds, *S. Turannius* Gertz; the principal MSS read *styrannius*] fuit exactae diligentiae senex, qui post annum nonagesimum, cum uacationem procurationis ab C. Caesare ultro accepisset . . ." (Griffin 1962: 106: "That Seneca adds *ultro* suggests that the resignation procedure was usual"). The identification as the same man in all three places, despite the confusion over his names, seems certain. Apart from *PIR* T 297 and *RE* 7a.1441–42, see Demougin (1992) 372–73. Other noteworthy cases in the context include L. Iulius Vestinus (*PIR*[2] I 622; Demougin 1992: 574–75), *amicus* of Claudius, Nero, Vespasian, and perhaps Titus, prefect of Egypt under Nero; and M. Oclatinius Adventus (*PIR*[2] O 9), *amicus* of Caracalla, then adlected to the senate by Macrinus and *cos. ord.* in 218—according to Dio 78.14 he was blind through extreme old age.

91. Crook (1955) 36. On the general subject, see also Mommsen (1887–88) 2.834–36; Syme (1956); Millar (1977) 110–22; Brunt (1988); and Eck in *CAH*[2] 11 (2000) ch. 4.

92. Thus R. P. Longden, *CAH* 11 (1936) 198; Longden, it should be noted, goes on to refer to two younger groups, lawyers and soldiers, advising Nerva. Cf. Crook (1955) 53; Syme (1958) 3, (1991) 546: "The reign of Nerva had been highly propitious for a whole group of elderly senators." Similarly under the aged Pertinax, Crook (1955) 78.

93. Crook (1955) 69: "[T]he old men who bring with them the traditions and policies of earlier reigns retire after a few years, and meanwhile new men are being trained within the circle, who will reach their maturity as counsellors of later emperors."

94. Millar (1977) 116–17; Halfmann (1986) 92–103, 245–53.

95. Herodian 6.1.2; Crook (1955) 87.

96. In particular Dio 52.15.1–4, and 52.33.3–4; cf. Brunt (1988), esp. 47–48.

97. Crook (1955) 113; see also Williams (1975) 70–71 on the *Tabula Banasitana* in this context.

98. Crook (1955) 53; also 63 for the time of Hadrian: "matters of small importance." Is this on account of our lack of knowledge, or is it reality? Domitian's council of *proceres,* presented in Juvenal 4, is a famous caricature on the theme.

99. See again Tacitus *Ann.* 14.54, Seneca's "retirement" speech in A.D. 62, in which he calls himself "senex et levissimis quoque curis impar." Tacitus has Seneca say hopefully, "possumus seniores amici quietem reposcere." Nero, of course, was not convinced.

100. On evolving modern conceptions of retirement, see, e.g., Donahue (1960), Goody (1976), and Moody (1998) 315–62; for very useful comparative perspectives, see also Gaunt (1983), Plakans (1989), and Laslett (1996) ch. 9. For assumptions about Roman retirement with which I would disagree, see, e.g., Dixon (1992) 149–57. Balsdon (1969) 169–92, though he uses the term "retirement," is well aware of its limited application to the ancient world and provides a useful collection of material on the subject.

101. E.g., Martial back to Bilbilis (10.96, etc.), or Statius, with his apparently reluctant wife, to Neapolis, *Silv.* 3.5.13: "patria senium componere terra" (he would have been in his early 40s at the time—note 4.4.70, and the frequency with which the prayer for old age is mentioned in Statius, as we saw in the previous chapter; cf. Coleman 1988: xix: "It is misleading to regard his return to Naples as 'retirement,'" because Naples was nearly as busy as Rome; Garthwaite 1989 argues, in my view convincingly, that Statius's withdrawal had nothing to do with old age and illness at all—any more, it might be said, than did Martial's—but was a result of his treatment at the hands of Domitian; one is reminded again of Seneca and Nero). One other case is worth mentioning: the equestrian writer of *mimi,* D. Laberius, "retired," only to be forced by Caesar to act in one of his own pieces at the age of 60 years (47/6 B.C.); he was not amused, especially as his piece did not win first prize but was defeated by that of a much younger rival (Macrobius *Sat.* 2.7.1–5, Aulus Gellius 8.15; for the context and some related difficulties, see Schwartz 1948; Krenkel 1994 has interesting speculations on the matter). For "retirement" on account of physical incapacity, one might note the dedicatory epigrams in *Anthologia Palatina* books 6 and 16, where it is often explicitly stated that old age is the cause and that the cessation of labor is anything but welcome: cases include a soldier, a schoolmaster (compare the case of Oppius Chares [Suetonius *Gramm.* 3.6] who persisted in teaching "ad ultimam aetatem et cum iam non ingressu modo deficeretur sed et visu"), fishermen (cf. the *seniculus* of Apuleius *Met.* 1.25), a hunter (6.93, Antipater of Sidon: he can no longer wield a spear and is all wrinkles, ὁ πρέσβυς, ὁ πᾶς ῥυτίς—for hunting being inappropriate to old age, cf. Symmachus *Ep.* 5.68 [*MGHAA* 6.1.144]), scribes, charioteers (cf. Cameron 1973: 178–79), and prostitutes (including 6.210 [Philetas of Samos], retirement at age 50—in Lucian *Dial. Meret.* 11.3, a 45-year-old prostitute has the nickname ἡ σορός; cf. Chapter 3 note 26; Lucilius, *Anthologia Palatina* 11.256 has a 100-year-old prostitute still active; contrast Sallust *Cat.* 24.3).

102. Zonaras 7.19. Talbert (1984) 153 cites Epictetus *Diss.* 3.24.36 (ἀεὶ βουλευτής) but this probably refers to the local town councillor.

103. See Dio 55.3.1 for this *lex Iulia de senatu habendo* of 9 B.C. (mentioned

above; note most recently Talbert in *CAH*² 10.328–29), and cf. Suetonius *Div. Aug.* 35. Suetonius also records that Augustus allowed equestrians "infirm with age [*senio*]" to be excused from taking part in the reintroduced *transvectio* on horseback, and that he subsequently allowed those over 35 years of age to relinquish their horses if they so wished (*Div. Aug.* 38.3; for the age of 35 years in this context—and not, as one might expect if we were dealing with *seniores,* 45 or 46 years—see too Dio 54.26.8 and 56.23.2; cf. Nicolet 1966: 79–80, and also Kleijwegt 1991: 215, following Veyne, on this "rite de passage"). Bonnefond-Coudry (1989) 369–74 deals in some detail with excuses under the republic for not attending senate meetings because of illness or infirmity, but has nothing to say on the subject of old age; there is brief discussion in Ryan (1998) 49. On the rigors of attending the Curia Julia in winter, see Talbert (1984) 126.

104. Pliny *Ep.* 4.23.3, and cf. 3.1.2 (discussed in Chapter 3, and quoted at the end of this section).

105. [Quintilian] *Decl. Min.* 306.16.

106. *Controv.* 1.8.4. Note the emphasis here on the fact that it was a matter of choice whether a senator over this age attended the house.

107. *De Brev. Vit.* 3.5 (Watt 1994: 238 suggests a change in punctuation, on the assumption that two different individuals are speaking, but this seems to me unnecessary—the same person is "retiring" in stages), 20.4; it is uncertain how much stress should be placed on the use of ordinal rather than cardinal numbers. The figure of 60 years is supported to some extent by the fact that from the age of 60 years a *vacatio* was granted from public life (see below). It is stated for a much later period by Saint Augustine *Quaest. Evang.* 1.9 (*PL* 35.1326 = *CCSL* 44b.13), that "solet enim otium concedi sexagenariis post militiam vel post actiones publicas." He is clearly condensing the facts here, however, to suit his argument: for the age limit of, at most, 50 (not 60) years in the army, see above.

108. Mommsen (1887–88) 3.917 n. 2.

109. McAlindon (1957).

110. See Stroux and Wenger (1928) 122; followed by O'Brien Moore in *RE* *Suppl.* 6.767.

111. For which see below. Talbert (1984) 153–54 likewise dismisses this idea, but he is wrong in stating that the age of 70 years "was taken from earlier Republican arrangements to hear these cases." The *lex Repetundarum* of 123/2 B.C., which he cites as evidence here, in fact set a maximum age for jurors of 60 years, not 70, as will be seen shortly.

112. *Laws* 6.755a–b; cf. *Rep.* 6.498b–c.

113. E.g., Dio 60.12.3. On the acoustics of the Curia Julia, see Talbert (1984) 125–26. For deafness as one of the characteristics of old age, see Lu-

cretius *de Rer. Nat.* 3.467–69; *Anthologia Palatina* 11.74 (Nicarchus); Lucian *Timon* 2, *Catapl.* 5; and (with typical acerbity) Juvenal 10.210–16. It is an age-old complaint: compare the grumblings of the octogenarian Barzillai to King David, 2 Samuel 19.35.

114. See above and, e.g., SHA *Sev. Alex.* 16.3: "fuit praeterea illi consuetudo, ut, si de iure aut de negotiis tractaret, solos doctos et disertos adhiberent, si vero de re militari, militares veteres et senes bene meritos . . ."

115. *Ep.* 4.23.2–4, 3.1.2 (I adapt Radice's translation of the latter).

116. See again Chapter 3 note 31.

117. As Lucian *pro Lapsu* 12–13 stresses (and he himself held a minor administrative post in Egypt in his old age), magistrates and men busy with political affairs depend on their physical vigor: if they lose their health, they are of little use.

118. Seneca *de Brev. Vit.* 20.4. Compare Horace's prayer, *Carm. Saec.* 45–47: "di, probos mores docili iuventae, di, senectuti placidae quietem . . . date."

119. Frag. 330 West: βίος δ' ἀπράγμων τοῖς γέρουσι συμφέρει, μάλιστα δ' εἰ τύχοιεν ἁπλοῖ τοῖς τρόποις ἢ μακκοᾶν μέλλοιεν ἢ ληρεῖν ὅλως, ὅπερ γερόντων ἐστίν. Cf. Falkner (1995) 227.

120. For the whole subject, see esp. Abbott and Johnson (1926) and Neesen (1981); to be used with caution are Langhammer (1973) and Drecoll (1997). The relevant articles in *RE* (9.1135 [Ziegler]) and *D&S* (3.2039 [Lécrivain]) are now too old to be useful, particularly on the question of exemption by age.

121. *Dig.* 50.2.12 (Callistratus), 50.5.5 (Macer, quoting Ulpian), 50.2.13.2 (Papirius Iustus, quoting a rescript of Marcus Aurelius and Verus). For further contrasts between *munera* and *honores,* see 50.4.12 (Iavolenus) and 50.4.17.1 (Hermogenian), showing that the distinction remained, at least in theory, to a very late period. It was not that the decurionate became a *munus* as such; it remained in name an *honor* but one which carried with it the obligation to perform specific burdensome *munera* as part of the job.

122. *Dig.* 49.4.1.2 (Ulpian), 50.4.14.3, 6 (Callistratus), and 50.6.2 (Ulpian), showing how compulsion was used in the case not just of *munera* but also of *honores.* Compare *CIL* 5.532 = *ILS* 6680 (Tergeste, reign of Antoninus Pius), 2.15: "munera decurionatus." In effect the decurionate became one of the most burdensome of all the *munera,* and the increasing difficulty in filling vacancies for the post is shown by the fact that certain otherwise ineligible classes of individuals could be drawn into service: e.g., bastards and those born of an incestuous union (*Dig.* 50.2.6.pr., Papinian), and illiterates (*Cod. Iust.* 10.32.6, A.D. 293). Furthermore, in times of shortage, all exemptions might be annulled (Modestinus, *Dig.* 50.4.11.2; *Cod. Iust.* 10.49.1–3, A.D. 408, 445, 472?). See also Eyben (1981) 339–40, with reference to other literature.

123. Compulsion to office: *Dig.* 50.4.12 (Iavolenus, early second century). From the second century compulsion appears to have become more common, as rescripts of Marcus Aurelius and Verus indicate: cf. *Dig.* 49.1.21.2 (Papirius Iustus), 50.1.38.6 (Papirius Iustus), 50.4.6.pr. (Ulpian); see also Jones (1940) 167–69, and Garnsey (1998) 4–15, 25.
124. Shortage of candidates: *Dig.* 50.2.3 (Ulpian), 50.2.12 (Callistratus), 50.4.6.pr. (Ulpian). Fugitives forced back: 50.2.1 (Ulpian), 50.4.4.3 (Ulpian). Fugitives subject to double term: *Cod. Theod.* 12.1.16 (= *Cod. Iust.* 10.32.18, A.D. 329); Evans Grubbs (1995) 25.
125. For definitions dating to ca. A.D. 300, see *Dig.* 50.4.1 (Hermogenian) and 50.4.18 (Arcadius Charisius), but note esp. the comments of Millar (1983) 78, and see now most fully Horstkotte (1996). The definitions of Callistratus, *Dig.* 50.4.14, are earlier (ca. A.D. 200) and more general in character. For the dangers (as here) in generalizing over the whole empire, however, see Abbott and Johnson (1926) 94–96; Millar (1983) 76, 80. Further theoretical definitions and distinctions as evidenced in Roman Egypt are outlined in Chapter 5.
126. Cf. *lex Urs.* (44 B.C.) 98.
127. *Dig.* 50.4.3.3 (Ulpian), 50.17.2 (Ulpian). But see *Cod. Iust.* 10.64.1 (Philip) for the case of wealthy women; Abbott and Johnson (1926) 87; Arjava (1996) 249–53.
128. Exemptions from patrimonial burdens very rare: *Dig.* 50.4.6.4 (Ulpian); *Cod. Iust.* 10.42 (age is mentioned as giving no immunity at 10.42.5 [Carus, Carinus, and Numerianus] and 10.42.7 [Diocletian and Maximian]). Exemption was granted (unavoidably but not always) to the poor, who nonetheless had to perform corporeal tasks since these need involve no expenditure: e.g., *Dig.* 27.1.7 (Ulpian), 27.1.40.1 (Paul), 50.4.4.2 (Ulpian), 50.4.6.pr. (Ulpian); *Cod. Iust.* 10.52.6.1 (= *Cod. Theod.* 12.17.1.1, A.D. 321/4). Contrast *Dig.* 50.5.10.3 (Paul).
129. *Dig.* 50.4.8. The principle of *annus coeptus* (see above) was also in operation here "but only for those offices in which no property of the *res publica* is entrusted to them," as Ulpian goes on to explain; hence the reference here to the 25th year ("ante vicensimum quintum annum") rather than to the age of 25 years.
130. Stated most explicitly in the case of *munera privata*: *Cod. Iust.* 5.30.5, A.D. 529; Justinian *Inst.* 1.25.13. On *Dig.* 26.2.32.2 (Paul) and 27.3.9.1 (Ulpian), see *Index Interpolationum* 2.120, 158.
131. E.g., *lex Urs.* 98; Flavian Municipal Law 83; *Dig.* 50.2.6.1 (Papinian), 50.2.11 (Callistratus), 50.5.2.pr., 50.6.3, 50.17.2 (Ulpian; on *iudices,* see below); *Cod. Theod.* 12.1.7 (A.D. 320), 12.1.19 (331), 12.1.58.2 (364). Cf. also *Cod. Iust.* 10.50.1–2 (Diocletian and Maximian). In this context, see most recently Horster (1996), citing earlier scholarship.

132. *Dig.* 50.6.4. Note also Fronto *Ep. ad Amic.* 2.7.17–18 van den Hout, ca. A.D. 165, unfortunately preserved in a fragmentary state (for the context, a man in his 70s who had served as a decurion for 45 years wishing to be reinstated with his honors after a period of exile, see Champlin 1980: 69–70 and van den Hout 1999: 441–43): "cui aetati omnium vacatio munerum [an exaggeration, or wishful thinking on Fronto's part?] data est, quam aetatem nulla lex, si sacramento adiguntur, res publica magis inter nullas se. . . . seni septuaginta annos olim egresso insignes maculas infligis, quando, oro te, abolendas?"

133. Note also *Cod. Iust.* 10.32.10 for an individual decision of A.D. 294 exempting an individual, the addressee's father, who proves himself to be "ultra septuagesimum annum aetatis," and *Dig.* 50.4.3.12 (Ulpian), stating that the age of 70 years confers exemption from the *munus* of *cura frumenti comparandi.*

134. *Dig.* 50.5.2.1 (Ulpian), 50.5.8.pr. (Papinian); Millar (1983) 77.

135. *Dig.* 50.6.6.pr. Tomulescu (1979) 117 takes Callistratus at face value and concludes that "les vieillards ont toujours été respecté à Rome." With Callistratus, contrast Pliny *Pan.* 38.6–7, praising Trajan for extending to *maiores* a privilege (exemption from the *vicesima hereditatum*) previously only accorded to the young—"for why should the younger generation be held in higher honour than the older one? And why should justice not equally apply to old and young alike?" (tr. Radice).

136. Financial means might obligate otherwise exempt persons to perform public services: Abbott and Johnson (1926) 102; Millar (1983) 82–83. Old age still subject to financial burdens: *Dig.* 50.4.6.4 (Ulpian), 50.5.11 (Hermogenian, with 50.4.18.29, Arcadius Charisius). This point is further discussed in the next chapter in the context of Roman Egypt (note esp. *P.Phil.* 1.18–34, early second century A.D.).

137. *Dig.* 50.2.11. Cf. *Cod. Iust.* 10.32.13, a rescript of Diocletian and Maximian stating that the age of 50 years affords no excuse. Incidentally, Dionysius of Halicarnassus *AR* 2.21.3 implies (cf. Chapter 9 note 104) that it was believed that in the time of Romulus the age of 50 years granted exemption, at least for those chosen to hold priesthoods, not just from military service (see chapter 4 note 14) but also τῶν κατὰ τὴν πόλιν ὀχληρῶν διὰ τὸν νόμον.

138. I.e., 30 years after the usual assumption of public duties: *Cod. Iust.* 10.32.58 = *Cod. Theod.* 12.1.191 (A.D. 436).

139. *Cod. Iust.* 10.50.3; Corcoran (1996) 103 n. 63. The reference to *munera personalia* here may indicate that the 55-year rule came to be applied to more than just the decurionate (which seems unlikely—see below), or it may be simply a confusion of the existing legislation in what was fast becoming a tortuously complicated matter. There is no need to amend the text, as suggested by, inter alios, Bonfante (1925) 434 n. 1.

140. *Cod. Iust.* 10.32.3, A.D. 285.

141. See further *Cod. Theod.* 7.22.7 (ca. A.D. 370) and 12.1.83 (380): someone "grandaevam praeferat senectutem" for release from *militia,* and cf. 1.15.12 (386): "nemo . . . annositatis se defendat obstaculo."
142. This is made clear in the legal texts repeatedly: e.g., in the *Digest,* at the very beginning of the section on *vacatio et excusatio munerum* (50.5.1.pr., Ulpian).
143. *Cod. Iust.* 10.32.41 (= *Cod. Theod.* 12.1.118), A.D. 387.
144. *Dig.* 50.5.1.3 (Ulpian): a man of 65 years is not exempt from *munera civilia.* It will be suggested in the next chapter that, while the age of 70 years remained the legal age for exemption, in practice it appears that this limit might be lowered to 65 or even 60 years in individual cases, from later in the third or early in the fourth century A.D. The evidence for this is largely papyrological, and perhaps the change may only apply to Roman Egypt.
145. *Dig.* 50.4.3.6 (Ulpian *Opiniones*).
146. *Dig.* 50.4.18.14 (Arcadius Charisius). The minimum age for serving as a *iudex* under the principate was in theory 25 years (as with the quaestorship, it had been 30 under the republic: *lex Repetundarum* 13, 17), but it is clear that this rule could be modified—or ignored—when insufficient candidates presented themselves: *Dig.* 4.8.41 (Callistratus, referring to a *lex Iulia*), 42.1.57 (Ulpian); *Cyrene Edicts* 1.16; Flavian Municipal Law 86; see also Suetonius *Div. Aug.* 32.3 (textual problems or an error?); *Oratio Claudii de aetate recuperatorum* (*FIRA*² 1.44), col. 1, lines 2–4 (presumably incorporating the rule of *annus coeptus*). Note too *CIL* 11.1437, the tombstone inscription from Pisae of C. Saturius Secundus (early third century A.D.?), the son of a *primipilus,* who lived only 19 years and 27 days but who nevertheless was able to have included among his list of honors the fact that he was "ex V decuris"—he had also been augur and "patronus coloniae Asculanorum"; see further Demougin (1975) 173–74.
147. *Lex Repetundarum* 17 (and cf. 13). Note Cornelius Nepos *Att.* 7.1: "incidit Caesarianum civile bellum, cum haberet annos circiter sexaginta. usus est aetatis vacatione . . ."; Festus 452L (drawing on Flaccus for the late republic or early empire; for the full context of this passage, see Chapter 9: *sexagenarios de ponte*): "sexagenari, qui iam nullo publico munere fungerentur"; and Varro *de Vita Pop. Rom.* 2, frag. 71 *ap.* Nonius Marcellus 842L (see further Chapter 1 on Varro's *gradus aetatum,* and Chapter 9 on *sexagenarii de ponte*): "cum in quintum gradum pervenerant atque habebant sexaginta annos, tum denique erant a publicis negotiis liberi atque otiosi." For the age limit of 60 years in this context, note also Chapter 4 note 107, and cf. [Cicero] *ad Heren.* 2.13.20. For such withdrawal in old age, note too Martial 4.78 (Afer the old *ardalio,* "busybody," an occupation better suited to younger men), and [Quintilian] *Decl. Maior.* 13.4 (the "iusta missio" of a *senex*). As Cicero has Cato

state—somewhat anachronistically, except in the context of military service—"et legibus et institutis vacat aetas nostra muneribus eis quae non
possunt sine viribus sustineri, itaque non modo quod non possumus,
sed ne quantum possumus quidem cogimur" (*de Sen.* 11.34).

148. *Cyrene Edicts* 5.112–13 (see above); Flavian Municipal Law 86, 87.

149. Ulpian, *Dig.* 50.5.13.pr. For exemptions from *munera* on the grounds of
illness from the second to fourth centuries, see, e.g., *Cod. Iust.* 10.51–
52: exemption was granted provided that the individual was considered
incapable (10.51.1: Gordian grants immunity from *munera personalia*,
on the application of the son, to a man blind in both eyes). Thus those
who were deaf and dumb were not excused from *munera* (*Dig.* 50.2.7.1
[Paul], 50.5.2.6 [Ulpian]). It is also stated that those "weighed down by
senium and *corporis inbecillitas*" are exempted only from *munera* involving physical labor (*Dig.* 50.5.2.7–7a [Ulpian]), not from mental or financial burdens. At *Cod. Iust.* 10.51.2–3, Diocletian and Maximian
grant immunity from *munera personalia* to a man crippled with arthritis
("articulari morbo debilitatum"), but not to a man suffering from gout
("podagrae valitudo"), though the latter may, on application to the *rec-
tor provinciae,* gain exemption from *corporalia munera*. Note also *Cod.
Theod.* 8.1.1 (given as A.D. 319 but it is clear that it should be dated to
343) where in regard to the administrative office *ad tabularios,* individuals may be exempted when age renders them incapable ("aetate . . . in-
pediente"); note that in this case no specific age limit is given: one continues for as long as one is capable (similarly *Cod. Iust.* 12.7.1 = *Cod.
Theod.* 6.10.1, A.D. 380, for the *notariorum nomen* retained in old age
without the duties). In the case of the *libitinarii* of Puteoli, however, the
physical duties required in their work apparently meant that only those
over the age of 20 years and no older than 50 years could do the job (*AE*
[1971] no. 88, 2.6).

150. *Dig.* 50.6.4 (Ulpian, quoted above), 27.1.2.pr. (Modestinus), 27.1.15.11
(Modestinus); *Cod. Iust.* 5.67.1 (A.D. 246); Justinian *Inst.* 1.25.13. Cf.
Frag. Vat. 238 (Ulpian); Bonfante (1925) 434 n. 1.

151. See further Abbott and Johnson (1926) 106–7; Millar (1983) 85–86;
Wolff (1986); Link (1989) 66–133.

152. *FIRA²* 1.56 = *W.Chr.* 462, 31 B.C. This is further evidence, incidentally,
that compulsion to office might occur from an early period.

153. *Cod. Theod.* 7.20.2 = *Cod. Iust.* 12.46.1, A.D. 320? (307 and 326 have
also been suggested: see Barnes 1982: 69 n. 102; the grammar of the
sentence is also somewhat suspect, glossed over in my translation: perhaps delete *sub* or replace *perfruantur*?); cf. *AE* (1937) no. 232 (= *FIRA²*
1.93, A.D. 311), with Corcoran (1996) 146–48.

154. *BGU* 180 = *W.Chr.* 396, lines 3–10; cf. Link (1989) 102–5. The five-
year ἀνάπαυσις is mentioned only here (Oertel 1917: 394–95; Johnson 1936: 612; Millar 1983: 85; Wolff 1986: 109); perhaps it is an

Egyptian peculiarity, or a result of this veteran's imagination, though the same period occurs (under different circumstances) in, e.g., Scaevola *Dig.* 50.4.5 (cf. 27.1.8.3, Modestinus).

155. For types of discharge, see *Dig.* 3.2.2.2 (Ulpian) and 49.16.13.3 (Macer). For privileges in old age granted only after an honorable discharge, note *Dig.* 49.18 (*de veteranis*); *Cod. Theod.* 7.20.4.3 (A.D. 325), 7.20.12.1–2 (A.D. 400); *Cod. Iust.* 10.55.2 (Diocletian and Maximian), but see also *Cod. Iust.* 10.55.3 (same emperors), with Millar (1983) 86, Wolff (1986) 106, 110, Corcoran (1996) 99.

156. *Cod. Theod.* 12.1.113 (A.D. 386): "nemo se annositate tueatur."

157. *Dig.* 22.4.6. According to Artemidorus *Oneirocrit.* 2.69, faith may be placed in the very young and the very old: the former because they have not yet learned to lie and cheat, the latter because they have only a short time left to live and therefore have no reason to deceive.

Chapter 5. Rules of Age in Roman Egypt

1. On the offices and archives of Roman Egypt, Cockle (1984) offers a good general survey. See further Reinmuth (1935); Jones (1940); Pierce (1968); Posner (1972); Brunt (1975); Wolff (1978), esp. §13; Burkhalter (1990); cf. also Duncan-Jones (1990) 67–73 and Drecoll (1997) 189–201. For an overview of bureaucracy (or the lack of it) in the Roman Empire, see Garnsey and Saller (1987) ch. 2.

2. *P.Oxy.* 2186, A.D. 260, referring to archives from as far back as A.D. 4/5; compare similarly *PSI* 457 (A.D. 275/6) with reference to the census of A.D. 173, and. *P.Mich.* 676 (A.D. 272), drawing on documentary evidence from the time of Nero, if not earlier (Nelson 1979: 26–35). For the existence and use of archive material from elsewhere in the empire, see Chapter 6.

3. E.g., *P.Oxy.* 1654 (ca. A.D. 150): a fee of ten obols.

4. Cockle (1984) 116.

5. The evidence was analyzed in depth by Hombert and Préaux (1952), but this study is now in most important respects superseded by Bagnall and Frier (1994); see now also Bagnall et al. (1997). There are currently extant over 380 copies of census declarations from Roman Egypt. We know of 17 censuses being held in Roman Egypt, every fourteen years, from A.D. 33/4 to 257/8; it remains uncertain if a census of this type was held in A.D. 19/20: see Bagnall and Frier (1994) 2–11, with Rathbone (1993) 89–90. On the census elsewhere in the empire, a subject for which primary source material is lacking, see Chapter 6.

6. On format, see Wallace (1938b) 100–104; Hombert and Préaux (1952) 100; Bagnall and Frier (1994) 20–26. For a convenient example, see *Sel. Pap.* 312 (= *P.Bad.* 75b, A.D. 147).

7. Hombert and Préaux (1952) 84–97.

8. *SB* 9050, A.D. 89; Cockle (1984) 121. Cf. Tomsin (1952) 503–5 for πρεσβύτεροι, "elders," acting as *komogrammateis* (and add *P.Oxy.* 4066, A.D. 183), a more humble occupation.

9. These papyri are further discussed later in this chapter in relation to the poll tax. Note the use made of the information about the men listed in these papyri by Hopkins (1980) 332–33 and Hobson (1985) 218–22. For other such tax lists, cf. Hombert and Préaux (1952) 135–41; Bagnall and Frier (1994) 27–28.

10. Originally published in part by Kenyon in 1898 as *P.Lond.* 260 and 261 but republished, in the correct order and with the addition of a papyrus from the Sammlung Erzherzog Rainer, by Wessely in *Stud. Pal.* 4 (1905) 62–78.

11. *P.Lond.* 260.43–59 = *Stud. Pal.* 4 (1905) 74, lines 550–66. It is strange that, while the ages in this specific list of over-aged individuals range from 63 to 80 years, three men, aged 62, 63, and 66 years, are included elsewhere in the roll among the general list (*P.Lond.* 260.14, 37, 39).

12. Wallace (1938b) 112–15.

13. On the registration of births in Roman Egypt (and in the empire as a whole), see Chapter 6. The crucial question of whether birth registration was compulsory is discussed there. It is also seen that the registration of the birth of a Greco-Egyptian was a quite separate process from the registration of the birth of a child to Roman citizens.

14. Wallace (1938b) 109–12; Taubenschlag (1955) 612–13; Mertens (1958) ch. 4; Nelson (1979).

15. Lists were also drawn up of those registered as having "disappeared," i.e., those who left their village in flight (cf., e.g., *P.Oxy.* 251–53, 2669, *P.Mich.* 580). It remains uncertain, however, whether the lists drawn up from the registration of births, deaths, and flight, and from the records of the *epikrisis*, were to be found outside the *poleis*. See now also Scheidel (1999), stressing our lack of precise knowledge of aspects of the bureaucratic process in this context.

16. *Gnom. Id. Log.* 44, 58–63. For a first-century (ca. A.D. 31–42?) edition of sections 35- 41, see *P.Oxy.* 3014.

17. *Gnom. Id. Log.* 63 presents something of a puzzle. It is stated there that those who have failed to register at the census are given three years within which to file a late return; thus it is interpreted by the principal editors (Schubart, Reinach, and Riccobono), as well as by Wallace (1938b) 103, Hombert and Préaux (1952) 98, and Lewis (1983) 157. The translation in *Sel. Pap.* 206, Johnson (1936) 715, and Johnson et al.'s *Ancient Roman Statutes* (Austin, 1961) 211, "if the additional subject for registration was under three years of age," meaning that infants under the age of three years did not have to be declared (the key word is προσθήκη), is not only an inaccurate translation but also a false statement: children of all ages had to be declared. It remains true, however,

that we possess no returns dated after the final day of the second year of a census, something we would surely expect to possess if a period of three years' grace was allowed. Perhaps late returns were routinely dated to the last official day of the census, whatever date they were eventually furnished. For census fraud in the provinces, see Brunt (1981) 167.

18. Over 100 different liturgical duties are known: Lewis (1997).

19. Cf. Thomas (1983) 36. It should be noted that in this chapter the term *munera* will generally be avoided, for the simple reason that the documents we are dealing with are in Greek and not in Latin. The English term "liturgies" (Greek λειτουργίαι) is preferable.

20. Lewis (1997) 89–97 offers a comprehensive list; Drecoll (1997) provides nothing new of note.

21. *P.Oxy.* 2754 (A.D. 111), lines 1–2.

22. See above regarding a γραφὴ ὑπερετῶν καὶ ἀσθενῶν, and cf. *P.Phil.* 5 (= *SB* 7192), with the comments of Scherer (1947).

23. *P.Flor.* 312.4–5, and 8 for use of the term ὑπερέτης. On this papyrus, note also Hagedorn (1985) 174 n. 21.

24. Scherer (1947) 15–16.

25. *P.Phil.* 1.19–22. Cf. again *Dig.* 50.6.6.pr. (Callistratus).

26. *SB* 10195. The dating is determined by reference to Volusius Maecianus, prefect in 161. On the petition, see also Haensch (1994) 517.

27. *P.Col.* 123 (*SB* 9526), *apokrima* 9, lines 35–39.

28. Westermann and Schiller (1954) 21–22.

29. MacMullen (1982).

30. See *P.Flor.* 382, lines 3 and 6, for the first statements; the text of the subsequent four rulings, lines 10–26, is badly fragmented. All six are republished in Oliver (1989) 481–83; see also Lewis (1996) 108 and Coriat (1997) 478–79, 488–91. For *P.Flor.* 382.17–23, the fifth ruling, see also *P.Mich.* 529.39–52 (A.D. 232–36). The repetition of the ruling presumably points to the failure of local officials to observe it. I am grateful to Simon Corcoran for his comments to me on the nature of the rulings in *P.Flor.* 382.

31. In the original edition (*PSI* vol. 10 [1932] p. 11) the date was given as the third century A.D., "certamente è del secolo III^p, piuttosto della seconda metà che non della prima," and so it was widely assumed to be, e.g., by Lewis (1963: 10, 1966: 519). S. Eitrem and L. Amundsen (*Papyri Osloenses* 3 [1936], on *P.Oslo* 111.152), however, argued for a late second- or early third-century date, largely on the evidence of *P.Flor.* 382. In fact, the editor of *PSI* vol. 10, in his *corrigenda,* stated that "III^p" appeared "per lapsum calami" and should have read "II^p." Further, Rea (1978) has dated the papyrus with certainty to between June or July A.D. 192 and 26 July 194, on the evidence of the *epistrategos* named in the petition.

32. Lewis (1966) 519.

33. *Dig.* 50.5.1.3 (see Chapter 4 note 144).
34. *Cod. Iust.* 10.32.10 (see Chapter 4 note 133), and compare Macrobius *Comm. in Somn. Scip.* 1.6.76 (ca. A.D. 400) where the age of 70 years is still mentioned (in a mathematical context, 7 X 10; see Chapter 1) as freeing someone "ab omni officio" and granting "aliorum munerum vacatio"; contrast *Comm. in Somn. Scip.* 1.6.74 where the age of 49 years (7^2) is said—presumably with undue optimism—to grant *remissio iusta* for most people, and age 42 (7 X 6) exemption from military service. Macrobius also notes, perhaps more astutely, that from age 42 to 70 each man's duties vary according to his capacities (1.6.76: "a septima usque ad decimam septimanam pro captu virium quae adhuc singulis perseverant variantur officia").
35. Compare also *P.Lond.* 1827 (early fourth century) where an inhabitant of a village in the Hermopolite nome applies to the *strategos* for release from unspecified duties for which he has passed the age; again, no age apart from old age is mentioned.
36. As is shown by *P.Panop.* 30 (= *SB* 11223). For the slow-moving nature of the Roman Egyptian bureaucracy, see also Hobson (1993) 210–15.
37. It seems likely that Apion was prefect prior to A.D. 328: *PLRE* 1.82.
38. Reading in line 6 ὑπερβὰς τὰ ἑξή[κοντα ἔτη. See *PSI* vol. 6 (1920) p. 101 and Lewis (1966) 520.
39. For the exemption of weavers, see Scherer (1947) 21–23 with *P.Phil.* 1.1–17, and cf. Katzoff (1972) 284–86.
40. Grenfell and Hunt (1908) 205.
41. Grenfell and Hunt (1908) 205–6.
42. J. D. Thomas (1976); Barnes (1976) 279–81. Subsequently Barnes, in collaboration with Thomas, published a revised version of the text: Barnes (1982) 234–37. Further adjustments in Barnes and Worp (1983); also published as *SB* 12306. Drecoll (1997) 43–44 remains unaware of the revised dating.
43. Barnes (1976: 280; 1982: 237). It is taken to be referring to liturgies by Lewis (1966) 519, Bowman (1971) 167, and Drecoll (1997) 43–44, as well as by Grenfell and Hunt (1908) 205, and Oertel (1917) 201 (with some hesitation). Cf. Corcoran (1996) 197, who supports my interpretation.
44. On *lex Rom. Burg.* 36.6, see above.
45. *Dig.* 50.2.2.8 (Ulpian), *Cod. Iust.* 10.50.3 (Diocletian and Maximian).
46. For the possible application of the "55-year-old rule" to the *boulai* of Roman Egypt, see firstly Wegener (1946) 176–77, who argues that it did not apply here because we have evidence of a senator who was 61 years of age (*P.Lond.* 348.4, A.D. 202–3). The absurdity of this argument is patent: there is nothing to say that our 61-year-old did not freely choose to serve. The man of 61 years in A.D. 202–3 was only 59 or so when the town councils were instituted and so he must have accepted the office

freely (cf. Lewis 1974: 44–46). Also, the "55-year-old rule" probably did not come into effect until a later date. In any case, "the position of *bouleutes,* once attained, lasted until death" (Bowman 1971: 25, and cf. Chapter 4 note 102; Bowman notes that "there seems to have been no maximum age," and cites *P.Lond.* 348 as evidence). As for the rule of 55 years in relation to *munera personalia,* no papyrus as yet has offered any example of its use in practice; cf. Lewis (1997) 92.

47. For the opposite theory, namely that the original age of exemption was 60 or 65 years and that this was subsequently raised to 70, see Berelson (1934) 53; Johnson (1936) 611; and Wegener (1956) 343–44; similarly Suder (1995a) 411 (= 1995b: 38): *privilegium aetatis* in the republic and early empire was from the age of 50–60 years, but by the end of the third century A.D. was from age 70. Such theories are not supported by the evidence presented here.

48. *Dig.* 27.1.15.11, 27.1.13.8 (both from Modestinus's work *de excusationibus*).

49. Brunt (1975: 137–38, 1981: 162); Lewis (1983) 159–60.

50. Wallace (1938b) 121–28; Rathbone (1993) 87. On the general subject of the poll tax in Roman Egypt, there are useful overviews in Wallace (1938b) ch. 8; Neesen (1980) 125–30; Rathbone (1993). That it was an Augustan innovation, not an inheritance from the Ptolemaic period, is now generally accepted; see Evans (1957) for the clearest arguments, with Tcherikover (1950), an excellent discussion, and Rathbone (1993) 90–99.

51. As is suggested, e.g., by Johnson (1936) 531–32 for the third century A.D.; cf. Oertel (1917) 374.

52. *Dig.* 50.15.3.pr. (*libro secundo de censibus*), with Millar (1993) 110.

53. Wilcken (1899) 242.

54. Kenyon (1898) 19–42 (quotations from p. 20); see also my note 9.

55. Wallace (1938b) 107.

56. First published in Wilcken (1906) 232–33 and subsequently as *W.Chr.* 63.

57. Wilcken (1906) 233: "die Kopfsteuerpflicht vom 14. bis zum 60. Jahre (inklusive)." Followed by Hombert and Préaux (1952) 137, among others.

58. Wessely in *Stud. Pal.* 4 (1905), as cited in note 10; Youtie (1964) 25–26.

59. For dead men still paying tax, see Wallace (1938b) 124–25 and, for possible parallels outside Egypt, Brunt (1981) 163. *P.Princ.* 1.9, a register of taxes from A.D. 31, records two such cases, while *P.Col.* 1 recto 3 of A.D. 135–45 cites another eight. See further Westermann and Keyes (1932) 82 and Scheidel (1999) 60.

60. See Oates (1976) 191 n. 4 for the difficulties here (also Browne on *P.Mich.* 577), though they do not affect our argument.

61. Cf. Oates (1976) 190–91.

62. Noted above. In the γραφὴ ὑπερετῶν καὶ ἀσθενῶν mentioned earlier, two 63-year-old men are noted as having been transferred to the list of those ὑπερετεῖς from the ἐλάσσωμα of the preceding year (*P.Lond.* 260.57–59), which might imply a lowering of the amount of tax due in the final year of liability. For "over-age" men still paying, at a reduced rate, see also below on *SB* 14710. In *P.Oslo* 124 (late first century A.D.), a weaver from Karanis applies for exemption from the weaver's tax; his grounds for exemption (lines 11–14) are his poor eyesight, his general state of health, and his old age (he says he is 80 years old). He also states that he is on the list of those classed as "over-age"; the phrase (lines 7–8) ὑπερετοῦς ἀρχαίου the editors here, probably correctly, take to mean "over-aged of old," i.e., for a long time on the list of those exempt.

63. *BGU* 1140 (*W.Chr.* 58), republished with discussion as *Corpus Papyrorum Judaicarum* 151 in Tcherikover and Fuks (1960) 29–33, and also in White (1986) 127–29; see too the comments of Tcherikover (1950) 201, and the important remarks of Kasher (1976) 148–51, refined in (1985) 200–207.

64. *BGU* vol. 4, p. 256. Tcherikover and Fuks (1960) 31 translate the phrase as "because of the age-limit of sixty."

65. Cf. Tcherikover and Fuks (1960) 30: the illogicality of Helenus's argument is obvious, "yet it is typical of Jews in this period, who went to all possible lengths in their struggle for emancipation."

66. Tcherikover (1950) 187, though he appears reluctant to accept this; his arguments are flawed, moreover, by only taking into account *P.Grenf.* 1.45 and overlooking 1.46. On these two papyri and the problems see also Grenfell and Hunt (1899) 209–10; Wilcken (1903) 395–96 (suggesting τελῶν); Wallace (1938a) 432 (questioning Wilcken's emendation; no mention in Wallace 1938b); Hombert and Préaux (1952) 51–52; Rathbone (1993) 90 n. 28; Bagnall and Frier (1994) 2–3.

67. *P.Princ.* 1.8, col. 7, line 1. The original editors dated this register of taxes to ca. A.D. 27-32, but Hanson (1974) 231 n. 9 has shown that it cannot be dated earlier than A.D. 40/1, and probably belongs to 46/7 (cf. Hanson 1984: 1108 n. 5). The same papyrus also records a man paying the tax at the age of 60 years (col. 1, line 24).

68. Wallace (1938b) 108. Alternatively, perhaps, there was some confusion as to whether exemption ended at the beginning or the end of one's 63rd year.

69. *P.Princ.* vol. 1 (1931) xx–xxii, and see again Tcherikover (1950) on *syntaxis, syntaximon,* and *laographia,* with Hobson (1984) 854–55.

70. *Stud. Pal.* 22 (1922) 93.12; see further Hobson (1984) for fuller publication (= *SB* 12816) and commentary. The list makes the age limit very clear (lines 12–16): the man has completed 62 years (i.e., turned 62) in the current year, and also died; for *both* reasons he has been "cut off" ([κεχωρ]ίσθαι).

71. Samuel et al. (1971) table 6.2, cols. 6, 9.
72. *P.Mich.* 223–25 (his age appears at 223.2416); see *Michigan Papyri* vol. 4.2 (1939) 85.
73. *P.Mich. inv.* 5806 = Sijpesteijn (1993a), with emendations by Bagnall (1995); cf. Bagnall and Frier (1994) 309–11; the quoted text is lines 28–29. Sijpesteijn comments (289) that Apronius is naturally exempt at age 61, quoting Hombert and Préaux (1952) as support—though, in fact, they assume (140) the age of exemption to be 62 years.
74. As Bagnall (1995) 253 notes, "the copyist was no perfectionist." Bagnall also comments (254) that "it would not be surprising if [Apronius] were really 62."
75. Van Minnen (1991) = *SB* 14710, a revised text of *Stud. Pal.* 20 (1921) 40 and 48.
76. Wessely, *Stud. Pal.* 20 (1921); Wallace (1938b) 108.
77. Thomas (1970) 176–77 argues on paleographical evidence, as well as the appearance of a certain name in the papyrus, that it dates from ca. A.D. 266; in this he is followed by van Minnen (1991) 122. Note that the poll tax is still being paid after the *Constitutio Antoniniana;* it is possible, however, that the regulations concerning who had to pay had changed. It is certainly true that evidence for the tax is sparser in the third century.
78. Doubts were raised by Thomas (1969) 349–50. Cf. van Minnen (1991) 122; at 125 he appears to conflate liturgies and the poll tax, as his assumption that the age of exemption rose from 60 to 65, then 70 years, shows. On the age limit for *laographia* increasing to 64 or 65 years, cf. Wallace (1938b) 108, 402; Neesen (1980) 122, 126, 128, 257.
79. Johnson (1936) 531–32 is guilty of overconfidence in this regard.
80. See Bagnall et al. (1997) 22–26 and 56 on provenance, 20 n. 3 and 92–93 on ὑπερετής, and 91–92 on age-guessing.
81. Hence, for example, on one notice of death (*P.Oxy.* 4480.15–16) the phrase "I present this notification so that you [the official] cannot allege ignorance (ἄγνοια) [of the death of my husband]."
82. Lewis (1997) 92.
83. See, e.g., *Dig.* 50.4.11.2 (Modestinus) and Chapter 4 note 122.
84. See references in my bibliography: Youtie (1966–75). Note now also Harris (1989), esp. 144–46, 276–81, and Hanson (1991).
85. Common, e.g., on census returns: Hombert and Préaux (1952) 40, 128–29.
86. Youtie (1971a, b; 1975a: 202–5).
87. Youtie (1971a) 169: "Sociologically speaking, scribes were indispensable, literacy was not"—but note also Harris (1989) 277 n. 502.
88. Youtie (1971a, 1975a).
89. Youtie (1975a) 221; Youtie even goes so far as to suggest (1975c: 108) that "for some the reputation of illiteracy in Greek, the language of the

alien and worldly bureaucracy, may have become a point of pride." Note also in this context Horsfall (1991) 71 on the fear engendered by writing.

90. Brunt (1975) 138.

91. Most frequently cited (recently by Drecoll 1997: 51) is the example of Aurelius Isidorus (from Boak and Youtie 1960) with his recorded ages in *P.Cair.Isid.* 81.5, 97.6, 125.14, 91.2, and 8.9, leading the editors to comment (394) that "the indifference of Egyptian villagers to precise statements of age is notorious." This may be true enough, but Egyptian administrators and officials, I would suggest, were rather more concerned with precision in these matters than were ordinary individuals. In any case, Isidorus's apparent indifference may be due not to innumeracy but to an inability to express his numeracy in Greek: cf. Hanson (1991) 184–87 and Scheidel (1996a) 88. It is also worth pointing out that other apparent examples of gross miscalculation of age in similar documents are in fact a result of errors in reading by the editors of the papyri: Youtie (1976a,b).

92. Schuman (1934–35). The suggestion I make here I first proposed in 1987. Farr (1993) 103 is clearly thinking along the same lines.

93. E.g., *P.Oxy.* 1469.24 (A.D. 298): ὑπὲρ αὐτῶν ἀξιωθεὶς ὑπ᾽ αὐτῶν φαμένων μὴ εἰδέναι γράμματα.

94. E.g., *P.Mich.* 166 II.12–13 and 168 II.7–8; cf. Schulz (1942) 87; Lanfranchi (1951) 105–7; Pescani (1961) 131–35; Lévy (1970) 447–48. The phrase is obviously a set one, of the form "professiones liberorum acceptae citra causarum cognitionem." For the phrase in the legal corpus, cf. *Dig.* 2.15.8.17 and 27.10.6 (Ulpian).

95. Duncan-Jones (1979); cf. also Duncan-Jones (1990) 79–81, 86–88, and see further Frier (1992) 287–88; Bagnall and Frier (1994) 44–47; Scheidel (1996a: ch. 2; 1996b). Scheidel's work, while justifiably challenging the notion that the accuracy of age statements must be directly correlated to levels of literacy (see Chapter 1), also serves to substantiate Duncan-Jones's most significant findings in regard to Roman Egypt as they relate to our analysis here.

96. With an apparent bias toward figures ending in 6, strangely enough. Spurious precision? More likely accidental.

97. Duncan-Jones (1979) 173–75; Scheidel (1996a) 71–72.

98. Samuel et al. (1971) 16; substantiated by Scheidel (1996a: ch. 2; 1996b), particularly in regard to declarants over the age of 40 years, interestingly enough.

99. Duncan-Jones (1979) 176.

100. Nothing could be further from the truth, then, than the statement by Carter (1967) 53 (see Chapter 1) that in Roman Egypt "age was not an important statistic in the eyes of the administrative bureaucracy." It

would also appear that the age-rounding noted in *P.Oxy.* 984A (see above) is an aberration.

101. Samuel et al. (1971) 5.

102. Parkin (1992) 22–27.

103. *Dig.* 50.6.6.pr. (discussed in the previous chapter).

104. Dio 51.17.4 (Αἴγυπτος μὲν οὕτως ἐδουλώθη); Tertullian *Apol.* 13.6, and similarly *ad Nat.* 1.10.23 (note also Lactantius *de Mort. Pers.* 23.5, 26.2, 36.1); Tcherikover (1950) 193. See also Brunt (1981) 170; McGinn (1989) 84; Rathbone (1993) 86–87.

105. See Parkin (1992) 31, where it is suggested, *pace* Frier (1982) 223 n. 25, that the age of 60 years as a limit in the customary and "Ulpianic" *formae* is derived from such a notion.

106. See still Poland (1909) 98–102, 577–87, for the background; Jones (1940) 225–26, arguing for the importance of birth and wealth rather than age as the criteria for membership; Oliver (1941), on the religious role, revised in 1958; Momigliano (1944) 114–15 on the *gerousia* of Alexandria, possibly a very special case; Magie (1950) 62–63, 855–60, an excellent overview, stressing the social function; el-Abbadi (1964), on Roman Egypt and the social function of the *gerousiai* there; van Berchem (1980), on the *gerousia* at Ephesus, one of the best documented, and hence, perhaps, the most controversial (note now also *SEG* 43.757–72); van Rossum (1988), the only full length study, in Dutch (he rightly stresses geographical differences but in the process, it seems to me, overlooks the paucity of evidence; he argues, chs. 3–4, that membership was based primarily on status, and that the *gerousia* was, in effect, an "old-boys' club," not a political institution); Roueché (1993) 162–65, astutely questioning the validity of a political-social distinction.

107. Rea (1975) 31–39, with Nelson (1979) viii–ix, 63–65. The papyri in question are *P.Oxy.* 3099–3102; the Greek phrase I quote appears at 3099.1.7–8, 3099.2.5–6, and 3101.10–11. Note still Turner (1937) on the evidence from *P.Ryl.* 599 (= *SB* 8032; A.D. 226) for the *gerousia* of Oxyrhynchus. Van Rossum (1988) 55–66 denies any old-age welfare aspect.

108. While I would in general emphasize, therefore, the difference between (i) the classical Spartan *gerousia* and its kind, and (ii) the type of *gerousia* we are describing here (cf. Chapter 4, esp. note 55), it must be noted that some *gerousiai* of the Roman era seem to have existed in towns that had no *boule,* and hence they may have had an explicit and legitimate, if not primary, *political* character. See, e.g., the cases of Casto[l]lus in Lydia (*OGI* 488, first or second century A.D.; Rhodes 1996: 400) and of Orcistus in Phrygia (A.D. 237; Rhodes 1996: 429–30). I intend to study the institution of the *gerousia* in much more depth at a later date.

Chapter 6. The Realities of Rules of Age

1. On *adrogatio* and marriage ages, see Chapter 7. On rules of age in relation to manumission (introduced by the *lex Aelia Sentia* of A.D. 4), see Buckland (1908) 537–44; note also the Flavian Municipal Law 28.
2. *Cod. Iust.* 4.19.9, A.D. 293; cf. *Dig.* 4.4.43 (Marcellus or Macer): "de aetate eius . . . probandum est."
3. Parkin (1992) 35–38; but see now also Virlouvet (1997).
4. See the collection of eighty-three Egyptian death notices (in Greek) in Casarico (1985), to which add *P.Sakaon* 50; *P.Tebt. frag.* 21016 (*ZPE* 77 [1989] 281–82); *P.Prag.* 1.19; three published in Duttenhöfer (1989); two in Hanson (1991) 194–98; and *P.Oxy.* 4478–80.
5. Montevecchi (1947); Mertens (1958) ch. 2. The most recent list appears in Cohen (1996); from that list, delete *P.Oxy.* 479 and add *P.Turner* 29 (Philadelphia?; after A.D. 195), *P.Turner* 30 (Philadelphia? A.D. 209), and *P.Oxy.* 3754 (Oxyrhynchus; A.D. 320). Cf. also Kruit (1998) 38 n. 3.
6. E.g., *P.Oxy.* 1030, *SB* 7359. Of the extant death notices, ten are of such over-age men.
7. E.g., *P.Oxy.* 2855, 3136; *P.Ups.Frid* 6 (see Llewelyn 1992: 137–40); *P.Corn.* 18.
8. Hombert and Préaux (1952) 135–36; Michael (1966) 85; Casarico (1985) 21: "Da conseguenza la presentazione della denuncia [sc. di morte] non poteva essere affidata alla buona volontà dei singoli abitanti."
9. Casarico (1985) 9, and cf. Youtie (1975b). There are some notices of birth for females: *BGU* 28, 2020; *P.Petaus* 1–2; *P.Berol.* inv. 25099; *P.Corn.* 18, *P.Oxy.* 3136; Montevecchi (1973) 179; Cohen (1996) 389.
10. Taubenschlag (1955) 625–26, 644.
11. Browne (1970) on *P.Mich.Mchl.* 10.18–19 (*SB* 11112), A.D. 48; see also Hanson (1991) 197. Casarico (1985) 18–19 adds the example of *P.Mert.* 9 (A.D. 12): "so that I may not be disturbed," and ("perhaps") *P.Oxy.* 3141 (A.D. 300) lines 14–16: "so that I may be free of molestation over matters pertaining to the trade of the wool sellers and over poll tax." Note similarly *PSI* 691 (A.D. 176). But in these examples the implication is not that the registration was required by law, but rather that the declaration was made in order to avoid further liability (expressed as "disturbance" or "molestation") to financial burdens.
12. Hopkins (1980) 313–14. By my calculations, there are extant today 94 Greek notices of death and 34 Greek notices of birth, a total of 128 documents.
13. Montevecchi (1947; 1973: 179–80).
14. Casarico (1985) 6 (my translation from the Italian); note too 18–19, 21; see now also Scheidel (1999) 63–65.
15. The best introduction remains Schulz (1942–43); note also Montevecchi

(1948), Lanfranchi (1951), Lévy (1952, 1970), Pescani (1961), and esp. Haensch (1992) 283–90, 306–13.

16. To the (still) standard list in Schulz (1942), add *Tabulae Heraculanenses* 1.5 (Herculaneum, A.D. 60), *P.Oxy.* 2565a–b (Oxyrhynchus, A.D. 224), and *P.Michael.* 61 (provenance unknown; second century A.D.?).

17. SHA *Marc. Aur.* 9.7–9. The evidence of Apuleius *Apol.* 89, as well as that of the Latin birth notices from Roman Egypt, is sufficient indication that in the Roman world the system long predates Marcus Aurelius.

18. Gardner (1986a: 2–3; 1986b: 144–46).

19. Schulz (1942) 80–81, while assuming that birth registration was obligatory, also remarks on "what an unreliable source the *Scriptores Historiae Augustae* are."

20. And, conversely, that fraudulent entries do not grant privileges to ineligible persons: *P.Tebt.* 285.

21. *Cod. Iust.* 4.21.6 (A.D. 286); cf. also 7.16.15 (293) and 4.21.11 (294), for the use of other evidence, written or oral, when a *professio* is not available. The term "natalis professio" in *Cod. Iust.* 4.21.6 leaves no doubt as to the type of document meant; generally, however, the word *professio* alone is used to indicate a birth notice, although *professio* can be used of any declaration before an official authority (e.g., *professio censualis/liberorum natorum/frumentaria*). For one very interesting case of *professiones* being mentioned as a means of checking someone's age—that of Lucius the ass at time of sale—see Apuleius *Met.* 8.24 (the plural probably reflects reference to both registration of birth and census returns; Apuleius's other uses of *professio* provide no further clue). Aging by teeth was a more common means, one imagines, of verifying the age of an animal: cf. *Met.* 8.23, with Columella 6.29.5, Pliny *NH* 11.64.168–69, and *Suda* A 59.

22. E.g., *Dig.* 1.5.8 (Papinian, recording a rescript of Antoninus Pius), *Cod. Iust.* 2.42.1 (A.D. 223). *Instrumentum* can broadly mean, inter alia, any type of evidence, but generally refers in this context to a written document rather than oral testimony (e.g., *Frag. Vat.* 168 [Ulpian, a rescript of Marcus Aurelius and Verus]: "si instrumentis probas habere te iustos tres liberos . . .").

23. E.g., *Cod. Iust.* 6.23.5 (A.D. 254), 2.42.2 (287), 4.19.14 (293): "ementita professione." Were the *tabulae* Apuleius presented in court in ca. A.D. 158 genuine?

24. *Cod. Iust.* 2.42.4 (A.D. 293).

25. E.g. *Dig.* 48.10 "de falsis." On the law of forgery in relation to written documents, see in particular 48.10.1.4 (Marcian), 48.10.13.pr. (Papinian), and 48.10.16 (Paul); note also Cicero *pro Arch.* 4.8, and cf. Champlin (1991) 72–73, 82–87.

26. Lévy (1952) 486. Of course, the announcement of a birth might be unofficial: from Pompeii, e.g., note *CIL* 4.294 and 4.8149, and cf. Cicero *ad Att.* 1.2.1.

27. *Dig.* 22.3.13 (Celsus); I presume that "Caesar noster" refers to Hadrian, though possibly Trajan is meant. It is stated here that "diversae professiones" have been put forward; this probably means "divergent official statements," rather than "divergent declarations of birth," unless the individual had had his birth registered more than once or confusion had arisen where persons of the same name had been registered.
28. *Dig.* 27.1.2.1 (for the context, see Chapter 4 note 150).
29. *Cod. Iust.* 2.44.2.pr.-1 (= *Cod. Theod.* 2.17.1.pr.-1, A.D. 321); cf. Chapter 4 note 5.
30. For Hadrian preferring the evidence of witnesses to *testimonia,* see Millar (1977) 236. For the late republic, note again Cicero *pro Arch.* 4.8.
31. *Dig.* 20.1.4 (Gaius) provides an interesting example of the relative value of written and oral evidence: in the case of mortgages (*hypothecae*), an agreement does not have to be in writing, so long as it can be proved (there is no need to suspect interpolation): "fiunt enim de his scripturae, ut quod actum est per eas facilius probari poterit: et sine his autem valet quod actum est, si habeat probationem: sicut et nuptiae sunt, licet testationes in scriptis habitae non sunt." This is precisely the point: written testimony may make proof an easier matter, but it is not essential. Note too *Dig.* 22.4.4, also Gaius.
32. Jolowicz and Nicholas (1972) 443, Bove (1985). The evolution of these principles is not always transparent and some rulings are contradictory. One plain case, however, involves the use of *epistulae uxoribus missae* as opposed to the evidence provided by witnesses or by *instrumenta* in general: cf. *Dig.* 22.3.29 (Scaevola, quoting a rescript of Marcus Aurelius and Verus) with *Cod. Iust.* 4.19.13 (A.D. 293); see also *Cod. Iust.* 4.1.6 (A.D. 291) on the use of oaths as evidence.
33. Written evidence preferable in third century: *Cod. Iust.* 4.20.1 (no date), 4.20.2 (A.D. 223), 2.42.3 (A.D. 293); for later rulings, see *Cod. Iust.* 4.21.15 (A.D. 317) and *Nov. Iust.* 73 (A.D. 538). Both types admissible: *Dig.* 22.4.5 (Callistratus, early third century), where it is noted that if a matter can be proved without recourse to writing (*litterae*), written documentation (*instrumentum*) is not essential. In the later third century Probus (*Cod. Iust.* 5.4.9) states that where a man has lived with a woman and had a daughter by her, both the marriage and the birth may stand as legitimate, even though "neque nuptiales tabulae neque ad natam filiam pertinentes factae sunt," so long as the man's neighbors or others can testify to the couple having cohabited.
34. *Dig.* 4.4.32 (Paul): a person under the age of 25 years convinced the *praeses* by his "aspectus corporis" that he was of "perfecta aetas." Note also Isidorus *Orig.* 9.3.36: *tirones* for military training are selected "non ex sola professione nativitatis, sed aspectu et valitudine corporis."
35. Hence, for example, in one *testatio* (*P.Diog.* 1, A.D. 127, Contrapollonospolis Magna) a soldier states that he has made the declaration "ut possit

post honestam missionem suam ad epicrisin suam adprobare filium suum naturalem esse."

36. It should be pointed out that the birth of children to prominent Roman citizens might be recorded in the "fasti actaque" (see, e.g., Suetonius *Tib.* 5, quoted in Chapter 1, for the use of such records to establish date of birth), but this would have been exceptional and does not constitute a register of births. It is also worth remarking in this context that anthropologists have shown that "even in societies where birth registration has become well-established, the social utility of chronometric age is still quite low" (Kaiser and Engel 1993: 835).

37. See Chapter 5 note 94.

38. Most scholarly attention has centered around the Roman census in republican times: e.g., Pieri (1968), Wiseman (1969a), Brunt (1971), Nicolet (1980). I know of no thorough, modern treatment of the Roman censuses of the imperial era, nor of the provincial censuses, apart from Unger (1887), which focuses on the epigraphical evidence for the mechanics of the census; Neesen (1980), which deals with taxation; and note also Aichinger (1992). See most recently on the general subject Nicolet (1988: 289–92; 1991: 123–47) and Lo Cascio (1999).

39. Note also the comments of Rathbone (1993), esp. 98.

40. The classic statements to this effect are Mommsen (1887–88) 2.416–17 and Schürer (1973) 399–427. A different viewpoint is adopted by Barnes (1982) 226–37, who also has a useful discussion of the census in the time of the late empire, though I disagree with his conclusion that the five-year cycle precedes Diocletian. On the provincial census, see also Jones (1974) 165; Brunt (1981); and Llewelyn (1992) 112–32.

41. For the early, traditional history of the Roman census, see Mommsen (1887–88) 2.334–39; Last (1945); Pieri (1968) part 2; Brunt (1971) 26–33 (and 13–14 for a list of census figures from 508 B.C. to A.D. 14).

42. The best and fullest discussion of the census figures is in Brunt (1971); note also Lo Cascio (1994, 1997, and his chapter in Scheidel 2001a), with Scheidel (1996a) 167–68. The other hotly contested question is exactly who was counted in the citizen census, which is of somewhat more relevance to this section of our study; for the problems, see Wiseman (1969a) with Brunt (1971), the latter heavily influenced, in this as in other areas, by Beloch (1886).

43. Cicero *de Leg.* 3.3.7; Dionysius of Halicarnassus *AR* 4.15.6. Ovid *Ars Amat.* 2.663–64 warns not to ask a woman how old she is—that is for the *rigidus censor* to work out (especially if she is past her girlish prime and already plucking those first white hairs).

44. As in Egypt; note also Ulpian, *Dig.* 50.15.3.pr. (*de censibus*): "aetatem in censendo significare necesse est, quia quibusdam aetas tribuit, ne tributo onerentur. . . . aetas autem spectatur censendi tempore"; *Tabula Heracleensis* (*lex Iulia Municipalis: FIRA*^{2} 1.13 = Crawford 1996: 355–91) lines

146–47, regarding local censuses in Italy in (presumably) late republican times: "quot annos quisque eorum habet." Age of slaves was also recorded: *Dig.* 50.15.4.5 (Ulpian). Lactantius *de Mort. Pers.* 23 provides an interesting reference to a later provincial census (of A.D. 306) where the officials are responsible, among other more serious misdemeanours, for the misrepresentation of age ("years were added to children and subtracted from the old") so as to ensure increased liability; "neither age nor infirmity granted exemption" (nulla aetatis, valitudinis excusatio) from the officials' harsh treatment (cf. Garnsey 1988: 246).

45. Cf. Chapter 4. On the division of citizens into tribes, classes, and centuries, according to wealth and age, see Pieri (1968) 58–75; Wiseman (1969a); Nicolet (1980) 51ff., 82ff.

46. For example, no *lustrum* (the religious ceremony held at the end of the census operation) was held between 70/69 and 28 B.C., although Brunt (1971) 104 is probably right to argue that registration must have continued in the interim (cf. Wiseman 1969a: 69–72). On phrases of the type "quinto quoque anno," see Chapter 1.

47. For the details, see Jones (1960) 21–26.

48. E.g., by Nicolet (1980) 65, quoted here; cf. Nicolet (1991) 132–33.

49. Sherwin-White (1963) 144–62; contrast the problems Petronia Iusta of Herculaneum had (e.g., Gardner 1986a: 1, and most recently Weaver in Rawson and Weaver 1997: 69–71).

50. Note Cicero *pro Arch.* 5.11 with Mommsen (1887–88) 2.374; Last (1945) 37–38; Nicolet (1980) 71; Gardner (1986a) 7.

51. Varro *de Ling. Lat.* 6.86, 88: "omnes Quirites"; Livy 1.44.1: "omnes cives Romani"; Mommsen (1887–88) 2.362; Brunt (1971) 15, 33.

52. Livy 3.3.9, *Per.* 59, 69.

53. *AR* 4.15.6 (adapted from E. Cary's trans.), and cf. 5.75.4; Livy 1.44.1 (who actually mentions the death penalty); Cicero *pro Caec.* 33.99; Gaius *Inst.* 1.160; Zonaras 7.19.

54. Wiseman (1969a) 60; Brunt (1971) 33–34; Nicolet (1980) 86.

55. Much has been made of the case of P. Annius Asellus who, it is claimed, was not registered on the census, and who therefore (according to Cicero) should not have been affected by the restrictions placed by the *lex Voconia* (on which see Crook 1986: 71) on his right to leave his estate to his daughter (Cicero *Verr.* 2.1.41.104: "P. Annius Asellus . . . cum haberet unicam filiam neque census esset, quod eum—natura hortabatur, lex nulla prohibebat—fecit ut filiam bonis suis heredem institueret"). But Nicolet (1980) 72 has shown that this cannot be so: "Sometimes a citizen . . . would conceal his wealth. Some time before 75—no doubt at the census of 86—the senator P. Annius Asellus did so because he wanted to appoint his daughter his heir, which the *lex Voconia* of 169 forbade in the case of inheritances of the first class. . . . But Annius could not possibly have made no declaration at all, if only because he was a senator

and had to figure on the Senate list drawn up by the censors. What the statement means is only that when he died in 75 there had been no census since 86 or perhaps 90–89, a lapse of 15 years, so that the property he wished to bequeath to his daughter escaped the provisions of the *lex Voconia.*"

56. Dio 59.22.3–4. Whether the reference is to the Roman or the provincial census is unclear, but one might presume the latter. That the story is probably apocryphal is of little consequence for our purposes. For the citizen census in this context, note *Cyrene Edicts* 1.4–5.

57. *Dig.* 22.3.10 (Marcellus, writing in the mid to later second century); Talbert (1984) 453, no. 166. *Monumenta* can refer to written records, not just buildings. For examples in the legal corpus, note, along with this passage, *Dig.* 22.5.3.2 (Callistratus, quoting a rescript of Hadrian: "publica monumenta," in the same sense of "public records"); *Frag. Vat.* 249.8 (Constantine and Licinius, A.D. 316: "monumenta iudiciorum ac populorum perscripta"); and cf. *VIR* 3.2 (1983) col. 1955. More generally, cf. Varro *de Ling. Lat.* 6.49: "ab eo cetera quae scripta ac facta memoriae causa monimenta dicta"; Paulus *ex* Festus 123L (emphasis added): "monimentum est, quod et mortui causa aedificatum est et quicquid ob memoriam alicuius factum est, ut fana, porticus, *scripta et carmina*"; Charisius *Ars Gramm.* 5 [434.6–7 Barwick]: "monimenta publica, annales, historiae, libri veteres, scrinia antiqua"; and see *TLL* 8.1464.28–1465.23. Note also Pliny *NH* 7.16.76: "invenimus in monumentis . . ."

58. See Chapter 2, in dealing with reported examples of longevity in the ancient world. Cf. also Parkin (1999).

59. Pliny *NH* 7.49.162–64; Phlegon *FGH* 257 F 37, translated with commentary in Hansen (1996).

60. As Gabriele Zerbi in his *Gerontocomia* of 1489 (see Chapter 9), ch. 15, assumes to be the case, a consequence of "the flowing air."

61. *NH* 7.48.159. Pliny adds the comment: "idque collatis censibus quos ante detulerat vitaeque argumentis—etenim curae principi id erat—verum apparuit." It is revealing that Pliny himself, apparently, did not check the figure: could he have done so had he wanted to? And perhaps the scholarly Claudius is Pliny's source here? Pliny does not list Claudius as one of his authorities for book 7 (though he is cited for several other books and his wife Agrippina is listed for book 7), but does cite him at 7.3.35 (cf. *HRR* 2.94).

62. *NH* 7.49.162. For the unusual (especially for this early period) term *vasaria* in the sense "public records" (rather than "record offices," as it is taken to mean in the *OLD*), cf. *Cod. Theod.* 13.11.13 (A.D. 412); Cassiodorus (sixth century) *Var. Lib.* 7.45. In listing (in book 1 of *NH*) his sources for book 7, Pliny mentions the *acta*.

63. Salomies (1987) 282–84 mentions Phlegon's list but makes no comment on the ordering of the names. Hansen (1996) 177 notes only that Phle-

gon "groups many persons together according to their first name." Cuntz (1888) 47 was more interested in the order of the names of the towns.

64. *Tabula Heracleensis* line 146; *CIL* 6.200 (= *ILS* 6049, *sine nominibus*). Cf. *CIL* 6.30983 (*ILS* 3840), and Daly (1967) 60–62.

65. For the limited use of archival material from the *aerarium* at Rome in the late republic, see Culham (1989), though this may be too pessimistic; note also Coudry (1994) and Moreau (1994). In any event the situation may have improved under the emperors, though more in the area of fiscal than archival developments: Millar (1964), Haensch (1992). That notices of birth were stored in the main archive in the temple of Saturn at Rome is stated by Servius *ad Georg.* 2.502, as well as by SHA *Marc. Aur.* 9.7 and *Gord.* 4.8; cf. Corbier (1974) 680–81.

66. For such grants, particularly the granting of citizenship on the petition of individuals, see Millar (1977) 477–90; on *commentarii* and the use made of them, cf. Millar (1977) 259–66, which includes a discussion of the *Tabula Banasitana*. Note also Sherwin-White (1973a) 314–16.

67. *Ep.* 10.95, 10.104–5; in neither case are the ages of the individuals given.

68. Sherwin-White (1973b) 87, with text. The quotation given here follows the emendation of Oliver (1972), reading *ann<o>s* and not the original editors' *ann<orum>*; but cf. Euzennat and Marion (1982) 78–81.

69. That such a register had actually existed under Julius Caesar is suggested by Cicero *ad Fam.* 13.36.1 (46/5 B.C.): "tabulam in qua nomina civitate donatorum incisa essent"; Caesar ordered it torn down.

70. The only other definite case we know of where civilians were given documentation to prove their citizenship is a troop of Greek ephebic dancers to whom Nero gave such documents (Suetonius *Nero* 12.1), clearly an unusual and remarkable instance. Note also Suetonius *Gaius* 38.1 (cf. H. Lindsay in his 1993 commentary *ad loc.*: "Although the evidence is sparse we must assume that civilians did have documentation to prove their citizenship." This is unnecessary.). See also Millar (1977) 480–81.

71. On the *diplomata militaria*, on the other hand, bronze plates recording grants of citizenship and of *conubium* to soldiers of the auxiliary forces on their discharge, age does not routinely appear (nor need it), only length of service.

Chapter 7. Old Age, Marriage, and Sexuality

1. Primary sources, principally legal, are usefully collected in Riccobono et al. (1945) 166–98. Raditsa (1980) provides a somewhat idiosyncratic survey of scholarship up to 1977. The most significant and innovative work to appear since then is that by Wallace-Hadrill (1981); note also Treggiari (1991) 60–80; Mette-Dittman (1991); Evans Grubbs (1995); and McGinn (1998) chs. 3–4.

2. Gaius *Inst.* 2.111, 144, 206–8, 286.

3. Riccobono et al. (1945) 186–87; Wallace-Hadrill (1981) 73–76.
4. The precise figures need not concern us here: [Ulpian] *Epit.* 16.1a; Parkin (1992) 117.
5. [Ulpian] *Epit.* 16.1, 3–4. See Parkin (2001).
6. Cf. Amundsen and Diers (1970), an incomplete collection; Diers (1974) 935 adopts a rather more critical approach. See also Parkin (1992) 123; Gourevitch (1996) 2097–98. Dean-Jones (1994) 105–8 discusses menopause but cites only Aristotle regarding age.
7. Pressat and Wilson (1985) 143.
8. Aristotle *Hist. An.* 7.5.585b. Scholars are divided as to whether book 7 is spurious; at any rate, it is no later than the third century B.C. Cf. *Pol.* 7.1335a9–10 for 50 years as the upper limit, and 7.1335a28–32 for a recommended age gap of some 20 years between husband and wife, so that the cessation of fertility in both partners coincides (on age gaps between spouses, see also Chapter 8). Aristotle also remarks that the children of older parents tend to be physically and mentally unsound (*Pol.* 7.1335b30–32) or female (*de Gen. An.* 4.3.766b29–31). See also Galen *de San. Tuenda* 2.2 (6.84K = *CMG* 5.4.2.39) and Columella 7.3.15.
9. *Coac. Praenot.* 5.30.502 (5.700L).
10. See again the summary in Censorinus *de Die Nat.* 14, where the age of 42 in particular is described as an *annus climactericus.* Our Hippocratic passage here has puberty at age 14, and old age commencing from age 63: seven's influence is omnipresent.
11. *Gynaec.* 1.4.20; cf. also 1.9.34.
12. Pliny *NH* 7.14.61; Solinus *Coll. Rerum Mem.* 1.59; cf. also Dionysius of Halicarnassus *AR* 4.6.5 for the 50th year being regarded as the upper limit of female fertility.
13. Oribasius (fourth century) *Ecl. Med.* 142.4 (*CMG* 6.2.2.301); Aetius (sixth century) *Lib. Med.* 16.4; Paul of Aegina (seventh century) 3.60 (*CMG* 9.1.274). Cf. Aristotle *de Gen. An.* 2.7.746b25–29, and Amundsen and Diers (1970) 82–83. For the inconvenience and undesirability of obesity in old age, not least because it speeds up the aging process, note Hippocrates *Aph.* 2.54 (4.486L), Celsus *de Med.* 2.1.23, Pliny *NH* 11.85.212, Galen *in Hipp. Aph.* 2.44, 2.54 (17B.547–48, 559–60K).
14. *Cod. Iust.* 6.58.12.pr.-1.
15. *Dig.* 19.1.21.pr. (Paul). On sterility in this context, cf. Parkin (1992) 114–15; for a definition of *sterilis,* see Columella 2.1.2–3, and cf. Pliny *NH* 17.3.35.
16. *Dig.* 38.1.35 (Paul *ad legem Iuliam et Papiam*). *Pace* Riccobono et al. (1945) 177 n. 6, Csillag (1976) 169, and Treggiari (1991) 69, there is no evidence that a similar rule existed for *liberti* from the age of 60 years; cf. Waldstein (1986) 174.
17. Polybius 36.16.1–5 (= *Suda* **M** 245, Plutarch *Mor.* 791f); Diodorus Siculus 32.16; Cicero *de Sen.* 10.34; Livy *Per.* 50; Valerius Maximus 5.2.ext.4,

8.13.ext.1; Pliny *NH* 7.14.61; Frontinus *Strat.* 4.3.11; Appian *Pun.* 106
(= *Suda* **M** 244); [Lucian] *Macr.* 17; Solinus *Coll. Rerum Mem.* 1.59 (gives
his age of fatherhood as the 76th year; this must be a simple copying mistake, unless another source—not Pomponius Mela—provided alternative evidence); Eutropius 4.11. On Masinissa's delight in his grandchildren, whom he himself reared until they were 3 years old, see Ptolemy
VIII Euergetes II *ap.* Athenaeus *Deipn.* 12.518f–19a (= *FGH* 234 F 8).
Such were the details that fascinated our ancient authors; for more historical considerations in regard to Masinissa, see *RE* 14.2154–65 (Schur),
Camps (1960), and Walsh (1965).

18. Pliny *NH* 7.14.61–62; Aulus Gellius 13.20.8, 13.20.15; Plutarch *Cato
Maior* 24; Valerius Maximus 8.7.1; Solinus *Coll. Rerum Mem.* 1.59; [Au-
relius Victor] *de Vir. Ill.* 47.9; Astin (1978) 105. Cf. also *Anthologia Palatina*
13.23 (Asclepiades) for a man of 80 losing a son of 9 years.

19. Aristotle *Hist. An.* 7.6.585b. Cf. *Pol.* 7.1335a8–9 for 70 years as the upper limit. As Falkner (1995) 310 remarks, Athenaeus *Deipn.* 2.69b implies (but note the comic context) sexual impotence for males from the
age of 60 years.

20. *NH* 7.14.62.

21. *Coll. Rerum Mem.* 1.59.

22. *Dig.* 1.7.15.2. Cf. *Dig.* 1.7.17.2 (Ulpian); Cicero *de Domo Sua* 13.34–
14.38; Aulus Gellius 5.19.4–6; Fayer (1994) 297–98; Gardner (1998)
128.

23. Nepos *Att.* 7.1. For details, see Chapter 4, esp. note 147.

24. Ovid *Amores* 1.9.4; Publilius Syrus *Sent.* 29W; Menander *Monost.* 146
Jaekel; Plautus *Merc.* 1015–26; Mimnermus frag. 1; Anacreon 13 (though
there is some scholarly debate about the meaning of this poem), 33–34
PMG; Propertius 3.5; Martial, e.g., 4.50, 11.71, 11.81; Sextus Empiricus
adv. Math. 7.239; Timon of Phlius *Silloi* frag. 17 Diels = *Suppl. Hell.* 791
(spoken by Dionysius of Heraclea and thus attributed to him at *Anth. Pal.*
10.38); [Lucian] *Amores* 10. See also, e.g., *Anthologia Palatina* 12.240
(Strato), Maximianus *Eleg.* 5, Arnobius *adv. Nat.* 3.37, and Chapter 3; on
young wives being considered unsuitable for elderly men, see Chapter 3
note 75 and Chapter 8 note 84. Stroh (1991) usefully collects material
from the poets *de amore senili* but his study is flawed through his determination to reach positive conclusions. Note also the chapter by Bertman
in Falkner and de Luce (1989), and for an excellent discussion of related
themes in early Greek poetry, see Falkner (1995) chs. 3–4.

25. *De Sen.* 9.27–14.49; see further Chapter 3 and cf. Pliny *Ep.* 2.3.6.

26. For the long tradition, see, e.g., Plato *Rep.* 1.328d, 329c–d; Seneca *de Brev.
Vit.* 1.3–4, 7.1–2, *Ep.* 26, 58.29–36, 68.13; Plutarch *Mor.* 788e–f; Juncus *ap.* Stobaeus *Flor.* 50.1.27 W-H.

27. Chapter 9 note 76. Hypereides *Pro Lyciphr.* 1.15 has the defense that af-

ter the age of 50 no man can begin to be a *moichos*. For modern scholarship, such as it is, on ancient "gerontosexuology" (as Suder dubs it), see Houdijk and Vanderbroeck (1987) on Greece, and Suder (1992) on Roman times.

28. Andreas Capellanus *de Amore* 1.5.2; Burrow (1986) 161; Shahar (1997) 16. Note the age limits, and for the medical tradition, see further Chapter 9.

29. See Parkin (2001) 228–32 for some evidence of a change in attitude in Christian times.

30. Pliny *Ep.* 4.19.5; Martial 4.13.9–10; see further Parkin (1997) 136–37, particularly for inscriptional evidence, and for elderly couples, note esp. *CIL* 8.12613 (= *ILS* 1680, Carthage; probably late first or early second century A.D.), a man who died at age 102, his wife at age 80; see also *CIL* 2.5464 (Baetica: 100 and 99 years), 6.8684 (= *ILS* 7375), 18758, 21303a, 21319, and 8.17084 (180 and 160 years, apparently). For long companionship without legal marriage, note *CIL* 6.26111: "A. Seio Fusco | Seia Thais fecit | patrono bene merenti cum | quo vixit annis L."

Chapter 8. Aging and the Roman Family

1. An earlier version of parts of this chapter appeared as Parkin (1997); for the sake of brevity, much supporting evidence cited there will not be repeated in notes here. For the importance of considering the life course in analyzing household structure and functions, see Kertzer (1986), Kertzer and Schiaffino (1986), Hareven (1996).

2. Cf. Homer (e.g., *Odyss.* 2.130–34); Pindar *Pyth.* 6; Theognis 821–22; the sayings of the Seven Sages (see Stobaeus *Ecl.* 3.1.172–173 [W-H vol. 3, pp. 111–28]; Tziatzi-Papagianni 1994: 134, 395, and re older people: 173, 311, 375, 386); Stobaeus *Flor.* 24–25 W-H; Polybius 6.4.5; Plutarch *Mor.* 479f–80b. One finds the same precept expressed, for example, in the traditions of the Jews (note the fifth commandment, *Exodus* 20.12, *Deut.* 5.16; and *Proverbs* 23.22: "Hearken to your father who begot you, and do not despise your mother when she is old"; Reinhold 1970: 351; Daube 1972: 41–52; Lambert 1982: 23–24); in the Koran (ch. 17); and traditionally among the Chinese (*ERE* 5 [1912] 731, 742; 9 [1917] 466–69; for the threat to the Chinese tradition as a result of [inter alia] modern demographic trends, see Jiang 1995, and, more generally, the excellent collection of essays in Formanek and Linhart 1997). On the general theme of honoring one's parents, see Lumpe and Karpp (1959); note also the chapters in Stol and Vleeming (1998). For more recent history, see esp. Thomson (1991) and, in a wider context, Horden and Smith (1998).

3. A story no doubt well known to the young of ancient Rome; cf. Naevius *Bell. Pun.* frag. 9 Buechner: "senex fretus pietatei"; Vergil *Aen.* 2.707–48,

3.480 ("o felix nati pietate"), 6.110–14 (the last line stressing Anchises' old age); Seneca *de Ben.* 3.37.1.

4. Pausanias 10.28.4; cf. Seneca *de Ben.* 3.37.2.
5. Xenophon *Mem.* 2.2.3; Seneca *de Ben. passim,* esp. 3.31–32. On the reciprocal nature of *patria potestas,* see esp. Saller (1988; 1994: 105–14).
6. See, e.g., Nugent (1985), Kendig et al. (1992), Clay and Vander Haar (1993), and Rendall and Bahchieva (1998).
7. In regard to care in old age in particular, cf. Homer *Iliad* 4.477–78, 17.301–2, *Odyss.* 2.130–31; Aeschylus *Choeph.* 750, 896–928; Sophocles *Ajax* 506–9, *Oed. Col.* 340–52 (see Daly 1986 on θρεπτήρια); Euripides *Iph. Aul.* 1230; Plato *Laws* 4.717b–718a, 11.927b–c (and note also 11.931a–e: aged and bedridden parents and grandparents as treasures or shrines in one's home; reproduced by, among others, the Pythagorean Pempelos [a curious name!—see Appendix C] of Thurii in his Περὶ γονέων [third or second century B.C.?] *ap.* Stobaeus *Flor.* 25.52 = Thesleff pp. 141–42); Aristotle *NE* 9.2.1165a; [Aristotle] *Oecon.* 1.1343b, 3.2 (frag. 184, Rose p. 143), 3.4 (p. 147); Xenophon *Oecon.* 7.12, 19; Menander *Monost.* 365 Jaekel: ἱκανῶς βιώσεις γηροβοσκῶν τοὺς γονεῖς; Longus *Daph. & Chl.* 3.9; Alciphron *Ep. Rust.* 13; *Anthologia Palatina* 7.647 (Simonides or Simias).
8. Pollux *Onom.* 3.12.
9. Parkin (1997) 124.
10. Lucretius *de Rer. Nat.* 4.1256; Cornelius Nepos frag. 59 (*HRR* 2.39). See further Columella 12.pr.1 and Parkin (1997) 124–25.
11. Parkin (1997) 125 n. 6. See also *GVI* 1823 (Naucratis, second century A.D., a father mourning his son, who would have nursed him in old age [γηρόκομος]); *CIL* 6.18086, a grandmother losing the support of her grandson, dead at the age of 2 years, "bacchillum [*sic*] summae senectae"); and see Sigismund Nielsen (1997) 193–98 on the use of *pientissimus* and *piissimus* in Roman epitaphs (of interest also is her observation, 202–3, that these epithets are rarely used of foster children). Note too the bizarre case (*BGU* 1024, Hermopolis, later fourth century A.D.) of an impoverished and elderly (τις γραῦς καὶ πένης, 7.9; cf. 8.12) mother of a murdered prostitute who successfully sues the alleged murderer for loss of support and solace in her old age. For childlessness in Roman society as an alleged source of power and influence, on the other hand, see below on *captatio.* That offspring should be there to provide support for an aged parent might also be used as a defense or mitigating circumstance when a son was being prosecuted in a court of law: see Chapter 9 note 10.
12. [Plutarch] *Mor.* 111e; Seneca *de Matr.* frag. 13.58, *ap.* Jerome *adv. Iovin.* 1.47 = Bickel (1915) 390.
13. Parkin (1997) 125 n. 8. Cf. Pliny *Pan.* 38.7: children's obedience to par-

ents is not due solely to *potestas,* but also to nature (*lex naturae*). See also Golden (1990) 92–94. As the wise Thales is said to have remarked, treat your parents as you would expect your children to treat you (Stobaeus *Ecl.* 3.1.172; Diogenes Laertius 1.37; Tziatzi-Papagianni 1994: 196).

14. *CIL* 10.1688 = *ILS* 1184, Puteoli; cf. *PIR²* C 762, 901.

15. Pliny *NH* 7.13.58–60. Augustus: contrast Plutarch *Mor.* 508a. Silanus: *PIR²* I 833. Metellus and his *felicitas:* cf. Cicero *de Fin.* 5.27.82, *Tusc. Disp.* 1.35.85; Valerius Maximus 7.1.1; Velleius Paterculus 1.11.5–7; Pliny *NH* 7.44.142; and note too his speech *de prole augenda* (Suetonius *Div. Aug.* 89.2; Livy *Per.* 59), on which see most recently Badian (1988 [1997]). On the joys of grandparenthood in this context, note also *Anthologia Palatina* 7.260 (Carphyllides); Herodotus 1.30 (Solon on Tellus the Athenian); *GVI* 545–46 (fourth century B.C.); *SEG* 8.497 = *SB* 5829 (Kom Abou Billou, second or first century B.C.); Pliny *NH* 7.43.139–41 (L. Caecilius Metellus, *cos.* 251, 247); Pliny the Younger *Ep.* 8.10, to his wife's grandfather on Calpurnia's miscarriage; and the case of Opramoas, the wealthy benefactor of Lycia in the second century A.D., who lived to see his descendants over several generations become Roman senators (*IGRom.* 3.735–36 = *Tituli Asiae Minoris* 2.3.915–16).

16. *Anthologia Palatina* 7.224; cf. 7.743 (Antipater of Sidon).

17. Parkin (1997) 125–26. Pietas, in human form, was depicted on some Roman coins attended by a stork: e.g., *RRC* 374/1 (81 B.C.), with Fears (1981) 881, and see also *LIMC* 8.1 (1997) 998–1003.

18. Parkin (1997) 126–27, to which add Sextus Empiricus *Pyrr. Hyp.* 3.210.

19. Namely those who had not been properly reared by their parents (the reciprocal nature of the arrangement is what matters); hence those who had not been taught a trade by their fathers, those born as bastards, and those hired out by their fathers as prostitutes were not regarded as legally bound to support their parents: Plutarch *Solon* 22.1–4; Vitruvius *de Arch.* 6.pr.3 (on which see below); Aeschines 1.13; Aelian *Var. Hist.* frag. 4 Hercher. Of related interest in a Roman context: Stoop (1995) argues that *XII Tables* 4.2, the oft-discussed mention of fathers selling their sons three times, refers to fathers prostituting their sons; for an Egyptian mother prostituting her daughter for financial support in old age, cf. *BGU* 1024 (cited above).

20. In Isaeus 2.10 it is stated that Menecles adopted a son in order to have someone to tend his old age (γηροτροφεῖν); see further Rubinstein (1993), esp. 66–68, and Pomeroy (1997) 122–23. For the Romans also adoption might be an effective means to ensure that there was someone there to tend one's old age; on *adrogatio* only being possible for those *in senectute,* see Chapter 7. For adoption as an inheritance strategy, cf., e.g., M. Corbier in Kertzer and Saller (1991) 127–44 and in Rawson (1991) 63–76, and note too Brettell (1991) 346 n. 6: "[A]dopted children show

greater humanity than legitimate ones toward the old in expression of gratitude for having been taken in." But note also Sigismund Nielsen (1997) 202–3 (mentioned above).

21. Hierocles *ap.* Stobaeus *Flor.* 25.53 (πῶς χρηστέον τοῖς γονεῦσιν: W-H p. 642 = von Arnim p. 58) and *Flor.* 22.1.24 (περὶ γάμου: W-H p. 503 = von Arnim p. 53).

22. *Wasps* 736–40 (with Parkin 1997: 127 n. 19), 1354–57. Amid much useful scholarly discussion, note most recently Menu (1992) and Slater (1996), the latter particularly stimulating on the theme of the young educating the old.

23. Otto (1890) no. 1625; Norden (1892) 268 n. 1 (= 1966: 2 n. 6); Cantarella (1971); Alfonsi (1970, 1976); Parkin (1997) 128. For an overview of its occurrence in Western culture, see also Covey (1992–93), who regards it as a sign of the devaluation of older people in certain periods. In a paper (as far as I am aware unpublished, although related themes are developed in Hockey and James 1993), delivered at the Association of Social Anthropologists conference in London in April 1988, entitled "Growing up and growing old: Metaphors of aging in contemporary Britain," Jennifer Hockey and Allison James discussed the infantilization of old people in modern British society and concluded that it is "a cultural strategy which gives a cyclical, rather than linear, quality to the passage from womb to tomb, in that the endpoint of human life, death, is distanced and transformed." By labeling old age as a second childhood, it is said, people attempt to disguise the fact that old age is the inevitable prelude to death by seeing life as being cyclical and therefore, by implication, continuous, since infancy and childhood are regarded as periods of safety. This may be true for modern Britain but it overlooks the history of the metaphor. In antiquity a different rationale must have operated, because infant mortality was particularly high. This is not, of course, to deny that old age, then and now, may in this context have a positive side, a reliving of "the pleasant days of my childhood" (Wagner 1995). The cyclical nature of this model may also be relevant to the idea of the ages of cities or of the world (see Chapter 1). Note too the proverb, linked to the *Ludi Capitolini,* "Sardi venales" ("Sardinians for sale"), and the appearance at those games of the mocked figure of a "senex cum toga praetexta bullaque aurea" (Festus 430L; cf. Plutarch *Rom.* 25.6, *Mor.* 277c), very evocative of a second childhood.

24. Alexis frag. 305 (Kassel and Austin; cf. frag. 282) *ap.* Vitruvius *de Arch.* 6.pr.3. It appears, from Plutarch *Mor.* 420d, that Alexis lived to be 104 or so years old (probably born 370s, died 270s B.C.), so perhaps he had a vested interest in the treatment of older people! Cf. Capps (1900) 59–60; Arnott (1996) 15–17.

25. Lerat (1943).

26. Cf. Taubenschlag (1932, 1956); Rupprecht (1998). Note also Chapter 2

on evidence from the Egyptian census returns for three- and four-generational households.

27. For a list of the relevant papyri, see Montevecchi (1935) 73; most recent updates in Sijpesteijn (1993b: 294–95; 1996: 163 n. 5), with *P.Mich.* 785. On the Roman law in this regard in relation to Egypt, see Husselmann (1957), citing earlier literature.

28. *P.Mich.* 321, 322a (A.D. 46); *P.Diog.* 11–12 (11.8: πρὸ μιᾶς ἡμέρας μου τοῦ θανάτου).

29. In general, see *Dig.* 39.6, *Cod. Iust.* 8.56, and, especially relevant to my arguments here, *Frag. Vat.* 294–96 (Papinian; A.D. 210; Papinian), with Voci (1980) 90, citing further relevant material. Note also Paola (1950, 1969); Amelotti (1953); Simonius (1958); Kaser (1971–75) 1.763–65, 2.564–67; Ankum (1994); Dropsie (1996). For the institution under Jewish law in relation to Roman law, see Yaron (1956, 1960, 1966); Cotton (1995) 183. For the difference between the *donatio mortis causa* and that *inter vivos,* note Paul *Dig.* 39.6.35.2.

30. *Dig.* 39.6.5 (Ulpian); Parkin (1997) 130.

31. It is stated in a rescript of Diocletian and Maximian that "senium quidem aetatis vel aegritudinem corporis sinceritatem mentis tenentibus testamenti factionem certum est non auferre" (*Cod. Iust.* 6.22.3.pr., A.D. 294); on *senium,* see below. On the *querela inofficiosi testamenti* and the (probably late) legal fiction that the testator is insane, when in reality he is just not acting according to *pietas,* see *Dig.* 5.2.1–2 (Ulpian, noting its frequency, and Marcian); Renier (1942); Watson (1971) 62–70; Champlin (1991) 15; and Gardner (1993: 64, 172; 1998: 37–39). For the limiting of testamentary power through old age in Athenian law, see [Aristotle] *Ath. Pol.* 35.2; Isaeus 2.13 (with Wyse *ad loc.*), 15, 18, 36; 4.16; 6.9, 21, 29, 35; [Demosthenes] 46.14; Harrison (1968) 152 n. 5.

32. Watson (1968) 51–53, 232; Kaser (1971–75) 2.395–97.

33. *P.Mil.Vogl.* 84 (= *P.Kron.* 50; cf. Hopkins 1980: 323, and note a not dissimilar—and passionately argued—case in *P.Cair.Masp.* 67353, village of Aphrodite, sixth century A.D.); *BGU* 1578 (on the date cf. Lewis 1970: 253 n. 9); *P.Enteux.* 26 (220 B.C.); *P.Lond.* 1708. Cf. also *P.Lond.* 1976 (Philadelphia, 253 B.C.): an elderly mother complaining to the estate manager Zenon that a married man has apparently eloped with her daughter and thus deprived her, the mother, of support in old age.

34. *P.Oxy.* 275, A.D. 66; note esp. lines 17–21.

35. *P.Oxy.* 1210, lines 4–5.

36. Wallace (1938b) 120 (but cf. Chapter 5 note 50). In *P.Flor.* 382 (discussed in Chapter 5), lines 38–40, an old man seems to be saying that his son should be exempt from a liturgy because he has to take care of his father (γηροτροφίαν). This is the father's wish; whether it was complied with is quite another matter.

37. *Pace* Taubenschlag (1932: 509–10; 1956: 175, 177).

38. But in this context note Saller (1994) 190, who convincingly argues, in the light of the relatively young age at which males on average became *sui iuris,* that "it would be wrong to imagine that old men in Rome owned the empire's wealth with the consequent political leverage." We must not assume that *patria potestas* automatically meant the older generation always controlled property. When a son, for example, was effectively the breadwinner in a family, an aged father without significant or tangible assets may have found his position as *paterfamilias* of little help or comfort.

39. Dixon (1988) 31, 47–51, 188–94; for comparative purposes, note esp. Kertzer and Karweit (1995). Regarding the widow in Greece, Schaps (1979) 84 observed: "Much can be surmised about the life of such women, but nothing is known." There has been some progress, however: Günther (1993); Pomeroy (1997), esp. 204–6. For Roman times, note Seneca *Cons. ad Marc.* 19.2 (even with wealth old-age security is a concern), and Pliny *Ep.* 8.23.7 (the elderly and now childless mother of Iunius Avitus). Modern sociohistorical scholarship on the subject of Roman widows is blossoming: see esp. Beaucamp (1990–92) and Krause (1994–95); the latter has provocative discussion, inter alia, on the age-spread of Roman widows, 1.67–73, as well as compelling arguments to show how numerous widows must have been, at least among the lower classes, and interesting material in vol. 2 re poverty. Apuleius provides some fascinating tales about solitary old women (cf. Callimachus's Hecale), such as the one (*Met.* 4.7) who looks after the robbers (who themselves spend their time raiding *aniles cellulas*; at least one old woman, *senile illud facinus,* gets the better of them, 4.12) in their cave: "anus quaedam curvata gravi senio," roundly abused by the young men ("busti cadaver extremum et vitae dedecus primum et Orci fastidium solum . . . quae diebus ac noctibus nil quicquam rei quam merum saevienti ventri tuo soles aviditer ingurgitare"—all images we have already seen associated with older people, particularly women). Note too *Met.* 9.15 for the aged *internuntia* who spends all her day drinking *vinum merum.*

40. Seneca *Controv.* 1.1, 1.7, 7.4 (the mother to be maintained, not just the father: 7.4.3-4; cf. 7.4.1 and 10: "If you won't feed your mother, at least bury her"); Quintilian *Inst. Or.* 5.10.97, 7.6.5; Quintilian *Inst. Or.* 7.1.55 (some parents may not deserve to be maintained at their children's expense if they have not treated them well in their turn); [Quintilian] *Decl. Min.* 368 ("patrem ali non solum oportet, verum etiam necesse est," 368.5); Ennodius (A.D. 473/4–521) *Dictio* 21 (*CSEL* 6.483–92 = *MGHAA* 7.260–65). In one case the "law" states that only "needy" parents must be maintained: [Quintilian] *Decl. Maior.* 5.pr.: "liberi parentes in egestate aut alant aut vinciantur." Cf. Lanfranchi (1938) 274–82; Bonner (1969) 95–96.

41. Seneca *Controv.* 1.7.10.
42. It may be noted that the declamatory "law" specifies imprisonment as the penalty for conviction, not loss of citizen rights (in Roman terms *capitis deminutio*). Cf. Plato *Laws* 11.932b (whipping and imprisonment for males under 30 and females under 40 who neglect their parents).
43. Albertario (1933) 251–79; Sachers (1951) 347–56; Zoz (1970); Gnilka (1985).
44. *Cod. Iust.* 5.25.1. The heading in the *Codex* is "de alendis liberis ac parentibus" (four brief extracts, all second century A.D.); thus, for example, *Cod. Iust.* 5.25.4 (A.D. 197) states that "si patrem tuum officio debito promerueris, paternam pietatem tibi non denegabit. quod si sponte non fecerit, aditus competens iudex alimenta pro modo facultatium praestari tibi iubebit. quod si patrem se negabit, quaestionem istam in primis idem iudex examinabit." Cf. *Dig.* 3.5.33(34) (Paul), where a grandmother is said to maintain her grandson "iure pietatis."
45. *Cod. Iust.* 5.25.2 (A.D. 161); cf. similarly 5.25.3 (A.D. 162).
46. *Iudex* seems to mean, and perhaps originally the text read, *consul*—the passage from Ulpian in the *Digest* cited below (25.3.5) comes from his *Libri tres de officio consulis*; on the other hand, *iudex* might be used to mean any officeholder giving judgment. Cf. *Index Interpolationum* 2.111–12; *Palingenesia* 2.953; W. Heumann and E. Seckel, *Handlexikon zu den Quellen des römischen Rechts*[10] (Graz, 1958) 293, s.v. *iudex* 3.a.‡; *VIR* 3.5.1349.35–43; Sachers (1951) 347 n. 4; Zoz (1970) 326 n. 19 (and note also the comments of Yaron 1974: 352).
47. *Dig.* 42.1.15; *Palingenesia,* 2.951–58 Honoré (1982) 175–90 argues for A.D. 215 as the date of composition.
48. *Dig.* 25.3.5.pr. For *exhibere* in the sense of providing support or maintenance, see *TLL* 5.2.1432–33; *VIR* 2.689–90.
49. *Dig.* 25.3.5.13: "iniquissimum enim quis merito dixerit patrem egere, cum filius sit in facultatibus." See further Gardner (1998) 74–85. At *Dig.* 25.3.5.16 Ulpian notes that it is stated in a rescript that the duty of a *filius* to support his parents is "ratione naturali" (on this phrase see Stein 1974: esp. 312, and note again Pliny *Pan.* 38.7, cited note 13), and does not extend as far as the payment of a father's debts. For the poverty of parents being a factor in this context, see *Dig.* 25.3.5.17 (cited immediately below), and [Quintilian] *Decl. Maior.* 5.pr. (cited note 40). Constantine introduced laws governing, in terms of *pietas,* the rights of a father over *bona materna* even when a child has been emancipated: *Cod. Theod.* 8.18.1–3; Evans Grubbs (1995) 115–16; Arjava (1996: 100–103; 1998: 151–53). It would appear that Constantine was confirming normal practice.
50. *Dig.* 25.3.5.15: "ratio pietatis" (cf. 37.15.1.pr. [Ulpian]).
51. *Dig.* 25.3.5.17, 25.3.5.2, 25.3.5.5. Cf. also 26.7.13.2 (Gaius), 27.3.1.4

(Labeo *ap.* Ulpian), 27.3.1.2 (Julian *ap.* Ulpian), and 27.2.4 (Julian): a needy mother or sister supported from the funds of a son; note also 25.3.8 (Marcellus): a daughter's child is not the liability of a maternal *avus* but of the father, unless the latter is *egens* himself or no longer alive. Seneca *Controv.* 9.5 (see Chapter 2) also implies that the ties felt between a maternal grandfather and his grandchildren are a result of nature rather than of laws.

52. *Cod. Iust.* 8.46.5 (A.D. 287); *Dig.* 24.3.20 (Paul), 23.3.73.1 (Paul). Cf. *P.Oxy.* 1121 (A.D. 295) where a woman states that she has cared for her ailing mother, as is her duty as a daughter; she complains that while she was seeing to her mother's funeral, two women living in her mother's house stole her property.

53. *Dig.* 25.3.5.4; see also *Nov. Iust.* 89.12.6, 13, 15 (A.D. 539).

54. Writing at Rome at the end of the first century B.C., he was, to quote Daube (1969) 86, "more Roman than most Romans" (cf. Gabba 1991: 148–51). The passage I refer to here is *AR* 2.26.

55. See, very briefly, Bolkestein (1939) 89–90, 128 (on Greece), and 296 (on Rome). His treatment has not stood the test of time well, particularly in regard to the alleged pagan/Judeo-Christian contrast.

56. Plato *Apol.* 36d; Plutarch *Mor.* 970b; Aelian *de Nat. Anim.* 6.49; Miller (1978) 4–11, 19–20.

57. Valerius Maximus 5.4.7; Pliny *NH* 7.36.121. In Solinus *Coll. Rerum Mem.* 1.124–25 (otherwise following Pliny closely), Festus 228L, and Tzetzes *Alleg. Iliad.* 24.331 (p. 340 Boissonade) the mother has become the father. For the Greek original, see Valerius Maximus 5.4.ext.1 and Hyginus *Fab.* 254, with *CIL* 4.6635 (= *CLE* 2048, Pompeii). See further Roscher (1897–1909) 2500–2501; *RE* 20.1223–24; Fears (1981) 880; *LIMC* 7.1.327–29; Saller (1994) 106–8; and for the long tradition, Raffaelli et al. (1997). Pliny also mentions (*NH* 16.5.13) that the winner of the *corona civica* won lifelong honor, and that he, his father, and his *avus* enjoyed a *vacatio munerum omnium*.

58. See, e.g., Plutarch *Solon* 31.2 (support for war invalids introduced by Peisistratus, apparently following Solon's example). On the Athenian pension (ἀργύριον) for an impoverished invalid (ἀδύνατος), cf. (pseudo-?) Lysias 24 (note that the invalid's old age features only slightly; see, most recently, Dillon 1995; Garland 1995: 37–38; Silk 1995: 182–85; and Menu 2000: 23–28); Aeschines 1.103–4; Harpocration s.v. ἀδύνατοι (οἱ ἐντὸς τριῶν μνῶν κεκτημένοι, τὸ δὲ σῶμα πεπηρωμένοι); and Rhodes (1981) on [Aristotle] *Ath. Pol.* 49.4. Plato, in the funeral speech of Aspasia which he has Socrates deliver, states (*Menex.* 248d–e) that one should expect the state to care for (γηροτροφεῖν) the aged parents of those killed in war; cf. [Demosthenes] 60.32; Bolkestein (1939) 282.

59. E.g., Tacitus *Dial.* 17.5 for old men at a *congiarium* under Vespasian (they had received the same under Augustus). Note that in the letter of Diony-

sius quoted by Eusebius (*Hist. Eccl.* 7.21.9–10, A.D. 261, discussed in Chapter 2) the implication seems to be that only those from 14 to 80 years of age received the grain distribution in Alexandria. While there is evidence that the minimum age at Rome was probably 10 or 14 years, this is the only reference of which I am aware to any imposition anywhere of a *maximum* age limit for eligibility. Wiedemann (1989) 45 n. 35 refers to an Aurelian panel on the Arch of Constantine, depicting Marcus Aurelius distributing largesse to women, children, and a bearded old man: all vulnerable or marginal members of society. But in fact Nash, Wiedemann's citation, makes no reference to this. Wiedemann must be referring to the Aurelian panel depicted in, e.g., Ryberg (1967) 71–76, figures 49–50 (also on the cover of Parkin 1992); in fact the largesse seems to be being made to two adult males, one man (old?—he has a beard, which proves nothing), two small children, and one woman. But the head of the "old" man, among others, has been restored. In any event, we never hear of a Roman emperor emulating Herod, who provided quite extensive aid to elderly people during a period of drought and plague in Judea and Syria in 25/4 B.C., according to Josephus *Ant. Jud.* 15.9.2.309–10.

60. Aristeides *Orat.* 24.42; de Leeuw (1939) 42–51. Aristeides, it is worth noting, lived to a quite advanced age, albeit not in the best of health; Philostratus *Vit. Soph.* 2.9.585 states that some sources give his age at death as 60, others nearly 70 years.

61. Aelian *de Nat. Anim.* 12.30: ἐς παραμυθίαν τοῦ γήρως. It may also be noted that Vitruvius *de Arch.* 2.8.10 reports that the *domus* of Croesus in Sardis was set up as a *gerusia* "ad requiescendum aetatis otio seniorum collegio." But this phrase is probably a later gloss, and the reference is merely to a standard *gerousia*, not to an old-age home in the modern sense, as Pliny *NH* 35.49.172 also states: "domum . . . Sardibus Croesi, quam gerusian fecere." Cf. Poland (1909) 582, no. 42; Roueché (1993) 162–64.

62. *Dig.* 30.122.pr.; Johnston (1985).

63. Tertullian *Apol.* 39.5–6; *Cod. Iust.* 1.2.22 (A.D. 529), 1.2.23 (530), 1.3.45.1b/3/3a (530), 1.3.55.2 (534); *Nov. Iust.* 7.1 (A.D. 535: γεροντοκόμος); cf. *SB* 4845 ("Byz. Zeit": γηροκομίον). See also Bolkestein (1939) 476; Talbot (1984) 275–78; Miller (1985) 24–26; van Hooff (1989); Constantelos (1991) 163–75; Roueché (1993) 165–69; van Minnen (1995). In the lexicographers occur terms like γηρωκομεῖον and γηροτροφεῖον, with no definition (*Suda* Γ 251; Herodian *Partit.* 205–6, 237 Boissonade; Zonaras *Lex.* 1.435 Tittman: γηρωκομεῖον μέγα, γηρωτροφεῖον μικρόν); their occurrence in such places need signify nothing more than their appearance in literature, perhaps in comic authors. In the context of Christianity, it is also worth noting that the Council of Gangra (in Paphlagonia, mid-fourth century) condemned—

"anathema sit"—not only parents who abandoned their children (*Canon* 15) but also *filii* who deserted their parents in order to serve their God (*Canon* 16).

64. Besides Cicero's *Laelius de Amic.*, note Aristotle *Rhet.* 1.15 (never befriend older people); *NE* 8.1.1155a (friends useful to tend aging individuals), 8.3.1156a (friendships of utility in old age, since in old age people pursue profit rather than pleasure), 8.5.1157b and 8.6.1158a (the old are not much given to friendship, because old age is unpleasant and no one enjoys the company of someone unpleasant). On this latter point note also Cicero *de Amic.* 10.33 and Maximianus *Eleg.* 1.282.

65. Horace *Sat.* 2.5, Seneca *de Brev. Vit.* 7.7, Pliny *NH* 14.1.2–7, and Tacitus *Ann.* 15.19, offer good introductions; Jerome *Epist.* 52.6 is particularly unpleasant. The features of old age, wealth, and childlessness tend to recur (e.g., Cicero *Parad. Stoic.* 39; Lucian *Dial. Mort.* 9.3; Tacitus *Hist.* 1.73; Epictetus *Diss.* 4.1.145–48). Compare the joy of an old man at the birth of a son to his daughter, thus frustrating the hopes of the vulture-like *gentilis*: Catullus 68.119–24 (with Pindar *Ol.* 10.86–90, and Chapter 2 note 60). Hopkins (1983) 96–97 warns against regarding literary references in this context as representative of general reality. Indeed Mansbach (1982) argues that *captatio* was more a literary topos than an historical reality. This may be true, but what is important here is that some of the elite class at Rome at least thought *captatio* was a real threat (or promise) in old age. On wills being used as a means of securing some form of old-age security, note Champlin (1989: 210–12; 1991: 22, and 87–102, on *captatio,* reliant on Mansbach's work and stressing, quite rightly, the moral import rather than the strictly legal or historical nature of the practice).

66. *Cons. ad Marc.* 19.2: "in civitate nostra plus gratiae orbitas confert quam eripit, adeoque senectutem solitudo, *quae solebat destruere,* ad potentiam ducit, ut quidam odia filiorum simulent et liberos eiurent, orbitatem manu faciant." Note also *Ep.* 19.4; Tacitus *Ann.* 3.25; Lucian *Dial. Mort.* 6.3.

67. See Martial 4.56 for Gargilianus sending "munera . . . senibus viduisque ingentia"; this does not, however, give Gargilianus the right to be called "munificus"—unless he also gives to Martial. Apuleius *Apol.* 91 suggests that it was a common assumption in the Roman world that an old widow could only secure a young husband by offering a substantial dowry (*uxor dotata*) or something similarly tempting (in fact, if we believe Apuleius, Pudentilla was only a few years older than him); for invective against *wealthy* old women, see Richlin (1992) 114. On the scurrilous subject of elderly wives and young grooms, note also Aristophanes *Lys.* 595–97; Plautus *Most.* 281; Seneca *Ep.* 47.17 ("consularem aniculae servientem"); Martial 9.80 (etc.); Juvenal 1.39; Lucian *Rhet. Praec.* 24; Apuleius

Apol. 67; Plutarch *Solon* 20.5, *Mor.* 749e, 754e; Treggiari (1991) 96–97 (and see also 102–3); Saller (1984: 202–4; 1994: 223); Krause (1994–95) 1.133–38 and cf. 1.114–22 and 2.252 (and 2.105–22 for widows' children as "Altersversorgung"). Martial 13.34 is characteristically blunt on the sexual boredom to be endured by a man married to an *anus coniunx;* cf. Varro *de Ling. Lat.* 7.28 (with Courtney 1993: 109–10) for more humor. An old woman with money, according to an anonymous poem in the *Anthologia Palatina* (11.425), is a rich tomb. Cicero *pro Scaur.* presents the case of a Sardinian, Aris, married to a "rich, old, ugly wife" whom he detests *propter foeditatem* (5.8; cf. 4.6: "it is well known that her ugliness was on a par with her old age") but whom he cannot divorce because of her dowry; she is found hanged in mysterious circumstances. On the veracity or otherwise of this story, see Treggiari (1991) 330–31; Saller (1994) 221–23; Krause (1994–95) 1.136. Stobaeus *Flor.* 22.5.109–17 W-H collects Greek literary references on the theme of age disparity between spouses. Note too Ovid *Ars Amat.* 2.663–702 on the benefits of older women as lovers: they have experience.

68. *Ep.* 8.18 (cf. 7.24 for the will of Ummidia Quadratilla, with Chapter 2 note 63, and see Syme 1985: 51–53). For a similar story, see Lucian *Dial. Mort.* 6: Thucritus, over 90 years of age, not only enjoys the attention of many legacy hunters but, because *captatores* lead such a stressful life, also outlives them (to the delight of everyone else); Pluto remarks that in their wills such old men tend to ignore the scavengers, and offspring and φύσις prevail, "as is δίκαιος." Compare also *Dial. Mort.* 5, 7–9.

69. Pliny *Ep.* 6.3 (the comments of Joshel 1986: 11 are useful). Analogous cases, fictional or otherwise, are few (unsurprisingly) even over the course of a millennium: note Callimachus *Epig.* 50 (= *Anthologia Palatina* 7.458), for Miccus caring for his old nurse Aeschra in her old age (γηροκομεῖ); [Demosthenes] 47.55 for an old nurse who returns to her former charge's house when her husband dies and she is old and alone; and Jerome *Ep.* 14.3 ("gerula quondam, iam anus, et nutricius, secundus post naturalem pietatis pater"). For an aged nurse still in the household after her charge has not only grown up but also died six months earlier, see Phlegon *Mirab.* 1 (*FGH* 257 F 36.1.2). *CIL* 6.29497 = *ILS* 8538 is the epitaph from Rome of a *nutrix assa,* aged 105 years. Note also Dixon (1988) 127–28; Bradley (1986: 220–21; 1991: 20, 22); Wiedemann (1996) 285. Cicero *de Amic.* 20.74 warns against showing uncalled-for kindness or gratitude to the *nutrices* or *paedagogi* of one's youth. Compare again Seneca's reaction on meeting an aged slave who had many years before been his favorite (*Ep.* 12.3). As Simone de Beauvoir (1977) 16–17 observed, "there is a great gulf between the aged slave and the aged patrician, between the wretchedly pensioned ex-worker

and an Onassis." On old slaves note again Tertullian's reference to *domestici senes,* quoted above, and see Wiedemann (1996); for imperial slaves and freedmen, cf. Chantraine (1973).

70. Cf. *Dig.* 7.1.12.3 (Pomponius *ap.* Ulpian), 29.5.3.7 (Ulpian). The painter Parrhasius apparently found one use for an aged slave: torturing him in order to produce a model for his picture of Prometheus Bound (Seneca *Controv.* 10.5—doubtless fictitious but of interest for attitudes to slaves; see Chapter 9 note 20). Protogenes, it was said, used an old woman to guard his easel when he was absent from his studio: Pliny *NH* 35.36.81. Pliny also notes, 13.47.132, that the animal-feed *cytisus* is so easy to reap that even a *puer* or an *anus* could do it (and he or she would presumably be cheap to hire); cf. similarly Columella 8.2.7 for "anus sedula vel puer" being used to watch over chickens. For an old woman guarding a man's *togula* at the baths, see Martial 12.70.2, and for an aged—and predictably bibulous—slave woman as doorkeeper, Plautus *Curc.* 76; we have met another elderly female with a job at Chapter 8 note 39. For more strenuous work, old slaves were at a disadvantage: see Varro *Res Rust.* 2.10.3, and Columella 1.8.3 for the recommendation that a *vilicus* not be too old nor too young. That Piso is tended by old, ugly slaves is used as a taunt by Cicero: *in Pis.* 27.67.

71. Cato *de Agri Cult.* 2.7; Plutarch *Cato Maior* 4–5; compare Martial 11.70.9–10: "vende senes servos, ignoscent, vende paternos; ne pueros vendas omnia vende miser." For the difficulty in selling old and infirm slaves, note Horace *Sat.* 2.3.281–87, *Epist.* 2.2.16; Varro *Res Rust.* 2.10.5; Cicero *de Off.* 3.71; *Dig.* 21.1.37 (Ulpian, on tricks used to sell a *veterator*). For one context where male and female slaves under the age of 8 years and over the age of 60 years were cheaper than those of 8–16, 16–40 (the most expensive), or 40–60 years, note the Aezani text of the Diocletianic Prices Edict (Crawford and Reynolds 1979: 177; Scheidel 1996c). One ploy may have been to sell aged slaves as "job lots"; cf. Plautus *Bacch.* 973–77 ("comptionalem senem"); Cicero *ad Fam.* 7.29.1 (Curius), "senes comptionalis," with Shackleton Bailey's comments *ad loc.* (no. 264). It should be added that the term might also have been used as abuse, if one reads "comptionali seni" for "contionali seni" at Livy 3.72.4. *Senes co[e]mptionales* feature in another sense, a legal device, at Cicero *pro Mur.* 12.27: to free herself from the obligation to maintain *sacra familiaria* in an inherited estate, a woman could apparently contract a *coemptio* marriage to a *senex;* he would then manumit her and by returning to her the estate as a gift, the *sacra* would lapse; see also Martini (1982). Both senses seem to be covered in *Glossae Codicis Vaticani 3321* (*CGL* 4.36.28), if the emendation is correct: "contemnalis (*coemptionalis,* Goetz) senex emptus manu[m] missus et tutor, auctor factus." For the sale of *parents,* see Chapter 9 note 121.

72. Nor need one attempt to exonerate him, *pace* Astin (1978) 261–66, 349–50.
73. Treggiari (1969) 16; Brunt (1971) 379–80, citing Dionysius of Halicarnassus *AR* 4.24.5: the manumitted, it is alleged, are made to take their grain handout back to their former masters.
74. See *Dig.* 38.1 (note 38.1.16.1 [Paul]: the nature of the services provided by the freedman to his patron will be affected by, inter alia, the age of both parties) and 37.15 "de obsequiis parentibus et patronis praestandis"); Watson (1967) 229–31; Treggiari (1969) 75–81; Fabre (1981); Waldstein (1986).
75. Parkin (1997) 135 n. 44. For slaves as a source of care in an owner's old age, note Domitius Tullus again, Statius *Silv.* 2.1.69 ("tu domino requies portusque senectae"), and *P.Oxy.* 3555 (first or second century A.D.), where a woman (ἀβοήθητον οὖσαν καὶ μόνην, "helpless and alone," lines 9–10; cf. Hobson 1993: 210 n. 1) complains to the *strategos* that her young slave girl, grievously injured on her way to a music lesson, will not now be able to tend her mistress in her old age (γηροβοσκόν, line 8). See also *SEG* 46.745, A.D. 223 (Macedonia): a male slave is to be manumitted on condition that he look after his owner, a woman, in her old age (γηροβοσκεῖν).
76. *Dig.* 33.2.33.2. Cf. *Dig.* 34.1 on *alimenta* left to freedmen in the will of a former master ("de alimentis vel cibariis legatis"), esp. 34.1.3 (rescript *ap.* Ulpian): "multi testamentis suis praestari libertis iubent necessaria." See further Treggiari (1969) 216–17, and generally Champlin (1991) 133–36. For a patron's duty (but not necessarily obligation, unless the freedman requests it) to maintain his freedman, see *Dig.* 25.3.6.pr. (Modestinus), 37.14.5.1 (Marcian), 38.2.33 (Modestinus).
77. Suetonius *Div. Claud.* 25.2; Dio 60.29.7; *Dig.* 40.8.2 (Modestinus); cf. *Cod. Iust.* 7.6.1.3 (A.D. 531, referring to Claudius's edict). For further discussion, see Fasciato (1949); Philipsborn (1950); Volterra (1956); Schmitt and Rödel (1974); Poma (1982) 160–63; Levick (1990) 124–25; Major (1994); Wiedemann (1996) 280–81. Of related interest: in the later fifth century, by the terms of the *Codex Euricianus* 277 (*MGH Leges* 1.1.5 = *Lex Visigothorum* 10.2.2, *MGH Leges* 1.1.392), fugitive slaves who had not been found within fifty (*sic!*) years could not be reenslaved. Cf. Buckland (1908) ch. 28.
78. *Dig.* 40.9.9.pr.; Columella 1.8.20 (and cf. 11.1.3 on the risk for an aged *vilicus*).
79. And indeed under later Roman law it is said that the infirmities of old age offer grounds for divorce; cf. *Dig.* 24.1.61 (Gaius): "propter . . . vel senectutem aut valetudinem aut militiam satis commode retineri matrimonium non possit." Plutarch for one expresses indignation at such grounds for divorce (*Mor.* 789b; cf. *Cic.* 41.6), which might suggest that

in his day it was not too uncommon. For the average length of married life, see Parkin (1992) 196 n. 190 and Saller (1994) 219–20.

80. Up until the age of 60 years for males and 50 for females, as discussed in the previous chapter. It is of related interest that Plato (*Laws* 11.930b) states that a man with no children whose wife dies must remarry so as to have children. When a couple are divorced but sufficient children already exist, new matches are to be aimed at companionship and mutual assistance in old age ('τῆς συγκαταγηράσεως ἕνεκα καὶ ἐπιμελείας ἀλλήλων τὴν διάζευξίν τε καὶ σύζευξιν ποιεῖσθαι χρεών'). On the possible advantages of concubinage over remarriage for elderly Roman males, see Saller (1987b) 74–76; Arjava (1996) 208; and the mass of detail in Friedl (1996). It was also possible for such support in sickness and in old age to be envisaged for a homosexual couple: [Lucian] *Amores* 46.

81. See Parkin (1997) 136, and contrast [Quintilian] *Decl. Min.* 306.20: "inter pares quoque annos citius femina senescit, neque amatur anus uxor nisi memoria." See Chapter 7 note 30 for testimony of enduring marriages.

82. Plutarch *Mor.* 983a–b; cf. Antigonus *Hist. Mirab.* 23, quoting lines from Alcman (26 *PMG*). See Thompson (1936) 139–40. The male bird, called the ceryl, is identified by Antigonus as simply the male halcyon; Aelian *de Nat. Anim.* 5.48, however, implies that it is a different species.

83. *De Nat. Anim.* 7.17. Cf. Seneca *de Rem. Fort.* 16.5 for old wives deserting their husbands ("veterum matrimoniorum repudia cognovimus et foediores divortio male cohaerentium rixas. quam multae quos in adulescentia amaverunt in senectute communi reliquerunt. quotiens anile divortium risimus"); Treggiari (1991) 476–77.

84. As we have seen, there appears to have been a common (literary) tradition that a young wife was not suited to an old man: see Chapter 7 note 24, and cf. also, e.g., Athenaeus *Deipn.* 13.559f–60a; Menander *Monost.* 168 Jaekel (= *Comp. Men. et Phil.* 1.236, and note 3.51): γέρων γενόμενος μὴ γάμει νεωτέραν, which has a very gnomic ring about it. Compare also again Pliny *Ep.* 8.18 (with Syme 1979: 254, and Chapter 3 note 74) for Domitius Tullus's wife caring for him in his very decrepit old age. It is interesting, as Bagnall and Frier (1994) 120 observe, that there are five cases in the census returns from Roman Egypt where women of or under the age of 25 years are married to quite considerably older men (gaps of 17, 17, 18, 19, and 28 years); in view of the relatively small size of the overall sample of census returns, this may have significance in terms of marriage patterns, at least for Egypt (where, as Bagnall and Frier have shown, remarriage for women was not the norm). See further Krause (1994–95) 1.21–34, 202–18.

85. Xenophon *Mem.* 2.8; [Demosthenes] 49.67.

86. *P.Lond.* 43 (= *Epist. Priv. Graec.* 59). Cf. Menander *Monost.* 227 Jaekel:

"Always lay aside an ἐφόδιον for old age." Bias (*ap.* Diogenes Laertius 1.88) expresses the sentiment—a not uncommon one, as we have seen—that σοφία is the best ἐφόδιον in preparing for old age; Aristotle (*ap.* Diogenes Laertius 5.21) advocates παιδεία, while Cicero *de Orat.* 1.60.255, in line with the *de Sen.,* has M. Antonius aver that "subsidium bellissimum existimo esse senectuti, otium." Cf. also [Plutarch] *de Lib. Educ.* 8c, and Chapter 8 note 92.

87. *Decl. Maior.* 5.4, 10–11. Compare the *inops senectus* of a father in similar circumstances, *Decl. Maior.* 9.9, 23; also 13.2–5, 17.2.
88. [Plutarch] *Mor.* 13b (ἐφόδια).
89. Horace *Sat.* 1.1.28–35; cf. 2.2.84–88, 2.3.117–23. For the madness of the miser, cf. Juvenal 14.135–37, and see Chapter 4 note 53. For the importance of a nest egg (*peculium . . . praesidii causa*), according to *rustici senes,* see *Dig.* 32.79.1 (Celsus quoting Proculus).
90. Either *iuvante* (with fate's help) or *iubente* (at fate's command); probably the latter, through betacism.
91. *CIL* 11.137 = *ILS* 1980. Note also the very touching and rather sad epitaph composed by an anonymous author (*Anthologia Palatina* 7.336): "Worn out by old age and poverty (γήραι καὶ πενίη τετρυμένος—the same phrase is used at 6.228, Addaeus of Macedon, of an ox), no one stretching out his hand to relieve my misery, on my tottering legs I went slowly to my grave, scarce able to reach the end of my wretched life . . . I died after my burial" (i.e., he went to a graveyard and died; cf. Martial 8.57 for a *senex* in a similar position).
92. Thus Cicero *de Sen. passim,* part of a long tradition (see Chapter 3). Musonius Rufus 17 (= Stobaeus *Flor.* 50.3.94) states that it is not wealth that is the best ἐφόδιον, παραμύθιον, or ἐπικούρημα of old age—witness the many rich men who are full of sadness and despair and think themselves wretched—but "to live according to φύσις, doing and thinking what one ought."
93. Cicero *de Sen.* 3.8; Powell (1988) 119–20.
94. *De Sen.* 5.14, describing Ennius at the age of 70 years; see further Parkin (1997) 137 with references, to which add Plato *Phaedr.* 267c; Lucian *Apol.* 10; *Anthologia Palatina* 6.30 (Macedonius Consul); Boissonade *Anec. Graec.* 1 p. 24 (γῆρας καὶ πενία, δύο τραύματα δυσθεράπευτα). For a comparative perspective, note Herlihy (1990).
95. Of some interest is Ausonius's bizarre and highly artificial letter written in a mixture of Greek and Latin to Paulus (*Epist.* 6 Green, who calls it a "macaronic masterpiece") complaining of the effects of old age, in which he states (lines 33–34) that "the helpless (ἀπάλαμνος) man gets no κουαιστωδέα [from *quaestus*] lucrov [*sic*] and the bedridden old man earns no golden μισθόν."
96. Juvenal 9.139–40; *Cod. Theod.* 14.18.1 (= *Cod. Iust.* 11.26.1), A.D. 382. For an (apparently) old, blind beggar in Ephesus in the first century A.D.,

see Philostratus *Vit. Apoll.* 4.10.130, and cf. Juvenal's *Iudaea tremens* (6.543); see also Epictetus *Diss.* 3.26.6 on very aged beggars. In the context of concessions granted to *infirmitas aetatis* in such contexts, note also *Dig.* 48.19.22 (a rescript of Antoninus Pius *ap.* Modestinus, on individuals "in metallum damnati"), with Solazzi (1930).

97. Stobaeus *Flor.* 50.2.85 (5.1051.17–22 W-H). On Juncus, see Chapter 3. That Juncus spoke from experience is, of course, unlikely.

98. 1051.23–1052.2 W-H.

99. See my Introduction. Nor, I should add, need it be assumed that things have always improved: cf., e.g., Smith (1984).

100. *W&D* 174–89; note also 331–32. Cf. Falkner (1989 = 1995: ch. 2), and note also, most recently, Most (1997). A millennium or so after Hesiod, St. Cyprian *ad Demetr.* 4 (*PL* 4.566 = *CCSL* 3a.37) observed in the context of an aging world ("mundo senescente"—cf. Chapter 1, with Parkin 1992: 60) that "canos videmus in pueris, capilli deficiunt antequam crescunt, nec aetas in senectutem desinit, sed incipit a senectute" (we see gray hairs on boys, the hairs fail before they begin to grow, and life does not finish in old age but begins from old age). Note also Ctesias *FGH* 688 F 45t (= Pliny *NH* 7.2.23; cf. Photius *Bibl.* 49b = *FGH* 688 F 45.49, Solinus *Coll. Rerum Mem.* 52.28, and cf. Chapter 1 note 39) for a race in India where the children turn gray immediately after birth.

101. For bibliographical references see Parkin (1997) 139–40, and note also Drerup (1933); Golden (1990) ch. 4; Eyben (1993) 47–49, 65–67; and Kleijwegt (1991) 63–67, who prefers the term "generational tension" and who remarks that the phenomenon is strikingly absent from ancient history, apart from fifth century B.C. Athens and the later Roman Republic. For the latter period, note also Bonnefond (1982) 217–22.

102. Gaunt (1983) 261. The tradition of such conflict can be seen, for example, in the mythologies of many cultures, such as in the Greek and Roman, with Uranus being overpowered by Cronus (Saturn) who was in turn overthrown by Zeus (Jupiter)—though Lucian reports in his *Saturnalia* (6–7) that Cronus handed power over voluntarily, burdened as he was by old age. In Maori creation mythology the two original gods, Rangi (the sky) and Papa (the earth), are in close embrace until their six male children (Tawhirimatea, the wind; Tane, the forests; Tu, war; Tangaroa, the sea; Rongo, the kumara or sweet potato; and Haumia, the fern root) plot to separate them; Tane accomplishes this by growing (as a tree) between them, pushing between them with his hands (the roots) and his legs and feet (the branches).

103. See Dixon (1997), esp. 153. For one particularly vivid portrayal of father-son conflict at a time of real crisis, note the *agon* at Euripides *Alc.* 614–746, with Thury (1988a) and, more generally, Zimmermann (1998). Familial tension between the generations may be glimpsed in the legal

corpus: e.g., *Cod. Iust.* 8.46.3–4 (A.D. 227, 259). Fraternal strife is also evident, but that of course tends not to cross generational lines.

104. Esp. Thucydides 6.13, 17–18; cf. Plutarch *Nic.* 11.3; Juncus *ap.* Stobaeus *Flor.* 50.3.95 W-H. For this and the threat felt to be posed to generational harmony by the sophistic movement (as well as, indeed, by democracy itself—Plato *Rep.* 8.563a-b, *Laws* 3.701b; cf. Cicero *de Rep.* 1.43.67), see Drerup (1933) 53–62; Roussel (1942), esp. 175–77, 183; note also de Romilly (1976), with Byl (1988a) 93 n. 65. Forrest (1975) is a particularly good discussion of the effect of a young political force in Athens; see also Ostwald (1986) 229–50; Carter (1986) ch. 5; Strauss (1993), esp. ch. 5; and, for republican Rome, Bonnefond (1982).

105. Eunapius *Vit. Soph.* 7.5.3.479; *PLRE* 1.814–17. For ideas on the relative merits of young versus old, note Seneca *Controv.* 7.7.13–14, a debate about the efficacy of a young, energetic general as compared with an elderly one with common sense; and two classic, epic cases: Nestor and Diomedes in the *Iliad* (book 8), and Entellus and Dares in the *Aeneid* (5.395–484, with Pavlovskis 1976 and Bertman 1976: ch. 11). The former example is used by Dio *Epit.* 78.40.4, citing *Iliad* 8.102–3, when he notes that the γέρων Macrinus (he was 53 years old at the time) was overthrown by the παιδάριον Elagabalus (ca. 13 years old) in A.D. 218.

106. Finley (1981) 170.

107. The *OLD* defines *senium* as (i) the condition of old age, usually implying decay or debility; (ii) the period of old age, senility, dotage, long life; (iii) melancholy, gloom, hypochondria. The negative element is omnipresent, as is usually the idea of old age. In the Latin legal corpus, *senium* is similarly used, without any special legal significance; it can refer to general ill-health or infirmity through age, without necessarily implying mental illness (*Dig.* 26.1.13.pr. [Pomponius, cited below]; 50.5.2.7 [Ulpian, cf. Chapter 4 note 149]; *Cod. Iust.* 6.22.3.pr. [A.D. 294; see Chapter 8 note 31]; 10.55.2 [Diocletian and Maximian]; 12.19.15.2 [A.D. 527]; 12.20.5.2 [Leo]; *Cod. Theod.* 7.20.12.2 [A.D. 400]), to the decrepitude of the ancient laws before the recodification under Justinian (*Cod. Iust.* 1.17.2.pr. [A.D. 533]), to the disrepair of old buildings (*Cod. Theod.* 15.1.15–16 [A.D. 365], 7.10.1.pr. [A.D. 405]; *Cod. Iust.* 8.11.16 = *Cod. Theod.* 15.1.44 [A.D. 406]), or to the enduring eloquence of a speaker despite his old age ("loquentia non ut aliae res senio deterioratur," *Nov. Theod.* 10.2.pr. [A.D. 439]; on this aspect of old age, cf. also Homer *Iliad* 1.249 [Nestor]; Euripides *Phoen.* 528–30; Lucian *Bacch.* 7, *Herc.* 4, 8; but on the weakened voice of older people, see Aristotle *de Audib.* 801b, Cicero *de Sen.* 9.28, *de Orat.* 1.60.254–55, Pliny *NH* 11.112.270, Quintilian *Inst. Or.* 12.11.2, and Chapter 3 on Juvenal 10.198). On the term *senium,* see also Slusanski (1974) 113, 352–54, 566–67; Powell (1988) 132.

108. *Orig.* 11.2.8, 30, following Jerome *Comm. in Amos* 2.pr. (*PL* 25.1021–23 = *CCSL* 76.255–56). Note similarly Isidorus *Diff.* 2.20.77 (*PL* 83.81: "inter senectutem et senium hoc differt, quod senectus vergens aetas a iuventute in senium, nondum tamen decrepita; senium vero est fessa atque extrema aetas, et vitam ultimam anhelans"; also *Diff.* 1.531 [*PL* 83.63]), Augustine *Enarr. in Psalm 70 Sermo* 2.4 (*PL* 36.894 = *CCSL* 39.962–63), and Jerome *Comm. in Hieremiam* 2.17.2 (*PL* 24.274 = *CCSL* 74.67); see Chapter 1 on Isidorus's *gradus aetatis,* and Eyben (1973b) 162. On *senium* in terms of old age ("senilis morbus"), note Nonius Marcellus 3L: "senium est taedium et odium: dictum a senectute, quod senes omnibus odio sint et taedio"; Paulus *ex* Festus 26L: "anatem dicebant morbum anuum, id est vetularum, sicut senium morbum senum"; Parkin (1997) 141.

109. Juvenal 10.232–33 (see Chapter 3); Galen *de Sympt. Caus.* 2.7 (7.200–201K); Plato *Phaedr.* 276d, with Galen *de Prop. Plac.* 3.2 (*CMG* 5.3.2.60, and Nutton's note *ad loc.*). For such signs of madness, cf. also Lucretius *de Rer. Nat.* 3.467–69; Cicero *in Pis.* 20.47 (with Nisbet's comments *ad loc.*); Seneca *Controv.* 2.4.2.

110. Various examples are collected in Parkin (1997) 142 n. 66, to which may usefully be added: Hippocrates *Prorrh.* 2.30 (9.64L); Herondas *Mim.* 1.67–68 (see Chapter 3 note 78); Sallust *Bell. Iug.* 11.5; Vergil *Aen.* 7.440; Statius *Silv.* 5.3.249; Plutarch *Lucull.* 43 (the case of Lucullus, at about the age of 60 years: Plutarch notes, however, that, according to Cornelius Nepos, Lucullus's mental decline was not a result of old age but of a love potion; see also Chapter 3 note 76); Lucian *pro Lapsu* 1, *Philops.* 20; Apuleius *Apol.* 53 ("misera insania crudae senectutis"); Herodian 7.8.5. Pollux *Onom.* 2.16 provides a list of insults used against older people in comedy, such as κρονόληρος (also at [Plutarch] *Mor.* 13b), μακκοῶν, παρανοῶν, and παραφρονῶν.

111. Cicero *de Sen.* 11.36. See also Diogenes of Oenoanda frag. 146 Smith for a similar argument, namely that madness (αἱ παρακοπαί) is not caused by old age "but by some other cause of natural origin"; like the elephant, the old man is slow in movement but intelligent (on this, note Pliny *NH* 8.5.15). Cf. also Diogenes of Oenoanda frag. 141 (the mind remaining active in old age) and 147 (some people survive into extreme old age with their senses unimpaired), and also NF 134 (Smith 1998: 165). On the theme of a sound mind in an unsound body in old age, see also Chapter 3 note 20.

112. Aretaeus 3.6.2 (*CMG* 2.41; the first-century dating, rather than the second century, is probably correct): τῇδε τῇ μανίῃ οὐδέ τι ἴκελον ἡ λήρησις, γήραος ἡ ξυμφορή· αἰσθήσιος γάρ ἐστι νάρκη καὶ γνώμης νάρκωσις ἤδε τοῦ νοῦ [Pigeaud (1987) 74 prefers τόνου] ὑπὸ ψύξιος· μανίη δὲ θερμόν τι καὶ ξηρὸν τῇ αἰτίῃ, καὶ ταραχῶδες τῇσι πρήξεσι. ἡ μὲν γὰρ λήρησις ἀρχομένη ἀπὸ γήραος οὔτε διαλείπει, καὶ ξυναπο-

θνῄσκει· μανίη δὲ καὶ διαλείπει καὶ μελεδῶνι ἐς τέλος ἀποπαύεται. In a medical context, see also Galen *Quod Animi Mores Corp. Temp. Seq.* 5 (4.786K), quoted below, in Chapter 9; and note Cassius Felix *de Med.* 63 on the subject of *lethargici* ("sensibus obtusis cum oblivione mentis"), a condition more common among *senes* than among *iuvenes*.

113. Hippocrates *Aph.* 5.16 (4.536L) has the same phrase, used of the effect of heat! For the term λήρησις, elsewhere used by Stoics of foolish talk associated with drunkenness, cf. Plutarch *Mor.* 504b, 716f; Diogenes Laertius 7.118; and Chrysippus *Frag. Mor.* 643 (*SVF* 3.163 = Stobaeus *Ecl.* 2.7 [W-H p. 109]). Note the nouns παράληρος and λῆρος, signifying delirium, and also the verb ὑποληρέω, clearly used by Aelian *Var. Hist.* 3.37 (cited Chapter 9 note 120) to refer to senile dementia.

114. Aristotle *Phys.* 4.12.221a, *de Mem.* 450b, 453b; Cicero *de Sen.* 7.21 ("memoria minuitur"; Powell 1988: 147); Lucretius *de Rer. Nat.* 3.1039–42 (of Democritus); Ovid *Met.* 12.182–84 (Nestor); Seneca *Controv.* 1.pr.2–3 (on the alleged demise in old age of Seneca's own prodigious memory); Maximianus *Eleg.* 1.123–26.

115. Pliny *NH* 7.24.90; Jerome *Chron.* p. 170–71H. Possibly he was older than 71, nor is there certainty re the year of death: see R. Hanslik, *RE* 8a.135–36, Jeffreys (1985), and Syme (1986) 219–20. For the forgetting of names, note also Seneca's description of a *vetulus nomenclator* at *Ep.* 27.5. On the other hand, special note was made of those who survived into old age with their memory intact: cf., e.g., Simonides *Eleg.* 89 West² (of himself at the age of 80 years; see Aristeides *Orat.* 28.60 for the context, with Lefkowitz 1981: 54–55 and Goldhill 1988; also Farrell 1997 for Simonides as "magnate/entrepreneur of artificial mnemonics"); Pliny *NH* 25.5.9 (of Castor the botanist); Philostratus *Vit. Soph.* 1.11.495–96 (of Hippias of Elis who had extraordinary powers of memory, even in old age, as, apparently, did most of the sophists; cf. *Vit. Soph.* 2.21.604, etc.). Cf. Seneca *Controv.* 2.6.13 ("vulgarem sensum satis vulgariter"): "the νοῦς blossoms (συνανθεῖ) in old age" (and cf. Seneca the Younger *Ep.* 26.2); Jerome *Ep.* 10.2: men of righteousness retain their memory into old age; any unrighteous men who enjoy a healthy old age have the devil to thank.

116. For other legal restrictions affecting older people within the family, note *Dig.* 26.1.13.pr. (Pomponius): a curator may be appointed for someone who has a tutor on account of the tutor's ill health or *senium aetatis;* and *Cod. Iust.* 6.22.3.pr. (A.D. 294), cited earlier in this chapter, notes 31 and 107.

117. Almost certainly a *graphe,* not a *dike:* Harrison (1968) 80–81.

118. Parkin (1997) 143.

119. Cicero *de Sen.* 7.22 ("quemadmodum nostro more male rem gerentibus patribus bonis interdici solet"); Anonymous *Vita Sophoc.* 13 (quoting Satyrus, third century B.C.); Plutarch *Mor.* 785a; [Lucian] *Macr.* 24 (the

son was convicted of insanity instead!); Apuleius *Apol.* 37; Jerome *Ep.* 52.3.6 (copying Cicero); cf. Valerius Maximus 8.7.ext.12. See also Mazon (1945); Lefkowitz (1981) 84–85; Powell (1988) 150–51.

120. As Lacey (1968) 106–7, 117–18, 130 argues, followed by Strauss (1993) 68–71; see also Golden (1981: 322 n. 21; 1990: 107–14).

121. Aristotle *Pol.* 7.1335a32–35 approves of just such a scheme in theory. Note too that in Aristophanes' *Wasps* it is Bdelycleon, not Philocleon, who runs the house. In Plato *Lysis* 209c, the young Lysis assumes that his father will hand over everything to him when he considers his son to "know better than himself." Lysis's father may have had something different to say on the subject.

122. Seneca *Controv.* 3.3; Bonner (1969) 106; Garnsey and Saller (1987) 141. See also above on *donationes,* with Shaw (1987) 21–26. For a valuable comparative study, see Gaunt (1983); note too Brettell (1991).

123. Gaius *Inst.* 1.55. Exceptions to the rule, *Inst.* 1.127–36; Parkin (1997) 144. It appears nonetheless that many, and probably most, Romans remained *in potestate* until their father, not to mention paternal grandfather, died.

124. Daube (1969) 75–76. The age differences, given that a Roman male on average married in his late 20s (see Saller 1987a), are probably not quite right, but the point remains just as valid.

125. Cicero *pro Rosc. Amer.* and the *senatusconsultum Macedonianum* (first century A.D., probably Vespasianic), on which see Daube (1947; 1969: 88–90); Hopkins (1983) 244–45; Gardner (1993: 63–66; 1998: 63). In a literary context note also Lucian *Dial. Mort.* 27.7, for a wealthy 90-year-old father poisoned by his dependent and deprived 18-year-old son: "οὐκ ἄδικα," comments Diogenes. Compare Ovid *Met.* 1.148–49, and Statius *Silv.* 3.3.14–16: "procul hinc, procul ite nocentes, si cui corde nefas tacitum fessique senectus longa patris. . . . " More generally, see Lassen (1992).

126. Compare Juvenal 16.51–56 for the case of a "tremulus pater" who courts ("captat") his son who earns a soldier's pay, a neat inversion of roles. See Daube (1953), and Gardner (1993) 57–62 on sons as their fathers' *institores.*

127. Discussed above; note also *Dig.* 10.2.20.3 (Ulpian), 10.2.39.5 (Scaevola); and re emancipated sons: 31.87.4 (Paul), 32.37.3 (Scaevola); cf. 45.1.107 (Iavolenus). See also Saller (1991: 40; 1994: 125–26, 172). *Dig.* 28.2.11 (Paul) even makes it sound as if in reality the distinction between father and son as property owners was minimal. One can imagine that in some households where two adult generations cohabited, the theory of legal property rights might have been modified in practice by day-to-day realities.

128. Saller (1986) 16, with Gardner (1993: 66–72; 1998: ch. 1), and cf.

Daube (1947) 303. The frequency of emancipation may have increased in later antiquity: see most recently Arjava (1998) 161–62.

129. Saller and Shaw (1984) 137; Saller (1986) 17.

130. *Dig.* 1.6.8 (Ulpian). On the whole subject of insanity in Roman law, see Nardi (1983), esp. 100–107; Lanza (1990); Gardner (1993) 167–78, in particular on the disadvantageous legal position of the son of a *furiosus pater;* Fayer (1994) 559–82.

131. *XII Tables* 5.7 (Crawford 1996: 643–46), with Diliberto (1984); cf. Cicero *de Inv.* 2.50.148, [Cicero] *ad Heren.* 1.13.23; *Dig.* 27.10; Paul *Sent.* 3.4a.7 (= 3.5.8 Liebs): "moribus per praetorem bonis interdicitur hoc modo: quando tibi bona paterna avitaque nequitia tua disperdis liberosque tuos ad egestatem perducis, ob eam rem tibi [ea re] <aere> commercioque interdico" (for the reading *aere,* see Watson 1967: 157).

132. *Dig.* 27.10.1.pr. (Ulpian), 27.10.13 (Gaius). Note also Columella 1.3.1 and Varro *Res Rust.* 1.2.8.

133. *Dig.* 26.5.12.1 (Ulpian, citing a rescript of Antoninus Pius, that a son, "si sobrie vivat," may be the *curator* of his father; this apparently went against the view of Celsus et al. that it was *indecorum* for a father to be ruled by his son), 27.10.1.1 (Ulpian, again citing Pius's rescript), 27.10.2 (Paul), 27.10.4 (Ulpian concerning a *furiosa mater,* referring to *pietas*). For the position of daughters in a related context, see 3.3.41 (Paul).

134. It is of interest, however, in the light of what we have said above about old age being regarded as a second childhood, that Gaius observed (*Inst.* 3.109) that "infans et qui infanti proximus est non multum a furioso differt, quia huius aetatis pupilli nullum intellectum habent."

135. Fayer (1994) 559 n. 680, 582 n. 766; Parkin (1997) 146–47. In a medical context, note the terminology used by Celsus *de Med.* 3.18 (*insania, furor, dementia, phrenesis*), with Stok (1996).

136. Note again the passage from Aretaeus cited above, and [Quintilian] *Decl. Min.* 349.3: "dementiam non posse curari." Renier (1950) 438 remarks that among the *furiosi* may be counted those "qui sont en état d'imbécillité ou de démence sénile."

137. Seneca *Controv.* 2.3, 2.4 (cf. Calpurnius Flaccus [second century A.D.] *Decl.* 30), 2.6. Other cases of relevance: *Controv.* 6.7, 7.6, 9.5.7, 10.3; [Quintilian] *Decl. Min.* 295 ("datum est hoc ius contra patrem. legum lator prospexit senectuti: ideo medicinam filiis imperavit," 295.4), 316, 328, 349, 367 (including a brief list of alleged symptoms of such *dementia;* cf. Winterbottom 1984 on *Decl. Min.* 349.4).

138. At *Inst. Or.* 11.1.82, Quintilian describes similar cases as "scholastica materia, sed non <quae in foro non> possit accidere."

139. Thus Quintilian *Inst. Or.* 7.4.11 (cf. 7.4.29); Seneca *Controv.* 2.3.13 ("ego [the speaker, Asinius Pollio, or Seneca himself?] scio nulli a praetore cu-

ratorem dari, quia iniquus pater sit aut impius, sed semper quia furiosus; hoc autem in foro esse curatorem petere, quod in scholastica dementiae agere").

140. Paul *Sent.* 3.4a.7, quoted note 131.
141. The solitary example is Seneca *Controv.* 2.6. As Bonner (1969) 94 says, the cases Seneca describes "seem to be as far-fetched as possible and in most of them a praetor would almost certainly have rejected the application." Cf. Gardner (1993) 172.
142. Parkin (1997) 147–48.
143. Thus is it imagined, as with the aged Philetas in Longus *Daph. & Chl.* 2.3, Laertes in Homer *Odyss.* 24.226–31 (cf. 11.195–96, Cicero *de Sen.* 15.54, and Pliny *NH* 17.6.50, in a discussion of *fimus:* "iam apud Homerum regius senex agrum ita laetificans suis manibus reperitur"), Vergil's *Corycius senex* (*Georg.* 4.125–46 with Servius *ad Georg.* 4.127; cf. *Enciclopedia Virgiliana* 1 [1984] 903–4 for a summary of scholarship, and see further esp. Clay in Falkner and de Luce 1989, and most recently Leigh 1994), Ovid's *senex* Hyrieus (*Fasti* 5.499), and Pliny's contemporary Antonius Castor (*NH* 25.5.9). Note also Valerius Maximus 7.1.2 (*de felicitate*) and Pliny *NH* 7.46.151 for Aglaus, the happy *senior* of Arcadia ("in angustissimo . . . angulo," remarks Pliny) in the time of Gyges, with a *praedium* sufficient to meet his needs.
144. Cicero *de Sen.* 11.38. Powell (1988) 177–78 detects some legal overtones here, particularly in *emancipata.* For advice not dissimilar to Cicero's, note also *Ecclesiasticus* 33.20–23.

Chapter 9. The Marginality of Old Age

1. Parkin (1998).
2. There is rich comparative material in this context in Simmons (1945, 1960), and Glascock and Feinman (1981; 1986: 286–87); note also Philibert (1984) and Stahmer (1978).
3. E.g., Isidorus *Orig.* 11.2.30, quoted in the previous chapter. According to Galen, certain of the Hippocratic school (ἔνιοι τῶν ὑπὸ Ἱπποκράτους) believed—incorrectly, as Galen asserts—that Hippocrates drew a similar distinction: Galen *in Hipp. Aph.* 3.31 (17B.648K).
4. Galen *de San. Tuenda* 5.12 (6.379–80K = *CMG* 5.4.2.167). For discussion of some ancient grammarians' interest in the terminology for such stages of old age, see further Appendix C.
5. Simmons (1945) provides many useful examples. See also the works cited in my Introduction, note 4.
6. Loraux (1975); Wiedemann (1989) 19–20.
7. E.g., Homer *Iliad* 15.660–66, 18.514–15; Thucydides 2.6; Xenophon *Anab.* 5.3.1, 7.4.5, *Hell.* 6.5.12, 7.1.30; Demosthenes 19.65; Lycurgus *in Leocr.* 39–40; Caesar *Bell. Gall.* 1.29.1; Strabo 6.3.3.279; Vergil *Aen.*

5.715, 12.131–32 (cf. Elftmann 1979, Martina 1988). For representations in Roman monumental art, note Wiedemann (1989) 20.

8. Sallust *Hist.* 4.21M; cf. Homer *Iliad* 22.71–76; Diodorus Siculus 14.74.1–2; Seneca *Controv.* 8.5; Petronius *Satyr.* 124.286; Tacitus *Germ.* 31; Plutarch *Phoc.* 24; Achilles Tatius 4.13.

9. E.g., Caesar *Bell. Civ.* 2.4 ("omnium seniorum, matrum familiae, virginum"); Diodorus Siculus 20.72.2; Livy 26.25.11 (the people of Acarnania in 211 B.C.: wives, children, and *seniores* over the age of 60 [*sic*— cf. Chapter 1] are evacuated; males aged 15–59 stay to fight); Seneca *Controv.* 10.4.14 (*mulier, senex,* and *pauper;* see my Introduction); Tacitus *Hist.* 3.33 (elderly men and women at the destruction of Cremona, of no value as booty), 4.52 ("innoxios pueros, inlustris senes, conspicuas feminas," *Ann.* 14.32; Phlegon *Mirab.* 2, *FGH* 257 F 36.2.9 (women, infant children, and the very old, τοὺς ὑπέργηρως, are taken to places of safety in a time of danger); Philostratus *Vit. Apoll.* 1.15.19. It was apparently proverbial (see *Suda* **M** 973 with Adler's notes) that "it is a waste of time to do a favor for an old man, a child, a woman, a neighbour's dog, a sleepy helmsman, or a chattering rower."

10. Quintilian *Inst. Or.* 4.1.13 and note also 6.1.24 with reference to *aetas;* Plato *Apol.* 34c–d; cf., e.g., Cicero *pro Cael.* 32.79–80, stressing the *senectus* of Caelius's father, and *Orator* 37.130–38.132 for Cicero's self-confessed skill at such appeals to pity (*miserationes*).

11. Livy 2.23 (cf. Saller 1994: 141). Note also Lucan 2.104–7. Plutarch *Tit. Flam.* 21.1 highlights the shame incurred by Titus in killing the aged Hannibal. In the early third-century A.D. work *Passio Perpetuae* (ch. 6), Perpetua's gray-haired father is publicly beaten with rods: "sic dolui pro senecta eius misera" (it is perhaps ironic that in the previous chapter Perpetua's father had begged her: "miserere, filia, canis meis"; cf. also 9: "ego dolebam pro infelici senecta eius").

12. Hesiod frag. 321 M-W; Aristophanes of Byzantium frag. 358 Slater; Apostolius 7.90 (*CPG* 2.419). Contrast Euripides *Melanipp.* frag. 508 (= Stobaeus *Flor.* 50.1.12) where, perhaps more conventionally, advice—a recurring feature, as we have seen—is assigned to older people; likewise *Appendix Proverbi* 4.6 (*CPG* 1.436 = *Suda* N 263): νέοις μὲν ἔργα, βουλὰς δὲ γεραιτέροις, and Pindar frag. 199 Snell *ap.* Plutarch *Mor.* 789e and *Lyc.* 21.6. Note too one of the maxims of the Delphic canon: παῖς ὢν κόσμιος ἴσθι, ἡβῶν ἐγκρατής, μέσος δίκαιος, πρεσβύτης εὔλογος, τελευτῶν ἄλυπος (Stobaeus *Ecl.* 3.1.173 [W-H p. 128.8–9], and see Robert 1968: 424- 26 for a third-century B.C. copy in Afghanistan [Aï-Khanum on the Oxus], said to have been dedicated by Clearchus). The proverb was also parodied, assigning πορδαί to older people: Strabo 14.5.14.675; Macarius 4.11 (*CPG* 2.167).

13. Though compare Chapter 3 note 92. For one particularly pathetic situ-

ation—the evacuation of Athens in 480 B.C. means the abandonment both of old people and of household pets—see Plutarch *Them.* 10.

14. *Amores* 1.9.4. Much earlier and much more poetic, but with the same pitiable force: Aeschylus *Agam.* 72–82. Cf. Ovid *Fasti* 5.59; Livy 6.23.4– 7; Tacitus *Ann.* 1.17–18, 34–35; also 3.43 (A.D. 21, trouble in Gaul: "Varro invalidus senecta vigenti Silio concessit," a telling juxtaposition between C. Visellius Varro, *cos. suff.* A.D. 12, and C. Silius, *cos. ord.* A.D. 13). On the upper age limit originally imposed for Roman military service (46–50 years), see Chapter 4. Of course, examples can be cited of old soldiers: e.g., from Rome *CIL* 6.33033, a centurion who died after 55 years of service and 85 years of life; and 6.2534 (= *ILS* 2050), a soldier who served twice and lived to be 80 years of age. See Birley (1988) 219–20 for long-serving centurions (twenty-one cases of 40 years or more service; the maximum is 61 years), and also 148–51 on equestrian officers and their ages; cf. also Dobson (1974) 411. The rugged Rutilians of every age fight: "canitiem galea premimus" (Vergil *Aen.* 9.612); Elizabeth Baynham has reminded me too of the Macedonian Silvershields, many of whom, in the years immediately following Alexander's death, "were 70 years of age, and none was younger than 60" (Plutarch *Eum.* 16.4; cf. Diodorus Siculus 19.30.6, 19.41.2: some were even older than 70). According to Suetonius *Tib.* 48, Tiberius saved money by refusing to discharge old soldiers; cf. Tacitus *Ann.* 1.80 for Tiberius's prolonging provincial governorships, keeping the same men till death, and note also SHA *Hadr.* 10.8.

15. E.g., Homer *Iliad* 4.321–23 (with 310), 2.370–71, 3.150–51, 11.667– 69, and for Nestor cf. also Cicero *de Sen.* 10.31, Juncus *ap.* Stobaeus *Flor.* 50.3.95 [W-H p. 1064], Apuleius *Soc.* 17, Diogenes of Oenoanda frag. 142 Smith. Curtius (1953) 170–72 is thought-provoking in this context; see also Silk (1995) on the characterization of Nestor through language, and Dickson (1995) 10–20 on "a typology of elders." More generally, note also, e.g., Plato *Rep.* 6.498b–c and SHA *Sev. Alex.* 16.3 (quoted in Chapter 4), as well as a variety of remarks by Cicero and Plutarch (as seen in Chapter 3). Sallust *Hist.* 2.87M observes the fact that old people may be keener for peace than are the young—and the latter, he goes on to note, may win out (2.92M). As well as military advisers, older people might hold themselves to be of value as general teachers and role models for the young; cf. Chapter 3 note 18; Eyben (1972b).

16. *Pol.* 3.1275a14–22 (tr. R. Robinson). Cf. Roussel (1942) 123–24; Mossé (1967); Whitehead (1991) 138. Aristotle concludes (3.1275b18–20) by defining a citizen as "whoever has a right to take part in deliberative and judicial office." Note also *Pol.* 4.1297b12–16: "In some places the political community consists not only of those who carry heavy arms but also of those who have done so. This was so among the Maleans, but they chose the officers (τὰς ἀρχὰς) from the active soldiers."

17. Stobaeus *Flor.* 50.2.85 [W-H p. 1051.3–14]; presumably the passage is anachronistic. Cf. Chapter 3, and Roussel (1942) 129–30. For the argument that the role of the young need not be confined solely to warfare (even in Sparta) but may also extend to politics, note already Isocrates 6.3–5.
18. E.g., Caesar *Bell. Gall.* 7.77.12, 7.78.1 ("aetate inutiles bello"); Vergil *Aen.* 2.509–10, the aged Priam and his useless sword ("arma diu senior desueta"); Martial 11.69.7; *Anthologia Latina* 929.1 ("utilis es nulli, cunctis ingrata, senectus"); Maximianus *Eleg.* 1.111; cf. Ovid *Met.* 10.396.
19. Cicero *pro Sest.* 10.24.
20. Herondas *Mim.* 6.54: ἦν μέν κοτ', ἦν τις, ἀλλὰ νῦν γεγήρακε; Cicero *ad Fam.* 7.3.4 (46 B.C.): "vetus est enim, ubi non sis qui fueris, non esse cur velis vivere"; Maximianus *Eleg.* 1.5: "non sum qui fueram: periit pars maxima nostri." Note that phrases of the type "I am not the person I was" were also used of the dead, as in *CLE* 1559.15 = *CIL* 6.13528.15, and cf. Ovid *Trist.* 3.11.25. See also Seneca *Controv.* 10.5.17, where one defense suggested for Parrhasius's torturing and killing an old slave as a model for a painting of Prometheus (see Chapter 8 note 70) is that the old slave was useless and was about to die anyway: "senem inutilem, expiraturum; si verum, inquit, vultis, non occidit illum, sed deficientis et alioqui expiraturi morte usus est." For the logic compare also Galen *de Caus. Procat.* 11.150 (*CMG* Suppl. 2.38). Publilius Syrus *Sent.* 360W puts it quite concisely: "mors infanti felix, iuveni acerba, nimis sera est seni" (cf. Chapter 2 note 30).
21. Cicero *de Sen.* 3.7, 8.25, 18.65. Cf. also, e.g., Lucian *Dial. Mort.* 6.2; Musonius Rufus 17 (Stobaeus *Flor.* 50.3.94 [W-H p. 1058]).
22. Maximianus *Eleg.* 1.281–88; cf. 1.55 for "miseranda senectus."
23. Cicero *pro Sest.* 52.111 (note also Pliny *Ep.* 1.14: an *adulescens/iuvenis* a year or two younger than Pliny reveres Pliny "ut senem"); Pliny *Ep.* 5.16.2 (cf. *CIL* 6.16631 = *ILS* 1030: "d. m. Miniciae Marcellae Fundani f. v. a. xii m. xi d. vii"); *GVI* 591; *CLE* 1388.6 (= *CIL* 6.8401, A.D. 577); Ausonius *Epigr.* 13 Green (cf. Ausonius *Epigr.* 14.2, "casta puella anus est," and contrast [Ausonius] *Mor. Var.* 41–42 [Green p. 676]: "grata senectus homini, quae parilis iuventae: illa iuventa est gravior, quae similis senectae"). Note also *CIL* 5.532 = *ILS* 6680 (Tergeste, reign of Antoninus Pius), 1.12–14, of L. Fabius Severus (*PIR*² F 66; *RE* 6.1868): "quamvis admodum adulescens senilibus tamen et perfectis operibus ac factis patriam suam nosque insuper sibi universos obstrinxerit." See esp. Gnilka (1972), with Curtius (1953) 98–105: Gnilka shows that the roots of the motif may be traced back as early as classical Greek times; note also Eyben (1973a) 237–38; Carp (1980); Burrow (1986), esp. ch. 3; Giannarelli (1988); Wiedemann (1989); Kleijwegt (1991) 125–31. Saints also not uncommonly die young (or else live to an extremely ripe old age); or as Martial (6.29.7) put it, "immodicis brevis est aetas et rara

senectus." Cato the Censor (*ap.* Pliny *NH* 7.51.171) declared that "senilem iuventam praematurae mortis esse signum"; cf. Quintilian *Inst. Or.* 6.pr.10; Seneca *Cons. ad Marc.* 23.3–5. Cicero has Cato aver that "nec enim umquam sum adsensus veteri illi laudatoque proverbio [otherwise unknown!: Otto 1890: no. 1626], quod monet mature fieri senem si diu velis senex esse; ego vero me minus diu senem esse mallem, quam esse senem antequam essem" (*de Sen.* 10.32). Cf. also Apuleius *Apol.* 85 on the negative image of a young man acting prematurely old ("viridi pueritia, cana malitia").

24. See Chapter 3. For the old women of Greece, see also Bremmer (1983a: 111; 1987); Henderson (1987); Just (1989) 112–13.

25. [Demosthenes] 43.62; cf. Lysias 1.15; Callimachus *Hymn* 6.124–30; Pausanias 2.35.7–8; *Homeric Hymn to Demeter* 101–2 (but see now also Pratt 2000); and Lefkowitz (1986) 44–45, 59, 125–26, for the comparative freedom of old women especially in religious contexts.

26. Garland (1990) 62; Cosminsky (1976) 231; Gélis (1991) 104–5. Plato's Socrates assumes it as common knowledge that midwives are beyond child-bearing age (*Theaet.* 149b). Soranus seems more concerned, on the other hand, with the midwife's physical and mental capacities than with her age; see further French (1986) sec. 2. Of the 16 *opstetrices* mentioned in *CIL* 6 (and not necessarily typical of their profession), only four have age at death recorded: 21 years (*CIL* 6.9723), 30 (6647), 31 (9724), and 75 (9720). For one example from Greek literature of an aged (and nefarious) midwife, see Aristophanes *Thesm.* 502–16; and from Roman law, *Dig.* 37.10.3.5 (Ulpian).

27. Lacey (1968) 117, 175; Schaps (1979) 41; Dixon (1988) 176–79, 228. See also Chapter 8 note 39 for further discussion and references.

28. See in similar vein Bremmer (1987) 206 (and note also Linton 1942: 594 for the formulation of the general sociological theory), and contrast with this the views of van Hooff (1983) and of Houdijk and Vanderbroeck (1987), who do not regard the elderly woman (or man) as marginalized at all. Of course, such freedom, whatever its negative sociological implications, might have been welcomed by an older woman. It is also perhaps worth remarking, somewhat contrary to what I have just been saying, that the virulence of some of the stereotypical images of elderly women in literature might suggest something more sinister than "minimal interest." For loss of esteem for women with increasing age, note also Xenophon *Oecon.* 7.42–43 (with Pomeroy *ad loc.*). See further Dean-Jones (1994) 108, who believes that the greater authority enjoyed by older Greek women in the classical world would have led to fewer menopausal disorders than women in the modern Western world experience. Whatever the truth of that, it is also worth remarking that in old age, with the loss of reproductive powers, the sharp distinctions typically drawn in antiquity between male and female might have been somewhat eroded.

29. *Amores* 1.8.113–14; see Chapter 3 note 119. According to Philostratus *Vit. Soph.* 2.18.599, εὔχομαί σοι γηρᾶσαι was a curse that all women shuddered at most anyway! The same author (*Vit. Soph.* 1.21.519) also indicates that the diminutive γραίδιον could be used as a term of abuse directed against men; in fact, to dream of a γραῦς was to foretell one's own death through sickness, because she "is a symbol of a corpse being carried out for burial": Artemidorus *Oneirocrit.* 5.40. It is of some related interest, perhaps, that γραῦς could also mean the scum on top of heated liquids—see *LSJ⁹* new suppl. s.v.; so could σῦφαρ (on which see Appendix C).

30. For brief but useful surveys of the history of "geriatric medicine" in the premodern period, cf. Steudel (1942), Grmek (1957; 1958: esp. 50–58), Lüth (1965), Demaitre (1990), Godderis (1998), Eckart (2000). One sociohistorical study that I have found particularly useful for comparative purposes in this context is Haber (1983) ch. 3. More specifically on the Greek literature, esp. the Hippocratic corpus, note Byl (1983, 1988b), Gnilka (1983) 1030–32, Corvisier (1985a) 146, Godderis (1989), Pisi (1995), Mazzini (1995). Zeman (1942–50) offers a series of papers surveying the medical history of old age, but on classical antiquity is very sketchy (particularly on the Roman material) and discusses much nonmedical evidence as well. Perhaps not surprisingly, the young have been rather better served: for the Roman context, see esp. Étienne (1976) and Bertier (1996), and note now Hummel (1999).

31. Aristotle *de Gen. An.* 5.4.784b32–34 (ὀρθῶς δ᾽ ἔχει καὶ λέγειν τὴν μὲν νόσον γῆρας ἐπίκτητον, τὸ δὲ γῆρας νόσον φυσικήν· ποιοῦσι γοῦν νόσοι τινὲς ταὐτὰ ἅπερ καὶ τὸ γῆρας); Democritus 296 D-K (quoted in note 44); Terence *Phorm.* 575 ("senectus ipsa morbus est"—Donatus in his commentary *ad loc.* quotes the comic poet Apollodorus of Carystus frag. 20: τὸ γῆράς ἐστιν αὐτὸ <νόσημα>); Cicero *de Sen.* 11.35 (with Powell 1988: 174); Vergil *Aen.* 6.275 (cf. *Georg.* 3.67); Pliny *NH* 7.50.169; Seneca *Ep.* 108.28 ("*insanabilis* morbus"); Juncus *ap.* Stobaeus *Flor.* 50.2.85 (W-H p. 1050.18–20); Philo *Abr.* 182 (ἡ μακρὰ καὶ ἀνίατος νόσος, τὸ γῆρας). Note also Cicero *Timaeus* 5.16–17 (≈ Plato 32–33a), where *morbus* and *senectus* are referred to in conjunction several times; similarly Pliny *NH* 11.94.231.

32. Cf. Aristotle *de Respir.* 17.479a; Cicero *de Sen.* 2.5, 19.71; and see Chapter 2, esp. note 30.

33. Galen *de San. Tuenda* 1.5.32–34 (6.20–21K = *CMG* 5.4.2.11: τὸν μὲν γὰρ τοιοῦτον ἐν νόσῳ τινὶ φήσομεν ὑπάρχειν, εἴπερ μὴ διὰ γῆρας ταῦτα πάσχοι· καίτοι καὶ τοῦτο νόσον εἶναι λέγουσιν ἔνιοι. τοὺς δ᾽ ἄλλους ἅπαντας, οἷς φύσει μήτ᾽ ὀξὺ βλέπειν μήτ᾽ ἀκούειν ὑπάρχει μήτε θέειν ὠκέως ἤ τι τοιοῦτον ἕτερον ἐνεργεῖν ἰσχυρῶς, οὔτε νοσεῖν οὔθ᾽ ὅλως παρὰ φύσιν ἔχειν ὑποληψόμεθα. πᾶσαι μὲν γὰρ αἱ νόσοι παρὰ φύσιν, οὐκ ἔχουσι δ᾽ οἱ τοιοῦτοι παρὰ φύσιν, ὥσπερ οὐδ᾽

417

οἱ γέροντες). See also *de San. Tuenda* 6.2 (6.388K = *CMG* 5.4.2.171), *Ars Med.* 21 (1.359K), and *de Marc.* 2, 4 (7.669, 680–1K). On modern theories, see Birren and Bengtson (1988) pt. 2, and Moody (1998) 82–88, 363–71; for the enduring assumption that old age is a disease, see, e.g., Sankar (1984).

34. Galen *de Marc.* 5 (7.681–82K), and note also *de Meth. Med.* 10.10 (10.721K) and *de San. Tuenda* 5.4, 6.2 (6.330, 389K = *CMG* 5.4.2.142, 171). Cf. Byl (1988b) 86–87. On the inescapable and incurable *marasmus* (or *marcor*) *senilis*, see *de Marc.* 1 (7.666K), and also von Kondratowitz (1991) 151–57 and Skoda (1994), esp. 116–17. Internal evidence indicates that the *de Marcore* was composed while Galen was writing the *de Sanitate Tuenda*.

35. On age as a factor in the treatment of patients, according to the Hippocratic corpus, cf. Lloyd (1983) 64 n. 12, Byl (1983) 85, and King (1998) 70–74. Contrast the Methodist school (Edelstein 1967: 180), though a similar regimen of health seems to have been recommended by, e.g., Asclepiades of Bithynia in the first century B.C. The Hippocratic author (*Aph.* 2.39, 4.480–82L) makes the observation that οἱ πρεσβῦται τῶν νέων τὰ μὲν πολλὰ νοσέουσιν ἧσσον· ὅσα δ᾽ ἂν αὐτοῖσι χρόνια νοσήματα γένηται, τὰ πολλὰ ξυναποθνῄσκει. Compare similarly Cicero *de Sen.* 19.67; Celsus *de Med.* 2.1.5, 5.26.6; Galen *in Hipp. Epid. 6 Comm.* 5.6 (17B.253 = *CMG* 5.10.2.2.274); Pliny *NH* 7.50.170. Presumably immunity to infection is built up if one survives.

36. I have omitted duplicate cases. Corvisier (1985a: 145; 1985b: 68) carried out a similar survey but came up with different, lower figures (in fact, his own figures differ in each case). For the use of the *Epidemics* as a statistical source, see Demand (1994). While some work has been done in recent years on the prosopography of the Hippocratic patients, there has been no significant analysis of their ages.

37. The not infrequent παῖς is ambiguous: slave or child? A παιδίσκη has a child (μειράκιον), 7.105 (5.456L); παῖς and παιδίον are used for the same individual, 5.100 and 7.113 (5.256, 460L); a παιδίον speaks, 7.117, 118 (5.462–64L). Hence I tend to favor "slave" in most cases; cf. Kudlien (1968) ch. 2. Also ambiguous is the comparative ἀφηλικέστερος, used at 7.101 (5.454L) of a woman; it probably means "fairly old" rather than "fairly young," if one may judge—quite likely one cannot—from its two other appearances in the Hippocratic corpus (*de Morb.* 1.22 [6.186L], of a man; *de Morb. Mul.* 2.120 [8.262L], of women).

38. Sixty-year-old patients are also mentioned at 3.2.4 (3.68L). It is worth remarking that age terms feature most frequently in books 5 and 7; these two books, perhaps by the same author, are now usually regarded as the latest in chronological order of the seven books. In reading the case studies, one must be careful not to make too many assumptions: *Epid.* 2.2.17

(5.90L) describes a woman as having lived many years (πολλὰ ἔτεα) but also mentions that she has just become pregnant (Littré takes it to mean that the woman's ailment, strangury, lasted many years, but this is clearly wrong, as the context alone shows).

39. Alexander of Tralles *de Febr.* 4, περὶ μαρασμοῦ (Puschmann 1.369); for similarly ruthless advice to doctors in another context, see Hippocrates *de Fract.* 36 (3.540L). Grmek (1958) 55–56 commented that such an attitude "has been fatal to the development of geriatrics. Unfortunately, it is not peculiar to the medical history of the past, but is a persisting attitude even of a number of physicians of our day."

40. Plutarch *Mor.* 136e26, 794b; cf. Tacitus *Ann.* 6.46. One is perhaps reminded in this context of the Tiberian *senatus consultum Persicianum,* mentioned in Chapter 7 and discussed further in Parkin (2001).

41. Galen *de San. Tuenda* 1.12 (6.63K = *CMG* 5.4.2.29).

42. Celsus *de Med.* pr.5.

43. On Zerbi's work, see Lind (1988), with Steudel (1942) 10; Grmek (1958) 59–61; Demaitre (1990) 6–7; and Godderis (1998). For the influence of Jupiter and Saturn, see esp. *Gerontocomia* chs. 1–4, 7, 9; also 16, on when to cut an elderly patient's fingernails (Wednesday) and toenails. The quotation on diet is from ch. 17. Unfortunately, Zerbi's Latin text has never been republished; I must rely on Lind's translation.

44. *Mor.* 791d; cf. Democritus 296 D-K: γῆρας ὁλόκληρός ἐστι πήρωσις· πάντ᾽ ἔχει καὶ πᾶσιν ἐνδεῖ.

45. Cicero *de Sen.* 11.36 (cf. 19.71) and Galen *de Marc.* 3 (7.673–75K; cf. *de Temp.* 3.2 [1.660K], *in Hipp. Aph.* 1.13, 14 [17B.403, 413]) use the effective image of a lamp that is running out of oil, on which see also Niebyl (1971), and cf. Aristotle *de Iuv. et Sen.* 5.469b and [Aristotle] *Probl.* 3.5.871b. Thus was the passing-away of the aged fisherman in *Anthologia Palatina* 7.295 (Leonidas of Tarentum). On the warm, moist child, see Bertier (1996), esp. 2164–75, and Hummel (1999) 98–100.

46. See Chapter 3 note 110.

47. As Galen notes, *de Temp.* 1.3 (1.522K). For Aristotle, see, e.g., *de Long. et Brev. Vit.* 5.466a (cold and dry); *de Iuv. et Sen.* 5.469b (cold); *de Respir.* 17–18.479a–b (cold); *de Gen. An.* 5.3.783b6–8, 5.4.784a30–34 (cold and dry); *Rhet.* 2.13.1389b29–32 (cold; see Chapter 3), *de Part. Anim.* 2.2.648b5; [Aristotle] *Probl.* 3.5.871a–b, 3.26.875a, 30.1.955a. Note already in the fifth century Hippon 38 A 11 D-K (dry). See further Egerton (1975) 309–10, and, more generally, Onians (1954) 214–21; Grmek (1958) 8–22; Eyben (1972a) 678–82 (an excellent introduction to, inter alia, the theory of the humors; note also Schöner 1964: esp. 86–93); Byl (1988b); and esp. Althoff (1992), a detailed analysis which is sensitive to the complexities inherent in Aristotle's treatment in various works. Note now also King (2001).

48. Among innumerable references to old age being cold and dry, note *de*

Temp. 2.2 (1.579–82K); *Quod Animi Mores Corp. Temp. Seq.* 5, 10 (4.786, 810); *de Plac. Hipp. et Plat.* 8.7 (cold; 5.703–4K = *CMG* 5.4.1.2.524); *de Marc.* 3, 4 (7.672, 679–80); *de Meth. Med.* 10.10 (10.721); *in Hipp. de Sal. Vict. Rat.* 7 (15.186–90K = *CMG* 5.9.1.94–96), *in Hipp. de Acut. Morb. Vict.* 22[25] (15.777K = *CMG* 5.9.1.293); *in Hipp. Aph.* 1.14 (17B.412–14), 3.18 (cold; 17B.613), 3.31 (17B.650); *adv. Lyc.* 7 (18A.239K = *CMG* 5.10.3.26); and extensively in his *de San. Tuenda,* such as 1.2 (dry; 6.6K = *CMG* 5.4.2.5; cf. *de Prop. Plac.* 7.3 [*CMG* 5.3.2.78]), and esp. in book 5 (6.319–20, 349–50, 357–58, 374K = *CMG* 5.4.2: 141, 151, 154, 165). Note also [Galen] *in Hipp. de Alim.* 11 (15.295K): old age is corruption, ἡ φθορά, through a drying-out process.

49. Hippocrates *de Victu* 1.33 (6.512L), *de Nat. Hom.* 17 = *de Salubr.* 2 (6.74L); cf. Lloyd (1964: 101, 103; 1966: 45, 60 n. 1). That old age is cold is frequently noted in the Hippocratic corpus: e.g., *Aph.* 1.14 (4.466L: γέρουσι δὲ ὀλίγον τὸ θερμόν), *de Victu* 1.25, 2.63 (6.498, 578). That older women are dry and with little blood is stated at *de Nat. Mul.* 1 (7.312L) and *de Morb. Mul.* 2.111 (8.238–40L).

50. Galen *de Temp.* 2.2 (1.580–82K); *de San. Tuenda* 5.8, 6.3 (6.349–51, 396–97K = *CMG* 5.4.2.151, 174); *de Sympt. Caus.* 3.10 (7.259K); *de Marc.* 3, 4 (7.672, 679–80); *de Simp. Med. Temp. ac Fac.* 1.8 (11.295–96K); *in Hipp. de Sal. Vict. Rat.* 7 (15.186–90 = *CMG* 5.9.1.94–96); note also *de Prop. Plac.* 5.6 (*CMG* 5.3.2.70). As for pseudo-Galenic works, note *Def. Med.* 107 (19.375K) and *in Hipp. de Humor.* 1.11 (16.101K) for the same counterargument, but contrast *Def. Med.* 104 (19.374K) and *de Humor.* (19.489K), where old age is said to be cold and humid. The image of a cold and humid old age remained popular in medieval depictions of the four ages: Burrow (1986) ch. 1.

51. See Chapter 3 on Juvenal 10.199 for medical references; cf. also Hippocrates *Aph.* 2.40 (4.482L), Macrobius *Sat.* 7.10.7–8, and Oribasius *Lib. Inc.* 3.6–8, 62.46 (*CMG* 6.2.2.77, 171). On the strong presence of the cold (and moist) *humor* phlegm—bringing sluggishness and forgetfulness—in old age, see Galen *de Temp.* 2.2 (1.580K), and cf. [Galen] *Def. Med.* 104 (19.374K) and *de Humor.* (19.489K): ἔστι δὲ καὶ τῷ γέροντι φλέγμα. νωθρὰ ἡλικία αὐτὴ καὶ ληθαργικὴ καὶ κωματώδης (followed by Bede *de Temp. Rat.* 35 [*PL* 90.459 = *CCSL* 123B.392–93]: "phlegmata dominantur in senibus. . . . phlegmata tardos, somnolentos, obliviosos generant"). The cold and dry *humor,* black bile, makes old age melancholic (cf. Celsus *de Med.* 3.18.17–18).

52. E.g., Juvenal 6.325: "iam frigidus aevo"; cf. *TLL* 6.1326.75–83, 1729.24–30 (*frigidus, gelidus*), and my Chapter 3.

53. Plautus *Mil.* 640–41 ("et ego amoris aliquantum habeo umorisque etiam in corpore | neque dum exarui ex amoenis rebus et voluptariis"); Accius frag. 56 ("quamquam exanguest corpus mi atque annis putret"); Cicero

de Sen. 10.34 (cf. Powell 1988: 172); Tacitus *Germ.* 31; Lucan 1.343; Statius *Theb.* 11.323; Seneca *Controv.* 8.5; Plutarch *Mor.* 450f; Valerius Maximus 3.8.5 ("exiguum senilemque sanguinem"); Juvenal 10.217–18, 11.5–6; Maximianus *Eleg.* 1.133–34. On a more scientific level, note Aristotle *Hist. An.* 3.19.521a; Hippocrates *de Morb. Sacr.* 9 (6.378L), *de Nat. Mul.* 1 (7.312L), *de Morb. Mul.* 2.111 (8.240L); Galen *de Temp.* 2.2 (1.582K); *Quod Animi Mores Corp. Temp. Seq.* 10 (4.810); *de Cur. Rat. Ven. Sect.* 13 (11.291); *adv. Lyc.* 7 (18A.238K = *CMG* 5.10.3.25–26). With the dryness of old age comes shrinkage: one thinks in particular of the Sibyl of Cumae, as well as of Tithonus.

54. Vergil *Aen.* 5.395–96; Isidorus *Orig.* 11.2.27.
55. Galen *Quod Animi Mores Corp. Temp. Seq.* 5 (4.786–87K); cf. [Aristotle] *Probl.* 30.1.955a: coldness of the brain leads to depression, hence older people are less cheerful and more prone to suicide. See also Chapter 8, esp. the passage quoted from Aretaeus, with Godderis (1989) 59–60.
56. Galen *de San. Tuenda* 6.3 (6.400K = *CMG* 5.4.2.176); contrast Hippocrates *de Victu* 1.32 (6.508–10L), where the opposite conclusion is reached because it is assumed that old age is cold and humid.
57. See Aristotle *de Gen. An.* 4.6.775a; *Hist. An.* 7.1.582a, 7.3.583b; Pliny *NH* 7.4.37, 9.48.89, 16.51.118; Hippocrates *de Oct. Part.* 9 (7.450L); Galen *in Hipp. Epid. 2 Comm.* 3.31 (*CMG* 5.10.1.298); cf. Dean-Jones (1994) 103–5. Aristotle *de Long. et Brev. Vit.* 5.466b (also 6.467a) states that as a rule in the animal kingdom males live longer than females, owing to the fact that the male is warmer than the female. He further observes that men who work hard age more quickly because work brings dryness (contrast Celsus *de Med.* 1.1.1); so, as a rule of nature, does reproduction: cf. Pliny *NH* 9.48.89, 16.51.117–19; Ovid *Ars Amat.* 3.80–82. Note also [Aristotle] *Probl.* 10.48.896a.
58. Particularly common as part of the Pythagorean doctrine of the four ages (mentioned in Chapter 1): Diogenes Laertius 8.10; Diodorus Siculus 10.9.5; Ovid *Met.* 15.199–236 ("senilis hiems," 212); Stobaeus *Flor.* 50.2.78 (Eratosthenes = Favorinus frag. 10 Baragazzi), 50.2.84 (Metrocles); Lucian *Sat.* 9; Hippocrates *de Humor.* 16 (5.496–98L), *de Morb. Sacr.* 10 (6.380L: τοῖσι πρεσβύτησιν ὁ χειμὼν πολεμιώτατός ἐστιν); Celsus *de Med.* 1.9.3–5 ("frigus inimicum est seni. . . . calor autem adiuvat omnia, quae frigus infestat"); Galen *de Plac. Hipp. et Plat.* 8.6 (5.693K = *CMG* 5.4.1.2.516), *in Hipp. de Sal. Vict. Rat.* 7 (15.186K = *CMG* 5.9.1.94–95); *in Hipp. Aph.* 3.18 (17B.612–14K); [Galen] *in Hipp. de Humor.* 1.1, 1.11, 2.38, 3.17 (16.26, 101–2, 345, 424K); Meletius *de Natura Hominis* (Cramer *Anec. Graec.* 3 p. 12), describing older people as cold and wet, like winter. At Hippocrates *Aph.* 3.23 and 31 (4.496, 500–502L), the diseases of old age and of winter coincide. Plutarch *Mor.* 736a, noting that old age is cold and dry, compares it to late autumn. The dangers of winter, but also of the height of summer, for older peo-

ple in Rome are highlighted by Shaw (1996) 119–21; cf. Scheidel (1996a) ch. 4.

59. Hippocrates *Aph.* 3.18 (4.494L; cf. 3.3, 4.486L), *Prorrh.* 2.39, 2.41 (9.68, 70L); Galen *in Hipp. Epid. 6 Comm.* 5.36[35] (17B.308K = *CMG* 5.10.2.2.319), *in Hipp. Aph.* 3.3, 3.18 (17B.567, 612–14K); Celsus *de Med.* 2.1.17. Cf. Aristotle *de Long. et Brev. Vit.* 1.465a.

60. *Probl.* 14.7.909b, 14.9–10.909b; cf. Chapter 2 notes 5 and 43. Hippocrates *de Aer. Aq. Loc.* 4 (2.20L), on the other hand, states that people who live in cities with cold winds live longer because they age more slowly.

61. Galen *de San. Tuenda* 5 (6.305–80K = *CMG* 5.4.2.135–67) and cf. 1.12 (6.62K = *CMG* 5.4.2.29); see also, e.g., Celsus *de Med.* 1.3.32–33; Oribasius *Synop. ad Eustath.* 5.18 (*CMG* 6.3.161), *Libri ad Eunap.* 1.11 (*CMG* 6.3.327–28); Aetius *Lib. Med.* 4.30 (*CMG* 8.1.372–75); Paul of Aegina 1.23 (*CMG* 9.1.19–20). On the subject, see also Orth (1963), and Wöhrle (1990), esp. 235–38 on *de San. Tuenda* 5. In the first century A.D. Rufus of Ephesus wrote on the regimen for old age but the work is not extant (cf. *ANRW* 2.37.2.1097). Compare [Lucian] *Macr.* 5–6 for factors such as diet, soil, climate, and exercise having an effect on longevity, and *Macr.* 18 for philosophers and all those concerned with παιδεία leading long lives, "doubtless because they take good care of themselves"; one is reminded again of Cicero's *de Senectute* (note in this context, e.g., 11.36, and cf. Finley 1981: 161). For the emerging theory, following Galen, of the "six nonnaturals" (air and environment, food and drink, evacuation and repletion, sleep and wakefulness, motion and rest, and passions of the mind) as the basis of regimens for the preservation of health, see García-Ballester (1993).

62. Galen *de San. Tuenda* 5.3 (6.322–23K = *CMG* 5.4.2.155). For exercise delaying the aging process, cf. Cicero *in Cat.* 2.9.20 (one type of Catilinarian adherent, Sulla's old soldiers, "aetate iam adfectum, sed tamen exercitatione robustum"); Aelian frag. 110 Hercher (see Chapter 1 note 42). An old man should not exercise too much (cf. again Cicero *de Sen.* 11.36, with Powell 1988: 174; Celsus *de Med.* 2.14.9; Seneca *Ep.* 83.3–4; see also Chapter 3 note 71), but *no* exercise is also dangerous (Hippocrates *de Artic.* 58 [4.254L]). Zerbi in his *Gerontocomia* devotes several pages to the subject (ch. 16), and has some interesting ideas on exercise for the aged infirm (including being carried in a litter or sitting in a boat) and the bedridden: "[I]f none of these conveyances is possible owing to the exceedingly weak condition of the old man, his bed should be suspended on ropes and moved back and forth. If this also is impossible, a rope should be attached to one leg of his bed and thus he can be pulled about here and there by hand, as Celsus prescribes." Presumably Zerbi has misunderstood *de Med.* 2.15.4, where Celsus means that the old patient should sleep in a hammock or rocker. For reading aloud and

horse-riding as exercises, also recommended by Zerbi, see Celsus *de Med.* 1.2.6, 1.8.1–3, 4.26.5, 4.32.1. For some discussion of ancient evidence regarding exercise in old age, see also Crowther (1990).

63. Cf. Galen *de San. Tuenda* 5.12 (6.373–79K = *CMG* 5.4.2.164–67) and *de Simp. Med. Temp. ac Fac.* 1.8 (11.395K). As to how frequently an aged patient should bathe, Galen gives few details, unlike Gabriele Zerbi (*Gerontocomia* ch. 16, elaborating on *de San. Tuenda* 5.12): "For those old people not completely decrepit a bath is necessary three or four times a month on account of the little exercise they take. Baths may be taken over a more extended period and thus less frequently by old men in their prime. For the weak and prostrate bathing is strictly forbidden." Presumably the Roman elderly who had ready access to the baths washed more frequently. Note Pliny *NH* 29.5.10 for the remarkable sight of "senes consulares" in cold baths, and cf. Seneca *Ep.* 53.3 and 83.5.

64. Galen *de Cur. Rat. Ven. Sect.* 13 (11.291K), while warning that a phlebotomy may be dangerous in the weakened state of old age (cf. Hippocrates *de Vict. Acut. (Spur.)* 2 [2.398L]; Galen *de Sect. ad Ingr.* 8 [1.89K], *de Meth. Med.* 8.4 [10.565], *ad Glauc. de Meth. Med.* 1.15 [11.46], *in Hipp. de Acut. Morb. Vict.* 17[19] [15.764K = *CMG* 5.9.1.287]), states that even a 70-year-old man, if he is robust enough, may be blood-let; likewise Celsus *de Med.* 2.10.1–4. See further Brain (1986), esp. 131.

65. E.g., Galen *de San. Tuenda* 5.6 (6.339–40K = *CMG* 5.4.2.147), where it is also noted that dried foods are preferable to fresh. On the benefits of cheese, however, note Pliny *NH* 11.97.242. Lean meat, especially young goat's flesh, is useful, apart from pork. Pliny *NH* 8.50.119 records that "quasdam modo principes feminas" ate venison every morning and suffered no fevers "longo aevo." Fish is generally good, as are some types of soft bread. Cf. also Galen *de Alim. Fac.* 1.2, 3.30 (6.485, 726K = *CMG* 5.4.2.219, 371–72). It was also noted in antiquity that as a rule old people need little food: see Chapter 3 note 108, with Eyben (1972a) 686.

66. This problem with milk is allegedly solved if honey is added: Galen *de Alim. Fac.* 3.15[14] (6.683K = *CMG* 5.4.2.346); but see also *de Marc.* 9 (7.701K) for the beneficial effects for an old man of milk drunk straight from a woman's breast (and note Herodotus 3.23; cf. Pliny *NH* 28.21.72–75 and Grmek 1958: 46) or, failing that, of warm donkey's milk. Galen *de San. Tuenda* 5.7 (6.343–44K = *CMG* 5.4.2.148) mentions the instance of one old farmer who survived beyond his 100th year thanks to goat's milk mixed with honey. For the benefits of honey for elderly individuals, since it produces blood (it is not beneficial for the young, since in their case it produces bile), see Galen *de Nat. Fac.* 2.8 (2.124K), *de Alim. Fac.* 3.39 (6.742K = *CMG* 5.4.2.381), *de Bon. et Mal. Alim. Suc.* 12 (6.809K = *CMG* 5.4.2.426).

67. On wine being good for older people, see Plato *Laws* 2.666b (wine, the gift of Dionysus, as an effective medicine [φάρμακον] against the crab-

bedness, αὐστηρότης, of old age); Galen *Quod Animi Mores Corp. Temp. Seq.* 10 (4.809–10K), citing Plato; much detail in *de San. Tuenda* 5.3, 5.5 (6.319, 334–38K = *CMG* 5.4.2.141, 144–46; some wines, however, are not suitable: 6.338K = *CMG* 5.4.2.146); Rufus *de Podagra* 13; Aristeides *Orat.* 41.7. Nor is excess recommended. Aristotle (*ap.* Athenaeus *Deipn.* 10.429c and Macrobius *Sat.* 7.6.15–21; cf. *de Anim.* 1.408b18–29) comments on the deleterious effect of too much wine on older people (because they are dry); noting the similarity of symptoms of old age and of drunkenness (cf. [Aristotle] *Probl.* 3.26.874b–75a, and my Chapter 3 on Juvenal 10.198), Aristotle *ap.* Macrobius remarks that drunk old men display double the negative effects; cf. Pliny *NH* 14.28.142; John Chrysostom *in Epist. ad Titum* 2.4.1 (*PG* 62.682–83). For a useful survey of the use of wine in Greek medicine, see Jouanna (1996), esp. 419–20.

68. For old men, wine, and dancing, note *Anacreontea* 39, 47; Aristophanes *Wasps* 1476- 81; also, of course, Teiresias and Cadmus in Euripides' *Bacch.* (188–89: ἐπιλελήσμεθ' ἡδέως | γέροντες ὄντες). For rejuvenation through wine, cf. Petronius frag. 21 (cited Chapter 3 note 121). For the proverb, see Athenaeus *Deipn.* 4.134c, 10.428a. On an old man dancing as a good omen ("salva res est, saltat senex"), incidentally, see Festus 436–38L (for *cantat* read *saltat*); Servius *ad Aen.* 3.279, 8.110; *Mythographus Vaticanus* 3.6.30 (*Scriptores Rerum Mythicarum Latini* 1.192–93); Otto (1890) no. 1628; Néraudau (1979) 348–50. Might this have something to do with the *Salii* (cf. Chapter 4 note 8)?

69. Pliny *NH* 14.8.60 ("Iulia Augusta LXXXII [*sic;* conventionally amended to read LXXXVI, the age at which Dio 58.2.1 says she died; this is probably right, but other possibilities exist: did Livia know how old she was? did Pliny? did Livia intentionally underestimate her own age? does the statement belong to A.D. 25? had Livia forgotten how old she was?!] annos vitae Pucino vino rettulit acceptos"), 22.53.114 ("multi senectam longam mulsi tantum intrita toleravere, neque alio ullo cibo").

70. *CIL* 14.914 = *CLE* 1318.

71. Cervilla et al. (2000). On Calment and the veracity (or otherwise) of claims of extreme longevity in history, see most recently Jeune and Vaupel (1995, 1999)

72. Hippocrates *Aph.* 3.31 (4.500–502L; note Galen's commentary *ad loc.,* 17B.648–51K, and also *de Plac. Hipp. et Plat.* 8.6 [5.696K = *CMG* 5.4.1.2.518]); Celsus *de Med.* 2.1.22 (tr. W. G. Spencer). Cf. also Galen *de Temp.* 2.2 (1.582K), *in Hipp. Epid. 6 Comm.* 3.1 (17B.5–6 = *CMG* 5.10.2.2.126).

73. See esp. Galen *de San. Tuenda* 6.2 (6.388–89K = *CMG* 5.4.2.171) and *de Temp.* 2.2 (1.582K). For the weak, slow pulse of older people, see Galen *de Marc.* 5 (7.685K), *de Puls.* 9 (8.464), *de Dig. Puls.* 2.3 (8.869), *de Caus. Puls.* 3.5 (9.118–25), *de Praes. ex Puls.* 2.4 (9.283); [Galen?]

Syn. de Puls. 15 (9.472); [Galen] *de Puls. ad Ant.* (19.635K); and cf. von Staden (1989) 280–81, 349–60 on Herophilus.

74. Celsus *de Med.* 5.26.31c, 7.26.1 (and cf. Maximianus *Eleg.* 1.170 on prostate problems). It is also startlingly unpleasant to note that, according to Pliny *NH* 28.13.52, scrapings from the walls of the gymnasia, said to have great warming properties, were applied as ointments "ulceribus senum puerorumque"; for other remedies for such *ulcera senilia,* see 22.23.48, 26.87.141–44, 31.47.126, 34.53.174.

75. Aristotle *de Gen. An.* 5.1.780a17–20, 31–33; Hippocrates *Epid.* 4.30 (5.174L); Galen *de Usu Part.* 10.5 (3.783–85K), *de Sympt. Caus.* 1.2 (7.100–101K), in *Hipp. Epid. 1 Comm.* 2.59 (17A.159K = *CMG* 5.10.1.81), in *Hipp. Epid. 6 Comm.* 1.26, 3.1 (17A.869, 17B.5K = *CMG* 5.10.2.2.42, 126); Celsus *de Med.* 6.6.32, 7.7.14b; Maximianus *Eleg.* 1.147–48. For the wider context, see Brothwell and Sandison (1967) 457–63 and Jackson (1996). To have survived to the age of 80 years with eyes undimmed was worthy of special mention: *GVI* 1379 (second or third century A.D.). On loss of vision through the alleged drying-out (as with old age) of the eye, see Roisman (1988) 28–29. Plutarch *Mor.* 625–26 gives some interesting theories on why old men need to hold reading material at a distance. Aesop (*Fabulae Graecae* 57 Perry) has the amusing tale of an old woman who called a doctor to treat her bad sight; the doctor applied an ointment, and while her eyes were thus covered he stole all her furniture; on removal of the ointment she refused to pay his bill, for she was adamant that her sight had not been cured—after all, she could not see her furniture.

76. Note Chapters 3 and 7 and Chapter 8 notes 67 and 84. See also Aristotle *de Gen. An.* 1.18.725b; Galen *Ars Med.* 24 (1.372K); *de Semine* 1.15 (4.578K); *de Venereis* (4.911K); *de San. Tuenda* 2.2, 6.3 (6.84, 398K = *CMG* 5.4.2.39, 398). Hippocrates *de Victu* 3.68 (6.596L), however, recommends sexual intercourse for older individuals in winter, to warm them up.

77. E.g., Galba: Suetonius *Galba* 21; Septimius Severus: Herodian 2.15.4, Dio 76.16.1, SHA *Sept. Sev.* 16.6; note also Corellius Rufus, Chapter 3 above; also, perhaps, Lucian: Lucian *de Merc.* 39; *Sat.* 7, 28, etc. Cf. also the poetic works *Podagra* and *Ocypus,* dubiously ascribed to Lucian; see *P.Oxy.* 2532v for an elegiac poem on gout (with similarities to the *Ocypus*). The scholar Tyrannio of Amisos was said to have died in old age (in 26 B.C.), paralyzed by gout (*Suda* A 1184: ἐτελεύτησε δὲ γηραιός, ὑπὸ ποδάγρας παραλυθείς). Note also Lucilius frags. 331–32M (quoted in Chapter 3 note 108). Gout only adds to the old man's unattractiveness in sex, as Tibullus 1.9.73–74 notes: "sed corpora foeda podagra | et senis amplexus culta puella fugit." Hippocrates *Prorrh.* 2.8 (9.26L) remarks that gout in old people is incurable "by the human art," though dysentery may cure it; for a magical incantation to cure gout, see Varro

Res Rust. 1.2.27, and cf. Pliny *NH* 22.57.120. Galen comments that gout is hereditary, and eunuchs do not get it: *in Hipp. Aph.* 6.28 (18A.43K); cf. *de San. Tuenda* 5.8 (6.349K = *CMG* 5.4.2.150); Celsus *de Med.* 2.8.28. See further Brothwell and Sandison (1967) 352–70; Byl (1983: 93–94; 1988a); Jackson (1988) 175–79 (particularly for skeletal evidence); Garland (1995) 19. Perhaps the amount of wine (if high in lead content) being drunk as a tonic for old age and, it was said, as a cure for gout, exacerbated the problem.

78. Cf. Hippocrates *Prorrh.* 2.23, 2.41 (9.52, 70L); Celsus *de Med.* 2.8.33; Galen *de Temp.* 2.2 (1.582K), *in Hipp. de Acut. Morb. Vict.* 22[25] (15.777K = *CMG* 5.9.1.293); Pliny *NH* 11.117.282 (and see 26.28.43: not just a problem for older people); Aetius *Lib. Med.* 3.159 (*CMG* 8.1.326–30). For diarrhea or related factors in old age, note the (potentially or actually) terminal cases of Atticus (Cornelius Nepos *Att.* 21), Augustus (Suetonius *Div. Aug.* 97.3, 98.5), and Vespasian (Suetonius *Div. Vesp.* 24).

79. Galen *de San. Tuenda* 5.9 (6.353K = *CMG* 5.4.2.152). Purging the body through daily vomiting was not regarded as conducive to a long life: Celsus *de Med.* 1.3.21.

80. Sciatica: see esp. Hippocrates *Prorrh.* 2.41 (9.70L). Insomnia, though mentioned in the passages from Hippocrates and Celsus quoted above, rarely recurs in the sources. Cicero *de Sen.* 13.44 may mean sleeplessness or bad dreams (Powell 1988: 190–91) and in any case implies its absence in old age, because one no longer indulges in the pleasures of excessive eating and drinking. Macrobius *Sat.* 7.10.9, however, assumes the presence of sleeplessness in old age. Galen mentions that he himself as an adult suffered from insomnia, which he found eating lettuce cured; now, however, he has problems with his teeth, so eats the lettuce boiled: *de Anim. Fac.* 2.40.4 (6.626K = *CMG* 5.4.2.309). He also cites insomnia in passing (*de Loc. Aff.* 3.6 [8.162K] and *in Hipp. Aph.* 3.31 [17B.650–1]) as a problem for some old men, caused both by the worry of old age (ὅτι φροντιστικόν πως ὑπάρχει τὸ γῆρας) and by the dryness of old men's bodies (cf. John Chrysostom *in Epist. ad Titum* 2.4.1 [*PG* 62.682]: old people are παράφρονες, οἱ μὲν ἀπὸ οἴνου, οἱ δὲ ἀπὸ λύπης). Note the remarks of Seneca *Ep.* 83.6 and the complaints of Maximianus *Eleg.* 1.249–56.

81. Rufus *de Renum et Vesicae Morbis* pr.4 (*CMG* 3.1.86); Galen *in Hipp. Aph.* 6.6 (18A.17K). In the Hippocratic *Epidemics* 6.8.4 (5.344L), it is stated that it is rare for kidney infections to heal in a patient over the age of 50 years; cf. also Hippocrates *Coac. Praenot.* 7.34.578 (5.718L), *de Morb.* 1.3 (6.144L).

82. Celsus *de Med.* 2.8.23; Aretaeus 1.10.6 (*CMG* 2.13; cf. Godderis 1989: 60–61); Cassius Felix *de Med.* 66; Brothwell and Sandison (1967) 474–88. A cough was regarded as a sure precursor of death: e.g., Martial 1.10,

5.39. For the old man's weakened respiration, cf. Galen *de Util. Respir.* 4.6 (4.500K), *de Diff. Respir.* 1.7 (7.771K); Pliny *NH* 11.115.277.

83. Hippocrates *Aph.* 3.31 (quoted above; cf. 6.57, with Galen's commentary [18A.96K]), *de Morb.* 2.21 (7.36L); Celsus *de Med.* 3.27.1a–b; Galen *de Loc. Aff.* 3.14 (8.208–14K), *in Hipp. Aph.* 3.16 (17B.602K); Aretaeus 3.7.8 (*CMG* 2.46; cf. Godderis 1989: 60); Cassius Felix *de Med.* 54. Two noteworthy stroke victims were L. Vitellius, father of the emperor and thrice *cos. ord.* (in A.D. 34, 43, 47; Suetonius *Vitell.* 3; Tacitus *Ann.* 12.42 describes him in A.D. 51 as "extrema aetate"; *PIR* V 500), and the emperor Trajan, who was left partly paralyzed by it (Dio 68.33.3).

84. In a medical context, note Hippocrates *de Artic.* 47 (4.200L); Galen *in Hipp. Aph.* 2.54 (17B.560K). Those already hunched over from an early age or from birth rarely survive to old age: Hippocrates *de Artic.* 41 (4.182L). More generally, see Terence *Eun.* 336 (of Archidemides: "incurvos, tremulus, labiis demissis, gemens"; cf. Aristophanes *Plut.* 266); Ovid *Ars Amat.* 2.670, *Met.* 3.276–77; [Tibullus] 3.5.16; Propertius 2.18.20; Tacitus *Ann.* 1.34 ("curvata senio membra"); Statius *Theb.* 4.419; Apuleius *Met.* 4.7 (quoted in Chapter 8 note 39); Lucian *de Luctu* 16 (cited in Chapter 3), *Sat.* 9 (in winter οἱ ἄνθρωποι ἐπικεκυφότες ὥσπερ οἱ πάνυ γεγηρακότες); *Anthologia Latina* 481.348; *CLE* 509.2 (= *CIL* 10.2598, Puteoli), 2075.1 (Capua); Maximianus *Eleg.* 1.211–24, 238, 261–62; Venantius Fortunatus *Carm.* 5.3.3. Thus also the common image of an elderly person with a stick: *CIL* 6.10213 (= *ILS* 6044, Rome, first century A.D.) for a 60-year-old "debilis inutilis baculi comes"; Calpurnius Siculus 5.12–13 ("aspicis ut nobis iam dudum mille querelas | afferat et baculum premat inclinata senectus"); Claudian *de Bell. Goth.* 483–84; Maximianus *Eleg.* 1.223; cf. Ausonius *Epicedion in Patrem* 61: "nonaginta annos baculo sine," and see *LSJ*[9] s.v. ἀσκίπων, with Poseidippus (as at Chapter 3 note 130) line 24. In Greek art, note the depiction of stooped Geras (Shapiro 1993: 93, with n. 92).

85. Juvenal 10.190–91. Cf. again also Saint Augustine *Sermo* 81.8 (*PL* 38.504, quoted in Chapter 3 note 105); Ausonius *Ecl.* 19.15–17 (Chapter 3 note 111).

86. Garland (1990) 249, and cf. (1995) 124–25, with Corvisier (1985b) 69–70. Edelstein (1967) 381 remarks that "it may at first glance seem strange that Greek medicine should pay little attention to the prolongation of life, to the old and their way of living," but adds that it is not so strange when one considers that to the Greeks old age was hateful; the Romans, on the other hand, apparently "cherished and respected it." For similarly simplistic generalizations, see Minois (1987) chs. 3–4. For useful discussion of comparative historical evidence for the age-based rationing of medical care (to the detriment of the elderly), see Edwards (1999).

87. Contrast the conclusion of Mazzini (1995) 363.

88. *NH* 7.50.168; cf. Chapter 3 *fin.* and Beagon (1992) 69–75, 236–39; note too the quite striking parallels (including "sensus hebescunt") in Eugenius Toletanus *Carm.* 14 (*MGHAA* 14.243 = *PL* 87.362–63; cf. Chapter 3 note 135) and in Pseudo-Cyprian/Augustine *XII Abus.* 2 (*PL* 4.948–49 = 40.1079–80). A sudden death is, according to Pliny, "summa vitae felicitas" (7.53.180), death is "praecipuum naturae bonum" (7.55.190), and a timely death is nature's greatest blessing (28.2.9). In the prologue to his *Gerontocomia,* Zerbi took Pliny to task over this.

89. Pliny *NH* 35.36.108; Dionysius of Halicarnassus *AR* 3.69.5; Livy 5.54.7 (see Ogilvie 1965: 750); Cicero *ad Att.* 1.18.3; Paulus 92L; Della Corte (1924); Néraudau (1979) 185–99. "Youth" will scarcely do as a translation, of course; "adulthood" is somewhat closer to the sense, since *iuventus* could extend at least to one's 40s (see esp. Chapters 1 and 4). As we have seen, such an age was the conventional ideal.

90. *Theog.* 211–25: Νύξ the mother of hateful old age, ether, day, destiny, sleep, dreams, sarcasm, fates, nemesis, deceit, discord. For *Senectus's* lineage, see also Cicero *de Nat. Deor.* 3.17.44 and Hyginus *Fab.* pr.1.

91. Vergil *Aen.* 6.275 ("tristis Senectus"; cf. Seneca *Ep.* 108.29); Seneca *Oed.* 594 ("gravis S."), *Herc. Fur.* 696 ("iners S."); Silius Italicus *Pun.* 13.583 ("queribunda S."); Claudian *in Rufin.* 1.31 ("Leto vicina S."). In his *Epithalamium* on the marriage of Honorius, Claudian has *Senium* excluded from the grove by "petulans Iuventas" (84–85)—a clever metaphor, perhaps, for social reality. Note also the evils released on the world by Pandora. For old age and the Underworld, see Panayotakis (1997).

92. Philostratus *Vit. Apoll.* 5.4.167; Eustathius *Comm. in Dionys.* 453 (Müller, *Geogr. Graec. Min.* 2.302). Altars to Heracles are also mentioned in Gades. It may be relevant that this hero is the only figure generally depicted (in art of the first half of the fifth century B.C., never in extant literature) as battling against personified old age, typically an emaciated figure with grotesquely swollen but flaccid genitals: see Richardson (1933) 72–77; Beazley (1949–51), with the closing comment (20): "To these Greek personifications of Old Age some may prefer the Chinese god of longevity, Shou-Lao, leering and obese. Others will find nothing to choose between them" (Beazley was 65 years old at the time); Brommer (1952); *Enciclopedia dell'arte antica* 3 (Rome, 1960) 839–40; *LIMC* 4.1.180–82, 4.2.100–101 (Shapiro); Shapiro (1993) 89–94, 238–39; Garland (1995) 118, 197; Grmek (1995) 262–64. Aside from this episode, Γῆρας plays little role in classical myths: *RE* 7.1240–42, *NP* 4 (1998) 949.

93. E.g., Sophocles *Oed. Col.* 607–8 (but contrast *Homeric Hymn to Aphrodite* 244–46: even the gods dread old age). Cf. McCartney (1925); Griffin (1980) 187; Janko (1981); Clay (1981–82). A tombstone might also de-

scribe the deceased as ἀγήρατος ἀθανάτη τε: *GVI* 357 (Rome, second or third century A.D.).

94. E.g., the Graeae, Fates (see Catullus 64.305–17, with Papanghelis 1994), and Furies: Billault (1980); Henderson (1987) 126–27; Garland (1990) 258.

95. For the folktale motif, see Thompson (1955–58) D 1880. For a survey of theories of prolongevity, see Gruman (1966), and note also Grmek (1958) 42–49.

96. Galen *de Marc.* 2 (7.670–71K); cf. *de San. Tuenda* 1.12, 6.3 (6.63, 399K = *CMG* 5.4.2.29, 176). Possibly he was Egyptian (cf. *de Marc.* 4, 7.678K). Aetius *Lib. Med.* 4.97 (*CMG* 8.1.407) quotes Galen and adds the name Philippos. If this is correct, at least two medical Philippoi of the second century A.D. could claim the honor: see *RE* 19.2367–69 and Korpela (1987) 189 no. 194. It is more likely, however, that Aetius has simply confused Galen's sophist with the physician Philippos whose work Galen discusses at length elsewhere (e.g., *de Marcore* 5–7, 7.685–94K; cf. also Juvenal 13.125; *PIR*² P 356). Such works with medical foundation may not have been uncommon: Clement of Alexandria *Paed.* 2.2.23.1 records that the doctor M. Artorius Asclepiades (Korpela 1987: 156 no. 6), in the time of Augustus, wrote a work on longevity (περὶ μακροβιοτίας).

97. *Iliad* 9.446; *Homeric Hymn to Aphrodite* 223–24. The rejuvenation of Aeson at the hands of Medea is perhaps the best-known story, to both Greeks and Romans (cf. McCartney 1925: 42–43, 55–57, with *Nostoi* frag. 6 [Davies; cf. Davies 1989: 84–85] and Ovid *Met.* 7.159- 293). Also well known was the story of Tithonus, with his gift of immortality at Eos's request but without eternal youth to accompany it; hence his increasing age and decrepitude (Horace *Odes* 2.16.30: "longa Tithonum minuit senectus"), till finally he became a cicada (see Chapter 2). The stories of such figures as Teiresias, Peleus, and Phineus are also of relevance. Aristophanes' play Γῆρας (some fragments of which survive) seems to have featured a chorus of old men who are rejuvenated.

98. On the shedding of skin by some reptiles and by arthropods, cf. Aristotle *Hist. An.* 8.17.600b; Hesychius Γ 26; Pliny *NH* 8.41.99, 8.49.111, 9.50.95, 20.95.254, 28.48.174, 29.32.101, 29.38.122, 29.39.137, 30.22.69, etc.; Aelian *de Nat. Anim.* 9.16; Athenaeus *Deipn.* 3.105d (Theophrastus); Lucian *Nav.* 44 (Timolaus wishes to live 1,000 years, shedding his old age like a snake about every 17 years); McCartney (1925: 61–63; 1929); Onians (1954) 291, 430. The old grandfather who pleads for the help of the robbers to save his grandson (Apuleius *Met.* 8.19–20) in fact turns out to be a hideous and vicious snake (see most recently the useful discussion in Brancaleone 1995). Dreaming of snakes, *pace* Freudian analysts, was said to signify rejuvenation (e.g., Artemi-

dorus *Oneirocrit.* 2.13–14, but note also 5.40: rejuvenation of the soul = death). On the medicinal qualities of snake skin, see, e.g., Dioscorides (first century A.D.) *de Mat. Med.* 2.17; Galen *de Simp. Med. Temp. ac Fac.* 11.19 (12.342K); *in Hipp. Aph.* 4.77 (17B.773K). For a diet of snake flesh leading to a very long life, see Pliny *NH* 7.2.27 and Gabriele Zerbi's *Gerontocomia* ch. 50.

99. Empedocles 31 B 111 D-K *ap.* Diogenes Laertius 8.59; Kingsley (1995) 222–23. See also *Homeric Hymn to Apollo* 193; Euripides *Suppl.* 1109–13 (how hateful for men to drag out their lives with food and drink and magic; they ought to die and make way for the young—quoted with approval by Plutarch *Mor.* 110c); Pliny *NH* 28.2.9.

100. Wiedemann (1989) 176–77.

101. Compare Kirk (1971) 123 with Finley (1981) 163. See, e.g., Horace *Sat.* 1.9.30 for an *anus* as fortune-teller.

102. Plato *Laws* 6.759d; Aristotle *Pol.* 7.1329a30–34. In Ptolemy I's edict to Cyrene (*SEG* 9.1, ca. 322/1 B.C.; referred to in Chapter 1 note 35 and Chapter 4 note 24), priests of Apollo are to be selected from the *gerontes,* who are 50 years of age or older. For aged priestesses in Greece, see Bremmer (1983a) 111; Garland (1990) 258 (and 281 for priests).

103. Vestal Virgins being one notable exception, whose (voluntary) "retirement" after thirty years would roughly coincide with the menopause; cf. Aulus Gellius 7.7.4; Dionysius of Halicarnassus *AR* 2.67.2 (who states that few take the option of retiring). See Tacitus *Ann.* 2.86 and *CIL* 6.2128 (= *ILS* 4923: "annis LXIIII") for two aged Vestals. Rives (1995b) 160 n. 104 notes that "eleven priestesses of the Cereres are attested in Africa: in six cases, their ages are given, and of these the youngest is 72 . . . , the oldest 97."

104. *Pontifex maximus:* Sallust *Cat.* 49.2; Festus 152L. Vestals: Ovid *Fasti* 4.639 (with Bömer and Fantham *ad loc.*). College of augurs: Cicero *de Sen.* 18.64. In an otherwise useful article, Morgan (1974) 138 cites Dionysius of Halicarnassus *AR* 2.21.3, where Romulus is said to have enacted a law that each *curia* should choose two men over the age of 50 to act as priests. Morgan regards this as highly atypical: "[F]or a Roman fifty was a very considerable age, and there was nothing to be gained by appointing a man whose health was such that he might need almost immediate replacement!" Despite citing Hopkins (1966–67) as evidence for the first statement, this is demographically naive.

105. Herondas *Mim.* 10 *ap.* Stobaeus *Flor.* 50.2.56; Lucian *de Mort. Pereg.* 10.

106. Porphyrius (who himself lived to his early 70s) *de Abst.* 4.21, in the context of arguing against the consumption of meat, provides perhaps the most comprehensive list from antiquity of the phenomenon; it was copied by Eusebius *Praep. Evang.* 1.4.7 (*PG* 21.40 = *GCS* Euseb. 3.1.16–17), and followed also by Jerome *adv. Iovin.* 2.7 (*PL* 23.309 =

Bickel 1915: 403) and by Theodoret *Graec. Affect. Cur.* 9.35–36; for Christian indignation, see also Eusebius *Laud. Const.* 13.14 (*GCS* Euseb. 1.240), *Theoph.* 2.81 (*GCS* 3.2.118). For noteworthy modern discussion (particularly regarding motivation—economic or religious? and on origins—real tradition and/or folk narrative?) and comparative material, see *ERE* 9 (1917) 465; Frazer (1929) 4.110; Dumézil (1950); Devoto (1956); Müller (1968); Gavazzi (1976); Moser-Rath (1977); Balsdon (1979) 245–49; Grassl (1982) 71–72; and Bremmer (1983a) 103–4; cf. also Thompson (1955–58) S 110.1, 140.1. One might in the context cite the alarming case of the prominent American physician, Sir William Osler (1849–1919), who, in 1905, at the age of 55 years, advocated (apparently with humorous intent) that old men over the age of 60 should be chloroformed, since the old were in his view "a burden to themselves and to others, and an obstacle to cultural and political progress" (Grmek 1958: 81; cf. Livesley 1975: 6–7; Cole 1992: 170–74; Laslett 1996: 125–26). One notes that Osler died at the age of 70 years. Some of his friends also, it seems, had a sense of humor: they presented him in 1905 with a copy of Cicero's *de Senectute.*

107. Hellanicus *ap.* Clement of Alexandria *Strom.* 1.15.72.2 = *FGH* 4 F 187b; Pomponius Mela *de Chorographia* 3.5.37, followed by Pliny *NH* 4.12.89 and Solinus *Coll. Rerum Mem.* 16.5; Pindar *Pyth.* 10.41–42.

108. Diodorus Siculus 2.57.4–5, 2.58.6; cf. Pliny *NH* 6.24.91 (100 years as a moderate life-span), 7.2.30 (Artemidorus) on Taprobane, with more detail on the island's inhabitants furnished by Palladius *de Gent. Ind. et Bragman.* 1.4 (ed. Berghoff): ἔνθα εἰσὶν οἱ λεγόμενοι Μακρόβιοι· ζῶσι γὰρ εἰς τὴν νῆσον ἐκείνην ἕως ἑκατὸν πεντήκοντα ἐτῶν οἱ γέροντες δι᾽ ὑπερβολὴν τῆς τῶν ἀέρων εὐκρασίας καὶ ἀνεξερευνήτου κρίματος θεοῦ.

109. *Paradoxographus Vaticanus* 65 Keller = 59 Giannini: Λίγυες τοὺς γονεῖς, ὅταν μηκέτι ὦσι διὰ γῆρας χρήσιμοι, κατκρημνίζουσιν. Cf. Tertullian *Apol.* 9.5: "maior aetas apud Gallos Mercurio prosecatur."

110. Pomponius Mela *de Chorographia* 3.7.65 (providing more detail than in Pliny *NH* 6.22.66 and Solinus *Coll. Rerum Mem.* 52.23); Philo *Abr.* 182 (quoted in note 31); cf. Curtius Rufus 8.9.32 on the Indian *sapientes*— by contrast, no honor is shown to the bodies of those who endure into and die of old age—and see also Strabo 15.1.68.717–18, on Calanus at the age of 72 years, and Solinus *Coll. Rerum Mem.* 52.22 (following Pomponius Mela *de Chorographia* 3.7.64): "sunt qui proximos parentesque priusquam annis aut aegritudine in maciem eant, velut hostias caedunt, deinde peremptorum viscera epulas habent: quod ibi non sceleris, sed pietatis loco numerant."

111. Porphyrius *de Abst.* 4.21.1 calls them "Troglodytes," as they are also called in many manuscripts of Strabo.

112. Herodotus 1.216; similarly Strabo 11.8.6.513. Cf. Porphyrius *de Abst.* 4.21.3, Jerome *adv. Iovin.* 2.7; Eusebius *Laud. Const.* 13.14 (*GCS* Euseb. 1.240).

113. Onesicritus *FGH* 134 F 5 *ap.* Strabo 11.11.3.517; Porphyrius *de Abst.* 4.21.4. Cf. Plutarch *Mor.* 328c: Alexander taught the Sogdians to support (τρέφειν) their parents and not to kill them; Eusebius *Laud. Const.* 13.14.

114. Aelian *Var. Hist.* 4.1; see also Strabo 11.11.8.520; Porphyrius *de Abst.* 4.21.3; Jerome *adv. Iovin.* 2.7.

115. Porphyrius *de Abst.* 4.21.4. Cf. Cicero *Tusc. Disp.* 1.45.108, Plutarch *Mor.* 499d, and Sextus Empiricus *Pyrr. Hyp.* 3.227, who all state that the parents are dead by this stage. Jerome *adv. Iovin.* 2.7 reports that they are still "semivivos."

116. Strabo 11.11.3.517, 8.520. Porphyrius *de Abst.* 4.21.4 (cf. also Jerome *adv. Iovin.* 2.7), in regard to the Caspians, mentions the latter detail but not the means of death, and contrasts this with the Hyrcanians, who, as has just been noted, left their parents *alive* to be so devoured.

117. Porphyrius *de Abst.* 4.21.4. Cf. Jerome *adv. Iovin.* 2.7: "Tibareni quos dilexerint senes suspendunt in patibulis"—this strange statement is perhaps to be explained by Jerome having misread κατακρημνίζουσι as κατακρημνῶσι; see Bickel (1915) 403. According to Theodoret *Graec. Affect. Cur.* 9.36, the Tibarenians gave up this νόμος when they converted to Christianity (likewise the Massagetae, 9.35).

118. See references in Jacoby's notes and in Adler's notes on *Suda* Σ 124, to which add *schol. ad* Lucian *Asin.* 24; note also Aelian *Var. Hist.* 4.1 (in Sardinia it was the νόμος that the children of aged parents beat them to death with clubs and bury them, since the very elderly are physically useless), and cf. Pittau (1991). See too Chapter 8 note 23 in the context of Sardinia and old age.

119. Heracleides Lembus *Excerpta Politiarum* 29.

120. Strabo 10.5.6.486; Aelian *Var. Hist.* 3.37 (a law that the very old should drink hemlock once they are no longer of use to the state because they are becoming insane [ὑποληρούσης—see Chapter 8 note 113 on the term]); *Anthologia Palatina* 7.470 (Meleager [?], referring to the Ceian law); Erasistratus frag. 3 Garofalo *ap.* Stobaeus *Ecl.* 3.7.57 (W-H vol. 3 pp. 325–26: Ἐρασίστρατος ὁ Κῷος ἤδη γηραιὸς ὢν ἕλκος ἐπὶ τοῦ ποδὸς δυσίατον ἔχων "εὖ γε" εἶπεν "ὅτι τῆς πατρίδος ὑπομιμνήσκομαι," καὶ κώνειον πιὼν κατέστρεψεν); Stephanus of Byzantium *Ethnic. s.v.* Ἰουλίς (a law that those over 60 be dosed with hemlock, to leave enough food for the others); Theophrastus *Hist. Plant.* 9.16.9 (the Ceians and hemlock). Cf. Schmidt (1903); Hirzel (1908) 82.

121. Valerius Maximus 2.6.8; cf. van Hooff (1990) 32. On the subject of the disposal of older people in the time of food shortages, it is of interest that according to *Nov. Valent.* 33 (A.D. 451; the text has been suspected),

"notum est proxime obscaenissimam famem per totam Italiam desae-
visse coactosque homines filios et parentes vendere [*homines homines et
parentes filios vendere* ?], ut discrimen instantis mortis effugerent." If the
text is to stand, one wonders who bought the parents, and why (my
thanks to Judith Evans Grubbs for the reference).

122. Darwin recorded (*Voyage of the Beagle,* ch. 10) that in Tierra del Fuego
the people there, in time of famine, "kill and devour the old women before they kill their dogs"; they are "held over smoke and choked." Note
the gender and the motivation. Cf. also Thomas (1993) 246, for the
Tlaxcalans offering to the Castilians four old women to sacrifice and eat;
Cortés insists, however, that he has come to put a stop to such practices—a modern-day Heracles or Alexander, it might be said, in the light
of what we shall presently discuss.

123. This age limit, incidentally, lends support to some conclusions we have
made in Chapter 1 in regard to ancient "definitions" of old age.

124. Frag. 797.2 K-T (unassigned, but it would surely make sense to assign
it to Menander's *Κωνειαζόμεναι*), quoted by Strabo and Stephanus of
Byzantium (as cited in note 120) in regard to the practice of senicide in
Ceos (line 1: καλὸν τὸ Κείων νόμιμόν ἐστι), and also quoted in Diogenianus (*ap.* L. Cohn, *Philologus* suppl. 6 [1891–93 = *CPG Suppl.*] 256,
268).

125. Compare Seneca's views on suicide, outlined in Chapter 3, and in similar vein Cicero *de Fin.* 3.18.60.

126. A young female virgin was more standard; cf. Parker (1983) 259. On the
subject note also Schwenn (1915) and Hughes (1991). For the ugly and
deformed as scapegoats, see most recently Garland (1995) 23–26.

127. Livy 22.57.6; Pliny *NH* 30.4.13 (citing a *senatus consultum* of 97 B.C. to
this effect, 30.3.12). *Pace* Fabre (1940), an influential article, it is not
just sacrifice involving bloodshed to which Livy refers, but any human
sacrifice. The fact that human sacrifices are mentioned by, e.g., Livy
27.11.6 (209 B.C.) and 27.37.4 (207 B.C.) shows only that before 97 B.C.
such rites, however un-Roman some may have felt them to be, did happen (or were later held to have happened) at Rome to avert unpropitious
omens. But what is more, according to Lactantius *Inst. Div.* 1.21.1, human sacrifice went on in Cyprus till the time of Hadrian. Note also Pliny
NH 28.3.12 for live human burial in the Forum Boarium: "nostra aetas
vidit" (other evidence, mainly relating back to the third century B.C., is
collected in Schwenn 1915: 148–49 and discussed by, inter al., Bémont
1960 and Ndiaye 2000). See also Mayor (1878–80) on Juvenal 15.116,
and Marquardt (1881–85) 3.297 n. 4, for many more references, particularly from Christian authors (e.g., Minucius Felix *Octav.* 30.4), to human sacrifice allegedly continuing well after 97 B.C. On the perceived
"foreignness" of human sacrifice, note Henrichs (1980) 233–34, and see
now Steel (1995) and Rives (1995a).

128. On Afranius, writing *fabulae togatae* in the second half of the second century B.C., see most recently *NP* 1 (1996) 215–16. On this fragment, note Daviault's comments in his Budé edition of the *togatae* (1981, p. 218): he favors the voting theory.

129. Cèbe (1998) 1900. Robinson (1976) 482 takes this satire as autobiographical, of Varro (as Epimenides) at the age of 60 years. In one of the other fragments a Marcus is indeed addressed, but the date of all these satires is quite uncertain, and in any case the fragments of the *Sexagesis* do not bear such a confident reconstruction. There are perceptive comments in Deschamps (1978) 94–96, arguing that Varro intentionally conflates the tradition of the 60-year-olds from the bridge with the tradition of the *Argei* (see also below).

130. Nonius defines *carnalis* as *edulis,* i.e. edible. *TLL* 3.474.62–66 comments re *carnalis:* "dubiae significationis. . . . fort. i.q. carnifices" (hence my suggested translation). Iunius, however, suggested the reading of *casnares,* which makes some sense; cf. Paulus *ex* Festus 41L: "casnar senex Oscorum lingua"; Varro *de Ling. Lat.* 7.29: "senem quod Osci casnar appellant" (cf. 7.28 on *cascus,* "ancient"). See also *TLL* 3.516.22–27; Néraudau (1978) 171–72; Deschamps (1978) 94–95 (defending *carnales;* followed by Cèbe 1998: 1930).

131. Müller added *non* before *mittendos* but was not followed by Lindsay. The addition is not essential and so should be omitted (note its absence in the passage from Fortunatianus quoted below). Lugli (1986) 61 would have Varro's words stop after *otiosi.* This I would also regard as unlikely.

132. Tomulescu (1979) 117 was not amused: "Il este [sic] absurde de penser que Cicéron a écrit ces mots. Cicéron qui est l'auteur de cet admirable livre: *De senectute.*"

133. The poem has, of course, been much discussed. For an up-to-date bibliography, see Thomson (1997) *ad loc.,* with Néraudau (1978) 174. Of particular relevance to our context are Birt (1926), who detects military overtones, and Quinn (1969), who seems to me to be more in tune with Catullus's humor. It is highly unlikely, however, that Catullus knew the true origin of the proverb when Varro for one did not. For dancing old men, see Chapter 9 note 68; it is perhaps of some interest that that proverb is linked by Festus with *parasiti Apollinis:* note the reference to Apollo in Lactantius *Inst. Div. Epit.* 18.2 below.

134. I give here an adaptation of the text, with *supplementa,* as printed in the editions of Festus by Müller and Lindsay; cf. also the text printed in *Glossaria Latina,* vol. 4, ed. J. W. Pirie and W. M. Lindsay (Paris, 1930) 425–26.

135. For the folktale motif, see Thompson (1955–58) J 151.1.

136. Macrobius *Sat.* 1.11.47 specifies the *pons Sublicius;* note too Varro *de Ling. Lat.* 7.44, with Radke (1990) 10 n. 20, and Nicholson (1984). The

oracle that Lactantius here quotes is also given by Dionysius of Halicarnassus *AR* 1.19.3 and Macrobius *Sat.* 1.7.28 (*ex* Varro). Cf. Ogilvie (1978) 24–26.

137. Macrobius *Sat.* 1.7.28 (following Varro) gives Ἄιδη, but Dionysius of Halicarnassus *AR* 1.19.3 has Κρονίδη, perhaps correctly; for Cronus in this context, note the Sardinian practice, quoted above, and cf. Sextus Empiricus *Pyrr. Hyp.* 3.208, 221, and Porphyrius *de Abst.* 2.27, where it is stated that in Carthage human victims are (even down to Porphyrius's own time) sacrificed to Cronus (see also Henrichs 1980: 196 and Steel 1995 on Punic child sacrifices).

138. It is noteworthy that in this rhetorical exercise, and implicitly in the following passage from Prudentius, the proverb is accorded a barbarian origin. Sextus Empiricus *Pyrr. Hyp.* 3.210 states that the Scythians cut the throats of their fathers when the latter reached the age of 60 years.

139. For *vietus,* "shriveled" or "wrinkled," in the context of old age, cf. Terence *Eun.* 688: "hic est vietus vetus veternosus senex"; Cicero *de Sen.* 2.5.

140. Néraudau (1978) is the most intelligent survey to date of the evidence; note also (1979) 318–22. Brief but useful is Gagé (1950) 41–42, who makes the suggestion that the practice could be seen as "superstition attachée à un âge 'climactérique'" (though the hebdomadal system plays no part here, I would add); he also draws attention to Livy 4.12.11, plebeians committing suicide (as a result of despair during a food shortage) by covering their heads and throwing themselves into the Tiber, and he raises some interesting ideas on Umbrian influences. Other discussions include Marquardt (1881–85) 3.194–95; Klotz (1923), though he overlooks the Ovidian passage; Berelson (1934) 55–57; Le Gall (1953) 84; Bömer (1957–58) 2.327–30; Balsdon (1969) 169, 392–93, (1979) 245–49; Radke (1975); Guarino (1979); Gnilka (1983) 1043; Lugli (1986); Ryan (1995); Suder (1995a) 405–9 = (1995b) 36–38.

141. Radke (1975) 154.

142. Frazer (1929) 4.81; likewise Berelson (1934) 57, "a pure piece of ratiocination." Ryan (1995) 189 points out that in relation to the *comitia* one would expect *pontes,* not *pons.* Even more to the point, the repeated references in the testimony to a bridge *on the Tiber* cannot be easily associated with the voting bridges (cf. Guarino 1979: 536), and the opposition of the *iuniores* would presumably be to the *seniores* (i.e., as we have seen, those 46 years of age and over), not merely those over the age of 60 years. However the "voting theory" has found favor with, e.g., Mommsen (1887–88) 2.408 n. 2, 3.401 n. 3; *L&S* s.v. *sexagenarius* II; Siber (1937) 262; Taylor (1966) 92; and Balsdon (1969) 169, (1979) 248, to name but a few. For slaves being thrown to their death from a bridge into the Tiber, or throwing themselves, note Gaius *Inst.* 3.219 and *Dig.* 21.1.17.6 (Celsus *ap.* Ulpian), in the context of the *lex Aquilia de*

damno, and cf. *Dig.* 9.2.7.7 (Caelius *ap.* Ulpian). For the plan to throw Julius Caesar from the bridge ("e ponte deicerent"), see Suetonius *Div. Iul.* 80.4.

143. Néraudau (1978), esp. 170; cf. Guarino (1979) 537–38.

144. Pliny *NH* 10.2.4–5: "Manilius [Mamilius?], senator ille maximis nobilis doctrinis doctore nullo" (that eminent senator, a most learned man, though he never had a teacher).

145. Dionysius of Halicarnassus *AR* 1.19.3; cf. Mommsen (1861) 284–87; Néraudau (1978) 161 n. 3; Schiebe (1999) 200 n. 35.

146. For the senator of 97 B.C, see *RE* 14.1115 (Manilius 4), for the consul of 149 B.C.; *RE* 14.1135–39 (Manilius 12).

147. Varro *de Ling. Lat.* 7.28; Courtney (1993) 110; on *cascus,* see also Chapter 9 note 130. Münzer *RE* 14.1115 assumes the senator of 97 B.C. again; see also Bardon (1952) 177–78.

148. For the assumption of antiquity note also "diu" in Nonius Marcellus 842L. Plautus *could* have referred to the proverb at, e.g., *Merc.* 1015–26 (cf. Chapter 7 note 24).

149. This is not the place for a detailed discussion of the Argei, on which the modern scholarship is vast; see the classic discussion in Frazer (1929) 74–113, and most recently Nagy (1985 [1993]); Radke (1990), esp. 12; *NP* 1 (1996) 1057–59; Schiebe (1999); Graf (2000).

150. Ovid *Fasti* 5.621, "priscorum . . . simulacra virorum," of course, only means that the Argei were effigies of men of old, not of old men.

151. E.g., Warde Fowler (1899) 112: "Apart from the theories of the learned [sc. regarding the Argei], it was the fact that the common people at Rome believed the puppets to be substitutes for old men, who at one time used to be thrown into the Tiber as victims" (he is a little more cautious at 116–19). Note also Nicholson (1984) 133: "A number of writers describe the ancient rite of the *sexagenarii de ponte,* in which, on a day in mid-May, straw dolls, representing old men, were cast from a bridge into the river Tiber." See further Klotz (1923) 2026; Néraudau (1978) 161–62, 168.

152. *Pace,* e.g., Berelson (1934) 57, who states, it seems to me rather naively, that "sexagenarians were held in higher esteem in Rome [sc. than to be sacrificed alive]; the strong patriarchal character of the Roman family would preclude any such treatment of its leading representative."

153. Cf. Valerius Maximus 3.2.7 for the "necessarium consilium" of leaving the *seniores* (who were on the point of death anyway and useless as soldiers, Livy 5.39.12–13 notes) "in plana parte urbis . . . quo facilius iuventus reliquias imperii tueretur."

154. I offer a few further possibly relevant details. Water is often regarded as a rejuvenating agent: Herodotus 3.23; *Anthologia Palatina* 11.256 (Lucilius); McCartney (1925); Grmek (1958) 42; cf. also G. Kaibel (ed.), *Epigrammata Graeca ex lapidibus conlecta* (Berlin, 1878) 366.5 ("Cotiaei,

infimae aetatis"): καὶ π[ηγαῖς] λοῦσα[ν] ἐν ἀθανάτοις, and note again the case of Pelias; perhaps there was some notion originally of old men being made young again in the process of entering the water. Second, congregating at bridges was a common practice of beggars: e.g., Seneca *de Vit. Beat.* 25.1; see also Courtney (1980) on Juvenal 4.116, and note Juvenal 14.134: "aliquis *de ponte*" signifies a beggar; the association of old men with bridges may have had some negative significance originally.

Final Remarks

1. See Eisenstadt (1971), with some discussion of classical antiquity (141–48, 204–6, 284–87); Stewart (1977); La Fontaine (1978); Bernardi (1985); Spencer (1990) 10–13.

2. See esp. Jeanmaire (1939). For age-groups in Sparta, see (briefly) Hodkinson (1983) 242–43 and MacDowell (1986) 159–67. For Athens's forty-two year-classes, see [Aristotle] *Ath. Pol.* 53.4–7. Sallares (1991) goes too far, it seems to me, in his claim that age-classes were the bases of Dark Age Greek societies. In any event, age categorization was, as we have seen, important in the Roman world, but that is far from making it an age-class system; the focus in Roman times was much more on rules of age than on classes of age.

3. On the "disengagement" theory, see the now classic and rather generalizing work by Cumming and Henry (1961). For critiques and opposing theories of the day, in particular the "activity" theory, cf. Maddox (1964); Havighurst (1963); Havighurst et al. (1964); and, for more balanced overviews, Hochschild (1975, 1976); Gutmann (1976); Victor (1987) ch. 2; Birren and Bengtson (1988) pt. 4; Moody (1998) 72–76.

4. Seneca *Herc. Oet.* 643 sums up the viewpoint neatly: "rarum est felix idemque senex." An imperial freedwoman, Claudia, dead at age 19, gleefully declared on her tombstone: "effugi crimen longa senecta tuum" (*CIL* 5.2931, Patavium).

5. Stobaeus *Ecl.* 3.1.173.113 = *Die Inschriften von Kyzikos und Umgebung* 2 (Bonn, 1983) no. 2, col. 2.24 (Miletopolis, fourth–third century B.C.); Servius *ad Aen.* 6.114: the lot of old age (*senectae sors*) is *quies et otium,* just as for childhood it is *ludus,* for *adulescentia amor,* and *ambitio* for *iuvenalis aetas.*

6. Menander *Monost.* 396 Jaekel had already put it simply: καλὸν τὸ γηρᾶν, ἀλλ᾽ ὑπεργηρᾶν κακόν (cf. *Monost.* 419). But another manuscript puts it differently: καλὸν τὸ γηρᾶν καὶ τὸ μὴ γηρᾶν πάλιν. *Ib., Sententiae ex pap.* 8.10 Jaekel is more realistic: καλὸν τὸ γηρᾶν, γηροβοσκὸν ἂν ἔχῃς.

7. Nonius Marcellus 3–4L: "aetatem malam senectutem veteros dixerunt. . . . bonam aetatem quoque dicimus adulescentiam vel iuventutem," citing for *mala aetas* Plautus *Menaec.* 758 (cf. also *Aul.* 43, *Rud.* 337), Ac-

cius frag. 85, Turpilius frag. 175, Pacuvius frag. 277–78, Afranius frag. 382 ("mala aetas nulla delenimenta ínuenit"); and for *bona aetas* Cicero *de Sen.* 14.48. Cf. *TLL* 1.1127.71–73, 1129.46–48. Ovid *ex Pont.* 1.4.1 describes old age as "deterior aetas." For *bona aetas*, see also Varro *Res Rust.* 2.6.2; Seneca *Controv.* 2.6.11; Seneca *Ep.* 47.12, 76.1. Contrast the Christian notion of καλόγηρος: Gnilka (1980).

Bibliography

Abbott, F. F., and Johnson, A. C. (1926). *Municipal Administration in the Roman Empire*. Princeton, N.J.

Afzelius, A. (1946). "*Lex annalis*." *C&M* 8: 263–78.

Aichinger, A. (1992). "Zwei Arten des Provinzialcensus? Überlegungen zu neupublizierten israelischen Papyrusfunden." *Chiron* 22: 35–45.

Albertario, E. (1933). *Studi di diritto romano, I.* Milan.

Alföldy, G. (1976). "Consuls and consulars under the Antonines: Prosopography and history." *AS* 7: 263–99. Reprinted in G. Alföldy, *Die römische Gesellschaft* (Stuttgart, 1986), 100–36, with Nachträge, 136–38.

——— (1977). *Konsulat und Senatorenstand unter den Antoninen*. Bonn.

——— (1985). *The Social History of Rome*. Tr. D. Braund and F. Pollock. London.

Alfonsi, L. (1970). "Il proverbio di Aristoph. *Nub.* 1417 e la sua diffusione nel mondo latino." *Dioniso* 44.3–4: 7–9.

——— (1976). "San Paolo e il 'ruolo' della età." *Sileno* 2: 331–32.

Algra, K. (1990). "Chrysippus on virtuous abstention from ugly old women." *CQ* 40: 450–58.

Allen, K. (1907). "The date of Cicero's *Cato Maior de Senectute*." *AJPh* 28: 297–300.

Alonso-Núñez, J. M. (1982). *The Ages of Rome*. Amsterdam.

Althoff, J. (1992). *Warm, kalt, flüssig und fest bei Aristoteles*. Stuttgart.

Amato, E. (ed.) (1999). *Per la ricostruzione del Περὶ γήρως di Favorino di Arelate*. Salerno.

Amelotti, M. (1953). *La "donatio mortis causa" in diritto romano*. Milan.

Amundsen, D. W., and Diers, C. J. (1970). "The age of menopause in classical Greece and Rome." *Human Biology* 42: 79–86.

André, J.-M. (1962). *Recherches sur l'otium romain*. Paris.

——— (1966). *L'otium dans la vie morale et intellectuelle romaine*. Paris.

——— (1989). "Sénèque: *De brevitate vitae, De constantia sapientis, De tranquillitate animi, De otio*." ANRW 2.36.3: 1724–78.

Andresen, C. (1979). "'Siegreiche Kirche' im Aufstieg des Christentums." *ANRW* 2.23.1: 387–459.

Ankum, H. (1994). "Donations in contemplation of death between husband and wife in classical Roman law." *Index* 22: 635–56.

Argetsinger, K. (1992). "Birthday rituals: Friends and patrons in Roman poetry and cult." *CA* 11: 175–93.

Arjava, A. (1996). *Women and Law in Late Antiquity*. Oxford.

——— (1998). "Paternal power in late antiquity." *JRS* 88: 147–65.

Armisen-Marchetti, M. (1995). "Sénèque et l'appropriation du temps." *Latomus* 54: 545–67.

Arnott, W. G. (ed.) (1996). *Alexis: The Fragments*. Cambridge.

Astin, A. E. (1958). *The* lex annalis *before Sulla*. Brussels.

——— *Cato the Censor.* Oxford.

Axelson, B. (1948). "Die Synonyme *adulescens* und *iuvenis*." In *Mélanges de philologie, de littérature et d'histoire anciennes offerts à J. Marouzeau*, 7–17. Paris.

Badian, E. (1964). *Studies in Greek and Roman History*. Oxford.

——— (1988 [1997]). "Which Metellus?" *AJAH* 13: 106–12.

Bagnall, R. S. (1995). "The people of P.Mich. inv. 5806." *ZPE* 105: 253–55.

Bagnall, R. S., and Frier, B. W. (1994). *The Demography of Roman Egypt*. Cambridge.

Bagnall, R. S., Frier, B. W., and Rutherford, I. C. (1997). *The Census Register P.Oxy. 984*. Brussels.

Balsdon, J. P. V. D. (1969). *Life and Leisure in Ancient Rome*. London.

——— (1979). *Romans and Aliens*. London.

Bardon, H. (1952). *La littérature latine inconnue, I*. Paris.

Barnes, T. D. (1968). "Philostratus and Gordian." *Latomus* 27: 581–97.

——— (1976). "Three imperial edicts." *ZPE* 21: 275–81.

——— (1982). *The New Empire of Diocletian and Constantine*. Cambridge, Mass., and London.

Barnes, T. D., and Worp, K. A. (1983). "P. Oxy. 889 again." *ZPE* 53: 276–78.

Bartelink, G. J. M. (1983). "Le thème du monde vieilli." *Orpheus* 4: 342–54.

Beagon, M. (1992). *Roman Nature*. Oxford.

Beaucamp, J. (1990–92). *Le statut de la femme à Byzance*. Paris.

Beaujeu, J. (1975) "Grammaire, censure et calendrier: *quinto quoque anno*." *REL* 53: 330–60.

Beazley, J. D. (1949–51). "Geras." *Bulletin van de Vereeniging tot Bevordering der Kennis van de antieke Beschaving te 's-Gravenhage* 24–26: 18–20.

Bibliography

Beloch, J. (1886). *Die Bevölkerung der griechisch-römischen Welt.* Leipzig.
Bémont, C. (1960). "Les enterrés vivants du Forum Boarium: essai d'interprétation." *MEFRA* 72: 133–46.
Béranger, J. (1964). "Les génies du sénat et du peuple romain et les reliefs flaviens de la Cancelleria." In M. Renard and R. Schilling (eds.), *Hommages à Jean Bayet,* 76–88. Brussels.
Berelson, L. (1934). "Old Age in Ancient Rome." Ph.D. dissertation, University of Virginia.
Bernardi, B. (1985). *Age Class Systems.* Tr. D. I. Kertzer. Cambridge.
Bertier, J. (1996). "La médecine des enfants à l'époque impériale." *ANRW* 2.37.3: 2147–2227.
Bertman, S. (ed.) (1976). *The Conflict of Generations in Ancient Greece and Rome.* Amsterdam.
Bettini, M. (1984). "'Pater,' 'avunculus,' 'avus' nella cultura romana più arcaica." *Athenaeum* 62: 468–91. Also published in *Sodalitas* (Naples) 2 (1984) 855–80.
——— (1991). *Anthropology and Roman Culture.* Trans. J. van Sickle. Baltimore and London.
Bickel, E. (1915). *Diatribe in Senecae Philosophi Fragmenta, I.* Leipzig.
Bickerman, E. J. (1980). *Chronology of the Ancient World*[2]. London.
Bienert, W. A. (1978). *Dionysius von Alexandrien: zur Frage des Origenismus im dritten Jahrhundert.* Berlin and New York.
Billault, A. (1980). "La vieille femme incarnation du mal." In J. Duchemin (ed.), *Mythe et Personification, Travaux et Mémoires,* 31–37. Paris.
Birley, A. R. (1981). *The Fasti of Roman Britain.* Oxford.
——— (1997). "Hadrian and Greek senators." *ZPE* 116: 209–45.
Birley, E. (1953). "Senators in the emperors' service." *PBA* 39: 197–214. Reprinted in Birley (1988) 75–92.
——— (1988). *The Roman Army: Papers, 1929–1986.* Amsterdam.
Birren, J. E., and Bengtson, V. L. (eds.) (1988). *Emergent Theories of Aging.* New York.
Birt, T. (1926). "*Pontifex* und *sexagenarii de ponte* (zu Catull c. 17)." *RhM* 75: 115–26.
Boak, A. E. R., and Youtie, H. C. (eds.) (1960). *The Archive of Aurelius Isidorus.* Ann Arbor.
Bolkestein, H. (1939). *Wohltätigkeit und Armenpflege im vorchristlichen Altertum.* Utrecht.
Boll, F. (1913). "Die Lebensalter. Ein Beitrag zur antiken Ethologie und zur Geschichte der Zahlen." *Neue Jahrbücher für das klassische Altertum* 31: 89–145. Reprinted in *Kleine Schriften zur Sternkunde des Altertums* (Leipzig, 1950), 156–224.
Bömer, F. (ed.) (1957–58). *Die Fasten.* Heidelberg.
Bonfante, P. (1925). *Corso di diritto romano, I.* Rome.

441

Bonnefond, M. (1982). "Le sénat républicain et les conflits de générations." *MEFRA* 94: 175–225.

Bonnefond-Coudry, M. (1989). *Le sénat de la république romaine de la guerre d'Hannibal à Auguste.* Rome.

———— (1993). "Le *princeps senatus:* vie et mort d'une institution républicaine." *MEFRA* 105: 103–34.

Bonner, S. F. (1969). *Roman Declamation in the Late Republic and Early Empire.* Liverpool.

Booth, A. D. (1979). "The date of Jerome's birth." *Phoenix* 33: 346–53.

Bourdelais, P. (1993). *Le nouvel âge de la vieillesse.* Paris.

Boutemy, A. (1939). "Notice sur le manuscrit 749 de la Bibliothèque municipale de Douai." *Latomus* 3: 183–206.

Bove, L. (1985). "Documentazione privata e prova. Le *tabulae ceratae.*" *Labeo* 31: 155–67.

Bowman, A. K. (1971). *The Town Councils of Roman Egypt.* Toronto.

Bradley, K. R. (1986). "Wet-nursing at Rome: A study in social relations." In Rawson (1986) 201–29.

———— (1991). *Discovering the Roman Family.* Oxford.

Brain, P. (1986). *Galen on Bloodletting.* Cambridge.

Brancaleone, F. (1995). "Il *senex/draco* in Apuleio, *Met.* VIII, 19–21." *Aufidus* 27: 45–72.

Braund, S. H. (1988). *Beyond Anger.* Cambridge.

Brecht, F. J. (1930). *Motiv-und Typengeschichte des griechischen Spottepigramms.* Leipzig.

Brelich, A. (1969). *Paides e Parthenoi, I.* Rome.

Bremmer, J. N. (1976). "Avunculate and fosterage." *Journal of Indo-European Studies* 4: 65–78.

———— (1983a). *The Early Greek Concept of the Soul.* Princeton, N.J.

———— (1983b). "The importance of the maternal uncle and grandfather in archaic and classical Greece and early Byzantium." *ZPE* 50: 173–86.

———— (1987). "The old women of ancient Greece." In J. Blok and P. Mason (eds.), *Sexual Assymetry,* 191–215. Amsterdam. Previously published as "Oude vrouwen in Griekenland en Rome," *Lampas* 17 (1984) 96–113; and as "La donna anziana: libertà e indipendenza," in G. Arrigoni (ed.), *Le donne in Grecia* (Bari, 1985), 275–98.

Brettell, C. B. (1991). "Property, kinship, and gender: A Mediterranean perspective." In Kertzer and Saller (1991) 340–53.

Brillante, C. (1987). "Il vecchio e la cicala, un modello rappresentativo del mito greco." In R. Raffaelli (ed.), *Rappresentazioni della morte,* 47–89. Urbino.

Brink, C. O. (ed.) (1971). *Horace on Poetry: The Ars Poetica.* Cambridge.

Briscoe, J. (1964). "Q. Marcius Philippus and *nova sapientia.*" *JRS* 54: 66–77.

Brisson, L. (1976). *Le mythe de Tirésias.* Leiden.

Brody, B. A. (ed.) (1989). *Suicide and Euthanasia.* Dordecht.

Brogan, O. (1962). "A Tripolitanian centenarian." In M. Renard (ed.), *Hommages à Albert Grenier*, 368–73. Brussels

Brommer, F. (1952). "Herakles und Geras." *Archäologischer Anzeiger* 67: 60–73.

Brothwell, D., and Sandison, A. T. (eds.) (1967). *Diseases in Antiquity*. Springfield, Ill.

Browne, G. M. (1970). *Documentary Papyri from the Michigan Collection*. Toronto.

Brunt, P. A. (1971). *Italian Manpower*. Oxford. Reissued with postscript, 1987.
——— (1975). "The administrators of Roman Egypt." *JRS* 65: 124–47. Reprinted in Brunt (1990) 215–54, with addenda, 514–15.
——— (1981). "The revenues of Rome." Review of Neesen (1980). *JRS* 71: 161–72. Reprinted in Brunt (1990) 324–46, with addenda, 531–40.
——— (1988). "The emperor's choice of *amici*." In P. Kneissl and V. Losemann (eds.), *Alte Geschichte und Wissenschaftsgeschichte*, 39–56. Darmstadt.
——— (1990). *Roman Imperial Themes*. Oxford.

Bruun, C. (1991). *The Water Supply of Ancient Rome*. Helsinki.

Buchheit, V. (1962). *Studien zum Corpus Priapeorum*. Munich.

Buckland, W. W. (1908). *The Roman Law of Slavery*. Cambridge.

Burckhardt, J. (1908). *Griechische Kulturgeschichte*⁶. Vol. 2. Berlin and Stuttgart.

Burkhalter, F. (1990). "Archives locales et archives centrales en Egypte romaine." *Chiron* 20: 191–216.

Burn, A. R. (1953). "*Hic breve vivitur*: A study of the expectation of life in the Roman empire." *P&P* 4: 2–31.

Burrow, J. A. (1986). *The Ages of Man: A Study in Medieval Writing and Thought*. Oxford.

Burstein, S. R. (1949). "Aspects of the psychopathology of old age revealed in witchcraft cases in the 16th and 17th centuries." *British Medical Bulletin* 6: 63–72.

Byl, S. (1974). "Platon et Aristote ont-ils professé des vues contradictoires sur la vieillesse?" *LEC* 42: 113–26.
——— (1975). "Lamentations sur la vieillesse dans la tragédie grecque." In J. Bingen, G. Cambier, and G. Nachtergael (eds.), *Le monde Grec*, 130–39. Brussels.
——— (1976). "Lamentations sur la vieillesse chez Homère et les poètes lyriques des VIIe et VIe siècles." *LEC* 44: 234–44.
——— (1977a). "Le vieillard dans les comédies d'Aristophane." *AC* 46: 52–73.
——— (1977b). "Plutarque et la vieillesse." *LEC* 45: 107–23.
——— (1978). "Lucien et la vieillesse." *LEC* 46: 317–25.
——— (1983). "La vieillesse dans le *Corpus hippocratique*." In F. Lasserre and P. Mudry (eds.), *Formes de Pensée dans la Collection Hippocratique*, 85–95. Geneva.

———— (1988a). "Rheumatism and gout in the *Corpus Hippocraticum.*" *AC* 57: 89–102.

———— (1988b). "La gérontologie de Galien." *History and Philosophy of the Life Sciences* (Naples) 10: 73–92.

———— (1996). "Vieillir et être vieux dans l'antiquité." *LEC* 64: 261–71.

Cameron, A. (1970). *Claudian.* Oxford.

———— (1973). *Porphyrius the Charioteer.* Oxford.

———— (1995). *Callimachus and His Critics.* Princeton, N.J.

Camps, G. (1960). "Massinissa ou les debuts de l'histoire." *Libyca: Bulletin du Service des Antiquités: Archéologie—Épigraphie* 8: 1–320.

Cantarella, R. (1971). "Aristofane, Erasmo e Shakespeare: storià di un proverbio." *RAL* 8.26: 113–30.

Capps. E. (1900). "Chronological studies in the Greek tragic and comic poets." *AJPh* 21: 38–61.

Carp, T. C. (1980). "*Puer senex* in Roman and medieval thought." *Latomus* 39: 736–39.

Carrick, P. (1985). *Medical Ethics in Antiquity.* Dordecht.

Carter, J. M. (1967). "Eighteen years old?" *BICS* 14: 51–57.

Carter, L. B. (1986). *The Quiet Athenian.* Oxford.

Cartledge, P., and Spawforth, A. (1989). *Hellenistic and Roman Sparta.* London and New York.

Casarico, L. (1985). *Il controllo della popolazione nell'Egitto romano. 1. Le denunce di morte.* Azzate.

Cèbe, J.-P. (ed.) (1972). *Varron, Satires ménippées.* Vol. 1. Rome.

———— (ed.) (1974). *Varron, Satires ménippées.* Vol. 2. Rome.

———— (ed.) (1980). *Varron, Satires ménippées.* Vol. 5. Rome.

———— (ed.) (1998). *Varron, Satires ménippées.* Vol. 12. Rome.

———— (ed.) (1999). *Varron, Satires ménippées.* Vol. 13. Rome.

Cervilla, J. A., Prince, M., Joels, S., Lovestone, S., and Mann, A. (2000). "Long-term predictors of cognitive outcome in a cohort of older people with hypertension." *British Journal of Psychiatry* 177: 66–71.

Champlin, E. (1980). *Fronto and Antonine Rome.* Cambridge, Mass.

———— (1985). "The glass ball game." *ZPE* 60: 159–63.

———— (1989). "'Creditur vulgo testamenta hominum speculum esse morum': Why the Romans made wills." *CPh* 84: 198–215.

———— (1991). *Final Judgments.* Berkeley.

Chantraine, H. (1973). "Außerdienststellung und Altersversorgung kaiserlicher Sklaven und Freigelassener." *Chiron* 3: 307–29.

Chevallier, R. (1976). *Αἰών: Le temps chez les Romains.* Paris.

Christes, J. (1998). "Lucilius *senex—vetus historia*—Epilog zu XXVI–XXX: drei alte Fragen neu verhandelt." *Philologus* 142: 71–79.

Clauss, M. (1973). "Probleme der Lebensalterstatistiken aufgrund römischer Grabinschriften." *Chiron* 3: 395–417.

Clay, D. (1990). "The philosophical inscription of Diogenes of Oenoanda." *ANRW* 2.36.4: 2446–559.

Clay, D. C., and Vander Haar, J. E. (1993). "Patterns of intergenerational support and childbearing in the Third World." *PS* 47: 67–83.

Clay, J. S. (1981–82). "Immortal and ageless forever." *CJ* 77: 112–17.

Cloud, J. D. (1989). "Satirists and the law." In S. H. Braund (ed.), *Satire and Society in Ancient Rome*, 49–67. Exeter.

Coale, A. J., Demeny, P. G., and Vaughan, B. (1983). *Regional Model Life Tables and Stable Populations*[2]. New York and London.

Cockle, W. E. H. (1984). "State archives in Graeco-Roman Egypt from 30 B.C. to the reign of Septimius Severus." *JEA* 70: 106–22.

Cody, J. M. (1976). "The *senex amator* in Plautus' *Casina.*" *Hermes* 104: 453–76.

Coffman, G. R. (1934). "Old age from Horace to Chaucer: Some literary affinities and adventures of an idea." *Speculum* 9: 249–77.

Cohen, N. (1996). "A notice of birth of a girl." In R. Katzoff, Y. Petroff, and D. Schaps (eds.), *Classical Studies in Honor of David Sohlberg*, 385–98. Ramat Gan.

Cole, T. R. (1992). *The Journey of Life.* Cambridge.

Coleman, K. M. (ed.) (1988). *Statius, Silvae IV.* Oxford.

Colmant, P. (1956). "Les quatre âges de la vie (Horace, *Art Poétique,* 153–175)." *LEC* 24: 58–63.

Colton, R. (1977). "Martial in Juvenal's tenth satire." *Studies in Philology* 74: 341–53.

Conrad, C., and von Kondratowitz, H.-J. (eds.) (1993). *Zur Kulturgeschichte des Alterns.* Berlin.

Constantelos, D. J. (1991). *Byzantine Philanthropy and Social Welfare*[2]. New York.

Corbier, M. (1974). *L'Aerarium Saturni et l'Aerarium militare.* Rome.

Corcoran, S. (1996). *The Empire of the Tetrarchs.* Oxford.

Coriat, J.-P. (1997). *Le Prince Législateur.* Rome.

Cornell, T. J. (1995). *The Beginnings of Rome.* London and New York.

Corvisier, J.-N. (1985a). *Santé et société en Grèce ancienne.* Paris.

——— (1985b). "La vieillesse en Grèce ancienne d'Homère à l'époque hellénistique." *ADH* 1985: 53–70.

——— (1991). "Les grands-parents dans le monde grec ancien." *ADH* 1991: 21–31.

Cosminsky, S. (1976). "Cross-cultural perspectives on midwifery." In F. X. Grollig and H. B. Haley (eds.), *Medical Anthropology,* 229–48. The Hague.

Cotton, H. M. (1995). "The archive of Salome Komaise daughter of Levi: Another archive from the 'Cave of Letters.'" *ZPE* 105: 171–208.

Coudry, M. (1994). "Sénatus-consultes et *acta senatus*: rédaction, conservation et archivage des documents émanant du sénat, de l'époque de César à celle des Sévères." In S. Demougin (ed.), *La mémoire perdue*, 65–102. Paris.

Courtney, E. (ed.) (1980). *A Commentary on the Satires of Juvenal.* London.

————— (ed.) (1993). *The Fragmentary Latin Poets.* Oxford.

Covey, H. C. (1989). "Old age portrayed by the ages-of-life models from the Middle Ages to the 16th century." *Gerontologist* 29: 692–98.

————— (1991). *Images of Older People in Western Art and Society.* New York.

————— (1992). "The definitions of the beginning of old age in history." *International Journal of Aging and Human Development* 34: 325–37.

————— (1992–93). "A return to infancy: Old age and the second childhood in history." *International Journal of Aging and Human Development* 36: 81–90.

Crawford, M. H. (ed.) (1996). *Roman Statutes.* London.

Crawford, M. H., and Reynolds, J. (1979). "The Aezani copy of the Prices Edict." *ZPE* 34: 163–210.

Crichton, A. (1991–93). "'The old are in a second childhood': Age reversal and jury service in Aristophanes' *Wasps*." *BICS* 38: 59–80.

Crisafulli, N. (1953). "L'idea della vecchiezza in Seneca." *Longevità* 2: 9–13.

Crook, J. (1955). *Consilium Principis.* Cambridge.

————— (1986). "Women in Roman succession." In Rawson (1986) 58–82.

Croon, J. H. (1981). "Het beeld van de oude mens in de literatuur van de oudheid." In J. H. Croon et al. (eds.), *De Lastige Ouderdom,* 9–28. Muiderberg.

Crowther, N. B. (1988). "The age-category of boys at Olympia." *Phoenix* 42: 304–8.

————— (1990). "Old age, exercise and athletics in the ancient world." *Stadion* 16: 171–83.

Csillag, P. (1976). *The Augustan Laws on Family Relations.* Budapest.

Culham, P. (1989). "Archives and alternatives in republican Rome." *CPh* 84: 100–115.

Cumming, E., and Henry, W. E. (1961). *Growing Old: The Process of Disengagement.* New York.

Cuntz, O. (1888). *De Augusto Plinii Geographicorum Auctore.* Bonn.

Curchin, L. (1980). "Old age in Sumer." *Florilegium* 2: 61–70.

Curtius, E. R. (1953). *European Literature and the Latin Middle Ages.* Tr. W. R. Trask. London.

Cuvigny, M. (ed.) (1984). *Plutarque, Oeuvres Morales 11.1, Traites 49–51.* Paris.

Dahlmann, H. (1959). "Bemerkungen zu Varros Menippea Tithonus, περὶ γήρως." In H. Dahlmann and R. Merkelbach (eds.), *Studien zur Textgeschichte und Testkritik,* 37–45. Cologne.

Dahlmann, H., and Heisterhagen, R. (1957). *Varronische Studien, I.* Wiesbaden.

Daly, J. (1986). "*Oedipus Coloneus:* Sophocles' *threpteria* to Athens." *QUCC* 22: 75–93; 23: 65–84.

Daly, L. W. (1967). *Contributions to a History of Alphabeticization.* Brussels.

Damsté, P. H. (1929). "De longaevitatis causis." *Mnem.* 57: 103–5.

Daube, D. (1947). "Did Macedo murder his father?" *ZRG* 65: 261–311.

————— (1953). "Actions between *paterfamilias* and *filiusfamilias* with *peculium castrense.*" In V. Arangio-Ruiz and G. Lavaggi (eds.), *Studi in memoria di Emilio Albertario, I,* 433–74. Milan.

———— (1969). *Roman Law: Linguistic, Social and Philosophical Aspects.* Edinburgh.

———— (1972). *Civil Disobedience in Antiquity.* Edinburgh.

David, E. (1991). *Old Age in Sparta.* Amsterdam.

Davies, M. (1989). *The Epic Cycle.* Bristol.

de Beauvoir, S. (1977). *Old Age.* Tr. P. O'Brian. Harmondsworth. Originally published as *La vieillesse* (Paris, 1970).

De Caria, F. (ed.) (1977). *L. Anneo Seneca. Il problema della vecchiaia.* Rome.

de Ghellinck, J. (1948). "*Iuventus, gravitas, senectus.*" In *Studia Mediævalia in Honorem Admodum Reverendi Patris R. J. Martin,* 39–59. Brugge.

de Leeuw, C. A. (1939). *Aelius Aristides als bron voor de kennis von zijn tijd.* Amsterdam.

de Luce, J. (1993). "*Quod temptabam scribere versus erat:* Ovid in exile." In A. M. Wyatt-Brown and J. Rossen (eds.), *Aging and Gender in Literature,* 229–41. Charlottesville and London.

———— (1994). "Ancient images of aging: Did ageism exist in Greco-Roman antiquity?" In D. Shenk and W. A. Achenbaum (eds.), *Changing Perceptions of Aging and the Aged,* 65–74. New York. Originally published in *Generations* 17 (1993) 41–45.

de Luce, J., Hendricks, J., Rodeheaver, D., and Seltzer, M. M. (1993). "Continuity and change: Four disciplinary perspectives on reading Cicero's *de Senectute.*" *Journal of Aging Studies* 7: 335–81.

de Romilly, J. (1976). "Alcibiade et le mélange entre jeunes et vieux: politique et médecine." *WS* 89: 93–105.

de Zulueta, F. (1953). *The Institutes of Gaius.* Vol. 2. Oxford.

Dean-Jones, L. (1994). *Women's Bodies in Classical Greek Science.* Oxford.

Degl'Innocenti Pierini, R. (1996). "*Venit ad pigros cana senectus* (Sen. *Herc. F.* 198). Un motivo dei cori senecani tra filosofia ed attualità." In L. Castagna (ed.), *Nove studi sui cori tragici di Seneca,* 37–56. Milan.

Delgado, J. J. (1961). "Concepto de 'adulescens' en Cicerón." In *Atti del I Congresso Internazionale di Studi Ciceroniani,* 2:433–52. Rome.

Delia, D. (1988). "The population of Roman Alexandria." *TAPhA* 118: 275–92.

Della Corte, M. (1924). *Iuventus.* Rome.

Demaitre, L. (1990). "The care and extension of old age in medieval medicine." In Sheehan (1990) 3–22.

Demand, N. (1994). *Birth, Death, and Motherhood in Classical Greece.* Baltimore and London.

Demougin, S. (1975). "Les juges des cinq décuries originaires de l'Italie." *AS* 6: 143–202.

———— (1992). *Prosopographie des chevaliers romains julio-claudiens.* Rome.

Deschamps, L. (1978). "Quelques clins d'oeil de Varron dans les *Satires Ménip-*

pées." In J. Collart (ed.), *Varron, grammaire antique et stylistique latine*, 91–100. Paris.

——— (1987). "Temps et histoire chez Varron." In S. Boldrini (ed.), *Filologia e forme letterarie. Studi offerti a Francesco della Corte, II*, 167–92. Urbino.

Develin, R. (1979). *Patterns in Office-Holding, 366–49 B.C.* Brussels.

Devoto, G. (1956). "L'uccisione dei vecchi e il lessico indeuropeo." In *MNHMHΣ XAPIN: Gedenkschrift Paul Kretschmer,* 93–99. Vienna. Republished as "I vecchi e l'uccisione dei vecchi," *Scritti minori* (Florence) 1 (1958) 119–25.

Dickson, K. (1995). *Nestor: Poetic Memory in Greek Epic.* New York and London.

Diers, C. J. (1974). "Historical trends in the age at menarche and menopause." *Psychological Reports* 34: 931–37.

Dietz, K. (1980). *Senatus contra principem.* Munich.

——— (1993). "Die beiden P. Mummii Sisennae und der Wiederaufbau der Basilike Stoa von Thera." *Chiron* 23: 295–311.

Diliberto, O. (1984). *Studi sulle origini della "cura furiosi."* Naples.

Dillon, M. P. J. (1995). "Payments to the disabled at Athens: Social justice or fear of aristocratic patronage?" *AS* 26: 27–57.

Dixon, S. (1988). *The Roman Mother.* London and Sydney.

——— (1992). *The Roman Family.* Baltimore and London.

——— (1997). "Conflict in the Roman family." In Rawson and Weaver (1997) 149–67.

Dobson, B. (1974). "The significance of the centurion and *primipilaris* in the Roman army and administration." *ANRW* 2.1: 392–434.

Donahue, W., Orbach, H. L., and Pollak, O. (1960). "Retirement: The emerging social pattern." In Tibbitts (1960) 330–406.

Dove, M. (1986). *The Perfect Age of Man's Life.* Cambridge.

Dover, K. J. (ed.) (1968). *Aristophanes: Clouds.* Oxford.

Drecoll, C. (1997). *Die Liturgien im römischen Kaiserreich des 3. und 4. Jh. n. Chr.* Stuttgart.

Drerup, E. (1933). *Das Generationsproblem in der griechischen und griechisch-römischen Kultur.* Paderborn.

Dropsie, M. A. (1996). *The Roman Law of Testaments, Codicils, and Gifts in the Event of Death* (mortis causa donationes). Littleton, Colo.

Duckworth, G. E. (1952). *The Nature of Roman Comedy.* Princeton, N.J.

Dumézil, G. (1950). "Quelques cas anciens de 'liquidation des vieillards': histoire et survivances." *RIDA* 4: 447–54.

Duncan-Jones, R. P. (1977). "Age-rounding, illiteracy and social differentiation in the Roman empire." *Chiron* 7: 333–53. Reprinted with addenda in H. Schneider (ed.), *Sozial- und Wirtschaftsgeschichte der römischen Kaiserzeit* (Darmstadt, 1981), 396–429.

——— (1979). "Age-rounding in Greco-Roman Egypt." *ZPE* 33: 169–77.

——— (1980). "Age-rounding in Roman Carthage." In J. H. Humphrey (ed.),

Excavations at Carthage, 1977, Conducted by the University of Michigan, 5:1–6. New Delhi.

———— (1990). *Structure and Scale in the Roman Economy.* Cambridge.

Duttenhöfer, R. (1989). "Drei Todesanzeigen." *ZPE* 79: 227–34.

Dyroff, A. (1937). "Junkos und Ariston von Keos über das Greisenalter." *RhM* 86: 241–69.

———— (1939). *Der Peripatos über das Greisenalter.* Paderborn.

Dyson, S. (1992a). *Community and Society in Roman Italy.* Baltimore and London.

———— (1992b). "Age, sex, and status: The view from the Roman rotary club." *EMC* 11: 69–85.

Ebling, F. J. (1980). "The physiology of hair growth." In M. M. Breuer (ed.), *Cosmetic Science,* 2:181–232. London and New York.

Eck, W. (1970). *Senatoren von Vespasian bis Hadrian.* Munich.

———— (1974). "Beförderungskriterien innerhalb der senatorischen Laufbahn, dargestellt an der Zeit von 69 bis 138 n. Chr." *ANRW* 2.1: 158–228.

———— (1979). *Die staatliche Organisation Italiens in der hohen Kaiserzeit.* Munich.

———— (1982a). "Jahres-und Provinzialfasten der senatorischen Statthalter von 69/70 bis 138/139." *Chiron* 12: 281–362.

———— (1982b). "Die Gestalt Frontins in ihrer politischen und sozialen Umwelt." In *Wasserversorgung im antiken Rom*, 47–62. Munich and Vienna.

———— (1983). "Jahres-und Provinzialfasten der senatorischen Statthalter von 69/70 bis 138/139." *Chiron* 13: 147–237.

———— (1985a). *Die Statthalter der germanischen Provinzen vom 1.-3. Jahrhundert.* Cologne and Bonn.

———— (1985b). "Statius *Silvae* 1.4 und C. Rutilius Gallicus als Proconsul Asiae II." *AJPh* 106: 475–84.

———— (1997). "Rome and the outside world: Senatorial families and the world they lived in." In Rawson and Weaver (1997) 73–99.

Eck, W., Caballos, A., and Fernández, F. (eds.) (1996). *Das* senatus consultum de Cn. Pisone patre. Munich.

Eckart, W. U. (2000). "Lust oder Last?—Alterskrankheit und Altersgesundheit in historischer Perspektive." *Zeitschrift für Gerontologie und Geriatrie* 33: 71–78.

Edelstein, L. (1967). *Ancient Medicine.* Ed. O. Temkin and C. L. Temkin. Baltimore.

Edwards, C. (1999). "Age-based rationing of medical care in nineteenth-century England." *Continuity and Change* 14: 227–65.

Eekelaar, J. M., and Pearl, D. (eds.) (1989). *An Aging World: Dilemmas and Challenges for Law and Social Policy.* Oxford.

Egerton, F. N. (1975). "Aristotle's population biology." *Arethusa* 8.2: 307–30.

Eisenstadt, S. N. (1971). *From Generation to Generation: Age Groups and Social Structure*[2]. New York and London.

el-Abbadi, M. A. H. (1964). "The *gerousia* in Roman Egypt." *JEA* 50: 164–69.

Elders, L. (1983). "Vieillesse, mort et mort volontaire dans l'antiquité classique." In J. Ries (ed.), *La mort selon la Bible dans l'antiquité classique et selon le manichéisme*, 91–133. Louvain-la-Neuve.

Elftmann, G. (1979). "Aeneas in his prime: Distinctions in age and the loneliness of adulthood in Vergil's *Aeneid*." *Arethusa* 12: 175–202.

Ernout, A., and Meillet, A. (1959). *Dictionnaire étymologique de la langue latine*. Paris.

Escalante Merlos, D. (1998). "La *anus* en la comedia greco-latina. Rasgos característicos y evolución." In J. Vincente Bañuls et al. (eds.). *El teatre clàssic al marc de la cultura grega i la seua pervivéncia dins la cultura occidental*, 133–46. Bari.

Estevez, V. A. (1966). "*Senex* as spouse in Plautus and Terence." *CB* 42: 73–76.

Étienne, R. (1959). "Démographie et épigraphie." In *Atti del Terzo Congresso Internazionale di Epigrafia Greca e Latina*, 415–24. Rome.

——— (1976). "Ancient medical conscience and the life of children." Tr. M. R. Morris. *Journal of Psychohistory* 4: 131–61.

Euzennat, M., and Marion, J. (eds.) (1982). *Inscriptions antiques du Maroc, 2*. Paris.

Evans, J. A. S. (1957). "The poll-tax in Egypt." *Aegyptus* 37: 259–65.

Evans, J. K. (1991). *War, Women and Children in Ancient Rome*. London and New York.

Evans, R. J., and Kleijwegt, M. (1992). "Did the Romans like young men? A study of the *lex Villia annalis*: Causes and effects." *ZPE* 92: 181–96.

Evans Grubbs, J. (1995). *Law and Family in Late Antiquity*. Oxford.

Évrard, É. (1978). "Vieux et ancien chez Tibulle." *Latomus* 37: 121–47.

Eyben, E. (1972a). "Antiquity's view of puberty." *Latomus* 31: 677–97.

——— (1972b). "The concrete ideal in the life of the young Roman." *AC* 41: 200–17.

——— (1973a). "Roman notes on the course of life." *AS* 4: 213–38.

——— (1973b). "Die Einteilung des menschlichen Lebens im römischen Altertum." *RhM* 116: 150–90.

——— (1977). *De jonge Romein volgens de literaire bronnen der periode ca. 200 v. Chr. tot ca. 500 n. Chr*. Brussels.

——— (1981). "Was the Roman 'youth' an 'adult' socially?" *AC* 50: 328–50.

——— (1993). *Restless Youth in Ancient Rome*. London and New York.

Fabre, G. (1981). *Libertus*. Rome.

Fabre, P. (1940). "*Minime romano sacro*: note sur un passage de Tite-Live et les sacrifices humains dans la religion romaine." *REA* 42: 419–24.

Falkner, T. M. (1985). "Old age in Euripides' *Medea*." *CB* 61: 76–78.

——— (1989). "Slouching towards Boeotia: Age and age-grading in the Hesiodic myth of the five races." *CA* 8: 42–60.

——— (1990). "The politics and the poetics of time in Solon's 'ten ages.'" *CJ* 86: 1–15.

——— (1995). *The Poetics of Old Age in Greek Epic, Lyric, and Tragedy.* Norman and London.

Falkner, T. M., and de Luce, J. (eds.) (1989). *Old Age in Greek and Latin Literature.* Albany, N.Y.

——— (1992). "A view from antiquity: Greece, Rome, and the elders." In T. Coll et al. (eds.), *Handbook of Humanities and Aging,* 33–39. New York.

Farr, J. (1993). "Manumission in the form of a *donatio mortis causa.*" *BASP* 30: 93–104.

Farrell, J. (1997). "The phenomenology of memory in Roman culture." *CJ* 92: 373–83.

Fasciato, M. (1949). "Note sur l'affranchissement des esclaves abandonnés dans l'île d'Esculape." *RHDFE* 27: 454–64.

Fayer, C. (1994). *La familia romana. Aspetti giuridici ed antiquari, I.* Rome.

Fears, J. R. (1981). "The cult of virtues and Roman imperial ideology." *ANRW* 2.17.2: 827–948.

Ferguson, J. (ed.) (1979). *Juvenal: The Satires.* London.

Finley, M. I. (1981). "The elderly in classical antiquity." *G&R* 28: 156–71. Reprinted in *A&S* 4 (1984) 391–408, in Falkner and de Luce (1989) 1–20, and in *Communications* 37 (1983) 31–45 (in French).

Fishelov, D. (1990). "The vanity of the reader's wishes: Rereading Juvenal's *Satire* 10." *AJPh* 111: 370–82.

Fitzgerald, W. (1988). "Power and impotence in Horace's *Epodes.*" *Ramus* 17: 176–91.

Forest, P. (1944). "La vieillesse chez Platon." In P. Gardette et al. (eds.), *Mélanges J. Saunier,* 21–25. Lyons.

Formanek, S., and Linhart, S. (eds.) (1997). *Aging: Asian Concepts and Experiences, Past and Present.* Vienna.

Fornara, C. W. (1966). "Sources of Plutarch's *An Seni Sit Gerenda Res Publica.*" *Philologus* 110: 119–27.

Forrest, W. G. (1975). "An Athenian generation gap." *YCS* 24: 37–52.

Fortes, M. (1984). "Age, generation, and social structure." In Kertzer and Keith (1984) 99–122.

Foulon, A. (1986). "Reflexions sur l'imitation: le cheval vieilli chez Ennius, Tibulle, Ovide." *Kentron* 2: 114–17.

Fowler, B. H. (1989). *The Hellenistic Aesthetic.* Bristol.

Frazer, J. G. (1929). *Ovid: Fasti.* London.

Freer, C. (1988). "Old myths: Frequent misconceptions about the elderly." In N. Wells and C. Freer (eds.), *The Ageing Population: Burden or Challenge?* 3–15. London and New York.

French, V. (1986). "Midwives and maternity care in the Greco-Roman world." In M. Skinner (ed.), *Rescuing Creusa,* 69–84. Lubbock, Tex.

Friedl, R. (1996). *Der Konkubinat im kaiserzeitlichen Rom.* Stuttgart.

Friedrich, P. (1978). *The Meaning of Aphrodite.* Chicago.

Frier, B. W. (1982). "Roman life expectancy: Ulpian's evidence." *HSCPh* 86: 213–51.

———— (1992). "Statistics and Roman society." *JRA* 5: 286–90.

Frösén, J., and Westman, R. (1997). "Quattro papiri Schubart." In *Papiri filosofici: miscellanea di studi, I,* 7–48. Florence.

Fry, C. L. (ed.) (1980). *Aging in Culture and Society.* New York.

———— (ed.) (1981). *Dimensions: Aging, Culture and Health.* New York.

Fry, C. L., and Keith, J. (eds.) (1986). *New Methods for Old-Age Research: Strategies for Studying Diversity.* South Hadley, Mass.

Fuà, O. (1979–80). "La dignità dell' anziano negli scrittori greci fino al IV secolo a.c." *Atti dell' Istituto di Scienze, Lettere ed Arti* 138: 397–414.

Gabba, E. (1991). *Dionysius and the History of Archaic Rome.* Berkeley.

Gagé, J. (1950). *Huit recherches sur les origines italiques et romaines.* Paris.

———— (1958). "Classes d'âge, rites et vêtements de passage dans l'ancien Latium." *Cahiers internationaux de sociologie* 24: 34–64.

Gallivan, P. A. (1974). "Confusion concerning the age of Octavia." *Latomus* 33: 116–17.

García-Ballester, L. (1993). "On the origin of the 'six non-natural things' in Galen." In J. Kollesch and D. Nickel (eds.), *Galen und das hellenistische Erbe,* 105–15. Stuttgart.

Gardner, J. F. (1986a). "Proofs of status in the Roman world." *BICS* 33: 1–14.

———— (1986b). *Women in Roman Law and Society.* London and Sydney.

———— (1993). *Being a Roman Citizen.* London.

———— (1998). *Family and Familia in Roman Law and Life.* Oxford.

Garland, R. (1987). "Greek geriatrics." *History Today* 37 (September): 12–18.

———— (1990). *The Greek Way of Life: From Conception to Old Age.* London.

———— (1995). *The Eye of the Beholder.* London.

Garnsey, P. (1988). *Famine and Food Supply in the Graeco-Roman World.* Cambridge.

———— (1998). *Cities, Peasants and Food in Classical Antiquity.* Ed. W. Scheidel. Cambridge.

Garnsey, P., and Saller, R. P. (1987). *The Roman Empire: Economy, Society and Culture.* London.

Garthwaite, J. (1989). "Statius' retirement from Rome: *Silvae* 3.5." *Antichthon* 23: 81–91.

Garver, E. (1994). "Growing older and wiser with Aristotle: *Rhetoric* II.12–14 and moral development." With commentary by M. Chaplin. *Proceedings of the Boston Area Colloquium in Ancient Philosophy* 10: 171–200.

Gaunt, D. (1983). "The property and kin relationships of retired farmers in northern and central Europe." In R. Wall, P. Laslett, and J. Robin (eds.), *Family Forms in Historic Europe,* 249–79. Cambridge.

Gavazzi, M. (1976). "The tradition of killing old people: Prolegomena to a revised methodical treatment of the subject." In L. Dégh, H. Glassie, and F. J. Oinas (eds.), *Folklore Today*, 175–80. Bloomington.

Gélis, J. (1991). *History of Childbirth*. Tr. R. Morris. Cambridge.

Giacomini, P. (1992–93). "La caratterizzazione della vecchiaia nei documenti epigrafici." *RSA* 22–23: 161–77.

Giannarelli, E. (1988). "Il παιδαριογέρων nella biografia cristiana." *Prometheus* 14: 279–84.

Gigon, O. (1968). "Jugend und Alter in der Ethik des Aristoteles." In J. Bursian and L. Vidman (eds.), *Antiquitas Graeco-Romana ac Tempora Nostra*, 188–92. Prague.

Gilbert, C. (1967). "When did a man in the Renaissance grow old?" *Studies in the Renaissance* 14: 7–32.

Glascock, A. P., and Feinman, S. L. (1981). "Social asset or social burden: Treatment of the aged in non-industrial societies." In Fry (1981) 13–31.

Glascock, A. P., and Feinman, S. L. (1986). "Treatment of the aged in nonindustrial societies." In Fry and Keith (1986) 281–96.

Gnilka, C. (1972). *Aetas spiritalis*. Bonn.

——— (1980). "Καλόγηρος. Die Idee des 'guten Alters' bei den Christen." *JAC* 23: 5–21.

——— (1983). "Greisenalter." *RAC* 12: 995–1094.

——— (1985). "Altersversorgung." *RAC*, suppl., 1–2: 266–89.

Godderis, J. (1989). "Περὶ γήρως: De antieke geneeskunde over de lichamelijke en psychische kwalen van de oude dag." *Kleio* 18: 51–66.

——— (1998). "A historical perspective on the care of the aged in medieval times." *Nursing Clinics of North America* 33: 557–68.

Golden, M. (1979). "Demosthenes and the age of majority at Athens." *Phoenix* 33: 25–38.

——— (1981). "Demography and the exposure of girls at Athens." *Phoenix* 35: 316–33.

——— (1990). *Children and Childhood in Classical Athens*. Baltimore and London.

——— (1992). "Continuity, change and the study of ancient childhood." *EMC* 11: 7–18.

Golden, M., and Toohey, P. (eds.) (1997). *Inventing Ancient Culture*. London and New York.

Goldhill, S. (1988). "A footnote in the history of Greek epitaphs: Simonides 146 Bergk." *Phoenix* 42: 189–97.

Gomme, A. W., and Sandbach, F. H. (eds.) (1973). *Menander: A Commentary*. Oxford.

Goody, J. (1976). "Aging in non-industrial societies." In R. H. Binstock and E. Shanas (eds.). *Handbook of Aging and the Social Sciences*, 117–29. New York.

Gorce, D. (ed.) (1962). *Vie de Sainte Mélanie*. Paris.

Gourevitch, D. (1996). "La gynécologie et l'obstétrique." *ANRW* 2.37.3: 2083–2146.

Gow, A. S. F., and Page, D. L. (eds.) (1965). *The Greek Anthology: Hellenistic Epigrams.* Vol. 2. Cambridge.

Graf, F. (2000). "The rite of the Argei—once again." *MH* 57: 94–103.

Grasby, R. D. (1975). "The age, ancestry, and career of Gordian I." *CQ* 25: 123–30.

Grassl, H. (1978–79). "Die älteste Römerin—eine Steirerin? Ein Beitrag zur Frage des Höchstalters in der Antike." *Schild von Steier* 15–16: 101–4.

———— (1982). *Sozialökonomische Vorstellungen in der kaiserzeitlichen griechischen Literatur.* Wiesbaden.

Grassmann, V. (1966). *Die erotischen Epoden des Horaz.* Munich.

Grasso, L. (1995). "Il linguaggio dei vecchi nelle commedie di Menandro (imprecazioni ed esclamazioni)." *Rudiae* 7: 231–43.

Grenfell, B. P., and Hunt, A. S. (eds.) (1899). *The Oxyrhynchus Papyri.* Vol. 2. London.

———— (eds.) (1908). *The Oxyrhynchus Papyri.* Vol. 6. London.

Griffin, J. (1980). *Homer on Life and Death.* Oxford.

Griffin, M. T. (1962). "*De brevitate vitae.*" *JRS* 52: 104–13.

———— (1976). *Seneca, a Philosopher in Politics.* Oxford.

Griffith, G. T. (1966). "*Isegoria* in the assembly at Athens." In E. Badian (ed.), *Ancient Society and Institutions*, 115–38. Oxford.

Grimaldi, W. M. A. (ed.) (1988). *Aristotle,* Rhetoric II. New York.

Grmek, M. D. (1957). "Les aspects historiques des problèmes fondamentaux de la gérontologie." *Le Scalpel* 110: 158–64.

———— (1958). *On Ageing and Old Age.* Den Haag.

———— (1995). "Les représentations figurées de la consumption et du corps émacié dans l'antiquité." *Medicina nei Secoli* 7: 249–72.

Gruen, E. S. (1992). *Culture and National Identity in Republican Rome.* Ithaca.

Gruman, G. J. (1966). "A history of ideas about the prolongation of life: The evolution of prolongevity hypotheses to 1800." *Transactions of the American Philosophical Society* 56.9: 1–102.

———— (ed.) (1979). *Roots of Modern Gerontology and Geriatrics.* New York.

Guarino, A. (1979). "*Depontani senes.*" *AAN* 90: 535–39.

Gubrium, J. F., and Holstein, J. A. (eds.) (2000). *Aging and Everyday Life.* Oxford.

Günther, L.-M. (1993). "Witwen in der griechischen Antike—zwischen Oikos und Polis." *Historia* 42: 308–25.

Gutmann, D. (1976). "Alternatives to disengagement: The old men of the Highland Druze." In J. F. Gubrium (ed.), *Times, Roles, and Self in Old Age*, 88–108. New York.

Haas, C. (1997). *Alexandria in Late Antiquity.* Baltimore and London.

Haber, C. (1983). *Beyond Sixty-Five: The Dilemma of Old Age in America's Past.* Cambridge.

Haensch, R. (1992). "Das Statthalterarchiv." *ZRG* 109: 209–317.

———— (1994). "Die Bearbeitungsweisen von Petitionen in der Provinz Aegyptus." *ZPE* 100: 487–546.

Hagedorn, D. (1985). "Zum Amt des διοικητής im römischen Aegypten." *YCS* 28: 167–210.

Halfmann, H. (1986). *Itinera Principum.* Stuttgart.

Halkin, L. (1948). "Le problème des 'decem menses' de la IVe églogue de Virgile." *LEC* 16: 354–70.

Hallett, J. P. (1984). *Fathers and Daughters in Roman Society.* Princeton, N.J.

———— (1992). "Heeding our native informants: The uses of Latin literary texts in recovering elite Roman attitudes toward age, gender and social status." *EMC* 11: 333–55.

Hamblenne, P. (1969). "La longévité de Jérôme: Prosper avait-il raison?" *Latomus* 28: 1081–1119.

Hambüchen, B. (1966). *Die Datierung von Senecas Schrift ad Paulinum de Brevitate Vitae.* Cologne.

Handley, E. W. (1993). "Aristophanes and the generation gap." In A. H. Sommerstein et al. (eds.). *Tragedy, Comedy and the Polis*, 417–30. Bari.

Hansen, M. H. (1987). *The Athenian Assembly in the Age of Demosthenes.* Oxford.

Hansen, W. (tr.) (1996). *Phlegon of Tralles' Book of Marvels.* Exeter.

Hanson, A. E. (1974). "Lists of taxpayers from Philadelphia." *ZPE* 15: 229–48.

———— (1984). "Caligulan month-names at Philadelphia and related matters." In *Atti del XVII Congresso internazionale di Papirologia*, 3:1107–18. Naples.

———— (1991). "Ancient illiteracy." In M. Beard et al., *Literacy in the Roman World*, 159–98. Ann Arbor.

Harcum, C. G. (1914). "The ages of man. A study suggested by Horace, *Ars Poetica,* lines 153–178." *CW* 7: 114–18.

Hareven, T. K. (ed.) (1996). *Aging and Generational Relations over the Life Course.* Berlin.

Harkness, A. G. (1896). "Age at marriage and at death in the Roman empire." *TAPhA* 27: 35–72.

Harris, R. (2000). *Gender and Aging in Mesopotamia.* Norman.

Harris, W. V. (1989). *Ancient Literacy.* Cambridge, Mass.

Harrison, A. R. W. (1968). *The Law of Athens, I.* Oxford.

Hartke, W. (1951). *Römische Kinderkaiser.* Berlin.

Häussler, R. (1964). "Vom Ursprung und Wandel des Lebensaltervergleichs." *Hermes* 92: 313–41.

———— (ed.) (1968). *Nachträge zu A. Otto, Sprichwörter und sprichwörtliche Redensarten der Römer.* Darmstadt.

Havas, M. L. (1992). "Le corps de l'empire romain vu par les auteurs latins et grecs." In M. Sordi (ed.), *Autocoscienze e rappresentazione dei popoli,* 239–59. Milan.

Havighurst, R. J. (1963). "Successful aging." In R. H. Williams, C. Tibbitts, and W. Donahoe (eds.), *The Process of Aging*, 1: 311–15. Chicago.

Havighurst, R. J., Neugarten, B. L., and Tobin, S. S. (1964). "Disengagement, personality and life satisfaction in the later years." In P. From Hansen (ed.), *Age with a Future*, 419–25. Munksgaard.

Haynes, M. S. (1962). "The supposedly golden age for the aged in ancient Greece (A study of literary concepts of old age)." *Gerontologist* 2: 93–98.

——— (1963). "The supposedly golden age for the aged in ancient Rome (A study of literary concepts of old age)." *Gerontologist* 3: 26–35.

Hazan, H. (1994). *Old Age: Constructions and Deconstructions*. Cambridge.

Henderson, J. (1987). "Older women in Attic old comedy." *TAPhA* 117: 105–29.

Henrichs, A. (1980). "Human sacrifice in Greek religion: Three case studies." *Fondation Hardt, Entretiens* 27: 195–235.

Hense, O. (ed.) (1909). *Teletis Reliquiae²*. Tübingen.

Herbert-Brown, G. (1999). "Jerome's dates for Gaius Lucilius, *satyrarum scriptor*." *CQ* 49: 535–43.

Herlihy, D. (1990). "Age, property, and career in medieval society." In Sheehan (1990) 143–58.

Herter, H. (1975). "Demokrit über das Alter." *Würzburger Jahrbücher für die Altertumwissenschaft*, n.s., 1: 83–92.

Herzig, H. E. (1994). "Der alte Mensch in der griechisch-römischen Antike." In K. Buraselis (ed.), *Unity and Units of Antiquity*, 169–79. Athens.

Highet, G. (1937). "The life of Juvenal." *TAPhA* 68: 480–506.

——— (1954). *Juvenal the Satirist*. Oxford.

Hillman, T. P. (1993). "When did Lucullus retire?" *Historia* 42: 211–28.

Hirzel, R. (1895). *Der Dialog*. Leipzig.

——— (1908). "Der Selbstmord." *Archiv für Religionswissenschaft* 11: 75–206.

Hobson, D. W. (1984). "*P.Vindob. Gr.* 24951 + 24556: New evidence for tax-exempt status in Roman Egypt." In *Atti del XVII Congresso internazionale di Papirologia*, 3:847–64. Naples.

——— (1985). "House and household in Roman Egypt." *YCS* 28: 211–29.

——— (1993). "The impact of law on village life in Roman Egypt." In B. Halpern and D. W. Hobson (eds.), *Law, Politics and Society in the Ancient Mediterranean World*, 193–219. Sheffield.

Hochschild, A. R. (1975). "Disengagement theory, a critique and proposal." *ASR* 40: 553–69.

——— (1976). "Disengagement theory: A logical, empirical, and phenomenological critique." In J. F. Gubrium (ed.), *Times, Roles, and Self in Old Age*, 53–87. New York.

Hockey, J., and James, A. (1993). *Growing Up and Growing Old: Ageing and Dependency in the Life Course*. London.

Hodkinson, S. (1983). "Social order and the conflict of values in classical Sparta." *Chiron* 13: 239–81.

Hofmann, J. B., and Szantyr, A. (1965). *Lateinisches Syntax und Stilistik.* Munich.

Hofmeister, A. (1926). "*Puer, iuvenis, senex.* Zum Verständnis der mittelalterlichen Altersbezeichnungen." In A. Brackmann (ed.), *Papsttum und Kaisertum,* 287–316. Munich.

Hohnen, P. (1988). "Zeugnisse der Altersreflexion bei Horaz." *Gymnasium* 95: 154–72.

Hombert, M., and Préaux, C. (1952). *Recherches sur le recensement dans l'Égypte romaine.* Leiden.

Honoré, T. (1982). *Ulpian.* Oxford.

Hopkins, M. K. (1966–67). "On the probable age structure of the Roman population." *PS* 20: 245–64.

——— (1980). "Brother-sister marriage in Roman Egypt." *CSSH* 22: 303–54.

——— (1983). *Death and Renewal.* Cambridge.

Horden, P., and Smith, R. (eds.) (1998). *The Locus of Care.* London and New York.

Horsfall, N. (1991). "Statistics or states of mind?" In M. Beard et al., *Literacy in the Roman World,* 59–76. Ann Arbor.

——— (1991–92). "Economia suburbana e tradizione bucolica: il *senex* di Claudiano." *Invigilata Lucernis* (Bari) 13–14: 169–77.

Horster, M. (1996). "Kinderkarrieren?" In C. Klodt (ed.), *Satura Lanx,* 223–38. Hildesheim.

Horstkotte, H. (1996). "Systematische Aspekte der *munera publica* in der römischen Kaiserzeit." *ZPE* 111: 233–55.

Houdijk, L. J. J., and Vanderbroeck, P. J. J. (1987). "Old age and sex in the ancient Greek world." *Wissenschaftliche Zeitschrift der Wilhelm-Pieck-Universität Rostock* 36: 57–61.

Howard, C. L. (1958). "*Quisque* with ordinals." *CQ* 8: 1–11.

Howell, N. (1986). "Age estimates and their evaluation in research." In Fry and Keith (1986) 57–76.

Howell, P. (ed.) (1980). *A Commentary on Book One of the Epigrams of Martial.* London.

Hübener, E. (1957). "Ciceros 'De senectute' in gerontologischer Schau." *Das Altertum* 3: 46–52.

Hughes, D. D. (1991). *Human Sacrifice in Ancient Greece.* London.

Hummel, C. (1999). *Das Kind und seine Krankheiten in der griechischen Medizin.* Frankfurt am Main.

Hummert, M. L., Garstka, T. A., Shaner, J. L., and Strahm, S. (1994). "Stereotypes of the elderly held by young, middle-aged, and elderly adults." *Journals of Gerontology: Psychological Sciences and Social Sciences* 49: 240–49.

——— (1995). "Judgments about stereotypes of the elderly: Attitudes, age associations, and typicality ratings of young, middle-aged, and elderly adults." *Research on Aging* 17: 168–89.

Husselmann, E. M. (1957). "*Donationes mortis causa* from Tebtunis." *TAPhA* 88: 135–54.

Jackson, R. (1988). *Doctors and Diseases in the Roman Empire*. London.

——— (1996). "Eye medicine in the Roman empire." *ANRW* 2.37.3: 2228–51.

Jacoby, F. (1902). *Apollodors Chronik*. Berlin.

Janko, R. (1981). "Ἀθάνατος καὶ ἀγήρως: The genealogy of a formula." *Mnem.* 34: 382–85.

Jeanmaire, H. (1939). *Couroi et Courètes*. Lille.

Jeffreys, R. (1985). "The date of Messalla's death." *CQ* 35: 140–8.

Jerphagnon, L. (1981). "Les mille et une morts des philosophes antiques." *Revue belge de philologie et d'histoire* 59: 17–28.

Jeune, B., and Vaupel, J. W. (eds.) (1995). *Exceptional Longevity*. Odense.

——— (eds.) (1999). *Validation of Exceptional Longevity*. Odense.

Jiang, L. (1995). "Changing kinship structure and its implications for old-age support in urban and rural China." *PS* 49: 127–45.

Johnson, A. C. (1936). *An Economic Survey of Ancient Rome*. Vol. 2: *Roman Egypt*. Ed. T. Frank. Baltimore.

Johnson, P., and Thane, P. (eds.) (1998). *Old Age from Antiquity to Post-Modernity*. London.

Johnston, D. (1985). "Munificence and *municipia:* Bequests to towns in classical Roman law." *JRS* 75: 105–25.

Jolowicz, H. F., and Nicholas, B. (1972). *Historical Introduction to the Study of Roman Law*[3]. Cambridge.

Jones, A. H. M. (1940). *The Greek City from Alexander to Justinian*. Oxford.

——— (1960). *Studies in Roman Government and Law*. Oxford.

——— (1964). *The Later Roman Empire, 284–602*. Oxford.

——— (1974). *The Roman Economy*. Ed. P. A. Brunt. Oxford.

Jones, B. W. (1984). "The age for the consulate." *La Parola del Passato* 217: 281–84.

——— (1992). *The Emperor Domitian*. London.

Jones, C. P. (1978). *The Roman World of Dio Chrysostom*. Cambridge, Mass.

Jones, J. W. (1853). "Observations on the origin of the division of man's life into stages." *Archaeologia* 35: 167–89.

Jones, W. H. S. (1946). *Philosophy and Medicine in Ancient Greece*. Baltimore.

Joshel, S. R. (1986). "Nurturing the master's child: Slavery and the Roman child-nurse." *Signs* 12: 3–22.

Jouanna, J. (1996). "Le vin et la médecine dans la Grèce ancienne." *REG* 109: 410–34.

Just, R. (1989). *Women in Athenian Law and Life*. London and New York.

Kádár, Z., and Berényi-Révész, M. (1986). "Die Anthropologie des Plinius Maior." *ANRW* 2.32.4: 2201–24.

Kahrstedt, U. (1936). *Untersuchungen zur Magistratur in Athen*. Stuttgart.

Kaiser, D. H., and Engel, P. (1993). "Time- and age-awareness in early modern Russia." *CSSH* 35: 824–39.

Kajanto, I. (1968). *On the Problem of the Average Duration of Life in the Roman Empire*. Helsinki.

Kannisto, V. (1988). "On the survival of centenarians and the span of life." *PS* 42: 389–406.

Karras, M., and Wiesehöfer, J. (1981). *Kindheit und Jugend in der Antike. Eine Bibliographie*. Bonn.

Kaser, M. (1971–75). *Das römische Privatrecht²*. Munich.

Kasher, A. (1976). "The Jewish attitude to the Alexandrian gymnasium in the first century A.D." *AJAH* 1: 148–61.

——— (1985). *The Jews in Hellenistic and Roman Egypt*. Tübingen.

Katzoff, R. (1972). "Precedents in the courts of Roman Egypt." *ZRG* 89: 256–92.

Kay, N. M. (ed.) (1985). *Martial Book XI: A Commentary*. London.

Keaveney, A. (1992). *Lucullus: A Life*. London and New York.

Kebric, R. B. (1983). "Aging in Pliny's *Letters:* A view from the second century A.D." *Gerontologist* 23: 538–45.

Kelly, J. N. D. (1975). *Jerome: His Life, Writings and Controversies*. London.

Kendig, H. L., Hashimoto, A., and Coppard, L. C. (eds.) (1992). *Family Support for the Elderly: The International Experience*. Oxford.

Kenyon, F. G. (ed.) (1898). *Greek Papyri in the British Museum*. Vol. 2. London.

Keogh, E. V., and Walsh, R. J. (1965). "Rate of greying of human hair." *Nature* 207: 877–78.

Kertzer, D. I. (ed.) (1986). *Current Perspectives on Aging and the Life Cycle*. Vol. 2: *Family Relations in Life Course Perspective*. Greenwich, Conn.

Kertzer, D. I., and Karweit, N. (1995). "The impact of widowhood in nineteenth-century Italy." In Kertzer and Laslett (1995) 229–48.

Kertzer, D. I., and Keith, J. (eds.) (1984). *Age and Anthropological Theory*. Ithaca and London.

Kertzer, D. I., and Laslett, P. (eds.) (1995). *Aging in the Past: Demography, Society, and Old Age*. Berkeley, Los Angeles, and London.

Kertzer, D. I., and Saller, R. P. (1991). *The Family in Italy from Antiquity to the Present*. New Haven and London.

Kertzer, D. I., and Schaie, K. W. (eds.) (1989). *Age Structuring in Comparative Perspective*. Hillsdale, N.J.

Kertzer, D. I., and Schiaffino, A. (1986). "Historical demographic methods of life-course study." In Fry and Keith (1986) 77–103.

King, H. (1986). "Tithonos and the tettix." *Arethusa* 19: 15–35. With comment by C. Segal, 37–47. Reprinted, without Segal's comment, in Falkner and de Luce (1989) 68–89.

——— (1998). *Hippocrates' Woman*. London and New York.

King, R. A. H. (2001). *Aristotle on Life and Death*. London.

Kingsley, P. (1995). *Ancient Philosophy, Mystery, and Magic*. Oxford.

Kirk, G. S. (1971). "Old age and maturity in ancient Greece." *Eranos Jahrbücher* 40: 123–58.

Kleijwegt, M. (1991). *Ancient Youth*. Amsterdam.

Klotz, A. (1923). *"Sexagenarii."* *RE* 2a: 2025–26.

Koliadis, M. G. (1988). *Die Jugend im Athen der klassischen Zeit*. Frankfurt am Main.

Konrad, C. F. (1994). "'Domitius Calvisius' in Plutarch." *ZPE* 103: 139–46.

Korpela, J. (1987). *Das Medizinalpersonal im antiken Rom*. Helsinki.

Koumakis, G. (1974). "Aristotle's opinions on old age from a social point of view" (in Greek, with an English summary). *Φιλοσοφία* 4: 274–85.

Krause, J.-U. (1994–95). *Witwen und Waisen im römischen Reich*. Stuttgart.

Krenkel, W. A. (1972). "Zur Biographie des Lucilius." *ANRW* 1.2: 1240–59.

——— (1994). *Caesar und der Mimus des Laberius*. Hamburg.

Kruit, N. (1998). "Age reckoning in Hellenistic Egypt." In A. M. F. W. Verhoogt and S. P. Vleeming (eds.), *The Two Faces of Graeco-Roman Egypt*, 37–58. Leiden.

Kudlien, F. (1968). *Die Sklaven in der griechischen Medizin der klassischen und hellenistischen Zeit*. Wiesbaden.

Kühner, R., and Stegmann, C. (1955). *Ausführliche Grammatik der lateinischen Sprache: Satzlehre³*. Hannover.

La Fontaine, J. S. (ed.) (1978). *Sex and Age as Principles of Social Differentiation*. London.

Lacey, W. K. (1968). *The Family in Classical Greece*. London.

Lambert, G. R. (1982). *Rhetoric Rampant*. Ontario.

Lamirande, E. (1982). "Les âges de l'homme d'après Saint Ambroise de Milan († 397)." *CEA* 14: 227–33.

Lane Fox, R. (1994). "Aeschines and Athenian democracy." In R. Osborne and S. Hornblower (eds.), *Ritual, Finance, Politics*, 135–55. Oxford.

Lanfranchi, F. (1938). *Il diritto nei retori romani*. Milan.

——— (1951). *Ricerche sul valore giuridico delle dichiarazioni di nascita in diritto romano*. Bologna.

Langhammer, W. (1973). *Die rechtliche und soziale Stellung der Magistratus municipales und der Decurions ... 2.-4. Jahrhundert der römischen Kaiserzeit*. Wiesbaden.

Lanza, C. (1990). *Ricerche su "furiosus" in diritto romano, I*. Rome.

Laroche, R. A. (1986). "Evidence of a forty-year generation value in Livy books I-X." In C. Deroux (ed.), *Studies in Latin Literature and Roman History IV. Collection Latomus* (Brussels) 196: 31–43.

Laslett, P. (1977). *Family Life and Illicit Love in Earlier Generations*. Cambridge.

——— (1983). *The World We Have Lost³*. London.

——— (1987). Review of Burrow (1986). *A&S* 7: 103–5.

——— (1988). "La parenté en chiffres." *Annales ESC* 43: 5–25.

——— (1990). Review of Minois (1989 [1987]). *SHM* 3: 461–62.

———— (1995). "Necessary knowledge: Age and aging in the societies of the past." In Kertzer and Laslett (1995) 3–77.

———— (1996). *A Fresh Map of Life*². London.

Lassen, E. M. (1992). "The ultimate crime. *Parricidium* and the concept of family in the late Roman republic and early empire." *C&M* 43: 147–61.

Lassère, J.-M. (1977). *Ubique Populus: peuplement et mouvements de population dans l'Afrique romaine*. Paris.

Last, H. (1923). "Αἰθίοπες μακρόβιοι." *CQ* 17: 35–36.

———— (1945). "The Servian reforms." *JRS* 35: 30–48.

Lauffer, S. (1983). "Annos undeviginti natus." In H. Heinen (ed.), *Althistorische Studien Hermann Bengston zum 70. Geburtstag dargebracht*, 174–77. Wiesbaden.

Le Gall, J. (1953). *Recherches sur le culte du Tibre*. Paris.

Lefkowitz, M. R. (1981). *The Lives of the Greek Poets*. London.

———— (1986). *Women in Greek Myth*. Baltimore.

Lehmann, Y. (1991). "Un exemple d'éclectisme médical à Rome: la théorie varronienne des âges de la vie." In P. Mudry and J. Pigeaud (eds.), *Les écoles médicales à Rome*, 149–57. Geneva.

Leigh, M. (1994). "Servius on Vergil's *senex Corycius:* New evidence." *Materiali e Discussioni per l'Analisi dei Testi Classici* 33: 181–95.

Lenkeit, P. (1966). *Varros Menippea "Gerontodidaskalos."* Cologne.

Lerat, L. (1943). "Une loi de Delphes sur les devoirs des enfants envers leurs parents." *Revue de Philologie* 17: 62–86.

Leschi, L. (1957). *Études d'épigraphie, d'archéologie et d'histoire africaines*. Paris.

Leunissen, P. M. M. (1989). *Konsuln und Konsulare in der Zeit von Commodus bis Severus Alexander*. Amsterdam.

Levick, B. (1966). "Drusus Caesar and the adoptions of A.D. 4." *Latomus* 25: 227–44.

———— (1990). *Claudius*. London.

Levison, W. (1898). "Die Beurkundung des Civilstandes im Altertum. Ein Beitrag zur Geschichte der Bevölkerungsstatistik." *Bonner Jahrbücher* 102: 1–82.

Lévy, J.-Ph. (1952). "Les actes d'état civil romains." *RHDFE* 30: 449–86.

———— (1970). "Nouvelles observations sur les *professiones liberorum*." In Y. Lobin (ed.), *Études offertes à Jean Macqueron*, 439–49. Aix-en-Provence.

Lewis, N. (1963). *Leitourgia Papyri*. Philadelphia.

———— (1966). "Exemption from liturgy in Roman Egypt: II, III." *Atti dell'XI Congresso Internazionale di Papirologia,* 506–41. Milan.

———— (1970). "On paternal authority in Roman Egypt." *RIDA*³ 17: 251–58.

———— (1974). "*Notationes legentis.*" *BASP* 11: 44–59.

———— (1983). *Life in Egypt under Roman Rule*. Oxford.

———— (1996). "*Notationes legentis.*" *BASP* 33: 61–66.

———— (1997). *The Compulsory Public Services of Roman Egypt*². Florence.

Lichtheim, M. (ed.) (1973). *Ancient Egyptian Literature*. Berkeley.

Lilja, S. (1978). "Descriptions of human appearance in Pliny's letters." *Arctos* 12: 55–62.

Lind, L. R. (tr.) (1988). *Gabriele Zerbi, Gerontocomia: On the Care of the Aged, and Maximianus, Elegies on Old Age and Love.* Philadelphia.

Link, S. (1989). *Konzepte der Privilegierung römischer Veteranen.* Stuttgart.

Linn, H. W. (1934). "Persius, Juvenal, and St. Jerome on old age." *CB* 10: 49–50.

Linton, R. (1942). "Age and sex categories." *ASR* 7: 589–603.

Livesley, B. (1975). *Galen, George III and Geriatrics.* London.

Liviabella Furiani, P. (1992). "I vecchi e la vecchiaia nei romanzi greci d'amore." In L. Rossetti and O. Bellini (eds.), *Mente ed esistenza*, 87–119. Naples.

Llewelyn, S. R. (ed.) (1992). *New Documents Illustrating Early Christianity, 6.* Sydney.

Lloyd, G. E. R. (1964). "The hot and the cold, the dry and the wet in Greek philosophy." *JHS* 84: 92–106

––––––– (1966). *Polarity and Analogy.* Cambridge.

––––––– (1983). *Science, Folklore and Ideology.* Cambridge.

Lloyd-Jones, H. (1963). "The seal of Posidippus." *JHS* 83: 75–99.

Lo Cascio, E. (1994). "The size of the Roman population: Beloch and the meaning of the Augustan census figures." *JRS* 84: 23–40.

––––––– (1997). "Le procedure di *recensus* dalla tarda repubblica al tardo antico e il calcolo della popolazione di Roma." In *La Rome impériale: démographie et logistique*, 3–76. Rome.

––––––– (1999). "*Census* provinciale, imposizione fiscale e amministrazioni cittadine nel Principato." In W. Eck (ed.), *Lokale Autonomie und römische Ordnungsmacht in den kaiserzeitlichen Provinzen vom 1. bis 3. Jahrhundert*, 197–211. Munich.

Loraux, N. (1975). "῞Ηβη et ἀνδρεία: deux versions de la mort du combattant athénien." *AS* 6: 1–31.

Lugli, U. (1986). "La depontazione dei sessagenari." *Studi noniani* 11: 59–68.

Lumpe, A., and Karpp, H. (1959). "Eltern." *RAC* 4: 1198–1203.

Lüth, P. (1965). *Geschichte der Geriatrie.* Stuttgart.

MacCary, W. T. (1971). "Menander's old men." *TAPhA* 102: 303–25.

Macdonell, W. R. (1913). "On the expectation of life in ancient Rome, and in the provinces of Hispania and Lusitania, and Africa." *Biometrika* 9: 366–80.

MacDowell, D. M. (1986). *Spartan Law.* Edinburgh.

MacMullen, R. (1982). "The epigraphic habit in the Roman empire." *AJPh* 103: 233–46.

Maddox, G. L. (1964). "Disengagement theory: A critical evaluation." *Gerontologist* 4: 80–82.

Maddox, G. L., et al. (eds.) (1995). *The Encyclopedia of Aging*^{2}. New York.

Magie, D. (1950). *Roman Rule in Asia Minor.* Princeton, N.J.

Maine, H. S. (1883). *Dissertations on Early Law and Custom.* London.

Major, A. (1994). "Claudius' edict on sick slaves." *Scholia* 3: 84–90.

Maltby, R. (1979). "Linguistic characterization of old men in Terence." *CPh* 74: 136–47.

Mansbach, A. R. (1982). "'Captatio': Myth and Reality." Ph.D. dissertation, Princeton University.

Mansfeld, J. (1971). *The Pseudo-Hippocratic Tract* Περὶ Ἑβδομάδων *ch. 1–11 and Greek Philosophy.* Assen.

Marquardt, J. (1881–85). *Römische Staatsverwaltung*². Leipzig.

Martin, D. B. (1996). "The construction of the ancient family: Methodological considerations." *JRS* 86: 40–60.

Martina, M. (1988). *"Senex."* Enciclopedia Virgiliana 4:768–72. Rome.

Martini, R. (1982). *"Coemptio fiduciae causa e senes coemptionales."* In F. Pastori (ed.), *Studi in onore di Arnaldo Biscardi,* 2:171–85. Milan.

Massaro, M. (1977). *"Aniles fabellae." Studi italiani di filologia classica* 49: 104–35.

Mastandrea, P., Tessarolo, L., and Sequi, C. (eds.) (1995). *Concordantia in Maximianum.* Hildesheim.

Mattingly, H. (1923). *Coins of the Roman Empire in the British Museum.* Vol. 1. London.

——— (1940). *Coins of the Roman Empire in the British Museum.* Vol. 4. London.

Mattioli, U. (1989). "Per la storia della vecchiaia." *Paideia* 44: 39–56.

——— (ed.) (1995). *Senectus.* Bologna.

Mayor, J. E. B. (ed) (1878–80). *Thirteen Satires of Juvenal*². London.

Mazon, P. (1945). "Sophocle devant ses juges." *REA* 47: 82–96.

Mazzini, I. (1995). "La geriatria di epoca romana." In Mattioli (1995) 2: 339–63.

McAlindon, D. (1957). "The senator's retiring age: 65 or 60?" *CR* 7: 108.

McCartney, E. S. (1925). "Longevity and rejuvenation in Greek and Roman folklore." *Papers of the Michigan Academy of Science, Arts and Letters* 5: 37–72.

——— (1929). "On the shedding of skins by human beings." *CW* 22: 176.

McGinn, T. A. J. (1989). "The taxation of Roman prostitutes." *Helios* 16: 79–110.

——— (1998). *Prostitution, Sexuality, and the Law in Ancient Rome.* New York and Oxford.

Menu, M. (1992). "Philocléon: une initiation de la vieillesse dans les comédies d'Aristophane?" In A. Moreau (ed.), *L'initiation,* 2:165–84. Montpellier.

——— (2000). *Jeunes et vieux chez Lysias.* Rennes.

Mercogliano, F. (1997). *"Tituli ex corpore Ulpiani": Storia di un testo.* Naples.

Merrill, E. T. (1900). "Note on a certain periodicity in vital statistics." *TAPhA* 31: xx–xxi.

Mertens, P. (1958). *Les services de l'état civil et le contrôle de la population à Oxrhynchus au IIIe siècle de notre ère.* Brussels.

Mette, H.-J. (1982). "Von der Jugend." *Hermes* 110: 257–68.

Mette-Dittman, A. (1991). *Die Ehegesetze des Augustus.* Stuttgart.

Meulder, M. (1991). "Platon peintre des âges de la vie humaine (*République,* VIII, 544a-IX, 580c)." *AC* 60: 102–29.

Meyer, M. (1989). "Alte Männer auf attischen Grabdenkmälern." *Mitteilungen des Deutschen Archäologischen Instituts: Athenische Abteilung* 104: 49–82.

Michael, E. M. (1966). "A Critical Edition of Select Michigan Papyri." Ph.D. dissertation, University of Michigan.

Millar, F. G. B. (1964). "The *aerarium* and its officials under the empire." *JRS* 54: 33–40.

———— (1977). *The Emperor in the Roman World.* London. (2nd ed., 1992.)

———— (1983). "Empire and city, Augustus to Julian: Obligations, excuses and status." *JRS* 73: 76–96.

———— (1993). *The Roman Near East.* Cambridge, Mass., and London.

Miller, S. G. (1978). *The Prytaneion.* Berkeley.

Miller, T. S. (1985). *The Birth of the Hospital in the Byzantine Empire.* Baltimore and London.

Minois, G. (1987). *Histoire de la vieillesse en occident de l'Antiquité à la Renaissance.* Paris. English translation by S. H. Tenison (Cambridge and Oxford, 1989).

Mitterauer, M., and Sieder, R. (1982). *The European Family.* Tr. K. Oosterveen and M. Hörzinger. Oxford.

Mócsy, A. (1966). "Die Unkenntnis des Lebensalters im römischen Reich." *Acta Antiqua Academiae Scientiarum Hungaricae* 14: 387–421.

Momigliano, A. (1944). Review of *CAH* 10. *JRS* 34: 109–16.

Mommsen, T. (1861). "Mamilius Sura, Aemilius Sura, L. Manilius." *RhM* 16: 282–87. Reprinted in *Gesammelte Schriften* 7 (Berlin, 1909) 70–76.

———— (1887–88). *Römisches Staatsrecht³.* Leipzig.

———— (1903). *Römische Geschichte⁹.* Vol. 1. Berlin.

Montevecchi, O. (1935). "Ricerche di sociologia nei documenti dell'Egitto greco-romano, I: I testamenti." *Aegyptus* 15: 67–121.

———— (1947). "Ricerche di sociologia nei documenti dell'Egitto greco-romano, VI: Denunce di nascita di greco-egizi." *Aegyptus* 27: 3–24.

———— (1948). "Ricerche di sociologia nei documenti dell'Egitto greco-romano, VII: Certificati di nascita di cittadini romani." *Aegyptus* 28: 129–67.

———— (1973). *La papirologia.* Turin.

Moody, H. R. (1998). *Aging: Concepts and Controversies².* Thousand Oaks, Calif.

Moreau, P. (1994). "La mémoire fragile: falsification et destruction des documents publics au 1er siècle av. J.-C." In S. Demougin (ed.), *La mémoire perdue,* 121–47. Paris.

Morgan, M. G. (1974). "Priests and physical fitness." *CQ* 24: 137–41.

Morizot, P. (1989). "Remarques sur l'âge du mariage des jeunes Romaines en Italie et en Afrique." *CRAI* 1989: 656–69.

Morris, J. (1964). "*Leges annales* under the principate. 1: Legal and constitutional." *Listy filologické* 87: 316–37.

——— (1965). "*Leges annales* under the principate. 2: Political effects." *Listy filologické* 88: 22–31.

Moser-Rath, E. (1977). "Altentötung." In K. Ranke (ed.), *Enzyklopädie des Märchens,* 1: 388–95. Berlin.

Mossé, C. (1967). "La conception du citoyen dans la *Politique* d'Aristote." *Eirene* 6: 17–21.

Mosshammer, A. A. (1976). "Geometrical proportion and the chronological method of Apollodorus." *TAPhA* 106: 291–306.

Most, G. W. (1997). "Hesiod's myth of the five (or three or four) races." *PCPhS* 43: 104–27.

Motto, A. L., and Clark, J. R. (1994). "Satire in Seneca's *de Brevitate Vitae.*" *AC* 63: 161–71.

Müller, K. E. (1968). "Zur Frage der Altentötung im westeurasiatischen Raum." *Paideuma* 14: 17–44.

Münzer, F. (1897). *Beiträge zur Quellenkritik der Naturgeschichte des Plinius.* Berlin.

Musso, O. (1968). "*Anus ebria.*" *Atene e Roma* 13: 29–31.

Musti, D. (1990). "La teoria delle età e i passaggi di *status* in Solone." *MEFRA* 102: 11–35.

Myers, K. S. (1996). "The poet and the procuress: The *lena* in Latin love elegy." *JRS* 86: 1–21.

Nagy, B. (1985 [1993]). "The Argei puzzle." *AJAH* 10: 1–27.

Nardi, E. (1983). *Squilibrio e deficienza mentale in diritto romano.* Milan.

Nash, L. L. (1978). "Concepts of existence: Greek origins of generational thought." *Daedalus* 107.4: 1–21.

Ndiaye, S. (2000). "*Minime Romano sacro,* à propos des sacrifices humains à Rome à l'époque républicaine." *Dialogues d'histoire ancienne* 26: 119–28.

Neesen, L. (1980). *Untersuchungen zu den direkten Staatsabgaben der römischen Kaiserzeit.* Bonn.

——— (1981). "Die Entwicklung der Leistungen und Ämter (*munera et honores*) im römischen Kaiserreich des zweiten bis vierten Jahrhunderts." *Historia* 30: 203–35.

Nelson, C. A. (1979). *Status Declarations in Roman Egypt.* Amsterdam.

Néraudau, J.-P. (1978). "*Sexagenarii de ponte* (Réflexions sur la genèse d'un proverbe)." *REL* 56: 159–74.

———. (1979). *La jeunesse dans la littérature et les institutions de la Rome républicaine.* Paris.

——— (1984). *Être enfant à Rome.* Paris.

——— (1987). "La loi, la coutume et le chagrin. Réflexions sur la mort des enfants." In F. Hinard (ed.), *La mort, les morts, et l'au-delà dans le monde romain*, 195–208. Caen.

Neuburger, M. (1947). "The Latin poet Maximianus on the miseries of old age." *BHM* 21: 113–19.

Nicholson, O. (1984). "Hercules at the Milvian bridge: Lactantius, *Divine Institutes*, I, 21, 6–9." *Latomus* 43: 133–42.

Nicolet, C. (1966). *L'ordre équestre à l'époque républicaine, I*. Paris.

——— (1976). "Le cens senatorial sous la république et sous Auguste." *JRS* 66: 20–38.

——— (1980). *The World of the Citizen in Republican Rome*. Tr. P. S. Falla. London.

——— (1984). "Augustus, government, and the propertied classes." In F. Millar and E. Segal (eds.), *Caesar Augustus: Seven Aspects*, 89–128. Oxford.

——— (1988). *Rendre à César*. Paris.

——— (1991). *Space, Geography, and Politics in the Early Roman Empire*. Ann Arbor.

Nicolova, A. B. (1986). "De la brièveté de la vie de Sénèque. Essai de chronologie par stylométrie." *Revue de l'Organisation internationale pour l'étude des langues anciennes par ordinateur* 22: 99–103.

Niebyl, P. H. (1971). "Old age, fever, and the lamp metaphor." *JHM* 26: 351–68.

Nilsson, M. P. (1920). *Primitive Time-Reckoning*. Lund.

Nisbet, R. G. M., and Hubbard, M. (eds.) (1970). *A Commentary on Horace: Odes, Book 1*. Oxford.

Nitecki, A. K. (1990). "Figures of old age in fourteenth-century English literature." In Sheehan (1990) 107–16.

Norden, E. (1892). "In Varronis saturas Menippeas observationes selectae." *Jahrbücher für classische Philologie,* suppl., 18: 265–352. Republished in *Kleine Schriften zum klassischen Altertum* (Berlin, 1966), 1–87.

Nugent, J. B. (1985). "The old-age security motive for fertility." *Population and Development Review* 11: 75–97.

Oakley, S. P. (ed.) (1997). *A Commentary on Livy Books VI–X*. Vol. 1. Oxford.

Oates, J. (1976). "Census totals: Nemesion's notes." In A. E. Hanson (ed.), *Collectanea Papyrologica: Texts Published in Honour of H. C. Youtie, I*, 189–96. Bonn

Ober, J. (1989). *Mass and Elite in Democratic Athens*. Princeton, N.J.

Öberg, C. S. (1999). *Versus Maximiani*. Stockholm.

O'Donnell, M. (1985). *Age and Generation*. London.

Oeri, H. G. (1948). *Der Typ der komischen Alten in der griechischen Komödie*. Basel.

Oertel, F. (1917). *Die Liturgie*. Leipzig.

Ogilvie, R. M. (ed.) (1965). *A Commentary on Livy, Books 1–5*. Oxford.

——— (1978). *The Library of Lactantius*. Oxford.

Oliver, J. H. (1941). *The Sacred Gerusia*. Athens.

———— (1958). "Gerusiae and Augustales." *Historia* 7: 472–96.

———— (1967). "Philosophers and procurators, relatives of the Aemilius Juncus of *Vita Commodi* 4, 11." *Hesperia* 16: 42–56.

———— (1972). "Text of the *Tabula Banasitana*, A.D. 177." *AJPh* 93: 336–40.

———— (1989). *Greek Constitutions of Early Roman Emperors from Inscriptions and Papyri*. Philadelphia.

Onians, R. B. (1954). *The Origins of European Thought²*. Cambridge.

Opelt, I. (1965). *Die lateinischen Schimpfwörter und verwandte sprachliche Erscheinungen*. Heidelberg.

Orentreich, D. S., and Orentreich, N. (1994). "Hair changes with aging as a parameter to utilize in the estimation of human biological age." In A. K. Balin (ed.), *Practical Handbook of Human Biologic Age Determination*, 375–88. Boca Raton, Fla.

Orth, H. (1963). "Δίαιτα γερόντων: die Geriatrie der griechischen Antike." *Centaurus* 8: 19–47.

Ostwald, M. (1986). *From Popular Sovereignty to the Sovereignty of Law*. Berkeley.

Otto, A. (1890). *Die Sprichwörter und sprichwörtlichen Redensarten der Römer*. Leipzig.

Panayotakis, S. (1997). "*Insidiae Veneris:* Lameness, old age and deception in the Underworld (Apul. *Met.* 6.18–19)." In H. Hofmann and M. Zimmermann (eds.), *Groningen Colloquia on the Novel*, 8:23–39. Groningen.

Paola, S. di (1950). *Donatio mortis causa*. Catania.

———— (1969). *Donatio mortis causa: Corso di diritto romano*. Naples.

Papanghelis, T. (1994). "Hoary ladies: Catullus 64. 305ff. and Apollonius of Rhodes." *SO* 69: 41–46.

Parke, H. W. (1988). *Sibyls and Sibylline Prophecy in Classical Antiquity*. Ed. B. C. McGing. London and New York.

Parker, R. (1983). *Miasma, Pollution and Purification in Early Greek Religion*. Oxford.

Parkin, T. G. (1992). *Demography and Roman Society*. Baltimore and London.

———— (1995). Review of Bagnall and Frier (1994). *BMCR* 6.2: 88–98.

———— (1997). "Out of sight, out of mind: Elderly members of the Roman family." In Rawson and Weaver (1997) 123–48.

———— (1998). "Ageing in antiquity: Status and participation." In Johnson and Thane (1998) 19–42.

———— (1999). "Clearing away the cobwebs: A critical perspective on historical sources for Roman population history." In J. Bintliff and K. Sbonias (eds.), *Reconstructing Past Population Trends in Mediterranean Europe*, 153–60. Oxford.

———— (2001). "On becoming a parent in later life: From Augustus to Antonio Agustín via St. Augustine." In S. Dixon (ed.), *Childhood, Class and Kin in the Roman World*, 221–34. London and New York.

Pavlovskis, Z. (1976). "*Aeneid* V: The old and the young." *CJ* 71: 193–205.

Peachin, M., and Preuß, G. (1997). "*CIL* VI 3836 (= 31747). Die Karriere des Aspasius Paternus?" *ZPE* 116: 176–92.

Pelling, M., and Smith, R. M. (eds.) (1991). *Life, Death, and the Elderly: Historical Perspectives.* London and New York.

Perelli, A. (1993). "Variazioni sul cavallo vecchio (Tibullo e altri)." *RCCM* 35: 119–36.

Pescani, P. (1961). "Osservazioni su alcune sigle ricorrenti nelle *professiones liberorum.*" *Aegyptus* 41: 129–40.

Pfisterer-Haas, S. (1989). *Darstellungen alter Frauen in der griechischen Kunst.* Frankfurt am Main.

Pflaum, H. G. (1950). *Les procurateurs équestres sous le Haut-Empire romain.* Paris.

Philibert, M. (1984). "Le statut de la personne âgée dans les sociétés antiques et préindustrielles." *Sociologie et sociétés* 16.2: 15–27.

———— (1986). "Discours des vieillards et discours sur la vieillesse chez Platon et aujourd'hui." In *Philosophie du langage et grammaire dans l'antiquité,* 137–52. Brussels.

Philipsborn, A. (1950). "L'abandon des esclaves malades au temps de l'empereur Claude et au temps de Justinien." *RHDFE* 28: 402–3.

Pierce, R. H. (1968). "*Grapheion,* catalogue and library in Roman Egypt." *SO* 43: 68–83.

Pieri, G. (1968). *L'histoire du cens jusqu'à la fin de la république romaine.* Paris.

Pigeaud, J. (1987). *Folie et cures de la folie chez les médecins de l'antiquité grécoromaine: la manie.* Paris.

Pisi, G. (1995). "La medicina greca antica." In Mattioli (1995) 1:447–87.

Pittau, M. (1991). "Geronticidio, eutanasia e infanticidio nella Sardegna antica." In A. Mastino (ed.), *L'Africa romana. Atti dell'VIII convegno di studio Cagliari,* 2: 703–11. Sassari.

Plakans, A. (1989). "Stepping down in former times: A comparative assessment of 'retirement' in traditional Europe." In Kertzer and Schaie (1989) 175–95.

Pokorny, J. (1959). *Indogermanisches Etymologisches Wörterbuch.* Bern.

Poland, F. (1909). *Geschichte des griechischen Vereinswesens.* Leipzig.

Poma, G. (1982). "Provvedimenti legislativi e attività censoria di Claudio verso gli schaivi e i liberti." *RSA* 12: 143–74.

Pomeroy, S. B. (1997). *Families in Classical and Hellenistic Greece.* Oxford.

Porzig, W. (1956). "*Senatus populusque Romanus.*" *Gymnasium* 63: 318–26.

Posner, E. (1972). *Archives in the Ancient World.* Cambridge, Mass.

Potter, D. S. (1990). *Prophecy and History in the Crisis of the Roman Empire.* Oxford.

Powell, A. (1994). "Plato and Sparta: Modes of rule and of non-rational persuasion in the *Laws.*" In A. Powell and S. Hodkinson (eds.), *The Shadow of Sparta,* 272–321. London.

Powell, J. G. F. (ed.) (1988). *Cicero: Cato Maior de Senectute.* Cambridge.

Pratt, L. (2000). "The old women of ancient Greece and the Homeric *Hymn to Demeter.*" *TAPhA* 130: 41–65.

Preisshofen, F. (1977). *Untersuchungen zur Darstellung des Greisenalters in der frühgriechischen Dichtung.* Wiesbaden.

Pressat, R., and Wilson, C. (1985). *The Dictionary of Demography.* Oxford.

Preston, S. H., McDaniel, A., and Grushka, C. (1903). "New model life tables for high-mortality populations." *Historical Methods* 26: 149–59.

Quinn, K. (1969). "Practical criticism: A reading of Propertius 1. 21 and Catullus 17." *G&R* 16: 19–29.

Rabenhorst, M. (1907). *Der ältere Plinius als Epitomator des Verrius Flaccus.* Berlin.

Raditsa, L. F. (1980). "Augustus' legislation concerning marriage, procreation, love affairs and adultery." *ANRW* 2.13: 278–339.

Radke, G. (1975). "*Sexagenarii.*" *Der kleine Pauly* 5: 153–54.

—— (1990). "Gibt es Antworten auf die 'Argeerfrage'?" *Latomus* 49: 5–19.

Raepsaet, G. (1971). "Les motivations de la natalité à Athènes aux Ve et IVe siècles avant notre ère." *AC* 40: 80–110.

Raffaelli, R., Danese, R. M., and Lanciotti, S. (eds.) (1997). *Pietas e allattamento filiale.* Urbino.

Rankin, H. D. (1964). *Plato and the Individual.* London.

Ranucci, G. (1976). "Due fonti di Plinio il Vecchio nel brano *de spatiis vitae longissimis* (*NH* 7, 153–159)." *Athenaeum* 54: 131–38.

Rathbone, D. W. (1993). "Egypt, Augustus and Roman taxation." *Cahiers du Centre G. Glotz* 4: 81–112.

Ratkowitsch, C. (1986). *Maximianus Amat.* Vienna.

—— (1990). "Weitere Argumente zur Datierung und Interpretation Maximians (zu vorliegenden Rezensionen)." *WS* 103: 207–39.

Rawson, B. (ed.) (1986). *The Family in Ancient Rome.* London and Sydney.

—— (ed.) (1991). *Marriage, Divorce, and Children in Ancient Rome.* Canberra and Oxford.

—— (1997a). "Representations of Roman children and childhood." *Antichthon* 31: 74–95.

—— (1997b). "'The family' in the ancient Mediterranean: Past, present, future." *ZPE* 117: 294–96.

Rawson, B., and Weaver, P. (eds.) (1997). *The Roman Family in Italy: Status, Sentiment, Space.* Canberra and Oxford.

Rawson, E. (1987). "*Discrimina ordinum:* The *lex Julia theatralis.*" *PBSR* 55: 83–114. Reprinted in *Roman Culture and Society: Collected Papers,* ed. F. Millar (Oxford, 1991), 508–45.

Rea, J. R. (ed.) (1972). *The Oxyrhynchus Papyri.* Vol. 40. London.

—— (ed.) (1975). *The Oxyrhynchus Papyri.* Vol. 43. London.

—— (1978). "Rutilius Achilles, epistrategus Heptanomiae in A.D. 194." *ZPE* 31: 143–44.

Rebert, H. F. (1926). "The literary influence of Cicero on Juvenal." *TAPhA* 57: 181–94.

Reinhold, M. (1933). "A contribution to biographical chronology." *CW* 26: 172–75.

———— (1970). "The generation gap in antiquity." *Proceedings of the American Philosophical Society* 114: 347–65. Reprinted in Bertman (1976) 15–54.

———— (1988). *From Republic to Principate*. Atlanta, Georgia.

Reinmuth, O. W. (1935). *The Prefect of Roman Egypt from Augustus to Diocletian*. Leipzig.

Rendall, M. S., and Bahchieva, R. A. (1998). "An old-age security motive for fertility in the United States?" *Population and Development Review* 24: 293–308.

Renier, E. (1942). *Étude sur l'histoire de la querela inofficiosi en droit romain*. Liège.

———— (1950). "Observations sur la terminologie de l'aliénation mentale." *RIDA* 5: 429–55.

Rhodes, P. J. (ed.) (1981). *A Commentary on the Aristotelian* Athenaion Politeia. Oxford.

———— (ed.) (1996). *The Decrees of the Greek States*. Oxford.

Riccobono, S., et al. (eds.) (1945). *Acta Divi Augusti I*. Rome.

Richardson, B. E. (1933). *Old Age Among the Ancient Greeks*. Baltimore.

Richardson, W. F. (1985). *Numbering and Measuring in the Classical World*. Auckland.

Richlin, A. (1992). *The Garden of Priapus*². New York and Oxford.

Richter, W. (1961). "Römische Zeitgeschichte und innere Emigration." *Gymnasium* 68: 286–315.

Riley, M. W. (1987). "On the significance of age in sociology." *ASR* 52: 1–14.

Rilinger, R. (1978). "Die Ausbildung von Amtswechsel und Amtsfristen als Problem zwischen Machtbesitz und Machtgebrauch in der Mittleren Republik (342 bis 217 v. Chr.)." *Chiron* 8: 247–312.

Rives, J. (1995a). "Human sacrifice among pagans and Christians." *JRS* 85: 65–85.

———— (1995b). *Religion and Authority in Roman Carthage from Augustus to Constantine*. Oxford.

Robert, L. (1968). "De Delphes à l'Oxus. Inscriptions grecques nouvelles de la Bactriane." *CRAI* 1968: 416–57.

Roberts, L. (1989). "Portrayal of the elderly in classical Greek and Roman literature." In P. von Dorotka Bagnell and P. S. Soper (eds.), *Perceptions of Aging in Literature*, 17–33. New York.

Robertson, B. G. (2000). "The scrutiny of new citizens at Athens." In V. Hunter and J. Edmondson (eds.), *Law and Social Status in Classical Athens*, 149–74. Oxford.

Robinson, L. (1976). "Marcus Terentius Varro, *Sexagesis* or born sixty years too late." In *Atti di congresso internazionale di studi varroniani*, 2: 477–83. Rieti.

Roesch, P. (1982). *Études béotiennes*. Paris.

Rögler, G. (1962). "Die *lex Villia annalis:* eine Untersuchung zur Verfassungsgeschichte der römischen Republik." *Klio* 40: 76–123.

Roisman, H. M. (1988). "Dry tearless eyes." *Mnem.* 41: 27–38.

Roscher, W. H. (1897–1909). *Ausführliches Lexikon der griechischen und römischen Mythologie*. Vol. 3. Leipzig.

——— (1903). *Die enneadischen und hebdomadischen Fristen und Wochen der ältesten Griechen*. Leipzig.

——— (1904). *Die Sieben-und Neunzahl im Kultus und Mythus der Griechen*. Leipzig.

——— (1906). *Die Hebdomadenlehren der griechischen Philosophen und Ärzte*. Leipzig.

——— (1911). *Über Alter, Ursprung und Bedeutung der hippokratischen Schrift von der Siebenzahl*. Leipzig.

——— (1913). *Die hippokratische Schrift von der Siebenzahl in ihrer vierfachen Überlieferung*. Paderborn.

——— (1916–24). *Ausführliches Lexikon der griechischen und römischen Mythologie*. Vol. 5. Leipzig.

——— (1919). *Die hippokratische Schrift von der Siebenzahl und ihr Verhältnis zum Altpythagoreismus*. Leipzig.

Rosenmayr, L. (1983). "Les étapes de la vie." *Communications* 37: 89–104.

Rosivach, V. (1994). "*Anus:* Some older women in Latin literature." *CW* 88: 107–17.

Roueché, C. (1993). "The ages of man." *Ktema* 18: 159–69.

Roussel, P. (1942). "Étude sur le principe de l'ancienneté dans le monde hellénistique du Ve siècle av. J.-C. à l'époque romaine." *Mémoires de l'Académie des Inscriptions et Belles-Lettres* 43.2: 123–227.

Rowland, B. (1979). "Exhuming Trotula, *sapiens matrona* of Salerno." *Florilegium* 1: 42–57.

Rowlands, A. (2001). "Witchcraft and old women in early modern Germany." *P&P* 173: 50–89.

Rubinstein, L. (1993). *Adoption in IV. Century Athens*. Copenhagen.

Rudd, N. (1986). *Themes in Roman Satire*. London.

Rupprecht, H.-A. (1998). "Die Sorge für die Älteren nach den Papyri." In Stol and Vleeming (1998) 223–37.

Russell, D. A. (ed.) (1990). *An Anthology of Latin Prose*. Oxford.

Rutherford, R. B. (1989). *Marcus Aurelius, a Study*. Oxford.

Ryan, F. X. (1995). "Sexagenarians, the bridge, and the *centuria praerogativa.*" *RhM* 138: 188–90.

——— (1996). "The minimum age for the quaestorship in the late republic." *MH* 53: 37–43.

——— (1998). *Rank and Participation in the Republican Senate*. Stuttgart.

Ryberg, I. S. (1967). *Panel Reliefs of Marcus Aurelius*. New York.

Ryder, K. C. (1984). "The *senex amator* in Plautus." *G&R* 31: 181–89.

Sachers, E. (1951). "Das Recht auf Unterhalt in der römischen Familie der klassischen Zeit." In *Festschrift Fritz Schulz, I,* 310–63. Weimar.

Sallares, R. (1991). *The Ecology of the Ancient Greek World.* London.

Saller, R. P. (1982). *Personal Patronage under the Early Empire.* Cambridge.

——— (1984). "Roman dowry and the devolution of property in the principate." *CQ* 34: 195–205.

——— (1986). "*Patria potestas* and the stereotype of the Roman family." *Continuity and Change* 1: 7–22.

——— (1987a). "Men's age at marriage and its consequences in the Roman family." *CPh* 82: 20–35.

——— (1987b). "Slavery and the Roman family." In M. Finley (ed.), *Classical Slavery,* 65–87. London

——— (1988). "*Pietas,* obligation and authority in the Roman family." In P. Kneissl and V. Losemann (eds.), *Alte Geschichte und Wissenschaftsgeschichte,* 393–410. Darmstadt.

——— (1991). "Roman heirship strategies in principle and in practice." In Kertzer and Saller (1991) 26–47.

——— (1994). *Patriarchy, Property and Death in the Roman Family.* Cambridge.

Saller, R. P., and Shaw, B. D. (1984). "Tombstones and Roman family relations in the principate." *JRS* 74: 124–56.

Salomies, O. (1987). *Die römischen Vornamen.* Helsinki.

Salomonson, J. W. (1980). "Der Trunkenbold und die trunkene Alte." *Bulletin Antieke Beschaving* 55: 65–135.

Samuel, A. E. (1972). *Greek and Roman Chronology.* Munich.

Samuel, A. E., Hastings, W. K., Bowman, A. K., and Bagnall, R. S. (1971). *Death and Taxes.* Toronto.

Sande, S. (1995). "An old hag and her sisters." *SO* 70: 30–53.

Sankar, A. (1984). "'It's just old age': Old age as a diagnosis in American and Chinese medicine." In Kertzer and Keith (1984) 250–80.

Schadewaldt, W. (1933). "Lebenszeit und Greisenalter im frühen Griechentum." *Die Antike* 9: 282–302. Reprinted in *Hellas und Hesperien* (Zurich and Stuttgart, 1960), 41–59; and in *Hellas und Hesperien*² (Zurich and Stuttgart, 1970), 1: 109–27.

Schaps, D. M. (1979). *Economic Rights of Women in Ancient Greece.* Edinburgh.

Scheidel, W. (1996a). *Measuring Sex, Age and Death in the Roman Empire.* Ann Arbor.

——— (1996b). "What's in an age? A comparative view of bias in the census returns of Roman Egypt." *BASP* 33: 25–59.

——— (1996c). "Reflections on the differential valuation of slaves in Diocletian's price edict and in the United States." *Münstersche Beiträge zur antiken Handelsgeschichte* 15: 67–79.

——— (1999). "The death declarations of Roman Egypt: A re-appraisal." *BASP* 36: 53–70.

——— (ed.) (2001a). *Debating Roman Demography.* Leiden.

———— (2001b). *Death on the Nile*. Leiden.

———— (2001c). "Roman age structure: Evidence and models." *JRS* 91: 1–26.

Scherer, J. (1947). *Papyrus de Philadelphie*. Cairo.

Schetter, W. (1970). *Studien zur Überlieferung und Kritik des Elegikers Maximian*. Wiesbaden.

Schiebe, M. W. (1999). "Lactanz, Varro und die Tradition des Argeer-Ritus." *RhM* 142: 189–209.

Schmidt, B. (1903). "Der Selbstmord der Greise von Keos. Ein kulturgeschichtliches Problem." *Neue Jahrbücher für das klassische Altertum* 11: 617–28.

Schmidt, M. G. (1999). "Ursus togatus (*CIL* VI 9797)." *ZPE* 126: 240–42.

Schmidt, R. (1955–56). "*Aetates mundi*. Die Weltalter als Gliederungsprinzip der Geschichte." *Zeitschrift für Kirchengeschichte* 67: 288–317.

Schmidt, W. (1908). *Geburtstag im Altertum*. Gießen.

Schmiel, R. (1974). "Youth and age: Mimnermus 1 and 2." *Rivista di filologia* 102: 283–89.

Schmitt, G., and Rödel, V. (1974). "Die kranken Sklaven auf der Tiberinsel nach dem Edikt des Claudius." *Medezin-historisches Journal* 9: 106–24.

Schneider, W. J. (1999). "Metamorphose einer *anus ebria*." *Philologus* 143: 87–100.

Schofield, M. (1986). "Euboulia in the *Iliad*." *CQ* 36: 6–31.

Schöner, E. (1964). *Das Viererschema in der antiken Humoralpathologie*. Wiesbaden.

Schulz, F. (1942–43). "Roman registers of births and birth certificates." *JRS* 32: 78–91; 33: 55–64.

Schuman, V. B. (1934–35). "The origin of the expression . . . ὡς ἐτῶν used in the papyri." *CW* 28: 95–96.

Schürer, E. (1973). *The History of the Jewish People in the Age of Jesus Christ*. Vol. 1. Ed. G. Vermes and F. Millar. Edinburgh.

Schwartz, J. (1948). "Sur quelques anecdotes concernant César et Cicéron." *REA* 50: 264–71.

Schwenn, F. (1915). *Die Menschenopfer bei den Griechen und Römern*. Gießen.

Scobie, A. (1983). *Apuleius and Folklore*. London.

Scullard, H. H. (1951). *Roman Politics, 220–150 B.C.* Oxford.

Sealey, R. (1957). "On coming of age in Athens." *CR* 7: 195–97.

Seaman, W. M. (1969). "On the names of old and young men in Plautus." *Illinois Studies in Language and Literature* 58: 114–22.

Sears, E. (1986). *The Ages of Man. Medieval Interpretations of the Life Cycle*. Princeton, N.J.

Segal, E. (1987). *Roman Laughter²*. New York and Oxford.

Shahar, S. (1997). *Growing Old in the Middle Ages*. Tr. Y. Lotan. London and New York.

Shapiro, H. A. (1993). *Personifications in Greek Art*. Zurich.

Shaw, B. D. (1973). "The *undecimprimi* in Roman Africa." *Museum Africum* 2 (1973) 3–10. Reprinted in Shaw (1995) ch. 2.

——— (1982). "The elders of Christian Africa." In P. Brind' Amour (ed.), *Mélanges offerts à R. P. Etienne Gareau*, 207–26. Ottawa. Reprinted in Shaw (1995) ch. 10.

——— (1987). "The family in late antiquity: The experience of Augustine." *P&P* 115: 3–51.

——— (1991a). "The cultural meaning of death: Age and gender in the Roman family." In Kertzer and Saller (1991) 66–90.

——— (1991b). "The structure of local society in the early Maghrib: The elders." *Maghrib Review* 16: 18–54. Reprinted in Shaw (1995) ch. 3.

——— (1995). *Rulers, Nomads, and Christians in Roman North Africa*. Aldershot, Hampshire, and Brookfield, Vt.

——— (1996). "Seasons of death: Aspects of mortality in imperial Rome." *JRS* 86: 100–38.

Sheehan, M. M. (ed.) (1990). *Aging and the Aged in Medieval Europe*. Toronto.

Sherwin-White, A. N. (1963). *Roman Society and Roman Law in the New Testament*. Oxford.

——— (1973a). *The Roman Citizenship*². Oxford.

——— (1973b). "The *Tabula* of Banasa and the *Constitutio Antoniniana*." *JRS* 63: 86–98.

Siber, H. (1937). "Die ältesten römischen Volksversammlungen." *ZRG* 57: 233–71.

Siegel, J. S. (1980). "On the demography of aging." *Demography* 17: 345–64.

Sigismund Nielsen, H. (1997). "Interpreting epithets in Roman epitaphs." In Rawson and Weaver (1997) 169–204.

Sijpesteijn, P. J. (1993a). "Settlement of a debt and extracts from census registers." *ZPE* 98: 283–91.

——— (1993b). "A donatio mortis causa." *ZPE* 98: 292–96.

——— (1996). "Marriage agreement with property division to take effect after death and other documents." *ZPE* 111: 163–70.

Silk, M. S. (1987). "Pathos in Aristophanes." *BICS* 34: 78–111.

——— (1995). "Nestor, Amphitryon, Philocleon, Cephalus: The language of old men in Greek literature from Homer to Menander." In F. De Martino and A. H. Sommerstein (eds.), *Lo spettacolo delle voci*, 165–214. Bari.

Simmons, L. W. (1945). *The Role of the Aged in Primitive Society*. New Haven.

——— (1960). "Aging in pre-industrial societies." In Tibbitts (1960) 62–91.

Simonius, P. (1958). *Die donatio mortis causa im klassischen römischen Recht*. Basel.

Sizoo, A. (1955). "Augustinus de senectute." In P. de Jonge et al. (eds.), *Ut Pictura Poesis*, 184–88. Leiden.

Skoda, F. (1994). "Le *marasme* dans les textes médicaux grecs. Sens et histoire du mot." *REG* 107: 107–28.

Slater, N. W. (1996). "Bringing up father: *paideia* and *ephebeia* in the *Wasps*."

In A. H. Sommerstein and C. Atherton (eds.), *Education in Greek Fiction*, 27–52. Bari.

Slusanski, D. (1973). "Varron et les *gradus aetatum.*" *Anal. Univ. Bucuresti. Limbi clasice si orientale* 22: 103–9.

———— (1974). "Le vocabulaire latin des *gradus aetatum.*" *Revue Roumaine de Linguistique* 19: 103–21, 267–96, 345–69, 437–51, 563–78.

Smith, J. E., and Oeppen, J. (1993). "Estimating numbers of kin in historical England using demographic microsimulation." In D. S. Reher and R. Schofield (eds.), *Old and New Methods in Historical Demography*, 280–317. Oxford.

Smith, M. F. (ed.) (1993). *Diogenes of Oinoanda: The Epicurean Inscription.* Naples.

———— (ed.) (1996). *The Philosophical Inscription of Diogenes of Oinoanda.* Vienna.

———— (1998). "Excavations at Oinoanda 1997: The new Epicurean texts." *Anatolian Studies* 48: 125–70.

Smith, R. M. (1984). "The structured dependence of the elderly as a recent development: Some sceptical historical thoughts." *A&S* 4: 409–28.

Solazzi, S. (1930). "*Infirmitas aetatis* e *infirmitas sexus.*" *Archivio Giuridico* 104: 3–31.

Sorabji, R. (1983). *Time, Creation and Its Continuum.* London.

Sourvinou-Inwood, C. (1995). "*Reading*" *Greek Death.* Oxford.

Spaltenstein, F. (ed.) (1983). *Commentaire des Élégies de Maximien.* Vevey.

Spencer, P. (ed.) (1990). *Anthropology and the Riddle of the Sphinx.* London and New York.

Stahmer, H. M. (1978). "The aged in two ancient oral cultures: The ancient Hebrews and Homeric Greece." In S. F. Spicker, K. M. Woodward and D. D. van Tassel (eds.), *Aging and the Elderly: Humanistic Perspectives in Gerontology*, 23–36. Atlantic Highlands, N.J.

Stamatakos, I. D. (ed.) (1957). Πλουτάρχου Εἰ πρεσβυτέρῳ πολιτευτέον. Athens.

Steel, L. (1995). "Challenging preconceptions of oriental 'barbarity' and Greek 'humanity.'" In N. Spencer (ed.), *Time, Tradition and Society in Greek Archaeology*, 18–27. London and New York.

Stein, P. (1974). "The development of the notion of *naturalis ratio.*" In A. Watson (ed.), *Daube Noster*, 305–16. Edinburgh and London.

Steudel, J. (1942). "Zur Geschichte der Lehre von den Greisenkrankheiten." *Sudhoffs Archiv für Geschichte der Medizin und der Naturwissenschaften* 35: 1–27. Reprinted in Gruman 1979.

Stevenson, T. (1998). "The 'problem' with nude honorific statuary and portraits in late republican and Augustan Rome." *G&R* 45: 45–69.

Stewart, F. H. (1977). *Fundamentals of Age-Group Systems.* New York.

Stok, F. (1991). "Catone e le età della vita." *RCCM* 33: 29–35.

—— (1996). "Follia e malattie mentali nella medicina dell'età romana." *ANRW* 2.37.3: 2282–2410.

Stol, M., and Vleeming, S. P. (eds.) (1998). *The Care of the Elderly in the Ancient Near East.* Leiden.

Stoop, B. (1995). "The sins of their fathers: *si pater filium ter venum duit.*" *RIDA*[3] 42: 331–92.

Strauss, B. (1993). *Fathers and Sons in Athens.* London.

Stroh, W. (1991). "De amore senili quid veteres poetae senserint." *Gymnasium* 98: 264–76.

Stroux, J., and Wenger, L. (1928). *Die Augustus-Inschrift auf dem Marktplatz von Kyrene.* Munich.

Suárez Martínez, P. M. (1984). "Horacio y las viejas libidinosas." *Estudios clásicos* 36: 49–62.

Subrenat, J. (ed.) (1987). *Vieillesse et vieillissement au Moyen-Age.* Aix-en-Provence.

Suder, W. (1978). "On age classification in Roman imperial literature." *CB* 55: 5–9.

—— (1987). "L'*initium senectutis* nell'impero romano e medio evo." In *Actes du 110e congrès national des sociétés savantes (Montpellier, 1985). Section d'histoire médiévale et de philologie. Tome I: Santé, médecine et assistance au moyen âge*, 65–79. Paris.

—— (ed.) (1991). *Geras. Old Age in Greco-Roman Antiquity: A Classified Bibliography.* Wroclaw.

—— (1992). "Old age and eros in the early Roman empire. Some opinions." In C. Deroux (ed.), *Studies in Latin Literature VI. Collection Latomus* (Brussels) 217: 228–36.

—— (1994). *Kloto, Lachesis, Atropos.* Wroclaw.

—— (1995a). "*Sexagenarios de ponte.* Statut juridique des vieillards dans la famille et dans la société romaine. Quelques remarques et opinions." *RIDA*[3] 42: 393–413.

—— (1995b). "La mort des vieillards." In F. Hinard (ed.), *La mort au quotidien dans le monde romain*, 31–45. Paris.

Sumner, G. V. (1967). "Germanicus and Drusus Caesar." *Latomus* 26: 413–35.

—— (1971). "The *lex annalis* under Caesar." *Phoenix* 25: 246–71, 357–71.

—— (1973). *The Orators in Cicero's Brutus.* Toronto.

Suolahti, J. (1963). *The Roman Censors.* Helsinki.

—— (1972). "*Princeps senatus.*" *Arctos* 7: 207–18.

Swain, S. (1996). *Hellenism and Empire.* Oxford.

Syme, R. (1939). *The Roman Revolution.* Oxford.

—— (1953a). "The proconsuls of Asia under Antoninus Pius." *ZPE* 51: 271–90. Reprinted in *Roman Papers* 4 (Oxford, 1988), 435–46.

—— (1953b). "Problems about proconsuls of Asia." *ZPE* 53: 191–208. Reprinted in *Roman Papers* 4 (Oxford, 1988), 347–65.

——— (1956). "Some friends of the Caesars." *AJPh* 77: 264–73. Reprinted in *Roman Papers* 1 (Oxford, 1979), 292–99.

——— (1958). *Tacitus*. Oxford.

——— (1971). *Emperors and Biography*. Oxford.

——— (1979). "Juvenal, Pliny, Tacitus." *AJPh* 100: 250–78. Reprinted in *Roman Papers* 3 (Oxford, 1984), 1135–57.

——— (1980). *Some Arval Brethren*. Oxford.

——— (1983a). "Domitian: The last years." *Chiron* 13: 121–46. Reprinted in *Roman Papers* 4 (Oxford, 1988), 252–77.

——— (1983b). "Eight consuls from Patavium." *PBSR* 51: 102–24. Reprinted in *Roman Papers* 4 (Oxford, 1988), 371–96.

——— (1983c). "Spanish Pomponii. A study in nomenclature." *Gerión* 1: 249–66. Reprinted in *Roman Papers* 4 (Oxford, 1988), 140–58.

——— (1985). "The *Testamentum Dasumii*: Some novelties." *Chiron* 15: 41–63. Reprinted in Syme (1988) 521–45.

——— (1986). *The Augustan Aristocracy*. Oxford.

——— (1988). *Roman Papers*. Vol. 5. Ed. A. R. Birley. Oxford.

——— (1991). *Roman Papers*. Vol. 7. Ed. A. R. Birley. Oxford.

Szövérffy, J. (1967). "Maximianus a satirist?" *HSCPh* 72: 351–67.

Talbert, R. J. A. (1984). *The Senate of Imperial Rome*. Princeton, N.J.

Talbot, A.-M. M. (1984). "Old age in Byzantium." *Byzantinische Zeitschrift* 77: 267–78.

Tansey, P. (2000). "The *princeps senatus* in the last decades of the republic." *Chiron* 30: 15–30.

Taubenschlag, R. (1932). "Die Alimentationspflicht im Rechte der Papyri." In G. Baviera (ed.), *Studi in onore di Salvatore Riccobono, I*, 505–18. Palermo. Reprinted in *Opera Minora* 2 (Warsaw, 1959), 539–55.

——— (1955). *The Law of Greco-Roman Egypt in the Light of the Papyri*². Warsaw.

——— (1956). "La γηροκομία dans le droit des papyrus." *RIDA*³ 3: 173–79, = *Opera Minora* 2 (Warsaw, 1959), 339–45.

Taylor, L. R. (1966). *Roman Voting Assemblies*. Ann Arbor.

Tazelaar, C. M. (1967). "Παῖδες καὶ ἔφηβοι: Some notes on the Spartan stages of youth." *Mnem.* 20: 127–53.

Tcherikover, V. (1950). "*Syntaxis* and *laographia*." *JJP* 4: 179–207.

Tcherikover, V. A., and Fuks, A. (eds.) (1960). *Corpus Papyrorum Judaicarum* Vol. 2. Cambridge, Mass.

Tengström, E. (1980). *A Study of Juvenal's Tenth Satire*. Göteborg.

Thane, P. (2000). *Old Age in English History*. Oxford.

Thibaut, A. (1824). "Über die *Senectus*." *Archiv für civilistische Praxis* 8: 74–90.

Thomas, H. (1993). *The Conquest of Mexico*. London.

Thomas, J. D. (1969). "The Nyctostrategia in the Egyptian metropolis." *CE* 44: 347–52.

——— (1970). "Chronological notes on documentary papyri." *ZPE* 6: 175–82.

——— (1976). "An unrecognised edict of Constantine (*P. Oxy.* 889)." *AS* 7: 301–8.

——— (1983). "Compulsory public service in Roman Egypt." In G. Grimm, H. Heinen, and E. Winter (eds.), *Das römischbyzantinische Ägypten,* 35–39. Mainz am Rhein.

Thomas, K. (1976). "Age and authority in early modern England." *PBA* 62: 205–48.

Thomas, R. (1989). *Oral Tradition and Written Record in Classical Athens.* Cambridge.

Thomasson, B. E. (1960). *Die Statthalter der römischen Provinzen Nordafrikas von Augustus bis Diocletianus.* Lund.

——— (1984). *Laterculi Praesidum.* Vol. 1. Arlöv.

——— (1991). *Legatus.* Stockholm.

——— (1996). *Fasti Africani.* Jonsered.

Thompson, D'A. W. (1936). *A Glossary of Greek Birds.* London.

Thompson, S. (1955–58). *Motif-Index of Folk-Literature.* Copenhagen.

Thomsen, R. (1980). *King Servius Tullius.* Copenhagen.

Thomson, D. (1991). "The welfare of the elderly in the past: A family or community responsibility?" In Pelling and Smith (1991) 194–221.

Thomson, D. F. S. (ed.) (1997). *Catullus.* Toronto, Buffalo, and London.

Thornton, H., and Thornton, A. (1962). *Time and Style.* London.

Thury, E. M. (1988a). "Euripides' *Alcestis* and the Athenian generation gap." *Arethusa* 21: 197–214.

——— (1988b). "A study of words relating to youth and old age in the plays of Euripides and its special implications for Euripides' *Suppliant Women.*" *Computers and the Humanities* 22: 293–306.

Tibbitts, C. (ed.) (1960). *Handbook of Social Gerontology.* Chicago.

Tomsin, A. (1952). "Étude sur les πρεσβύτεροι des villages de la χώρα égyptienne." *Bulletin de l'Académie royale de Belgique, Classe des Lettres* s. 5, 38: 95–130, 467–532.

Tomulescu, C. St. (1979). "Quelques petites études de droit romain." *BIDR*[3] 21: 95–117.

Toner, J. P. (1995). *Leisure and Ancient Rome.* Cambridge.

Treggiari, S. (1969). *Roman Freedmen during the Late Republic.* Oxford.

——— (1991). *Roman Marriage.* Oxford.

Troyansky, D. G. (1989). *Old Age in the Old Regime.* Ithaca and London.

——— (1996). "The history of old age in the western world." *A&S* 16: 233–43.

Turner, E. G. (1937). "The *gerousia* of Oxyrhynchus." *Archiv für Papyrusforschung* 12: 179–86.

Twigg-Porter, G. (1962–63). "Cicero, classic gerontologist." *CB* 39: 1–4.

Tziatzi-Papagianni, M. (ed.) (1994). *Die Sprüche der sieben Weisen.* Stuttgart and Leipzig.

Ugolini, G. (1995). *Untersuchungen zur Figur des Sehers Teiresias.* Tübingen.

Ullman, B. L. (1933–34). "Life begins at forty." *CJ* 29: 456–59.

Unger, J. J. (1887). "De censibus provinciarum romanarum." *Leipziger Studien zur classischen Philologie* 10: 1–76.

van Berchem, D. (1980). "La gérousie d'Ephèse." *MH* 37: 25–40.

van den Berghe, P. L. (1973). *Age and Sex in Human Societies.* Belmont, Calif.

van den Hout, M. P. J. (1999). *A Commentary on the Letters of M. Cornelius Fronto.* Leiden.

van Gennep, A. (1909). *Les rites de passage.* Paris.

van Hooff, A. J. L. (1983). "Oud-zijn in het oude Hellas." *Tijdschrift voor Gerontologie en Geriatrie* 14: 141–48.

——— (1989). "Caring for the old: 'quid pro quo' or 'omnia pro Deo'?" In A. A. A. Bastiaensen, A. Hilhorst, and C. H. Kneepkens (eds.), *Fructus centesimus,* 325–32. Sint-Pietersabdij and Dordrecht.

——— (1990). *From Autothanasia to Suicide.* London.

van Minnen, P. (1991). "Eine Steuerliste aus Hermupolis: Neuedition von *SPP* XX 40 + 48." *Tyche* 6: 121–29.

——— (1995). "Medical care in late antiquity." In P. J. van der Eijk, H. F. J. Horstmanshoff, and P. H. Schrijvers (eds.), *Ancient Medicine in its Socio-Cultural Context,* 1:153–69. Amsterdam.

van Ooteghem, J. (1959). *Lucius Licinius Lucullus.* Brussels.

van Rossum, J. A. (1988). *De gerousia in de Griekse steden van het Romeinse Rijk.* Den Haag.

Venini, P. (1960). "La vecchiaia nel *de Senectute* di Cicerone." *Athenaeum* 38: 98–117.

Vessey, D. W. T. C. (1973). "Prudentius, Shakespeare, and the seven ages of man." *CPh* 68: 208–11.

Victor, C. R. (1987). *Old Age in Modern Society: A Textbook of Social Gerontology.* London.

Vidman, L. (1982). "Osservazioni sui *praefecti urbi* nei primi due secoli." *Atti del Colloquio Internazionale AIEGL su Epigrafia e Ordine Senatorio, I,* 289–303. Rome.

Vílchez, M. (1983). "Sobre los períodos de la vida humana en la lírica arcaica y la tragedia griega." *Emerita* 51: 63–95, 215–53.

Virlouvet, C. (1997). "Existait-il des registres de décès à Rome au Ier siècle ap. J.-C.?" In *La Rome impériale: démographie et logistique,* 77–88. Rome.

Vitucci, G. (1956). *Ricerche sulla prefectura urbi in età imperiale (sec. I–III).* Rome.

Voci, P. (1980). "Storia della *patria potestas* da Augusto a Diocleziano." *Iura* 31: 37–100.

Vogel-Weidemann, U. (1982). *Die Statthalter von Africa und Asia in den Jahren 14–68 n. Chr.* Bonn.

Volterra, E. (1956). "Intorno a un editto dell'imperatore Claudio." *RAL* 8.11: 205–19.

———— (1969). "*Senatus consulta.*" *Novissimo Digesto Italiano* 16: 1047–78.

von Kondratowitz, H.-J. (1991). "The medicalization of old age." In Pelling and Smith (1991) 134–64.

von Staden, H. (1989). *Herophilus.* Cambridge.

Wackernagel, W. (1862). *Die Lebensalter.* Basel.

Wagner, A. (1995). "Second childhood (On turning 80) (A piece of my mind)." *Journal of the American Medical Association* 274: 606.

Walde, A., and Hofmann, J. B. (1954). *Lateinisches etymologisches Wörterbuch*[3]. Heidelberg.

Waldstein, W. (1986). *Operae libertorum.* Stuttgart.

Wall, R. (1995). "Elderly persons and members of their households in England and Wales from preindustrial times to the present." In Kertzer and Laslett (1995) 81–106.

Wallace, S. L. (1938a). "Census and poll-tax in Ptolemaic Egypt." *AJPh* 59: 418–42.

———— (1938b). *Taxation in Egypt from Augustus to Diocletian.* Princeton, N.J.

Wallace-Hadrill, A. (1981). "Family and inheritance in the Augustan marriage laws." *PCPhS* 27: 58–80.

Walsh, P. G. (1965). "Massinissa." *JRS* 55: 149–60.

Waltz, R. (1949). "Ordinal et cardinal: une 'règle' caduque." *REA* 51: 41–53.

Warde Fowler, W. (1899). *The Roman Festivals of the Period of the Republic.* London.

Waters, W. E. (1922). "The old age of a horse." *CPh* 17: 87–88.

Watson, A. (1967). *The Law of Persons in the Later Roman Republic.* Oxford.

———— (1968). *The Law of Property in the Later Roman Republic.* Oxford.

———— (1971). *The Law of Succession in the Later Roman Republic.* Oxford.

Watt, W. S. (1994). "Notes on Seneca, *de Beneficiis, de Clementia,* and *Dialogi.*" *HSCPh* 96: 225–39.

Webster, R. (ed.) (1900). *The Elegies of Maximianus.* Princeton, N.J.

Wegener, E. P. (1946). "The βουλευταί of the μητροπόλεις in Roman Egypt." In M. David, B. A. van Groningen, and E. M. Meijers (eds.), *Symbolae ad jus et historiam antiquitatis pertinentes Julio Christiano van Oven dedicatae,* 160–90. Leiden.

———— (1956). "The *entolai* of Mettius Rufus." *Eos* 48: 331–53.

Welsh, D. (1977). "The age of majority in Athens." *EMC* 21.3: 77–85.

West, M. L. (1971). "The cosmology of 'Hippocrates,' *de Hebdomadibus.*" *CQ* 21: 365–88.

Westermann, W. L., and Keyes, C. W. (eds.) (1932). *Tax Lists and Transportation Receipts from Theadelphia.* New York.

Westermann, W. L., and Schiller, A. A. (1954). *Apokrimata.* New York.

White, J. L. (ed.) (1986). *Light from Ancient Letters.* Philadelphia.

Whitehead, D. (1991). "Norms of citizenship in ancient Greece." In A. Molho,

K. Raaflaub, and J. Emlen (eds.), *City States in Classical Antiquity and Medieval Italy*, 135–54. Stuttgart.

Wiedemann, T. (1989). *Adults and Children in the Roman Empire*. London.

——— (1996). "*Servi senes:* The role of old slaves at Rome." *Polis* 8: 275–93.

Wilamowitz-Moellendorff, U. von (1893). *Aristoteles und Athen*. Vol. 1. Berlin.

Wilcken, U. (1899). *Griechische Ostraka aus Aegypten und Nubien, I.* Leipzig and Berlin.

——— (1903). "Papyrus-Urkunden." *Archiv für Papyrusforschung* 2: 385–96.

——— (1906). "Neue Nachträge zu P. Lond. II." *Archiv für Papyrusforschung* 3: 232–46.

Wilhelm, F. (1907). "Maximianus und Boethius." *RhM* 62: 601–14.

——— (1911). *Die Schrift des Juncus περὶ γήρως und ihr Verhältnis zu Ciceros Cato maior.* Breslau.

Wilkinson, L. P. (1974). *The Roman Experience.* New York.

Williams, W. (1975). "Formal and historical aspects of two new documents of Marcus Aurelius." *ZPE* 17: 37–78.

Winterbottom, M. (ed.) (1984). *The Minor Declamations Ascribed to Quintilian.* Berlin and New York.

Wirszubski, C. (1954). "Cicero's *cum dignitate otium:* A reconsideration." *JRS* 44: 1–13.

Wiseman, T. P. (1969a). "The census in the first century B.C." *JRS* 59: 59–75.

——— (1969b). *Catullan Questions.* Leicester.

Wöhrle, G. (1990). *Studien zur Theorie der antiken Gesundheitslehre.* Stuttgart.

Wolff, H. (1986). "Die Entwicklung der Veteranenprivilegien vom Beginn des 1. Jahrhunderts v. Chr. bis auf Konstantin d. Gr." In W. Eck and H. Wolff (eds.), *Heer und Integrationspolitik*, 44–115. Cologne.

Wolff, H. J. (1978). *Das Recht der griechischen Papyri Ägyptens in der Zeit der Ptolemäer und des Prinzipats, 2.* Munich.

Wortley, J. (1997). "Aging and the aged in Aesopic fables." *International Journal of Aging and Human Development* 44: 183–203.

——— (1998). "Aging and the aged in 'The Greek Anthology.'" *International Journal of Aging and Human Development* 47: 53–68.

Wuilleumier, P. (ed.) (1961). *Cicéron: Caton l'Ancien (de la Vieillesse)³.* Paris.

Yamagata, N. (1993). "Young and old in Homer and in Heike monogatari." *G&R* 40: 1–10.

Yaron, R. (1956). "Some remarks on 'donatio mortis causa.'" *RIDA³* 3: 493–512.

——— (1960). *Gifts in Contemplation of Death.* Oxford.

——— (1966). "'Donatio sola cogitatione mortalitatis.'" *RIDA³* 13: 369–75.

——— (1974). "Semitic elements in early Rome." In A. Watson (ed.), *Daube Noster,* 343–57. Edinburgh and London.

Youtie, H. C. (1964). "Notes on papyri." *BICS* 11: 15–30.

——— (1966). "Pétaus, fils de Pétaus, ou le scribe qui ne savait pas écrire." *CE* 81: 127–43.

———— (1971a). "Ἀγράμματος: An aspect of Greek society in Egypt." *HSCPh* 75: 161–76.

———— (1971b). "Βραδέως γράφων: Between literacy and illiteracy." *GRBS* 12: 239–61.

———— (1975a). "Ὑπογραφεύς: The social impact of illiteracy in Graeco-Roman Egypt." *ZPE* 17: 201–21.

———— (1975b). "A record of deaths on a Michigan ostracon." *ZPE* 18: 77–79.

———— (1975c). "Because they do not know letters." *ZPE* 19: 101–8.

———— (1976a). "*P. Mich.* III 176–178." *ZPE* 20: 284–87.

———— (1976b). "Εὔτυχος Εὐτύχου." *ZPE* 21: 207–8.

Zanker, P. (1989). *Die trunkene Alte*. Frankfurt am Main.

———— (1995). *The Mask of Socrates*. Tr. A. Shapiro. Berkeley.

Zeman, F. D. (1942–50). "Life's later years: Studies in the medical history of old age." *Journal of the Mount Sinai Hospital* 8 (1942) 1161–65; 11 (1944–45) 45–52, 97–104, 224–31, 300–7, 339–44; 12 (1946) 783–91, 833–46, 890–901, 939–53; 13 (1947) 241–56; 16 (1950) 308–22; 17 (1950) 53–68. All reprinted in Gruman (1979).

Zimmermann, B. (1998). "Generationenkonflikt im griechisch-römischen Drama." *Würzburger Jahrbücher für die Altertumswissenschaft*, n.s., 22: 21–32.

Zocca, E. (1995). "La *senectus mundi*. Significato, fonti e fortuna di un tema ciprianeo." *Augustinianum* 35: 641–77.

Zoz, M. G. (1970). "In tema di obbligazioni alimentari." *BIDR*³ 12: 323–55.

Index

Roman names generally follow the ordering of OCD^3.

Reference is only made to the notes where it is deemed useful to refer to particular items to which the reader might not otherwise be led by the main text. An *index locorum* is available at ⟨http://www.clas.canterbury.ac.nz/oldancients .html⟩

ANCIENT SOCIETY AND HISTORY

The series Ancient Society and History offers books, relatively brief in compass, on selected topics in the history of ancient Greece and Rome, broadly conceived, with a special emphasis on comparative and other nontraditional approaches and methods. The series, which includes both works of synthesis and works of original scholarship, is aimed at the widest possible range of specialist and nonspecialist readers.

Published in the Series: